C0-AWT-051

Arthur Miller's Life and Literature

An Annotated and Comprehensive Guide

Stefani Koorey

The Scarecrow Press, Inc.
Lanham, Maryland, and London
2000

SCARECROW PRESS, INC.

Published in the United States of America
by Scarecrow Press, Inc.
4720 Boston Way, Lanham, Maryland 20706
www.scarecrowpress.com

4 Pleydell Gardens, Folkestone
Kent CT20 2DN, England

British Library Cataloguing-in-Publication Information Available

Library of Congress Cataloging-in-Publication Data

Koorey, Stefani, 1959–
Arthur Miller's life and literature : an annotated and comprehensive guide / Stefani Koorey. p. cm. Includes index.
ISBN 0-8108-3869-9 (alk. paper)
1. Miller, Arthur, 1915—Bibliography. 2. Miller, Arthur, 1915—Chronology. I. Title.
Z8574.88 .K67 2000 [PS3525.I5156]
016.812'52—dc21 00-041000

The paper used in this publication meets the minimum requirements of American National Standard for Information Sciences—Permanence of Paper for Printed Library Materials, ANSI/NISO Z39.48–1992.
Manufactured in the United States of America.

This book is dedicated to
the memory of my father
Alfred Joseph Koorey
(1925-1987)
and my mother
Betty Zane Donaldson Koorey
(1923-1999)

Contents

PART IV: APPENDIXES

Preface

I spent two years conducting research for my doctoral dissertation on Arthur Miller. The majority of this twenty-four month period was consumed with searching thousands of bibliographic resources and data bases (books, journal articles, newspaper indexes, periodical guides, archives, dissertations, internet sites) for material germane to my study. I distinctly remember feeling both overjoyed and delighted when I came across Tetsumaro Hayashi's *An Index to Arthur Miller Criticism*, 2nd. ed. (1976), hoping that I had at last discovered the magical short-cut to my long ordeal.

My sense of relief was soon followed by deep despair as I realized that Hayashi's index was outdated. Undaunted, I began my search anew for another edition. When I was forced to face the cruel reality that such a tool was nonexistent, I knew in my heart that I had to immediately cease my whining, accept my plight, and forge ahead, or I would never begin my writing.

That brief moment of disappointment has now blossomed into a project—namely, the creation of a comprehensive index to Arthur Miller's life and literature. It is my wish that future generations of Miller scholars, theatre practitioners, educators, and academics like myself, will not have to think of the library as their primary residence. Instead of doing months of bibliographic research, they can take their kids to the beach.

Since this bibliography is a work of research, I am greatly indebted to a number of librarians and research collections around the country who have made this book possible by saving me untold hours and dollars with their considerable involvement. Primary among these individuals and institutions is Linda Gabriel and her staff in the Interlibrary Loan Department at the Orange County Library System in Orlando, Florida. She has been with this project the longest, since it was only a germ of an idea, and has ordered and processed literally thousands of requests on my behalf. This project owes its comprehensiveness to her diligence, speed, and commitment to excellence. I am also greatly indebted to Ruth Wu at Valencia Community College for her quick and accurate work in handling my vast quantities of requests for books through her interlibrary loan department.

The research collections and staffs of a number of libraries have also been indispensable, and among these are Barbara Hall at the Margaret Herrick Library at the Academy of Motion Picture Arts and Sciences, Joseph A. Puccio in the Collection Management Division at the Library of Congress, Susan Brady at the Beinecke Rare Book and Manuscript Library at Yale University, Susan Halpert at Harvard University, Cynthia Earman at the Rare Book and Special Collections Reading Room at the Library of Congress, Kathleen Kienholz at the American Academy of Arts and Letters, the staff at the American Film Institute, the Harry Ransom Humanities Research Center at the University of Texas at Austin, the Billy Rose Theatre Collection at the New York Public Library for the Performing Arts, and the Museum of Radio and Television.

I am particularly grateful to a number of colleagues who offered their advice or graciously supplied me with copies of their work when all other avenues were unavailable. These special individuals include, Kate Egerton, Susan C. W. Abbotson, George Jensen, Joseph Valente, Jonathan Witt, Steven R. Centola, and Stephen Marino. A large debt of thanks also goes to several theatre companies for their always quick response to my queries, including, The Long Wharf Theatre, The Guthrie Theater, The Lyric Opera of Chicago, and the Goodspeed Opera House.

This project was completed without funding of any kind. In my dogged determination to provide as comprehensive a work as was humanly possible, I hired two research assistants and I wish to thank them here for their speed and accuracy. They are Cliff Farrington, who examined the Arthur Miller Collection at the University of Texas at Austin, and Peter J. Apel, who was my assistant at the University of Michigan at Ann Arbor.

Personal thanks go to my friends and family who suffered through my three-year obsession for detail and comprehensiveness with this project. They include, Kat Koorey, Mike Worrell, Sandi Levi, Cheryl Beck, Ardith Gumbert, Charlie Hoeck, Reba R. Gordon, and Crystal Sullivan.

Grateful acknowledgment is made to Dr. Tetsumaro Hayashi for permission to use information contained in *Arthur Miller Criticism 1930-1967* (1969) and *An Index to Arthur Miller Criticism* (1976).

As the subject of this bibliography, I also owe an incalculable debt to Arthur Miller for living a life of such fascinating accomplishment, both personally and professionally. It is an honor to contribute in some way to the body of scholarship that surrounds this preeminent playwright, novelist, essayist, poet, political activist, and both American and world citizen.

Scope, Methodology, Organization, and Use of This Book

Arthur Asher Miller is one of the most produced, and therefore one of the most studied, American dramatists. He has been writing plays for the Broadway stage since 1944—over fifty-six years. The Miller canon includes not only his work as a dramatist, but his prolific output as a man of letters. As of 1999, Miller has authored fifteen original full-length plays, two full-length stage adaptations, one musical, one volume of nine short stories plus various short stories published in magazine format, one novel, one "cinema-novel," three novellas, numerous radio plays, seven one-act plays, one children's book, one television adaptation of his own short story, an expansive autobiography, five personal-experience journals, four screenplays (three of which have been produced), one teleplay based on another's memoir, over one hundred essays on subjects ranging from theatre history and dramatic theory to his personal political involvements, and countless letters to the editor. Most recently, he has collaborated on an opera version of one of his stage plays. Additionally, Miller has participated in well over one hundred interviews with scholars, critics, authors, and journalists worldwide—this producing, literally, thousands of pages of commentary, opinions, and insight.

Yet, despite the plethora of essays, interviews, critical commentary, news items, and book-length studies by and about Arthur Miller, there are less than a handful of published bibliographic reference texts and supplemental articles available to the modern researcher—all but the most recent of which are grossly out of date and in dire need of extensive revision, and none of which are comprehensive.

Since the issuance of the two most recent bibliographic works solely dedicated to Miller studies, Tetsumaro Hayashi's *An Index to Arthur Miller Criticism* (1976) and John Ferres's *Arthur Miller: A Reference Guide* (1979), enormous quantities of scholarly articles, books, dissertations, interviews, magazine articles, and newspaper essays and reviews (electronic and print) have been published and many more are forthcoming. Miller's own continued and substantial output as a man of letters since 1979 further mandates an updated bibliographic study. Now that Miller is nearing his eighty-fifth birthday and still actively writing works for the stage, an updated and inclusive annotated bibliography of the life and the literature of one of America's premiere social dramatists is warranted.

Arthur Miller's Life and Literature: An Annotated and Comprehensive Guide is designed for the modern researcher, be he theatre historian, social historian, secondary educator, or an interested student of literary criticism. Both professional and amateur theatre practitioners will find a work such as this an invaluable tool when electing to produce a Miller work. As one who has worked for many years in the capacity of dramaturg, I clearly see this work providing a practical means for production research and reviews so vital to that endeavor.

As an educational tool for secondary schools, this bibliography will also prove useful. Middle and high school drama and English teachers are forever in need of information regarding video resources and internet sites. Moreover, in some instances, this reference guide will be helpful to history teachers studying HUAC and the McCarthy era in American political history. Since *The Crucible* is perhaps the most studied Miller play at this educational level, this reference tool will also aid those educators who are searching for documentary, literary, or theatrical evidence regarding this masterpiece.

This work is the first bibliographic study of Arthur Miller to:

- ❖ Present an exhaustive inventory of published materials about, relating to, and by Arthur Miller
- ❖ Include citations for general appraisals, literary criticism, and doctoral dissertations
- ❖ Incorporate in a comprehensive fashion both literary criticism and production reviews for all of Miller's dramatic works (full-length and one-act)
- ❖ Provide a detailed catalogue of Arthur Miller manuscript and typescript archive collections nationwide
- ❖ Identify media-related materials, including CD-ROM products, internet sites, film and video productions, and sound recordings
- ❖ Include listings for unpublished conference papers that are germane to Arthur Miller studies

Scope and Approach

Arthur Miller's Life and Literature takes up where all other Miller bibliographic works have left off—namely, besides the standard inclusion of literary criticism and production reviews, this text includes citations for all matter relating to Miller, including his personal life and political involvements. Some of these most interesting topics encompass, but are not limited to, Miller's presidency of PEN (Poets, Essayists, Novelists—the international writers's organization dedicated to fighting censorship and the defense of persecuted writers around the world), his marriage to Marilyn Monroe, his involvement in the Peter Reilly murder case, his opposition to and testimony before the House Committee on Un-American Activities (HUAC), his service as a delegate to Democratic conventions in 1968 and 1972, his awards and honors, etc. This approach will enable this guide to be useful not only to those who wish to gain access to particular sources but also to anyone searching for general period surveys and resources for study. It also provides, in and of itself, a most interesting read of Miller's life in an annotated format.

Only works written in English are included in this study. This decision not only reflects my own limitations in the area of world languages, but also since this book is well over 800 pages in length, dramatically illustrates the massive profusion of writings about Miller. Knowledge of that fact should serve as a useful guide for anyone considering compiling a text of non-English language sources.

Although this guide depends heavily on American publications, a large quantity of the essays in English are from books, journals, and newspapers that are published outside the U.S. (including England and Canada). With the advent of online research sites and fee-based indexes, it has become relatively easy to locate significant sources in Miller studies, both scholarly and nonacademic, without much travel or expense.

The periodicals selected in this guide reflect a wide-range of interdisciplinary studies, and they include news magazines and daily newspapers (both local and national), professional theatre journals, scholarly publications, nonacademic periodicals, general interest magazines, and special-interest periodicals (such as *The Advocate* and *Christopher Street*). In many cases, a news item regarding Miller would appear in several newspapers concurrently, such as the Tony or Academy Award nominations. In these instances, and primarily to save space, I have elected to list and annotate only one source per biographical item.

There is a noted absence, however, of significant articles from the *New York Journal-American*, the *Daily Worker*, and the *New Masses*. While each publication is represented by a few entries, the bulk of Miller material from these sources was impossible to obtain, even through the interlibrary loan departments of two institutions. What articles were available generally had a price tag attached, some as high as $20—for just a two-column photocopy. It is my one regret that this guide could not include the important items relating to Miller's controversial involvement in the juvenile delinquency film for the New York City Youth Board and early commentary on the playwright's political life that is contained within these sources.

Unless of some significance (important interview, quote not captured elsewhere, lengthy profile), smaller regional newspaper articles and news items are not included. This omission also covers regional productions (including college productions) of Miller's plays, unless, of course, they were deemed important either because of the stature of its cast or Miller's own personal interest in the production. This is not an arbitrary choice on my part, but rather reflects my effort to offer citations for important, but not all, productions of Miller's plays. For those Miller scholars who are interested in smaller regional productions, a database exists for this category of reportage—*DataTimes*—available online and on CD-ROM at some public, and most academic, libraries.

This guide includes a listing of all unpublished doctoral dissertations in English from American universities. Each of the 111 works included have been annotated from either their respective DAI entries or from actual hands-on perusal on my part. They are presented chronologically and, in such order, offer an interesting examination of the evolutionary development of Miller studies.

Book-length studies in English are also represented in this guide, regardless of their place of publication. Excluded from this study are the plethora of published literature guides and student study guides and notes (such as *Bloom's Notes*, *Cliffs Notes*, *Monarch Notes*, *Penguin Study Notes*, *MaxNotes*, *York Notes*, and *Brodie's Notes*). While they are useful in their fashion, they are on the whole comprised of excerpts of longer critical studies—and each of those *are* included within these pages.

The manuscript collections portion of the guide is drawn from American repositories only. The media resources and recordings listed are from English-speaking productions and every effort has been made to indicate where copies of the items are housed so that the reader will be able to access them. Generally speaking, most libraries, both academic and public, do not interlibrary loan audio-visual material, so if the reader is interested in these all-important recordings and video tapes, a personal visit to the holding institution will often be necessary.

Comprehensiveness

I have made every attempt to construct an exhaustive study of Millerania. Unfortunately, many sources remained inaccessible to the end and others were, as mentioned above, cost-prohibitive to obtain. I also encountered a quantity of misleading citations from extremely reputable indexes and printed bibliographies. For instance, I came across a feature article in the *Chicago Tribune* that detailed actor Tim Gregory's rise from college performer to featured actor in an acclaimed production of *The Woman in Black*. The article makes mention of a work called *Arthur(Miller): The Musical* with which Gregory was involved. After contacting the Goodspeed Opera House for further information, I received back a jolly reply that the show was about the Dudley Moore film and not the playwright, along with the friendly reminder that you should not believe everything you read. While this proved to be a humorous moment, it highlights the ever-present problem of the reliability of source material and the (sometime) lack of confirmation of content, even by a major American newspaper. Wild goose chases aside, it is important to state that I in no way guarantee the information contained in the items that I have annotated, only that the annotation accurately reflects the content of the article, essay, interview, or commentary as I found it.

In the often overlooked area of dustjacket commentary, there are few tools available to locate Miller's writings in support of other authors. Some of the most helpful resources in this pursuit proved to be antiquarian, rare book, and out of print book search engines—each providing much-needed detailed information that included bibliographic citations, annotations, and real people contacts for questions and queries. Those most helpful included Bibliofind, Powell's Books in Portland, Oregon, Abebooks, Book Finder, and Alibris book search.

Reviews of books about Miller, Marilyn Monroe, or other individuals in the playwright's life are excluded from this bibliography. Also excluded are death notices and features on prominent actors, directors, and friends from Miller's life, unless the essay offers some new or interesting piece to the Miller puzzle heretofore unpublished. Additionally, encyclopedic sources such as *Who's Who*, *Contemporary Authors*, *Writers Directory*, and *Contemporary Literary Criticism* have not been included. As of 1999, Miller is prominently listed in over 250 of these various sources and reference volumes.

Methodology

The appendixes not only contain the production records and cast lists from the first American and British production of each Miller work, but also present a detailed listing of both the indexes and the periodicals that were consulted in the construction of this bibliography. In some cases, a new source was discovered only after reading an essay or news item, which might make a brief mention of another essay or event not yet encountered. More like a grand scavenger hunt, the methodology of this book evolved into one big cross-reference experience. Every effort was made to confirm that an essay was, in fact, a reprint of an earlier work, an excerpt was indeed from the source listed, and the all-important page numbers were accurately recorded.

Online searching has not been without its own brand of problems. For instance, there are more than a handful of individuals named "Arthur Miller" in the news. I have discovered an art critic Miller who lived in the early part of the twentieth century (which was particularly problematic since Miller also contributed forewords and introductions to several artists and photographers of his acquaintance), a famed Harvard law professor and television host, an American playwright in the early 1930s (this one stumped Hayashi), a writer of park ranger books, a noted cinematographer, a physicist, a sports portrait artist, a clinical assistant professor at the NYU School of Medicine, local government officials, and even several small-time criminals.

I am most proud to note that almost all of the items in this bibliography were personally examined for annotation, and only a relatively small number of citations were annotated from abstracts. It became my mission to track down even the smallest mentioning of Miller and I am happy to report that I only had to eliminate a tiny percentage of citations that I could not locate or obtain.

In this pursuit, I have amassed eight banker's boxes filled with photocopies, playbills, journal issues, and reprints of articles, interviews, essays, and blurbs. In addition, I have filled two floor-to-ceiling shelves with books about the Salem witch trials, the Holocaust and its aftermath, the McCarthy era, American theatre history, and works by and about Miller, Elia Kazan, and Marilyn Monroe. If you are likewise inclined to craft a comprehensive and annotated bibliography, be forewarned—your vocation *will* become your avocation and your home will become a small library.

Style

Print citations in this work follow the *Chicago Manual of Style*, 14th ed. (1993) and online citations follow *The Columbia Guide to Online Style* (Walker and Taylor, 1998). Listed here are a few important style choices of which the reader should be aware:

- ❖ Stage plays, radio plays, fiction, nonfiction, and essays by Miller are presented alphabetically.
- ❖ Interviews (both in print and electronic), general critical appraisals and literary criticism, and bibliographies and checklists are alphabetized by the name of the author. (Please note that an "interview" is defined as any item in which Miller is extensively quoted.)
- ❖ Biographical items, dissertations, critical analysis of stage plays, fiction, nonfiction, film, and television productions of Miller's works are listed chronologically. (Please note that the chronological sequencing of the stage plays refers only to the order in which the plays are listed, not the organization of the citations relating to each play).
- ❖ Manuscript collections and conference papers are presented alphabetically by venue with individual citations listed alphabetically by author or content.
- ❖ Publisher information has been abbreviated to omit words such as "Publisher," "Press," and "Incorporated." Additionally, a list of abbreviations used in this bibliography is included in the prefatory matter.
- ❖ The spelling of the word "theatre" conforms to the preferred usage of each production company, publication, author, critic, and journalist represented in this work. Usage in the narrative portion of the bibliography, and when not a direct quote, is my own preferred "re" spelling.

Consistency being a priority, every effort was made to list the details of each citation as specified by the source. However, periodicals have been known to make mistakes, omit page numbers, change their titles, and alter the format and the frequency of their publications. Please note that any discrepancy in the citations reflects the circumstances of that particular publication, and they were not arbitrarily augmented by this bibliographer.

Organization and Presentation

Arthur Miller's Life and Literature: An Annotated and Comprehensive Guide is divided into three main sections:

I. Primary Sources, which includes all works by Miller as well as interviews and manuscript collections of his original material
II. Secondary Sources, which includes bibliographies and checklists, doctoral dissertations (USA/unpublished), biographical items, general appraisals and literary criticism, stage play criticism, film, radio, and television criticism, fiction and nonfiction criticism, and conference papers (unpublished)
III. Media Resources, which includes film and television productions of Miller's plays, documentaries, tributes, and biographical film, sound recordings and Internet sources and CD-ROM products

In crafting a listing of Miller's stage plays, screenplays, teleplays, and smaller dramatic works, I have elected not to include all imprints or reprints of a particular work. Instead, I have provided the reader with information regarding first publication, first acting edition, significant reprints, periodical publications, and special editions.

The general appraisals and literary criticism section of Part II is further divided into five subareas. These include: book length studies; critical essays in books; critical essays in journals and magazines; critical essays in newspapers; and brief mentions in books, journals, and newspapers. Unlike other Miller bibliographies, the critical commentary in these subareas is arranged by author and not presented in a chronological fashion. This facilitates the grouping of works by the same author-critic, which, I will venture to say, is what the researcher is looking for in the first place.

Over the years, this work went through many organizational changes. I studied other bibliographies for guidance, but ultimately made decisions on arrangement and organization based on how such an item might be accessed—in other words, where someone might first look to find what they wanted. My aim was to create a user-friendly reference tool that also could be read for content.

Likewise, the critical commentary for each play in chapter 5, part II, is similarly divided into the following subcategories of material: book length studies; critical essays in books; critical essays in journals and magazines; critical essays in newspapers; production reviews; related interviews and profiles not with Miller; and news reports, letters to the editor, and related material. It must be noted that not all of Miller's plays have had critical commentary written about them in all of these categories, so you will find that subsections have been eliminated when there was an absence of items of that description.

It was a definite challenge to decide exactly where a certain citation belonged once I had created these subcategories. In many cases, an item that first appeared biographical in nature (for instance, a news item regarding the opening of a significant foreign production) on closer examination actually related more directly to the stage play than Miller's life, and was therefore placed in the news items section for the play. On the other hand, news items that focused on Miller traveling to a particular country to attend rehearsals of his play were placed in the biographical section of Part I.

The greatest challenge, by far, to this decision-making process came with the abundance of critical commentary and news reports regarding the Wooster Group's production of *L.S.D.*, which used portions of Miller's *The Crucible* in this experimental work. A great controversy grew from this with Miller threatening suit if the group's artistic director, Elizabeth LeCompte, did not cease from using Miller's text. While certainly biographical in nature, I chose to place almost all of the Wooster Group material with *The Crucible* in part II of the bibliography. It was more important, in this case, to keep the material relating to this event in one place, tied to Miller's play rather than his life.

All possible attempts have been made to eliminate any bias on my part in the selection of source material and in the composition of the annotations. In reading nearly everything written by and about Miller in English, I must admit that there is a great deal of overlap when it comes to the critical commentary of his works. You might find that I have been particularly excited by a fresh approach or truly fascinating account and I have indicated as such in my annotations. This is not to imply that every other source not so designated is dull or repetitious, but, rather, that this particular author has crafted a new way of looking at the topic and I wanted the reader to recognize this.

The annotations are, on the whole then, descriptive rather than evaluative. Often experts will argue whether a work is important or ground breaking and I elected to leave that decision to those who obtain the full essay or article for their own considered opinion.

As a note of disclaimer, I must acknowledge that despite my best efforts there are bound to be errors, both typographical and human, and omissions within these pages. I can only promise the reader that every attempt has been made to verify and confirm the material in this work.

Key to Abbreviations and Explanatory Notes

A	Autographed
ALS	Autographed letter, signed
AMS	Autographed Manuscript
ANS	Autographed Note, signed
APCS	Autographed Postcard, signed
D	Document
Dir.	Director
Diss.	Dissertation
DPS	Dramatists Play Service
Ed.	Editor
FTP	Federal Theatre Project
GB	Great Britain
HUAC	House Committee on Un-American Activities
Illus.	Illustrator or Illustrated by
Inc.	Incomplete
Mimeo.	Mimeographed
Misc.	Miscellaneous
MS	Manuscript
Narr.	Narrator
N.B.	*Nota bene*, take notice
n.d.	No date identified or known
N.J.	New Jersey
n.p.	No page numbers identified
n.v.	No volume number identified
N.Y.	New York
P	Press
PC	Post Card
PEN	International organization of Poets, Essayists, Novelists
Perf.	Performer
pp.	Pages

Prod.	Producer
Rpt.	Reprinted
S	Signed
Sec.	Section
T	Typed
T/cc	Typed copies
TLS	Typed Letter, signed
TMS	Typed Manuscript
TMSS	Typed Manuscript Signed
Tr.	Translator or translated by
U	University
unpub.	Unpublished
UP	University Press
U.S.	United States
vol.	Volume
[ ]	Information between brackets is supplied from source other than manuscript itself

Chronology

1915 Arthur Asher Miller is born on 17 October at East 112th Street in Harlem, to Isadore and Augusta Barnett Miller. Arthur is the second of three children; Kermit, older by three years, will become a salesman, and Joan, born in 1921, will eventually appear on the stage under the professional name of Joan Copeland.

1928 The Miller family is forced to move to Schermerhorn Street in the Midwood section of Brooklyn when his father's coat making firm fails in 1928. Arthur attends James Madison High School, later to transfer to Abraham Lincoln High nearer to his home. While at ALHS, young Arthur receives a football injury, which will later prevent him from military service.

1932 After graduating from Abraham Lincoln High School in Brooklyn, Miller works at various jobs, including truck driver, singer on a local radio station, and shipping clerk in a car parts warehouse on Tenth Avenue in Manhattan for more than a year at $15 a week.

Miller writes his first short story entitled "In Memoriam," depicting an aging salesman. Miller discovers serious literature, including Dostoyevsky's *The Brothers Karamazov*.

Miller is turned down twice for admission to the University of Michigan because of his poor academic record (he failed algebra three times and was expelled from class on several occasions).

1934 Miller is finally accepted for conditional admission to the University of Michigan, convincing the dean that he is ready to become a serious student. Miller enrolls in journalism.

To support himself, Miller works in the cafeteria washing dishes and earns a small salary as night editor of *The Michigan Daily*.

1936 Miller composes *No Villain*, his first play, in six days during spring vacation; the play receives the Hopwood Award in Drama at the University of Michigan.

Miller revises *No Villain* for the Theatre Guild's Bureau of New Plays Contest with new title, *They Too Arise.*

1937 Miller enrolls in Kenneth Rowe's playwriting class at the University of Michigan.

They Too Arise garners $1250 as winner of the Theatre Guild Award from Bureau of New Plays.

Honors at Dawn wins Hopwood Award in June.

Miller starts writing *The Great Disobedience* for the 1938 Hopwood Contest.

1938 Miller revises *They Too Arise* with a new title, *The Grass Still Grows.*

The Great Disobedience wins second place in the Hopwood Contest.

Miller graduates in June with a B.A. in English from the University of Michigan.

Miller joins the Federal Theatre Project in New York City; composes radio plays, scripts, and stage plays for The Project, Columbia Workshop (CBS), and Cavalcade of America (NBC).

1940 After the Federal Theatre Project is abolished, Miller goes on relief. Travels to North Carolina to collect dialect speech for the folk division of the Library of Congress.

August 5 — Miller marries Mary Grace Slattery, whom he had met at the University of Michigan. She works as a waitress and then as a literary editor at Harper & Brothers while Miller writes.

1944 Miller visits army camps for background data for *The Story of G. I. Joe*, a screenplay. Instead, publishes *Situation Normal*, a journal of his army tour.

The Man Who Had All the Luck is produced on Broadway but closes after only six performances, losing $55,000.

September 7 — a daughter, Jane, is born.

1945 *Focus*, a novel about anti-Semitism, is published. In a short article in *New Masses* magazine, Miller attacks Ezra Pound for his pro-fascist activism.

1947 January 29 — *All My Sons*, directed by Elia Kazan, opens on Broadway and runs 328 performances. Later published, *All My Sons* receives New York Drama Critics Circle Award, winning out over Eugene O'Neill's *The Iceman Cometh*.

May 31 — a son, Robert, is born.

Miller's name appears in an ad in the *Daily Worker* protesting the treatment of German anti-fascist refugees like Gerhard Eisler.

Miller auctions off the manuscript of *All My Sons* on behalf of the Progressive Citizens of America. His name appears as a sponsor of the World Youth Festival under the aegis of the communist-dominated World Federation of Democratic Youth in Prague.

1949 *Death of a Salesman*, directed by Elia Kazan, is produced and published; runs 472 performances; receives both the Pulitzer Prize and the Antoinette Perry Award (Tony).

Miller publishes "Tragedy and the Common Man" and "Arthur Miller on the Nature of Tragedy" in the *New York Times*. These are the first of many essays on politics, drama, theatre, social issues, theatre history, and social theory that are to appear in the years to come.

1950 Miller meets Marilyn Monroe at Twentieth Century-Fox on a visit to Hollywood with Kazan. Miller later writes of their parting: "Flying homeward, her scent still on my hands, I knew my innocence was technical merely, and the fact blackened my heart, but along with it came the certainty that I could, after all, lose myself in sensuality." (*Timebends*, 307)

In November, *Death of a Salesman* closes after 742 performances. In December, *An Enemy of the People*, an adaptation of Ibsen's play, is produced and runs thirty-six performances. It is published in 1951.

1952 Elia Kazan testifies before HUAC, at first refusing to cooperate. He then changes his mind and returns to testify fully in executive session, confirming some dozen names of people he had known in his months as a member of the Communist Party.

Miller begins research in Salem for new play about witchcraft trials of 1690s.

1953 *The Crucible* is produced and published; runs 197 performances to mixed reviews, and wins both the Antoinette Perry and the Donaldson awards as best play of the year.

1954 Miller is denied a passport by the State Department to visit Brussels for the European premiere of *The Crucible* on the grounds that his presence would not be in the best interests of the country.

Marilyn Monroe divorces Joe DiMaggio.

1955 Marilyn Monroe moves to New York City.

In May, Miller and Monroe begin to see each other secretly and regularly, after meeting again at a party.

Miller is charged with left-wing activities by Scripps-Howard reporter Frederick Woltman in the *New York World-Telegram* and is investigated by the New York City Youth Board for possible Communist associations.

In September, Miller's plays *A View from the Bridge* and *A Memory of Two Mondays* (one-act plays) are produced and published; they run for a disappointing 149 performances.

Miller spends six weeks in Reno establishing residency required for Nevada divorce from Mary Grace Slattery.

Miller writes short story, "The Misfits."

1956 June 11 — Miller wins uncontested divorce in a five-minute hearing, charging his wife with "extreme cruelty, entirely mental in nature."

Miller receives honorary doctorate from the University of Michigan.

June 21 — Miller testifies before the House Committee on Un-American Activities.

June 27 — Miller is given ten days to answer HUAC's questions on past Communist-front associations or face citation for contempt of Congress.

June 29 — Miller marries Marilyn Monroe. Miller is nearing forty and Monroe had just turned twenty-nine years old.

July 6 — State Department issues six-month passport to Miller after he answers questions regarding "derogatory information" that had kept him from getting a passport two years previously.

July 7 — Miller refuses to give House Investigators names of persons who attended a Communist writers' meeting in 1947.

July 10 — Miller is charged with contempt of Congress by HUAC.

July 25 — The House votes 373 to 9 to cite Miller for contempt of Congress.

September — Marilyn suffers miscarriage.

In October, *A View from the Bridge* (two-act version) is staged in London and runs 220 performances.

1957 February 18 — Federal grand jury indicts Miller on charges of contempt of Congress.

March 1 — Miller pleads not guilty in Federal District Court to an indictment charging contempt of Congress.

May 14 — Miller's trial for contempt of Congress begins.

May 21 — Federal Judge Charles F. McLaughlin rules that Arthur Miller's romance with Marilyn Monroe is "irrelevant and immaterial" to his trial for contempt. Joseph L. Rauh Jr., Miller's defense attorney, charges that HUAC had called Miller as a witness in an effort to get some of the publicity he was receiving as Miss Monroe's suitor.

May 23 — Miller trial ends, verdict postponed.

May 31 — Arthur Miller is found guilty on two counts of contempt of Congress.

June 28 — One count of contempt is dropped.

July 16 — Attorneys for Miller ask for acquittal from Federal District Judge Charles F. McLaughlin, citing a recent action setting aside the contempt conviction of Cornell University President, Marcus Singer.

July 19 — Miller is fined $500 and given a suspended one month jail sentence for contempt of Congress.

July 25 — Miller's lawyer urges U.S. Court of Appeals to reverse the playwright's contempt of Congress conviction "without further legal formalities."

August 1 — Monroe suffers second miscarriage (from ectopic pregnancy).

Arthur Miller's Collected Plays is published.

1958 February 21 — attorneys for Miller contend that HUAC had used his romance with Marilyn Monroe to seek publicity for itself. His counsel argues that the committee was after headlines, not information for legislation, when the playwright was called as a witness in June 1956.

August 7 — Miller's conviction for contempt of Congress is reversed by the U.S. Court of Appeals for the District of Columbia. The full nine-man court holds unanimously that the House Committee on Un-American Activities had not sufficiently warned the playwright of the risk of contempt if he elected to refuse to answer its questions.

December 16 — Monroe miscarries for third and final time.

Miller is elected to the National Institute of Arts and Letters.

1959 Miller is awarded Gold Medal for Drama, National Institute of Arts and Letters. In December, *Esquire* publishes his short story, "I Don't Need You Any More."

1960 *The Misfits* begins filming in Reno, Nevada.

Miller meets Ingeborg Morath on the set of *The Misfits*. She is present as a staff photographer for Magnum to document the filming.

"Please Don't Kill Anything" (short story) appears in *Noble Savage*.

November — Marilyn Monroe announces that she and Miller have separated and she is filing for divorce.

1961 January 24 — Marilyn Monroe travels to Juarez, Mexico, to obtain her divorce from Miller on the grounds of "incompatibility of character."

The Misfits (film) is released and the screenplay is published.

March 6 — Miller's mother, Augusta, dies of a heart ailment at the age of 70.

1962 May 19 — Marilyn Monroe takes Isadore Miller (Arthur's father) as her escort to John F. Kennedy's birthday party in Madison Square Garden and introduces him to the president.

February 17 — Miller marries Inge Morath.

August 4 — Marilyn Monroe dies in the early morning hours in her home in Los Angeles of either a suicide or an accidental drug overdose.

September 15 — Miller and Morath have daughter, Rebecca Augusta.

1964 *After the Fall* is produced and published. *Fall* was written as the inaugural production for the newly established Lincoln Center Repertory Theater. Elia Kazan directs, Robert Whitehead produces.

Incident at Vichy is produced and, one year later, published.

1965 Miller is elected president of PEN, an international literary organization (term expires in 1969).

1966 *Death of a Salesman* is presented on CBS to an audience of seventeen million.

Isadore Miller dies on the day Miller makes the opening speech at the 1966 New York PEN Congress.

1967 *I Don't Need You Any More*, a collection of nine short stories, is published.

In April, *The Crucible* is produced on television.

1968 *The Price* is produced and published.

Miller serves as Eugene McCarthy delegate to the Democratic National Convention in Chicago.

Miller petitions the Soviet government to lift the ban on the works of Aleksandr Solzhenitsyn.

1969 *In Russia* (with photographs by Inge Morath), a travel journal is published.

In February, *The Price* closes after 425 performances.

Miller refuses to allow his works to be published in Greece in protest of that government's oppression of writers.

1970 In February, Miller supports a Roxbury, Connecticut, high school teacher who refuses to say the Pledge of Allegiance in her classroom.

At the end of the year, the Soviet Union, reacting to *In Russia* and to Miller's advocacy of freedom for writers worldwide, bans all of Miller's works.

1971 Miller helps to free Brazilian playwright Augusto Boal from prison; Boal visits the U.S. following his release.

Miller is elected to the American Academy of Arts and Letters.

1972 *The Creation of the World and Other Business* is produced and published; runs for twenty performances.

Miller serves as a delegate to Democratic National Convention in Miami.

1974 *Up from Paradise* (musical version of *Creation of the World*) is produced.

1975 Miller appears with a panel before the Senate Permanent Subcommittee on Investigations to support the freedom of writers throughout the world.

Czech poet and playwright Pavel Kohout addresses an open letter to Miller and other noted writers to assure their continuing help to further the cause of human rights.

1976 November 24 — Charges against Peter Reilly in the murder of his mother are dropped after the new State's Attorney of Connecticut announces that he has discovered evidence in the files of his predecessor that tended to clear the youth. Miller had become deeply involved in the case earlier in the year, at one point hiring a private detective who discovered much of the new evidence presented.

1977 In January, *In the Country* (with photographs by wife Inge Morath), a journal, is published.

In April, *The Archbishop's Ceiling* is produced for a limited run at Washington's Kennedy Center to negative reviews.

1978 *The Theater Essays of Arthur Miller* is published.

In November, NBC produces the comedy *Fame* to lukewarm reviews.

1979 *Chinese Encounters* (with photographs by Inge Morath), a journal, is published.

1980 *Playing for Time*, a film adapted from the memoir by Fania Fénelon, is produced for television and published. Miller is criticized by the author and many liberals for his defense of CBS's choice to cast Vanessa Redgrave in the leading role.

The American Clock is produced and published. With his sister Joan playing Rose Baum, a character based on their mother Augusta, the play closes after only twelve performances.

Miller is hospitalized several days in Waterbury Hospital Health Center in December with a broken leg.

1981 *Arthur Miller's Collected Plays, Volume II* is published.

1982 *Some Kind of Love Story* and *Elegy for a Lady*, two short plays, are produced at the Long Wharf Theatre in New Haven to unremarkable reviews. Later in the year both are published.

1983 *Salesman in Beijing* is published. In May, *Salesman* wins standing ovations and high praise from Chinese audiences. While in China, fire extensively damages the Miller's home in Roxbury, Connecticut.

1984 Miller awarded the Kennedy Center Honors for distinguished lifetime achievement At the opening banquet in the Cannon Building, he appreciates the irony, pointed out by friend and lawyer Joe Rauh, of being honored in the same room in which his HUAC hearing had been held twenty-eight years earlier.

Miller is involved in a dispute with the experimental off-off-Broadway Wooster Group over their unauthorized use of scenes from *The Crucible* in a play entitled *L.S.D.*

1985 Miller travels to Istanbul with Harold Pinter to lend solidarity to Turkish writers.

Death of a Salesman, with Dustin Hoffman, is aired on CBS to a television audience of twenty-five million people.

1986 *The Archbishop's Ceiling* is produced and published.

1987 *Clara* and *I Can't Remember Anything*, two one-act plays are published as *Danger: Memory!*, and produced.

Timebends, Miller's autobiography, is published.

1989 The Arthur Miller Centre for American Studies at the University of East Anglia, Norwich, is established to encourage the study of all aspects of the United States in Britain. The Centre's Director: Christopher Bigsby.

1990 Miller writes screenplay *Everybody Wins*. It is filmed, starring Nick Nolte and Debra Winger, directed by Karel Reisz.

1991 *The Ride Down Mount Morgan* is produced and published. World premiere in London closes after three months.

1992 First ever International Arthur Miller Conference is held in April at Millersville University in Pennsylvania.

Arthur Miller Society is founded.

1993 *The Last Yankee* (full-length) is produced and published.

Miller is awarded the National Medal of the Arts by President Clinton.

1994 *Broken Glass* is produced and published. *Broken Glass* receives nomination as Best Play, losing to Kushner's *Angels in America: Perestroika.*

Miller is awarded a one year appointment as Professor of Contemporary Theatre at Oxford University.

1995 Arthur Miller celebrates his eightieth birthday.

Miller receives an honorary doctorate from Oxford University in October.

2nd International Arthur Miller Conference is held in April at Millersville University in Pennsylvania.

Homely Girl, A Life and Other Stories, a collection of three novellas set in pre- and post-war Manhattan is published by Viking to mark his birthday on October 17.

Miller becomes involved in the appeal of Richard Lapointe, a brain-damaged dishwasher, who was convicted of raping and killing his wife's eighty-eight-year-old grandmother after a nine-hour interrogation in which Lapointe made three contradictory confessions. "This is a great problem," says Miller. "It ought to interest people that when they get a confession from an innocent man, a murderer gets a passport to freedom."

While dining at a New York restaurant with family and friends, a photographer/paparazzi, apparently resembling Joe DiMaggio, interrupts the party and asks Miller if he still dreams about former wife Marilyn Monroe. Reportedly, believing this man to be DiMaggio, Miller gets extremely upset and "punches out the reporter." Later, in an interview, Miller says he merely asked the man to leave the restaurant.

1996 *The Crucible* is made into a film. Directed by Nicholas Hytner and starring Daniel Day-Lewis, Winona Ryder, Joan Allen, and Paul Scofield. Film is produced by Miller's son Robert.

The Crucible: Screenplay is published by Penguin.

Miller's daughter, Rebecca, marries actor Daniel Day-Lewis.

Third International Arthur Miller Conference is held on 18 September 1996 at Utica College.

1997 Arthur Miller receives an Academy Award nomination for his screenplay of *The Crucible.*

Miller undergoes eye surgery on his retina to correct his vision.

1998 Critically acclaimed revival of *A View from the Bridge* opens Off Broadway by the Roundabout Theatre Company. Production moves to the Neil Simon Theatre on Broadway and receives numerous Tony Award nominations and wins as Best Revival and Best Actor in a Play for Anthony La Paglia.

Fourth International Arthur Miller Conference, "Arthur Miller's Dramatic Theory and Strategy," is held at Millersville University, Millersville, Pennsylvania.

Premiere of Miller's first new play in five years, *Mr. Peters' Connections*, Off Broadway by the Signature Theatre Company. The production stars Peter Falk and Anne Jackson.

Miller named the winner of the first PEN/Laura Pels Foundation Award to a master American dramatist.

Miller is named the recipient of the Lucille Lortel Award for Lifetime Achievement at the 13th annual awards ceremony.

Arthur Miller Symposium held 17 April 1998 at the University of Evansville in Indiana.

1999 February 10—*Death of a Salesman* opens on Broadway, exactly fifty years after the original production and stars Brian Dennehy and Elizabeth Franz, directed by Robert Falls. It receives mostly positive reviews.

Miller appears as a Martha Heasley Cox lecturer at the 1998-99 Major Authors Series, held 22 April, at the Morris Dailey Auditorium at San Jose State University Center for Literary Arts.

Fifth International Arthur Miller Conference is held at St. Francis College in Brooklyn Heights, New York.

2000 March 19 — Miller and fellow-author William Styron sign autographs and chat with Cuban students in Havana on a visit to Cuba aimed at strengthening U.S. cultural links with the island nation.

Introduction: Miller and His Critics

Near the end of Arthur Miller's *Broken Glass* (1994), Dr. Harry Hyman suggests to a physically sick and emotionally weak Phillip Gellburg that he will find the simple solution to his ills, as well as the cure for his wife's paralysis, by taking a long hard look at himself in a mirror. "You hate yourself, that's what's scaring her to death," Hyman lectures. "That's my opinion. How it's possible I don't know, but I think you helped paralyze her with this 'Jew, Jew, Jew' coming out of your mouth and the same time she reads it in the paper and it's coming out of the radio day and night? You wanted to know what I think. . . . that's what I think."[1]

Hyman is asserting that only through an examination of his own soul will Gellburg come to understand his kinship with his persecutors; only then will he realize that there is no one left to blame. Indeed, the doctor's prescription for what ails Phillip and Sylvia Gellburg might very well serve as a remedy for the afflictions of nearly every one of Arthur Miller's protagonists. It is also, quite possibly, the reason why Miller has received both laudatory praise and vociferous attacks for his works. Miller demands of his characters and, by implication, his audiences and critics, to look within themselves to find the enemy.

Miller's protagonists, at once both complex and contradictory, are most often male and traditionally carry the moral burden of the play. Their suffering, sacrifice, and deliberate acts of passive resistance are presented as ideals with which the audience is meant to identify and respect. Miller crafts his characters to attain their allotment of personal heroism only through the acceptance of their social guilt. Each man's tragedy ultimately reveals itself as a loss of private honor in the face of a more public responsibility.

Typically, investigations and critical analysis of the works have centered on Miller as a social and moral dramatist, reworking and reevaluating Miller's own professed theme of man's relation to community and self. These socio-politico-economic approaches to Miller's plays attempt to foreground the central crisis of survival and personal identity amid the backdrop of modern American social drama. While some explore the psychological processes and implications of the actions of his protagonists in relation to larger social issues (Weales, Murray, and Moss), others evaluate Miller on the basis of his public commitment to correcting the problems of society and his preoccupation with defining a moral existence for oneself in an ultimately immoral world (Hayman, Welland, and Corrigan).

James J. Martine endorses what he sees as Miller's greatest strength—his virile and otherwise heroic capacity to know what he means and fearlessly mean what he says. He proclaims Miller a "courageous writer" who has repeatedly demonstrated for the world his personal and political mettle. Miller's essays are particularly valuable, Martine continues, "because they reveal him to be a humanistic and humane human being concerned with the 'community' of the theater and the world, and they express his vision *clearly*." Steven Centola designates Miller's tragic vision as "distinctly American," that his dramas convey "an optimistic toughness," and that "he has been as fearless in tackling hard issues and in facing adversity in his private life as he has been in his artistic one." Ultimately, Centola contends, Miller's plays "offer real hope" that can be reclaimed "if the individual, recognizing his imperfections and capacity to commit the most horrible atrocities, accepts the freedom to choose and takes responsibility for all willfully chosen actions."[2]

It is important to note that critical commentary of Miller's drama often includes references to the playwright's controversial political life and socially responsive commitments. In addition to his literary output, then, part of Arthur Miller's renown stems from the manner in which he has chosen to conduct his public life beyond the theatre—his civically conscious actions on behalf of those unable, or otherwise not in the position, to speak for themselves. Since his early days as a writer, Miller has publicly lent his name as well as his finances to numerous causes, mainly those involving the victimization of the individual either at the hands of government, both foreign and domestic, local and national, or organizations dedicated to opposing free speech or other constitutionally sanctioned rights.

As early as 1941, as a newly discovered essay proves ("Hitler's Quarry" in *Jewish Survey*), Miller attempted to draw attention to the persecution of Jews worldwide and publicly condemned the U.S. State Department's failure to help the thousands of Jews who were attempting to escape Nazism. In 1944, with the publication of his only novel *Focus*, Miller became one of the first American authors to write a book in which anti-Semitism played a pivotal role.

More recently, in 1970 Miller publicly supported a Roxbury high school teacher who refused to say the Pledge of Allegiance in her classroom. In 1972, Miller, through the press, attacked the three-year sentence imposed on publisher Ralph Ginzburg for a 1963 obscenity conviction. During 1975 and 1976, he was deeply involved in the Peter Reilly murder case—personally hiring a detective who eventually uncovered new evidence that overturned Reilly's conviction of the first degree murder of his mother. In 1980, Miller was heavily criticized in the media by author Fania Fénelon and many liberals for his defense of CBS's choice to cast Vanessa Redgrave in the leading role of a Jewish woman organizing an orchestra in Auschwitz in *Playing for Time*, in view of Redgrave's controversial and much-publicized support of the Palestine Liberation Organization. More recently, Miller has involved himself in the criminal appeal of Richard Lapointe, a brain-damaged dishwasher, who was convicted of raping and killing his wife's 88-year-old grandmother after a nine-hour interrogation in which Lapointe made three contradictory confessions.

At the epicenter of his much publicized political life stands his one defining moment: Miller's refusal to name names in 1956 before the House Committee on Un-American Activities. With the recent release of the American film version of *The Crucible* (1996), and the debate regarding the awarding of an Academy Award for Lifetime Achievement to Miller's old friend and colleague Elia Kazan, a new generation of Americans is learning of Miller's courageous personal and political stand against the committee.

Yet no matter how honorably he has conducted himself in his public life, Miller has forever experienced a disquieting love-hate relationship with his critics. While being hailed as a dramatist of universal relevance, adept at depicting the common Everyman, he as been attacked for his use of subject matter, dramatic structure, character, and language in his literature.

To his champions, he is lauded as "one of the three or four leading playwrights of the American Theatre" (Neil Carson), "an unquestionable master of the family drama" (Allan Lewis), "a central figure in the drama and consciousness of our time" (Raymond Williams), "the most socially conscious of all major American Dramatists" (Dennis Welland), "one of the two playwrights of the post-war American theater who deserve any consideration as [a] major dramatist" (Gerald Weales), and "an authentic Wunderkind, the ablest writer of stage tragedies since Eugene O'Neill" (Robert Sylvester).[3]

To his detractors, Miller is "old fashioned" (Simon), "dreary" (Nightingale), "tiresome" (Brustein), "overrated" (Macaulay), and considered an old-school playwright whose dramas are primarily concerned with investigating masculine issues and, according to Iska Alter, defining the constituents of male identity within their respective, and decidedly patriarchal, systems of culture. Kenneth Tynan pointedly states that, "Miller's plays are hard, 'patrist,' athletic, concerned mostly with men." Arthur Oberg calls Miller's art "masculine and craggy," while David Savran says Miller personifies "masculine playwriting."[4]

While they will perpetually argue over the caliber of his writing, most critics will acknowledge that one of Miller's greatest strengths as a dramatist is his penetrating insight into the American family, however dated that insight is thought to be. In his early plays, Miller's protagonists were viewed by audiences, scholars, and commentators as generalized middle-class American common men who are confronted throughout the action of the dramas with the problems of everyday life. His focus on the father-son conflict is considered by many to be the most universal of his thematic qualities and one of his greatest contributions to the development of American social drama.

Another distinguishing trait of Miller's writing is his interest in translating the larger social concerns of perseverance and public prominence into a crisis of private identity and a personal quest for forgiveness. Embedded deep within his literary canon is a fundamental tension between the protagonist and the society in which he inhabits, between his private consciousness and his public responsibility. The Miller hero always has a double debt to pay: the one he owes to himself, and the one he owes to the greater social order of mankind. In Miller's drama, this conflict between the public and the private can manifest as a character who is powerless to stop a series of events that he has unconsciously set in motion (Eddie Carbone, John Proctor, Joe Keller), a character who is struggling for individual or collective self-realization (Gay Langdon, Sylvia Gellburg, Quentin), or a character who, in striving to define himself, is ready to pay with his life for a measure of personal integrity (Willy Loman, Von Berg).

Miller's plays are very closely tied to the personal and/or political events in his life. Issues of betrayal, guilt, loss of identity, and self-destruction caused by the refusal to connect with the outside world haunt Miller's canon. As Miller looked back at national and international catastrophes, it became evident that issues such as personal survival and identity were at the root of all economic, cultural, and political disasters. In *Timebends*, Miller contextualizes his life in relation to world history and the effects incidents such as the Great War, World War II, the Holocaust, HUAC, the Vietnam conflict, the Nazi war crimes trials, not to mention the Salem witch hunts, have had on configuring his current sensibilities. Specifically, the events surrounding the Great Depression frame Miller's perceptions regarding American democratic society as well as his early ideological beliefs.

It must be noted that critical response to Miller's dramas is more positive abroad, especially in England, than in his home country. Contemporary commentary unceasingly points this out but offers little in the way of a definitive explanation. The reason could involve a simple difference in sensibilities or because, as has been argued by cultural anthropologists, England is a country that enjoys all things American. Perhaps the reaction is tied to the large number of critics who report on productions abroad; their sheer numbers guaranteeing a more even-handed evaluation.

As the length and scope of this bibliography demonstrates, there is an extensive and substantial body of Miller scholarship in print, including comparative analyses, genre considerations, thematic and structural evaluations, theatrical perspectives, and gender studies. The first dissertation on Miller was written in 1952 and traced the ideological and artistic developments of post-depression American drama, concluding that Miller exhibited a bond with preceding generations of American writers "by continuing the tradition of protest against the dominant standards of materialism and success."[5] In addition to literary and theatrical approaches to the Miller canon, an impressive number of interdisciplinary studies exist. These include those from such disparate fields of study as sociology, marketing, theology, psychology, business, law, history, science, and statistics.

Recently, a new examination is taking place among feminist critics who view Miller and his use of the female character as evidence of female power determined by masculine authority. Some of the most interesting work in the area of female character analysis and gender role stereotyping (both male and female) and its relation to the Miller canon can be found in studies by Iska Alter, June Schlueter, David Savran, Sue-Ellen Case, Elin Diamond, Gayle Austin, Jeffrey D. Mason, Charlotte Goodman, Kay Stanton, John Clum, and Jill Dolan. They comprise but of a few of the feminist critics currently exploring Miller's use of female icon (Mother, Wife, Mistress, Whore, Golden Girl) as an important new evaluative methodology.

Throughout the Miller canon, man's vital need to know himself and identify his relationship to the prevailing social order serves as the overall thematic impetus of his dramas, and, in turn, frames the psychic action of his plays. To drive home his point, Miller employs this theme on three different levels at the same time: as an unmasking that occurs within the textual reality of his dramas whereby Miller forces his protagonists to come to terms with their varying degrees of guilt; as an autobiographical recognition of Miller's own life and political concerns dramatized within his literature, producing a radical mimesis of life imitating art imitating life; and, lastly, as a metatextual enlightenment that takes place beyond the drama as the audience members identify personally with Miller's characters and their psychic dilemmas. The metaphor of the mirror, then, as a surface that forms images of true representation by reflection, most closely describes Miller's complex and active literary technique of dramatizing mankind's, as well as his own, passionate struggle for understanding.

With few exceptions, Miller's *oeuvre* contains deeply American themes, stories, and characters—the salesman, Puritan farmer, longshoreman, cowboy, Yankee, detective, Jewish-American businessman, G.I., housewife. His works expose the flaws and cracks in the foundations of social and political order. Indeed, Miller is a man of many passions—and passionate people have a tendency to offend, not necessarily by what they say and do, but by the absolute determination and moral certainty with which they conduct their lives and craft their art.

Harold Clurman accurately labels Miller a moralist and defines that trait as "a man who believes [that] he possesses the truth and aims to convince others of it."[6] American critics, on the main, seem to resist a moralist theatre, and charge that, while having its rightful place in theatre history, it is not a truly relevant way of presenting plays in a contemporary world. Yet the paradox continues, for not only are Miller's plays in continual production around the world but also a recent spate of highly successful and critically acclaimed revivals points to Miller having, finally, the last laugh.

Notes

1. Arthur Miller, *Broken Glass* (New York: Penguin, 1994), 151.

2. James J. Martine, *Critical Essays on Arthur Miller* (New York: G. K. Hall, 1979), xi.

3. Neil Carson, *Arthur Miller* (New York: Grove, 1982), 1; Allan Lewis, *American Plays and Playwrights of the Contemporary Theatre* (New York: Crown, 1970), 52; Raymond Williams, "The Realism of Arthur Miller," *"Death of a Salesman": Text and Criticism*, ed. Gerald Weales (New York: Viking, 1967), 325; Dennis Welland, *Miller the Playwright* (London: Methuen, 1983), 12; Gerald Weales, "Arthur Miller: Man and His Image," *"Death of a Salesman": Text*

and Criticism (New York: Penguin, 1977), 350; Robert Sylvester, "Brooklyn Boy Makes Good," *Saturday Evening Post*, 16 July 1949: 26-27.

4. John Simon, "Settling the Account," *Commonweal*, 1 March 1968: 655-56; Benedict Nightingale, "Family Sores," *New Statesman*, 14 March 1969: 384-85; Robert Brustein, "Still Searching for Theatre," *New Republic*, 3 August 1998: 29-30; Alastair Macaulay, "*Broken Glass*," *Financial Times*, 1 March 1995, *Theatre Record* 15.4 (1995): 225-26; Iska Alter, "Betrayal and Blessedness: Explorations of Feminine Power in *The Crucible*, *A View from the Bridge*, and *After the Fall*," *Feminist Rereadings of Modern American Drama*, ed. June Schlueter (Cranbury, N.J.: AUP, 1989), 116; Kenneth Tynan, "American Blues: The Plays of Arthur Miller and Tennessee Williams," *Encounter* 2.5 (1954): 13-19; Arthur Oberg, "*Death of a Salesman* and Arthur Miller's Search for Style," *Criticism* 9 (1967): 303-11; David Savran, *Communists, Cowboys, and Queers* (Minneapolis: U of Minnesota P, 1992), 5.

5. William J. Fisher, "Trends in Post-Depression American Drama: A Study of the Works of William Saroyan, Tennessee Williams, Irwin Shaw, and Arthur Miller," Diss. New York U, 1952.

6. Harold Clurman, "Arthur Miller: Theme and Variations," *Theater, The Annual of the Repertory Theater of Lincoln Center, Volume One*, ed. Barry Hyams (New York: Repertory Theater Pub./Playbill, 1964), 15.

PART I
PRIMARY SOURCES

1. Stage Plays, Screenplays, Teleplays, and Smaller Dramatic Works (published)

After the Fall. [periodical] *Saturday Evening Post* 1 February 1964: 34–36, 40–41, 44–59. [final stage version, revised to cut eighteen minutes] New York: Viking, 1964. London: Secker and Warburg, 1965. [acting edition, revised stage version] New York: DPS, 1965. Rpt. in *Arthur Miller's Collected Plays: Vol. 2*. New York: Viking, 1981, 125–242. Rpt. in *Arthur Miller Plays: Two*. London: Methuen, 1988. Rpt. in *The Portable Arthur Miller*. Ed. Christopher Bigsby. New York: Penguin, 1995. 259–358.

After the Fall [television adaptation]. New York: Bantam, 1974.

All My Sons: A Play in Three Acts. New York: Reynal and Hitchcock, 1947. [acting edition] New York: DPS, 1947. Rpt. in *Arthur Miller's Collected Plays*. New York: Viking, 1957. 57–127. Rpt. in *Arthur Miller Plays: One*. London: Methuen, 1988.

The American Clock. [acting edition] New York: DPS, 1982. [revised stage version] *The Archbishop's Ceiling* and *The American Clock*. New York: Grove, 1989. Rpt. in *Arthur Miller Plays: Three*. London: Methuen, 1990. Rpt. as *The American Clock: A Vaudeville*. New York: DPS, 1992. Rpt. in *The Portable Arthur Miller*. Ed. Christopher Bigsby. New York: Penguin, 1995. 359–446.

The Archbishop's Ceiling. [revised stage version] London: Methuen, 1984. [acting edition] New York: DPS, 1985. [revised stage version] Rpt. with *The American Clock*. New York: Grove, 1989. Rpt. in *Arthur Miller Plays: Three*. London: Methuen, 1990.

Arthur Miller Plays: Five. London: Methuen, 1995.

Contains *The Last Yankee*, *The Ride Down Mount Morgan*, and *Almost Everybody Wins* [screenplay].

Arthur Miller Plays: Four. London: Methuen, 1994.
Contains *The Golden Years*, *The Man Who Had All the Luck*, *I Can't Remember Anything*, and *Clara*.

Arthur Miller Plays: Three. London: Methuen, 1990.
Contains *The American Clock*, *The Archbishop's Ceiling*, and *Two-Way Mirror* [two one-act plays *Elegy for a Lady* and *Some Kind of Love Story*].

Arthur Miller's Adaptation of "An Enemy of the People" by Henrik Ibsen. New York: Viking, 1951. [acting edition] New York: DPS, 1951. Rpt. in *Seeds of Modern Drama*. Ed. Norris Houghton. New York: Dell, 1963. [paperback edition] New York: Penguin, 1977.

Arthur Miller's Collected Plays. New York: Viking, 1957. Rpt. as *Arthur Miller Plays: One*. London: Methuen, 1988.
Contains "The Introduction to the *Collected Plays*," *All My Sons*, *Death of a Salesman*, *The Crucible*, *A Memory of Two Mondays*, and *A View from the Bridge* [two-act version].

Arthur Miller's Collected Plays: Vol. 2. New York: Viking, 1981. Rpt. as *Arthur Miller Plays: Two*. London: Methuen, 1988.
Contains "Introduction," *The Misfits* [cinema-novel], *After the Fall*, *Incident at Vichy*, *The Price*, *The Creation of the World and Other Business*, and *Playing for Time* [screenplay adaptation].

Broken Glass. [acting edition] New York: DPS, 1994. New York: Penguin, 1994. Rpt. in *The Portable Arthur Miller*. Ed. Christopher Bigsby. New York: Penguin, 1995. 489–568.

The Creation of the World and Other Business. New York: Viking, 1973. Excerpt rpt. in *Vogue* January 1973: 132–33. [acting edition] New York: DPS, 1973. Rpt. in *Arthur Miller's Collected Plays: Vol. 2*. New York: Viking, 1981. 375–446. Rpt. in *Arthur Miller Plays: Two*. London: Methuen, 1988.

The Crucible: A Play in Four Acts. New York: Viking, 1953. [periodical] Rpt. with additional scene [Act II, Scene II] in *Theatre Arts* 37 (October 1953): 35–67. [acting edition] *The Crucible: Drama in Two Acts*. New York: DPS, 1954 [Act I of first edition becomes Act I, Scene I; Act II becomes Act I, Scene II; added scene becomes Act II, Scene I; Act II of first edition becomes Act II, Scene II; Act IV becomes Act II, Scene III]. Rpt. in *Arthur Miller's Collected Plays*. New York: Viking, 1957. 223–329. Rpt. in *The Portable Arthur Miller*. Ed. Harold Clurman. New York: Viking, 1971. 134–282. Rpt. in *"The Crucible": Text and Criticism*. Ed. Gerald Weales. New York: Viking, 1971. New York: Penguin, 1996. "A Private Meeting of John and Abigail" [added scene to Act II]. Rpt. in *Twentieth Century Interpretations of "The Crucible": a Collection of Critical Essays*. Ed. John H. Ferres. Englewood Cliffs, N.J.: Prentice-Hall, 1972. 109–12. Rpt. in *Arthur Miller Plays: One*. London: Methuen, 1988. Rpt. in *The Portable Arthur Miller*. Ed. Christopher Bigsby. New York: Penguin, 1995. 132–258.

The Crucible: Screenplay. New York: Penguin, 1996.

Danger: Memory! [*I Can't Remember Anything* and *Clara*]. New York: Grove, 1986. London: Methuen, 1986.[acting edition] New York: DPS, 1987. Rpt. in *Arthur Miller Plays: Four*. London: Methuen, 1994.

Death of a Salesman: Certain Private Conversations in Two Acts and a Requiem. New York: Viking, 1949. [periodical] Rpt. in *Theatre Arts* 35 (March 1951): 50–91. [acting edition] New York: DPS, 1952. [paperback edition] New York: Bantam, 1951, 1955. Rpt. in *New Voices in the American Theatre*. New York: Random House, 1955. 111–226. Rpt. in *Arthur Miller's Collected Plays*. New York: Viking, 1957. 129–222. Rpt. in *"Death of a Salesman": Text and Criticism*. Ed. Gerald Weales. New York: Viking, 1967. 11–139. New York: Penguin, 1996. 11–139. Rpt. in *The Portable Arthur Miller*. Ed. Harold Clurman. New York: Penguin, 1977. 3–133. Rpt. in *Arthur Miller Plays: One*. London: Methuen, 1988. Rpt. in *The Portable Arthur Miller*. Ed. Christopher Bigsby. New York: Penguin, 1995. 19–131. [paperback edition] New York: Penguin, 1998.

Death of a Salesman: 50th Anniversary Edition. New York: Penguin, 1999.

Elegy for a Lady. [acting edition] New York: DPS, 1980. [periodical] *Esquire* December 1980: 98–104. Rpt. in *Arthur Miller Plays: Three*. London: Methuen, 1990. Rpt. in *EST Marathon '96: The One-Act Plays*. Lyme, N.H.: Smith and Kraus, 1998.

Everybody Wins [screenplay]. New York: Grove Weidenfeld, 1990.

The Golden Years [radio play 1939–40, produced in 1987 for BBC Radio] and *The Man Who Had All the Luck* [1944]. London: Methuen, 1989. Rpt. in *Arthur Miller Plays: Four*. London: Methuen, 1994. *The Golden Years* excerpt in *The Portable Arthur Miller*. Ed. Christopher Bigsby. New York: Penguin, 1995. 3–18. [acting edition] New York: DPS, 1996. *The Golden Years* also known as *Montezuma the King*. MS in the Harry Ransom Humanities Research Center, The University of Texas at Austin.

I Can't Remember Anything. *Telling Tales: New One-Act Plays*. Ed. Eric Lane. New York: Penguin, 1993. Rpt. in *Arthur Miller Plays: Four*. London: Methuen, 1994.

"An Immigrant's Land" [Aria from Act II, Scene 5, for opera version of *A View from the Bridge*]. Rpt. in Bruce Weber, "Birth of an Opera: From Words to Music." *New York Times* 4 August 1999: P1.

Incident at Vichy. New York: Viking, 1965. [acting edition] New York: DPS, 1966. London: Secker and Warburg, 1966. Rpt. in *The Portable Arthur Miller*. Ed. Harold Clurman. New York: Penguin, 1977. 283–342. Rpt. in *Arthur Miller's Collected Plays: Vol. 2*. New York: Viking, 1981. 243–91. New York: Penguin, 1985. Rpt. in *Arthur Miller Plays: Two*. London: Methuen, 1988.

"I Think about You a Great Deal" [monologue]. *Václav Havel: Living in Truth. Twenty-Two Essays Published on the Occasion of the Award of the Erasmus Prize to Václav Havel*. Ed. Jan Vladislav. London: Faber and Faber, 1986. 263–65. Rpt. in *Literary Cavalcade* (September 1990): 24–25.

A short poignant monologue "written as an expression of solidarity with Václav Havel, for performance at the International Theatre Festival in Avignon on 21 July 1982." The WRITER speaks to a memory of the IMPRISONED ONE about his thoughts regarding freedom and writing, incited by his receiving a bundle of mail, each letter requesting help to "save" something.

The Last Yankee. [one-scene acting version]. New York: DPS, 1991.

The Last Yankee. [two-scene version] London: Methuen Drama, 1993. [acting edition] New York: DPS, 1993. New York: Penguin, 1994. Rpt. in *The Portable Arthur Miller*. Ed. Christopher Bigsby. New York: Penguin, 1995. 447–88. Rpt. in *Arthur Miller Plays: Five*. London: Methuen, 1995.

Let's Make Love [revisions to screenplay].

Revised final shooting script, dated 30 December 1959, private owner. On second page it states, "This version by Hal Kanter, Arthur Miller, George Cukor, and Jerry Wald."

The Man Who Had All the Luck. *Cross-Section: A Collection of New American Writing*. Ed. Edwin Seaver. New York: Fischer, 1944. 486–552. Revised in *The Golden Years* and *The Man Who Had All the Luck*. London: Methuen, 1989. Rpt. in *Arthur Miller Plays: Four*. London: Methuen, 1994. [acting edition] New York: DPS, 1996.

A Memory of Two Mondays. *A View from the Bridge: Two One-Act Plays*. New York: Viking, 1955. [acting edition] *A Memory of Two Mondays: Play in One Act*. New York: DPS, 1956. [periodical] Rpt. in *Theatre Arts* September 1956: 33–68. Rpt. in *Arthur Miller's Collected Plays*. New York: Viking, 1957. 331–76. Rpt. in *Arthur Miller Plays: One*. London: Methuen, 1988.

The Misfits [cinema novel]. New York: Viking, 1961. [paperback edition] New York: Dell, 1961. London: Secker and Warburg, 1961. Excerpt rpt. in *The Portable Arthur Miller*. Ed. Harold Clurman. New York: Viking, 1971. 481–94. Rpt. in *Arthur Miller's Collected Plays: Vol. 2*. New York: Viking, 1981. 5–124. Rpt. in *Arthur Miller Plays: Two*. London: Methuen, 1988.

The Misfits [screenplay]. *Film Scripts Three*. Eds. George P. Garrett, O. B. Hardison Jr., and Jane R. Gelfman. New York: Irvington, 1989. 202–382.

Mr. Peters' Connections. [acting edition] New York: DPS, 1998. New York: Penguin, 1999.

Playing for Time [teleplay, produced in 1980 for CBS television]. New York: Bantam, 1981. Rpt. in *Arthur Miller's Collected Plays: Vol. 2*. New York: Viking, 1981. 447–531. Rpt. in *Arthur Miller Plays: Two*. London: Methuen, 1988.

Playing for Time [full length stage play adapted from teleplay by Miller and based upon the book of the same title by Fania Fénelon]. Chicago: Dramatic Publishing Company, 1985. London: N. Hern, 1990.

The Portable Arthur Miller. Ed. Harold Clurman. New York: Viking, 1971. New York: Penguin, 1977.

Contains: "Biographical Notes" and "Editor's Introduction" by Clurman; texts of *Death of a Salesman*, *The Crucible*, *Incident at Vichy*, and *The Price*; full text of the short stories "The Misfits," "Fame," and "Fitter's Night"; excerpts from *In Russia* and *The Misfits* [cinema novel]; "Lines from California" [poem]; and a bibliography of works by Arthur Miller.

The Portable Arthur Miller. Ed. Christopher Bigsby. New York: Penguin, 1995.

Contains: "Biographical Notes" and "Introduction to the Original Edition" by Harold Clurman; "Introduction to the Revised Edition" by Bigsby; full texts of *Death of a Salesman*, *The Crucible*, *After the Fall*, *The American Clock*, *The Last Yankee*, and *Broken Glass*; excerpts from *Timebends* [autobiography, 1987] and *The Golden Years* [play, 1939]; and bibliography.

The Price. [periodical, condensed] *Saturday Evening Post* 10 February 1967: 40–45, 48–52, 54–59. New York: Viking, 1968. [acting edition] New York: DPS, 1968. Rpt. in *The Portable Arthur Miller*. Ed. Harold Clurman. New York: Penguin, 1977. 343–444. Rpt. in *Arthur Miller's Collected Plays: Vol. 2*. New York: Viking, 1981. 293–373. New York: Penguin, 1985. Rpt. in *Arthur Miller Plays: Two*. London: Methuen, 1988.

The Ride Down Mount Morgan. London: Methuen Drama, 1991. [revised stage version] New York: Penguin, 1992. [acting edition] New York: DPS, 1999. Rpt. in *Arthur Miller Plays: Five*. London: Methuen, 1995.

The Ryan Interview, or How It Was Around Here. *EST Marathon '95: The Complete One-Act Plays*. Ed. Marisa Smith. Lyme, N.H.: Smith and Kraus, 1995. 139–50. Rpt. in *Michigan Quarterly Review* 37.4 (Fall 1998): 803–16.

Some Kind of Love Story. [acting edition] New York: DPS, 1983. Rpt. in *Arthur Miller Plays: Three*. London: Methuen, 1990.

That They May Win. *The Best One-Act Plays of 1944*. Ed. Margaret Mayorga. New York: Dodd, Mead, 1945. 45–59.

Produced on 21 December 1943 for the Victory Committee of Welfare Center 67 at Albemarle Road, Brooklyn, by the Stage for Action theatre group in New York.

The Two-Way Mirror: Some Kind of Love Story and *Elegy for a Lady*. London: Methuen, 1984. Rpt. in *Arthur Miller Plays: Three*. London: Methuen, 1990.

Up from Paradise [musical version of *The Creation of the World and Other Business*]. [acting edition] New York: Samuel French, 1984. Full conductor's score [154 p.] located in the Library of Congress, Performing Arts Reading Room.

Produced in Ann Arbor, Michigan, 1974. Book and lyrics by Arthur Miller, music by Stanley Silverman.

A View from the Bridge [one-act play]. In *A View from the Bridge: Two One-Act Plays*. New York: Viking, 1955. [periodical] Rpt. in *Theatre Arts* 40 (September 1956): 31–68.

A View from the Bridge [full length play]. [acting edition] New York: DPS, 1957. London: Cresset Press, 1957. Rpt. in *Arthur Miller's Collected Plays*. New York: Viking, 1957. 377–439. New York: Viking, 1966. New York: Penguin 1977. Rpt. in *Arthur Miller Plays: One*. London: Methuen, 1988.

2. Radio Plays and Unpublished Works

Radio Plays

The Four Freedoms [radio play, 1942]. TMS in the Library of Congress.

Grandpa and the Statue [radio play, 1945, produced 26 March 1945 by Du Pont "Cavalcade of America"]. *Radio Drama in Action: Twenty-Five Plays of a Changing World*. Ed. Erik Barnouw. New York: Rinehart, 1945. 267–81. Rpt. in *Plays from Radio*. Eds. A. H. Lass, Earle L. McGill, and Donald Axelrod. Cambridge, Mass.: Houghton Mifflin, 1948. 236–52. Excerpt in *Drama on the Air*. Ed. David R Mackey. New York: Prentice-Hall, 1951. 361, 363–64, 377–78.

The Guardsman by Ferenc Molnar (1924) [radio play, produced 20 September 1945]. Adapted by Miller from translation by Hans Bartsch and Grace I. Colbron. *Theatre Guild on the Air*. Ed. H. William Fitelson. New York: Rinehart, 1947. 65–97. Excerpt in *Drama on the Air*. Ed. David R. Mackey. New York: Prentice-Hall, 1951. 328–29, 341–46. Excerpt in *Introduction to Radio and Television*. David C. Phillips, John M. Grogan, and Earl Hiryan. New York: Ronald, 1954. 148.

Joe, the Motorman [radio play, n.d.]. TMS at the Harry Ransom Humanities Research Center, The University of Texas at Austin.

Listen for the Sound of Wings [radio play, produced 19 April 1943]. Recording in the Museum of Television and Radio in New York.

Pride and Prejudice by Jane Austin; adaptation by Miller [radio play, 1945, produced on 10 November 1945]. Cataloged in the *Cavalcade of America* program log in the Library for the Performing Arts at Lincoln Center.

The Pussycat and the Expert Plumber Who Was a Man [radio play, Columbia Workshop]. *One Hundred Non-Royalty Radio Plays*. Ed. William Kozlenko. New York: Greenberg, 1941. 20–30. Rpt. in *Prose and Poetry of the World*. Ed. James K. Agnew and Agnes L. McCarthy. Syracuse: Singer, 1954.

The Story of Gus [radio play, unproduced]. Written for the OWI Domestic Radio Bureau to be part of a series depicting the lives of those who served as Merchant Marines. *Radio's Best Plays*. Ed. Joseph Liss. New York: Greenberg, 1947. 307–19.

Three Men on a Horse by George Abbott and John Cecil Holm; adaptation for radio by Miller [radio play, produced 6 January 1946]. *Theatre Guild on the Air*. Ed. William H. Fitelson. New York: Rinehart, 1947. 203–38.

Thunder from the Mountains [radio play, 1942, produced 28 September 1942]. Recording in the Museum of Television and Radio in New York.

William Ireland's Confession [radio play, Columbia Workshop]. *One Hundred Non-Royalty Radio Plays*. Ed. William Kozlenko. New York: Greenberg, 1941. 512–21.

Unconfirmed Radio Plays

The following nine radio plays are listed in *The Theater Essays of Arthur Miller* (Da Capo, 1996: 590–91) as held by the New York Public Library, Library for the Performing Arts, Lincoln Center.

The Battle of the Ovens [unpub. radio play, 1942, produced 22 June 1942]. MS in the Library for the Performing Arts at Lincoln Center.

Bernadine, I Love You [unpub. radio play, 1945, produced 5 March 1945]. MS in the Library for the Performing Arts at Lincoln Center.

Captain Paul [unpub. radio play, 1941, produced 27 October 1941]. MS in the Library for the Performing Arts at Lincoln Center.

The Eagle's Nest [unpub. radio play, 1942, produced 28 December 1942]. MS in the Library for the Performing Arts at Lincoln Center.

I Was Married in Bataan [unpub. radio play, 1942, produced 5 October 1942]. MS in the Library for the Performing Arts at Lincoln Center.

Joel Chandler Harris [unpub. radio play, 1941, produced 23 June 1941]. MS in the Library for the Performing Arts at Lincoln Center.

The Philippines Never Surrendered [unpub. radio play, 1945, produced 30 April 1945]. MS in the Library for the Performing Arts at Lincoln Center.

The Story of Canine Joe [unpub. radio play, 1944, produced 21 August 1944]. MS in the Library for the Performing Arts at Lincoln Center.

Toward a Farther Star [unpub. radio play, 1942, produced 2 November 1942]. MS in the Library for the Performing Arts at Lincoln Center.

Unpublished Other Works

Difficult Years [Italian motion picture, 1950].

According to William J. Fisher in his 1952 dissertation, "Trends in Post-Depression American Drama: A Study of the Works of William Saroyan, Tennessee Williams, Irwin Shaw, and Arthur Miller," Miller wrote the commentary for this film about fascism concerning an average Italian citizen during Mussolini's rise, reign, and fall. Plot: A likable little man who wants to be left alone is pressured to join the fascists in order to obtain a promotion. He yields, only to be trapped by the guilt of his association when the fascists are defeated.

Fame [play, produced in 1970 at The New Theater Workshop]. One-act play in a double-bill with *The Reason Why*.

Fame [play, produced in 1978 for NBC television]. Revised two-act version.

The Grass Still Grows [play, 1939, unproduced revision of *They Too Arise*]. TMS at the Harry Ransom Humanities Research Center, The University of Texas at Austin and in the Special Collections Library, Harlan Hatcher Graduate Library, The University of Michigan.

The Great Disobedience [play, 1938, produced as a laboratory production in 1938 at the University of Michigan]. MS in the Special Collections Library, Harlan Hatcher Graduate Library, The University of Michigan.

The Half-Bridge [play, 1941–43, unproduced]. TMS in Harry Ransom Humanities Research Center, The University of Texas at Austin.

Honors at Dawn [play, 1937, unproduced]. Original MS in the Hopwood Room, University of Michigan. Microfilm copy in the Special Collections Library, Harlan Hatcher Graduate Library, The University of Michigan.

The Hook [screenplay, 1951, unproduced]. TMS at Harry Ransom Humanities Research Center, The University of Texas at Austin.

"In Memorium" [sic] [short story, c.1932]. TMS in Harry Ransom Humanities Research Center, The University of Texas at Austin.

Listen My Children ["comedy satire with music," 1939, unproduced]. Written with Norman Rosten. TMS in the Library of Congress.

No Villain [play, 1936, produced 12 March 1937 at the University of Michigan]. Original MS in the Hopwood Room, University of Michigan. Microfilm copy in the Special Collections Library, Harlan Hatcher Graduate Library, The University of Michigan.

The Reason Why [produced in 1970 at The New Theater Workshop]. One-act play in a double bill with *Fame*. Made into a film in 1962, 14 min. in length, starring Eli Wallach, Robert Ryan. Produced by Gino Giglio.

One-act play asking basic questions into the nature of man and his violent tendencies. Also explored are issues relating to the causes and consequences of, and possible solutions to, war.

"Speech to the Neighborhood Watch Committee" in *Urban Blight* (monologue in musical review), based on an idea by John Tillinger, music by David Shire, lyrics by Richard Maltby Jr. Produced in New York, 1988.

Review of production: Winer, Linda. "Revue with Urban Bite." *Newsday* 20 June 1988: II: 7. "On the sobering side are Arthur Miller's monologue about the destructive effects of material possessions."

They Too Arise [play, 1936]. Revision of *No Villain*, produced in 1937 at the Lydia Mendelssohn Theatre. TMS at George Mason University. TMS in the Theatre Collection, New York Public Library. Excerpts appear in Benjamin Nelson's *Arthur Miller: Portrait of a Playwright*. New York: David McKay, 1970. 31–38.

Two Years ["unpublished memoir," n.d.]. TMS at the Harry Ransom Humanities Research Center, The University of Texas at Austin.

3. Fiction and Poetry (published)

"Bees [short story]." *Michigan Quarterly Review* 29.2 (Spring 1990): 152–57.

Subtitled "A Story to Be Spoken," "Bees" details a summer during his first marriage when Miller discovered a large colony of bees living in the wall of his Connecticut farmhouse and his ultimately futile efforts to eliminate them.

"Fame" [short story, original title "Recognitions"]. *I Don't Need You Any More*. New York: Viking, 1967. 166–74. Rpt. in *The Portable Arthur Miller*. Ed. Harold Clurman. New York: Viking, 1971. 495–502. Rpt. in *Yale Literary Magazine* 54.4 (March 1971): 32–40. Rpt. in Miller, *The Misfits and Other Stories*. New York: Scribner's, 1987. 166–74. Rpt. in Miller, *Homely Girl, A Life, and Other Stories*. New York: Viking, 1995. 49–58.

A playwright enjoying his new found financial and popular success stops in a bar for a drink only to meet an old friend from high school who does not recognize him as the famous man he has become. When the friend realizes that this is *the* Meyer Berkowitz, he acts as though they have just met for the first time.

"Fitter's Night" [short story]. In Miller, *I Don't Need You Any More*. New York: Viking, 1967. 175–223. Rpt. in *The Portable Arthur Miller*. Ed. Harold Clurman. New York: Viking, 1971. 503–49. Rpt. in Miller, *The Misfits and Other Stories*. New York: Scribner's, 1987. 175–223. Rpt. in Miller, *Homely Girl, A Life, and Other Stories*. New York: Viking, 1995. 61–115.

An evening in the life of shipfitter Tony Calabrese on the docks at the New York Naval Shipyard.

Focus [novel]. New York: Reynal and Hitchcock, 1945. London: Victor Gollancz, 1949. New York: Dell, 1959. New York: Penguin, 1978. New York: Arbor House, 1984. Syracuse: Syracuse UP, 1997.

Story of Lawrence Newman, an anti-Semite, who, after donning a pair of eyeglasses, is mistaken for a Jew and treated as such. Newman loses his job and his girlfriend and eventually comes to understand responsibility and the evils of hatred.

"Glimpse at a Jockey" [short story]. *Story* 5 (1962): 130–40. Rpt. in *The Noble Savage* 5 (October 1963): 138–40. Rpt in Miller, *I Don't Need You Any More*. New York: Viking, 1967. 114–17. Rpt. in Miller, *The Misfits and Other Stories*. New York: Scribner's, 1987. 114–17.

Monologue of a jockey talking about sex, his newly found father, and the horse-racing racket.

"Ham Sandwich" [fragment of a short story]. *Boston University Quarterly* 24.2 (1976): 5–6.

Homely Girl, A Life [novella]. *Grand Street* 2.1 (January 1992): 119–27. Rpt. in signed limited edition as *Homely Girl, A Life*. [Illustrated by Louise Bourgeois]. New York: Peter Blum Books, 1992. Rpt. in extract form as "Pages from 'Homely Girl, A Life'" in *Cimaise* April/May 1995: 57–66, with illustrations by Louise Bourgeois. Published in Great Britain as *Plain Girl, A Life*. London: Methuen, 1995. Rpt. in *Homely Girl, A Life, and Other Stories*. New York: Viking, 1995. 3–46.

Story of Janice Sessions, defined as an unattractive woman, who discovers true happiness in a relationship with a blind man. The story is told in a flashback as Janice wakes up beside the dead body of her blind lover and learns to survive despite her looks.

Homely Girl, A Life, and Other Stories [short stories]. New York: Viking, 1995.

Contains three short stories, all previously published: "Homely Girl, A Life," "Fame," and "Fitter's Night."

I Don't Need You Any More: Stories by Arthur Miller [short stories]. New York: Viking, 1967.

Contains foreword by Miller entitled, "About Distances" plus nine short stories: "I Don't Need You Any More," "Monte Sant' Angelo," "Please Don't Kill Anything," "The Misfits," "Glimpse at a Jockey," "The Prophecy," "Fame," "Fitter's Night," and "A Search for a Future."

"I Don't Need You Any More" [short story]. *Esquire* December 1959: 270–71, 274, 276, 278, 280, 283–84, 288, 290–92, 295–96, 298–309. Rpt. in Miller, *I Don't Need You Any More: Stories by Arthur Miller*. New York: Viking, 1967. 3–52. Rpt. in Miller, *The Misfits and Other Stories*. New York: Scribner's, 1987. 3–52.

Story that depicts the private world of a five-year-old Jewish boy.

"In Memoriam" [short story]. *New Yorker* 25 December 1995 and 1 January 1996: 80–81. Rpt. in *Sales and Marketing Management* 148 (August 1996): 56–57.

Discovered by critic John Lahr in 1995 while hunting in the Harry Ransom Humanities Research Center at the University of Texas at Austin for a suitable way for *The New Yorker* to honor Miller on the occasion of his 80th birthday, "In Memoriam" was written while Miller was seventeen years old. The short story foreshadows *Death of a Salesman* and centers on a salesman named Schoenzeit who worked for Miller's father and threw himself in front of a train.

"It Takes a Thief" [short story]. *Collier's* 8 February 1947: 23, 75–76. Rpt. in *Crime and Crime Again*. Eds. Bill Pronzini, Barry N. Malzberg, and Martin H. Greenberg. New York: Bonanza Books, 1986. 283–91.

Story that tells of the robbery of Mr. and Mrs. Shelton, a middle-class couple, who strangely stand mute when asked if the $91,000 in cash recovered with their jewelry was also a part of their missing items. Because of its unlawful origin, Shelton must deny that the money is his, losing his life savings in the process.

Jane's Blanket [children's story, ages 4–6; illustrated by Al Parker]. New York: Crowell-Collier, 1963. Rpt. with illustrations by Emily A. McCully. New York: Viking, 1972.

Story of a child being weaned from her blanket.

"Lines From California: Poem." *Harper's* May 1969: 97. Rpt. in *The Portable Arthur Miller*. Ed. Harold Clurman. New York: Viking, 1971. 561–62.

Collection of thoughts on the superficiality of life in California. Writes Miller, "Tragedy is when you lose your beat./Life is a preparation for retirement./The sun is good for business./Al Jolson left a trust fund which pays to floodlight his tomb at night forever; even in death a man should have bills."

"Lola's Lament" [poem]. *Unleashed: Poems by Writers' Dogs*. Eds. Amy Hempel and Jim Shepard. New York: Crown, 1995. 60–61.

Miller writes as if his dog Lola is speaking: "I worry. I have to because nobody else does. . . . Between the dangers and the greetings I'm simply exhausted."

The Misfits [short story]. *Esquire* October 1957: 158, 160–66. Rpt. in Miller, *I Don't Need You Any More*. New York: Viking, 1967. 79–113. Rpt. in *The Portable Arthur Miller*. Ed. Harold Clurman. New York: Penguin, 1977. 447–80. Rpt. in *Great "Esquire" Fiction: The Finest Stories from the First Fifty Years*. New York: Penguin, 1983. 127–44. Rpt. in Miller, *The Misfits and Other Stories*. New York: Scribner's, 1987. 79–113.

Story of three "misfit" men living in the new American west who rope and capture wild mustangs for sale as dog food.

"Monte Saint Angelo" [short story]. *Harper's* March 1951: 39–47. Rpt. in *Prize Stories of 1951*. Ed. Herschel Brickell. New York: Doubleday, 1951. Rpt. in *These, Your Children*. Ed. Harold Ribalow. New York: Beechhurst Press, 1952. Rpt. in *Stories of Sudden Truth*. Ed. Joseph Greene and Elizabeth Abell. New York: Ballantine, 1953. 167–80. Rpt. in *A Treasury of American Jewish Stories*. Ed. Harold U. Ribalow. New York: Thomas Yoseloff, 1958. 707–24. Rpt. as "Monte Sant' Angelo" in Miller, *I Don't Need You Any More*. New York: Viking, 1967. 53–70. Rpt. in *The Literature of American Jews*. Ed. Theodore L. Gross. New York: Free Press, 1973. 240–53. Rpt. in Miller, *The Misfits and Other Stories*. New York: Scribner's, 1987. 53–70. Rpt. in *A Treasury of Jewish Literature from Biblical Times to Today*. Ed. Gloria Goldreich. New York: Holt, 1992. 213–28.

Story of an American Jew who gradually develops an awareness of his ethnic identity.

"The 1928 Buick." *Atlantic* October 1978: 49–51, 54–56.

"The Plaster Masks" [short story]. *Encore: A Continuing Anthology* 9 (April 1946): 424–32.

A writer attempts to come to an understanding of the impact of war injuries on the veterans of World War II.

"Please Don't Kill Anything" [short story]. *Story* (1960): 126–31. Rpt. in *Noble Savage* 1 (March 1960): 126–31. Rpt. in *Redbook* October 1961: 48–49. Rpt. in Miller, *I Don't Need You Any More*. New

York: Viking, 1967. 71–78. Rpt. in *Avant Garde* 4 (September 1968). Rpt. in Miller, *The Misfits and Other Stories*. New York: Scribner's, 1987. 71–78.

Story of a couple walking on the beach and the woman's desperate attempt to save the throw-away fish discarded by fishermen.

"The Poosidin's Resignation" [fragment of a play]. *Boston University Quarterly* 24.2 (1976): 7–13.

"The Prophecy" [short story]. *Esquire* December 1961: 140–41, 286–87. Rpt. in Miller, *I Don't Need You Any More*. New York: Viking, 1967. 118–66. Rpt. in Miller, *The Misfits and Other Stories*. New York: Scribner's, 1987. 118–66.

Containing themes of loveless despair and aging, "The Prophecy" tells the story of Cleota Rummel, 49, and her small dinner party on the evening that her famous architect husband has gone on a trip. A Jewish fortuneteller/prophet offers Cleota some insight into her life and its lack of "climaxes." Moody and richly descriptive, we learn about the characters through their complex inner dialogue.

"Rain in a Strange City" [poem]. *Travel and Leisure* September 1974: 8.

"Recognitions" [short story]. *Esquire* July 1966: 76, 118. Rpt. as "Fame" in Miller, *I Don't Need You Any More.* New York: Viking, 1967. 118–74. Rpt. as "Fame" in *The Portable Arthur Miller.* Ed. Harold Clurman. New York: Viking, 1971. 495–502. Rpt. as "Fame" in Miller, *The Misfits and Other Stories*. New York: Scribner's, 1987. 118–74.

"A Search for a Future" [short story]. *Saturday Evening Post* 13 August 1966: 64–68, 70. Rpt. in *The Best American Short Stories, 1967.* Ed. Martha Foley and David Burnett. Boston: Houghton Mifflin, 1967. Rpt. in Miller, *I Don't Need You Any More.* New York: Viking, 1967. 224–40. Rpt. in Miller, *The Misfits and Other Stories*. New York: Scribner's, 1987. 224–40.

Story of an elderly actor who regrets his career and admires his ailing father.

"Waiting for the Teacher: On Israel's Fiftieth Anniversary" [poem]. *Harper's* July 1998: 56–57.

Miller interweaves memories of waiting for Gromyko in 1948

and speaking with Dayan in the sixties in this prose poem addressing the need for Israel to "call the Teacher from the desert" and end its violent ways. "For unless he is summoned/He will not come. He is unable/To idly enter the city;/Unless he is called by those who love him,/He will sit in the dust beside the gate. . . ."

"White Puppies." *Esquire* July 1978: 32–36.

4. Nonfiction

Books

Chinese Encounters [with Inge Morath]. New York: Farrar, 1979. Excerpt as "In China." *Atlantic Monthly* March 1979: 90–117. Excerpt as "China Scenes, China Voices." *Reader's Digest* July 1979: 58–64.

With photographs by wife Inge Morath, this lengthy essay examines Miller's own experiences and insights gained from his trip to China in the fall of 1978.

In the Country [with Inge Morath]. New York: Viking, 1977.

Fascinating and often humorous sketches of the politics, people, and simple country life of rural Connecticut. Morath's tender photographs accompany a text by Miller. Includes commentary and a photograph of Alexander Calder, a neighbor and friend of the Millers, and a photo taken at a dinner party with Fredric March and Leonard Bernstein. A single photograph of Miller appears on page 172.

In Russia [with Inge Morath]. London: Secker and Warburg, 1969. New York: Viking, 1969. Except in *Harper's* September 1969: 37–78. Excerpt rpt. in *The Portable Arthur Miller*. Ed. Harold Clurman. New York: Viking, 1971. 550–60. Excerpt rpt. in *The Theater Essays of Arthur Miller*. New York: Viking, 1978. 319–46. Excerpt rpt. in *The Theater Essays of Arthur Miller*. Revised ed. Eds. Robert A. Martin and Steven R. Centola. New York: Da Capo, 1996. 319–46.

Account of Miller and wife Morath's visit to Russia in 1968, that, according to Miller, "reports the images which underlie the Russian cultural consciousness—the images evoked by novels, poems, paintings, and plays and by their creators." Morath's photographs accompany a text by Miller.

Salesman in Beijing. New York: Viking, 1983. Excerpted in *The Theater Essays of Arthur Miller*. Revised ed. Eds. Robert A. Martin and Steven R. Centola. New York: Da Capo, 1996. 384–95.

Miller's journal, kept while directing *Death of a Salesman* in China, focusing on the problems of staging the play in Chinese and the effects of the Cultural Revolution.

Situation Normal. New York: Reynal and Hitchcock, 1944. Excerpt in condensed form as "Their First Look at Live Bullets." *Science Digest* 17 (April 1945): 73–76.

Dedicated to Miller's brother, Lieutenant Kermit Miller, *Situation Normal* details in nine chapters Miller's experiences touring army camps "to go among the soldiers and pick up enough facts, honest-to-God true facts, to make a soldier picture [for Lester Cowan who had secured the rights to Ernie Pyles's book, *The Story of G.I. Joe*] which soldiers would sit through until the end without once laughing in derision."

Timebends: A Life [autobiography]. New York: Grove, 1987. New York: Penguin, 1995. Excerpt in "Cover Story: Once in Love with Marilyn, Arthur Miller Looks at His Life, Loves and Writing." *Newsday* 13 December 1987: Magazine: 14+. Excerpt in *Writing Our Lives: Autobiographies of American Jews, 1890–1990*. Ed. Steven Joel Rubin. New York: Jewish Pub. Society, 1991. 209–17. Excerpt in *The Portable Arthur Miller*. Ed. Christopher Bigsby. New York: Penguin, 1995. 569–70. Excerpt in *The Theater Essays of Arthur Miller*. Revised ed. Eds. Robert A. Martin and Steven R. Centola. New York: Da Capo, 1996. 436–53.

Forewords and Introductions

"About Distances." *I Don't Need You Any More: Stories by Arthur Miller*." New York: Viking, 1967. ix–xiii. Rpt. in Miller, *The Misfits and Other Stories*. New York: Scribner's, 1987. ix–xiii.

Short essay in which Miller discusses the differences between the short story and the dramatic form. Says Miller, all literary forms "are degrees of distance writers need to take between themselves and the dangerous audience which they must cajole, threaten, and, in one way or another, tame."

"About Theater Language." *The Last Yankee*. New York: Penguin, 1994. 75–98. Rpt. in *Arthur Miller Plays: Five*. London: Methuen, 1995. Rpt. in *The Theater Essays of Arthur Miller*. Revised ed. Eds. Robert A. Martin and Steven R. Centola. New York: Da Capo, 1996. 526–43.

Miller discusses his development as a playwright from the 1930s to *The Last Yankee* and the importance of creating dramas that are aimed at both the mind and the flesh. The aim of modern drama, he says, is "to show what life now *feels like*."

"Conditions of Freedom: Two Plays of the Seventies—*The Archbishop's Ceiling* and *The American Clock*." *The Archbishop's Ceiling and The American Clock*. New York: Grove, 1989. vii–xx. Rpt. in *The Theater Essays of Arthur Miller*. Revised ed. Eds. Robert A. Martin and Steven R. Centola. New York: Da Capo, 1996. 472–84.

Miller examines the social and political contexts of both plays, saying that for *The Archbishop's Ceiling* the 1970s were "an era of the listening device," and *The American Clock* with its look back at the Great Depression and the 1930s was capturing the "essential chaos" of that era.

"Foreword to *After the Fall*." *Saturday Evening Post* 1 February 1964: 32. Rpt. in *The Theater Essays of Arthur Miller*. Ed. Robert A. Martin. New York: Viking, 1978. 255–57. Rpt. in *The Theater Essays of Arthur Miller*. Revised ed. Eds. Robert A. Martin and Steven R. Centola. New York: Da Capo, 1996. 255–57.

Miller counters his critics who have attacked *After the Fall* for its sordid representation of former wife Marilyn Monroe by insisting that it is not "about" something—"it is something. And primarily it is a way of looking at man and his human nature as the only source of the violence which has come closer and closer to destroying the race."

"Foreword to *America in Passing*" by Henri Cartier-Bresson. Boston: Bulfinch, 1996. 6–7.

Miller praises Cartier-Bresson's photography as "painfully ironical pictures of the United States before Reagan's 'it's morning in America' made it so difficult, if not impermissible, to take a straight look at real life on this continent . . . Faith is working through these pictures, and that may be the hidden reason why they seem so ageless." On page 88, Cartier-Bresson includes a photograph of Marilyn Monroe taken on the set of *The Misfits*.

"Foreword to *The Arena Adventure: The First 40 Years.*" Ed. Laurence Maslon. Introduction by Zelda Fichandler. New York: Applause, 1990. 4–5.

While praising the Arena Stage as "one of the oldest and finest" regional theatres in America, Miller laments on the lack of federal subsidy of theatre in the United States, a situation he finds "unfortunate." "To put on valuable plays that are not necessarily widely popular is part of the art theatre's reason for existence whereas it is definitely not part of the commercial management's ideology at all."

"Foreword to *Cold Spring in Russia*" by Olga Chernov Andreyev. Trans. Michael Carlisle. Ann Arbor: Ardis, 1978.

Miller praises Andreyev's first-hand account of the Russian revolution and of the Russian Civil War as having "the feel of life," and her writing as "a literary accomplishment" and "a book which will enter the record and remain for a very long time."

"Foreword to *The Haunted Fifties: 1953–1963. A Nonconformist History of Our Times*" by I. F. Stone. Boston: Little, 1989.

Short essay in which Miller praises Stone as a reporter with "common sense, fairness, and social conscience" who "spoke for freedom and truth in a delusionary time." Most notable for his assessment of the 1950s: "that hurricane of corrupted speech, ritualized patriotism, paranoid terror, and sudden conversions to acceptability."

"Foreword to *Love and Freedom: My Unexpected Life in Prague*" by Rosemary Kavan. New York: Hill and Wang, 1988. ix–x.

Miller praises Kavan's book as "a direct and unpretentious account of the Czechoslovakian tragedy" and "a warm and human witness to what amounts to the surreal transformation of a Western people and civilization into something quite different—perhaps a colony of not Moscow exactly but Istanbul."

"Foreword to *Nostalgia for the Present*" by Andrei Voznesensky. Eds. Vera Dunham and Max Hayward. Trans. Robert Bly, et al. New York: Doubleday, 1978. xi.

Miller praises Voznesensky as "a marvelously lyrical poet" who has "carved out a private speech for public occasions, an intimacy which is yet open-armed toward the world."

"Foreword to *Thoughts on Human Dignity and Freedom*." New York: Universe, 1991. v.

A collection of fifty photographs that "show the many faces of the human race," *Thoughts on Human Dignity* is published by Amnesty International, with all proceeds of the book sales benefiting that organization. Miller's foreword praises Amnesty International for its effective application of "the same standards to all countries regardless of their social and political systems." He offers the hope that while "everything is going from bad to worse these days," at least there has been an improvement in the level of awareness worldwide to human rights, as evidenced by diplomatic considerations and foreign relations agendas.

"Foreword to *Toward the Radical Center: A Karel Capek Reader*." Ed. Peter Kussi. Highland Park, N.J.: Catbird, 1990: n.p.

Miller charts his own introduction to the Czechoslovakian writer as a student at the University of Michigan, his understanding of this writer's place in eastern European literature, and his estimate of Capek's talent as "a wonderfully surprising teller of some fairly astonishing and unforgettable tales."

"Introduction to *Chapters from My Autobiography: Mark Twain*." New York: Oxford UP, 1996. xxxi–xliii.

Lengthy introductory essay to a volume of reprints of twenty-five installments published in the *North American Review* from September 1906 to December 1907 under the title "Chapters from My Autobiography." Miller lauds Twain as "plainspoken," an American "treasure," and an artist of universal popularity who "refused to pander to the loyalists of any party" yet "was clearly passionate about the need for honest men in government in an age when corruption was rife. . . ."

"Introduction to *Collected Plays*." *Arthur Miller's Collected Plays*. New York: Viking, 1957. 3–55. Excerpt rpt. in *Playwrights on Playwriting: The Meaning and Making of Modern Drama from Ibsen to Ionesco*. Ed. Toby Cole. New York: Hill and Wang, 1960. 261–75. Excerpt rpt. as "The 'Real' in Ibsen's Realism." *Discussions of Henrik Ibsen*. Ed. James Walter McFarlane. Boston: Heath, 1962. 104–5. Excerpt rpt. in *Aesthetics and the Philosophy of Criticism*. Ed. Marvin Levich. New York: Random House, 1963. 204–9. Rpt. in *"Death of a Salesman": Text and Criticism*. Ed. Gerald Weales. New York: Viking, 1967. 155–71. Excerpt rpt. in *Representative Men: Cult Heroes of Our Time*. Ed.

Theodore L. Gross. New York: Free Press, 1970. 278–83. Rpt. in *"The Crucible": Text and Criticism*. Ed. Gerald Weales. New York: Viking, 1971. 161–69. Rpt. in *The Theater Essays of Arthur Miller*. Ed. Robert A. Martin. New York: Viking, 1978. 113–70. Excerpt rpt. in *Major Literary Characters: Willy Loman*. Ed. Harold Bloom. New York: Chelsea, 1991. 33–42. Rpt. in *The Theater Essays of Arthur Miller*. Revised ed. Eds. Robert A. Martin and Steven R. Centola. New York: Da Capo, 1996. 113–70.

Miller's most extensive analysis of his own writing processes. Also addressed are the critical reactions to his works, his definition of drama, and the nature of tragedy.

"Introduction to *Collected Plays 2*." *Arthur Miller's Collected Plays: Vol. 2*. New York: Viking, 1981. 1–2.

While recognizing his reputation as a realistic playwright, Miller resists the label stating, "The truth is that I have never been able to settle upon a single useful style."

"Introduction to *Focus*." Syracuse, N.Y.: Syracuse UP, 1984. v–x. Rpt. and adapted as "The Face in the Mirror: Anti-Semitism Then and Now." *New York Times Book Review* 14 October 1984: 3.

Essay exploring the conditions of anti-Semitism at the time Miller wrote the book in 1945 to the present day. *Focus* "was written when a sensible person could wonder if [the right of Jews to exist] had reality at all. . . . It's central image is the turning lens of the mind of an anti-Semitic man forced by his circumstances to see anew his own relationships to the Jew."

"Introduction to *The Golden Years and The Man Who Had All the Luck*." London: Methuen, 1989. 5–10. Rpt. in *The Theater Essays of Arthur Miller*. Revised ed. Eds. Robert A. Martin and Steven R. Centola. New York: Da Capo, 1996. 466–71.

On rereading two of his early works reprinted in this volume, Miller sees them as expressing his reactions to that time in his life and articulates his surprise at their metaphorical nature considering that realism was the only tradition he was aware of at the time he penned them.

"Introduction to *Inge Morath: Life as a Photographer*." New York: Gina Keyahoff, 1999.

Brief five-line introduction to wife Morath's collection of photographs that praises her "subjective celebration of life in all its permutations."

"Introduction to *Kesey's Garage Sale*" by Ken Kesey. New York: Viking, 1973. xiii–xviii. Revised and rpt. as "Miracles." *Esquire* September 1973: 112–15, 202–4.

Lengthy essay comparing the American cultural revolutions of the thirties and the sixties. Finding both similarities and differences between them, Miller laments that "evidently, we are not fated to be wise, to be still in a contemplation of our cyclical repetitiousness, but must spawn new generations that refuse the past absolutely and set out yet again for that space where evil and conflict are no more."

"Introduction to *Arthur Miller Plays: Four*." London: Methuen, 1994: vii–xii.

Miller introduces this mixed collection of early and later works by detailing their genesis and meaning.

"Introduction to *Arthur Miller Plays: Three*." London: Methuen, 1990. ix–xiii. Rpt. in *The Theater Essays of Arthur Miller*. Revised ed. Eds. Robert A. Martin and Steven R. Centola. New York: Da Capo, 1996. 509–13.

In a rather convoluted essay, Miller attacks what he sees as the "two distinct kinds of theatre in our time, the Majority one and the Other. The Majority includes the musicals, light comedies, melodramas of reassurance and farces—anything that takes people's minds off their troubles. The Other, in contrast, is devoted to generating anxiety rather than reassurance, or escape through hermetically circular ironies."

"Introduction to *Portraits*" by Inge Morath. New York: Aperture, 1986. 6–7.

In his introduction to wife Inge Morath's photographs, Miller praises her for her "definite sense of composition" which appears "entirely impromptu and unarranged. . . . She has discovered with a painter's eye the environments that people tend to arrange around themselves and their facial gestures." Of note is a photograph of Miller and another of Marilyn Monroe from the set of *The Misfits*.

"Introduction to *Sean O'Casey: Plays 2*." London: Faber and Faber, 1998. vii–xi.

Calling O'Casey "a real poet" that had a "gift of laughter that left you in tears for the human race," Miller discusses O'Casey's influence on young writers of the thirties and relates a story from the early 1950s when O'Casey's last play was denied production on Broadway under pressure from veteran's groups and "right-wing hysterics." As a member of the board of the Dramatists Guild, Miller offered a resolution that American playwrights insist on O'Casey's right to be heard and mount a counter picket line.

"Introduction to *A View from the Bridge*." New York: Viking, 1960. v–x. Rpt. in *The Theater Essays of Arthur Miller*. Ed. Robert A. Martin. New York: Viking, 1978. 218–22. Rpt. in *The Theater Essays of Arthur Miller*. Revised ed. Eds. Robert A. Martin and Steven R. Centola. New York: Da Capo, 1996. 218–22. Rpt. in *A View from the Bridge*. New York: Penguin, 1997. v–x.

Miller explains his reasoning and process in expanding his play from its original one-act format to its current full-length version. "I think it can be said that by the addition of significant psychological and behavioral detail the play became not only more human, warmer and less remote, but also a clearer statement."

"New Introduction to *Timebends: A Life*." New York: Penguin, 1995.

For the reprint edition of Miller's autobiography, the playwright recalls some of the "unimportant matters" that he omitted in the original work, published eight years previously, including his "adolescent lust for sports."

"A Note on the Historical Accuracy of *The Crucible*." *The Crucible: A Play in Four Acts*. New York: Viking, 1953. Rpt. as "A Note on the Historical Accuracy of *The Crucible*; with an excerpt from *The Crucible*." Eds. John Gassner and R. G. Allen. *Theatre and Drama in the Making, Vol. 2: The Nineteenth and Twentieth Centuries*. Boston: Houghton, 1964. 848–57.

Preface of sorts to *The Crucible*, included here for its assertions regarding the changes that Miller has made to the historical texts in order to best fashion the dramatic line of his play.

"Notes on *The Crucible* as Film." *The Crucible: Screenplay*. New York: Penguin, 1996. vii–xi.

After admitting a pronounced bias of playwriting over screen writing, Miller relates his excitement at finally seeing *The Crucible* made into a film and his happiness over director Nicholas Hytner's theatrical background that preserved him "from the fear of language, especially archaic-sounding language, which he saw as a strength rather than something from which to flee."

"On Screenwriting and Language." *Everybody Wins: A Screenplay by Arthur Miller*. New York: Grove, 1990. Rpt. in *The Theater Essays of Arthur Miller*. Revised ed. Eds. Robert A. Martin and Steven R. Centola. New York: Da Capo, 1996. 514–22.

Miller discusses the differences between the two literary forms of screen writing and playwriting, noting that, in film, language is a "servant to the images."

"On Social Plays." *A View from the Bridge*. New York: Viking, 1955. 1–18. Rpt. in *The Theater Essays of Arthur Miller*. Ed. Robert A. Martin. New York: Viking, 1978. 51–68. Rpt. as "A View of One-Acters." *New York Times* 25 September 1955: II: 1, 3. Rpt. in *Two Modern American Tragedies: Reviews and Criticism of "Death of a Salesman" and "A Streetcar Named Desire."* Ed. John D. Hurrell. New York: Scribner's, 1961. 41–48. Rpt. in *The Theater Essays of Arthur Miller*. Ed. Robert A. Martin. New York: Viking, 1978. 51–68. Excerpt rpt. as "Viewing *A View from the Bridge*," *Theatre Arts* 40 September 1956: 31–32. Rpt. in *The Theater Essays of Arthur Miller*. Revised ed. Eds. Robert A. Martin and Steven R. Centola. New York: Da Capo, 1996. 51–68.

This is one of Miller's most important essays, often reprinted and quoted, which discusses the relevance of social drama ("the drama of the whole man") as an art form.

"Preface to an Adaptation of Ibsen's *An Enemy of the People*." New York: Viking, 1951. *An Enemy of the People*. New York: Viking, 1951. 7–12. Rpt. in *The Theater Essays of Arthur Miller*. Ed. Robert A. Martin. New York: Viking, 1978. 16–21. Rpt. in *The Theater Essays of Arthur Miller*. Revised ed. Eds. Robert A. Martin and Steven R. Centola. New York: Da Capo, 1996. 16–21.

Miller explains his reasons for adapting Ibsen's work for modern audiences—"to demonstrate that Ibsen is really pertinent today," and "to buttress the idea that the dramatic writer has, and must again demonstrate, the right to entertain with his brains as well as his heart"—as well as the particulars of his alterations to the original script.

"Preface to *The Guardsman*." *Theatre Guild on the Air*. Ed. H. William Fitelson. New York: Rinehart, 1947. 67–68.

In an essay introducing Miller's radio play adaptation of a play by Ferenc Molnar, the playwright discusses his efforts to turn a stage play into a radio drama, including adding locations, shortening scenes, and being conscious of the economy of language. Also included are Miller's observations of the similarities between the radio and film mediums.

"Preface to *Mr. Peters' Connections*." New York: Penguin, 1999. vii–viii. Also "Preface for *Mr. Peters' Connections*." *Mr. Peters' Connections*. New York: DPS, 1999. 3.

Short preface to the first edition of Miller's play in which the playwright explains that the action takes place inside the mind of Mr. Peters—"from where it is still possible to glance back toward daylight life or forward into misty depths"—what characters are alive, dead, or a Mr. Peters's construct, how Miller imagines the set, and a description of the action of the play.

"Preface to 1988 Edition of *Liberty Denied: The Current Rise of Censorship in America*" Revised. ed. by Donna A. Demac. New Brunswick, N.J.: Rutgers UP, 1990. xi–xii.

Short preface in which Miller relates his own experiences with "thoughtless lies" and "savage portrayals" that have pictured him "as everything from a terrorist and communist traitor to an anti-Semite, plagiarist, and pimp." Instead of suing those who would defame him, Miller has chosen to ignore them, for "suing a writer seemed to cross a principle that I respect and cherish more than even my own reputation: the freedom to speak and print—yes, even to speak lies and print them. It cannot be right to defend liberty by limiting its use, even by those who really care little about it."

"Preface to *Three Men on a Horse*." *Theatre Guild on the Air*. Ed. H. William Fitelson. New York: Rinehart, 1947. 205–6.

In this essay introducing Miller's radio adaptation of a play by John Cecil Holms and George Abbot, Miller discusses the process by which he followed "the logic of the play's own movements" to enlarge its "physical scope" and make it workable as a radio play.

"Preface to *A View from the Bridge*" [two-act version]. New York: Compass, 1960, v–x. Excerpted as "Viewing *A View from the Bridge*." *Theatre Arts* 40 (September 1956): 31–32.

Miller details his reasons for revising and expanding the one-act play into a full-length piece.

"Prefatory Remarks to *Castrated: My Eight Months in Prison*" by Ralph Ginzburg. New York: Avant-Garde Books, 1973. 13.

Miller remarks on "the folly, the menace of all censorship—it lays down rules for all time which are ludicrous a short time later."

"A Question of Relatedness." Excerpt from Miller's "Introduction to the *Collected Plays*." *Arthur Miller's Collected Plays*. New York: Viking, 1957. 12–22. Rpt. in *Modern Critical Interpretations of Arthur Miller's "All My Sons."* Ed. Harold Bloom. New York: Chelsea, 1988. 5–14.

This lengthy section of the "Introduction to the *Collected Plays*" details Miller's process in writing *All My Sons* and the subsequent critical reaction to his first successful Broadway play.

"*Salesman* at Fifty." *Death of a Salesman, 50th Anniversary Edition*. New York: Penguin, 1999. ix–xiii.

Miller discloses his incredulity over the passage of time since writing *Death of a Salesman* and its fiftieth anniversary. He additionally discusses the role of critics in the American theatre, the state of the theatre both past and present, and the positive reception his works have enjoyed in countries very different from his own. "It is satisfying and gratifying that people everywhere react pretty much the same in the same places in the play."

"The Sin of Power." *Index on Censorship* May–June 1978: 3–6. Rpt. as "Foreword to *Since the Prague Spring: The Continuing Struggle for Human Rights in Czechoslovakia*." Ed. Hans-Peter Riese. Trans. Eugen Loebl. New York: Vintage, 1979. ix–xiv. Rpt. in *An Embarrassment of Tyrannies: Twenty-Five Years of Index on Criticism*. Eds. W. L. Webb and Rose Bell. New York: Braziller, 1998. 76–81.

Miller relates images of repression that he has encountered around the world, especially in Czechoslovakia, and the importance of the continuing and endless struggle against the "sin of power."

"Sorting Things Out." *The Theater Essays of Arthur Miller*. Ed. Robert A. Martin. New York: Viking, 1978. xli–xliv. Rpt. in *The Theater Essays of Arthur Miller*. Revised ed. Eds. Robert A. Martin and Steven R. Centola. New York: Da Capo, 1996. lv–lviii.

Miller's introduction to a large collection of his theatre essays in which he expresses his regret for ever having brought up the tragic nature question of *Death of a Salesman*, explains the tone of his essays, and expresses his intent in writing them as an attempt to "objectify the social situation of our theatre . . . rather than leaving these matters—as our critics normally did—to temperament and taste without deeper reason or cause."

Essays

"After Kefauver—What?" *Sunday Compass* 25 March 1951: 9–10, 17.

Miller says he sees a serious threat to personal privacy and reputation in the "trial by public opinion" (wide coverage in the media). Just as significant was the assumption by many witnesses that private or personal loyalty superseded social responsibility. He concludes by calling for a third political party, a nonconformist party, that would not have ties to "gangsters."

"Again They Drink from the Cup of Suspicion." *New York Times* 26 November 1989: Sec. 2: 5, 36. Rpt. in *The Theater Essays of Arthur Miller*. Revised ed. Eds. Robert A. Martin and Steven R. Centola. New York: Da Capo, 1996. 460–65.

Miller offers his motives for writing *The Crucible* (as an "opposition to the madness") and his thoughts on the reasons for the play's universality.

"The Age of Abdication." *New York Times* 23 December 1967: 22.

Miller describes his feelings of watching a television news story in which fifteen thousand Vietnamese peasants were forced out of their villages by Americans who then proceeded to burn down their thatched houses to deny shelter to the Vietcong.

Agel, Jerome. "First Memory." *New York Times* 26 October 1975: VI: 111.

Compilation of first memories of notable artists and writers. In a passage that will later appear in his autobiography, Miller writes, "I was probably 2 or 3. I don't know. I was on the floor; my mother, in a long woolen dress that reached to her ankles, was speaking into a wall telephone. I tugged at her arm: a shaft of sunlight crossed her shoe."

"An American Reaction." *World Theatre* I (1951): 21–22.

Short essay that is a reply to the article in the same issue titled "Can the Craft of Playwriting Be Learned?" by Walter Prichard Eaton. Miller's response is that while college courses can help develop a writer's talent, "a man is born with a sense of play structure. . . . It seems to me that the man who is born with the dramatic point of view cannot lose by attending such a school, and just conceivable [sic] he may gain a great deal in the formation of his talent, and the strengthening of his will to keep it." Black-and-white head shot of Miller accompanies the text.

"The American Theater." *Holiday* January 1955: 90–104. Rpt. in *"Death of a Salesman": Text and Criticism*. Ed. Gerald Weales. New York: Viking, 1967. Penguin, 1996. 151–55. Rpt. in *The Pursuit of Learning*. Ed. Nathan Comfort Starr. New York: Harcourt, 1956. Rpt. in *Passionate Playgoer*. Ed. George Oppenheimer. New York: Viking, 1958. 13–32. Rpt. in *A Contemporary Reader: Essays for Today and Tomorrow*. Ed. Harry William Rudman and Irving Rosenthal. New York: Ronald, 1961. 184–98. Rpt. in *The Theater Essays of Arthur Miller*. Ed. Robert A. Martin. New York: Viking, 1978. 31–50. Rpt. in *The Theater Essays of Arthur Miller*. Revised ed. Eds. Robert A. Martin and Steven R. Centola. New York: Da Capo, 1996. 31–50.

Miller discusses the glamour of the theatre, the importance and power, albeit undeserved, of the Broadway theatre to the success or failure of a new work, and the differences between show business and the theatre.

"Are We Interested in Stopping the Killing?" *New York Times* 8 June 1969: Sec. 2: 21.

Op-ed piece in which Miller shares his surprise at Averell Harriman's comments that it is the United States, and not the Vietnamese, who are on the offensive in Vietnam, contradicting the president's position on the matter. Miller poses the blunt question: "Are we or are we not interested in stopping the killing?"

"Arthur Miller." *Antaeus* 73/74 (Spring 1994): 33–35. Rpt. in *Who's Writing This? Notations on the Authorial I with Self-Portraits*. Ed. Daniel Halpern. Hopewell, N.J.: Ecco, 1995. 129–31.

Short essay that comments on the critical misunderstanding of literature as autobiography and Miller's own identity being at odds with his public and literary selves. A self-portrait accompanies the text.

"Arthur Miller: How the Nazi Trials Search the Hearts of All Germans." *New York Herald Tribune* 15 March 1964: 24. Rpt. in "Arthur Miller's Neglected Article on Nazi War Criminals' Trials: A Vision of Evil." Robert Lee Feldman. *Resources for American Literary Study* 15 (Autumn 1985): 187–96.

Miller reports his experiences witnessing the Nazi war-crimes trials in Frankfurt, Germany, in 1964. "Perhaps the deepest respect we can pay the millions of innocent dead is to examine what we believe about murder, and our responsibility as survivors for the future."

"Arthur Miller on *The Crucible*." *Audience* 12 (July–August 1972): 46–47. Rpt. in *The Theater Essays of Arthur Miller*. Revised ed. Eds. Robert A. Martin and Steven R. Centola. New York: Da Capo, 1996. 365–67.

Miller relates his impression of the French film version of *The Crucible*, saying "it was weakened and made less actual, rather than more pointed, by Sartre's overly Marxist screenplay. . . . Yet despite all this I found it a stimulating and even gripping picture which was finally deeply moving and quite beautiful. It is not, to me, *The Crucible* but a version of it, and a strong film in its own right."

"Arthur Miller Speaks Out on the Election." *Literary Cavalcade* (November 1984): 4–5.

While admitting that he doesn't "think either political party has found men of the imagination and character the times need," Miller urges the "individual-as-citizen" to take an active part in American democracy to help make politics "mean hope and intelligence at work in the human situation of our time."

"Arthur Miller vs. Lincoln Center." *New York Times* 16 April 1972: II: 1, 5. Rpt. as "Challenge the Lincoln Center Board: Can or Will They Create Repertory?" *Dramatists Guild Quarterly* 8 (Winter 1972): 6–11. Rpt. in *Playwrights, Lyricists, Composers on Theater*. Ed. Otis L. Guernsey Jr. New York: Dodd, Mead, 1974. Rpt. in *The Theater Essays of Arthur Miller*. Ed. Robert A. Martin. New York: Viking, 1978. 354–61. Rpt. in *The Theater Essays of Arthur Miller*. Revised ed. Eds. Robert A. Martin and Steven R. Centola. New York: Da Capo, 1996. 354–61.

Miller discusses the problems encountered by those who wished to establish a repertory theatre at Lincoln Center in New York. He accuses the board of directors of arrogance and stupidity at the firing of Robert Whitehead. "I think it is time the Lincoln Center board is called to account. . . . They must no longer be allowed to fob off their failure on the artists working for them."

"Art and Commitment." *Anvil and Student Partisan* 11 (Winter 1960): 5.

Short essay in which Miller expresses his views that it is a writer's job to reveal reality, not mask it.

"Authors on Translators." *Translation* 2 (1974): 5–8.

Short piece in which Miller remarks that he is unaware of the quality of translations of his works, except French, which he can read, and German, which he "can sort of hear." He admits a feeling of gratitude to translators for the playwright feels that "a conscientious translator must feel he has never finished, never quite got it."

"Autobiographical Statement." *Cross-Section: A Collection of New American Writing*. Ed. Edwin Seaver. New York: Fischer, 1944. 556.

Autobiographical note for a collection of plays by various playwrights that includes Miller's *The Man Who Had All the Luck*. Of note is Miller's comment regarding the possibility of having two plays in production at the same time at the age of twenty-eight [it didn't materialize]. "Why everything had to happen at once I don't know. There have been months of my life when I did nothing but sit in Brooklyn with my feet on the radiator, whole rainy months."

"Autobiographical Statement." *Twentieth Century Authors: A Biographical Dictionary of Modern Literature, First Supplement*. Ed. Stanley J. Kunitz. New York: Wilson, 1955. 669–70.

Miller discusses his early educational failures, his first writing (a description of a fountain pen), the book that changed his life (*The Brothers Karamazov*), his writing awards at the University of Michigan, the only story of his that he likes ("Monte Saint Angelo"), and his aim "to bring to the stage the thickness, awareness, and complexity of the novel."

"Autobiographical Statement." *World Authors, 1900–1950*. New York: Wilson, 1996.

After making brief mention of his literary influences, or early lack thereof, Miller relates that, while he cares about all of his plays, "the only story I like is 'Monte Saint Angelo.'" "My aim is what it has been from the beginning—to bring to the stage the thickness, awareness, and complexity of the novel."

"The Bangkok Prince." *Harper's* July 1970: 32–33.

Miller details his visit and interview with the seventy-year-old Prince of Thailand, whom he found "very tough, his reincarnation will be as a stern ferret."

"Banned in Russia." *New York Times* 10 December 1970: 47.

Miller relates his shocked surprise to learn that his works have been banned in Russia, as "part of a new campaign to liquidate ideological slackness and stop the infiltration of liberal ideas into literary and scientific thinking."

"The Battle of Chicago: From the Delegates' Side." *New York Times Magazine* 15 September 1968: 29–31, 122, 124, 126, 128. Rpt. in excerpt form as "Eyewitness" in *Law and Disorder: The Chicago Convention and Its Aftermath*. Ed. Donald Myrus. Chicago: Donald Myrus and Burton Joseph, 1968. Rpt. as "From the Delegate's Side." *Telling It Like It Was: The Chicago Riots*. Ed. Walter Schneir. New York: New American Library, 1969. 43–56.

Miller served as a McCarthy delegate at the 1968 Democratic Convention in Chicago. In this lengthy essay, he details his experiences as a delegate and his reactions to the violence on both the inside and the outside of the International Amphitheater.

"Before Air Conditioning." *New Yorker* 22–29 June 1998: 144–47. Rpt. in *The Best American Essays 1999*. Ed. Edward Hoagland. Boston: Houghton, 1999. 185–87.

Miller recounts his memories of September 1927 in New York City, an unusually hot month, including how the residents and the workers in his father's coat factory coped with the heat and how the young Miller first came in contact with air-conditioning.

"The Birth of *Death of a Salesman*." *Playbill* (February 1988): n.p.

In this except from Miller's autobiography *Timebends: A Life* (1987), the playwright discusses the writing, casting, and the initial response of *Death of a Salesman.*

"The Bored and the Violent." *Harper's* November 1962: 50–56. Rpt. in *First Person Singular*. Ed. Herbert Gold. New York: Dial, 1963. 173–84.

Based on his experience on the New York streets with gang youth, Miller shares his "impressions" regarding the causes of delinquency, which he defines as boredom. "People no longer seen to know why they are alive; existence is simply a string of near-experiences marked off by periods of stupefying spiritual and psychological stasis, and the good life is basically an amused one."

"A Boy Grew in Brooklyn." *Holiday* March 1955: 54–55, 117–24.

Billed as the "fourth in a series of nostalgic home-town stories by America's great writers," Miller looks back on his childhood "in New York's lustiest borough." Notable for the playwright's detailed depiction of his father. Large photo of Miller accompanies the text.

"Brewed in the Crucible." *New York Times* 9 March 1958: II: 3. Rpt. in *The Theater Essays of Arthur Miller*. Ed. Robert A. Martin. New York: Viking, 1978. 171–74. Rpt. in *"The Crucible": Text and Criticism*. Ed. Gerald Weales. New York: Viking, 1971. Penguin, 1996. 169–73. Rpt. in *The Theater Essays of Arthur Miller*. Revised ed. Eds. Robert A. Martin and Steven R. Centola. New York: Da Capo, 1996. 171–74.

Miller comments on the new off-Broadway production of *The Crucible*, which, "appearing in a warmer climate, may, I hope, flower, and these inner petals may make their appropriate appearance." His disappointment at the reaction to the premiere production was that "no critic seemed to sense what I was after." Rather than being about McCarthyism, his play is about "the conflict between a man's raw deeds and his conception of himself."

"Bridge to a Savage World." *Esquire* October 1958: 185–90.

Film treatment of sorts for Miller's unproduced documentary on juvenile delinquency and youth gangs in New York City, which includes his own experiences with living for two months with various gangs and his thoughts on how the film should be structured. It is Miller's considered belief that gangs are made up of "scared kids" who "have never known life excepting as a worthless thing; they have been told from birth that they are nothing, that their parents are nothing, that their hopes are nothing."

"Broadway." *The Atlas of Literature*. Ed. Malcolm Bradbury. New York: Stewart, Tabori and Chang, 1996. 244–47. Rpt. as "Death of the Dramatist." *Electronic Telegraph* 21 September 1996. http://www.telegraph.com.uk (11 April 1999).

Miller discusses the Broadway theatre from the position of a writer of serious American drama and laments the lack of new plays in production, citing commercial financial considerations as the culprit. "I can't think of a writer who liked Broadway—a writer that is, who was trying to open up the country to itself." Color photograph from the premiere production of *Death of a Salesman* accompanies the text. Of note is the photograph of a young Miller on the cover of the book.

"Broadway Cornered." *Interview* April 1997: 70, 72.

Miller interviews Scott Elliott, director of the Williamstown Theatre Festival production of *The Ride Down Mount Morgan*. Elliot responds to questions relating to the important subjects dealt with through film as opposed to theatre, his thoughts on the function of the director, and the state of the American theatre.

"Broadway, from O'Neill to Now." *New York Times* 21 December 1969: Sec. 2: 3, 7. Rpt. in *The Theater Essays of Arthur Miller*. Ed. Robert A. Martin. New York: Viking, 1978. 347–53. Rpt. in *The Theater Essays of Arthur Miller*. Revised ed. Eds. Robert A. Martin and Steven R. Centola. New York: Da Capo, 1996. 347–53.

Miller makes a call for public subsidy of theatre if it is to survive—"A subsidized theater, a theater no longer competing with industry for the right to occupy land, would be relieved at least of the particular kinds of pressure which this unacknowledged competition generates."

"By Arthur A. Miller." *Michigan Daily* 24 May 1935: 1. Rpt. in *Special to the* Daily*: The First One Hundred Years of Editorial Freedom at the* Michigan Daily. Ed. Susan Holtzer. Ann Arbor: Gaddo Cap, 1990. 23.

In an essay appended to an Associated Press article, "Anti-Red Bill Sent to Senate," Miller reports on the passage in the House of the anti-violent overthrow measure.

"Concerning the Boom." *International Theatre Annual*, No. 1. Ed. Harold Hobson. London: John Calder, 1956. 85–88.

Miller looks at the 1956 New York theatre season, which he sums up as "the usual trendless jumble."

"Criticisms of Government Relief Are Offered by Social Workers." *Michigan Daily* 11 December 1935: 2.

News item in which Miller reports on the criticisms and suggestions for revision of the Federal Relief Administration programs by delegates under the national coordinating committee of rank-and-file social workers.

"Dan Weiner." *The Fifty Stars of the USA: U.S. Camera, 1960*. Ed. Tom Maloney. New York: U.S. Camera Publishing, 1959. 316, 354. Rpt. in *Dan Weiner, 1919–1959*. New York: Grossman, 1974. 10–11.

Miller eulogizes photographer Weiner as a friend and praises his childlike quality, "the way an artist must always be until he is finished, a child who is fanatically pursuing the complicated toy of beauty."

"Death in Tiananmen." *New York Times* 10 September 1989: Sec. 4: 31.

Op-ed piece written to call attention to the coming march [October 1] by the Federation of Chinese Students on the Chinese embassy in Washington. Miller relates his experiences working in China six months previously to direct his *Death of a Salesman* with Chinese actors in Beijing's People's Art Theater.

"Dinner with the Ambassador." *Nation* 18 May 1985: 577, 593–95.

Miller offers an absorbing account of his visit (with Harold Pinter) to Turkey on behalf of the International PEN Club, during which both men were the dinner guests of U.S. ambassador Robert Strausz-Hupé. Miller and Pinter spoke out against the imprisonment and torture of political prisoners in Turkey.

"Educators of Four Countries Aid Middle English Dictionary." *Michigan Daily* 19 December 1935: 6.

Miller reports that a dictionary of Middle English words is being compiled by members of sixty American colleges and universities, and institutions in Canada, England, and Sweden, as a part of a program financed by the American Council of Learned Societies and the Rockefeller Foundation.

"Faculty Men Welcome Controversial Social Questions in Class Discussions." *Michigan Daily* 1 March 1936: 1.

Miller interviews four University of Michigan professors regarding their report to the congress of the National Education Association that studied the question whether it is appropriate for teachers to foster discussion of controversial subjects in the classroom.

"The Family in Modern Drama." *Atlantic Monthly* April 1956: 35–41. Rpt. in *The Theater Essays of Arthur Miller*. Ed. Robert A. Martin. New York: Viking, 1978. 69–85. Rpt. in *Modern Drama:*

Essays in Criticism. Eds. Travis Bogard and William I. Oliver. New York: Oxford UP, 1965. 219–33. Rpt. in *The Theater Essays of Arthur Miller*. Revised ed. Eds. Robert A. Martin and Steven R. Centola. New York: Da Capo, 1996. 69–85.

Miller investigates how a playwright chooses a form and how all theatre, whether realism, verse drama, expressionism, or the poetic play, deals with issues of human relations, primarily family. Says Miller, all plays we call great have one thing in common, they all ask the question: "how may a man make of the outside world a home?"

"Fat Rolls Off for University Scientists in New Experiment." *Michigan Daily* 23 April 1935: 6.

Miller reports for his university's newspaper on weight loss experiments conducted by Dr. L. H. Newburgh of the University Hospital Nutrition Department. The experiments involve measuring the oxygen burned and carbon dioxide given off by the body, creating an index of that loss, and using that index as an exact basis for an accurate diet that permits the regulation of body weight.

"A Genuine Countryman." *Blair & Ketchum's Country Journal* (January 1978): 34–38. Rpt. in condensed form as "Legacy from a Simpler Time." *Reader's Digest* June 1978: 146–50.

Excerpts from *In the Country*.

"Get it Right. Privatize Executions." *New York Times* 8 May 1992: A31.

Tongue-in-cheek op-ed piece in which Miller makes the case for allowing executions of convicted criminals to be carried out in sports stadiums, charging admission, and theatricalizing the event. "My proposal would lead us more quickly to boredom and away from our current gratifying excitement—and ultimately perhaps to a wiser use of alternating current."

"Global Dramatist." *New York Times* 21 July 1957: II: 1.

Miller discusses the critical reception of his dramas worldwide.

"Griggs Locates Messages by Haiti Emperor." *Michigan Daily* 29 February 1936: 2.

News item by Miller reporting the findings by Professor Earl L. Griggs of the English Department, who, in researching his book *Thomas Clarkson, the Friend of Slaves*, discovered letters between Clarkson and Henry Christophe, "the Negro emperor of

Haiti," which showed the latter to be "an enlightened, noble-spirited leader of Negro peoples."

"Hitler's Quarry." *Jewish Survey* 1.1 (1941). Rpt. in "Arthur Miller's Unheard Plea for Jewish Refugees: 'Hitler's Quarry.'" George W. Crandell. *ANQ* 13.1 (Winter 2000): 33+.

Essay appearing in the inaugural issue of *The Jewish Survey*. Miller tries to draw attention to the then current persecution of the Jews in Transylvania, Romania, Luxembourg, Poland, Bulgaria, France, Algeria, Norway, Holland, Belgium, Canada, Africa, and South America and condemns the U.S. State Department's failure to help the thousands of Jews who are "attempting to escape Nazism."

"Holding Company Act Termed Too Severe by Prof. Waterman." *Michigan Daily* 17 December 1935: 6.

News item by Miller reporting Professor Merwin H. Waterman's reaction to the extinction of the Holding Company Act.

"Ibsen and the Drama of Today." *The Cambridge Companion to Ibsen*. Ed. James McFarlane. London: Cambridge UP, 1994. 227–32. Rpt. in *The Theater Essays of Arthur Miller*. Revised ed. Eds. Robert A. Martin and Steven R. Centola. New York: Da Capo, 1996. 544–51.

While admitting that Ibsen's technique is considered "old fashioned," Miller praises the playwright for the organic nature of his art—"It wasn't that things fit together but that *everything* fit together . . . His works have an organic intensity making them, or most of them, undeniable. To me he was the reincarnation of the Greek dramatic spirit."

"Ibsen's Message for Today's World." *New York Times* 24 December 1950: II: 3, 4.

In this condensed version of his foreword to the published play, Miller explains his reasons for adapting Ibsen's work: to demonstrate its pertinence and the writer's "right to entertain with his brains as well as his heart."

"Ibsen's Warning." *Index on Censorship* (London) 18 July–August 1989: 74–76.

Miller reflects on *An Enemy of the People* and the importance and pertinence of Ibsen's warnings of danger for the environment to modern audiences.

"The Inspiration for Willy Loman." *Playbill* (February 1988): n.p.
In this lengthy excerpt from Miller's autobiography *Timebends: A Life* (1987), the playwright focuses on cousin Manny, a salesman from his childhood, and his role as one of the models for Willy Loman in *Death of a Salesman.*

"In the Ayes of the Beholders: With Congress Debating Obscenity in Federally Funded Art, What Will Happen to Free Expression?" *Omni* February 1991: 10.
"First Word" column by Miller in which he states that the current debate over NEA funding has become a "far-Right campaign" that "is dragging us straight into political censorship." "Congress ought to give up trying to kid itself—laying down orthodox lines of taste in matters of art, means censorship."

"It Could Happen Here—And Did." *New York Times* 30 April 1967: II: 17. Rpt. in *The Theater Essays of Arthur Miller*. Ed. Robert A. Martin. New York: Viking, 1978. 294–300. Rpt. in *The Theater Essays of Arthur Miller*. Revised ed. Eds. Robert A. Martin and Steven R. Centola. New York: Da Capo, 1996. 294–300.
Miller discusses the reasons for the longevity of *The Crucible* which was "generally dismissed as a cold, anti-McCarthy tract, more an outburst than a play" when it premiered in 1953, and has since become his most produced play worldwide.

"Journey to *The Crucible*." *New York Times* 8 February 1953: II: 3. Rpt. in *The Theater Essays of Arthur Miller*. Ed. Robert A. Martin. New York: Viking, 1978. 27–30. Rpt. in *The Theater Essays of Arthur Miller*. Revised ed. Eds. Robert A. Martin and Steven R. Centola. New York: Da Capo, 1996. 27–30.
Miller details his trip to Salem and his examination of town records to piece together his story of a people who had "such belief in themselves and in the rightness of their consciences as to give their lives rather than say what they thought was false."

"Kazan and the Bad Times." *Nation* 22 March 1999: 6.
Essay in support of Elia Kazan's receiving a special Academy Award for lifetime achievement in film despite the fact that he named names before HUAC. While admitting that he is "perhaps overly sensitive to any attempts to, in effect, obliterate an artist's name because of his morals or political actions," Miller says he hopes that one can "find it in one's heart praise for what a man has done well and censure for where he has tragically failed."

"Kidnapped." *Saturday Evening Post* 25 January 1969: 40–42, 78–82.
Lengthy essay relating Miller's visit to Rome in the 1960s. During the drive to the hotel, he remembers his last visit to Italy (Sicily) in the 1940s when he met Lucky Luciano.

"Let's Privatize Congress: The Legal Way to Buy Senators." *New York Times* 10 January 1995: A19. Rpt. as "The Best Congress Money Can Buy." *San Francisco Chronicle* 12 January 1995: A23.
In a humorous op-ed piece, Miller offers the suggestion that each representative and senator should have his salary paid by whatever business group wants to buy his/her vote. That way, America could do away with congressional hypocrisy by privatization.

"Limited Hang-Out: The Dialogues of Richard Nixon as a Drama of the Anti-Hero." *Harper's* September 1974: 13–14, 16, 20.
After reading Nixon's presidential transcripts, Miller likens them to a good play whose dialogue springs "from conflict surrounding a paradox." Miller feels "confronted with the decay of a language, of a legal system; in these pages what was possibly the world's best hope is reduced to a vaudeville, a laugh riot."

"Lincoln Repertory Theater—Challenge and Hope." *New York Times* 19 January 1964: Sec. 2: 1, 3.
Far away from the pressures of commercial Broadway theatre, Miller describes the new Repertory Theater at Lincoln Center as an ideal: "an attempt to create a human bridge across the gap between individual psychology and those areas of life we find so hard to react to humanly, our moral existence, our political existence and, above all, perhaps, our passion to understand our own responsibility and our guilt for this world we cannot quite believe we made."

"Lost Horizon." *American Theatre* July/August 1992: 68.
After admitting that he is "not a proper estimator of theatre in America because I see too few productions," Miller laments that while the country is bursting with talent, "it is being wasted like so much else that is human among us" on television and film. Miller concludes, "It seems to me we don't have an American theatre but only the shards of one, some of the broken pieces reflecting lights, others covered with the dust where they have fallen."

"Making Crowds." *Esquire* November 1972: 160–61, 216, 218, 220, 222, 224, 226, 228.

In a lengthy essay, Miller discusses his experiences as a McGovern delegate to the 1972 Democratic Convention in Miami.

"Many Writers: Few Plays." *New York Times* 10 August 1952: Sec. 2: 1. Rpt. in *The Theater Essays of Arthur Miller*. Ed. Robert A. Martin. New York: Viking, 1978. 12–15. Rpt. in *"The Crucible": Text and Criticism*. Ed. Gerald Weales. New York: Viking, 1971. Penguin, 1996. 169–73. Rpt. in *The Theater Essays of Arthur Miller*. Revised ed. Eds. Robert A. Martin and Steven R. Centola. New York: Da Capo, 1996. 12–15.

Miller ruminates on the possible reason why there are so few great plays in America at the present time. He defines a great play as a great thought that has been thrust outward—this, in itself, a daring act and the proper quality of creative art. Miller feels that, unfortunately for the theatre, "playwrights have become more timid with experience and maturity, timid in ethical and social idea, theatrical method, and stylistic means." Blaming "the knuckleheadedness of McCarthyism," Miller finds guardedness, suspicion, and aloof circumspection as the strongest traits he sees around him, "and what have they ever had to do with the creative act?"

"The Measure of the Man." *Nation* 11 February 1991: 151–54.

Fascinating account of Miller's interview with Nelson Mandela in which the playwright attempts to gain insight about Mandela's roots and his remarkable lack of bitterness after almost twenty-eight years in a South African prison.

"The Measure of Things Is Man." *Theatre 4*. New York: International Theatre Institute, 1972. 96–97. Rpt. in *The American Theatre, 1970–71*. New York: Scribner's, 1972. 96–97.

Miller ponders whether man is the measure of things in contemporary society or if the measure is "the reigning artistic style in which man sees himself."

"Men and Words in Prison." *New York Times* 16 October 1971: 31.

In an op-ed piece, Miller discusses the work of PEN to free writers held in prisons both in the East and the West.

"Michigan Bank Failure Called Fault Of Incompetent Officials." *Michigan Daily* 6 October 1935: 1.

Miller reports on the analysis of Prof. Robert G. Rodkey,

called "State Bank Failures in Michigan," that states that 35 percent of the combined capital and gross deposits of the 163 Michigan banks which failed during the depression were frozen as far back as 1928.

"Miller on Miller, Life and Marilyn." *Times Union* (Albany) 21 January 1988: A8.

In this the third of five installments on best-selling authors, Miller discusses the form of autobiographical writing, details the contents of his autobiography, including anecdotes regarding his childhood, his literary career, the dismal state of commercial theatre in New York, European views of literature, and Marilyn Monroe's impact on his writing.

"Miracles." *Esquire* September 1973: 112–115, 202–204.

Lengthy essay in which Miller discusses the "revolutions" of the thirties and the sixties, including his memories of the depression and his "sense that we were in the grip of a mystery deeper and broader and more interior than an economic disaster."

"A Modest Proposal for Pacification of the Public Temper." *Nation* 3 July 1954: 5–8.

A "Swiftian" satire that proposes "a method of obtaining final assurance in the faithfulness of any citizen toward his country."

"My Wife Marilyn: Playwright Pays Affectionate Tribute to Her Feat." *Life* 22 December 1958: 146–47.

Miller relates his early misgivings, and later affection, for his then-wife Marilyn Monroe's photographic series by Richard Avedon where Monroe was made up to look like various cinematic stars. Of note is the playwright's oft-quoted assessment of the childlike qualities of his wife and "her quick sympathy and respect for old people, for whatever has endured." Large close-up photograph by Avedon of Monroe hugging a smiling Miller from behind accompanies the text.

"The Nature of Tragedy." *New York Herald Tribune* 27 March 1949: Sec. 5: 1, 2. Rpt. in *The Theater Essays of Arthur Miller*. Ed. Robert A. Martin. New York: Viking, 1978. 8–11. Rpt. in *The Theater Essays of Arthur Miller*. Revised ed. Eds. Robert A. Martin and Steven R. Centola. New York: Da Capo, 1996. 8–11.

This is one of Miller's most quoted essays, and written in defense of criticism attacking *Death of a Salesman*'s claim that it is a tragedy of the common man. Miller frames his work as a Socratic argument proving the need for a redefinition of tragedy based upon our more modern understandings and sensibilities.

"A New Candor at Issyk-Kul." *Newsweek* 19 January 1987: 8.

"My Turn" essay that details Miller's journey to Russia, along with fifteen other American and European writers and scientists, at the invitation of "a lone Soviet novelist, the purpose of which was 'to talk, free of ideologies, about how we are to get into the Third Millennium.'" Miller expresses his happy but cautious surprise at the two-and-a-half hour meeting with Gorbachev and the possibility of a more open line of communication both with and within Russia.

"A New Era in American Theater?" *Drama Survey* 3 (Spring 1963): 70–71.

Short essay in which Miller derides Broadway as "so encrusted with commercial considerations that now even the quality of the plays themselves is damaged," and applauds the new Tyrone Gutrie Theater, "a first-class, professional, noncommercial theatre," which has decided to produce *Death of a Salesman* in its inaugural season.

"New Pamphlet Lists 500 Books for College Men and Women." *Michigan Daily* 17 November 1935: 2.

News item in which Miller reports on the publication of a pamphlet, compiled by three University of Michigan English department professors, that lists five hundred books that should be read.

"The Night Ed Murrow Struck Back." *Esquire* December 1983: 460–62, 465, 467–68.

Lengthy essay detailing Edward R. Murrow's broadcast in 1953. which proved to be the beginning of the end for Joseph McCarthy. "There was no doubt that night that Murrow's was the voice of decency, and if he and CBS had not struck at McCarthy until his decline had begun . . . it still demonstrated . . . the persistence of scruple as a living principle. . . this nation is in Murrow's eternal debt."

"1956 and All This." *The Theater Essays of Arthur Miller*. Ed. Robert A. Martin. New York: Viking, 1978. 86–109. Originally published as "The Playwright and the Atomic World." *Colorado*

Quarterly 5 (Autumn 1956): 117–37. Rpt. with same title in *Tulane Drama Review* 5 (June 1961): 3–20. Rpt. in *Theatre in the Twentieth Century*. Ed. Robert Corrigan. New York: Grove, 1963. 29–48.

Lengthy essay in which Miller details his understanding of world affairs based on varying foreign reactions to works written for the American audiences. Miller calls for "an entirely new approach" to "the whole problem of what the future is to be."

"Note by Arthur Miller." [album notes] *Beethoven Symphonies 5 & 7*. Philharmonic Orchestra conducted by Vladimir Ashkenazy. New York: Penguin Classics, 1998.

Miller relates an experience that occurred on the afternoon before the first performance of *Death of a Salesman* in Philadelphia when director Elia Kazan suggested that he, Miller, and Lee J. Cobb attend a performance of Beethoven's Seventh Symphony and "relax." After "being struck for the first time by the series of near-climaxes, each reined in until the final ingathering explosion," Miller whispered in Cobb's ear: 'This is the last ten minutes.' Says Miller, "He understood; as Willy, he had often yielded to the temptation of blowing all his forces well before his final climaxes. He was a terribly edgy horse, and sometimes, because he wanted every moment to count, nearly gave way to his own emotions rather than the controlled arc of the play."

"A Note from Arthur Miller." *New Theater Review* (Winter 1988): 2. Rpt. in *New Theater Review* 15 (Fall/Winter 1996): 9.

Brief essay in which Miller relates his earliest awareness of Samuel Beckett's dramatic work ("terribly private, for too philosophical to be of use") and his later surprise at their "vaudeville" nature—"I'm sorry I couldn't know this when I needed such reassurance most. But it's never too late, is it."

"Okay, But Who Was I?" *Life* 10 November 1987: 72–88.

Lengthy excerpt from Miller's autobiography *Timebends: A Life*.

"On Broadway: Notes on the Past and Future of American Theater." *Harper's* March 1999: 37–45.

Lengthy essay in which Miller decries the current state of American commercial theatre, where the risk of financial loss controls both the quality and the style of new theatrical productions, and examines "a tiny bit of the history of age-old stylistic strategies employed by playwrights to trap reality on the stage."

"Once in Love with Marilyn, Arthur Miller Looks at His Life, Loves and Writing." *Newsday* 13 December 1987: Magazine: 14+.

Lengthy excerpt from Miller's autobiography *Timebends: A Life.*

"On Censorship." *Censored Books: Critical Viewpoints*. Eds. Nicholas J. Karolides, Lee Burress, and John M. Kean. Metuchen, N.J.: Scarecrow, 1993. 3–10.

After lamenting that many Americans still do not have an understanding of the threats of censorship to the freedom of the state, Miller considers historical attempts to revise Shakespeare and current practice of omitting segments of the Bard's plays from educational texts. He further relates his own experiences with censors and censorship and reflects on current international censorship practices.

"On the Shooting of Robert Kennedy." *New York Times* 8 June 1968: 30.

Op-ed piece in which Miller challenges the nation, in the wake of the assassination of Robert Kennedy, to "wipe out the disgrace of poverty in this richest of all nations" and "begin to construct a civilization, which means a common consciousness of social responsibility, or the predator within us will devour us all."

"On True Identity." *New York Times Magazine* 13 April 1975: 111.

Editorial piece attacking the proposal that every American be required to carry a national card of identity.

"Our Bloodless Coup." *Nation* 1 November 1999: 6.

Opinion piece in which Miller admonishes the American people for their current outrage "at the spectacle of an American President refusing to confess that he touched it," when they have fallen asleep over much more important issues that face us as a nation: poverty, abortion clinic bombings, and the "U.S. complicity in installing Pinochet and the CIA's supporting his murders."

"Our Guilt for the World's Evil." *New York Times Magazine* 3 January 1965: Sec. 6: 10–11, 48.

Lengthy essay detailing the provenance of the story and the meaning behind Miller's new play, *Incident at Vichy*. He also explores the meaning of guilt as it relates not only to liberalism but also to the work at hand.

"Oxygen, Usually One of Man's 'Best Friends,' Can Be Harmful." *Michigan Daily* 5 December 1935: 2.

Miller reports on experiments by the physiology department of the medical school on the study of "the physological [sic] effects of oxygen pressure on dogs."

"The Parable of the Stripper." *New Republic* 3 January 1994: 30.

Miller comments on the current ethnic problems in Yugoslavia by relating an experience in a local nightclub during his trip there in the sixties to preside over the International PEN Congress.

"The Past and Its Power: Why I Wrote *The Price*." *New York Times* 14 November 1999: Sec. 2: 5.

Lengthy essay in which Miller explains the plot and context of *The Price*, a play written, he says, in reaction to the "morally agonizing Vietnam War" and the "surge of avant-garde plays" that were produced in the sixties.

"Picking a Cast." *New York Times* 21 August 1955: Sec. 2: 1.

Essay in which Miller bemoans the fact, after having sat through three months of casting for his new play *A View from the Bridge*, that auditions for the theatre are "barbaric, and time-consuming, and ought to be replaced by "a permanent American theatre" whose ultimate boon will be to "make it easier for the actor to be charming, which is to say, himself, unafraid."

"The Playwright and the Atomic World." *Colorado Quarterly* 5 (1956): 117–37. Rpt. in *TDR* 5 (June 1961): 3–20. Rpt. in *Theatre in the Twentieth Century*. Ed. Robert Corrigan. New York: Grove, 1963. 29–48. Rpt. as "1956 and All This" in *The Theater Essays of Arthur Miller*. Ed. Robert A. Martin. New York: Viking, 1978. 86–109. Rpt. in *The Theater Essays of Arthur Miller*. Revised ed. Eds. Robert A. Martin and Steven R. Centola. New York: Da Capo, 1996. 86–109.

Lengthy essay in which Miller details his understanding of world affairs based on varying foreign reactions to works written for American audiences. Miller calls for "an entirely new approach" to "the whole problem of what the future is to be."

"A Playwright's Choice of 'Perfect' Plays." *New York Times* 14 January 1979: II: 10.

Short essay in which Miller names *Oedipus Rex* by Sophocles as his choice for a "perfect" play because it is "about political tyranny and at the same time an implacable confrontation with the processes of personal guilt, innocence and the human claim to justification."

"Politics as Theater." *New York Times* 4 November 1972: 33.

Op-ed piece about the theatricality of the recent Democratic Convention held in Miami, where we were "trying to cast the part of President."

"The Prague Winter." *New York Times* 16 July 1975: 37.

Lengthy op-ed piece in which Miller details the political oppression of writers in Prague, Czechoslovakia.

"Program Note." *Stagebill* for *Mr. Peters' Connections*. The Guthrie Lab. 29 October–21 November, 1999: n.p.

Brief essay describing the "suspended state of consciousness" in which *Mr. Peters' Connections* takes place. Many candid photographs of Miller at the play's read-through and rehearsals accompany the text.

"R." *Hockney's Alphabet*. New York: Random House, 1991. 61–63.

In a book published to raise money for people living with AIDS, Miller contributed an essay on the letter R after being provided with a Hockney drawing of the letter meant to inspire. Miller's brief essay draws a comparison between denial of the current epidemic with his recollections as a young boy of the shame associated with contracting tuberculosis, since it was "the common idea that the disease came from poverty, with which decent people were in no hurry to be associated if they could help it."

"Red and Anti-Red Curbs on Art Denounced by U.S. Playwright." *New York Times* 13 February 1956: 9.

In honor of the 75th anniversary of Dostoyevsky's death in 1881, Miller protests the artistic and political suppression of writers in the United States and the Soviet Union.

"Reflections on Butterflied Legs of Lamb and Other Things." *The Great American Writers Cookbook*. Ed. Dean Faulkner Wells. Oxford, Miss.: Yoknapatawpha, 1981. 66.

Brief entry in which Miller relates his culinary repertoire, including butterflied legs of lamb, broiled chicken, and fried eggs "with a little garlic."

"A Remarkable Hostility." *New Theater Review* 15 (Fall/Winter 1996): 30.

In a retrospective on the founding of the Lincoln Center Repertory Theater, Miller remarks on the open hostility from the press, academics, and "self-appointed artistic types" who finally "got to the board, and they pulled the rug out, and Kazan and Whitehead never had a chance to do anything."

"The Role of Men of the Mind in the World Today." *New York Herald Tribune*, 1961. Rpt. in *The Nonconformers: Articles of Dissent*. Eds. David Evanier and Stanley Silverzweig. New York: Ballantine, 1961. 137–43.

Never before documented essay by Miller on the occasion of his being invited, along with 154 other writers, scientists, and artists, to attend the inauguration of President-elect John F. Kennedy. Miller comments on the role of the intellectual in American society and political life, concluding, "In any case, it seems we will soon be looking at or at least glancing toward our poets, writers, and men of the mind for more than a laugh."

"Sakharov, Detente and Liberty." *New York Times* 5 July 1974: 21.

Essay that criticizes President Richard Nixon's silence regarding Soviet persecutions and refers to the hunger strike by Soviet scientist Andrei Sakharov who is protesting the jailing of dissidents in the Soviet Union. Says Miller, "a detente that suppresses liberty is a travesty and cannot endure."

"Salem Revisited." *New York Times* 15 October 1998: A31. Rpt. as "Return of the Witch Hunt; Hysteria Over Clinton's Sex Scandal Has Roots in Old Salem." *Los Angeles Times* 16 October 1998. Also printed simultaneously in *Los Angeles Daily News* 16 October 1998.

Miller's op-ed piece in which he finds parallels between the pursuit of President Clinton by Congress for sexual misconduct and the Salem witch trials of 1692. Miller also admits to important differences, such as public reaction and self-identification producing "sympathy for their leader."

"Salesman Has a Birthday." *New York Times* 5 February 1950: Sec. 2: 1, 3. Rpt. in *The Theater Essays of Arthur Miller*. Ed. Robert A. Martin. New York: Viking, 1978. 12–15. Rpt. in *"Death of a Salesman": Text and Criticism*. Ed. Gerald Weales. New York: Viking, 1967. Penguin, 1996. 147–50. Rpt. in *The Theater Essays of Arthur Miller*. Revised ed. Eds. Robert A. Martin and Steven R. Centola. New York: Da Capo, 1996. 12–15.

Short article in which Miller relates snippets of memories from the writing and the production of *Salesman* and details his feelings regarding the success of the play on the occasion of the production's first anniversary.

"School Prayer: A Political Dirigible." *New York Times* 12 March 1984: 31.

Op-ed piece that criticizes those who would enforce a mandate of silent school prayer in the schools, when "clearly the procedure is not according to the Constitution, a document that once was pretty close to biblical in its sacredness for conservatives." Miller recounts his automatic recitation of the Pledge of Allegiance as a boy, convinced the line was "One Nation in a Dirigible, with Liberty and Justice for All."

"Scientists See and Hear What Dog's Brain Cells Are Doing." *Michigan Daily* 9 November 1935: 1.

News item in which Miller reports on experiments to produce photographs and sounds of nerve centers in the brains of dogs, being conducted by Dr. Robert Gesell, head of the department of physiology at the University of Michigan.

"Sellars, Slosson, Shepard Speak on Fascism, Naziism and Hearst." *Michigan Daily* 12 March 1936: 1.

Miller reports on a symposium sponsored by the Student Alliance on War and Fascism.

"Should Ezra Pound Be Shot?" *New Masses* 25 December 1945: 5–6.

Miller is among five writers contributing to a debate regarding the treason trial of poet Ezra Pound. Miller, in the longest essay of the group, calls Pound's views "straight fascism with all the anti-Semitism, anti-foreignism included" and Pound himself "a Mussolini mouthpiece." He attacks those writers and critics who would allow Pound to speak irresponsibly because he is "a fine poet." Concludes Miller, "In a world where humanism must conquer lest humanity be destroyed, literature must nurture the conscious of man."

"Schubert's Loves Are Displayed in Art Cinema's Latest Picture." *Michigan Daily* 30 October 1935: 6.

In a news item announcing the screening of *Unfinished Symphony* by the Art Cinema League, Miller offers a positive review of the foreign film, praising the acting and the lack of "Hollywood's 'playing up' to the musical sequences."

"Simplicity of Aran's Life and People Described by Stephens." *Michigan Daily* 10 October 1935: 3.

Miller reports on the talk delivered by Irish poet James Stephens at the Lydia Mendelssohn Theatre at the University of Michigan.

"Snips about Movies." *Michigan Quarterly Review* 34.4 (Fall 1995): 592–94. Rpt. in *The Movies: Texts, Receptions, Exposures*. Eds. Laurence Goldstein and Ira Konigsberg. Ann Arbor: U of Michigan P, 1996. 133–35.

Essay in which Miller makes various comments on the movies (that "unalienated art designed for the masses")—his experiences in working with Russell Metty (cinematographer for *The Misfits*), the worldwide appeal of the American commercial film, his first-ever memories of watching a movie as a small child, his perception regarding the lack of respect for writers of film, and his thoughts on film as a medium that invites trickery, reflecting, perhaps, the truth that the whole of civilization "is about performances rather than the real thing."

"Soliloquys." *Playwrights, Lyricists, Composers on Theater*. Ed. Otis L. Guernsey Jr. New York: Dodd, Mead, 1974. 217–18.

Miller discusses his early career as a writer of radio plays.

"Some Would Forge Ahead in Space, Others Would Turn to Earth's Affairs." *New York Times* 21 July 1969: 7.

In an article composed of reactions to man's landing on the moon by notable Americans, Miller expresses his hope that, now that the United States has accomplished this great thing, Congress will turn its attention to authorize funds to make expeditions to needy places on the earth.

"The Story of Adam and Eve." *Genesis: As It Is Written: Contemporary Writers on Our First Stories*. Ed. David Rosenberg. Calif.: Harper San Francisco, 1996. 35–41.

Lengthy essay in which Miller explains not only his first

youthful reactions to the first book of the Bible, but his later attempts to dramatize its story in *The Creation of the World and Other Business*. Additionally, he draws a parallel between various "literal-minded" interpretations of Genesis and similar reactions to his play *Death of a Salesman.*

"*Story of G.I. Joe*: A Sequence from the Film." *Theatre Arts* (September 1945): 514–20.

In an editor's introduction to an excerpt from the film script *The Story of G.I. Joe*, Miller's piece on Ernie Pyle, written for *New Masses* after the journalist's death, is quoted at length.

"Subsidized Theater." *New York Times* 22 June 1947: Sec. 2: 1.

Two-column essay by Miller in which he makes a case for a privately subsidized New York City theatre that would eliminate competitive business practices while enabling playwrights to create important dramatic art. Says Miller, "We do have the playwrights. What we don't have is a Theater."

"Suspended in Time." *Life* May 1983: 104–8.

Photographic essay with Miller's accompanying text in which the playwright offers his thoughts, reactions, and memories of the Brooklyn Bridge, including a harrowing near-fatal automobile encounter in the early 1950s.

"Tan, Blue, Brown Mice? Sure, the University Owns Hundreds." *Michigan Daily* 12 October 1935: 1, 2. Rpt. in *Special to the* Daily*: The First One Hundred Years of Editorial Freedom at the* Michigan Daily. Ed. Susan Holtzer. Ann Arbor: Gaddo Cap, 1990. 134.

Miller reports on the little-known Laboratory of Vertebrate Genetics on the campus of the University of Michigan, which houses all manner and color of mice for research in heredity. Although not mentioned in this article, according to various sources Miller himself supposedly worked part-time in the mice lab while a student.

The Theater Essays of Arthur Miller. Ed. Robert A. Martin. New York: Viking, 1978.

Includes "Author's Foreword: Sorting Things Out," "Tragedy and the Common Man," "The Nature of Tragedy," "The *Salesman* Has a Birthday," "Preface to an Adaptation of Ibsen's *An Enemy of the People*," "Many Writers: Few Plays," "Journey to *The Cruci-*

ble," "The American Theater," "On Social Plays," "The Family in Modern Drama," "1956 and All This," "Introduction to the *Collected Plays*," "Brewed in *The Crucible*," "The Shadows of the Gods," "Morality and Modern Drama," "On Adaptations," "Introduction to *A View from the Bridge* (two-act version)," "The State of the Theater," "On Recognition," "Foreword to *After the Fall*," "What Makes Plays Endure?" "Arthur Miller: An Interview," "It Could Happen Here—And Did," "The Contemporary Theater," "On the Theater in Russia," "Broadway, from O'Neill to Now," "Arthur Miller vs. Lincoln Center." Also includes a chronology, play casts and production information, and a bibliography of works by Miller.

The Theater Essays of Arthur Miller. Revised ed. Eds. Robert A. Martin and Steven R. Centola. New York: Da Capo, 1996.

This edition contains all of the essays from the original edition published in 1978 plus "Arthur Miller on *The Crucible*," "The American Writer: The American Theater," "*Salesman* in Beijing," "The Will to Live," "The Mad Inventor of Modern Drama," "An Interview with Arthur Miller," "From *Timebends: A Life*," "A Fabulous Appetite for Greatness," "Again They Drink from the Cup of Suspicion," "Introduction to *The Golden Years* and *The Man Who Had All the Luck*," "Conditions of Freedom: Two Plays of the Seventies—*The Archbishop's Ceiling* and *The American Clock*," "A Conversation with Arthur Miller," "Arthur Miller: An Interview," "Introduction to *Plays: Three*," "On Screenwriting and Language: Introduction to *Everybody Wins*," "About Theater Language: Afterword to *The Last Yankee*," and "Ibsen and the Drama of Today." Also included are a list of casts and production information, bibliography of works by Arthur Miller, chronology, and indexes to both editions.

"Thoughts on a Burned House." *Architectural Digest* November 1984: 44+. Excerpt rpt. in *Architectural Digest* April 1999: 52.

Miller relates his experience of coming back from his trip to China to find that his house had burned down. Color photo of Miller accompanies the excerpt.

"Tragedy and the Common Man." *New York Times* 27 February 1949: Sec. 2: 1, 3. Rpt. in *"Death of a Salesman": Text and Criticism*. Ed. Gerald Weales. New York: Viking, 1967. Penguin, 1996. 143–47. Rpt. in *Theatre Arts* 35 (March 1951): 48, 50. Rpt. in *Literature for Our Time*. Eds. Harlow O. Waite and Benjamin P.

Atkinson. New York: Holt, 1953. Rpt. in *Tragedy Plays, Theory and Criticism*. Ed. Richard Levin. New York: Harcourt, Brace, 1960. Rpt. in *Two Modern American Tragedies: Reviews and Criticism of "Death of a Salesman" and "A Streetcar Named Desire."* Ed. John D. Hurrell. New York: Scribner's, 1961. 38–40. Rpt. in *Aspects of Drama*. Ed. Sylvan Barnet, et al. New York: Little, Brown, 1962. Rpt. in *The Modern Theatre*. Ed. Robert W. Corrigan. New York: MacMillan, 1964. Rpt. in *American Playwrights on Drama*. Ed. Horst Frenz. New York: Hill and Wang, 1965. 79–83. Rpt. in *The Play and the Reader*. Eds. Stanley Johnson, Judah Bierman, and James Hart. Englewood Cliffs, N.J.: Prentice-Hall, 1966. Rpt. in *The Theater Essays of Arthur Miller*. Ed. Robert A. Martin. New York: Viking, 1978. 3–7. Rpt. in *The Theater Essays of Arthur Miller*. Revised ed. Eds. Robert A. Martin and Steven R. Centola. New York: Da Capo, 1996. 3–7.

Miller's most controversial essay, sparking decades of debate regarding modern dramatic theory. It appeared in print soon after the opening of *Salesman*. In it Miller justifies the common man as "apt a subject for tragedy in its highest sense as kings were."

"20 Per Cent Cut in Local Relief Seen by Wagg." *Michigan Daily* 3 March 1936: 1, 2.

Miller reports on a cut in state relief appropriations, which will reduce by 20 to 25 percent payments to individuals on state aid.

"Uneasy about the Germans." *New York Times Magazine* 6 May 1990: 46, 77, 84–85.

Lengthy essay in which Miller asks the questions "Do Germans accept responsibility for the crimes of the Nazi era?" and "Is their repentance such that they can be trusted never to repeat the past?" Miller concludes by inviting modern Germany to "relinquish denial and take to heart the donations of history to one's character and the character of one's people."

"University of Michigan." *Holiday* December 1953: 68–71, 128–32, 136–37, 140–43. Rpt. in *Points of Departure*. Eds. A. J. Carr and W. R. Steinhoff. New York: Harpers, 1960. Excerpt rpt. as "Going to College" in *The Thirties, A Time to Remember*. Ed. Don Congdon. New York: Simon and Schuster, 1962. 400–401.

Miller revisits the scenes of his college days, remembering events and people, while comparing his memories with current conditions. Miller calls his time at U of M as "the testing ground for all my prejudices, my beliefs and my ignorance, and it helped to lay out the boundaries of my life. For me it had, above everything else, variety and freedom."

"The War between Young and Old, or Why Willy Loman Can't Understand What's Happening." *McCalls* July 1970: 32.

Miller places the Kent State massacre in the context of a war between old and young, casting Nixon and Agnew into the role of Willy Loman's brother Ben—they "don't waste time on introspection beyond the moment when they must once again appear before the natives looking stern and right and, if necessary, furious."

"What Makes Plays Endure." *New York Times* 15 August 1965: Sec. 2: 1, 3. Rpt. in *The Theater Essays of Arthur Miller*. Ed. Robert A. Martin. New York: Viking, 1978. 258–63. Rpt. in *The Theater Essays of Arthur Miller*. Revised ed. Eds. Robert A. Martin and Steven R. Centola. New York: Da Capo, 1996. 258–63.

Miller discusses the genesis of *A View from the Bridge* and *A Memory of Two Mondays* in order to "throw some light on theatrical conditions and one man's reaction to them ten years ago, and possibly on the play itself."

"What's Wrong with This Picture?" *Esquire* July 1974: 124–25, 170.

Miller discusses Soviet repression of both artists and intellectuals in Prague, Czechoslovakia.

"When Life Had at Least a Form." *New York Times* 24 January 1971: Sec. 2: 17.

Miller believes that the initial failure of *A Memory of Two Mondays* in its premiere in the "glamour-time" of 1955 was because it was written to evoke the memory of the depression.

"White Soles' Burden." *Travel Holiday* June 1991: 59.

In response to a question regarding the author's most vivid memory of a travel encounter, Miller humorously recounts the time, in 1950, that he had a lunch appointment in London with a publisher and everyone stared at him as he entered the restaurant because he did something that simply wasn't done—he wore white shoes in July.

"Why Elia Should Get His Oscar." *Guardian* (London) 6 March 1999: 2. Rpt. as "Kazan and the Bad Times" in *Nation* 22 March 1999: 6.

Brief essay in which Miller cites personal examples of censorship of his dramas as evidence of his sensitivity "to any attempts to, in effect, obliterate an artist's name because of his morals or political actions." He states that he feels Kazan should be honored with the Academy Award for his "exemplary work in theater and film" rather than dismissed for "where he has tragically failed."

"Why I Wrote *The Crucible*: An Artist's Answer to Politics." *New Yorker* 21 and 28 October 1996: 155–64.

On the occasion of the filming of the American film version of Miller's *The Crucible*, the playwright discusses the genesis of his stage play, including the work's political source, his research in Salem in the spring of 1952, his discovery of the play's dramatic form, his interest in writing a play using "a new language" of seventeenth-century New England, his memories of opening night, his decision to direct another production of the play a year later, and his thoughts regarding the play's universal appeal.

"With Respect to Her Agony—But with Love." *Life* 7 February 1964: 66.

In an essay that follows Tom Prideaux's ambiguous review, Miller defends *After the Fall* by stating unequivocally that "the character of Maggie, which in great part seems to underlie the fuss, is not in fact Marilyn Monroe." He appeals to audiences and critics not to play "Find the Author," and, instead, view the work as a "dramatic statement of a hidden process which underlies the destructiveness hanging over this age."

Speeches

"The American Writer: The American Theater." *Michigan Quarterly Review* 21 (Winter 1982): 4–20. Rpt. in *The Writer's Craft: Hopwood Lectures, 1965–81*. Ed. Robert A. Martin. Ann Arbor: U of Michigan P, 1982. 254–70. Rpt. in *The Theater Essays of Arthur Miller*. Revised ed. Eds. Robert A. Martin and Steven R. Centola. New York: Da Capo, 1996. 368–83. Excerpt rpt. in *Avery Hopwood: His Life and Plays*. Jack F. Sharrar. Ann Arbor: U of Michigan P, 1998. 214–15.

Speech given on the fiftieth anniversary of the Avery Hopwood award at U of M, Miller's alma mater. Miller discusses his memories of winning the award, his indebtedness to Professor Rowe, the development of his writing style, and the state of the theatre in the United States, which he calls "more hostile to serious work than it was a half-century ago, but all is not by any means lost."

"Arthur Miller on McCarthy's Legacy." *Harper's* July 1984: 11–12.

Portion of a speech given on 30 April 1984 called "The Interrogation of Angel Rama" given at a program on "Forbidden Writers" sponsored by PEN American Center and the Fund for Free Expression. While discussing the case and reading from the interrogation transcript of Angel Rama, a Uruguayan literary critic who "chose to go into exile after the military destroyed democracy in his country," Miller is reminded of his own trial for contempt of Congress in 1956. Miller speaks out against the McCarran-Walter Act, a law he calls "one of the pieces of garbage left behind by the sinking of the great scow of McCarthyism."

Bordens, William. "Democrats Begin Hartford Battle." *New York Times* 22 June 1968: 19.

News item reporting on a meeting of the resolutions committee of the Democratic Party in Connecticut. Miller's resolution calling for the immediate cessation of American bombing of North Vietnam and asking for peace negotiations to begin is quoted.

"Clurmania: Address, May 6, 1979." *Nation* 26 May 1979: 606–607.

Publication of Miller's remarks on the occasion of a tribute to Harold Clurman held at the opening of the Harold Clurman theatre in New York City. Miller says of his colleague and friend, Clurman was "a man of honor who admired the brave, a greatly tolerant fellow who could abide almost any thing excepting those truths which cannot work the lock that opens the door to poetry in this, the most vulgar of the arts."

"Crowd Here Hails Monk from Vietnam." *New York Times* 10 June 1966: 9.

Before a town hall audience of 1,200, Miller and Robert Lowell pay tribute to Vietnamese monk Thich Nhat Hanh, at an event organized by the International Committee of Conscience on Vietnam. Miller denounces the U.S. presence in Vietnam, saying "no sane person any longer believes that President Ky is any more than an American creation."

"Even Galileo Confessed." *Convicting the Innocent: The Story of a Murder, a False Confession, and the Struggle to Free a 'Wrong Man.'"* Ed. Donald S. Connery. Cambridge, Mass.: Brookline Books, 1996. 86–88.

Speech given by Miller at a symposium on Convicting the Innocent, held in Hartford, Connecticut, in June of 1994, in which the playwright discusses famous cases of coerced confessions, attempts at coerced confessions, and the use of confessions as evidence in 1692 at the Salem Witch Trials and the Peter Reilly murder case, in which he was personally involved.

"Harold Clurman Memorial Meeting." "The Invisible Director: The Stage Direction of Harold Clurman as Witnessed by Actors, Stage Managers, Producers, Playwrights and Critics from Three Representative Productions." Bruce Sweet. Diss. New York U, 1981. 222–23.

Remarks made by Miller on 18 September 1980 at the Shubert Theatre for a memorial to honor the late Harold Clurman. After praising Clurman as one who "made so few enemies" and "had no peer among the theatre critics and commentators in this country," Miller speaks on his belief that "in all justice, criticism should have been his avocation, rather than the main work of only lecturing the last third of his life."

"Miller Condemns 'Total Diplomacy.'" *New York Times* 8 May 1957: 5.

News article quoting at length from Miller's speech to the National Assembly of the Authors League of America the day before in which the playwright denounced "total diplomacy" as a threat to "the soul of art and the people themselves." Says Miller, "The mission of the written word is not to buttress high policy but to proclaim the truth, the truth for whose lack we must surely die; it is a mission not lightly to be cast aside for temporary advantage."

"Miller Sees PEN Growing Mightier." *New York Times* 6 July 1965: 30. Lengthy extract appears as "Literature and Masse Communications." *World Theatre* 15 (1966): 164–67.

Miller speaks on the subject of mass communication at the PEN Club Congress in Bled, Yugoslavia. Miller discusses the political power of the writer. Of note are his comments regarding critics and reporters and their job to keep the machine fed. "I daresay, that if the authors' names were removed from every new book and play and poem in the next six months, and critics had to evaluate them intrinsically, blindly, there would be chaos which would take years to sort out. For suddenly we would be confronted with the works themselves rather than the mythology surrounding authors and their lives, and reputations, a mythology in very large part created by reportage." Photo of Miller accompanies the *World Theatre* excerpt reprint.

"Miller Speaks." *Theater Week* 16 April 1990: 31.

Extract from Miller speech given on the occasion of the opening of the Arthur Miller Centre for American Studies at the University of East Anglia, Norwich, England, in May 1989. Miller tells his British audience that the best hope for theatre is with them because of their subsidized system—"The theater of the bottom line—meaning what pays big goes and what doesn't pay big does not deserve to live—is a catastrophe."

"The New Insurgency." *Nation* 3 June 1968: 717.

Excerpts from a speech given on 19 May 1968 at a rally for Senator Eugene McCarthy at Madison Square Garden. Miller predicts that the next president will have to make decisions based on the will of the people and not continue to support institutions that are "dead and inhuman and must be dismantled."

On Censorship and Laughter [pamphlet]. Chicago: Illinois Humanities Council, 1990.

Miller's keynote address at the "Expressions of Freedom" symposium exploring the role that art, literature, and music have played in the "preservation and pursuit of liberty over the past two centuries," held in Chicago on 11 November 1990. Finding that "when you step back a bit there is something comically Lilliputian" about censorship, Miller offers what he calls "a brief sketch of one writer's experience with repression" in which he relates censorship incidences with *Focus*, *All My Sons*, and *The Misfits*, as well as government control of the arts in countries such as the [former] Soviet Union and China.

"On Recognition." *Michigan Quarterly Review* 2 (Autumn 1963): 213–20. Rpt. in *The Theater Essays of Arthur Miller*. Ed. Robert A. Martin. New York: Viking, 1978. 237–51. Rpt. in *To The Young Writer* (Hopwood Lectures, 2nd Series). Ed. Arno L. Bader. Ann Arbor: U of Michigan, 1965. Rpt. in *The Theater Essays of Arthur Miller*. Revised ed. Eds. Robert A. Martin and Steven R. Centola. New York: Da Capo, 1996. 237–51.

In an address at the University of Michigan on 23 May 1963 at the Hopwood Awards ceremony, Miller offers his advice to young writers to speak for and to their society instead of seeking recognition, stressing self-satisfaction in an ethical sense over outward recognition. He warns against mistaking oneself for a finished product when, in fact, one has only begun the struggle of the artist.

"The Role of PEN." *Saturday Review* 4 June 1966: 16–17. Excerpt rpt. as "Arthur Miller: PEN, Politics, and Literature." *Publisher's Weekly* 18 July 1966: 32–33.

Miller's first address as president of PEN to an international PEN congress of 600 writers from more than fifty countries in New York. He defended the organization against is many critics and dealt principally with the interaction of the worlds of literature and politics. "To universalize culture is our ultimate aim. It is our particular business as writers simply because no other group is in a position to care as much as we can care about it, and because it is in the nature of writing to reach out to the whole world." Photo of Miller by wife Inge Morath accompanies the text.

"The Shadows of the Gods." *Harper's* August 1958: 35–43. Rpt. in *The Theater Essays of Arthur Miller*. Ed. Robert A. Martin. New York: Viking, 1978. 175–94. Rpt. in *American Playwrights on Drama*. Ed. Horst Frenz. New York: Hill and Wang, 1965. 134–53. Rpt. in *The Theater Essays of Arthur Miller*. Revised ed. Eds. Robert A. Martin and Steven R. Centola. New York: Da Capo, 1996. 175–94. Excerpt rpt. as "Influences on Miller's Writing" in *Readings on Arthur Miller*. Ed. Thomas Siebold. San Diego, Calif.: Greenhaven, 1997. 49–55.

Lengthy essay based on a talk that Miller delivered to the New Dramatists Committee in which he relates various literary influences on his work, including Tolstoy, Dostoevsky, Ibsen, "the Greeks and the German Expressionists," and Chekhov.

"A Talk on Peace and Justice." *Jewish Currents* 48.6 (June 1994): 4–6, 34.

Full text of Miller's speech presented at the annual Peace and Justice Service of Congregation Mishkan Israel in Hamden, Connecticut, on 25 March 1994, honoring his friend Rabbi Goldburg. Miller mentions his current production of *Broken Glass* and then speaks on the subject of "the violent tribalism of mankind."

"Toward a New Foreign Policy." *Society* March-April 1976: 10, 15–16.

Essay edited for written publication from a speech delivered by Miller before the Senate Permanent Subcommittee on Investigations on 18 November 1975. Miller forcefully argues for a solution to our international loss of prestige as one in which the Senate and the House "inform the present administration [Nixon], and administrations to come, that the hard-won wealth, resources, and talents of the American people are not to be travestied in supporting antidemocratic dictatorships regardless of how anticommunist they advertise themselves to be."

"Tribute to Pascal Covici." *Pascal Covici, 1888–1964*. Quill and Brush, 1964. 9–11.

Tribute by Miller to Covici, senior editor at Viking Press, given at a service at the Riverside Memorial Chapel, New York City, on 16 October 1964. Other tributes are by Saul Bellow, Malcolm Cowley, Joseph Campbell, John Steinbeck, and Pascal Covici Jr.

"We're Probably in an Art That Is—Not Dying." *New York Times* 17 January 1993: Sec. 2: 5. Rpt. in *The Theater Essays of Arthur Miller*. Revised ed. Eds. Robert A. Martin and Steven R. Centola. New York: Da Capo, 1996. 523–25.

In an article adapted from Miller's comments following a reading of *The Last Yankee* at the 92nd Street Y, Miller assesses the current state of theatre in the United States and the art of drama in Europe.

"The Writer in America." *Mainstream* 10 (July 1957): 43–46. Rpt. as "The Writer's Position in America" in *Coastlines* 2 (Autumn 1957): 38–40. Excerpt rpt. in *New York Times* 8 May 1957: 5.

In May of 1957, a three-day meeting of several hundred members of the National Assembly of Authors and Dramatists was held in New York City. Principal matters discussed were censorship, the position of the writer in America, and writer-publisher relations. Miller spoke on "the question of the integration of the writer into the domestic and foreign policies of the nation at any particular moment," strongly insisting that a free press and a free literature be preserved.

"Writers in Prison." *Encounter* June 1968: 60–62.

Miller's address to a meeting in London sponsored by the International PEN Defense Committee for Soviet and Greek Writers in Prison. Speaking from a position as one who was himself "hauled up before the House Committee on Un-American Activities a decade ago," Miller protested the censorship and jailing of Soviet writers, a penalty "normally reserved for desperate criminals."

"Can or Will We Support Repertory? Let's Get the Facts." *Playwrights, Lyricists, Composers on Theater*. Ed. Otis L. Guernsey Jr. New York: Dodd, Mead, 1974. 285–90.

Article prepared from comments made by Miller at a symposium, the playwright addresses the controversy surrounding the New York City Center proposed takeover of the Vivian Beaumont and Forum Theaters from the financially ailing Repertory Theater of Lincoln Center. Miller was a member of the Ad Hoc Committee to Save the Theater at Lincoln Center. After summarizing the "origin of this disaster," Miller calls the board of the Lincoln Center "to account," and invites theatre professionals and interested persons to "to go in and challenge those men, to face the realities together, and decide what is to become of a potentially great theater that belongs to all of us."

Letters

"Assail Repression of Soviet Jews." *New York Times* 30 December 1970: 24.

Letter to the editor of the *New York Times*, signed by Miller and sixteen other scholars, scientists, and writers, protesting the Soviet government's sentencing to death or harsh prison terms of thirty-four Jews for "having planned to hijack an airplane and divert it to Finland" when in fact they "were tried for the crime of being Jews."

"Flash: Clear All Wires!" *Michigan Daily* 7 December 1934: 4.

Letter to the editor in which Miller complains of "sartorial rubbish-dealing" in the gossip-type content of the school newspaper. Says Miller, "With the world scampering gaily toward an uncertain fate, the colors of new shoe laces sort of lose their appeal, except of course, for those children who insist on remaining with us to exhibit their pettiness and shallow minds." Reply by the editor follows Miller's letter and defends the paper's policy—"The truth, Mr. Miller, is that quite as large—and certainly far more audible—a group reads Page 5 as reads Page 4. Miss So-'n-So's shoe laces must continue to be duly reported as long as Miss So-'n-So and her friends remain so breathlessly interested in them."

"The Hero's Last Sigh." *New York Times* 17 March 1996: Sec. 6: 14.

Miller writes to protest Michiko Kakutani's column on Salman Rushdie, which stated that Miller almost alone among prominent American writers had refused to protest the Iranian government's threat to murder Rushdie. In fact, Miller had joined in statements by PEN condemning the fatwa.

"Letter: Persecution of Turkish Journalists." *Independent* (London) 14 June 1994: 15.

Miller is among fifteen signed artists and writers protesting the persecution of Turkish journalists.

"On Adaptations." *New York Times* 29 November 1959: II: 13. Rpt. in *The Theater Essays of Arthur Miller*. Ed. Robert A. Martin. New York: Viking, 1978. 215–17. Rpt. in *The Theater Essays of Arthur Miller*. Revised ed. Eds. Robert A. Martin and Steven R. Centola. New York: Da Capo, 1996. 215–17.

In a letter to the Radio-Television editor of the *New York Times*, Miller protests the "digesting" of classics of literature for the television because they then become superficial. "We are breaking the continuity of culture by passing on its masterpieces through mutilated distortions. . . . You cannot digest a work of art because it is digested in the first place; it is the ultimate distillation of the author's vision by definition."

"Reply to John Gassner." *World Theatre* 4 (Autumn 1955): 40–41.

In a reply to John Gassner's article titled "Modern Drama and Society," Miller contends that "social drama is only another way of saying Whole Drama."

"Repression in Brazil." *New York Times* 24 April 1971: 28.

Letter to the editor, signed by Miller and fourteen others, dated 2 April 1971, protesting the repression of Brazilian theatre artists and writers.

"Sheriff Andres: A Rebuttal." *Michigan Daily* 31 March 1937: 4.

Lengthy letter to the editor in which Miller vexatiously attacks a Mr. C.B.C., who in the previous day's paper had defended Sheriff Andres's decision to break up a sit-in by Washtenaw Republicans. Miller calls C.B.C. a "Fascist" and a "liar."

"Symposium: Playwriting in America." *Yale/Theatre* 4 (Winter 1973): 19–21.

Miller's response to a letter sent to "a number of prominent people involved in the theatre and cultural affairs" by the editors of *Yale/Theatre*. The letter asks if the recipient agrees with their conclusion that the American stage has returned "to a theater primarily of text rather than one incorporating text into a spectacle of increasingly more exotic, non-verbal proportions." Miller admits his hope that *Yale/Theatre*'s conclusion is correct because among all theatre professionals, it is the playwright alone who can, "if he has the talent, lift spectacle to that coherency which creates a world rather than the disparate effects of feeling alone."

"Talk vs. Action." *Michigan Daily* 2 April 1935: 4.

In this letter to the editor, signed "A.M.," Miller makes a rousing call for the students at the University of Michigan to attend the April 4th rally against war. Says Miller, "We must show our numbers so that the lords of war will think more than twice before they buck such live, tangible, moving opposition."

"To Newt on Art." *Nation* 31 July/7 August 1995: 118. Rpt. as "We Spend Less on the Support of Our Fine Arts than Almost Every Other Advanced Country" in *Chronicle of Higher Education* 18 August 1995: B5.

On hearing that Newt Gingrich had made the comment that Miller "had effected great works without the benefit of government fellowships" to a contingent of artists at a breakfast to lobby for continued congressional support of the arts, Miller sent a letter to Gingrich that was later printed. Miller attempts to correct Gingrich's impression by reporting his own reliance on federal funds at two points in his life. While opposing government funding of all arts and artists (for therein lies control of the arts), Miller appeals for government support, for "the act of supporting its arts, Congress demonstrates a pride in our arts which I know will move most American artists to tape their highest artistic ideals in return."

"University and Student Workers." *Michigan Daily* 26 January 1937: 4.

Letter to the editor in which Miller calls for the the administration of the university to allow and encourage the League workers to bargain as a unit for higher wages. Says Miller, "For to do otherwise is to teach liberty with invalidating reservation, to laugh in the face of the University's own teachers, to demand social responsibility on commencement day and to forbid it all the days before then."

"Wants Supplement." *Michigan Daily* 18 January 1938: 4.

Letter to the editor, signed by Miller and Norman Rosten, among others, supporting the suggestion that the *Michigan Daily* issue a literary supplement. Not only will the student body enjoy such a section, they argue, but it is imperative that a connection be reestablished between the writer and for "those for whom he writes."

"We Have Done Nothing." *Michigan Daily* 21 March 1935: 4.

Letter to the editor, signed "A.M.," in which Miller warns of the impending possibilities of war in Europe. Says Miller, "The World has obviously forgotten the lesson it swore to remember and it appears that the American student, the man who shoulders the gun, is intent upon purging his mind of pertinent but uncomfortable thoughts. . . . It is our selfish duty to delve into the actual causes of modern wars, to find what makes them and then to formulate a plan to break them, finally to act."

Statements

"Al Hirschfeld's Secret." *Hirschfeld on Line*. New York: Applause, 1999. 29. Caricatures of Miller appear on pages 29, 176, 302.

Miller praises Al Hirschfeld as a man who "knows the secret of all theater" and possesses the simple gift of making "all these people look interesting. Because they probably are to him."

"Statement." *Louise Bourgeois: The Locus of Memory, Works 1982–1993*. Eds. Charlotta Kotik, Terrie Sultan, and Christian Leigh. New York: Brooklyn Museum, 1994. 76.

Miller praises the work of sculptor/artist Louise Bourgeois—"whatever else her work may be, it seems full of an implacable truthfulness to her recall, her dreams, her most private vision, and in that there is a beauty of integrity, which informs her art."

"Statement." *The Work of Robert Kaufmann (1913–1959)*. New York: Thistle, 1961. 28.

In a book of appreciations and reprints of paintings by Robert Kaufmann, Miller praises the artist for his "constant growth toward a humane rendering of what he saw without sentimentality or softening his vision."

Advertisements, Book Reviews, and Dustjacket Commentary

Ash, Timothy Garton. *The File: A Personal History*. New York: Random House, 1997.

Blurb: "No population was as closely watched for signs of dissidence, although Hoover's FBI came fairly close at times."

Bernstein, Walter. *Inside Out: A Memory of the Blacklist*. New York: Knopf, 1996.

Blurb: "Walter Bernstein has written the best book on the blacklist I have read. It is also a sharp insight into that terrible period" (inside front flap).

Binyan, Liu. *A Higher Kind of Loyalty: A Memoir of China's Foremost Journalist*. New York: Random House, 1990.

Blurb: "Liu Binyan's autobiography is the gripping story of a journalist-writer who made the fatal mistake of trying to tell the truth in Mao's China. But it is not quite the now-familiar tale of tortures and endless persecution, for there is a powerful stylistic directness, a wealth of detailed observation, and the passionate humanity of a witness and victim of the most surrealistic tyranny of this or any other age. Despite everything, it is a book of hope, for Liu Binyan, truth can still save us."

"Commemorations by Hans Herlin" [advertisement]. *Atlantic Monthly* October 1975: 110.

Advertisement that quotes Miller's comments on the novel. Writes Miller, the book reads "like a thriller and relentlessly illuminates the whole tragedy of Germany wrestling with a history it can neither forget or remember."

"A Fabulous Appetite for Greatness." *New York Times Book Review* 6 November 1988: 12–13. Rpt. in *The Theater Essays of Arthur Miller*. Revised ed. Eds. Robert A. Martin and Steven R. Centola. New York: Da Capo, 1996. 455–59.

Positive review of *The Selected Letters of Eugene O'Neill*, edited by Travis Bogard and Jackson R. Bryer. Miller calls the book "essential" because they demystify O'Neill.

"Farrell: Seething Slums Strangle Their Spawn." *Michigan Daily* 2 February 1936: 6.

Book review of *Studs Lonigan: A Trilogy* by James T. Farrell in which Miller calls "written with unquestionable honesty and convincingness."

Forché, Carolyn, ed. *Against Forgetting: Twentieth-Century Poetry of Witness*. New York: W. W. Norton, 1993.

Blurb: "From every continent comes the news that our age is an age of murder and repression on a scale unimagined before. And yet I can't peruse this book without marveling at what beauty these writers have made of the calamity called the Twentieth Century. I would not have thought a poetry anthology could be so stirring."

Gotham Book Mart and Gallery Bookmark. 41 West 47th St.. New York, 10036.

Blurb: "Invaluable as a source of books for research of all kinds."

Halliday, Ernest Milton. *John Berryman and the Thirties: A Memoir*. Amherst: U of Massachusetts P, 1987.

Blurb: "I lived through this time, yet found much [here] that was new and richly evocative. It is a very good read and respectful of chaos—the normal writer's condition and Berryman's especially."

"A Hero of Our Time." *Los Angeles Times* 29 June 1997: 5. Rpt. as book review for *The Courage to Stand Alone: Letters from Prison and Other Writings* by Wei Jingsheng. New York: Viking, 1997 in the *Los Angeles Times* 14 December 1997: 6.

Letter to the editor praising writer Wei Jingsheng's "incredible courage" and condemning his "horrifying treatment" by the Chinese government in giving the writer another lengthy prison sentence for speaking his thoughts.

Leverich, Lyle. *Tom, the Unknown Tennessee Williams*. New York: Norton, 1995.

Blurb: "Plainly a work of distinction . . . I think it will be of great service to Williams' reputation."

"Lippman." *Michigan Daily* 5 April 1936: 10.

Book review of *Interpretations* by Walter Lippman, which Miller calls "so inconsistent as to be almost whimsical."

"The Mad Inventor of Modern Drama." *New York Times Book Review* 6 January 1985: 1, 30. Rpt. in *The Theater Essays of Arthur Miller*. Revised ed. Eds. Robert A. Martin and Steven R. Centola. New York: Da Capo, 1996. 414–18.

Positive book review of an "absorbing and profound" biography of August Strindberg by Olaf Lagercrantz.

Meisner, Sanford, and Dennis Longwell. *Sanford Meisner on Acting*. New York: Vintage, 1987.

Blurb: "This book should be read by anybody who wants to act or even appreciate what acting involves. Like Meisner's way of teaching, it is the straight goods."

"Ralph Ginzburg Enters Prison Today" [advertisement]. *New York Times* 17 February 1972: 21.

Full-page protest by artists, authors, and notable professionals protesting the jailing of Ralph Ginzburg on obscenity charges. Writes Miller, in part, "After all the legal, moral, and psychological arguments are done, the fact remains that a man is going to prison for publishing and advertising stuff a few years ago which today would hardly raise and eyebrow in your dentist's office. . . . Compared to the usual run of entertainment in this country, Ginzburg's publications and his ads are on a par with *National Geographic*."

"A Review of *In Hiding: The Life of Manuel Cotes* by Ronald Fraser." *New York Times* 9 July 1972: VII: 1, 34.

Positive review of a book about a Spaniard's passive resistance to Franco. Says Miller, the story shows "what the Spanish Civil War was really about."

Riccio, Vincent, and Bill Slocum. *All the Way Down*. New York: Simon and Schuster, 1962.

Inside flap: "Arthur Miller says that Vincent Riccio is the only man he has ever met who has the three qualities required to work with juvenile delinquents: a deep love for kids, a psychological understanding of their needs, and the guts to walk into battlefield conditions unarmed. Blurb: "This book has a virtue, a very great and real one, I think, in that it conveys the endless, leaden, mind-destroying boredom of the delinquent life. Its sex is without romance or sexuality, its violence is without release or gratification—unlike the movies but exactly like the streets. This is no story of the hoodlum priest who saves the worthy but misguided good boy. It is, rather, the story of the man who would like to help, hardly manages to at all, and is nearly worn out in the attempt. But his thoughts are real thoughts and not borrowed, and his vision is made not of what he wishes but of what he saw."

Timerman, Jacobo. *Prisoner without a Name, Cell without a Number*. New York: Knopf, 1981.

Blurb: "A lyrical outcry, riveting to read and chilling to contemplate. . . ."

"What Are You Doing Out There?" [advertisement]. *New York Times* 15 January 1951: 9.

Half-page advertisement, funded by donations from Miller and other notables, denouncing the pamphlet "Red Channels" for judging and convicting artists for their political beliefs, supporting First Amendment rights of those writers and directors who have appeared before HUAC, and protesting loyalty oaths that have been instituted on college campuses. Say the ad, "Speak up for freedom! It doesn't matter how—it may be done in a letter to your Congressman, to a radio network or sponsor, or to your school or college. It may be in conversation in your own home. But speak up!"

Yevtushenko, Yevgeny. *Don't Die before You're Dead*. Trans. Antonia W. Bouis. New York: Random, 1995.

Blurb: "Yevtushenko has been one of Russia's most adventurous writers for more than thirty years. His work has played an important part in Russia's historic struggle to open herself up to the modern world."

5. Interviews

Print

Abbotson, Susan C. W. "An Afternoon with Arthur Miller." *The Arthur Miller Society Newsletter* (June 1999): 13.

Abbotson reports on a question-and-answer session held on 15 July 1996 at the Clark Art Institute in Williamstown, Mass., in honor of the American premiere of *The Ride Down Mount Morgan* at the Williamstown Theatre Festival. Miller responds to questions regarding his new play, writing plays and formulas for success, and "his own frequently ambivalent reception in America."

Alex, Patricia. "Arthur Miller Stands the Test of Time." *The Record* (Bergen County, N.J.) 22 March 1996: A3.

At an appearance at Fairleigh Dickinson University in Hackensack in March 1996, Miller responds to questions regarding the state of the American theatre. Miller comments on the continuing relevancy of *Death of a Salesman*, the film production of *The Crucible*, and what he considers to be the biggest achievement in his career as a writer—learning to spell.

Allsop, Kenneth. "A Conversation with Arthur Miller." *Encounter* 13 (July 1959): 58–60. Rpt. in *Conversations with Arthur Miller*. Ed. Matthew C. Roudané. Jackson: UP of Mississippi, 1987. 52–55.

From his working space in his New York apartment that he shares with wife Marilyn Monroe, Miller talks "about present-day metropolitan society and the theatre that that society produces."

"American Playwrights Self-Appraised." *Saturday Review* 3 September 1955: 18–19.

In a short answer to a questionnaire, Miller gives a general response on his techniques and goals.

"AOL Chat with Arthur Miller." 21 February 1999. http://www.deathofasalesman.com/aol-chat-miller.htm (27 February 1999).

Miller answers questions regarding his original inception of the role of Willy Loman, the financial constraints placed on straight plays on Broadway, what has made *Death of a Salesman* endure for fifty years, his memories of *Salesman*'s first opening, his creative process as a writer, and the relevance of *The Crucible* to modern sensibilities.

Applebome, Peter. "Present at the Birth of a Salesman." *New York Times* 29 January 1999: B1.

Lengthy interview in which Miller discusses his feelings regarding the opening of the fiftieth anniversary production of *Death of a Salesman*, the actors who have played the role of Willy Loman, the state of the professional Broadway theatre, and the displaced role of the writer in American culture (theatre, film, and television).

Armitstead, Claire. "Double Visionaries." *Guardian Weekly* (London) 7 August 1994: 27.

Interview with Miller and director David Thacker discussing the production of *Broken Glass*, including the details of their working relationship. Miller praises English actors over Americans as artists who "can switch tracks very quickly without falling apart. They're more used to working with language." Miller concludes by lauding the National Theatre as having "a sense of community and dignity that doesn't exist in New York."

"Arthur Miller." *Vanity Fair* March 1999: 280.

Miller answers a series of questions relating to his idea of perfect happiness, his greatest fear, the historical figure he most admires, the trait he deplores in himself and others, his greatest extravagance, his favorite journeys, words or phrases he feels are overused, and his greatest achievements.

"Arthur Miller." *For the Love of Books: 115 Celebrated Writers on the Books They Love Most.* Ed. Ronald B. Schwartz. New York: Grosset/Putman, 1999. 183–84.

In response to the question "What books have left the greatest impression on you, and why?" Miller answers with three titles: *A High Wind in Jamaica* by Richard Hughes (the "finest description of a hurricane I've ever read"), *The Castle* by Franz Kafka ("a lesson in how to do more with less"), and *The Brothers Karamazov* ("it opened up a dark subterranean world which was utterly strange in Brooklyn and began a lifelong love affair with Russian literature").

"Arthur Miller Ad-Libs on Elia Kazan." *Show* January 1964: 55–56, 97–98. Rpt. in *Conversations with Arthur Miller*. Ed. Matthew C. Roudané. Jackson: UP of Mississippi, 1987. 68–79.

In an interview devoted to *After the Fall*, Miller discusses (at length) the Lincoln Center Repertory Theater system, Elia Kazan's strategies as director of this new play, and his method of revising and finishing the play during the rehearsal process.

"Arthur Miller on His Plays at the Lincoln Centre." *Times* (London) 23 January 1965: 5.

Interview conducted in London during rehearsals for the National Theatre production of *The Crucible*. Miller discusses his work, the current state of the commercial American theatre, and his displeasure with the interference of the Board in the artistic decisions at the Lincoln Center.

"Arthur Miller Talks." *Michigan Quarterly Review* 6 (Summer 1967): 153–84. Contains three items: (1) "Arthur Miller Talks: The Contemporary Theater" [Speech], 153–63. Rpt. in *The Theater Essays of Arthur Miller*. New York: Viking, 1978. 301–18. Rpt. in *Conversations with Arthur Miller*. Ed. Matthew C. Roudané. Jackson: UP of Mississippi, 1987. 112–27. (2) "Arthur Miller Talks: Freedom in the Mass Media" [panel discussion], 163–78. (3) "Arthur Miller Talks Again: A Chat with a Class in Stage Directing" [interview], 178–84. Rpt. in *Conversations with Arthur Miller*. Ed. Matthew C. Roudané. Jackson: UP of Mississippi, 1987. 128–36. Rpt. in *The Theater Essays of Arthur Miller*. Revised ed. Eds. Robert A. Martin and Steven R. Centola. New York: Da Capo, 1996. 301–18.

"Arthur Miller Talks: Freedom in the Mass Media" [panel discussion]. *Michigan Quarterly Review* 6 (Summer 1967): 163–78.

Panel discussion with Mike Wallace, Arnold Gingrich, and Arthur Miller, followed by questions by students, in which Miller expresses his dissatisfaction with most U.S. newspapers and television news departments and their focus on what he sees as entertainment rather than the truth. Miller also discusses censorship issues as they relate to the TV premiere of *The Crucible*, and the network's request that Miller remove "four pages of expressions" before it could be produced for television.

"Arthur Miller Talks: The Contemporary Theater." *Michigan Quarterly Review* 6 (Summer 1967): 153–63. Rpt. in *The Theater Essays of Arthur Miller*. New York: Viking, 1978. 301–18. Rpt. in *Conversations with Arthur Miller*. Ed. Matthew C. Roudané. Jackson: UP of Mississippi, 1987. 112–27. Rpt. in *The Theater Essays of Arthur Miller*. Revised ed. Eds. Robert A. Martin and Steven R. Centola. New York: Da Capo, 1996. 301–18.

Part of an informal talk delivered at the University of Michigan on 28 February 1967. Miller speaks about "the situation of the theater these days, rather than about plays and about the art of the theater, because there won't be any art of the theater if the situation doesn't change. . . . We have shows in New York, but we don't have any theater in New York."

"Arthur Miller Talks Again: A Chat with a Class in Stage Directing." *Michigan Quarterly Review* 6 (Summer 1967): 178–84. Rpt. in *Conversations with Arthur Miller*. Ed. Matthew C. Roudané. Jackson: UP of Mississippi, 1987. 128–36.

Miller discusses the playwright's relationship to the director and offers details regarding his own working relationship with Elia Kazan.

Atlas, James. "The Creative Journey of Arthur Miller Leads Back to Broadway and TV." *New York Times* 28 September 1980: Sec. 2: 1, 32.

On the occasion of the television premiere of *Playing for Time* and the New York opening of *The American Clock*, Miller discusses how he came to write both works, the controversy surrounding the casting of Vanessa Redgrave in the role of Fania Fénelon, his memories of growing up in the depression, his recollections of the opening of *Salesman* in 1949, and his thoughts on his satisfaction with his career as a playwright.

Balakian, Janet. "A Conversation with Arthur Miller." *Michigan Quarterly Review* 29 (Spring 1990): 158–70. Rpt. in *The Theater Essays of Arthur Miller*. Revised ed. Eds. Robert A. Martin and Steven R. Centola. New York: Da Capo, 1996. 483–99.

Lengthy interview in which Miller answers questions regarding comparisons of his current work and his earlier writing, issues of illusion and reality in the canon, Miller's interest in the bending of time, and memory as a thematic concern.

———. "An Interview with Arthur Miller." *Studies in American Drama 1945 to the Present* 6.1 (1991): 28–47. Rpt. as "Arthur Miller" in *Speaking on Stage: Interviews with Contemporary American Playwrights*. Eds. Philip C. Kolin and Colby H. Kullman. Tuscaloosa, Ala.: U of Alabama P, 1996. 40–57.

Miller discusses *The American Clock* and *The Archbishop's Ceiling*, socialism, the Great Depression, the social and personal in his plays, and his most recent works.

Barber, John. "Guilt Edged Miller." *Daily Telegraph* (London) 10 September 1979. 13.

Interview conducted on the occasion of the National Theatre production of *Death of a Salesman*, starring Warren Mitchell. Miller discusses the impact of his play, the theme of guilt that runs through his cannon, his literary silence during his years of marriage to Marilyn Monroe, and his latest, as yet unnamed, play.

Barnouw, Eric, ed. *Radio Drama in Action: Twenty-Five Plays of a Changing World.* New York: Farrar and Rinehart, 1945. 268.

Brief explanation by Miller as to his intentions behind the writing of *Grandpa and the Statue*, a radio play written in 1945 for *Cavalcade of America*. "If people get the idea from the show that, Jew, Irish, Italian or what not, we were all welcome here once, that will be a great satisfaction to me."

Barthel, Joan. "Arthur Miller Ponders *The Price*." *New York Times* 28 January 1968: II: 1, 5.

In an interview that appeared ten days prior to the opening of *The Price*, Miller responds to questions regarding the new work's themes, the usual casting and staging problems he encountered with this production, and his views on his literary career and the Vietnam war protests.

Bentley, Eric. *Thirty Years of Treason: Excerpts from Hearings before the House Committee on Un-American Activities, 1938–1968*. New York: Viking, 1971. 790–825.

Fairly complete transcript of Miller's testimony/interview before HUAC on 21 June 1956. Bentley precedes the transcript with a brief retelling of Miller's political involvements which led to his investigation by the Committee.

Bigsby, Christopher. "Arthur Miller: The Art of the Theatre II, Part II." *Paris Review* 152 (Fall 1999): 208–24.

Transcript of an interview conducted in 1998 at the 92nd Street YMHA in New York. Miller discusses his views on political theatre, the theme of the past in *The Price*, what lead him to write *The Creation of the World and Other Business*, themes of betrayal in his dramas, his approach to the Holocaust as a subject, the genesis of *Mr. Peters' Connections*, his meeting with Gorbachev in 1984, and his sense of dramatic structure.

———. "Arthur Miller: An Interview." *The Theater Essays of Arthur Miller*. Revised ed. Eds. Robert A. Martin and Steven R. Centola. New York: Da Capo, 1996. 500–508. Excerpt rpt. as "An Interview with Arthur Miller" in *Readings on Arthur Miller*. Ed. Thomas Siebold. San Diego, Calif.: Greenhaven, 1997. 32–38. [From *Arthur Miller and Company*. Ed. Christopher Bigsby. London: Methuen, 1990. 55–62.]

Miller responds to questions on *Death of a Salesman*—its lyrical quality, its perceived pessimism, Linda's role, the pathology of Willy Loman, the character of Ben, and Miller's assessment of the various actors who have portrayed Willy.

———. "14 October 1991, Olivier Theatre." *Platform Papers 7: Arthur Miller*. London: Royal National Theatre, 1995. 15–21.

On the occasion of the world premiere of *The Ride Down Mount Morgan* in London, Miller responds to questions concerning his decision to produce the play first in England, the story of the play, the idea behind the structure of the play, his move toward comedy, the theme of betrayal, what prompted him to write his autobiography, and his thoughts on whether suicide feeds the tragic sensibility or neutralizes it.

———. "3 August 1994, Olivier Theatre." *Platform Papers 7: Arthur Miller*. London: Royal National Theatre, 1995. 23–31.

Miller discusses the structure, genesis, themes, and historical element of *Broken Glass*, the part his Jewishness plays in his writing, how the depression has proven resonant to his work, and his feelings on the indomitability of the human spirit.

———. "3 July 1984, Lyttelton Theatre." *Platform Papers 7: Arthur Miller*. London: Royal National Theatre, 1995. 7–13.

After Miller reads from *Salesman in Beijing*, he answers questions regarding the consequences of McCarthyism in America, his views on the position of censorship in China, the reaction of Chinese audiences to *Death of a Salesman*, the influence of Greek tragedies on his plays, the commercialism of the American theatre, and his feelings regarding the Lord Chamberlain's strictures on his *A View from the Bridge*.

———. "Why Willy Loman Goes on Selling." *Daily Telegraph* (London) 4 February 1999: 24.

Miller discusses the differences between the design of the 1949 and 1999 productions of *Death of a Salesman*, his relationship with his environment that has led to carpentry as a hobby, and the social relevance that his fifty-year-old work still enjoys.

———, ed. *Arthur Miller and Company*. London: Methuen, 1990. Excerpt rpt. as "Arthur Miller: An Interview" in *The Theater Essays of Arthur Miller*. Revised ed. Eds. Robert A. Martin and Steven R. Centola. New York: Da Capo, 1996. 500–508. Excerpt rpt. as "An Interview with Arthur Miller" in *Readings on Arthur Miller*. Ed. Thomas Siebold. San Diego, Calif.: Greenhaven, 1997. 32–38.

Published to commemorate Miller's seventy-fifth birthday, this lengthy interview is intercut with commentary by actors, designers, directors, critics, and fellow writers, all expressing their praise or memories of "America's greatest living playwright." Miller talks about his youth, experiences, influences, techniques, and the moral and political issues of his plays. Miller discusses his father's financial ruin in the 1920s and the Great Depression's influence on his views of society, family, and the individual, including its impact on his writing.

Boasberg, Leonard W. "In Latest Miller Play, Characters Are Jews, the Subject Denial." *Philadelphia Inquirer* 3 March 1996: G1.

Telephone interview with Miller for a piece on the Philadelphia Theatre Company production of *Broken Glass*. Miller discusses his play's themes, its setting, the subject of anti-Semitism then and now, and what he sees as the problem with the economic nature of American theatre.

Brandon, Henry. "A Conversation with Arthur Miller and Marilyn Monroe." *Sunday Times* (London) 20 March 1960: 14–15. Rpt. as "The State of the Theater: A Conversation with Arthur Miller." in *Harper's* November 1960: 63–69. Expanded version rpt. as "Sex, Theater, and the Intellectual." *As We Are*. New York: Doubleday,

1961. 102–31. Abridged as "A Conversation with Arthur Miller." *World Theatre* 11 (Autumn 1962): 229–40. Expanded version rpt. in *Conversations with Henry Brandon*. Boston: Houghton Mifflin, 1968. 182–213. Rpt. in *The Theater Essays of Arthur Miller*. Ed. Robert A. Martin. New York: Viking, 1978. 223–36. Rpt. in *Conversations with Arthur Miller*. Ed. Matthew C. Roudané. Jackson: UP of Mississippi, 1987. 56–67. Rpt. in *The Theater Essays of Arthur Miller*. Revised ed. Eds. Robert A. Martin and Steven R. Centola. New York: Da Capo, 1996. 223–36.

Interview conducted in Hollywood at the Beverly Hills Hotel in March 1960. Miller responds to questions regarding his relationship with wife Marilyn Monroe, the role of the artist in modern society, the evolution of American drama, and his writing processes.

Breit, Harvey. "In and Out of Books: Politics II." *New York Times* 19 May 1957: Sec. 8: 8.

Interview conducted for an article on the release of Miller's *Collected Plays* in which the playwright discusses the protracted nature of his contempt of Congress hearings and the role of the writer in society. Cartoon of Miller accompanies the text.

Breslauer, Jan. "The Arthur Miller Method." *Los Angeles Times* 19 June 1994: Calendar: 8.

Lengthy interview in which Miller discusses the issues of ethnic separatism and anti-Semitism raised by *Broken Glass*, the conditions of the nonmusical theatre in New York City, the reasons for his high regard in Britain, and the modern relevance of *Death of a Salesman*. Included are comments by Robert Whitehead, Jack O'Brien, and Stanley Kaufmann. Five photographs accompany the text.

Buckley, Tom. "In the Beginning Miller's Creation. . . ." *New York Times* 5 December 1972: 49, 67.

Buckley interviews Miller, Harold Clurman, and others involved with *The Creation of the World and Other Business* for the reasons behind the play's failure. Reasons cited include communication problems between Clurman and his actors, the lack of the proper amount of rehearsal time, the unprofessional conduct of the actors, and the incomplete condition of Miller's play.

———. "Miller Takes His Comedy Seriously." *New York Times* 29 August 1972: 22. Rpt. in *Conversations with Arthur Miller*. Ed. Matthew C. Roudané. Jackson: UP of Mississippi, 1987. 249–52.

Interview conducted at the start of rehearsals for *The Creation of the World and Other Business* at ANTA in which Miller discusses the play's process and his religious and biblical interests. Of note are the personal details revealed in this interview, including the whereabouts of his first two children and his new role of grandfather to his son Robert's child.

Bunce, Alan N. "Intelligence Resisted, Says Arthur Miller." *Christian Science Monitor* 10 June 1967: 6.

News article reporting Miller's participation in the twelfth biannual congress of the International Theatre Institute in New York. In his address to the convention, Miller remarks on the state of the American professional theatre and says it is "perfect proof of the resistance of the theatre to the application of intelligence. . . . It's terribly hard to convince anyone here that it's more than a way of passing an evening."

Calta, Louis. "Miller Defends Theme of *Price*." *New York Times* 5 March 1968: 32.

Interview in which Miller defends himself against the accusation by critics that he has been insulated from the events of the day and therefore cannot write about them.

"Can Great Books Make Good Movies? 7 Writers Just Say No!" *American Film* 12.9 (July/August 1987): 36–40.

In a composite round table created from several evenings of America's literary figures talking about the challenges of translating literature into film held at the 92nd St. YMHA in New York City, Miller comments on the passive nature of film, the "inescapable" set of a theatre production that creates dramatic pressure in a live performance, his memories of making the film version of *All My Sons*, and money as being the only reason to make his plays into films.

Carlisle, Olga, and Rose Styron. "Arthur Miller: An Interview." *Paris Review* 10 (Summer 1966): 61–98. Rpt. in *Writers at Work: The Paris Review Interviews, Third Series*. Ed. George Plimpton. New York: Viking, 1972. 197–230 (includes a copy of a page of manuscript for *The Price*). Rpt. as "The Art of the Theatre II: Arthur Miller, an Interview." *Conversations with Arthur Miller*. Ed.

Matthew C. Roudané. Jackson: UP of Mississippi, 1987. 85–111. Rpt. in *The Theater Essays of Arthur Miller*. Ed. Robert A. Martin. New York: Viking, 1978. 264–93. Rpt. in *The Theater Essays of Arthur Miller*. Revised ed. Eds. Robert A. Martin and Steven R. Centola. New York: Da Capo, 1996. 264–93.

Lengthy interview covering an extremely wide range of issues, including: Miller's early career, his early influences, his "notion of tragedy," his relationship with his father, his opinions about Russian and European theatre, his thoughts on the failure of the Lincoln Center Repertory Theater, his views on various acting methods, his interests in screenwriting, his memories of writing radio plays, his feelings regarding various productions of *After the Fall*, Eugene O'Neill, theatre critics and their influence on playwriting in America, his creaative methodology regarding the genesis of *The Crucible*, and his views on politics.

Carr, Jay. "Arthur Miller Revisits Salem Reshaping His Play." *Boston Globe* 15 December 1996: N1.

Interview with Miller and director Nicholas Hytner on the occasion of the release of the American film version of *The Crucible*. Hytner discusses working with Miller and the formidable shooting logistics on Hog Island, Massachusetts. Miller discusses the differences between the film and the play ["the movie follows the line of the play through images, whereas the play is purely language"], themes of sexuality and betrayal, modern witch-hunt mentalities, Miller's own brush with HUAC, his censorship by the U.S. Army, and Sartre's screenplay for *The Witches of Salem*, filmed in 1956.

Carroll, James, and Helen Epstein. "Seeing Eye to Eye." *Boston Review* 14 (February 1989): 12–13.

Miller responds to questions regarding the meaning of memory in his work, his "tragic sense," his tendency to write out of a "fierce moral argument," the autobiographical nature of his plays, his identity as a Jew, the Chinese reaction to *Death of a Salesman*, and where he finds the faith to keep on writing.

Centola, Steven R. "Introduction." *Arthur Miller in Conversation*. Dallas, Tex.: Contemporary Research, 1993. 9–20.

Includes reprints of previously published interviews, "'The Will to Live': An Interview with Arthur Miller," and "'Just Looking for a Home': A Conversation with Arthur Miller" [see below for annotations], plus a summary of Miller's major dramatic works and a selected bibliography. In his introductory essay to his two interviews with Miller, Centola examines the "ironic" circumstance in which "one of the literary giants of the twentieth century" deservedly enjoys immense contemporary popularity abroad while critics in his home country laud him "exclusively on accomplishments that came very early in his career."

———. "'Just Looking for a Home': A Conversation with Arthur Miller." *American Drama* 1.1 (Fall 1991): 85–94. Rpt. as "August 2, 1990" in Centola's *Arthur Miller in Conversation*. Dallas, Tex.: Contemporary Research, 1993. 45–54.

Centola focuses his questions around issues involving the characters in several of Miller's later plays (*Clara*, *The Archbishop's Ceiling*, *I Can't Remember Anything*, and *Elegy for a Lady*).

———. "The Last Yankee: An Interview with Arthur Miller." *American Drama* 5.1 (Fall 1995): 78–98.

Lengthy interview in which Miller discusses the works of which he is most proud, his difficulties in working with American actors, directors and audiences, his attraction to nonrealistic styles in theatre, as well as specific comments regarding *Broken Glass*, *The Last Yankee*, and *The Ride Down Mount Morgan*.

——— "'The Will to Live': An Interview with Arthur Miller." *Modern Drama* 27 (September 1984): 345–60. Rpt. in *Conversations with Arthur Miller*. Ed. Matthew C. Roudané. Jackson: UP of Mississippi, 1987. 343–59. Rpt. as "June 25, 1985" in Centola's *Arthur Miller in Conversation*. Dallas, Tex.: Contemporary Research, 1993. 21–43. Rpt. in *The Theater Essays of Arthur Miller*. Revised ed. Eds. Robert A. Martin and Steven R. Centola. New York: Da Capo, 1996. 396–413.

Lengthy interview in which Centola queries Miller regarding his vision of the human condition as expressed in several of his plays (*After the Fall*, *Incident at Vichy*, and *The Price*).

Century, Douglas. "Miller's Tale of 'Tribalism': The Playwright Returns to His Roots." *Forward* 22 April 1994: 1, 10.

On the occasion of the Broadway premiere of *Broken Glass*, Miller discusses his problem with Broadway, the relevance of *Broken Glass* to modern audiences, his own memories of 1938, Jewish identity in his plays, and the cycles of hatred that inspired the writing of *Broken Glass*.

Cheever, Susan. "Arthur Miller: The One Thing That Keeps Us from Chaos." *New Choices for Retirement Living* October 1994: 22–25.

After a biographical sketch, Miller discusses the importance of family in his drama, as well as his relationships with his parents, his three children, and his wife Inge Morath.

Choy, Marguerita. "It All Comes Together for Arthur Miller at 84." *Times of India* 21 October 1999. http://www.timesofindia.com/211099/21worl19.htm. (12 December 1999). *Reuters* 19 October 1999.

On the occasion of Miller winning the Dorothy and Lillian Gish Prize, Miller comments on his plans to put the $200,000 prize "to good use," the lack of opportunities for new playwrights, and his experience with writing an opera version of *A View from the Bridge*.

Christiansen, Richard. "Arthur Miller's Verdict on Willy: He Has Elements of Nobility." *Chicago Tribune* 15 January 1984: Sec. 13: 19.

On the occasion of the opening in Chicago of the Dustin Hoffman *Death of a Salesman*, Miller discusses the tragic nature of the play, the origins of the character of Willy Loman, the issue of reality in the play, the film version of his play, and the state of the theatre in New York today.

———. "Dustin Hoffman and the Rebirth of a Classic *Salesman*." *Chicago Tribune* 15 January 1984: Sec. 13: 18–19.

Interview during the rehearsal of the Chicago opening of *Death of a Salesman*, starring Dustin Hoffman. It is reported that the production will run five weeks, move to Washington, D.C., and then Broadway from 19 March through June. Miller discusses his views on Hoffman as Willy Loman and his satisfaction with this production. Says Miller, "I'm starting to get excited all over again . . . We're doing it right, and there's nothing like doing it right."

———. "Long-Lived Success." *Chicago Tribune* 9 January 2000: 1.

Miller discusses "his miraculous year of 1999," which saw several award-winning revivals of his works and the premiere of the opera version of *A View from the Bridge*. Topics range from the influence of the depression on his works, his early attempts at playwriting, his success in England, and the commercial theatre in New York. Three photographs accompany the text.

Christy, Marian. "The Imperturbable Arthur Miller." *Boston Globe* 22 March 1987: B29.

Miller discusses his interest in social and moral dilemmas, his writing technique, and criticism and the artist.

Clark, John. "A Classic at Stake." *Los Angeles Times* 8 December 1996: Calendar: 5.

Interview with Miller and director Nicholas Hytner conducted on the occasion of the opening of the American film version of *The Crucible*. After a series of mutual admiration comments, the playwright and the director discuss the casting of Daniel Day-Lewis as John Proctor, the community effort to help build the set on Hog Island, and the cinematic quality of the original play.

Colford, Paul D. "Perpetual Arthur Miller: Entering His 80th Year." *Newsday* 28 September 1995: B2. Rpt. as "Not Your Average 80th Birthday." *Los Angeles Times* 29 September 1995: E9.

On the occasion of Miller's honor by friends and admirers at the New York Public Library to celebrate his 80th birthday, Miller discusses his busy year, his writing routine, and his being "troubled by what he sees as a hostile standoff between voices on the left and right of the political debate" in the United States.

Connery, Donald S., ed. *Convicting the Innocent: The Story of a Murder, a False Confession, and the Struggle to Free a 'Wrong Man.'* Cambridge, Mass.: Brookline, 1996. 88–94.

Excerpt of transcript of a question-and-answer session at a symposium on "convicting the innocent," held in Hartford, Connecticut, in June of 1994. Miller and other panelists, including Peter Reilly, answer questions regarding Peter Reilly's case and the subsequent lack of an investigation into the murder of his mother.

"Conversation at St. Clerans between Arthur Miller and John Huston." *Guardian* (London) 25 February 1960: 6.

Lengthy and important interview with the screenwriter and the director of *The Misfits* conducted in John Huston's Irish home during the film's early planning stage. Subjects discussed include, how Huston chooses his film subjects, each man's awareness of his own style, Miller's inclination to write plays that deal with "what is in the air," why Miller has not written a novel since *Focus*, the collaborative aspects of film and theatre, the plans for *The Misfits*, the differences between English and American writers,

Miller's feelings regarding the "great" medium of film, and the future artistic plans of both men beyond the film.

Cook, Jim. "Their Thirteenth Year Was the Most Significant." *Washington Post and Times Herald* 10 July 1956: 24.

After a biographical profile of Miller and wife Marilyn Monroe, Cook interviews Miller and his sister Joan Copeland on their childhood memories. Miller is quoted as saying that his thirteenth year was his most significant because it was in that year that the depression hit and his life changed forever.

Corrigan, Robert W. "Arthur Miller: Interview." *Michigan Quarterly Review* 13 (Fall 1974): 401–5. Rpt. in *Conversations with Arthur Miller*. Ed. Matthew C. Roudané. Jackson: UP of Mississippi, 1987. 253–57.

In this excerpt from a longer interview, conducted on 16 November 1973, Miller is asked to comment on what Corrigan sees as the playwright's new mode of dramatizing ideas rather than actions, tragic form and his explorations of dramatic form, and his views on man's relation to society and vice versa.

"Critics' Award Pleases Author of *All My Sons*." *New York Herald Tribune* 23 April 1947: 27.

Brief biography and interview with Miller on the occasion of his winning the New York Drama Critics' Circle Award for *All My Sons*, in which the playwright expresses his gratitude and sense of validation for the award which proved that a playwright "could say what you wanted on Broadway without having to sugar-coat it or slick it up."

Dahlby, Tracy. "Arthur Miller Says Chinese Understand His *Salesman*." *Washington Post* 1 May 1983: 1.

Lengthy interview/profile with Miller in Beijing directing *Death of a Salesman* with an all-Chinese cast. Miller discusses cross-cultural differences and similarities between the U.S. and China, the transfer of acting styles, and the complexities of translating an American play for Chinese audiences.

"*Death of a Salesman*: A Symposium." *Tulane Drama Review* 2.3 (May 1958): 63–69. Rpt. in *Two Modern American Tragedies: Reviews and Criticism of "Death of a Salesman" and "A Streetcar Named Desire."* Ed. John D. Hurrell. New York: Scribner's, 1961. Rpt. in *Major Literary Characters: Willy Loman*. Ed.

Harold Bloom. New York: Chelsea, 1991. 43–49. Rpt. in *Conversations with Arthur Miller*. Ed. Matthew C. Roudané. Jackson: UP of Mississippi, 1987. 27–34.

Symposium on "Ideas and the Theatre" that includes Miller, Gore Vidal, Richard Watts, John Beaufort, Martin Dworkin, David W. Thompson, and Phillip Gelb as moderator. They discuss the tragic nature of *Death of a Salesman*'s Willy Loman, whether the play "still stands up," its sentimental nature, Willy Loman's value system, and his Everyman status.

Deedy, John. "Critics and the Bible." *Commonweal* 5 January 1973: 290.

Miller is asked his reaction to the negative critical commentary on *The Creation of the World and Other Business*. He believes that the bulk of the criticism was based on their faulty understanding of the Bible and contends that the play "needs to be produced again" to insure that the work will get a fair reading and the critics "will discuss what the play is about."

Dodds, Richard. "An Unexpected Phone Call from a Great Writer." *Times-Picayune* 8 November 1990: E1.

Telephone interview with Miller on the occasion of a production of *The Crucible* at the Lee Petit Theatre du Vieux Carre in New Orleans. Miller responds to questions concerning the play's continued relevance, his reaction to negative criticism of his works, and his view of life ("It's a war. You fight it and try to survive it. But I've enjoyed most of it.").

Dorman, Michael. "Still Unpredictable at 72." *Newsday* 13 December 1987: 17.

Interview with Miller on the occasion of the publication of *Timebends*. Miller discusses his feelings regarding being "misunderstood," his working habits, current projects, the nature of his work, and his hopes for how he will be remembered.

Dreifus, Claudia. "Arthur Miller on TV." *TV Guide* 21 August 1993: 24–27. Rpt. as "Arthur Miller" in Dreifus's *Interview*. New York: Seven Stories, 1997. 255–65.

On the occasion of the premiere on TNT of his *The American Clock*, Miller speaks with Claudia Dreifus on the genesis of the play, his views on violence on television, and his recollections regarding former wife Marilyn Monroe. For the publication of her book *Interview*, Dreifus includes material added from the original transcript of her conversation that was not included in the earlier *TV Guide* version.

Dunham, Mike. "Playwright Finally Visits His Metaphor." *Anchorage Daily News* 9 August 1996: H7.

Brief phone interview with Miller and Inge Morath in which they express their excitement over their future, first-ever, trip to Alaska to attend the Prince William Sound Theatre Conference in Valdez. Miller will receive the Edward Albee Last Frontier Playwright Award and Morath will lecture on photography.

———. "Society, Art and Obligations: Conversations with Arthur Miller." *Anchorage Daily News* 1 September 1996: H3.

Lengthy and important feature article containing three excerpts from the fourth annual Prince William Sound Theatre Conference in Valdez, Alaska. In the first, Miller responds to questions on the state of the arts in America; in the second, a one-on-one interview with *Daily News* reporter Mike Dunham, Miller discusses subsidy of the arts and the tragic personality; and in the third, Dunham offers a description of Miller's acceptance of the Edward Albee Last Frontier Playwright Award. After thanking his hosts, Miller is quoted as saying, "I'm just another citizen who has a technique for saying what others are feeling."

Edwards, Brian. "Arthur Miller: After the Canonization." *In the Vernacular: Interviews at Yale with Sculptors of Culture*. Ed. Melissa E. Biggs. Jefferson, N.C.: McFarland, 1991. 139–44.

In an interview conducted in Miller's Roxbury studio in the spring of 1989, and originally published in *The Yale Vernacular*, Miller discusses the social phenomenon of McCarthyism, his delight over the British production of *A View from the Bridge*, which, he says, was "closer to his meaning" than the production in New York, Harold Pinter's economy of language, dramatic conversation, and theatrical form.

Emery, Fred. "The Meeting of St. George and the Godfather." *Times* (London) 6 November 1972: 12.

In an article on the political race for president between Richard Nixon and George McGovern, Miller is quoted as offering his opinion as to McGovern's campaign. Says Miller, McGovern should realize that "we are not casting the Moses to lead us out of the desert but the chief officer of a bank to which we are all depositors."

Evans, Everett. "'I Just Go on Writing.'" *Houston Chronicle* 17 March 1996: Z9.

Miller discusses his latest work *Broken Glass*, set during World War II, the play's thematic implications for contemporary political life, the screenplay of *The Crucible*, his admiration for Robin Baitz, David Mamet, and John Guare, and the state of American commercial theatre.

Evans, Richard I. *Psychology and Arthur Miller*. Dialogues with Notable Contributors to Personality Theory, Vol. 5. New York: Dutton, 1969. Excerpt rpt. as "The Writer and Society" in *Conversations with Arthur Miller*. Ed. Matthew C. Roudané. Jackson: UP of Mississippi, 1987. 152–72. Repub. as *Dialogue with Arthur Miller*. New York: Praeger, 1981.

Book-length interview divided into three sections ("The Writer as Creator," "The Writer and Psychology," and "The Writer and Society") in which Miller discusses with Evans, a professor of psychology, his views on the impact of the play on society, artistic subjectivity, creativity, character development, human behavior, dramatic themes, and personality and cultural determinism. Of particular importance is the preface by Robert Whitehead in which he refutes Miller's oft-repeated claim that he did not have an awareness that people would perceive of the Maggie character in *After the Fall* as resembling his late wife Marilyn Monroe. According to Whitehead, Miller realized this some "two months prior to rehearsal."

"Every Play Has a Purpose." *Dramatists Guild Quarterly* 15 (Winter 1979): 13–20. Rpt. as "Arthur Miller: Purposes." *Broadway Song & Story: Playwrights, Lyricists, Composers Discuss Their Hits*. Ed. Otis L. Guernsey Jr. New York: Dodd, Mead, 1985. 210–16.

Essentially a transcript combining two conversations between Miller and Dramatists Guild Special Projects gatherings of dramatists, including a question-and-answer session at the November 1978 meeting, Miller discusses his belief that a theatre's purpose "springs directly out of the kind of society it finds itself in at the time," his timing with writing *Death of a Salesman*, which contributed to its critical and popular success, details of his experiences working on *Up from Paradise*, the stresses of being successful at an early age, his progression as an artist, and the state of the commercial theatre in America.

Evett, Marianne. "Tallying Cost of American Dream; Arthur Miller Still Sees Drive for Success Destroying Families." *Plain Dealer* 1 May 1994: J1.

Interview in which Miller discusses the universality of the themes in *Death of a Salesman*, the alienation that comes from industrialization, and his interests in family relationships in his dramas.

Fallaci, Oriana. "A Propos of *After the Fall*." *World Theatre* 14 (1965): 79, 81, 83–84, 87.

Excerpts from an interview with Miller in which he angrily responds to the negative critical reaction to *After the Fall*. Says Miller, "I did not expect such a narrow-minded reaction, so cruelly and miserably mean. I did not expect such incredible and degrading short-sightedness. . . . In my opinion, this is the best play I have ever written. . . . You ask why so many people bear a grudge against me: they resent it because I remind them that for thirty, forty, perhaps sixty years of their lives, they have never stopped to wonder why they are alive. Well, I have stopped to wonder."

Fariello, Griffin. "Arthur Miller." *Red Scare: Memories of the American Inquisition: An Oral History*. New York: Norton, 1995. 340–45.

Telephone interview in which Miller details his experiences with anti-communist sentiment in the 1950s—including public attacks on *Death of a Salesman* in the Midwest, the studio short subject made to accompany the release of *Salesman* in movie theatres, Roy Brewer and Joe Ryan asking him to change the mob characters to communists in *The Hook*, being attacked by the *Journal-American* and *World-Telegram* for his alleged communist affiliations, the opening of *The Crucible* that was met with silence yet has become his most produced play, his appearance before HUAC, and his views regarding the state of the theatre in America.

Feldberg, Robert. "Sitting Pretty." *The Record* (Bergen County, N.J.) 14 November 1999: Y1.

Interview conducted in Miller's New York apartment where the playwright is asked for his thoughts on his success, his popularity with foreign audiences, and the new Broadway revival of *The Price*. Three photographs accompany the text.

Feldman, Robert. "Arthur Miller on the Theme of Evil: An Interview." *Resources for American Literary Study* 17 (Spring 1990): 87–93.

Feldman queries Miller about his reactions to the Nazi war crimes trials and his views on the problem of evil in society and drama.

Feron, James. "Miller in London to See *Crucible*." *New York Times* 24 January 1965: 82. Rpt. in *Conversations with Arthur Miller*. Ed. Matthew C. Roudané. Jackson: UP of Mississippi, 1987. 83–84.

Brief interview in which Miller talks about the relevance of *The Crucible* to modern audiences, the controversy surrounding the autobiographical nature of *After the Fall*, the language difficulties in England, and the Lincoln Center turmoil.

Fosburgh, Lacey. "Styron and Miller Defend Yevtushenko Against Charges in British Press of Hypocrisy." *New York Times* 25 November 1968: 15.

Miller defends Soviet poet Yevgeny Yevtushenko against criticism in the British press that he is a propagandist for the Soviet Union and pretends to be an "exponent of freedom." Says Miller, "To be sure, he is a patriotic Soviet citizen, but it doesn't follow that he has lent himself to oppressive forces within or outside his country. He opposes the regime so strongly and so sincerely just because he loves his country so much."

Frank, Stanley. "A Playwright Ponders a New Outline for TV." *TV Guide* 8 October 1966: 8.

In an interview conducted within months of the CBS television premiere of *Death of a Salesman*, starring Lee J. Cobb, Mildred Dunnock, and George Segal, Miller discusses the play's universality and his views on the popular and critical success of the television production. Additionally, Miller suggests that the television networks each devote one hour of programming time each week to "creative programming" to help make television an "authentic art form on a par with the theatre and movies."

Freedman, Samuel G. "Miller Tries a New Form for an Old Play." *New York Times* 23 October 1983: H: 3, 5.

Interview conducted during rehearsals for the Jewish Repertory Theatre proudction of *Up from Paradise*. Miller discusses the adaptation of his work, what he has learned from Eugene O'Neill's disrepute in the 1930s, and his satisfaction with the work.

Frymer, Murry. "Arthur Miller Reflects on a Half-Century of Conscience." *San Jose Mercury News* 2 December 1987: E1.

Lengthy newspaper interview/feature on the occasion of the publication of Miller's autobiography, *Timebends: A Life*, in which Miller discusses his surprising economic success, former wife Marilyn Monroe, his popularity in Great Britain, and the effects of his writing worldwide.

Funke, Lewis. "Interview with Arthur Miller." *Playwrights Talk about Writing*. Chicago: Dramatic, 1975. 175–95.

Lengthy interview in which Miller discusses in depth the nature of art and drama, his writing processes, critics and the theatre, and modern dramatic forms. The drama's ultimate function, says Miller, "is probably to make human beings more civilized in the sense of making them more of a community, if only for the time they are in the theatre, but hopefully, this sentiment remains in the mind."

———. "Miller—Before the Fall." *New York Times* 3 October 1971: II: 1, 8.

Miller discusses his new play, inspired by Studs Terkel's *Hard Times*, that takes place during the depression, and denies the connection between the comic character of Solomon in *The Price* and his recent *The Creation of the World and Other Business*.

———. "Stars Help Arthur Miller Film TV Antiwar Allegory." *New York Times* 17 November 1969: 58.

Interview held on Miller's Roxbury, Conn., farm, during the shooting of *The Reason Why*, a one-act script for television, starring Eli Wallach and Robert Ryan. Miller comments on the influence of the Vietnam war on the film and its somewhat autobiographical nature.

———. "Thoughts on a Train Bound for Wilmington." *New York Times* 18 January 1953: II: 1, 3.

Interview with Miller and Jed Harris, the director of *The Crucible*. Harris comments on the play's value as a theatrical experience and his refusal to see Miller as a social playwright or "a sort of Brooklyn Ibsen."

———. "A Zestful Miller Starts Rehearsal." *New York Times* 6 December 1967: 40.

Funke interviews Miller in his home in Roxbury as *The Price* goes into rehearsal. Miller reveals that he usually has "run into feelings of despair and exhaustion" after writing a play, but he "has had a lot of joy writing this one."

Gelb, Barbara. "Question: Am I My Brother's Keeper?" *New York Times* 29 November 1964: II: 1, 3. Rpt. in *Conversations with Arthur Miller*. Ed. Matthew C. Roudané. Jackson: UP of Mississippi, 1987. 78–82.

In an interview devoted to *Incident at Vichy*, Miller discusses the play's plot, themes, and characters, his happiness with his script ("it very successfully does what I want it to do"), and his new lack of concern for public reaction to his plays.

Gelb, Phillip. "A Matter of Hopelessness in *Death of a Salesman*: A Symposium with Arthur Miller, Richard Watts, John Beaufort, Martin Dworkin, David W. Thompson and Phillip Gelb (Moderator)." *Tulane Drama Review* 2 (May 1958): 63–69. Rpt. in *Two Modern American Tragedies: Reviews and Criticism of "Death of a Salesman" and "A Streetcar Named Desire."* Ed. John D. Hurrell. New York: Scribner's, 1961. 76–88. Complete Miller interview printed as "Morality and Modern Drama." *Educational Theatre Journal* 10 (October 1958): 190–202. Rpt. in *Conversations with Arthur Miller*. Ed. Matthew C. Roudané. Jackson: UP of Mississippi, 1987. 35–51. Rpt. in *"Death of a Salesman": Text and Criticism*. Ed. Gerald Weales. New York: Viking, 1967. 172–86. Rpt. in *The Theater Essays of Arthur Miller*. Ed. Robert A. Martin. New York: Viking, 1978. 195–214. Rpt. in *The Theater Essays of Arthur Miller*. Revised ed. Eds. Robert A. Martin and Steven R. Centola. New York: Da Capo, 1996. 195–214.

This symposium is the transcript of a radio program made up of excerpts from several interviews recorded by Gelb for a series entitled "Ideas and the Theatre." In it, critics from the *New York Post* (Watts), *Christian Science Monitor* (Beaufort), and *Progressive* (Dworkin) magazine discuss their reactions to Willy Loman and *Death of a Salesman*. Following their conversation, Miller responds to their comments. In the full-length interview Miller chiefly discusses what Gelb terms "the apparent lack of moral values in modern drama," including commentary regarding the drama of Tennessee Williams and G. B. Shaw. In response to several statements posited by Gelb, Miller defends various critical reactions to Willy Loman in *Salesman*.

Gilroy, Harry. "Bellow Assails Literary 'Elite.'" *New York Times* 14 June 1966: 52.

News item reporting the details of the opening of the PEN Congress at New York University that quotes, at length, Miller's views on the absence of the Soviet delegation, the condemnation of the prison sentences of Andrei D. Sinyavsky and Yuli M. Daniel for smuggling anti-Soviet works abroad, the necessity of welcoming writers as writers rather than political ambassadors, and the role of PEN in offering "a kind of sanctuary" to writers to express their views that are "always in danger of being brought down by things, by technology, by suppression or sheer ignorance."

———. "A Million Sales for Willy Loman." *New York Times* 8 March 1968: 36.

On the occasion of receiving a gold copy of the title page from *Death of a Salesman* from Viking Press to mark the millionth copy sold of his play, Miller chides critics for misunderstanding *The Price.*

———. "PEN Convenes Today at N.Y.U." *New York Times* 12 June 1966: 38.

Miller is quoted from a press conference held at the opening of International PEN Congress on his views of opening a PEN center in Russia. Miller remarks that such a center "might help to bring about a time when there would be absolute freedom there, just as PEN wants to see in all the rest of the world."

Gollub, Christian-Albrecht. "Interview with Arthur Miller." *Michigan Quarterly Review* 16 (Spring 1977): 121–41. Rpt. in *Conversations with Arthur Miller*. Ed. Matthew C. Roudané. Jackson: UP of Mississippi, 1987. 273–90.

Interview conducted in Roxbury, Connecticut, in August of 1975. Miller responds to elementary questions regarding his favorite playwrights (O'Neill and Pinter), his early literary influences, his feelings on seeing his works produced, his views on why the public identifies with his plays, his popularity abroad, the commercial nature of American theatre, the musical version of *The Creation of the World and Other Business*, his current reading habits, and his views on privacy. Of note is Miller's comment concerning his own role as a playwright—"I am a dispassionate observer of the ongoing disaster of the human race."

Gordinier, Jeff. "Casting a Spell." *Entertainment Weekly* 6 December 1996: 18–27.

Lengthy profile/interview/essay with Miller on the making of the American film version of *The Crucible*. Both color and black-and-white photographs and production stills of Miller, Daniel Day-Lewis, Winona Ryder, and Nicholas Hytner accompany the text. Cover of this issue is devoted to the film.

Goyen, William. "Arthur Miller's Quest for Truth." *New York Herald-Tribune Magazine* 19 January 1964: 35.

Miller responds to questions concerning the repertory theatre system and the Lincoln Center Theater, his playwriting techniques, and the themes of *After the Fall*.

Green, Blake. "A Literary Lion Still Roars." *Newsday* 17 January 1993: 15.

On the occasion of the New York premiere of *The Last Yankee*, Miller discusses the play's impetus, the "impoverished" state of the American theatre, the reasons behind his resurgence in popularity in Great Britain, his reluctance to work in film, the themes in *The Last Yankee*, and the nation's lasting obsession with ex-wife Marilyn Monroe.

Greenfeld, Josh. "Writing Plays Is Absolutely Senseless, Arthur Miller says, 'But I Love It. I Just Love It.'" *New York Times Magazine* 13 February 1972: 16–17, 34–39. Rpt. in *Conversations with Arthur Miller*. Ed. Matthew C. Roudané. Jackson: UP of Mississippi, 1987. 233–48. Rpt. in *Norton Book of Interviews: An Anthology from 1859 to the Present Day*. Ed. Christopher Silvester. New York: Norton, 1996. 537–50.

After being shown around Miller's 350-acre Roxbury, Connecticut, farm, Greenfeld asks Miller questions concerning his writing and reading habits, his views on the current theatre in New York, his political stance, what his alternate career might have been had he not become a playwright (carpenter), and his current and future reputation.

Griffin, John and Alice. "Arthur Miller Discusses *The Crucible*." *Theatre Arts* 37 (October 1953): 33–34. Rpt. in *Conversations with Arthur Miller*. Ed. Matthew C. Roudané. Jackson: UP of Mississippi, 1987. 24–26.

Miller discusses the dramatic appeal of the true story of the Salem witch trials that led him to write *The Crucible*, including the historical basis for the play. "The moral size of these people drew me . . . they didn't whimper." In relation to *Salesman*, Miller admits that Willy Loman "lacks sufficient insight," which "would have made him a greater, more significant figure."

Gritten, David. "Miller's Crossing." *Los Angeles Times* 4 November 1991: F1.

On the occasion of the world premiere of *The Ride Down Mount Morgan* at the Wyndham Theatre in London's West End, Miller discusses the reasoning behind his not opening this play in New York, the "out of sight" Broadway ticket prices, the play's themes, going to Stockholm to direct *Death of a Salesman*, and his hopes for the American film version of *The Crucible* which is soon to begin production.

Gruen, John. "Portrait of a Playwright at Fifty." *New York* 24 October 1965: 12–13. Rpt. as "Arthur Miller." *Close-Up*. New York: Viking, 1968. 58–63.

Miller interview in which he discusses his reasons for declining President Johnson's invitation to the White House to look on as he signs the Art and Humanities Act, a bill that grants government subsidy to the arts—a concern of Miller's for decades. Miller also addresses critical reaction to *After the Fall* by stating, "If it *were* Marilyn . . . it would be a tribute to the depth and reality of her suffering," as well as comments on the off-off-Broadway theatre of the day.

Guernsey, Otis L. "Conversation with Arthur Miller." *Dramatists Guild Quarterly* 24.2 (Summer 1987): 12–21.

Miller discusses the definition of drama, his career, his training, the economics of being a playwright, and the reception of his plays worldwide.

———, ed. "*Death of a Salesman*." *Broadway Song & Story: Playwrights, Lyricists, Composers Discuss Their Hits*. New York: Dodd, Mead, 1985. 16–23.

Session recorded for the *Dramatists Guild Quarterly*. Participants Garson Kanin (moderator), Mildred Dunnock, Alan Hewitt, Elia Kazan, and Arthur Miller reminisce on their involvement with the original production of *Salesman*.

Gussow, Mel. "Arthur Miller Returns to "Genesis" for First Musical." *New York Times* 17 April 1974. 37.

During rehearsals for *Up from Paradise* in New York, before the musical's opening 23 April at the University of Michigan, Miller discusses the transformation of his stage play *The Creation of the World and Other Business* into the musical form, the "joyful playfulness" of this production, and his excitement in working outside the commercial theatre.

———. "Arthur Miller: Stirred by Memory." *New York Times* 1 February 1987: H: 1, 30.

Lengthy interview conducted on the occasion of the opening of two one-act plays (*Clara* and *I Can't Remember Anything*) at Lincoln Center. Miller discusses the thematic elements of both dramas, the writing of his autobiography, his marriage to Marilyn Monroe, Monroe's acting talent, his dislike for Lee Strasberg's acting approach, his memories of working with Lee J. Cobb and Elia Kazan on *Death of a Salesman*, his durability as a playwright, and his faith in the possibilities of theatre.

———. "Dustin Hoffman's *Salesman*." *New York Times* 18 March 1984: Sec. 6: 36–38, 40, 46, 48, 86.

Lengthy profile and interview of Dustin Hoffman on the occasion of his performing the role of Willy Loman in *Death of a Salesman*. Hoffman discusses his career, his approach to the role of Loman, his relationship with Miller, and his now-famous obsessive personality. Miller is quoted on Hoffman's approach—"He has that kind of feisty quickness that I always associated with Willy, changing directions like a sailboat in the middle of a lake with the wind blowing in all directions. He's a cocky little guy overwhelmed by the size of the world and trying to climb up to the top of the mountain. Dustin will create a new Willy. It ain't going to be the other one. It'll be his Willy."

———. "From Broadway to Peking. It's Miller Time." *New York Times* 15 October 1982: C2.

In an article discussing the wealth of Miller revivals in the new theatre season, including mention of Miller's impending trip to Peking to direct *Death of a Salesman*, Miller discusses the ideas behind his two new one-acts, *Elegy for a Lady* and *Some Kind of Love Story*, and his views on the inhospitable nature of Broadway.

Hattersley, Roy. "Arthur Miller: A View from the Barricades." *Guardian* (London) 24 October 1998: Features: 6.

Lengthy feature profile and interview of Miller on the occasion of his being voted "Playwright of the Century," in which the playwright discusses his marriage to Marilyn Monroe, his father Isadore, the drama of Tennessee Williams, American commercial theatre, and the McCarthy era.

Hayman, Ronald. "Arthur Miller." *Playback 2*. New York: Horizon, 1973. 7–22.

Miller discusses the theatre of Ibsen, Beckett, and Brecht, playwriting courses, the role of the critic, reasons for the lasting appeal of his plays, what he sees as a self-destruction in modern society, and modern playwrights who confuse journalism with theatre.

———. "Arthur Miller Talks about His Play." *Times* (London) 15 February 1969: 19.

In an interview focusing on *The Price*, Miller discusses the origins of the character of Gregory Solomon, the role of the past in his play, and he discloses that, among his unfinished works, there are about fifty plays and "more poetry than most of the poets write."

———. "Interview with Arthur Miller." *Arthur Miller*. New York: Ungar, 1972. 3–21. Rpt. in *Conversations with Arthur Miller*. Ed. Matthew C. Roudané. Jackson: UP of Mississippi, 1987. 187–99.

Miller responds to questions regarding his reactions to various productions of his plays, his conscious use of language and dialect, his impressions of himself as a screenwriter, Freudian interpretations of his plays, the use of guilt in *All My Sons*, and the processes involved in writing *After the Fall* and *A View from the Bridge*.

Heaton, C. P. "Arthur Miller on *Death of a Salesman*." *Notes on Contemporary Literature* 1 (1971): 5.

Miller responds to questions regarding *Death of a Salesman* from students at Florida State University who had read his play and essay on "Tragedy and the Common Man" and still needed some clarification on several points. Asked "On what do you base your deviation from the classical concept of tragedy?" Miller responded with "Sheer willfulness."

Herbert, Edward T. "Eugene O'Neill: An Evaluation by Fellow Playwrights." *Modern Drama* 6.3 (December 1963): 239–40.

Short item listing quoted comments by five noted playwrights on their views on Eugene O'Neill. Miller praises O'Neill's ability to challenge his audiences and for possessing "a kind of conscience to many writers." Says Miller, "It was easier to write knowing such a man existed."

Hewes, Henry. "American Playwrights Self-Appraised." *Saturday Review* 3 September 1955: 18–19.

In response to a questionnaire regarding what he sees as important trends in theatre today, Miller praises the theatre of Bertold Brecht.

———. "Broadway Postscript: Arthur Miller and How He Went to the Devil," *Saturday Review of Literature* 31 January 1953: 24–26. Rpt. in *Conversations with Arthur Miller*. Ed. Matthew C. Roudané. Jackson: UP of Mississippi, 1987. 19–23. Rpt. in *"The Crucible": Text and Criticism*. Ed. Gerald Weales. New York: Viking, 1971. 182–88.

During a rehearsal for the premiere production of *The Crucible*, Miller discusses his use of period language and themes, his responsibility for the play's historical accuracy, the work's lack of an historical allegory, and the importance of making the right alterations during the rehearsal process.

Hill, Logan. "Priceless." *New York* 1 November 1999: 147.

On the occasion of the opening of an acclaimed Broadway revival of *The Price*, Miller describes the play's genesis and themes and concludes that "*Salesman* proved that there was an audience for something other than a musical. And I always believed that." Current photograph of Miller accompanies the text.

Hills, Rust. "Conversation: Arthur Miller and William Styron." *Audience* 1.6 (November–December 1971): 4–21. Rpt. in *Conversations with Arthur Miller*. Ed. Matthew C. Roudané. Jackson: UP of Mississippi, 1987. 206–32.

Interview conducted in Roxbury, Connecticut, in June of 1971, with Miller and William Styron. The writers discuss critics and critical reaction to their works, working with editors and producers, and teachers who have inspired them.

Hirschhorn, Clive. "Memories of a Salesman." *Plays and Players* (London) July 1986: 7–10.

Miller answers questions regarding his one-act plays *Clara* and *I Can't Remember Anything*, the state of Broadway theatre, and Miller's coping strategies following his early success with *Death of a Salesman*.

Holland, Bernard. "Arthur Miller Play Set to Stanley Silverman Music Resurfaces." *New York Times* 2 October 1981: C3.

Miller is interviewed on the occasion of the concert version of *The Creation of the World and Other Business*, called *Up from Paradise*, at the Whitney Museum. Miller and collaborator Stanley Silverman adapted the play as a narrated concert, featuring woodwind quintet, Miller narrating, and starring Austin Pendleton and Len Cariou. Miller discusses the reworking of the script, the leitmotifs that run through the music, his early career as a singer, and his work on a new play called *The Ride Down Mount Morgan*.

Huftel, Sheila. "Miller's Questioning by the House Un-American Activities Committee" in *Readings on Arthur Miller*. Ed. Thomas Siebold. San Diego, Calif.: Greenhaven, 1997. 56–62. [From Huftel's *Arthur Miller: The Burning Glass*. New York: Citadel, 1965. 31–53.]

Section of Huftel's book that focuses on Miller's appearance before HUAC in 1956, including excerpts from the playwright's testimony.

Hulbert, Dan. "Arthur Miller: A Dramatist for the Ages." *Atlanta Journal-Constitution* 9 January 2000: L4.

On the occasion of the television broadcast of the Showtime presentation of *Death of a Salesman*, starring Brian Dennehy and Elizabeth Franz, Miller answers questions regarding whether he feels that the play has lost any of its "power" since its premiere fifty years ago, the universal qualities of the play, the range of actors who have played Willy Loman, his desire to see *After the Fall* produced as a "first-class revival" in New York, and the secret to his stability.

Hutchens, John K. "Mr. Miller Has a Change of Luck." *New York Times* 23 February 1947: Sec. 2: 1, 3. Rpt. in *Conversations with Arthur Miller*. Ed. Matthew C. Roudané. Jackson: UP of Mississippi, 1987. 3–5.

Lengthy profile of Miller's career up to and including *All My Sons*, detailing the origins of the drama's plot and Miller's reaction to his play's success.

Hyams, Barry. "A Theater: Heart and Mind." *Theater: Annual of the Repertory Theater of Lincoln Center, Volume One*. New York: Repertory Theater Publications/Playbill, 1964. 48–77.

Detailing the evolution of the Repertory Theater of Lincoln Center, Hyams introduces the reader to essays with various participants in the Center's first season: Miller, Ellia Kazan, Robert Whitehead, Jo Mielziner, Jose Quintero. Miller discusses the physical traits of the theatre and how they have determined the style of his production of *After the Fall*, encouraging a naturalistic writing. He praises the Repertory concept for its generosity to the artist: this is the first time he will be able to use lead actors in all roles, have the luxury of a longer rehearsal time, and be able to read the script aloud to his actors and participate fully in the rehearsal process. Several candid photographs of Miller, Kazan, and Whitehead working on *After the Fall* accompany the text.

Kakatani, Michiko. "Arthur Miller: View of a Life." *New York Times* 9 May 1984: Sec. 3: 17. Rpt. as "Arthur Miller" in *The Poet at the Piano: Portraits of Writers, Filmmakers, Playwrights, and Other Artists at Work*. New York: Times Books, 1988, 161–64.

Lengthy article that chronicles Miller's theatrical career and personal controversies while briefly discussing his chagrin at the dearth of Tony nominations for his revival of *Death of a Salesman*, starring Dustin Hoffman.

Kaplan, James. "Miller's Crossing." *Vanity Fair* November 1991: 218–21, 241–48.

Lengthy profile/interview conducted on the occasion of the opening of *The Ride Down Mount Morgan* in London. Miller discusses his love of his country home, his financial ruin following his divorce from Marilyn Monroe in 1960, his marriage to Monroe, the character of Lyman Felt in *Mount Morgan*, *The Misfits*, wife Inge Morath, and his views on modern playwrights.

Kelly, Kevin. "Arthur Miller Emerges Again on Several Fronts." *Boston Globe* 12 October 1980: 81–82.

During a break in rehearsals for *The American Clock*, Miller discusses his writing habits, finding early fragments of what would later become *Death of a Salesman* in a trunk during a move, the themes and structure of *The American Clock*, critical response to his plays, and shares an anecdote about walking out of a Robert Brustein and John Simon lecture at Yale on the demise of the American theatre.

———. "Miller Is Proud of the Product." *Boston Globe* 30 September 1980.

Interview with Miller on the occasion of the CBS telecast of his *Playing for Time* starring Vanessa Redgrave. Miller discusses the details of filming the project, his working relationship with Redgrave, his work as adaptor to Fania Fénelon's memoir, and his views on writing for television.

Kerson, Jennie F. "Miller Time." *Brown Daily Herald* 2 March 1998. http://www.herald.netspace.org/issues/030298/miller.f.html (3 April 1999).

Interview conducted at Trinity Repertory Theatre in Providence, R.I., on 1 March 1998. Miller discusses the changes in American theatre over the span of his career and the importance of a play script as an "instrument for the actor."

Kilian, Michael. "Maryann Plunkett May Not Be a 'Star,' But She Could Be Our Finest Actress." *Chicago Tribune* 21 March 1993: Sec. 5: 3.

In a feature profile of Maryann Plunkett, the resident leading lady of Tony Randall's National Actors Theatre, Miller is quoted as praising her performance in *The Crucible*.

King, Susan. "Arthur Miller's *Enemy* Has Found a Friend." *Los Angeles Times* 11 June 1990: F1.

On the occasion of the read-through of the *American Playhouse* production of *An Enemy of the People*, starring John Glover and George Grizzard, Miller comments on the cast, his collaboration with director Jack O'Brien, his early experiences with film versions of his plays, and his feelings about writing screenplays. A photograph of Miller accompanies the text.

Kissel, Howard. "Standing on the Corner of Broadway and Miller." *Daily News* 7 February 1999.

Interview conducted during and following the unveiling of "Miller Way," the stretch of road between 49th and Eighth Avenue, renamed in honor of the fiftieth anniversary revival of *Death of a Salesman*. Miller discusses the international relevance of the play and the importance of the work's lack of ethnic particularity. Says Miller, "All my plays are involved with high moral issues. The idea of simply replicating life is the farthest thing from my concerns."

Kroll, Jack. "Rebirth of a Salesman." *Newsweek* 22 February 1999: 54.

Miller discusses the success of *Death of a Salesman*, the development of Willy Loman as a character, his marriage to Marilyn Monroe, his enormous popularity in Great Britain, and the impact, after fifty years, of *Salesman.*

Kuchwara, Michael. "Doyen of Drama Persists." *Orlando Sentinel* 5 June 1994: F10.

In this interview with "the American theater's longest-running living playwright," Miller discusses the commercial New York theatre as "increasingly resistant" to drama, especially his own.

Kullman, Colby H. "*Death of a Salesman* at Fifty: An Interview with Arthur Miller." *Michigan Quarterly Review* 37.4 (Fall 1998): 624–35.

Interview conducted 17 September 1997 in Miller's East Side New York City apartment. Miller responds to questions regarding his thoughts on his masterpiece at fifty, his views on crosscultural casting, Willy's appeal as a universal type, working with directors (esp. Kazan), the characters in *Death of a Salesman* and their effects on audiences, his influence from Tennessee Williams, Linda Loman as co-dependent, and advice he might give to young playwrights.

Lambert, Angela. "An Intellect at Ease." *Independent* (London) 2 August 1994: 17, 19.

While in London for the final rehearsals for *Broken Glass*, Miller responds to questions concerning the importance of his Jewishness, the difficulties his non-Jewish wives have encountered in his family, Monroe's conversion to Judaism, the reason why *Broken Glass* is being previewed at the National, his preoccupations apart from writing, his views on the art form of film, and his opinions regarding the improvement of the human condition.

Lamos, Mark. "An Afternoon with Arthur Miller." *American Theatre* 3.2 (May 1986): 18–23, 44. Rpt. in *Conversations with Arthur Miller*. Ed. Matthew C. Roudané. Jackson: UP of Mississippi, 1987. 376–88.

Miller discusses *Death of a Salesman* and *The Crucible* and how his works have been translated to video and film.

Lardner, James. "Arthur Miller—Back in Control at 65." *Washington Post* 26 October 1980: L: 1, 5.

Interview in which Miller expresses his happiness at being back in the theatre after working in television and film, primarily because he has more control over theatrical productions of his work.

Lemon, Brendon. "Arthur Miller by Brendon Lemon: The Greatest Living American Playwright." *Interview* May 2000.

Brief interview in which Lemon asks Miller about his dog Lola and the reasons why *The Ride Down Mount Morgan* has taken so long to open on Broadway, to which Miller responds, "Because it comes from deep down inside me, so it took a long time to get right."

Liss, Joseph. "*The Story of Gus* by Arthur Miller." *Radio's Best Plays*. New York: Greenberg, 1947. 305–306.

In this foreword to Miller's radio play, Liss quotes Miller regarding his thoughts on radio as a medium of dramatic expression and the reasons why his radio play was never produced. Says Miller: "Radio today is in the hands of people most of whom have no taste, no will, no nothing but the primitive ability to spot a script that does not conform to the format. Give the medium to the artists and something might happen. As it is—death in the afternoon and into the night."

Loney, Glenn Meredith. *Playwrights Talk about Writing: Interviews with Lewis Funke*. Chicago: Dramatic, 1974. 19–28.

Lesson plans and class questions for use with interview cassettes of Jean Kerr, Arthur Miller, John Osborne, Neil Simon, and Douglas Turner Ward. See Funke, Lewis, *Playwrights Talk about Writing*. Includes a literary biography, interview summary, discussion questions, and possible projects linked to the interviews for further study.

Lovell, Glenn. "Playing on a Classic; '*Salesman* Relevant Today,' Playwright Says." *San Jose Mercury News* 22 April 1999: B1.

Interview with Miller on the occasion of both his wife's [Inge Morath] photo exhibit at the Art-Tech gallery in San Jose and Miller's speaking engagement at San Jose State University. Miller discusses his latest play, *Mr. Peters' Connections*, the modern relevance of *Death of a Salesman*, gun control and violence, and his views on the controversy surrounding Elia Kazan receiving a special Oscar for lifetime achievement.

Maas, Willard. "Poetry and The Film: A Symposium." *Film Culture* 29 (Summer 1963). Rpt. in *Film Culture Reader*. Ed. P. Adams Sitney. New York: Praeger, 1970. 171–200. Rpt. in *Poetry and Film*. New York: Gotham Book Mart, 1972. n.p.

Excerpt of a symposium held 23 October 1953 by Cinema 16, with Maya Deren, Parker Tyler, Dylan Thomas, Arthur Miller, and moderated by Willard Maas. Fascinating discussion in which several avant-garde filmmakers attempt to define poetry in film, only to find Miller strongly disagreeing on the subject. Miller argues, "The possibility for the poet or the writer to tell a story or to transmit an emotion in their films, it seem [sic] to me, is contained within the image, so that I'm afraid, even though I'm much in sympathy with Willard's desire to join poetic speech with images, that, possibly, in the long run, it will be discovered to be a redundancy—that the poetry is in the film just as it is in the action of the play first."

MacBeath, Innis. "Miller Defends Yevtushenko." *Times* (London) 26 November 1968: 5.

In response to attacks on Yevgeny Yevtushenko as a "hack propagandist" and "squalid pseudo-liberal abhorred by all of his liberal colleagues" by Kingsley Amis in the *New Statesman*, Miller and William Styron defend the Soviet poet on the grounds that Yevtushenko "has been a voice of conscience among his colleagues."

McGinniss, Joe. Untitled. *Heroes*. New York: Viking, 1976. 120–21.

In an interview in Miller's home, McGinniss questions the playwright about his views on heroes and his continuing need to create. To the latter issue Miller responds, "it's because you need to try to make something beautiful. To give form to the chaos of feeling that is your life."

McIntyre, Alice T. "Making *The Misfits* or Waiting for Monroe or Notes from Olympus." *Esquire* March 1961: 74–81.

Lengthy first-hand account of the filming of *The Misfits* that quotes Miller, Monroe, Gable, and John Huston on issues relating to the script, the difficulty of the shoot, approaches to character, and Monroe's now-legendary and expensive tardiness and illnesses that caused many delays in shooting.

Mandell, Jonathan. "Renaissance Man." *Newsday* 28 October 1997: B3.

Interview conducted during rehearsals for the Signature Theatre Company's production of *The American Clock*. Miller discusses his recent eye operation, his current productivity, his views on what he sees as the "drifting confusion on the part of the people," the theme of his new, as yet untitled and unfinished, play, and the American theatre's hostility to straight plays.

Marino, Stephen. "Arthur Miller at Queens College: 'I Have No Wisdom beyond My Plays.'" *The Arthur Miller Society Newsletter* (June 1999): 15–16.

Marino reports on a question-and-answer session at The Evening Reading Series of Queens College of the City University of New York on 29 October 1996. Miller responded to questions regarding his early writing career, the connection between *The Crucible*, the Salem witch trials, the contemporary political climate, and the various actors who have played Willy Loman.

Martin, Robert A. "Arthur Miller and the Meaning of Tragedy." *Modern Drama* 13 (May 1970): 343–49. Rpt. in *Conversations with Arthur Miller*. Ed. Matthew C. Roudané. Jackson: UP of Mississippi, 1987. 200–205.

Miller discusses his current views on tragedy, Quentin's relationship with God in *After the Fall*, and the play's ultimate meaning.

———. "Arthur Miller—Tragedy and Commitment." *Michigan Quarterly Review* 8 (Summer 1969): 176–78. Rpt. in *Conversations with Arthur Miller*. Ed. Matthew C. Roudané. Jackson: UP of Mississippi, 1987. 173–76.

Miller is asked if *After the Fall* "fell into place" for him as a playwright as *Death of a Salesman* had, if he considers Quentin an extension of Chris Keller and Biff Loman, if he sees a hopelessness in the human condition, and if he agrees with John F. Kennedy's description of himself as "an idealist without illusions."

———. "The Creative Experience of Arthur Miller: An Interview." *Educational Theatre Journal* 21 (October 1969): 310–17. Rpt. in *Conversations with Arthur Miller*. Ed. Matthew C. Roudané. Jackson: UP of Mississippi, 1987. 177–86.

Miller responds to questions concerning his early influences, the ideas in his plays, the autobiographical nature of *After the Fall*, his views of critics who accuse him of writing "crypto-Jewish characters," and the importance of being Jewish to his work as a playwright. Of note is Miller's assertion that if he had not written *The Crucible* "that period would be unregistered in our literature, on any popular level . . . when one says 'It was in the air,' I *made* it in the air . . . I nailed it to the historical wall."

Martin, Robert A., and Richard D. Meyer. "Arthur Miller on Plays and Playwriting." *Modern Drama* 19 (December 1976): 375–84. Rpt. in *Conversations with Arthur Miller*. Ed. Matthew C. Roudané. Jackson: UP of Mississippi, 1987. 262–72.

Lengthy interview between Miller and undergraduate students in a class in American drama which took place between rehearsals for the premiere production of *Up from Paradise* at the University of Michigan in the spring of 1974. Miller answers a wide range of questions, including the degree of his involvement in the productions of his plays, whether he believes in God, if Linda Loman in *Death of a Salesman* contributed to Willy's demise, his views on O'Neill's legacy, and the appeal of family settings to his dramatic work.

Martine, James J. "All in a Boiling Soup: An Interview with Arthur Miller." *Critical Essays on Arthur Miller*. Boston: G. K. Hall and Co., 1979. 177–88. Rpt. in *Conversations with Arthur Miller*. Ed. Matthew C. Roudané. Jackson: UP of Mississippi, 1987. 291–306.

Interview conducted in New York City, on 13 February 1979, in which Miller responds to questions concerning his early influences, his current reading habits, the one consistent factor that all great playwrights share, Willy Loman's relevancy to current audiences, the role of the critic, his working habits, his television watching habits, his legacy, and the relationship of his protagonists to their communities.

Max, D. T. "Double Trouble." *Harper's Bazaar* January 1997: 92–95.

Lengthy profile of Daniel Day-Lewis and Winona Ryder, Proctor and Abigail from the film version of *The Crucible*. Of note are the actor's feelings regarding their roles, their thoughts on Miller's screenplay, and the importance of the film for future generations. Miller comments on both actors and the universal qualities of the work that make it applicable to current audiences.

Meyer, Michael R. "A Playwright's Crusades." *Maclean's* 16 September 1985: 6+.

Miller discusses his involvement with PEN, his revival of *Salesman*, his current work, his autobiography, and the state of the professional theatre in America.

"Miller Decries U.S. Theater as Superficial." *Atlanta Constitution* 25 January 1990: E4.

In an article devoted to excerpts of Miller's interview conducted during a break in rehearsals for *The Price* at the Young Vic Theatre in London, the playwright is quoted as accusing U.S. theatre of being superficial and finds the success of the British theatre is dependent on government subsidies.

"Miller's Tales." *New Yorker* 11 April 1994: 35–36.

Profile of Miller on the occasion of the premiere of *Broken Glass* at the Long Wharf Theatre in New Haven. Miller discusses the genesis of the play, his writing schedule, the state of the commercial Broadway theatre, the lack of mature actors, and for whom he writes plays.

Millstein, Gilbert. "Ten Playwrights Tell How It All Starts." *New York Times Magazine* 6 December 1959: 63, 65.

Miller is interviewed regarding the source of his dramatic inspiration, citing a conversation as the source for *All My Sons*, an idea that "rose to the surface from his subconscious one spring night" for *Death of a Salesman*, and his interest in the Salem witch trials while a student at the University of Michigan as leading to his writing *The Crucible* in later years.

Morley, Sheridan. "Miller on Miller." *Theatre World* 61 (March 1965): 4–8.

Brief interview with Miller on the occasion of the National Theatre's production of *The Crucible*. With mostly negative responses to the questions put to him, Miller discusses McCarthyism, *After the Fall*, and his current projects. Photograph of Miller plus nine others from the production accompany the text.

"Mosaic of Marilyn." *Coronet* February 1961: 58–69.

Miller is interviewed regarding his creation of the role of Roslyn Tabor in *The Misfits* for then-wife Marilyn Monroe. Says Miller, "To understand Marilyn best, you have to see her around children. . . . The thing is, Marilyn has become a sort of fiction for writers; each one sees her through his own set of pleasures and prejudices."

Moss, Leonard. "Lack of Tension: An Interview with Arthur Miller." *Foreign Literature* (1987): 23–30. Rpt. as "The Absence of Tension: A Conversation with Arthur Miller." *Arthur Miller*. Revised ed. Boston: Twayne, 1980. 107–22. Rpt. in *Conversations with Arthur Miller*. Ed. Matthew C. Roudané. Jackson: UP of Mississippi, 1987. 315–31.

Interview conducted in Roxbury, Connecticut, on 27 July 1979. Miller is asked about his views on various productions of *The Price*, the play's examination of "the architecture of sacrifice," whether the idea of dying worries him, his views on political and dramatic tension, if he has a personal model in the moral world, his recent work on *Playing for Time*, and his memories of his mother.

Neill, Heather. "Hands across the Sea." *Sunday Times* (London) 31 January 1993: Sec. 8: 21.

Interview with Miller and director David Thacker during their collaboration on Miller's *The Last Yankee*, being produced in England at the Young Vic. Miller answers questions regarding his inspiration for the play and Thacker discusses his working relationship with the "greatest living playwright."

———. "Leading Role." *Times Educational Supplement* (London) 9 August 1994: A15.

Interview in which Miller discusses his work, methodology, and philosophy, including the plot of *Broken Glass*. Miller expresses his belief in the power of writing to change people, his opinion on individual and collective experiences, and his attitudes on strongly felt issues.

Newmark, Judith. "A View from the Greatest Living American Playwright." *St. Louis Post-Dispatch* 6 September 1998: F1.

Lengthy interview in which Miller discusses his belief in justice as an ideal worth striving for, his use of time in *Salesman*, his sense of himself as a Jewish writer, and his need to push the theatre in new directions. Nine photographs accompany the text. Note: there are several instances of incorrect biographical information.

"On Creativity." *Playboy* December 1968: 139.

In response to the question, "Do creative people have any characteristics in common, in their backgrounds or their personalities, that can be identified as wellsprings of that creativity?" Miller offers his view that "a case can be made for art as a response to the death or spiritual bankruptcy of the father; but since many non-artists experience the same disaster, we are back where we started: What in the artist creates the artistic response?"

"Our Most Widespread Dramatic Art Is Our Most Unfree." *New York Times* 26 November 1978: II: 1, 33.

On the occasion of his first television play, *Fame*, Miller asks and answers these two questions: "How did I come to write a play for television?" and "Why have established American playwrights just about ceased to write for the medium?"

Papatola, Dominic P. "Mr. Miller's *Connections*." *Saint Paul Pioneer Press* 28 October 1999: E1.

Miller discusses his latest play, *Mr. Peters' Connections*, appearing at the Guthrie Theater Lab, and the creative experience of the rehearsal process. Three photographs accompany the text.

"People." *Newsday* 27 March 1989: 8.

Miller is interviewed regarding the filming of *Everybody Wins*, his first screenplay since his 1961 *The Misfits*. Miller discusses the form of filmmaking, the film's themes, and his views on the casting of Debra Winger and Nick Nolte.

"Playwright/Co-Librettist's Note." *Stagebill* for *A View from the Bridge*. Lyric Opera of Chicago. 45th Season, 1999–2000: 42–43.

In the program for the world premiere of William Bolcom's *A View from the Bridge*, Miller answers questions regarding his interest in opera, his previous work with composers, the characteristics that make his play *A View from the Bridge* operatic, his relationship with Bolcom and Weinstein, his role in the creation of the new opera, his interest in the song "Paper Doll," his opinions as to the chorus's role and the work's enduring appeal. Candid photographs of Miller working on the opera and at home in Connecticut accompany the text.

"Playwrights at the Cliff-Edge." *Economist Financial Report* 9 July 1988: 85.

Arthur Miller, Tom Stoppard, Tina Howe, Athol Fugard, and Lanford Wilson discuss playwriting at the Graduate Center at the City University of New York.

Poetry and Film. New York: Gotham Book Mart, 1972.

Excerpts from a symposium held at Cinema 16 on 18 October 1953, with Miller, Dylan Thomas, et al.

Preston, Rohan. "Miller Time." *Star Tribune Online* (Minneapolis) 31 October 1999: F1.

Telephone interview on the occasion of the 3 November opening of his play *Mr. Peters' Connections* at the Guthrie Theater Lab in Minneapolis. Miller discusses the play's meaning and its genesis, including his use of time, which has no fixed existence in this play. Says Miller, "No other play uses such a technique—I don't know any that exist, to tell you the truth. It's a completely different and experimental work."

Rajakrishnan, V. "After Commitment: An Interview with Arthur Miller." *Indian Journal of American Studies* (Hyderabad) 9.1 (1979): 54–64. Rpt. in *Theatre Journal* 32 (May 1980): 196–202. Rpt. in *Conversations with Arthur Miller*. Ed. Matthew C. Roudané. Jackson: UP of Mississippi, 1987. 332–42.

Often quoted interview in which Miller answers questions regarding the metaphysical focus of his later plays, the silence in his dramatic career from 1955 to 1964 and whether this absence influenced his shift in focus, the autobiographical nature of *After the Fall*, Camus's *The Fall* and Miller's use of it as a point of departure for *After the Fall*, the differences between Miller's theatre and the Theatre of the Absurd, the nature of Von Berg's gesture in *Incident at Vichy*, the double movement in *The Price*, and his use of stage metaphors in *Death of a Salesman* and *The Price*.

Rasky, Harry. "Arthur Miller On Home Ground." *Nobody Swings on Sunday, the Many Lives and Films of Harry Rasky*. Don Mills, Ontario: Collier Macmillan, 1980. 246–56.

Excerpts from Rasky's 1977 documentary film on Miller [see Part 3: Media] in which Miller discusses his memories of his childhood in Brooklyn, his parents influence on his writing, the character of Willy Loman, the character of Roslyn Tabor from *The Misfits*, and his memories of first hearing of Marilyn Monroe's death. Of note are the descriptive portions of the interview that includes details regarding Miller's home in Connecticut and Rasky's method of convincing Miller to do the film.

Raymont, Henry. "Miller and Freed Brazilian Discuss New Satire Genre." *New York Times* 25 June 1971: 16.

Article that details the meeting between Miller and Augusto Boal, a leading Brazilian director, and their talk about a form of revolutionary satire that is gaining popularity in Latin America called "newspaper theatre." Miller is quoted on his understanding of the situation in Brazil where theatre artists are "using the theatre as a means of keeping alive some spark of freedom."

"Response to Audience Questions & Answer Session." *Michigan Quarterly Review* 37.4 (Fall 1998): 817–27.

At a question-and-answer session at the Miller Symposium at the University of Evansville in Indiana on 18 April 1998, Miller responds to questions concerning his impressions of various Willy Lomans, the origin of his ideas, the level of his involvement in the rehearsal process of his plays, his memories of working on the film *The Misfits*, his views on the character of Linda Loman in *Death of a Salesman* and her appeal to modern audiences, the autobiographical nature of his works, his thoughts on working in a repertory system, his relationship with and influence from Tennessee Williams, and the reasons why he had made so few films.

"The Responsible Man." *Economist* 14 July 1990: 91.

Profile of Miller framed by the following question: "How can honesty survive the falsehoods and claustrophobia of society?" Miller says the focus of his plays has been shifting from unconscious characters created by society to conscious beings responsible for their own actions.

Romano, Carlin. "America's Playwright at 80, Arthur Miller Is Awash in Acclaim, and Not Just on This Side of the Atlantic." *Philadelphia Inquirer* 27 December 1995: C1.

Miller discusses his views on the survival of the theatre as an art, the greatest problem facing American theatre [the "bottom line"], and the modern relevance of his dramas. Five photographs accompany the text.

Roudané, Matthew C. "An Interview with Arthur Miller." *Michigan Quarterly Review* 24 (Summer 1985): 373–89. Rpt. in *Conversations with Arthur Miller*. Ed. Matthew C. Roudané. Jackson: UP of Mississippi, 1987. 360–75. Rpt. in *The Theater Essays of Arthur Miller*. Revised ed. Eds. Robert A. Martin and Steven R. Centola. New York: Da Capo, 1996. 417–35.

Interview conducted on 7 November 1983 in Miller's New York City apartment in which the playwright is asked to discuss the plays that hold the fondest memories for him, the continued relevance of *Death of a Salesman*, the influence of the American Dream on his work, his creative process, the form-shift of the role of the narrator/chorus in *A View from the Bridge* from the one-act to the two-act play, whether he considers himself a dramatic innovator, the differing receptions of his plays through time, the role of women in his dramas, his revision of Ibsen's *An Enemy of the People*, his rehearsal procedure, and his views on the role of the theatre in an ideal world.

———, ed. *Conversations with Arthur Miller*. Jackson: UP of Mississippi, 1987.

Collection of thirty-five interviews, conducted from 1947 to 1986, with various critics, journalists, scholars, writers, and other professionals. All entries are annotated in this section of the bibliography.

Rudman, Michael. "Michael Rudman in Conversation with Arthur Miller." *Plays and Players* (London) October 1979: 20–21, 26–27.

In this interview conducted by Michael Rudman, the director of the National Theatre production of *Death of a Salesman*, Miller comments on the play, Stanislavsky, David Belasco, and his own advancing age. Of note is the lengthy anecdote by Miller, not printed before or since, regarding the "broken man" who appeared one day on the playwright's lawn, soon after *Salesman* opened in 1949, claiming that Willy's story was his story. A two-page photo spread from Rudman's production, starring Warren Mitchell and Ursula Smith, appears on the later pages.

Samachson, Dorothy and Joseph. "Why Write a Play?" *Let's Meet the Theatre*. New York: Abelard-Schuman, 1955. 15–20.

Interview aimed at the amateur theatre practitioner in which Miller discusses his reasons for choosing theatre over nondramatic forms of writing, his views on critics, and his advice to the young playwright and noncommercial theatre group. Production photograph of *Death of a Salesman* accompanies the text.

Sanoff, Alvin. P. "The Theatre Must Be Bread, Not Cake." *US News and World Report* 11 January 1988: 54–55.

Miller discusses his new autobiography, his previous works, the New York theatre, the European view of literature, and the lasting mystery of Marilyn Monroe.

Scavullo, Francisco. "Arthur Miller, Playwright." *Scavullo on Men*. New York: Random House, 1977. 134–37.

Miller responds to various off-beat questions regarding his writing habits, the kind of women he likes, his marriage to Marilyn Monroe and his thoughts on her abilities as an actress, his feelings regarding women's liberation, his views on the American male, what it is like to grow older, his health, his views on religion, his thoughts on American theatre, his experiences with drugs, the importance of sex to his creative life, and whether he is worried that his daughter is growing up in a word of violence, drugs, and pornography. Full-page photographic portrait of Miller by Scavullo accompanies the text.

Schumach, Murray. "Arthur Miller Grew in Brooklyn." *New York Times* 6 February 1949: II: 1, 3. Rpt. in *Conversations with Arthur Miller*. Ed. Matthew C. Roudané. Jackson: UP of Mississippi, 1987. 6–8.

In an interview conducted just days before the premiere of *Death of a Salesman* at the Morosco Theatre, Miller discusses the motifs of the play, his dramatic technique, how the idea of the play came to him, his dislike of hotels, and his need to continue to work for a few weeks each year in a factory. Says Miller, "Anyone who doesn't know what it means to stand in one place eight hours a day doesn't know what it's all about. It's the only way you can learn what makes men go into a gin mill after work and start fighting. You don't learn those things in Sardi's."

———. "Miller Still a *Salesman* for a Changing Theater." *New York Times* 26 June 1975: 32–33. Rpt. in *Conversations with Arthur Miller*. Ed. Matthew C. Roudané. Jackson: UP of Mississippi, 1987. 258–61.

On the occasion of the opening of a revival of *Death of a Salesman* at the Circle in the Square Theatre, directed by and starring George C. Scott, Miller reflects on changes in himself, the theatre, and the world in the past twenty-five years since the play's premiere in 1949.

Seymour, Gene. "Of Crucibles, Blacklists, Scoundrels and Toads." *Newsday* 24 November 1996: C14.

Transcript of a telephone conversation between Miller and Walter Bernstein, a writer during the Hollywood blacklist and currently a teacher of screenwriting at Columbia University, in which they discuss the film version of Miller's *The Crucible* and the changes that the playwright made in adapting the script into a screenplay, the modern relevance of the play, and memories of the McCarthy era.

Shanley, John P. "Miller's Focus on TV Today." *New York Times* 21 January 1962: II: 19.

Miller states that he is unenthusiastic about commercial television in general.

Shepard, Richard F. "Lincoln Theater Talks Collapse." *New York Times* 16 December 1964: 52.

In a lengthy article detailing Robert Whitehead's discharge as head of the Lincoln Center Repertory Theater, Miller is interviewed by telephone from his home in Connecticut on his thoughts on the developments. Says Miller, "Mr. Whitehead's departure just makes it absolutely definite that beyond the two plays I have given the repertory company, I won't be giving any more. . . . I don't believe that any artistic enterprise can be run if there is so narrow a freedom as the board has demonstrated through the past few weeks."

———. "Work Begins in City College Arts Hall." *New York Times* 13 May 1975: 30.

News item reporting on the symposium held at City College on "Theatre in the University," with panelists Miller, Edward Albee, Peter Shaffer, and moderator Alan Schneider. Miller is quoted as praising universities for their theatres but criticizing them for "not knowing what to do with their buildings." It is Miller's contention that university theatres should be producing new works instead of established successes.

Mr. Showbiz. "*J-PEGGED*: Arthur Miller." *Mouthoff Celebrity Lounge* (10 January 1996). http://showbiz.starwave.com/showbiz/audio/WAV/MILLER3. WAV (10 February 2000).

In this lengthy interview with RealAudio files for downloading. Miller responds to eighteen posted questions on various topics, including his views on politics today, why he thinks *Death of a Salesman* has universal appeal, how the depression influenced his writing, why Marilyn Monroe has remained an enduring icon, advice to the aspiring playwright, and his creative relationship with his daughter Rebecca.

Siegel, Ed. "CBS to Film *Death of a Salesman*." *Boston Globe* 13 October 1984: N57.

Details of a press conference attended by eighty television critics for the CBS production of Miller's *Death of a Salesman*, starring Dustin Hoffman and John Malkovich. When asked what prompted him to write the play, Miller responds, "The collapse of the entire world." Miller also mentions that he was dissatisfied with working on *Playing for Time* because they did not have time to film the script as written and he was forced to rewrite on the set. Remarks Miller, "If the subject hadn't been so important, I would have walked away from it."

———. "Miller Still Writes Plays Addressed to Anybody." *Boston Globe* 14 July 1996: B22.

Profile/interview in which Miller discusses *The Ride Down Mount Morgan* on the occasion of the play's opening at the Williamstown Theatre Festival and his work on the screenplay for *The Crucible.*

Simonson, Robert. "Values, Old and New." *Theater Week* 18 January 1993: 13–18.

Interview with Miller and director John Tillinger, focusing on their collaboration for *The Last Yankee*, including an analysis of the themes and characters of the play and a brief discussion of their careers. Miller is on the cover of this issue.

Smith, Wendy. "PW Interviews: Arthur Miller." *Publisher's Weekly* 6 November 1987: 51–52.

Miller responds to questions regarding his views on the importance of continuity with the past, the origins of his political activism, and the contemporary American theatre.

Sorensen, Holly. "Millers' Crossing." *Premiere* March 1996: 41.

Miller and his daughter Rebecca discuss his American film version of *The Crucible* and her film *Angela*.

Span, Paula. "Miller's Dialogue with the World." *Washington Post* 15 December 1996: G: 1, 6.

Lengthy feature article profiling Miller's career as a playwright on the occasion of the premiere of the film version of *The Crucible*. Also quoted are Miller's son Robert Miller, Nicholas Hytner, Steven Centola, and Edward Albee. Various photographs of Miller and his productions accompany the text.

Stafford, Richard D. "Who Owns It?: Arthur Miller, A. J. Antoon Share Thoughts on Play Ownership and Creative Control." *Southern Theatre* 33.4 (Summer 1992): 18–22.

Interview with Miller and Antoon on the subject of play ownership.

Stark, Susan. "A Milestone for Miller: *The Crucible* Goes to Hollywood." *Detroit News & Free Press* 26 October 1996: C1.

At a press conference held prior to the opening of the American film version of *The Crucible*, Miller discusses the universality of the play in cultures as diverse as China, Russia, Chile, and America—"To generalize, we're all living at the edge of the unknown in every society. And when people come up with an easy, quasi-logical explanation for things we don't understand it's devastating. Or it can be devastating."

Stearns, David Patrick. "Timeless Arthur Miller." *USA Today* 7 January 2000: E: 1–2.

Profile of Miller on the occasion of the television premiere of *Death of a Salesman* on Showtime, starring Brian Dennehy. Miller discusses his current work in progress and the continued popularity of former wife Marilyn Monroe. Eleven black-and-white photographs, some production stills, accompany the text.

Stevens, Virginia. "Seven Young Broadway Artists." *Theatre Arts* 31 June 1947: 52–56.

Miller is interviewed about his career, his objectives as a playwright, the economics of the Broadway theatre, and the themes of *All My Sons*.

Strickland, Carol. "Arthur Miller's Latest Message to Humanity." *Christian Science Monitor* 26 April 1994: 12.

In a telephone interview conducted on the occasion of the opening of *Broken Glass* at the Booth Theatre in New York, Miller discusses the play's purpose, the work's implications, the universal nature of his characters, and his satisfaction with the outcome of his script.

Sullivan, Dan. "A Few Lines from Arthur Miller with Characteristic Simplicity." *Philadelphia Inquirer* 5 December 1987: D1.

Miller discusses his feelings regarding the state of American theatre, critical reaction in America and abroad to his plays, the British theatre system, and his staying power. Three photographs accompany the text.

Sweet, Bruce. "The Invisible Director: The Stage Direction of Harold Clurman as Witnessed by Actors, Stage Managers, Producers, Playwrights and Critics from Three Representative Productions." Diss. New York U, 1981. 106–62, 222–23.

In a chapter devoted to Harold Clurman's direction of *Incident at Vichy*, author Sweet interviews Robert Whitehead (producer for *Vichy*), actors Joseph Wiseman (LeDuc), Michael Strong (Le Beau), Ira Lewis (the Boy), and Miller. Miller discusses Clurman's directing style, his memories of rehearsals, and his assessment of Clurman's character, especially in relation to Elia Kazan.

Sylvester, Robert. "Brooklyn Boy Makes Good." *Saturday Evening Post* 16 July 1949: 26–27, 97–98, 100. Rpt. in *Conversations with Arthur Miller*. Ed. Matthew C. Roudané. Jackson: UP of Mississippi, 1987. 9–18.

Biographical sketch interspersed with quips by Miller and then-wife Mary Grace Slattery. Of note is the plethora of financial details regarding royalties and production costs for *Death of a Salesman*.

Terkel, Studs. "Studs Terkel Talks with Arthur Miller." *Saturday Review* September 1980: 24–27. Rpt. in *Conversations with Arthur Miller*. Ed. Matthew C. Roudané. Jackson: UP of Mississippi, 1987. 307–14. Rpt. as "Arthur Miller." *The Spectator: Talk about Movies and Plays with the People Who Made Them*. New York: New Press, 1999. 76–83.

On the occasion of the premiere of *The American Clock* (a play inspired by Terkel's book *Hard Times*) at the Spoleto Festival in Charleston, S.C., Miller discusses the play's motifs and themes, including the Great Depression, guilt, and society's effect on "the inner life of a man." Says Miller of his play, "It's the story of the United States talking to itself."

Terry, Clifford. "Arthur Miller, Area Code 203." *Chicago Tribune Magazine* 24 January 1965: 38.

On the occasion of the opening of the touring company production of *After the Fall* at the Blackstone Theatre in Chicago, Miller responds to questions regarding the positive response from audiences to his controversial play, the ease with which the show transferred to a touring production without much revision, the themes and structure of *Incident at Vichy*, his decision to abandon

Lincoln Center following the internal management dispute, critics, and the state of the commercial Broadway theatre.

"The Testimony of Arthur Miller, Accompanied by Counsel, Joseph L. Rauh Jr." United States House of Representatives, Committee on Un-American Activities. *Investigation of the Unauthorized Use of United State Passports, 84th Congress, 2d Session, Congressional Record*, Part 4, June 21, 1956. Washington: United States Government Printing Office, November 1956, pp. 4660–4690. See also "Proceedings against Arthur Miller," *Congressional Record*, Report # 2922, July 25, 1956. 1–38.

Miller's testimony before HUAC where he declines to name those who had been present at a meeting of Communist Party writers in 1947.

"The Testimony of Arthur Miller, Author and Playwright." United States Senate, Committee on Government Operations. *Negotiation and Statecraft, Hearings Before the Permanent Subcommittee on Investigations, 94th Congress, First Session, Congressional Record*, Part 4, November 18, 1975, pp. 159–64.

Miller's testimony before the Permanent Subcommittee on Investigations on 18 November on the United State's obligation to guarantee freedom of author's everywhere, "to insure their work without peril of suppression, harassment, torture, or death." Includes Miller's prefatory remarks followed by a copy of his prepared statement. Concludes Miller, "The Senate and the Congress, it seems to me, have the obligation to decide whether Czech repression is in contravention of the Helsinki accords. If it is, then the State Department should be instructed to ask the Soviet Government what it intends to do about the matter as a signatory to the agreement."

Toubiana, Serge. "Something Burning Up: An Interview with Arthur Miller." *The Misftis: The Story of a Shoot*. London: Phaidon, 2000. 6–48.

Lengthy interview with both Miller and wife Inge Morath concerning their memories of the making of *The Misfits*, including the break-up of Miller's marriage to Marilyn Monroe, the genesis of the film project, working with Gable, Clift, and Huston, and critical response to the film. Of note are the dozens of black-and-white photographs, some never seen before now, by Magnum photographers Eve Arnold, Henri Cartier-Bresson, Inge Morath, Bruce Davidson, and Cornell Capa, among others.

Trussell, Robert. "Arthur Miller Heads for Kansas." *Kansas City Star* 21 April 1995: P13.

Interview conducted on the occasion of Miller's trip to Independence, Kansas, to receive the William Inge Festival Award for Distinguished Achievement in the American Theatre. Miller discusses his memories of Inge, the long wait for *The Crucible* to be made into an American motion picture, and the state of the theatre in America.

Tyler, Christian. "The People's Playwright." *Financial Times* (London) 2 November 1991: 24.

On the occasion of the London opening of *The Ride Down Mount Morgan*, Miller discusses his reasons for writing, his competitive nature, his goal of delivering "up a human being and a society" in the same moment, the universal qualities of his plays, and his sense of his own mortality.

Tyler, Ralph. "Arthur Miller Says the Time Is Right for *The Price*." *New York Times* 17 June 1979: II: 1, 6.

Interview in which Miller discusses *The Price* and its recent successful revival.

Unger, Arthur. "Arthur Miller Talks of His Holocaust Drama." *Christian Science Monitor* 19 September 1980: 19.

On the occasion of the casting of *The American Clock*, Miller discusses the controversy surrounding the casting of Vanessa Redgrave in *Playing for Time*, his own experiences with being fired from writing a film on juvenile delinquency for the New York City Youth Board because of his politics, his disagreement with Redgrave's political stand but his determination that she not be dismissed because of her beliefs, and his belief that the things will work out fine. Says Miller, "I am a great believer in the long run. I've had to be because in the short haul I usually lose but in the long run, as often as not, I win. And I believe that what an artist *does* in his work, not what he says, is for the long run."

"University Needs Lab Theatre, Miller, Play Prize Winner." *The Michigan Daily* 6 March 1937: 1.

A student at the University of Michigan, the twenty-one-year-old Miller is interviewed on the occasion of the first production of his first play *They Too Arise*, presented on 12 and 13 March in Ann Arbor. Miller discusses the need for a laboratory theatre on campus, that four agents of the Federal Theatre Project are going to attend a performance to "examine the possibilities of their producing it," and his delight at finding that the Hillel Players "happen to fit the roles better than I thought any college group could." Article states that Miller is a junior, majoring in English composition. Of special note is the fact that this is Miller's first interview in print.

Vajda, Miklós. "Playwriting in America Today: A Telephone Interview with Arthur Miller." *New Hungarian Quarterly* 77 (1980): 123–24.

Taped 17 March 1979 and aired on World Theatre Day (27 March 1979) as a part of a series of telephone interviews with leading theatrical artists for Hungarian Radio's First Programme, Miller responds to questions regarding his views on writing in the seventies compared to previous decades, the lack of new talent emerging on the current theatre scene, and if the present is less suitable for dramatic presentation than the past.

Wadler, Joyce. "Adventurer with Brightly Colored Stories." *New York Times* 18 March 1998: B2.

Interview/profile of Inge Morath on the occasion of her retrospective exhibit at the Leica Gallery in New York. Of note are her comments regarding Marilyn Monroe and her thirty-five year marriage to Arthur Miller.

Wager, Walter. "Arthur Miller." *Playwrights Speak*. New York: Delta, 1967. 1–24. Rpt. in *Conversations with Arthur Miller*. Ed. Matthew C. Roudané. Jackson: UP of Mississippi, 1987. 137–51.

In an interview conducted at the Chelsea Hotel on 10 November 1964, Miller comments on a wide range of topics, including his writing technique and routine, the Anglo-Saxon audience's resistance to "objective knowing," the subject matter of *Incident at Vichy*, his "silent" period preceding *After the Fall*, drama as an expression of profound social needs, and his role in the casting of his plays.

Wain, John. "Literature and Life—I: Arthur Miller." *Observer* (London) 8 September 1957: 5.

Miller responds to questions regarding his views on social realism, the social responsibility of the writer in today's society, criteria for good playwriting, and the themes of *A View from the Bridge*.

Weber, Bruce. "A Long Day of Talking and a Big Night of Singing." *New York Times* 11 October 1999: E1.

In an article offering the details of the opening day activities of the opera version of *A View from the Bridge*, commissioned by the Lyric Opera of Chicago, Weber includes portions of a public symposium on the creation of the opera held in the morning with panelists Miller, Dennis Russell Davies (conductor), Robert Bolcom (composer), Arnold Weinstein (co-librettist with Miller), and Frank Galati (director). Speaking infrequently during the symposium, Miller admits to his lack of knowledge about opera, discusses his early singing career and his memories of his visit to Italy after World War II, and remarks on the origin of the story as based on one he had heard in Brooklyn.

Wertham, Frederic. "Let the Salesman Beware." *New York Times Book Review* 15 May 1949: 4, 12.

Miller believes that the reason for the popular success of *Death of a Salesman* stems from the audience's identification with Willy's insecurities and his male need for an "efficient, successful, praiseworthy personality."

Whitcomb, Jon. "Marilyn Monroe—The Sex Symbol versus the Good Wife." *Cosmopolitan* December 1960: 52–57.

Interview with Miller and Marilyn Monroe on the set of *The Misfits*, in which Miller discusses why he wrote the film for his wife, his role in the production of the movie, and the challenges of being married to a Hollywood celebrity.

"Who Killed Kennedy?" *Fact* 3.6 (November/December 1966): 6.

In a poll of celebrities and authorities on their opinions as to who killed President John F. Kennedy, Miller contributes a brief item stating that enough evidence exists to believe that there was more than one gunman.

Wolf, Matt. "Arthur Miller's Latest for London in Fall." *Philadelphia Inquirer* 29 August 1991: D3.

In an article announcing the world premiere in London of *The Ride Down Mount Morgan*, starring Tom Conti, Miller is quoted in a telephone interview as being pleased with the production and its premiere in a city with more "theatre culture" and "actors of a certain caliber."

———. "An Exile of Sorts Finds a Welcome." *New York Times* 13 October 1991: H6.

Lengthy interview/essay in which Wolf investigates the "special relationship" between Miller and the British theatre and its audiences. The playwright discusses the "dark defeatism over the whole New York scene," his views on the market-driven Broadway stage, and the theatregoing habits of audiences in England "which is all but lost, he said, in his home city."

Wolfert, Ira. "Arthur Miller, Playwright in Search of His Identity." *New York Herald Tribune* 25 January 1953: IV: 3.

Brief profile/interview in which Miller discusses his career and the genesis of *The Crucible*.

Zolotow, Sam. "Miller to Trim *After the Fall*." *New York Times* 11 August 1964: 37.

Zolotow reports that Miller has decided to revise *After the Fall* to shorten its running time by eighteen minutes, even though the production as been running since 23 January of this year. When asked about what prompted Miller to make the changes, Miller responded that he "couldn't find them earlier. I discovered that the scenes themselves were dramatized sufficiently so that in some cases Quentin's speeches could be reduced and in some cases eliminated. The basic process amounted to threading the play to eliminate any excess words or sentences." In addition, Miller notes that the touring company of the show has his permission to make changes necessary to conform to the requirements of proscenium theatres.

Electronic Media

Adams, Noah. "Current Opera Production of *The Crucible* Playing to Rave Reviews." *All Things Considered*. NPR. 15 January 1999. Broadcast transcript.

In a piece on the opera version of *The Crucible* at the Washington Opera, Miller responds to questions regarding the relevance of *The Crucible* to modern audiences.

Alexander Calder. American Masters. PBS. 17 June 1998.

Miller is one of many friends of the artist interviewed regarding Calder.

Arthur Miller. Prod. Kevin Loader. Interviewed by Alan Yentob. BBC-TV. Chicago: Films Incorporated, 1989. Rereleased in 1997 by Films for the Humanities and Sciences.

In a program that first appeared on the British television series "Omnibus," Miller gives a candid interview about his life and work. He discusses his most famous works, his personal and literary evolution, his marriage to Marilyn Monroe, and his current work and interests.

Arthur Miller. BBC. Films Inc., Chicago, 1988.

Production that, through interviews and film clips, explores the connection between Miller's life and his literature.

Arthur Miller: A Conversation with Mike Wallace. CBS News. Films for the Humanities and Sciences. 1999.

Miller discusses his youth, his relationship with his father, critical reaction to his plays, and his marriage to Marilyn Monroe.

Arthur Miller: Interview and Profile. Prod, Kevin Loader. *Sunday Afternoon with Peter Ross*. Sydney: A.B.C. 1989.

Miller discusses his childhood and upbringing, personal and political views, including his life with Marilyn Monroe.

Arthur Miller: Today's Theatre. University of Michigan Video Film Library, 1975.

Miller talks about his new play, *Up from Paradise*, and offers his view of problems that plague Broadway.

Baker, Russell. *Interview with Russell Baker*. *Masterpiece Theatre*. PBS. WGBH/Boston. 1996.

Bigsby, Christopher, and Leonard Kingston. *Arthur Miller and The Crucible: Naming Names* Prod. Andree Molyneux. BBC. 1981. Films for the Humanities, 1997.

Parallels dramatized scenes from the BBC production of *The Crucible* with Miller's recorded testimony before the House Committee on Un-American Activities, revealing Miller's concern for personal and group freedom and the fundamental themes in common with both.

Bragg, Melvyn. "Arthur Miller." *The South Bank Show*. Dir. and Prod. Hilary Chadwick. London Weekend TV, 1980. Bravo Cable Network, 1991.

Conan, Neal. "Arthur Miller's 17th Play Premieres in New York." *Morning Edition*. NPR. 10 February 1993. Broadcast transcript.

Interview conducted by Phyllis Joffee of Connecticut Public Radio in which Miller discusses the hero of *The Last Yankee*, his reasons for choosing the format of a short piece, and the commercialism of New York theatre.

Conversations with Playwrights Arthur Miller and Israel Horovitz. Prod. and dir. Ralph Curtis. Host James MacAndrew. *Camera Three*. CBS. Creative Arts Television, 1960.

A conversation with Miller and Israel Horovitz about the role of the artist in society, focusing on the artist as a private, public, and political being. Copy located in the Creative Arts Television Archive Collection at the Library of Congress.

"*Death of a Salesman* on Showtime." *Showbiz Today*. CNN. 6 January 2000. Broadcast transcript.

Short profile of the taping of the fiftieth anniversary production of *Death of a Salesman*, directed by Robert Falls and starring Brian Dennehy, for Showtime. The playwright was uncertain as to the play's abilities to be filmed for television without losing something in the translation but, says Miller, he found the taping "surprisingly rich."

Dowell, Pat, and Bob Edwards. "*The Crucible*." *Morning Edition*. NPR. 29 November 1996. Broadcast transcript.

In a piece reviewing the American film version of *The Crucible*, Miller discusses the motivating reasons for writing the story and the universal issues that make the work relevant from generation to generation.

Evans, Richard. *Psychological Dialogue with Playwright Arthur Miller*. "Notable Contributors to the Psychology of Personality." Pennsylvania State University Audio-Visual Services, 1980, 1989.

Evans interviews Miller at his home in Roxbury, Connecticut, in 1965. Part 1 deals with motivations, psychological analysis of the author through his works, impact on audiences, and various psychological theories. Part 2 shows Miller's reactions to major personality theories, his views on personality growth, identity and role conflict, and contemporary problems.

Final Cut. Discovery People Channel. 5 December 1999. Broadcast transcript.

Full tape of interview with Mike Wallace for *60 Minutes* segment, taped in 1987. Miller disscusses his HUAC testimony, his marriage to Marilyn Monroe, and his writing routine.

John Huston: the Man, the Movies, the Maverick. Prod. Joni Levin. Dir. Frank Martin. A Point Blank Production. Turner Home Entertainment, 1988.

Biographical study of John Huston told through interviews with family and friends. Also discusses his professional life through scenes from his most famous films and interviews and stars who worked with him. Contributors include, among others, Paul Newman, Lauren Bacall, Miller, Anjelica Huston, Michael Caine, and Robert Mitchum.

Interview with Arthur Miller. A&E Network. 9 January 1985. Melvyn and Bragg, 1980.

Contains readings from *The American Clock*, *The Crucible*, and *Death of a Salesman*.

Interview with Howard Bay. Interviewed by Brendan Gill. The New York Public Library's Theatre on Film and Tape Archive at The New York Public Library for the Performing Arts. 20 March 1984.

Bay discusses his career as a scenic and lighting designer. Included are his comments regarding his work on *Death of a Salesman.*

Kurnis, Jay. "Arthur Miller Talks about Depression, Economic Pressures, and the Opening of His New Play *An American Clock*." PBS. November 1980.

Miller talks about the Great Depression and the critical reaction of his new play *The American Clock*. Held by Michigan State University Library.

Moyers, Bill. "Willy Loman Comes to China." *Our Times with Bill Moyers*. CBS. 1983.

Interview/profile of Miller on the occasion of his traveling to Peiking to direct a production of *Death of a Salesman* with an all-Chinese cast.

Private Conversations on the Set of "Death of a Salesman." Dir. and prod. Christian Blackwood. PBS. 15 September 1985. Karl-Lorimar Home Video, Castle Hill Prods., 1986

Offers a unique perspective of the 1985 Schlondorff revival and "reveals the complexity of moving from text to content, from script to spectacle."

Rasky, Harry. *Arthur Miller on Home Ground. Spectrum Series.* Canadian Broadcasting Corporation. 24 October 1979. PBS. 8 October 1980.

Rather, Dan. "*Death of a Salesman* Opens on Broadway." *CBS Evening News with Dan Rather.* CBS. 9 February 1999. Broadcast transcript.

Interview for CBS News on the occasion of the opening of the fiftieth anniversary production of *Death of a Salesman.* In short sound bites, Miller discusses the meaning of the play, the modern relevance of the fifty-year-old play, and his enthusiasm over the Robert Falls's production, starring Brian Dennehy.

———. *60 Minutes Classics Special.* CBS. 3 March 1999. Broadcast transcript.

Second part of *60 Minutes Classics* is new interview with Dan Rather in which Miller discusses the differences between the original and revival productions of *Death of a Salesman*, the character of Linda Loman, and the universal appeal of the play.

Research Conversations with Arthur Miller, Playwright. "Studies of Significant American Artists" series. Boston University Productions, 1997, 1987.

Conversations recorded 25–26 April 1987. Includes chronological list of works by Miller. Biographical discussion with Sigmund Koch (tape 1), work process and craft discussion with Jacques Cartier and Sigmund Koch (tapes 2 and 3), trends, problems, and achievements of theatre in the twentieth century discussion with Peter Altman and Sigmund Koch (tape 4).

Rose, Charlie. *The Charlie Rose Show.* PBS. 13 May 1994.

Rose, Charlie. *The Charlie Rose Show.* PBS. 31 August 1994.

Stamberg, Susan. "*Streetcar* Anniversary Part II." *All Things Considered.* NPR. 1 February 1997. Broadcast transcript.

In a piece devoted to the fiftieth anniversary of *A Streetcar Named Desire*, Miller is quoted as to his memories of Williams and the latter's influence on the language of *Death of a Salesman.*

Vitale, Tom. "Arthur Miller's *Death of a Salesman*." *All Things Considered*. NPR. 10 February 1999. Broadcast transcript.

Miller discusses the inital audience reaction to *Death of a Salesman* and the character of Willy Loman. Also included are comments by critics Douglas Watt and Ben Brantley, and actors Dustin Hoffman, George C. Scott, Brian Dennehy, and Elizabeth Franz.

Wallace, Mike. *60 Minutes Classics Special*. CBS. 3 March 1999. Broadcast transcript.

Broadcast on the occasion of the fiftieth anniversary production of *Death of a Salesman*, directed by Robert Falls and starring Brian Dennehy. First part of segment is the rebroadcast of an interview conducted in 1987 for *60 Minutes*. In it Miller discusses his early success at thirty-three, his marriage to Marilyn Monroe, and his thoughts on an epitaph.

Wilson, Ed. *Spotlight*. Dir. William D. Schempp. City University of New York, 1990, 1991.

Interviews with celebrities, including Miller, Jessica Tandy and Hume Cronyn, Emanuel Azenberg, Henry David Wang, Lloyd Richards, Larry Gelbart, Robert Whitehead, Lanford Wilson, August Wilson, Wendy Wasserstein, George Abbott, Edward Albee, Arthur Kopit, John Guare, A. R. Gurney, Garson Kanin, Marsha Norman, Harold Prince, Jerry Zacks, and Christopher Durang.

William Styron: The Way of the Writer. Written and directed by Variety Moszynski. Narrated by Mary MacDowell. *American Masters*. Thirteen/WNET New York Center for Visual History and Little Bear/France. Inner Dimension, 1997.

Part of "Voices and Visions" series. Commentators include Meryl Streep, Arthur Miller, Peter Matthiesen, Carlos Fuentes, and William Styron. They discuss many factors that influence Styron's writing.

Writers of Today. First Run/Icarus Films, 1990, 1950.

Originally produced in the 1950s as a segment of "Writers of Today." Miller interview in which the playwright expresses his views on the role of the theatre and of the playwright in society. He also criticizes the business nature of theatre in New York City. Copy held by George Mason University.

6. Manuscript, Correspondence, Recording, Photographic, and Miscellaneous Collections

Academy of Motion Picture Arts and Sciences

Lester Cowan Collection. Margaret Herrick Library, Academy of Motion Picture Arts and Sciences.

Unprocessed collection that contains script material, production information, and correspondence related to Arthur Miller's uncredited work on the film *The Story of G.I. Joe*.

George Cukor Collection. Margaret Herrick Library, Academy of Motion Picture Arts and Sciences.

Miller's involvement with rewriting *Let's Make Love* (20th Century-Fox, 1960) is represented by the following five items:

1. Script: test scenes and script pages 6–12; 31 December 1959 and n.d.

2. Script: second revised shooting final script by Norman Krasna; 15 January 1960, with changes through 13 June 1960; 139 pages.

3. Script: second revised shooting final script by Norman Krasna; 15 January 1960, with changes through 13 June 1960; 139 pages [bound].

4. Correspondence 1960. Contains a copy of a letter from Arthur Miller regarding Marilyn Monroe, 30 April 1960.

John Huston Collection. Margaret Herrick Library, Academy of Motion Picture Arts and Sciences.

Miller material primarily relates to *The Misfits* (United Artists, 1961).

1. Script, first draft "play for the screen" by Arthur Miller (based upon the author's story published in Esquire Magazine, October 1957); 18 October 1957; 164 pages [lightly annotated].

2. Script, revised screenplay by Arthur Miller; 15 June 1959; pages 1–50 [inc.; includes photocopy of letter from Mr. Miller, 16 June 1959].

3. Script, revised screenplay by Arthur Miller; September 1959; 163 pages.

4. Script, revised screenplay by Arthur Miller; September 1959; 159 pages [inc.; heavily annotated].

5. Script, revised screenplay by Arthur Miller; March 1960; 147 pages [lightly annotated].

6. Script, screenplay by Arthur Miller; [March 1960], with revisions through 18 July 1960; approximately 147 pages [medium annotations].

7. Script, revised pages; 13 July 1960, 16 July 1960, 18 July 1960, 28 August 1969, and 19 September 1960.

8. Script, screenplay by Arthur Miller; n.d., with revisions through 2 November 1960; approximately 146 pages [medium annotations; bound copy].

9. Script, book of screenplay by Arthur Miller; New York: The Viking Press, 1961; 132 pages [inscribed by Mr. Miller to John (Huston), January 1961].

10. Erickson, C.O. (Doc) 1959–1961. Includes letter from Mr. Erickson saying how pleased he was to handle production of *The Man Who Would Be King*, 17 August 1959; copy of a letter from Mr. Huston regarding Bill Hornbeck, 29 January 1960; letter from Mr. Erickson discussing costumes and stating he was opposed to hiring Jack Cardiff, 11 March 1960; letter from Mr. Erickson reporting on the Reno premiere of *The Misfits*, 8 February 1961.

11. General 1959–1961. Includes telegram from John Huston stating that Robert Mitchum would like to see the script of *The Misfits*, 4 August 1959; menu for company dinner at the Mapes Hotel, 18 October 1960; note from David O. Selznick praising the film, 2 March 1961; distribution statement, 1 April 1961; staff lists.

12. Miller, Arthur 1958–1960. Includes copy of a letter from John Huston to Mr. Miller, 23 July 1958; handwritten letter from Mr. Miller, 14 July 1959; letter from Mr. Miller, ca. 1961.

13. Publicity 19[61]. contains: narration for a featurette.

14. Publicity clippings 1960–1961.

15. Reviews 1961.

16. Sketches. n.d., Contains folder with horse-roping sequence storyboards by S. Grimes.

17. *The Story of "The Misfits"*, 1963. Galleys of this book by James Goode; photocopy of reviews.

18. Wardrobe files. n.d. Contains wardrobe plot for Clark Gable; photostatic copies of costume sketches for Marilyn Monroe—change 1 [includes swatch]; change 2 [includes swatch]; change 2A; change 3 [includes swatch]; change 4 [includes swatch]; change 5 [includes swatch]; change 6 [includes swatch]; change 7; change 7A [includes swatch]; change 8; change 8A [includes swatch].

Alex North Collection, Margaret Herrick Library, Academy of Motion Picture Arts and Sciences.

Collection contains: *(a)* material relating to North's involvement with *The Misfits* (United Artists, 1961), including a thank-you note from Arthur Miller [photocopy] 1961; *(b) Death of a Salesman* (CBS-TV, aired 15 September 1985), including clippings, continuity files, correspondence, instrumental breakdowns, music breakdowns, notes, playscript with notations by North, playscript with stage directions by Rudman, clippings, and playbills; *(c) After the Fall* (Unrealized, Paramount, circa 1965–1969), screenplay by Arthur Miller; n.d.; 155 pages; and *(d) Playing for Time* (CBS-TV telefeature, aired 30 September 1980), script by Arthur Miller; n.d.; 118 pages [with a cover letter from Linda Yellen, Syzygy Productions, 19 July 1979].

Martin Ritt Collection. Margaret Herrick Library, Academy of Motion Picture Arts and Sciences.

Collection contains material relating to *A View from the Bridge* (Coronet Theatre, 1955) including playscripts of *A View from the Bridge*, approximately 86 pages [medium annotations], and two of *A Memory of Two Mondays*, 72 pages, second script heavily annotated by Martin Ritt, clippings, and reviews, playbills, legal files, and a correspondence file, which includes a copy of a letter from Mr. Ritt to Arthur Miller stating that he would have to pass on making *The Price* 4 November 1968.

William Wyler Collection. Margaret Herrick Library, Academy of Motion Picture Arts and Sciences.

Miller content in political file and includes letter from Arthur Miller, 10 October 1950, soliciting support for proposed ad [text attached].

Fred Zinnermann Collection. Margaret Herrick Library, Academy of Motion Picture Arts and Sciences.

Collection contains material relating to "Juvenile Delinquency Film" (Combined Artists, Inc. United Artists, unrealized), including a script and notes ("Memorandum on Juvenile Delinquency Film") by Arthur Miller; copyright 1955; 30 pages [typed; cover: "to be produced by Richard Saunders for Combined Artists, Inc."], correspondence that includes two letters from Richard Saunders regarding the project and attachment of Gene Kelly, both mentioning Miller's involvement with the project, and correspondence relating to *Playing for Time*, August–September 1978.

Alabama Department of Archives and History

Virginia Foster Durr, Papers, 1904–1991. Alabama Department of Archives and History, State of Alabama, Montgomery, Alabama. 4 archive boxes, 1 oversized folder; 1.3 cubic feet.

Collection contains correspondence, letters, clippings, photographs, awards, certificates, ephemera, and printed material of Virginia Foster Durr, civil rights activist. Miller is included as a prominent correspondent.

American Academy of Arts and Letters

Various Items, 1958–1998. American Academy and Institute of Arts and Letters.

Collection that includes administrative material such as RSVP forms, etc., and correspondence, telegrams, and tributes by Miller, who has been a member of the Academy since 1958.

1. TLS, 31 January 1958, to Louise Bogan, accepting election to membership in the National Institute of Arts and Letters.
2. TLS, 17 December 1970, to Babette Deutsch.
3. TLS, 28 March 1972, to Mrs. Eloise Segal.
4. ALS, 3 July 1972, to Felicia Geffen (Executive Director).
5. 2 TLS, 11 June 1973, and 23 November 1973, to Joseph Mitchell (Secretary of the Institute).
6. 4 TLS, 17 July 1973, 9 May 1975, 6 September 1975, and 15 December 1975, to Margaret Mills (Executive Director).
7. Transcript of Institute Dinner "An Evening with Arthur Miller," where he reads from *Up from Paradise*.
8. ALS, 20 November 1975, to William Meredith.
9. ALS, 9 February 1975, to Miss Larson.

Correspondence while serving on Literary Awards Committee 1976–1977.

1. TLS, 15 December 1976, to William Meredith.

2. TLS, 8 January 1977, to Jacques Barzun (President of the Academy).

3. Telegram, 30 January 1977, to Margaret Mills.

4. 4 TLS, rec'd 28 April 1977, 6 March 1980, 16 July 1981, 26 February 1985, to Margaret Mills.

5. TLS, 11 September 1978, to George Rickey.

6. TLS, 27 September 1977, to Jack Levine.

7. ALS, 2 March 1980, to Margaret Mills.

8. Written tribute to Louis Untermeyer, c. 6 March 1980.

9. T/ccLS, 21 March 1980, to William Maxwell.

10. TLS, 20 June 1980, to John Updike and William Meredith.

11. 2 ALS, red'd 2 June 1982, and 6 October 1983, to Margaret Mills.

12. Tribute to Tennessee Williams, 2 December 1983.

13. Tribute to Harrison Salisbury, 4 November 1993.

14. ALS, 21 January 1995, to Kevin Roche (President of the Academy).

American Film Institute

Charles K. Feldman Collection. Louis B. Mayer Library, American Film Institute. 14 filing cabinets.

Collection of scripts, correspondence, client records, and financial and legal material relating to Feldman's career as a lawyer, agent, and producer from the 1930s to the 1960s, which includes daybooks that document Miller and Elia Kazan's trip to Hollywood in 1951.

Columbia University

Harold Clurman, Papers, 1922–1980. Rare Book and Manuscript Library, Columbia University. 13 items in one box; .5 linear feet.

Collection of correspondence, notebooks, and photocopies of manuscripts. Letters from Miller are included in this collection.

Greenberg Collection. Rare Book and Manuscript Library, Columbia University.

Collection of materials relating to the publishing company that includes two letters by Miller. 1. TDS [1p], Brooklyn, March

1941, letter of agreement for Miller's play *The Pussycat and the Expert Plumber Who Was a Man* to appear in a Greenberg anthology. 2. TDS [1p], Brooklyn, March 1941, letter of agreement for Miller's play *William Ireland's Confession* to appear in a Greenberg anthology.

Arthur Miller, Manuscripts, 1952–1953. Rare Book and Manuscript Library, Columbia University. ca. 50 items; 1 box.

Collection of playbills, playscripts, notes, caricatures, rehearsal lists, files, and newspaper reviews and clipping for *The Crucible*. The playscripts show the working notes of Miller and director Jed Harris.

Reminiscences of Arthur Miller: Oral History. Oral History Research Office, Columbia University. Transcript; 44 leaves.

Transcript of interview by Joan and Robert Franklin. Miller discusses the depression as an influence on his life and literature, working on the Federal Theatre Project, *All My Sons*, *Death of a Salesman*, post-World War II theatre, the red scare, and his response to McCarthyism in *The Crucible*.

Isidor Schneider, Papers, 1925–1975. Rare Book and Manuscript Library, Columbia University. Ca. 5,000 items; 21 boxes.

Manuscripts and correspondence of Isidor Schneider, American poet and novelist. Literary correspondence includes letters from Miller.

Dartmouth College Library

Death of a Salesman by Arthur Miller. Dartmouth College Library, Dartmouth College. 1 box.

Typescript of Miller's play "with significant variations from the published text" belonging to Alan Hewitt who played Howard Wagner in the original 1949 production of *Death of a Salesman*.

George Mason University

Federal Theatre Project Collection. Special Collections and Archives, Fenwick Library, George Mason University.

Collection of Federal Theatre Project papers, administrative reports, audio tapes, playscripts, radio scripts, photographs, playbills, and lectures. Includes a copy of Miller's "They Too Arise" in the playscript collection.

Georgetown University

James P.J. Murphy Papers. Special Collections Division: Archives, Manuscripts, Rare Books and Fine Prints, Lavinger Library, Georgetown University.

Autograph collection containing correspondence and signed photographs of the 1930s and 1940s. Contains the following Miller material: 1 ALS/PC from Miller to JPJM, in response to a request by JPJM for an autograph [19 December 1953 postmark], with 1 TLS from Miller's secretary to JPJM regarding the same.

Ned O'Gorman Papers. Special Collections Division: Archives, Manuscripts, Rare Books and Fine Prints, Lavinger Library, Georgetown University.

Collection contains correspondence, manuscripts, notes, and diaries of poet-author Ned O'Gorman. Contains the following Miller material: 2 TLSs from AM, dated 25 August 1977 and 9 September 1977, signed for him by his secretary, to Ned O'Gorman, both turning O'Gorman down for a speaking engagement to raise money for the Children's Storefront.

Leonard Reed Collection. Special Collections Division: Archives, Manuscripts, Rare Books and Fine Prints, Lavinger Library, Georgetown University. 2 boxes; .75 linear feet.

Collection of mimeo. typescripts and review copies of plays. Contains 1 mimeo. typescripts of *Death of a Salesman*, as prepared for production, including music and sound cues at end. Dated September 1948.

Harvard University

Letters [3]. Manuscript Department, Houghton Library, Harvard University.

1. TLS, 1950, to John Mason Brown
2. TLS, 1950, to John Mason Brown
3. TLS, 1969, to John Updike

Indiana University, Lilly Library

Rust Hills, Manuscripts, 1954–1996. Manuscripts Department, Lilly Library, Indiana University. Ca. 3,000 items.

Collection consists of papers belonging to L. Rust Hills, author and editor. Box 1 contains six items of correspondence to

Hills from Miller: 1964, 9 March; 28 September [PC]. 1973, 24 October; 25 November [sec'y signed]. 1978, 2 February; 30 May. Items concern articles and short stories submitted to Hills for inclusion in the various magazines for which he worked.

"The Hook: A Play for the Screen." Manuscripts Department, Lilly Library, Indiana University.

Frank Taylor, Manuscripts, 1932–1984. Manuscripts Department, Lilly Library, Indiana University. Ca. 1,650 items.

Collection consists of correspondence, papers, business files, and memorabilia of Frank Taylor, independent publisher and film producer. Taylor was a friend of Miller's, having "discovered" him while editor-in-chief of Reynal and Hitchcock and publishing *Focus*, as well as having served as producer for *The Misfits*. Collection contains files relating to the production of *The Misfits*.

Library of Congress

"Arthur Miller Delivering the Theodore D. Spencer Lecture at Harvard University, February 18, 1953." Archive of Recorded Poetry and Literature, Library of Congress. 1 sound reel tape.

In a speech originally broadcast over radio station WGBH, Boston, Miller discusses contemporary drama, dramatic form, and other techniques.

"Arthur Miller, Half-Length Portrait, Facing Right, with Pipe in His Mouth." *New York World-Telegram & Sun* Collection. Library of Congress.

United Press photograph dating from between 1960–1970.

"Arthur Miller, Half-Length Portrait, Seated at Typewriter, Facing Left, Left Hand Under Chin." 1 photoprint. Prints and Photographs Reading Room, Library of Congress.

Photograph of Miller dating from between 1945–1960.

Henry Brandon Papers, 1939–1994. Manuscript Division, Library of Congress. Ca. 20, 400 items; 32.2 linear feet.

Collection consists of correspondence, essays, articles, and related mater of journalist and author Henry Brandon. Miller content includes Brandon's typed transcripts and handwritten notes from joint interview with Miller and Monroe, located in Box 18 and 19 of the "Interview File" and Box 28 of the "Reference File."

"Children of the Sun." [n.d. 193* TMS]. Rare Books Division, Library of Congress. 1 v. [various pagings].

"Dance Drama." [n.p., c.1942 TMS]. Rare Books Division, Library of Congress. 1 v.

"*Death of a Salesman* Poster." Prints and Photographs Division, Library of Congress.

Poster for play produced at the Cape Theatre, Cape May, N.J., showing the silhouetted back of a walking man by artist Joseph Hirsch.

Martha Dodd Papers, 1950–1990. Manuscript Division, Library of Congress. 4,900 items in 16 containers; 7.2 linear feet.

Collection of author and political exile Dodd that includes correspondence, writings, research materials, memoirs, genealogical materials, clippings, and other papers relating to Dodd's life. Correspondence between Miller and Dodd is included.

Federal Theatre Project Papers, 1932–1943. Music Division. Library of Congress. Ca. 525,000 items in 43 file cabinets; 522 linear feet.

Massive collection of the Federal Theatre Project that includes seven playreader's reports, both signed and unsigned, plus synopsis, for Miller's play *They Too Arise*.

"The Four Freedoms." [n.p., 1942 radio play TMS]. Rare Books Division, Library of Congress. 18 leaves.

"From Under the Sea; A Play in One Act." [n.p., 1955 TMS]. Rare Books Division, Library of Congress. 69 leaves.

"The Grass Still Grows; A Play in Three Acts." [193* TMS]. Rare Books Division, Library of Congress. 1 v. [various pagings].

"The Great Disobedience; A Play in Three Acts." [n.p. 193* TMS]. Rare Books Division, Library of Congress. 1 v. [various pagings].

"The Half-Bridge; A Play in Three Acts." [n.d. 194* TMS]. Rare Books Division, Library of Congress. 1 v. [various pagings].

"Head-and-Shoulders Portraits of Marilyn Monroe with Husbands; on Left with Joe DiMaggio, on Right with Arthur Miller." *New York World-Telegram & Sun* Newspaper Photograph Collection, Library of Congress.

Associated Press photographic print taken 1954, 1956; printed 1962.

"Listen My Children; A Comedy Satire with Music." [1939 TMS]. Written with Norman Rosten. Rare Books Division, Library of Congress.

Rudolph Maurice Loewenstein Papers, 1919–1975. Manuscript Division, Library of Congress. 9,600 items in 24 containers; 10.3 linear feet.

Loewenstein was Miller's psychoanalyst. Collection includes correspondence files between Loewenstein and Miller. Forms part of the Sigmund Freud Collection.

"The Man Who Had All the Luck; A Play in Three Acts." [194* TMS]. Rare Books Division, Library of Congress. 1 v. [various pagings].

"A Memory of Two Mondays; A Play in One Act." [195* TMS]. Rare Books Division, Library of Congress. 85 leaves.

"Monroe and Miller Depart for London." *New York World-Telegram & Sun* Collection, Library of Congress.

United Press photograph taken in 1956. Notes: "Marilyn Monroe and her new husband, playwright Arthur Miller leave her New York apartment for Idlewild Airport."

Joseph Rauh Jr. Papers, 1913–1988. Manuscript Division, Library of Congress. 105,900 items in 284 containers; 113.6 linear feet.

Collection includes legal files, personal and general correspondence, subject files, appointment books, and other records relating to Rauh's career. Rauh was Miller's lawyer during his HUAC years.

"The Sign of the Archer; A Play." [n.p., 194* TMS]. Rare Books Division, Library of Congress. 1 v. [various pagings].

"They Too Arise; A Play in Three Acts and Eight Scenes." [n.p., 193* TMS]. Rare Books Division, Library of Congress. 44 leaves.

"Thomas Chalmers, Gene Lockhart, and Howard Smith in *Death of a Salesman.*" Encyclopaedia Britannica Collection, Library of Congress.

Photographic print taken in 1949 from the premiere production of *Death of a Salesman.*

"Those Familiar Spirits." [n.d. 195* TMS]. Rare Books Division, Library of Congress. 1 v. [various pagings].

Frederic Wertham Papers, 1818–1986. Manuscript Division, Library of Congress. 82,200 items in 216 containers; 85.1 linear feet.

Collection includes correspondence, memoranda, writings, speeches, lectures, reports, research notes, patient case files, tests, transcripts of court proceedings, biographical info, clippings, drawings, photographs and other materials pertaining to Wertham's career in psychiatry. Includes correspondence between Wertham and Miller.

"William Ireland's Confession; A Play for Radio." [n.d. 193* radio play TMS]. Rare Books Division, Library of Congress. 31 leaves.

Museum of Television and Radio, New York

The Museum of Television and Radio has an extensive collection of recorded works by and about Arthur Miller, including early radio plays and works in which Miller appeared as a guest or voice-over.

Listen for the Sound of Wings [unpub. radio play, produced on 19 April 1943], 1943.

Thunder from the Mountains [unpub. radio play, produced 28 September 1942], 1942.

The National Archives

"American Playwright Arthur Miller." Motion Picture, Sound, and Video Branch, National Archives at College Park.

Unidentified sound recording with broadcast date of 29 July 1966 for the Voice of America, United States Information Agency.

"Glimpses of America: Arthur Miller and the American Scene." Motion Picture, Sound, and Video Branch, National Archives at College Park.

Unidentified sound recording with broadcast date of 25 June 1968 for the Voice of America, United States Information Agency.

"Perspective #281: A Conversation with Arthur Miller." Motion Picture, Sound, and Video Branch, National Archives at College Park.

Unidentified sound recording with broadcast date of 23 October 1968 for the Voice of America, United States Information Agency.

"Perspective #282: A Conversation with Arthur Miller." Motion Picture, Sound, and Video Branch, National Archives at College Park.

Unidentified sound recording with broadcast date of 30 October 1968 for the Voice of America, United States Information Agency.

New Haven Colony Historical Society Library

Congregation Michkan Israel (Hamden, Conn.), Records, 1843–[ongoing]. New Haven Colony Historical Society Library, New Haven, Connecticut. 10, 626 items; 31 linear feet.

Records of the reform congregation organized in 1840 in New Haven, which moved to Hamden, Connecticut, in 1960. Miller was a speaker there and is included in a subject file of major speakers and correspondents.

The New York Public Library

Luther Adler Papers, 1903–1984. Billy Rose Theatre Collection, The New York Public Library for the Performing Arts. 5 boxes; 2 linear feet.

The collection contains clippings, contracts, correspondence, photographs, programs, scripts, and other material that document Luther Adler's career on stage, screen, and television, covering Adler's involvements with the Group Theatre and his problems with blacklisting. Miller's *A View from the Bridge* is represented in the subject listing for the collection.

"*After the Fall*." [TMS]. Billy Rose Theatre Collection, New York Public Library for the Performing Arts.

"*All My Sons*" [Chester Erskin cinema adaptation of Miller's play]. Billy Rose Theatre Collection, New York Public Library for the Performing Arts.

All My Sons theatre stills collection. Photographs and Prints Division, Schomburg Center for Research in Black Culture, The New York Public Library.

2 photoprints from two productions of Miller's *All My Sons* featuring Alfonso Sherman, Madelyn Brewer, Singer Buchanan, Robert Tucker, Inez Crutchfield, Raoul Settle, Gladys Canter, and Leon Van Hattan.

"*The American Clock: A Play*." Billy Rose Theatre Collection, New York Public Library for the Performing Arts.

T/ccMS, 1980, 49 leaves. This version probably produced, Biltmore Theatre, N.Y., 20 November 1980.

"*The American Clock: A Mural for Theatre.*" Billy Rose Theatre Collection, New York Public Library for the Performing Arts.

T/cc, 1980, 121 leaves. This version probably produced, Harold Clurman Theatre, N.Y., 29 April–17 May 1980. Includes T/ccL, 15 March 1983, to Dorothy Swerdlove, Billy Rose Theatre Collection, New York Public Library, from Bridget Aschenberg, International Creative Management.

"*The American Clock: A Mural for Theatre.*" Billy Rose Theatre Collection, New York Public Library for the Performing Arts.

T/ccMS, with emendations, 1975–1980, 102 leaves. "Corrections incorporated in final copy" on title page. First production: University Players, University of Michigan, Ann Arbor, 24–27 April 1974.

Brooks Atkinson Papers, *T MSS 1968–001, Billy Rose Theatre Collection, The New York Public Library for the Performing Arts. 46 boxes; 11.25 linear feet.

Collection consists of correspondence, awards, personal papers, photographs, ephemera, scrapbooks, date books, clippings and subject files that document the life and career of the drama critic for the *New York Times*. Includes correspondence with Miller from 1959–1961, and an article written by John Steinbeck about Miller.

Roman Bohnen Papers, *T-MSS 1994–028, Billy Rose Theatre Collection, The New York Public Library for the Performing Arts. 8 boxes, 2 lin. ft.

Collection that documents the career of Roman Rohnen, his life as a New York actor and member of the Group Theatre, his motion picture years, and the establishment of the Actors' Lab. In Series II: Personal and Professional Correspondence, 1918–1949, Box 3, Folder 3, there is a letter from Miller to Bohnen.

Bourgeois, Louise. *Etchings for Homely Girl, a Life*. New York: Peter Blum, 1992.

One of fifty-four copies printed by Harlan and Weaver Intaglio, New York, on Somerset Soft White paper, of which 44 arabic-numbered copies were offered for sale. Composed of ten prints, issued in light grayish green cloth portfolio. Each print numbered 36/44 and initialed in pencil.

Montgomery Clift Papers, *T-MSS 1967–006, Billy Rose Theatre Collection, The New York Public Library for the Performing Arts. 30 boxes; 12.3 lin. ft.

Collection contains correspondence, scripts, photographs, notes, and scrapbooks. Clift collection contains the following Miller related items: script of *The Crucible* by Arthur Miller[with unidentified annotations]; script for play *From Under the Sea* by Arthur Miller; script of play *Incident at Vichy* by Arthur Miller; screenplay of *Focus* by Ruth Messina based on novel by Arthur Miller [with unidentified annotations] and a clean copy of same script; a folder of miscellaneous correspondence with Miller; and 4 drafts of the screenplay of *The Misfits* with Clift's holograph annotations.

Harold Clurman Papers, 1938–1975. Billy Rose Theatre Collection, The New York Public Library for the Performing Arts. 10 boxes; 4 linear feet.

Collection documents the years 1938–1978 of the theatrical career of Clurman, noted director, author, and teacher, and consists of notebooks, journals, director's annotated scripts, writings, and photographic scrapbooks. Includes the director's script for Miller's *Incident at Vichy* and the director's notebook for same play.

"*The Crucible*." [TMS, three versions]. Billy Rose Theatre Collection, New York Public Library for the Performing Arts.

"*Death of a Salesman*." [TMS]. Billy Rose Theatre Collection, New York Public Library for the Performing Arts.

Homely Girl, a Life. New York: Peter Blum Edition, 1992. Preferred edition, 2 vols.

Twelve hundred copies printed at the Stinehour Press, Lunenburg, Vt., on Mohawk Superfine paper from Monotype Emerson type, issued with 10 reproductions of drawings by Louise Bourgeois. One of 100 "preferred edition" copies, signed by Miller, Bourgeois, and Inge Morath. Vol. 1 contains the Miller story. Vol. 2 contains the same story, printed in light gray, with sentences selected by Bourgeois printed in red.

Homely Girl, a Life. New York: Peter Blum Edition, 1992. Special edition, 2 vols.

One hundred copies printed at the Stinehour Press, Lunenburg, Vt., on Mohawk Superfine paper, issued with 10 original drypoint prints by Louise Bourgeois. No. 35/100, signed by Miller and Bourgeois. Vol. 1 contains story by Miller, printed in black, with the prints by Bourgeois. Vol. 2 contains the same story, printed in light gray, with sentences selected by Bourgeois printed in red.

"*Incident at Vichy*." [TMS]. Billy Rose Theatre Collection, New York Public Library for the Performing Arts.

Interview with Arthur Miller. The Billy Rose Collection, Theatre on Film and Tape Archive, New York Public Library for the Performing Arts.

U-matic format, 3/4 inch, 60 min. Videotaped at The New York Public Library's Theatre on Tape and Film Archive at The New York Public Library for the Performing Arts, New York City, 14 December 1981. Interviewed by John Stix. Miller discusses his career as a playwright, his attitudes toward the professional theatre, and his writing approach.

"*The Man Who Had All the Luck*." [1943 TMS]. Billy Rose Theatre Collection, New York Public Library for the Performing Arts.

New Dramatists Playwright Lecture Series, *L (Special) 90.14, The Rogers and Hammerstein Archives of Recorded Sound, The New York Public Library for the Performing Arts. 31 sound recordings.

Collection that contains recordings and lectures presented at the New Dramatists Playwright Lecture Series recorded during the years of 1951 and 1960. Item *LT-7 3134 is 1 sound tape reel: analog, 3 3/4 ips, item titled "Lecture/Arthur Miller, May 19, 1958." This is the tape of Miller's lecture given at the Morosco Theatre.

Production Files, Repertory Theatre of Lincoln Center, 1963–1973. Billy Rose Theatre Collection, The New York Public Library for the Performing Arts. 30 linear feet.

Collection consists of production files, containing playbills, prompt books, scripts, set and costume design drawings for the years 1963–1973. Files included *After the Fall*, *Incident at Vichy*, and *The Crucible*.

"They Too Arise." [c1936 TMS]. Revision of "No Villain." Billy Rose Theatre Collection, New York Public Library for the Performing Arts.

"*A View from the Bridge*." [TMS]. Billy Rose Theatre Collection, New York Public Library for the Performing Arts.

Princeton University

Kimon Friar Papers, 1926–1988. Seeley G. Mudd Manuscript Library, Princeton University. 124 boxes; 48.50 cubic feet.

Collection of correspondence, manuscripts, poetry, lectures, sound recordings, articles, and miscellaneous materials from Greek-American poet, translator, editor, and manager of the Circle in the Square Theatre in New York. Contains unidentified Miller correspondence.

Osip Mandelshtam Collection. Seeley G. Mudd Manuscript Library, Princeton University. 20 boxes.

Collection contains correspondence, Russian language works, and printed matter of Russian author Osip Mandelshtam. In correspondence file, this collection contains a letter by Miller and Inge Morath, typewritten with handwritten addenda n.d. [late 1960s].

PEN American Center Archives. Seeley G. Mudd Manuscript Library, Princeton University. 261 boxes, 10 oversized flat cases; 130 linear feet.

Collection of correspondence, publications, newspaper clippings, manuscripts, audio-visual material, grants, programs, committee meetings minutes, governance files, membership information. and office files dating from the founding of PEN Center in 1922 until 1992. Contains a great deal of material relating to Miller as an active member and president of PEN International from 1965–1968.

State Historical Society of Wisconsin

Alvah Cecil Bessie, Papers, 1929–1985. Archives Division, Statue Historical Society of Wisconsin, Madison. 42 archive boxes and 1 card box; 17.2 cubic feet.

Collection documents the career of Alvah Bessie, novelist, screenwriter, literary and film critic, and member of the Hollywood Ten. Letters to Bessie from Miller are included in this collection.

Kermit Bloomgarden, Papers, 1938–1977. Archives Division, State Historical Society of Wisconsin, Madison. 63.8 cubic feet of materials. Portions presented and portions placed on deposit by Kermit

Bloomgarden and his estate.

Collection includes correspondence, scripts, promotion materials and reviews, and production files of Kermit Bloomgarden, producer of many award-winning Broadway plays and musicals. Correspondence with Miller is included as are items relating to *Death of a Salesman.*

Herman Shumlin, Papers, 1930–1968. Archives Division, State Historical Society of Wisconsin, Madison. 21 boxes, 1 flat box, oversized items, microfilm reels; 8.6 cubic feet.

Collection includes correspondence, production and publicity materials, financial and legal records, clippings, scripts, directors' prompt books, and miscellaneous production materials of Herman Shumlin, producer and director of Broadway dramas. There is a Miller subject file in this collection containing unspecified documents.

University of Iowa

Letters [2]. Special Collections Department, University of Iowa Libraries, Iowa City, Iowa.

1. ALS, 6 March 1946, to Capt. Robert C. Murphy Jr. of Brooklyn, N.Y., thanking him for his letter concerning *Focus*.

2. ALS, 21 May 1946, to Capt. Robert C. Murphy Jr. of Brooklyn, N.Y., discussing the relationships between and the responsibilities of science and society as a whole.

University of Michigan, Ann Arbor

Alternative Perspectives on Vietnam Sound Recording Series, 1965. Bentley Historical Library, University of Michigan, Ann Arbor.

Fifteen sound tape reels. An international conference on alternative perspectives on Vietnam held at the University of Michigan, 14–18 September 1965. Recordings of the conference proceedings include plenary sessions featuring study group reports and papers by Fenner Brockway, Emil Mazey, Arthur Miller, and others. Forms part of the Alternative Perspectives on Vietnam papers, 1965–1966. Recordings of conference proceedings [partial].

Alternative Perspectives on Vietnam papers, 1965–1966. Bentley Historical Library, University of Michigan, Ann Arbor.

Includes correspondence, minutes, clippings, and printed materials from the International Conference on Alternative Perspectives on Vietnam held at the University of Michigan on 14–18 September 1965. Miller correspondence dated 27 August 1965 and 30 September 1965.

Arthur Miller Collection, 1936–1979. Special Collections Library, University of Michigan, Ann Arbor. 27 items.

In part, photocopies. Consists of 4 playscripts ("The Grass Still Grows" 1939; "The Great Disobedience" 1938; "Honors at Dawn" 1937; and "No Villain" 1936, 1 lecture "On Recognition" 1963), correspondence dealing with permissions to use the above manuscripts, photocopy of "The Golden Years" 1939–1940, and 2 photos.One exchange of letters concerns an assessment of Miller's promise as a writer, offered in 1941 by Professor R. W. Cowden, then chairman of the Hopwood Awards Committee.

Correspondence. With H. C. Jameson, 1967. Arthur Miller Collection, 1936–1979, Special Collections Library, University of Michigan, Ann Arbor. 4 items.

Letters, 11 May and 15 August [T/cc] from H. C. Jameson to Miller; reply, 18 August [TLS, with envelope]; and permission letter [n.d.] from Miller to H. C. Jameson [TLS]; with photocopy of the permission letter. Concerns the authenticity of the photocopy of letter granting permission to microfilm "No Villain" and "Honors at Dawn" for Dwain Manske.

Esquire, Inc. Records, 1933–1977. Bentley Historical Library at the University of Michigan, Ann Arbor.

Manuscripts of published articles and poetry, research and legal notes, correspondence with authors, and letters to the editors. Miller content includes 4 folders in Box 4 in "Subseries 1933–1959" and 4 folder in Box 12 in "Subseries, 1960–1977."

Federal Theatre Project Correspondence, 1936–1938. Special Collections Library, The University of Michigan, Ann Arbor. 25 items.

Collection is part of the Kenneth Thorpe Rowe, Student Play Collection and contains letters that relate to cooperation between the Federal Theatre Project and Rowe on behalf of his playwriting students, including Miller and Norman Rosten.

"The Grass Still Grows; A Comedy." Arthur Miller Collection, 1936–1979, Special Collections Library, The University of Michigan, Ann Arbor. 141 leaves.

1939, T/ccMSS. Manuscript notation on title page: "Revised

3–6–39." Reports the UM record: "This is an entirely rewritten version substituted in Prof. K. T. Rowe's files for a 1938 version originally submitted in Rowe's creative writing course." Photocopy in the Rowe student play collection, 1974.

"The Great Disobedience." Arthur Miller Collection, 1936–1979, Special Collections Library, The University of Michigan, Ann Arbor. 108 leaves.

1938, T/ccMSS, with holograph and typescript corrections. Lacks title page. Also referred to as "the Jackson Prison Play" because it grew out of Miller's visit to the Jackson prison. Produced as part of a bill by University of Michigan Theatre Department in a laboratory production, 1938. Photocopy in the Rowe student play collection, 1974.

"Honors at Dawn; A Play in Three Acts." Arthur Miller Collection, 1936–1979, Special Collections Library, The University of Michigan, Ann Arbor. 1 v. (iii, 98, [i.e., 100] leaves).

1937 TMSS with some holograph corrections. Copy filmed from original script onto microfilm, 2 reels, on reel with "No Villain."

Hopwood Awards Collection, 1930–. Special Collections Library, The University of Michigan, Ann Arbor. 8,111 items.

Consists of correspondence relating to the annual University of Michigan student contests in creative literature for the Avery Hopwood and Julie Hopwood Prizes funded by income from the Avery Hopwood bequest. Collection includes Miller correspondence.

Letter. 13 November 1965, Roxbury, Conn., to Chloe Aaron. Arthur Miller Collection, 1936–1979, Special Collections Library, The University of Michigan, Ann Arbor. 1 p. TLS [n.p.].

Grants permission to use Miller's "Honors at Dawn" for a thesis.

Letter. 25 January 1968, to Harriet Jameson, Ann Arbor. Arthur Miller Collection, 1936–1979, Special Collections Library, The University of Michigan, Ann Arbor. 1 p. TLS [n.p.].

Grants permission for Mrs. Barbara Priddy to receive photocopies of "Honors at Dawn" and "No Villain."

Letter. 1969?, to Chloe Aaron. Arthur Miller Collection, 1936–1979, Special Collections Library, The University of Michigan, Ann Arbor. 1 p. TLS [n.p.].

Concerns galleys and layout of wife Morath's photos for unnamed book. References several acquaintances, including Milan Kundera.

"No Villain; A play." Arthur Miller Collection, 1936–1979, Special Collections Library, The University of Michigan, Ann Arbor. 1 vol. (iv, 60 [i.e., 61] leaves).

1936 TMS. University of Michigan Collection of Avery Hopwood Award Winners. Copy filmed from original manuscript onto 2 reels, 35 mm. microfilm. On reel with Miller's "Honors at Dawn."

Office of the President. University of Michigan.

Presidential records includes correspondence concerning Miller's honorary degree of L.H.D. in 1956.

"On Recognition: Lecture." Arthur Miller Collection, 1936–1979, Special Collections Library, The University of Michigan, Ann Arbor. 17 leaves.

T/ccMS with holograph corrections of speech given in 1963. Published in the *Michigan Quarterly Review* 2.4 (October 1963).

Pamphlets and Reprints. Bentley Historical Library, The University of Michigan, Ann Arbor. 1 box

Collection of undetermined materials by and about Miller held in storage in Bentley Historical Library.

Student Play Collection, 1928–1970. Special Collections Library, The University of Michigan, Ann Arbor. 1,354 items.

Collection comprises 1,181 original plays, scenarios, and radio scripts, some in more than one version, submitted by students in playwriting courses; 22 skits and one-act plays submitted for the Armed Services recreation program in World War II; and continuities for two patriotic song services for use in war bond drives. Forms part of the K.T. Rowe Student Play Collection.

WUOM Sound Recording Series. Bentley Historical Library, The University of Michigan, Ann Arbor. 8 sound cassettes, 289 sound tape reels, 17 sound disks.

Radio station of the University of Michigan; formerly University of Michigan Broadcasting Service. Undetermined Miller contribution. Recordings of programs produced and broadcast by WUOM, including recordings of interviews, lectures, conferences, and ceremonial events that occurred at the University of Michigan. Forms part of WUOM (Radio Station: Ann Arbor, Michigan} Records, 1913–1986.

University of Michigan Media Resources Center, 1948–1986. Bentley Historical Library, The University of Michigan, Ann Arbor. Ca. 2,500 items; 6 linear feet.

Photographs, films, and videotapes. Undetermined Miller contribution.

University of Texas at Austin, Harry Ransom Humanities Research Center

Boris Aronson Scenic Design Papers, 1939–1977. Harry Ransom Humanities Research Center, The University of Texas at Austin. 5 boxes; 2.1 linear feet, plus 3 oversize boxes, 2 flat file drawers.

Collection contains original sketches, photostats, and copy prints of sketches, photographs and reproductions, scripts, technical drawings, and a model, documenting Boris Aronson's work as set designer for thirty-one plays written or produced between 1939 and 1977. Includes Miller subject file and files for four premiere productions. Contents include, *The Crucible* (1953): sketches with watercolor (5), PC (3), art reproductions (2), photos (29), color prints of sketches (3); *A Memory of Two Mondays* (1955): photos (15), script: *A View from the Bridge* (1955): sketches with watercolor (5), photos (2), script; *Incident at Vichy* (1964): technical drawings (7), stage model, photos (43), copy print of sketch; and *The Creation of the World and Other Business* (1972): sketches, some with watercolor, pastel, and paint (9), collage, assembled piece photos (7), copy prints of sketches (6).

Pascal Covici, Correspondence, 1924–1966. Harry Ransom Humanities Research Center, The University of Texas at Austin. 1 box, 1 oversize folder; .5 linear feet.

Collection of correspondence, bulk 1938–1964, of Pascal Covici, publisher and editor. Covici was Miller's editor at Viking Press. Miller is listed as among the significant correspondents in this collection.

English Stage Company at the Royal Court Theatre, Correspondence, 1955–1959. Harry Ransom Humanities Research Center, The University of Texas at Austin. .5 box, 13 files.

Collection includes a file containing Miller correspondence for the year 1956, negotiating textural changes with the office of Lord Chamberlain, translations, rights, permissions, scheduling of *The Crucible.*

John Gassner Collection. Hobitzelle Theatre Arts Library, The University of Texas at Austin.

Collection includes a file of correspondence from Miller.

Arthur Miller Collection, 1935–1980. Harry Ransom Humanities Research Center, The University of Texas at Austin.

Collection is in two sections—the first part, owned by the HRHRC, was given to the center in 1961 and 1962; and is 4 linear feet of material; the second part is uncatalogued, was placed on deposit in 1984, and consists of approximately 35 linear feet of material. Taken together, the entire collection includes working notebooks, scripts, manuscripts (of plays, essays, poems, short stories, and film scripts), drafts, correspondence, production files, interviews, programs, and photographs of American and European productions of Miller's plays.

Materials Owned by HRHRC

Manuscripts

Address to PEN Congress. Corrected TS, unbound (7pp).

All My Sons. Mimeo. with ANS by Miller on title page. 14 July 1947.

All My Sons. TMS, T/cc MS, and mimeo./printer's copy with ANS by Miller on title page. n.d.

[All My Sons]. Tr. into the Italian: Tutti meiei figli. T/cc MS with ANS by Miller on title page. [1947].

[All My Sons] The Sign of the Archer. T/cc MS with Miller's note: "early version of All My Sons," n.d.

Collected Plays (Introduction). 11 discarded versions, all TMS/inc with A revisions, n.d.

Concerning the Boom [essay]. T/cc MS/ final. n.d.

Concerning the Boom [essay]. TMSS. n.d.

The Crucible. T/cc MS with few A revisions and with ANS by Miller on title page. n.d.
The Crucible. TMS/final revised script. n.d.
[The Crucible]. TMS/first typed draft with extensive A revisions. 11 September 1952.
The Crucible. TMS S/first version with ANS by Miller on title page. n.d.
The Crucible: Act I, Scenes I and II. TMS with A revisions. n.d.
[The Crucible]/inc. TMS/misc pp of different versions with many A revisions. n.d.
The Crucible: Act I, Scene II. T/cc MS with ANS by Kermit Bloomgarden attached: "Carbon used by Hart Stenographic." 22 November 1952.
The Crucible: Act I, Scene I. T/cc MS with ANS by Kermit attached: "Copy used by Anne Meyerson." 22 November 1952.
The Crucible: Act I, Scenes I and II. TMS and T/cc MS final revision with A revisions. 22 November 1952.
The Crucible: Act II, Scene I. TMS with A revisions. n.d.
[The Crucible]. Adaptation cinematographique by Jean-Paul Sartre. Mimeo. with ANS on title page by Miller. n.d.
[The Crucible], adapted and translated into the French by Marcel Ayme. Mimeo. with ANS by Miller on first page. n.d.
[The Crucible]/inc. scenes from Les sorciéres de Salem by Sartre. Mimeo. with 2 ANS by Miller. n.d.
The Crucible. Jean-Paul Sartre, "la chasse aux sorciéres" (prologue). Mimeo. with ANS by Miller on first page. n.d.

Death of a Salesman. T/cc MS/final script with A revisions and ANS by Miller on first page. n.d.
Death of a Salesman. T/cc MS/second version. n.d.
[Death of a Salesman]. "In Memorium," TMS/photostat of story which became play with ANS by Miller attached. c.1932.
Death of a Salesman. Mimeo./final draft with ANS by Miller on title page. 3 August 1951.
Death of a Salesman. Mimeo. with ANS by Miller on title page. n.d.
Death of a Salesman: Final Manuscript But One. TMS with A revisions with ANS by Miller, "includes some obvious work that did not survive rehearsals and scenes which were later added and reshaped."

Focus. TMS and T/cc MS/pp from intermediate draft with A revisions. n.d.
Focus. TMS with many A revisions. n.d.

[Focus] Some Shall Not Sleep. T/cc MS/early draft with A additions and emendations (246 pp with pp 175–185 missing). n.d.
[Focus] Mr. and Mrs. Goldsmith. TMS with many A revisions. n.d.

[The Golden Years] Montezuma the King. Act I: Scenes I and II. T/cc MS. n.d.
The Golden Years. T/cc MS (108 pp) c.1939. Unpub.
The Golden Years. T/cc MSS with his ANS by Miller on title page, "unpublished, unproduced, written 1939–1940, for the WPA Theatre Project which was disbanded before the play could be done."

[The Grass Still Grows] They Too Arise. T/cc MS with A revisions and his ANS on title page. This version was produced by the Hillel Players at the University of Michigan 12–13 March 1937.
The Grass Still Grows. TMSS. n.d. Revision of They Too Arise.
The Grass Still Grows. T/cc MS with his ANS on title page. 8 June 1939.

The Half-Bridge: A Play in Three Acts. TMS and T/cc MSS with his ANS on title page. 1941–1943.

The Hook: A Play for the Screen. T/cc MSS with his ANS on title page. 1951. Included with this is TMS/fragments for shooting script (6pp).

[I Don't Need You Any More]. 5 TMS and Tcc/MS/early version/inc with many A revisions. n.d.
[I Don't Need You Any More] Forbidden Vision. TMS/first draft/inc with A revisions. 3 December 1958.
[I Don't Need You Any More]. 12 TMS and T/cc MS/inc versions with A revisions. n.d.
[I Don't Need You Any More]. 12 TMS and T/cc MS/inc versions with A revisions. n.d.
[I Don't Need You Any More]. T/cc MS/pp 1–39. n.d.
I Don't Need You Any More. TMS with many A revisions. 17 March 1959.

Intellectuals [The Role of Men of the Mind in the World Today] (essay). TMS with A revisions. 1960.

Joe the Motorman: A Radio Sketch. TMS with ANS by Miller on first page, "This is my first radio play—as well as the first writing for which I was paid—$100 from the *Rudy Vallee Variety Show*. Edward Everett Horton played Joe." n.d.

The Man Who Had All the Luck. T/cc MS/Stage manager's copy with some A notes in Miller's hand. n.d.

The Man Who Had All the Luck. T/cc MS with 4 AMS pp. inserted. n.d.

The Man Who Had All the Luck: A Play in 3 Acts. T/cc MS with ANS by Miller on title page, "unpublished in this version. My first play produced on Broadway for or five performances. Based entirely on an unpublished novel of mine." n.d.

[The Man Who Had All the Luck] Something Like a Fable. TMS with A revisions. n.d.

A Memory of Two Mondays. Mimeo./printer's copy with ANS by Miller. n.d.

A Memory of Two Mondays. Mimeo. with A revisions and T inserts. n.d.

[A Memory of Two Mondays] Two Years. TMS with ANS by Miller, "unpublished memoir, written probably in the middle Forties. A Memory of Two Mondays, ten years or so later, takes up the same material." n.d.

A Memory of Two Mondays: An Improvisation on a Bygone Year. Mimeo. with A revisions and one T p. inserted. n.d.

A Memory of Two Mondays: An Improvisation of a Bygone Year. TMS with A revisions. n.d.

A Memory of Two Mondays: A Play in One Act. TMS with extensive A revisions. n.d.

[The Misfits]. TMS fragment with A emendations, 5 pp. n.d. Intermediary workings that follow the screenplay and precede the cinema novel. Included in this: T/ccMS fragment with A emendations. 7 pp. n.d. Composed later intermediary material.

The Misfits. (N.B.: This version has many pages missing (probably rejected), many pages that are deleted (as though to be rejected), and several inserts which are on a different kind of paper).

The Misfits. TMS and T/ccMS (second) draft of cinema novel with A emendations (168 pp). "Revision . . . September 1959") Date deleted: 15 June 1959.

The Misfits. T mimeo (third) draft of cinema novel version with A emendations (176pp).

[The Misfits]. The (first) draft/inc of cinema novel version with A emendations. 36 pp. n.d.

The Misfits. TMS (second) draft with A emendations. 149 pp. October 1957. This version labeled "1st draft . . . October 1957."

The Misfits. TMS (third) draft with A emendations and ANS by Miller on title page. 165 pp. "First draft, October 28, 1957." Bound.
The Misfits. TMS (fourth) draft with A emendations and insertions. 115 pp. "First draft, October 28, 1947." (Typographical error; should be October 28, 1957).
The Misfits. T mimeo (fourth) draft of cinema novel version with TMS inserts and A emendations (199pp). "Revision . . . March 1960." Bound.
[The Misfits]. Composite TMS, TccMS, T mimeo., and T thermofax/Movie version with extensive revisions. 236 pp. 13 July 1960–22 October 1960. Signed in several places. Bound.
[The Misfits]. TMS (first draft/inc with A emendations. 116 pp. n.d.
[The Misfits]. AMS fragment ending of cinema novel version 2 pp. n.d.
[The Misfits]. TMS fragment of cinema novel version with A emendations. 2pp. n.d.
[The Misfits: Rejected pp. I]. TMS fragments with A emendations (N.B.: MSS pagination by cataloger).
[The Misfits: Final Rejects for Viking version]. TMS fragments with A emendations. 30 pp. n.d.
[The Misfits: Rejected pp III]. TMS fragments with A emendations. 35 pp. n.d. (N.B.: MSS pagination by cataloger).
[The Misfits: Rejected pp II]. TMS fragments with A emendations (N.B.: MSS pagination by cataloger).

A Modest Proposal. T/cc MS/"published in *The Nation*." n.d.
[A Modest Proposal] A Peek into the Future. TMS/first draft with A revisions. n.d.

One of the Brooklyn Villages (Autobiographical sketch). TMSS with A and T emendations. 18pp. n.d.

Please Don't Kill Anything. TMS with A revisions. n.d.
Please Don't Kill Anything. T/cc MS with A revisions. n.d.

Social Plays: What Are They? (Introduction to A View from the Bridge). TMS with extensive A revisions. n.d.

Speech to New Dramatists Committee. TMS with A revisions. c.1956–1957.

The University of Michigan (essay). TMSS with A revisions. n.d.

[A View from the Bridge] From Under the Sea. TMS with extensive A revisions with ANS on title page. 28 February 1955.
A View from the Bridge. A notes. n.d. Written in working notebook Death of a Salesman.
[A View from the Bridge] From Under the Sea. Mimeo/early version with 20pp of TMS inserted. n.d.
A View from the Bridge. Mimeo with ANS from Miller to Kay Brown. Mimeo inserts for British version. n.d.
[A View from the Bridge]. Mimeo with Miller's A notes on actors' performances and A revisions. n.d.
A View from the Bridge. Motion picture script by Norman Rosten. T/cc MS with ANS by Miller on title page. n.d.
A View from the Bridge. Printer's copy/pp 74–155. Mimeo with ANS by Miller on title page. n.d.
A View from the Bridge. Tr. into French by Marcel Ayme. Mimeo with T/cc MS inserts and ANS by Miller on title page. n.d.
A View from the Bridge. TMS with A revisions. 28 February 1955.

William Ireland's Confession. TMSS/cut version of published play. "This was edited & cut by" with arrow pointing to the typed words: "Radio Teatro de America." 5 January 1944.
William Ireland's Confession: A Historical Play. T/cc MS with ANS by Miller on first page. n.d.

Working Notebooks

[After the Fall]. Early working draft with many suggestions for title throughout, [33pp], 27 January 1958. [included within the second Misfits notebook]
[All My Sons]. [43pp], n.d.
The Crucible. [92pp], n.d.
[The Crucible] Those Familiar Spirits [244pp], n.d.
Death of a Salesman. [66pp], n.d. Also written in notebook: Notes for A View from the Bridge.
[The Hook]. [62pp], n.d.
The Misfits. [119pp], n.d.
The Misfits. 27 January 1958 [contains early version of After the Fall].

Correspondence

1. 2 T/ccL to Arthur Miller from Robert Downing, 22 August 193, 25 November 1964.
2. ALS to Mrs. Dean, n.d.
3. TLS (by secretary) to Robert Spira, 23 January 1957.
4. TLS to Dame Edith Sitwell, 24 May 1957.

5. TLS to Arthur Miller from *The Christian Science Monitor*, 9 February 1956.
6. TLS to James Donald Adams, 3 October 1958.
7. TLS to Arthur Miller from Viking Press, 21 December 1955; includes amendment to their contract re: *A View from the Bridge*, signed also by Miller.
8. TLS/xerox to Mordecai Gorelik, 26 February 1975.
9. TLS to Peter Owen, Ltd, 16 October 1957.
10. TLS/photostat to Willard Maas and Marie Menken, 12 July 1956.
11. ALS and APCS to Pascal Covici, n.d. and 15 March 1954.
12. TLS/photocopy to Willard Maas, 12 July 1956, directed also to Marie Mencken.
13. T/ccL to Miller re: Joseph Giles, 9 October 1950, from *Harper's*.

Materials on Deposit at HRHRC

NOTE: Among the items in boxes 54–66 are fragments of unfinished plays, essays, poems, and short stories, including these titled by Miller in his hand:

Essays: "1949"; "Colliers' War"; "Dangerous Thoughts"; "Inside the Outside/A Jungle Ramble"; "A Note on the Mood Play"; "The King's Way."

Plays: "The Bomb"; "Behind the Times: A Play in One Act"; "The Friend"; "The Reason Why"; "Design for a Play" (dialogue fragment); "Terror Play"; "Rojas Play"; "Morning, Noon, and Night" (complete manuscript of "All My Sons" before final rehearsal version).

Short Stories: "Barcelona, Aristotle, and the Death with Tragedy"; "The Day Before Dying"; "Dedication"; "The Dispensation"; "Ditchy, a Short Story"; "The Girls from New York"; "The Independents"; "A Glimpse at Andrew"; "Glimpse at the Maid"; "The Intruder"; "A Regular Death Call"; "The Test for It"; "Wilde Strawberries"; "Yankee Day"; "Winter Crossing."

Manuscripts

Major Works

Box	1–7	After the Fall
	1	Oversize vol. After the Fall
Box	8	All My Sons
	9–11	American Clock
	12	The Archbishop's Ceiling
	13–14	The Chinese Encounter
	15–18	The Creation of the World and Other Business

	19–22	The Crucible
	23–26	Death of a Salesman
	27	Earlier workings of After the Fall and The Price
	28	Enemy of the People
	29	Fame
	30–31	Focus
	32	The Half-Bridge, The Hook
	33	In Russia
	34–35	Incident at Vichy
	36	Man Who Had All the Luck
	37–41	The Misfits
	42	Montezuma
	43	Playing for Time
	44–49	The Price
	50	Up from Paradise
	51–53	A View from the Bridge
Smaller Works		
Box	54	Misc. - A
	55	A (cont.)
	56	B - F
	57	G -
	58	K - L
	59	M - N
	60	0 - Pq
	61	Pr - Radio scripts
	62–63	Radio scripts
	64	S
	65	T - Wq
	66	Wr - Z

Working Notebooks

After the Fall. [190pp], Fall/September–November 1962.

After the Fall. [129pp], Fall/End/August 3, 1963.

After the Fall. [41pp], Begun August 18/63 (For cutting "Fall")

American Clock. [148pp], July 6/70.

The Creation of the World and Other Business. 2 notebooks. The first is labeled "First Creation Book/A Piece of String/ (American Clock, 3rd)/Feb. 10/71" and is 199 pp. long. The second is labeled "Creation (2nd Bk)" and is 71 pp. long.

Correspondence

Box	67	A - I
		Agents
		Allied Maintenance Corporation
		Benton, William
		Blake, James
		Clurman, Harold
		Controversy
		Fellowship of Reconciliation
		Fan Mail
		Greece Invitations
	68	J - Q
		Jews in Russia
		Kazan, Elia
		Kurtz, Maurice
		Leary, Dr. Timothy
		Martin, Robert A.
		Meyer, Richard
		Mexican Trip, 1968
		Navasky, Victor
		Nixon, Richard
		O'Grady, Gerald
		Osborne, Robert (Two folders)
		Oz, Amos
		PEN Club Political Campaign, 1972
	69	R - Requests
		Rauh, Joe
		Repression—Writers in Prison
		Requests (twelve folders)
		Revueltas, José
	70	Requests (cont.) - Z
		Russia
		Stone, J.F.- Weekly

Printed Material

Carton	71	Scrapbooks and unsorted
	72	Unsorted
	73	Unsorted

Yale University

Death of a Salesman by Arthur Miller. Yale Collection of American Literature, Beinecke Rare Book and Manuscript Library, Yale University. 170 leaves.

T/ccMS, with annotations in holograph by Elia Kazan, dated 1948 September.

A. B. Guthrie, Jr. Papers. Yale Collection of American Literature, Beinecke Rare Book and Manuscript Library, Yale University. 54 boxes; 35 linear feet.

Collection of correspondence, writings, personal papers, subject files, and printed material spanning the life and literary career of A. B. Guthrie, Jr., author of western novels and environmental writings. Miller is included in the collection as named file dated 1950.

Matthew Josephson Papers. Yale Collection of American Literature, Beinecke Rare Book and Manuscript Library, Yale University. 21 boxes, 8.50 linear feet.

Collection that documents the life and career of Matthew Josephson—poet, reporter, and author of works on nineteenth-century French literature and twentieth-century American economic history. Letter general folders contain single letter by Miller.

Eugene O'Neill Papers. Yale Collection of American Literature, Beinecke Rare Book and Manuscript Library, Yale University. 185 boxes; 92.60 linear feet.

Collection of materials, documents, scripts, photographs, correspondence, clippings—both personal and professional—of Eugene O'Neill. Miller letter of 22 February 1940 is listed in correspondence file.

Pamphlets by and about Arthur Miller. Beinecke Rare Book and Manuscript Library, Yale University. 31 cm.

According to Yale, this collection is a "small box of newspaper clippings [mostly *New York Times*], several theatre programs for productions, and 4 magazines with articles about Miller."

Theatre Guild Correspondence. Yale Collection of American Literature, Beinecke Rare Book and Manuscript Library, Yale University. 159 boxes; 63.75 linear feet.

Collection of uncatalogued Theatre Guild Correspondence. Folder listing notes Miller correspondence included.

PART II
SECONDARY SOURCES

1. Bibliographies and Checklists

Ahearn, Allen and Patricia. "Author Price Guide: Arthur Miller." Dickerson, Md.: Author PriceGuides, December 1993.

Seven-page price guide that includes facsimile of Miller's signature, brief biographical sketch, and a list of Miller's first editions (American and British) with entries for limited and trade editions.

Basi, Carol Lynn Papadopoli. "An Arthur Miller Bibliography with a Focus on the Sixties and an Introduction Seeking to Establish Miller's Present Critical Stature." Masters Thesis. U of Louisville, 1992.

A study that attempts to include all available sources relating to Miller's published works for the 1960s, including articles, interviews, production reviews, addresses by Miller, critical books, dissertations and theses, foreign critical articles, and bibliographies, "thus indicating the direction of critical thought about [Miller's] artistic status." Includes list of foreign translations of Miller's plays through *Vichy* and an introductory analysis "seeking to establish Miller's present critical stature in the literary and theatrical world." Some annotation. Many typing errors and omissions.

"Bibliography of Works (1936–1996) by Arthur Miller." *The Theater Essays of Arthur Miller*. Revised ed. Eds. Robert A. Martin and Steven R. Centola. New York: DaCapo, 1996. 585–612.

Chronological listing of Miller material by genre. Selected list of interviews. Includes listings of recordings, television productions, and videography. Not annotated.

Bigsby, C. W. E. *File on Miller*. London: Methuen, 1988.

Published as part of the "Writers-Files" series, this small volume offers a Miller chronology, a section on Miller's plays (*No Villain* to *Playing for Time*) that includes information on first performances, major revivals, publication, brief synopsis, and representative critical response, including Miller's own comments, a section on Miller's nondramatic works, a section entitled "The Writer on His Work," and a final bibliographical guide to other primary and secondary sources for further reading. Not annotated or comprehensive.

Carpenter, Charles. "Arthur Miller." *Modern Drama: Scholarship and Criticism, 1981–1990. An International Bibliography*. Toronto: U of Toronto P, 1997. 66–69.

International bibliography of works in Roman-alphabet languages. Lists 158 selective citations of criticism and scholarship of Miller's works. Subheadings include: works by Miller (including works and interviews), reference sources, collections of essays, and works about Miller. Not annotated.

———. "Studies of Arthur Miller's Drama: A Selective International Bibliography, 1966–1979." *Arthur Miller, New Perspectives*. Ed. Robert A. Martin. Englewood Cliffs, N.J.: Prentice-Hall, 1982. 205–19.

With almost two-hundred entries, this selected list includes books, parts of books, and articles published since 1966 in "Roman-alphabet language." Excluded: biographical summaries, review of performances, unpublished dissertations, and Miller statements. Supplements Ferres. Not annotated.

Dyer, James Joseph. "An Instructor's Handbook to Six Major Plays of Arthur Miller." Diss. Indiana U of Pennsylvania, 1983.

Accompanying each chapter in Dyer's handbook (*All My Sons*, *Death of a Salesman*, *The Crucible*, *A View from the Bridge*, *After the Fall*, and *The Price*) is an annotated bibliography containing "key articles by Miller's critics germane to the play."

Eissenstat, Martha Turnquist. "Arthur Miller: A Bibliography." *Modern Drama* 5.1 (May 1962): 93–106.

Sections on individual plays ending with *A View from the Bridge*. No articles after 1962. Those interested in a specific play can find essays and reviews arranged for that purpose. Includes foreign language materials, both books and articles. Not annotated.

Ferres, John H. *Arthur Miller: A Reference Guide*. Boston: G. K. Hall, 1979.

Contents are divided as follows: Arthur Miller's major works, writings about Miller (1944–1977), and index. The entire work is arranged in chronological order. Foreign language items are excluded, unless translated into English. "Books, pamphlets, dissertations, reviews, and articles dealing wholly or in part with Miller are included, whether published in the United States or abroad." Each numbered entry includes summary abstract.

Goldfarb, Alvin. "Arthur Miller." *American Playwrights since 1945: A Guide to Scholarship, Criticism, and Performance*. Ed. Philip C. Kolin. New York: Greenwood, 1989. 309–38.

Covers Miller's works through 1987. Includes essay entitled "Assessment of Miller's Reputation," primary bibliography of Miller's works, essay on production history, essay surveying secondary sources and future research opportunities, and a listing of selected secondary sources arranged alphabetically by author.

Haedicke, Susan. "Arthur Miller: A Bibliographic Essay." *Cambridge Companion to Arthur Miller*. Ed. Christopher Bigsby. Cambridge: Cambridge UP, 1997. 245–66.

As her title describes, Haedicke offers a bibliographic essay of selected secondary works about Miller, divided into bibliographies, biographical dimensions, critical studies, interdisciplinary approaches, fiction and screenplays. Does not include primary sources or production reviews.

Hayashi, Tetsumaro. *Arthur Miller and Tennessee Williams: Research Opportunities and Dissertation Abstracts*. Jefferson, N.C.: McFarland, 1983.

Lengthy essay surveying doctoral dissertation research in the field of Arthur Miller studies, followed by abstracts of forty-six dissertations that include discussions of Miller's work, written between 1952 and 1980.

———. *Arthur Miller Criticism (1930–1967)*. Metuchen, N.J.: Scarecrow, 1969.

Bibliography covering Miller's work through *The Price*, with an emphasis on "all the known published and unpublished works." Arranged into three main parts: Primary Works, Secondary Material, and Audio-Visual Material. An author index is included. Of special note is the section on unpublished works, including manuscripts and letters. Now outdated; contains some errors.

———. "Arthur Miller: The Dimension of His Art and a Checklist of His Published Works." *Serif* 4 (June 1967): 26–32.

Checklist that Hayashi says attempts "to include all of the

known published works of Arthur Miller." Divided by genrre: Plays, Adaptations, Novels and Short Stories, Articles and Essays, and Reports. Now dated. Includes farce written in 1930 (*Marry the Girl*) that does not belong to this Miller's canon.

———. *An Index to Arthur Miller Criticism*, 2nd ed. Metuchen, N.J.: Scarecrow, 1976.

Updated edition of *Arthur Miller Criticism (1930–1967)*, with an attempt to arrange items for functional use. Includes Miller chronology and index. Arranged into three main parts: primary sources through *Creation of the World and Other Business*; secondary sources including books, essays in books, dissertations, master's theses, interviews, periodical articles, newspaper articles and news, and bibliographies; and appendices for standard reference guides consulted, newspapers and periodicals indexed, and Miller's unpublished manuscripts, letters, and postcards. Not annotated.

Henderson, Cathy. "Twentieth-Century American Playwrights: Views of a Changing Culture." Austin, Tex.: Harry Ransom Humanities Research Center, 1994. Also published as *Library Chronicle* 25.1.

Of interest to Miller scholars is this guide to the Harry Ransom Center's Miller holdings. Not complete.

Jensen, George H. *Arthur Miller: A Bibliographic Checklist.* Columbia, S.C.: Faust, 1976.

Descriptive bibliography listing editions, printings, states, and issues of Miller books through *Creation of the World and Other Business*. Includes list of first book appearances, Miller's contributions to periodicals, speeches, interviews, testimony, recordings, and doubtful attributions. Of note is the inclusion of Miller's student writings from the *Michigan Daily* published by the University of Michigan.

Manske, Dwain Edgar "A Study of the Changing Family Roles in the Early Published and Unpublished Works of Arthur Miller, to Which Is Appended a Catalogue of the Arthur Miller Collection at the U of Texas at Austin." Diss. U of Texas, Austin, 1970.

Included here for the work's appendix, that lists, in detail, all items until 1970 in the Arthur Miller Collection at the University of Texas at Austin. Arranged alphabetically, related drafts are listed in order of composition. Manuscripts are described, content noted, and date of composition recorded along with date of first publication and/or performance.

Martin, Robert A. "Bibliography of Works (1936–1977) by Arthur Miller." *Theater Essays of Arthur Miller*. New York: Viking, 1978: 379–92.

Selected listing of primary sources, including recordings and manuscript collections. Not annotated.

Martine, James J. "Introduction." *Critical Essays on Arthur Miller*. Boston: G. K. Hall, 1979. ix–xxii.

Lengthy bibliographic essay evaluating selected sources and materials available to the Miller scholar. Includes information on bibliographic sources, editions, biography, criticism (books and articles), and studies of individual works (books and articles). *Critical Essays* includes thirty reviews, articles, interviews, and essays that examine and evaluate the Miller canon, from *The Man Who Had All the Luck* to *The Creation of the World and Other Business*, including Miller's lesser known short stories.

Moss, Leonard. "Selected Bibliography." *Arthur Miller*. Revised ed. Boston: Twayne, 1980. 144–79.

Annotated bibliography containing primary and secondary source listings printed in English through *The Price*. Critical books and articles separated for *Death of a Salesman* but are lumped together for all other Miller works indexed.

Salem, James M., ed. "Arthur Miller." *A Guide to Critical Reviews: Part I: American Drama, 1909–1982*. 3rd ed. Metuchen, N.J.: Scarecrow, 1984. 359–67.

Simple listing of citations of production reviews for Miller's major works through *American Clock*. Not annotated, some repetition.

Schlueter, June. "Arthur Miller." *Contemporary Authors Bibliographical Series. Vol. 3: American Dramatists*. Ed. Matthew C. Roudané. Detroit: Gale, 1986. 189–270.

Lengthy bibliographic section that offers a thirty-nine page bibliographic checklist of primary and selected secondary materials plus a narrative bibliographic essay that covers published bibliographies and checklists, selected interviews, and critical essays on Miller's plays. Only narrative section annotated.

Ungar, Harriet. "The Writings of and about Arthur Miller: A Check List 1936–1967." *Bulletin of the New York Public Library* 74 (1970): 107–34.

Self-titled as a "bio-bibliography," Ungar limited work to material "which concerns Arthur Miller from a literary point of view, published in English and Western European languages." No personal (Marilyn Monroe, HUAC) references. Listing includes anthologies of major plays, foreign translations, films, recordings. Some annotation.

Wilkinson, Richard Thomas. "Arthur Miller Manuscripts at the University of Texas." MLS Report, University of Texas, 1964.

Seventy-eight page report detailing the Miller manuscripts held by the University of Texas at Austin. Superseded by Manske dissertation.

2. Doctoral Dissertations

1952

Fisher, William J. "Trends in Post-Depression American Drama: A Study of the Works of William Saroyan, Tennessee Williams, Irwin Shaw, and Arthur Miller." Diss. New York U, 1952.

Fisher traces the ideological and artistic developments of post-Depression American drama, concluding that William Saroyan, Tennessee Williams, Irwin Shaw, and Arthur Miller all exhibit a bond with preceding generations of American writers "by continuing the tradition of protest against the dominant standards of materialism and success."

1959

Carson, Herbert L. "Modern Tragedy and Its Origins in Domestic Tragedy: A Study of Selected English and American Domestic Tragedies from Elizabethan to Modern Times." Diss. U of Minnesota, 1959.

In an investigation into the use of language, thought, and character in domestic tragedy and the contribution of these qualities to the tragic experience, Carson examines Miller's *Death of a Salesman* as a modern example of a genre in which the characters are not elevated, the surroundings are simple and familiar, the stories are personal and familial and presented in a generally realistic manner, with endings involving death or a personal catastrophe.

Geier, Woodrow Augustus. "Images of Man in Five American Dramatists: A Theological Critique." Diss. Vanderbilt U, 1959.

Geier studies various images of man (Liberal Man, Natural Man, Imperfect Man, and Materialistic Image) as presented in the plays of Eugene O'Neill, Paul Green, Maxwell Anderson, Tennessee Williams, and Arthur Miller.

1960

Staub, August William. "The Subjective Perspective; Aspects of Point of View in Modern Drama." Diss. Louisiana State U, 1960.

Staub examines eight "significant point-of-view experiments in drama," including *Death of a Salesman*, in an effort to demonstrate that the subjective perspective is the "primary and most distinctive feature of modern dramaturgy."

1962

Johnson, Vernon Elso. "Dramatic Influences in the Development of Arthur Miller's Concept of Social Tragedy." Diss. George Peabody College for Teachers, 1962.

In an attempt to show the development of the playwright's concept of social tragedy, including the primary influences of Henrik Ibsen, Anton Chekhov, and expressionism, Johnson examines six Miller works: *All My Sons*, *Death of a Salesman*, *The Crucible*, *A Memory of Two Mondays*, *A View from the Bridge*, and *Enemy of the People*.

1963

Johnson, Robert Garrett. "A General Semantic Analysis of Three of Arthur Miller's Plays: *Death of a Salesman*, *The Crucible*, and *All My Sons*." Diss. U of Denver, 1963–64.

Applying the principles of general semantics set forth by Alfred Korzybski, Johnson evaluates Miller's works in an effort to "discover if a conceptual framework which is based upon a knowledge of structure, symbolic processes, and consciousness of abstracting might supply a systematic method for the analysis of a play."

Sheldon, Neil. "Social Commentary on the Plays of Clifford Odets and Arthur Miller." Diss. New York U, 1963.

After determining the important social problems in the periods in which Odets and Miller wrote, Sheldon identifies, charts, and compares social trends in the work of both writers and examines the extent to which each dealt with them.

1964

Calvery, Catherine Ann. "Illusion in Modern American Drama: A Study of Selected Plays by Arthur Miller, Tennessee Williams, and Eugene O'Neill." Diss. Tulane U, 1964.

Calvery studies the nature of illusion in selected plays: Miller's *Death of a Salesman*, Williams's *The Glass Menagerie* and *A Streetcar Named Desire*, and O'Neill's *A Touch of the Poet* and *The Iceman Cometh*. Of *Salesman*, the author finds that while Loman's dreams of being well liked protect him from the truth of his failure, his realization that he can preserve his dreams by dying for them destroys him in the end.

Van Allen, Harold. "An Examination of the Reception and Critical Evaluation of the Plays of Arthur Miller in West Germany from 1950–1961." Diss. U of Arkansas, 1964.

Studying newspaper clippings and production statistics, Van Allen examines the critical reception of Miller in West Germany in the years 1950–1961.

1965

Beltzer, Lee. "The Plays of Eugene O'Neill, Thornton Wilder, Arthur Miller and Tennessee Williams on the London Stage, 1945–1960." Diss. U of Wisconsin, 1965.

Researching newspapers, journals, books, and interviews with theatre artists, Beltzer examines the critical reception of eighteen commercial productions of O'Neill, Wilder, Miller (*All My Sons*, *Death of a Salesman*, *View from the Bridge*, and *The Crucible*), and Williams.

Martin, Robert Allen. "The Major Plays and Critical Thought of Arthur Miller to the 'Collected Plays.'" Diss. U of Michigan, 1965.

Martin offers a close textual comparison and analysis of Miller's plays and essays to chart his development as a playwright based on textual evidence rather than critical evaluation.

1966

Murray, Edward James. "Structure, Character, and Theme in the Plays of Arthur Miller." Diss. U of Southern California, 1966.

After description, analysis, and interpretation, Murray offers a close analytical study of Miller's plays "as plays" in an effort "to offer evidence in support of Miller's right to be considered, along with Tennessee Williams, as the only American dramatist worthy to be mentioned with Eugene O'Neill."

Roberts, Kenneth Harris. "The Lincoln Center Repertory Theater, 1958–1965." Diss. Ohio State U, 1966.

Roberts investigates the major dispute between business and the arts at the Lincoln Center's Repertory Theater and citing William Schuman, president of Lincoln Center, as the catalyst of the conflict. Since Miller's *After the Fall* was the premiere production at the Repertory, his involvement with the fledgling company figures throughout this study.

1967

Long, Madeleine J. "Sartrean Themes in Contemporary American Literature." Diss. Columbia U, 1967.

Long applies the themes of existentialism to a study of Ellison's *Invisible Man*, Hemingway's *The Old Man and the Sea*, and Miller's *Death of a Salesman* in this study intended to assist high school students and teachers of literature.

1968

West, Constance Catherine. "The Use of Persuasion in Selected Plays of Arthur Miller." Diss. U of Minnesota, 1968.

With a focus on *Death of a Salesman* and *The Crucible*, West examines Miller's use of persuasive methodologies in an effort to provide an "added dimension to the study of his drama."

1969

Epstein, Arthur David. "Arthur Miller's Major Plays: A Critical Study." Diss. Indiana U, 1969.

Epstein offers a close literary reading of seven Miller plays to "suggest that Miller's view of man's relationship to himself and his world has become increasingly complex and less certain."

Dieb, Ronald Kenneth. "Patterns of Sacrifice in the Plays of Arthur Miller, Tennessee Williams, and Edward Albee." Diss. U of Denver, 1969.

Dieb analyzes the ritualistic sacrificial patterns of each playwright to determine how effectively they "have expressed the meaning and methods of the ancient ritual of sacrifice in modern terms." Dieb concludes that "Miller's use of the sacrificial resolution lacks the poetic sensitivity of Williams and the emotional vitality of Albee, but it is infinitely more substantial since it delineates responsibility as the only valid source of sacrificial action."

Miller plays examined: *Death of a Salesman*, *A View from the Bridge*, *The Crucible*, and *Incident at Vichy*.

Flanagan, James K. "Arthur Miller: A Study in Sources and Themes." Diss. U of Notre Dame, 1969.

Flanagan examines the themes of family, society, and women in Miller's life and literary works. "The focus of this study is upon both the major factors in Miller's life which influence his writings and the manner in which this influence is expressed in his writings."

1970

Ashley, Franklin Bascom. "The Theme of Guilt and Responsibility in the Plays of Arthur Miller." U of South Carolina, 1970.

With a concentration on the protagonist in each work, Ashley charts the development of the major themes of guilt and responsibility in Miller's plays from *All My Sons* to *The Price*.

Harrow, Kenneth Joseph. "The Transformation of the Rebel: A Comparative Study of the Works and Development of Albert Camus, Arthur Miller, and Ignazio Silone." Diss. New York U, 1970.

Harrow compares the thematic development of the works of Camus, Miller, and Ignazio Silone and traces their transformations from rebels to mature humanists. Miller plays studied: *All My Sons*, *Death of a Salesman*, and *After the Fall*.

Manske, Dwain Edgar. "A Study of the Changing Family Roles in the Early Published and Unpublished Works of Arthur Miller, to Which is Appended a Catalogue of the Arthur Miller Collection at the U of Texas at Austin." Diss. U of Texas, Austin, 1970.

Manske examines the father-son relationships in Miller's early unpublished works, finding that although Miller had discovered the conflict in his first play, *No Villain* (1936), he had spent "ten years trying to work with plots which tend to prevent any confrontation between father and son." It was not until *All My Sons* and *Death of a Salesman*, argues Manske, that Miller was able to dramatize the conflict effectively and learn that "the knowledge of self is knowledge of how to act with both justice and mercy."

Scanlan, Tom. "The American Family and Family Dilemmas in American Drama." Diss. U of Minnesota, 1970.

Scanlan examines the way in which the family is represented in American drama, illuminating a pattern of value and ideology "which has implications for American literary and intellectual history."

1971

Blades, Larry Thomas. "Williams, Miller, and Albee: A Comparative Study." Diss. St. Louis U, 1971.

Blades studies five thematic relationships (Society, the Individual, Guilt and Atonement, Sex and Marriage, and the Family) in selected plays of Williams, Miller, and Albee. Miller works examined include *Death of a Salesman*, *The Misfits*, *After the Fall*, *The Price*, and *A View from the Bridge*.

Higgins, David M. "Existential Valuation in Five Contemporary Plays: Miller, Pinter, Beckett, Albee, and Genet." Diss. Bowling Green U, 1971.

After examining critical response, Higgins evaluates the "problems and consequences of existential valuation" in five plays: Genet's *The Balcony*, Beckett's *Waiting for Godot*, Pinter's *The Homecoming*, Albee's *Box-Mao-Box*, and Miller's *The Price*. "In the section on *The Price*, which centered upon a conflict of extremist points of view regarding guilt and innocence, responsibility and self-affirmation, doubt and belief, martyrdom and murder, and so on, it was found that the character representing synthesis was the wisest, most complete, and most dramatic in the play."

Lavi, Gay Heit. "Children of Civilization Fall Together: A Study of Style and Language in the Plays of Arthur Miller." Diss. U of Pittsburgh, 1971.

By centering on Miller's dramatic works, Lavi traces what she sees as the playwright's "growing pessimism as it leads him to accept compromise in what he comes to know as a fallen world." Also examined are Miller's themes, his problems of expression, his method of characterization, his poetic approach, and his "use of mythological super-structures to give universal significance to themes in his drama." In-depth analysis is provided for *Death of a Salesman* and *After the Fall*.

Leopold, Vivian Ruth. "Man and Society in the Plays of Arthur Miller." Diss. New York U, 1971.

Leopold seeks to determine whether Miller's concern for the individual in relation to society, as presented in his essays written between 1949 and 1968, is reflected in his dramatic works.

1972

Bettenhausen, Elizabeth Ann. "'Forgiving the Idiot in the House': Existential Anxiety in the Plays of Arthur Miller and Its Implications for Christian Ethics." Diss. U of Iowa, 1972.

Using the theory of existential analysis by Paul Tillich, Bettenhausen examines five Miller plays (*All My Sons*, *Death of a Salesman*, *After the Fall*, *Incident at Vichy*, *The Price*) to prove "Tillich's contention that the anxiety of emptiness and meaninglessness is characteristic of this century" and "is reinforced by the evidence of the plays."

Fleming, William P., Jr. "Tragedy in American Drama: The Tragic Views of Eugene O'Neill, Tennessee Williams, Arthur Miller, and Edward Albee." Diss. U of Toledo, 1972.

This study examines the modern American tragic form in selected works of four playwrights. Says Fleming, "Even though the results show that the characteristics for American tragedy differ only slightly from accepted modern definitions, still the fact remains that these American playwrights have presented a type of tragedy unique to America, but by its very nature, becomes universal."

McMahon, Helen Marie. "Arthur Miller's Common Man: The Problems of the Realistic and the Mythic." Diss. Purdue U, 1972.

McMahon examines Miller's common man in order to reveal "what appears to be an inconsistency between the question his protagonist asks at the moment of crisis which begins each drama and the answer which is provided at the end of the play."

Stephens, Suzanne Schaddelee. "The Dual Influence: A Dramaturgical Study of the Plays of Edward Albee and the Specific Dramatic Forms and Themes Which Influence Them." Diss. Miami U, 1972.

Concerned with the manner in which the form of Albee's plays shapes his themes, Stephens studies the ways in which Albee presents his characters, structures his episodes, and uses language. Of note to Miller studies is chapter two, in which Stephens analyzes plays by Miller and Williams in an attempt to establish the realist-expressionistic concepts and devices used by these playwrights.

Welch, Charles Arnold. "Guilt in Selected Plays of Arthur Miller: A Phenomenological Inquiry and Creative Response." Diss. United States International U, 1972.

Welch examines the experience of guilt in three Miller plays (*The Crucible*, *After the Fall*, and *Incident at Vichy*) in an effort "to determine whether a phenomenological analysis of Arthur Miller's drama gives heightened meaning to an understanding of guilt."

1973

Slavensky, Sonia Wandruff. "Suicide in the Plays of Arthur Miller: A View from Glory Mountain." Diss. Loyola U of Chicago, 1973.

This study examines ten works by Miller to highlight the playwright's dependence on suicide as a dramatic form. Concludes Slavensky, "suicide is used by Miller as the metaphorical embodiment of the psycho-social and cultural predicament of his hero's struggle to die honorably."

Zurcher, Carl Donald. "An Analysis of Selected American Criticism of the Plays of Arthur Miller in the Light of His Own Commentary on Drama." Diss. Purdue U, 1973.

Zurcher applies Miller's own views on art and theatre as expressed in articles, speeches, essays, interviews, and news reports to all of his produced plays from *The Man Who Had All the Luck* to *The Price* in order to assess the playwright's success in fulfilling his stated goals.

1974

Jacobson, Irving Frederic. "The Fallen Family: A Study in the Work of Arthur Miller." Diss. U of California, Los Angeles, 1974.

Jacobson charts the function of the family within Miller's plays and nondramatic works.

Roderick, John Machado, III. "Arthur Miller and American Mythology: The Dream as Life-Force in Twentieth-Century American Drama." Diss. Brown U, 1974.

Roderick examines the Dream impulse in Miller's protagonists in order to underscore its mythic dimension and reveal "a significant metaphysical statement by a major American playwright."

Thippavajjala, Dutta Ramesh. "The Heroes of Arthur Miller." Diss. U of Kansas, 1974.

This study examines Miller's work from *All My Sons* to *The Price*, including his unpublished plays, early drafts of major plays, and other manuscripts, in an effort to trace his hero's struggles for identity—and thus revealing Miller's own moral vision.

1975

Cummings, Dorothy Stacey. "Major Themes in the Plays of Antonio Buero Vallejo and Arthur Miller: A Comparative Study." Diss. U of Arkansas, 1975.

Cummings defines the major themes of each playwright as expressed in their plays from the late 1940s to the early 1970s and compares these treatments "in order to reach a clearer understanding of the questions asked about the human condition and the answers implied in their dramatic works."

Feldman, Jack. "The Plays of Arthur Miller: Theory and Practice." Diss. U of Wisconsin at Madison, 1975.

This study uses Miller's theory of drama as an evaluative tool in the study of his plays, revealing that while the playwright developed great skill in the dramatic form, which allowed him to express his philosophy in his dramatic works, Miller did not always follow his own precept.

Thompson, John Lee. "Self-Realization in the Major Plays of Arthur Miller." Diss. U of Nebraska at Lincoln, 1975.

Thompson analyzes the degree of self-realization experienced by each of the main characters in his major plays from *All My Sons* (1947) to *The Price* (1968). The studies of each play include a critical introduction, plot synopsis, information regarding critical controversies, and a discussion of each main character's self-realization with textual support.

Wonzong, Randy Lee. "A Structural Analysis of Arthur Miller's Major Plays." Diss. Northwestern U, 1975.

Without the use of external criteria such as biographic or social criticism, Wonzong presents a structural analysis of Miller's plays, from *All My Sons* to *Incident at Vichy*.

1976

McKay, Charles Eugene. "The Themes of Awareness, Self-Knowledge, and Love in Arthur Miller's Major Dramatic Works." Diss. U of Mississippi, 1976.

McKay examines the qualities of self-knowledge, awareness, and love in Miller's plays from *All My Sons* to *The Creation of the World and Other Business* as components of Miller's new moral code based on experience rather than religion.

1977

Gold, Ronald Lester. "A Comparative Analysis of Arthur Miller's *Death of a Salesman* by Means of Dramatic Criticism and the Sereno and Bodaken Trans-Per Model." Diss. U of Southern California, 1977.

Applying the Bodaken-Sereno Trans-Per Model as well as established dramatic criteria, Gold attempts to resolve the debate over whether *Death of a Salesman* is a psychological or sociological play.

Groski, Leonard Dennis. "A Course of Study Inquiring into the Nature of Dramatic Tragedy." Diss. Carnegie-Mellon U, 1977.

Applying Artistotle's theory of tragedy, Groski presents an instructor's guide focusing on the reading and analysis of eight dramatic works (including Miller's *Death of a Salesman*).

Pahnichaputt, M. L. Ananchanok. "The Image of Home in Five American Literary Works." Diss. U of Denver, 1977.

Selecting literary works that contain a variety of American geographical localities and historical periods, Pahnichaputt surveys each author's "ambivalent attitude toward home" and their "often pejorative aspects of family relationships." Works evaluated: Hawthorne's *The House of Seven Gables*, Ole Rolvaag's *Giants in the Earth*, Faulkner's *Absalom, Absalom!*, O'Neill's *Long Day's Journey into Night*, and Miller's *Death of a Salesman.*

1978

Castro, Donald Frank. "A Phenomenological Approach to the Concept of Genre." Diss. Washington State U, 1978.

Castro presents four essays on a phenomenological approach to genre. Miller's work *After the Fall* is studied along with Williams's *The Glass Menagerie* and O'Neill's *Long Day's Journey into Night* in the essay entitled "Autobiographical Drama: A Phenominological Description."

Garcia, Ana Lucia Almeida Gazolla de. "Tragedy and Value: A Study of Dias Gomes' *O Pagador de Promessas* and *O Santo Inquérito* and Arthur Miller's *Death of a Salesman*." Diss. U of North Carolina at Chapel Hill, 1978.

In applying the principles of phenomenology as defined by Hegel, Max Scheler, and Eugene H. Galk to two works by Brazilian playwright Alfredo Dias Gomes and one work by Miller (*Death of a Salesman*), Garcia concludes that while Gomes's works are tragic, in Miller's play "the sense of failure and desperation creates a feeling of pathos which excludes any possibility of manifestation of the tragic."

Gray, Cecilia Delores. "Achievement as a Family Theme in Drama." Diss. Oregon State U, 1978.

Gray charts the development and maintenance of the theme of family achievement in O'Neill's *Long Day's Journey into Night* and Miller's *Death of a Salesman.*

Hagy, Boyd Frederick. "A Study of the Changing Patterns of Melodrama as They Contributed to American Playwriting From 1920–1950." Diss. Catholic U of America, 1978.

Hagy studies the setting, plot development, characterization, acting style, and music of fourteen plays by American playwrights in an effort to illuminate the development of melodrama from its nineteenth-century origins to its current state as a sub-genre "appropriately designated as realistic melodrama." Miller play studied: *All My Sons.*

1979

McGlinn, Jeanne Blain. "The Bible in Modern American Drama." Diss. U of Kansas, 1979.

McGlinn investigates the use of the Bible as source material for modern American drama. Included in her study is a survey of American drama from 1900 to 1979 that lists every biblical play professionally produced, including statistical information and critical reaction, and a detailed examination of the biblical plays of seven major American playwrights: Philip Barry, Maxwell Anderson, Marc Connelly, Clifford Odets, Archibald MacLeish, Paddy Chayefsky, and Arthur Miller.

Talbert, Linda Lee. "Witchcraft in Contemporary Feminist Literature." Diss. U of Southern California, 1979.

Talbert examines "the psychological dimensions of the myth of feminine evil and the socio-sexual, religious, and political relationship that exists between patriarchy and fear of women." She offers a comparison analysis of Miller's *The Crucible* and Ann Petry's *Tituba of Salem* "because their works treat the significance of the slave in the trials."

1980

Greenfield, Thomas Allen. "Standing Before Kings: Work and the Work Ethic in American Drama, 1920–1970." Diss. U of Minnesota, 1980.

Greenfield traces the theme of work in modern American drama, focusing a third of his study on Williams and Miller as the two playwrights who "brought to fruition the drama of the American working man." Both had presented the dilemma of an American middle class trapped between the belief that daily work had value and the frustration over the meaninglessness of the daily routine.

Sippl, Diane Marie. "The Family in American Drama." Diss. U of California, Irvine, 1980.

Sippl examines Pulitzer Prize-winning plays produced between 1920 and 1950, plays which mostly portray the family as the seat of conflict—an ironic and unsettling depiction considering that the purpose of the Pulitzer Prize was to recognize plays "which seemed to best represent the educational value and power of the stage in raising the standard of good morals, good taste and good manners." Of note to Miller studies is Sippl's analysis of *Death of a Salesman* as a play that "lacks a true conflict and offers only the soliloquy of a mentally disturbed man."

Swenson-Davis, Anna Marcia. "From Sex Queen to Cultural Symbol: An Interpretation of the Image of 'Marilyn Monroe.'" Diss. U of Michigan, 1980.

Stating that Marilyn Monroe functions as a symbol, a mythic figure, and a cultural icon and can therefore be 'read' like any other 'text' informing it, Swenson-Davis investigates what Monroe the vital image reveals about Americans between 1930 and 1980. Miller's works concerning Monroe are discussed.

Todras, Arthur. "The Liberal Paradox: Clifford Odets, Elia Kazan, and Arthur Miller." Diss. Indiana U, 1980.

Todras examines representational works of Odets, Kazan, and Miller in relation to each artist's liberal politics and involvement with the American leftist movement of the 1930s through the 1950s. He concludes that their dramas "are marked, inscribed, by this historical context."

1981

Centola, Steven Ronald. "Freedom and Responsibility After the Fall: A Sartrean Perspective of Arthur Miller's Existential Humanism." Diss. U of Rhode Island, 1981.

Working from a framework of the philosophy of Jean-Paul Sartre, Centola examines the existential nature of Miller's dramaturgy, giving special emphasis to three of his works: *After the Fall*, *Incident at Vichy*, and *The Price*. "In these plays, [Miller's] vision crystallizes into a sharply focused vision of the metaphysical anguish which lies at the heart of the human condition."

Denby, Priscilla Lee. "The Self Discovered: The Car in American Folklore and Literature." Diss. Indiana U, 1981.

This study explores the automobile as a complex and powerful symbol of self that "augments basic polarities of our experience that help shape our self-image." Denby uses notable works of American literature (Miller included) as part of her source material for information about and insight into cars.

Kelly, Kay Elizabeth. "A Values-Centered Approach to the Teaching of Literature on the College Level." Diss. U of Georgia, 1981.

Based on a transactional model of reader response, Kelly formulates an instructional model for a values-centered approach to literature on the college level. In addition to Camus's short story "The Guest" and a selection of poetry, Kelly summarizes and evaluates the values in Miller's *Death of a Salesman*.

Sweet, Bruce. "The Invisible Director: The Stage Direction of Harold Clurman as Witnessed by Actors, Stage Managers, Producers, Playwrights and Critics from Three Representative Productions." Diss. New York U, 1981.

Using selected productions from each era of Clurman's long career (Odets's *Awake and Sing*, McCullers's *The Member of the Wedding*, and Miller's *Incident at Vichy*), Sweet investigates the director's rehearsal procedures and their subsequent performance results. Major emphasis is placed on Clurman's preparatory work, casting, setting, auditions, and preview performances.

1982

Lindholm, Karl Lambert. "Anticlimax: The Sporting Hero in Modern American Literature." Diss. Case Western Reserve U, 1982.

This study examines the psychologically crippled ex-sporting hero as an American archetype of some of this country's best fiction. "Modern American writers [including Miller] have used the sporting hero in his disillusioned and nostalgic adult persona to demonstrate the immense human battle against time, as a vital symbol of the presence of death in the midst of our lives and the struggle to find meaning in a random and chaotic world."

Sobrinho, Miguel Joao. "O Teatro Consciente de Arthur Miller e Jorge Andrade." Diss. Tulane U, 1982.

Comparative study of Brazilian playwright Jorge Andrade and Arthur Miller, focusing primarily on their similar themes and reliance on real events for dramatic content. Miller plays examined include *Death of a Salesman* (the use of the past as a determinant of the present), *A View from the Bridge* (groups in social transition), and *The Crucible* (an attack on social injustice).

Wilcox, Robert Harland. "The Poetry of Realistic Drama." Diss. The U of Wisconsin at Madison, 1982.

This study utilizes Aristotle's six categories of poetics (plot, character, thought, language, rhythm, and spectacle) to examine the "web of metaphoric relationships" in four realistic American plays: O'Neill's *Long Day's Journey into Night*, Williams's *Cat on a Hot Tin Roof*, Miller's *The Crucible*, and Albee's *Who's Afraid of Virginia Woolf?*

1983

Dyer, James Joseph. "An Instructor's Handbook to Six Major Plays of Arthur Miller." Diss. Indiana U of Pennsylvania, 1983.

Designed for use in high school and junior college, Dyer developed a "compact yet thorough" instructor's manual for *All My Sons*, *Death of a Salesman*, *The Crucible*, *A View from the Bridge*, *After the Fall*, and *The Price*. Includes play synopsis, critical reaction with annotated bibliography, and Dyer's analysis. Dyer concludes that "while Miller has experimented with form, his thematic concerns have remained fairly consistent."

Lewis, Jonathon Roy. "The Comedy Films of Jerry Lewis and Marilyn Monroe: A Narratological Study and an Introduction to the Social/Ideological Project." Diss. U of California at Los Angeles, 1983.

Focusing his study on eight selected comedy films of Jerry Lewis and Marilyn Monroe, Lewis attempts to "address the problematic relationship between cinema and culture" as well as cinema and history. Strangely, the author includes a chapter discussing Monroe's "comedy" film *The Misfits*, offering an in-depth analysis of the film's story, theme, character-star, and spectator-text dynamic.

Neiheiser, Thomas Neil. "Heroes and Fools: Characterizations in Holocaust Drama." Diss. U of Utah, 1983.

This work charts the development of the hero and fool roles in Holocaust plays. Miller's works *Incident at Vichy* and *Playing for Time* are included among the forty-nine works analyzed.

Schroeder, Patricia Richards. "The Presence of the Past in Modern American Drama." Diss. U of Virginia, 1983.

Schroeder examines the dramatic structure experimentations of O'Neill, Wilder, Miller, and Williams as attempts "to portray a past that influences and partially constitutes present stage reality." Schroeder concludes that Miller's revision of linear causality places his "evolving notion of 'process' at the heart of each play."

1984

Briskin, Alan Mark. "Institutionalization of the Soul: Reflections on the Concepts of Management and Shadow (Authority, Autonomy)." Diss. The Wright Institute, 1984.

Beginning with an analysis of the theories of Michel Foucault and the management practices of Horace Mann and Frederick Taylor, Briskin examines what he calls the "shadow of American management practice." *Death of a Salesman* is discussed as an example of the destructive consequences of "the individual who identifies too closely with the dictates of management and the human dilemmas that ensue."

1985

Feldman, Robert Lee. "The Problem of Evil in Five Plays by Arthur Miller." Diss. U of Maryland at College Park, 1985.

Tracing Miller's definition of evil through such works as *An Enemy of the People*, *The Crucible*, *After the Fall*, and *Incident at Vichy*, Feldman concludes that the "implicit message in these plays is that evil is a moral problem for which there are no easy solutions."

Mahmoud, Mohamed A. W. "A Stylistic, Sociolinguistic, and Discourse Analysis of Linguistic Naturalism in Selected Plays of Arthur Miller and Eugene O'Neill." Diss. U of Delaware, 1985.

Noting a dearth of studies relating to language in modern drama, Mahmoud relies on the work of sociolinguistics and discourse analysis on orality and literacy to highlight the appropriateness of both playwright's choice of language in the depiction of their illiterate and uneducated characters. Concludes Mahmoud, "What Miller and O'Neill have produced is not linguistically poor characters, but characters who are naturalistically portrayed."

Vineberg, Steve Edward. "Method in Performance: Fifty Years of American Method Acting." Diss. Stanford U, 1985.

Vineberg explores the development of method acting in America, specifically in the Group Theatre and Actors Studio. Miller content includes a comparison of Lee J. Cobb's and Dustin Hoffman's performances in productions of *Death of a Salesman*.

1986

Kihn, Patricia Lenehan. "Kenneth Tynan and the Renaissance of Post-War British Drama." Diss. Wayne State U, 1986.

Kihn examines Tynan's reactions to dramatists of the post-war era, including Miller, as proof of the critic's "total commitment toward change."

Long, Deborah Marie. "The Existential Quest: Family and Form in Selected American Plays." Diss. U of Oregon, 1986.

Long studies O'Neill's *Long Day's Journey into Night*, Miller's *Death of a Salesman*, and Williams's *Cat on a Hot Tin Roof* in order to "prove that each of these plays presents an identical vision of reality which is translated into concrete form such that subject, theme, dramatic action, characterization, dialogue, symbol, set design, lighting and sound are all projections of an existential ideology."

Ngwang, Emmanuel Njegani. "Survival and Personal Identity in Arthur Miller's Major Plays." Diss. Oklahoma State U, 1986.

Ngwang examines Miller's novel, major plays, and theatre essays in an effort to trace "the origins of Miller's democratic humanism to his personal experience and the historical events that helped in shaping his ideology." The underlying conflict in all of these works, concludes Ngwang, is between survival and personal identity that reflects Miller's own private "concern for a society in which personal identity and survival could fuse in a single human goal."

Sabinson, Eric Mitchell. "Script and Transcript: The Writings of Clifford Odets, Lillian Hellman and Arthur Miller in Relation to Their Testimony Before the U. S. House Committee on Un-American Activities." Diss. State U of New York at Buffalo, 1986.

Sabinson examines the relationship between the works of Hellman, Odets, and Miller and their testimony before HUAC as a "confrontation between discourses." In each playwright's works leading up to and following their appearances, the issues of interrogations, acts of faith, the nature of truth, responsibility for the past, and the individual under pressure from the community were explored in, what Sabinson determines, preparation for their testimony in their fictional works.

1987

Bavaria, Richard Ernest. "A Value Analysis of Four Fathers from Secondary School Literature: Pap, Atticus, Willy, and Walter." Diss. U of Maryland at College Park, 1987.

Employing content analysis to identify the patriarchal values of principal characters from works frequently taught in secondary education, Bavaria highlights the influence each father has had on his children—those that served as negative examples (such as Willy Loman in Miller's *Death of a Salesman*) tended to drive their children away, while those with positive values, taught their offspring the importance of a life led through courage, tolerance, civility, and the importance of the family.

1988

Austin, Gayle. "Feminist Theory and Postwar American Drama." Diss. City U of New York, 1988.

After outlining the stages of development of feminist criticism, Austin investigates sixteen plays, by both male and female playwrights, written between 1945–1985, using various feminist critical perspectives—anthropology (Gayle Austin), psychology (Nancy Chodorow), literary criticism (Sandra M. Gilbert and Susan Gubar), and film theory (Laura Mulvey).

Proehl, Geoffrey Scott. "Coming Home Again: American Family Drama and the Figure of the Prodigal (O'Neill, Miller, Williams)." Diss. Stanford U, 1988.

Proehl examines the figure of the prodigal husband or son as a representation of the family in American drama. Miller's *Death of a Salesman* is used to illustrate male prodigality in American domestic drama, the use of brother pairs, and the role of the mother grace figure whose calling is to wait and forgive.

1989

Doherty, Lynn. "The Art of Producing: The Life and Work of Kermit Bloomgarden." Diss. City U of New York, 1989.

Doherty presents a chronological survey of the career of independent theatre producer Kermit Bloomgarden based on primary source material, including the Bloomgarden collection at the State Historical Society of Wisconsin and interviews with several key employees and family members. Bloomgarden produced Miller's first major hit, and *Death of a Salesman* is among the forty plays included in this five chapter discussion of the years 1940 to 1974.

Heidt, Edward R. "Narrative Voice in Autobiographical Writing." Diss. U of Southern California, 1989.

Applying speech act and narrative theory, as well as Edmund Husserl's phenomenology and Jacques Derrida's language philosophy, to a broad variety of autobiographical documents, including Miller, Heidt studies each narrative's "mimetic/diagetic voices which express acts and states of consciousness unique to the autobiographer" in an effort to contribute to "an understanding of how autobiographical writing might stand a single genre."

Horner, Carl Stuart. "The Boy Inside the American Businessman: Corporate Darwinism in Twentieth Century American Literature (Salinger, Vonnegut, Miller, Heller, Updike)." Diss. Florida State U, 1989.

In this socioeconomic study of twentieth-century American literature, Horner explores various literary works in an attempt to illustrate how "mainstream businessmen must either discipline, suppress, or kill boyish tendencies that collide with the expectations of American business or suffer the frustration, demotion, or demolition of corporate Darwinism." Willy Loman in Miller's *Death of a Salesman*, according to Horner, cannot realize success despite his fanatic struggles to "suffocate his boyish love of freedom and adventure in order to force-fit himself to corporate expectations."

Tuttle, Jon Wilson. "Arthur Miller's Revision of America." Diss. U of New Mexico, 1989.

Relying primarily on Miller's commentary on his art and ethics, Tuttle explores Miller as humanist—his emphasis on the democratic ideals of individual freedom and social justice, brotherly love, family unity, and good faith—in an effort to "synthesize Miller's ideas about American value and to chart the changes in those ideas."

Tyson, Lois Marie. "The Commodification of the American Dream: Capitalist Subjectivity in American Literature." Diss. The Ohio State U, 1989.

Tyson employs five critical tools—psychoanalysis, Marxism, feminism, existentialism, and post-structuralism—to analyze Edith Wharton's *House of Mirth*, F. Scott Fitzgerald's *The Great Gatsby*, Arthur Miller's *Death of a Salesman*, and Joseph Heller's *Something Happened* in an effort to "learn how the individual and the group are dialectically related in contemporary American society."

1990

Wang, Qun. "On the Dramatization of the Illusory World in Tennessee Williams, Arthur Miller and Edward Albee's Major Plays." Diss. U of Oregon, 1990.

Wang examines the differing ways in which the three playwrights approach the conflict between illusion and reality. While Miller "defines truth in terms of his characters' moral soundness," Williams divulges a reality which is either overlooked or obliterated by his characters' nostalgia, and Albee objectifies "the detrimental consequence of a character's willingness to substitute for reality a self-created unreality in order to protect his/her individual or emotional integrity."

1991

Antoniadis, Maria V. "Tragedy and the Family: Existentialism and Family Therapy." Diss. The Wright Institute, 1991.

For her Ph.D. in clinical psychology, Antoniadis explores the usefulness of connecting existential thought to the family therapy field, especially in the areas of family crisis and tragedy. The tragic aspects of Miller, Williams, and Shakespeare are examined to show the commonalities between the field of existential psychotherapy and literature.

Balakian, Janet Nafena. "The Evolution of Arthur Miller's Dramaturgy 1944 to the Present." Diss. Cornell U, 1991.

Through an extensive analysis of the canon through 1987, Balakian contends that Miller "has been incorrectly perceived as a realistic playwright." She focuses on Miller's dramatic experiments with Ibsenesque Realism, Greek tragedy, German Expressionism, vaudeville, and the fable to demonstrate "an organic connection between form and content in his work" and the variety of literary idioms that Miller "has created in order to come to terms with special artistic problems."

Cline, Gretchen Sarah. "The Psychodrama of the 'Dysfunctional' Family: Desire, Subjectivity, and Regression in Twentieth-Century American Drama." Diss. Ohio State U, 1991.

Using psychoanalytic, feminist, and existential theories, Cline examines the families of O'Neill's *A Long Day's Journey into Night*, Miller's *Death of a Salesman*, Williams's *A Streetcar Named Desire*, and Marsha Norman's *Getting Out* in order to study "the restrictions that exist within emotional patterns and interactions of the Tyrones, Lomans, Kowalskis, and Howsclaws."

Erickson, Steven Craig. "The Drama of Dispossession in Selected Plays of Six Major American Playwrights." Diss. U of Texas at Dallas, 1991.

Through analysis of selected works of O'Neill, Miller (*Death of a Salesman*), Albee, Williams, Mamet, and Shepard, Erickson examines the condition of the American experience of dispossession—the result a character attempting to realize the ideal of possession—"as it manifests itself within three thematic areas: the self, the home, and the environment."

Redfield, Catherine Erin. "The Fallen." Diss. U of Southwestern Louisiana, 1991.

This dissertation is a collection of six original short stories, "each a tragedy according to the definition Arthur Miller details in his essay 'Tragedy and the Common Man.'"

Shalaby, Nadia Abdelgalil. "Assertion of Power: A Sociolinguistic Analysis of *Death of a Salesman*, *The Caretaker*, and *Look Back in Anger*." Diss. U of South Carolina, 1991.

This study examines each drama's use of linguistic strategies in which characters achieve power in situations of conflict. Shalaby hopes that her effort will equip critics with an interactive approach to discourse, "thus helping to account for the way certain characters are perceived both by other characters in the plays and by readers/viewers."

Stafford, Richard Dobson. "Play Ownership and the Struggle for Creative Control in Theatrical Productions." Diss. Texas Tech. U, 1991.

From interviews with various theatrical artists, including Miller, Stafford explores the struggle for creative control the problem of ownership in theatrical productions while offering several possible solutions to the problem presented, including open communication, a system of interpretation limits between publishers and directors, and the development of a New Play Contract between playwrights and directors.

1992

Bergeron, Jill Stapleton. "Codependency Issues in Selected Contemporary American Plays." Diss. The Louisiana State U and Agricultural and Mechanical College, 1992.

This study explores the nature of codependency and the importance of its use as an evaluative tool in understanding many plays, their characters, and relationships, including *Death of a Salesman.*

Fletcher, Anne. "The Theory and Practice of Mordecai Gorelik: Emblem for the Changing American Theatre." Diss. Tufts U, 1992.

Fletcher details Gorelick's legacy of "integrity, scholarship, and vision" in this study of the designer/theorist. Of note to Miller scholarship is the inclusion of Gorelick's work on *All My Sons*, Miller's first Broadway success.

Fox, Larry Phillip. "A Comparative Analysis of Selected Dramatic Works and Their Twentieth Century Operatic Adaptations." Diss. U of South Carolina, 1992.

Comparative analysis of three dramatic works (Hellman's *The Little Foxes*, Miller's *The Crucible*, and Georges Bernanos's *Dialogues des Carmelites*) and their operatic adaptations, including their transformation processes, methodology of adaptation, and musical idiom as intensifying element. Of note to Miller studies, Fox offers a scene-by-scene study of the Miller/Ward works, with a final summary commentary on each act and the effects of music on text.

Myers, Mary Kay Zettl. "Closure in the Twentieth-Century American Problem Play." Diss. U of Delaware, 1992.

Myers identifies major closural devices of the problem play and determines how they function within the play's formal and thematic structures by examining three plays about materialism (including Miller's *The American Clock*), to three plays about alienation, to three plays about racism, to three plays about war.

1993

Babcock, Francis Granger. "Rewriting the Masculine: The National Subject in Modern American Drama." Diss. The Louisiana State University and Agricultural and Mechanical College, 1993.

Tracing the development of "an American masculinity" through three stages of American capitalism, Babcock attempts to "construct a genealogy of American maleness and then examines how this genealogy was altered and reconstructed during times of economic crisis and technological innovation." Analyzing the dramas of O'Neill, Williams and Miller, the author notes how each playwright challenges "the dominant version of the national subject by offering a counter-discourse to the consumerism and nationalism advocated by popular conceptions of American masculinity."

Campo, Carlos Alejandro. "The Role of Friendship in Arthur Miller: A Study of Friendship in His Major Dramatic and Non-Dramatic Writing." Diss. U of Nevada, Las Vegas, 1993.

Campo examines Miller's central and recurrent use of friendship "as a means to unify our increasingly individual society." Works examined include: *Situation Normal*, *Focus*, "I Don't Need You Any More," "Monte Sant' Angelo," "Fitter's Night," *All My*

Sons, *Death of a Salesman*, *After the Fall*, and *The Ride Down Mount Morgan*.

Fallows, Randall Jonathan. "Dramatic Realities: The Creation and Reception of American Political and Fictional Dramas of the Late 1940's and Their Influence on Gender Role Construction." Diss. U of California, San Diego, 1993.

Fallows "explores the influence of cold war political language on the formation of gender roles, as represented in a few paradigmatic dramas of the late 1940s"— Miller's *Death of a Salesman*, Hellman's *Another Part of the Forest*, Capra's *It's a Wonderful Life*, Chaplin's *Monsieur Verdoux*, and the texts of the House Un-American Activities Committee as drama. Fallows concludes that "a cultural approach to understanding literature is more fruitful than those approaches based on following a canon, for the former not only shows more accurately how a text is constructed and reconstructed in various readings, but also provides us with a personal power of discernment over those images which could lead to social conformity."

Rosefeldt, Paul Nagim. "The Absent Father in Modern Drama." Diss. The Louisiana State U and Agricultural and Mechanical College, 1993.

The quest for the absent father—a character that not only propels the action but also initiates the quest, spawns imitators or doubles who trace his path, and becomes the ultimate goal of a destructive quest—is examined in selected works of various classical and modern dramatists (including Miller).

1994

Cleary, Kathleen Colligan. "Playing God in Live Theatre: The Politics of Representation." Diss. Ohio State U, 1994.

Following a discussion on the difficulty and controversy in portraying the Christian God in the theatre, Cleary moves to an analysis of several twentieth-century plays: Connelly's *The Green Pastures*, Miller's *The Creation of the World and Other Business* and *Up From Paradise*, and Tony Harrison's *The Mysteries*, and suggests parallels between the portrayals of God and contemporaneous issues.

1995

Baard, Ronald William. "Beyond Illustration: A Method for Using Drama and Film in Pastoral Counseling." Diss. School of Theology at Claremont, 1995.

Using a theoretical foundation from Susan Langer's philosophy of art and theory of drama, this study attempts to show the value of integrating drama into pastoral counseling. Miller's *Salesman* is used as part of a case study in which a "Euro-American male" interacted with the drama "in order to move to deeper levels of understanding and healing with respect to his 'father-wound.'"

1996

Caruso, Cristina Claudia. "White Corrassable Bond-(age): *Lost in America* as Textual Escape." Diss. State U of New York at Albany, 1996.

Using John Winthrop's 1630 lay sermon "A Model of Christian Charity" as starting point, Caruso examines the "nomadic" nature of American cultural production in an "effort to deterritorialize the reifying matrices of textual bondage" present in each work. Miller work examined: *The Crucible.*

Mason, Carol Ann. "Fundamental Opposition: Feminism, Narrative, and the Abortion Debate." Diss. U of Minnesota, 1996.

Mason examines nineteenth-century feminist and fundamentalist writings and three twentieth-century discourses (literature, cinema, and media accounts of anti-abortion terrorism) in an effort to put "issues of narratology in the contemporary, political arena of U.S. feminist and Christian fundamentalist conflict." Miller work examined: *The Crucible.*

Miller, Lance Barry. "Gone West: Landscapes of the Imaginary in Modern American Drama." Diss. Stanford U, 1996.

Miller uses the theories of poet Charles Olson, Jacques Lacan, Roberto Calasso, and Rene Girard to examine the drama of William Vaughn Moody, Eugene O'Neill, John Steinbeck, Arthur Miller (specifically *Death of a Salesman*), and Sam Shepard in an effort to argue that "the 'west' has been a problem of representation in response to crises in the mediation of imaginary desiring and historical narrative, a problem that becomes itself a subject of American drama as it enters postmodernity."

Proctor, Susan Kay Anthony. "A Semiotic Reading of Arthur Miller's *Death of a Salesman*." Diss. U of Oklahoma, 1996.

With an end result geared toward developing a "definitive text or metatext," Proctor presents a semiotic reading of six theatre (1949–1984) and three film/video productions of *Death of a Salesman* in an effort "to discover the differences that diverse theatre practices tend to create in the interpretation and growth of a text."

Solomonson, Michael C. "An Archetypal Study of the Fertility Angel Paradigm in Dramatic Literature." Diss. U of Nebraska, 1996.

In light of historical and literary antecedents, Solomonson analyzes (in the fourth chapter of her study) the fertility angel character (a figure that exhibits power over the human natal process and promotes agricultural fecundity) as it appears in the works of Brecht, Kushner, Miller, and Wilder.

Witt, Jonathan Ronald. "Fearless Audiences: How Modern American Literature Flatters Us." Diss. U of Kansas, 1996.

Working from the preposition that much of modern American literature portrays pride as virtue, thus reinforcing the audience's pride by way of flattery, Witt devotes a portion of her dissertation to examining *Death of a Salesman* (among other literary works by Williams, O'Neill, Shakespeare, and Sophocles) and the problems created by what she calls the "audience's paradox"— "that tension created when a work employs an obscure, lowly character as protagonist and so makes that obscure person the center of our attention," thus making him famous.

1997

Abbotson, Susan Claire Whitfield. "Towards a Humanistic Democracy: The Balancing Acts of Arthur Miller and August Wilson." Diss. U of Connecticut, 1997.

This study explores the thematic similarities between the works of Miller and Wilson in an effort to illustrate how their plays "form an affirmation of American potential and spirit, which reveals the playwrights' mutual, humanistic, and democratic vision of America."

Koorey, Stefani. "Attention Must Be Paid: The Misinvention of Women in the Life and Literature of Arthur Miller." Diss. The Pennsylvania State U, 1997.

Koorey presents a materialist feminist approach that identifies and inspects Miller's unique pattern of female gender icon construction as represented in nine of his works: *All My Sons*, *Death of a Salesman*, *The Crucible*, "Please Don't Kill Anything," *The Misfits*, *After the Fall*, *Playing for Time*, *Broken Glass*, and "Homely Girl, A Life." Concludes Koorey, with no privileged female characters in the canon, Miller instead crafts a highly fractured and fraudulent picture of American domestic life.

Marino, Stephen A. "Arthur Miller's Language: The Poetic in the Colloquial." Diss. Fordham U, 1997.

Marino examines the often overlooked and rather sophisticated poetic elements (metaphor, symbol, and imagery) of Miller's canon, suggesting that the playwright has "created a unique dramatic idiom in twentieth-century American drama."

Wilkins, John Robinson. "The Problem of the American Playwright: The Successes and Failures of e. e. cummings, Arthur Miller and Sam Shepard." Diss. U of California, Berkeley, 1997.

Wilkins concentrates on e. e. cummings, Arthur Miller, and Sam Shepard's attempts "to create an authentic American theatrical aesthetic" and the difficulty each encountered in "writing not only for an audience unconcerned with and untutored in the conventions of their art, but the daunting task of teaching that audience how to understand their work."

1998

Lavoie, Bernard. "Arthur Miller in Montreal: Cultural Transfer of American Plays in Quebec (1965–1997)." Diss. The Louisiana State U and Agricultural and Mechanical College, 1998.

This study surveys all productions of Miller plays presented in Montreal, supported with interviews of the artists involved, in an attempt to "identify and explain how the translative and the appropriation practices of American plays have evolved and developed in Quebec from the 1960s to the 1990s."

2000

Egerton, Katherine E. "'Sick in Twos and Threes and Fours': Representation, Redemption, and Mental Illness in Arthur Miller's Later Plays." Diss. U of North Carolina, 2000.

This study traces the development of Miller's use of the language of illness and health "as remedies for the diseases of society." Egerton argues that in Miller's later "chamber-scale plays," men emerge as moral failures while the women are labeled as possessing mental illnesses, concluding that "Miller bifurcates by gender the crises in these people's lives in order that the perspectives embodied by the women and the men may clash, combine, and heal both the one and the many." Miller works examined include: *The Price*, *The Archbishop's Ceiling*, *Some Kind of Love Story*, *The Last Yankee*, *The Ride Down Mount Morgan*, and *Broken Glass*.

3. Biographical News Articles, Essays, Profiles, and Features

1946

"Words Like Tracer Bullets." *New York Post Week-End Magazine* 27 April 1946: 2, 8.

Biographical profile of Miller on the occasion of the publication of his novel *Focus*. Of note is the journalist's view that "People often find themselves confused as to [Miller's] nationality—a fact which has important bearing on the theme of *Focus*." Includes lengthy excerpts from Miller's book.

Weiler, A. H. "By Way of Report." *New York Times* 21 July 1946: II: 3.

News item announcing the recent purchase of the rights to *Focus* by King Brothers, who have engaged Jerome Cholorov to write the scenario. Columbia or Monogram might be the releasing company.

1947

Atkinson, Brooks. "Season's Best Play." *New York Times* 27 April 1947: II: 1. See also Louis Calta, "*All My Sons* Wins Critics' Laurels." *New York Times* 22 April 1947: 33.

Lengthy article announcing Miller's play *All My Sons* as the New York Drama Critics Circle Award winner and its presentation later that day (Sunday) at a cocktail party at the Algonquin. The citation is awarded for the "frank and uncompromising presentation of a timely and important theme, because of the honesty of the writing and the cumulative power of the scenes, and because it reveals a genuine instinct for the theatre in an intelligent and thoughtful new playwright."

"To Sell *All My Sons* Script." *New York Times* 14 May 1947: 31.

News item announcing the auctioning off of Miller's script for *All My Sons* on Sunday at the Hotel Brevoort by the Progressive Citizens of America. Also on the auction block will be letters and manuscripts by Hemingway, Henry Wallace, FDR, and Albert Maltz.

"The Dance: Prague Festival." *New York Times* 25 May 1947: II: 6.

Miller is mentioned as among the notables sponsoring the U.S. Committee for the World Youth Festival. Other sponsors on this committee include Ingrid Bergman, Helen Hayes, Cornelia Otis Skinner, and Thomas Mann.

"Miller, Playwright, Buys Brooklyn Home." *New York Times* 1 June 1947: Sec. 8: 1.

Brief news item detailing Miller's purchase of a two-family home at 31 Grace Court in the Heights section of Brooklyn from Irving Bussing, and Miller's plans to convert part of the house into a studio.

"Miller Fails in Plea." *New York Times* 11 June 1947: 33.

News item announcing that the U.S. State Department has refused to sponsor a production of Miller's *All My Sons* at the World Youth Festival in Prague. Appealing the decision, Miller is quoted in a wire signed by others that the "participants have no special political affiliations."

Bernstein, Lester. "Miller Rejects Hollywood's Bid." *New York Times* 17 July 1947: 15.

News item reporting that Miller has turned down an offer by Hollywood to write a film to be directed by Alfred Hitchcock.

———. "Ferrer Is Sought by Company of 12." *New York Times* 22 July 1947: 30.

Brief mention is made that *All My Sons* has been acquired by the United States Army for production in Germany, to star Helena Timik, widow of Max Reinhardt. Also of note is the statement regarding Miller's next play, "now described as a comedy, set on the lower East Side in the twenties, and involving an Italian-American worker. It is called 'Plenty Good Time.'"

1948

"Book Ban Protested." *New York Times* 16 February 1948: 23.

News item reporting that the teachers at the De Witt Clinton high school in the Bronx are protesting the banning of Miller's book *Focus* from their school library on the grounds that it "offends the Catholic Church."

1949

MacKey, Joseph. "Brooklyn Literary Tree Blooms." *New York Sun* 1 March 1949: 7.

Fascinating item reporting that the same house at 102 Pierrepont Street in Brooklyn, once home to both Arthur Miller and Norman Mailer, was the location of the writing of both *All My Sons* and *The Naked and the Dead*. Photographs of the outside entrance and an inside room, once belonging to Miller, accompany the text. Of note is the mention of the size of Miller's duplex: seven rooms.

"Page One Awards Made by Newspaper Guild." *New York Times* 29 March 1949: 21.

Brief item reporting that the New York Newspaper Guild has chosen *Death of a Salesman* as the recipient of their Drama Award.

"Miller's Play Wins Stage Prize." *New York Times* 4 April 1949: 26.

Brief item announcing *Death of a Salesman* as the winner of the Theatre Club prize for "outstanding play of the season."

"Red Visitors Cause Rumpus." *Life* 4 April 1949: 39–43.

Article detailing the events at the Cultural and Scientific Conference for World Peace held at the Waldorf-Astoria Hotel in New York City. Miller is pictured in a group of fifty individuals under the heading "Dupes and Fellow-Travelers Dress Up Communist Fronts." Among those pictures are Norman Mailer, Lillian Hellman, Clifford Odets, Leonard Bernstein, Aaron Copeland, Albert Einstein, Dorothy Parker, Langston Hughes, Charles Chaplin, and Thomas Mann. The article describes this group as fifty "prominent people who, wittingly or not, associate themselves with the Communist front organization and thereby lend it glamour, prestige, or the respectability of American liberalism."

Zolotow, Sam. "Miller Play Wins Critics Plaudits." *New York Times* 13 April 1949: 40.

News item announcing Miller's *Death of a Salesman* being awarded the New York Drama Critics' Circle Award as one of three outstanding plays of the 1948–49 Broadway season, followed by a profile of Miller's life and literary career.

"Miller Receives Award." *New York Times* 17 April 1949: 63.

News item reporting Miller's acceptance of the New York Drama Critics' Circle Award for *Death of a Salesman*, given to him by John Mason Brown. Miller praises his cast as responsible, in a large measure, for the play's success.

"*Salesman, Kate* Win Perry Award." *New York Times* 25 April 1949: 19.

News item announcing the triple win for *Death of a Salesman* at the Antoinette Perry Awards (the Tony): Miller winning for best drama, Elia Kazan for best director, and Arthur Kennedy (Biff) awarded a prize for acting.

"The Pulitzer Prizes." *New York Times* 3 May 1949: 24.

Opinion piece that congratulates Miller for winning the Pulitzer Prize for *Death of a Salesman.*

"Sketches of Pulitzer Prize Winners." *New York Times* 3 May 1949: 22.

Miller is included in this biographical sketch of the Pulitzer Prize winners.

Grutzner, Charles. "*Salesman* is Pulitzer Prize; Sherwood Cozzens Cited." *New York Times* 3 May 1949: 1, 22.

Lengthy item which mentions Miller as making a sweep of the three major drama prizes for *Death of a Salesman*: the Pulitzer Prize, the New York Drama Critics' Circle Award, and the Antoinette Perry Award (the Tony).

"Pulitzer Prizes Announced at Columbia University." *Publishers Weekly* 7 May 1949: 1877.

Item announcing that Miller's *Death of a Salesman* has been named as recipient of the 1949 Pulitzer Prize, awarded for an "original American play, which shall represent in marked fashion the educational value and power of the stage."

"Named 'Father of the Year.'" *New York Times* 26 May 1949: 5.
News item reporting that Miller is among ten outstanding fathers recognized by the National Father's Day Committee.

"Miller Gets Writers Award." *New York Times* 1 June 1949: 43.
Short item announcing Miller as the recipient of the Writer's Award for *Death of a Salesman* from the American Committee of Jewish Writers, Artists and Scientists for "a permanent contribution to contemporary literature."

Freedley, George. "The Theatre." *Library Journal* 15 June 1949: 100–101.
Item reporting that Miller's *Death of a Salesman* is the first play to be chosen for publication by the Book-of-the-Month Club.

Calta, Louis. "*Salesman* Tops Theatrical Poll." *New York Times* 12 July 1949: 31.
News item announcing the slew of Donaldson Awards announced for *Death of a Salesman*—Best Play of the 1948–49 Broadway season, Lee J. Cobb for best actor, Arthur Kennedy and Mildred Dunnock for best supporting actors, Elia Kazan for direction, and Jo Mielziner for "best background."

1950

Ribalow, Harold U. ed. "The Jewish Short Story in America." *This Land, These People*. New York: Beechhurst Press, 1950. 1–10.
In the introduction of a collection of Jewish short stories, Miller is quoted from a 1947 speech explaining his reasoning for not concerning himself with Jewish subjects as a fear that "even an innocent allusion to the individual wrong-doing of an individual Jew would be . . . twisted into a weapon of persecution against Jews."

1951

Warfel, Harry R. *American Novelists of Today*. New York: American Book Company, 1951. 301.
Short biographical essay of Miller's life and literature to date that includes a lengthy quote by Miller on the need for social change. "We ought to be struggling for a world in which it will be possible to lay blame. Only then will great tragedies be written, for where no order is believed in, no order can be breached, and thus all disasters of man will strive vainly for moral meaning."

"What Are You Doing Out There?" *New York Times* 15 January 1951: 9.

Signed by Miller and a dozen other writers, educators, and artists, this advertisement asks for resistance to the encroachments of mass hysteria and injustice on individual liberty. "We only ask you to raise your voice for freedom. . . If the voices of decency and courage remain silent, the right of everyone to live and work in peace and freedom may be lost . . . *Speak Up For Freedom*!"

1953

"Letter to Christopher Fry, 29 January 1953." *Kenneth Tynan Letters*. Ed. Kathleen Tynan. New York: Random House, 1994. 193.

In the reprint of a letter to Christopher Fry in New York City, dated 29 January 1953, critic Kenneth Tynan comments on Miller refusing to speak with Elia Kazan after the director "squealed to the Un-American Activities Tribunal . . . with such political bickerings do our authors waste their time."

1954

"Playwright Arthur Miller Refused Visa to Visit Brussels to See His Play." *New York Times* 31 March 1954: 16.

News item detailing Miller's denial of a visa by the U.S. State Department on the grounds that he is "believed to be supporting the Communist movement." Miller denied the charge and withdrew his application because the passport would have come too late for him to attend the opening in Brussels of *The Crucible.*

1955

Grutzner, Charles. "39 TV Films Based on City Planned." *New York Times* 25 October 1955: 1, 21.

Front page column detailing a million dollar program by the city of New York for producing thirty-nine commercial television films based on city files. Briefly mentioned is Mayor Wagner's decision to conduct an investigation into the charges that Miller, who had written a film script on the city's youth gangs, "had some left-wing affiliations." Also of note is Wagner's assertion that "nothing of a derogatory nature has come up yet—we are not having a witch hunt or anything, we are just trying to find out."

Grutzner, Charles. "Mayor Hails City TV Plans." *New York Times* 26 October 1955: 1, 62.

New York Mayor Wagner is criticized by the New York Civil Liberties Union for investigating the political affiliations of Miller in connection with the film he is writing for the New York City Youth Board.

Fast, Howard. "I Propose Arthur Miller as the American Dramatist of the Day." *Daily Worker* 8 November 1955: 6.

In this Communist newspaper, Fast compares Miller to other "left-wing" writers Clifford Odets and Lillian Hellman, and praises *The Crucible* as a tribute to the courage of Ethel and Julius Rosenberg. He also sees *A View from the Bridge* as a story of betrayal that represents the problems the playwright faced during the Cold War. Fast congratulates Miller for "fighting with all the wit and skill at his command for his survival as an artist."

Bennett, Charles G. "City Hall Dodges Youth Film Issue." *New York Times* 30 November 1955: 38.

News report detailing the controversy swirling around Miller's left-wing activities and its impact in the decision-making process of the Board of Estimate in awarding the contract for the production of a film that Miller has written portraying the work with street gangs of the Youth Board.

"Youth Board Set to Approve Film." *New York Times* 5 December 1955: 33.

News item announcing that the New York City Youth Board is soon to ratify a contract with Miller, signed in July, for a film about street gangs.

"City Drops Plans for a Youth Film." *New York Times* 8 December 1955: 47.

Brief item reporting that the Board of Estimate has voted not to make the film about youth gangs that Miller was to write because of the playwright's "association with some subversive groups at one time."

"Miller Hits Back at Youth Agency." *New York Times* 9 December 1955: 29.

Item reporting Miller's displeasure with the Board of Estimate for overriding the subcommittee's recommendation that the film on youth gangs be made. Says Miller, "Let us see whether fanaticism . . . can perform a creative act. Let it take its club in hand and write what it has just destroyed."

Molarsky, Osmond. "Miller Protest Queried." *New York Times* 15 December 1955: 36.

Letter to the editor, dated 9 December from Westport, Connecticut, protesting the American Legion for preventing Miller from "donating his services as script writer" to a proposed film on juvenile delinquency, "thus leaving the job to some possibly fourth-rate writer at a fee of a couple of thousand dollars." Molarsky questions whether they should wait to see if there is anything "subversive" in the script before they oppose Miller's writing of it.

Goodman, Walter. "How Not to Produce a Film." *New Republic* 26 December 1955: 12–13.

Article detailing the controversy surrounding Miller's attempt to make a film on juvenile delinquency for the New York City Youth Board, which revoked its contract for the production of a film because of Miller's so-called left-wing activities. The project was canceled after the Board was pressured by the American Legion, the Catholic War Veterans, and the New York Police Department.

1956

Schwartz, Harry. "Red and Anti-Red Curbs on Art Denounced by U.S. Playwright." *New York Times* 13 February 1956: 9.

News article announcing Miller's appeal to both Soviet Communists and United States anti-Communists to "recognize that true art is above politics and any interference with its freedom is 'an act against mankind itself.'" A photograph of Miller accompanies the text.

"Cultural Group Rebukes Miller." *New York Times* 14 February 1956: 5.

News item reporting the denial of the American Committee for Cultural Freedom that it invited Miller to write an appeal for cultural freedom in the United States and the Soviet Union. Further, they object to Miller placing the two countries on a par in their suppression of writers and artists.

"Soviet Challenged to Reveal Criticism." *New York Times* 15 February 1956: 28.

News item reporting that the Radio Liberation and the American Committee for Cultural Freedom are banding together to challenge the Soviet Union to publish Miller's written statement denouncing their political interference with all artistic freedom in their country.

Farrell, James. "Curbs on Art Opposed." *New York Times* 21 February 1956: 32.

News item reporting that the chairman of the American Committee for Cultural Freedom has denied that Miller was invited to issue an appeal for cultural freedom on the occasion of Dostoevski's death. The chairman additionally denies Miller's implication that the committee was "attempting to draw the memory of Dostoevski onto a political platform."

Breit, Harvey. "Dostoevsky." *New York Times* 26 February 1956: Sec. VII: 8.

While Breit chastises Miller for equating the Soviet Union's suppression of artistic freedom with the United States, he praises the playwright for refusing the Soviet Union's invitation to visit, knowing that Miller would be denied a passport and thus making a political statement against the United States.

"Arthur Miller Gets Divorce." *New York Times* 12 June 1956: 24.

Three-sentence news item announcing Miller's uncontested divorce from first wife, Mary Grace Slattery, on the basis of "extreme cruelty, entirely mental in nature."

"Michigan U Honors Nine." *New York Times* 17 June 1956: 8.

Miller is mentioned as receiving an honorary degree from the University of Michigan, his alma mater.

Drury, Allen. "Arthur Miller Admits Helping Communist-Front Groups in the 1940's," *New York Times* 22 June 1956: 1, 9.

Front page news story detailing Miller's first day of testimony before the House Committee on Un-American Activities and his recess announcement of his impending marriage to Marilyn Monroe. Photo of Miller accompanies text. Photo of Monroe appears on page 9.

"Miller Ordered to Reveal Names." *New York Times* 28 June 1956: 10.

News article detailing HUAC's vote to give Miller ten days to answer questions on his past Communist-front associations "or face a citation for contempt of Congress."

Rovere, Richard H. "The Monroe Doctrine," *Spectator* 29 June 1956: 877.

Oft-quoted opinion essay in which Rovere calls Miller's announcement of his betrothal to Marilyn Monroe during a short recess at his hearing before HUAC "more than odd, it was symbolic, portentous, rich in paradoxes and fulfillments. And of course it was, as it should have been, full of good theatre. What a backdrop! What timing! What a way to steal a scene! . . . Though one does not wish Mr. Miller any bad luck now that he has had such good luck, it would be interesting and instructive to see what would happen if the public were to be torn between Congress in all its dignity and Miss Monroe in all hers."

"Arthur Miller Weds Marilyn Monroe." *New York Times* 30 June 1956: 19.

News item reporting Miller's marriage to Marilyn Monroe in White Plains, New York.

"Engagement Party." *Newsweek* 2 July 1956: 21–22.

Article detailing Marilyn Monroe's confirmation of her engagement to Miller. Photo of the couple accompanies the text.

"Millers Remarried." *New York Times* 3 July 1956: 16.

Brief news item announcing the second marriage ceremony "in the Jewish faith" between Miller and Monroe.

"Miller Granted European Passport." *New York Times* 7 July 1956: 15.

News item reporting that Miller has been granted a six-month passport by the U.S. State Department for a European honeymoon with Marilyn Monroe. Apparently, affidavits that Miller submitted with his application convinced the State Department that the playwright was not now pro-Communist.

"Miller Declines to Identify Reds." *New York Times* 8 July 1956: 25.

News report announcing Miller's refusal to give HUAC the names of persons who had attended a Communist writers' meeting in 1939 or 1940. Also of note is the State Department's announcement that they had issued Miller a six-month passport "after he answered questions regarding 'derogatory information' that had kept him from getting a passport two years ago."

"People." *Time* 9 July 1956: 36.

Brief article detailing Miller's marriage to Marilyn Monroe and their return to their home in Connecticut.

"Reds Linked to Film." *New York Times* 9 July 1956: 3.

News item reporting that an East German newspaper has reported that a French-East German group will film *The Crucible* with a screenplay by Jean-Paul Sartre. Miller is noted as commenting that the East German company's connection with the project is in violation of his French contract.

"German Link to Movie Denied." *New York Times* 10 July 1956: 26.

The French film company that is to make a movie of *The Crucible* denies that it has made a deal with an East German company to co-produce.

Lewis, Anthony. "House Unit Asks Miller Citation." *New York Times* 11 July 1956: 10.

News article detailing Miller being charged with contempt of Congress by HUAC for declining "for reasons of conscious" to name other persons who had been present at meetings he had attended.

"Arthur Millers Leave for London." *New York Times* 14 July 1956: 33.

Short news piece announcing Miller and bride Monroe's departure for a honeymoon and business trip to London where she is making *The Prince and the Showgirl* with Laurence Olivier. Large photo of the couple accompanies text.

"Wedding Wine for Marilyn." *Life* 16 July 1956: 113–15.

Photographic essay of Miller and Marilyn Monroe's wedding ceremony in Connecticut. Includes seven black-and-white candid shots by Milton Greene.

Drury, Allen. "House Votes 373–9 for Citing Miller." *New York Times* 26 July 1956: 7.

Single column news piece announcing the House vote (373 to 9) to cite Miller for contempt of Congress, resulting from Miller's refusal to give HUAC the names of persons who had attended Communist writers meetings in 1947.

Johnson, Gerald W. "Undermining Congress." *New Republic* 6 August 1956: 10.

Opinion piece in which Johnson claims to understand why Miller "refused to answer the question put to him by the House Un-American Activities Committee. The substance of that question was, 'Who else was as big a fool as you were in 1947?'" Miller, he says, refused to name names because to do so would be "indecent," and "if the Congress of the United States has put pressure on an American citizen to do an indecent thing, then Congress itself has acted indecently."

Melese, Gilbert. "Viewing the Miller Case Abroad." *New York Times* 8 August 1956: 24.

Letter to the editor, dated 26 July from Sèvres, France, offering a foreign viewpoint to Miller's prosecution on contempt of Congress charges. Melese believes that the playwright's ordeal is the "result of Senator McCarthy's hysteria."

"Arthur Miller on Way Here." *New York Times* 27 August 1956: 15.

Three-sentence news item announcing Miller's trip alone to the United States for a vacation to see his children by a previous marriage while bride Monroe remains in London.

"Playwright Flies Here from London for Visit." *New York Times* 28 August 1956: 13.

News item reporting that while Miller is in the United States he will be taking his two children by his first wife, Mary Grace Slattery, on a trip. After this excursion, he will return to London to attend rehearsals of a production of *A View from the Bridge.*

Bentley, Eric. "The Miller Case." *New Republic* 10 September 1956: 23.

Bentley rebuts Gerald Johnson's assertion in the *New Republic* piece ("Undermining Congress") that Miller was not that involved with Communist-front groups. Instead, Bentley insists that Miller had "deep involvement of a large class of persons in a movement inadequately defined by words like giddy."

"Marilyn Monroe Here." *New York Times* 22 November 1956: 50.

Item reporting that Miller and wife Marilyn Monroe have retuned to the United States following the completion of Monroe's film *The Prince and the Showgirl.*

1957

Loftus, Joseph A. "Arthur Miller and Dr. Nathan Indicted on Contempt Charges." *New York Times* 19 February 1957: Sec. 1: 1, 14.

News article announcing a Federal grand jury's indictment of Miller on charges of contempt of Congress for refusing to name names before HUAC. Also indicted was Otto Nathan, an associate professor at NYU and executor of the estate of Albert Einstein. Large photos of Miller and Otto accompany text.

"Moscow Backs Miller." *New York Times* 20 February 1957: 2.

News item announcing that Radio Moscow has reported that there is a connection between Miller's contempt of Congress charge and his writing of *The Crucible*.

"Miller and Nathan Disavow Contempt." *New York Times* 2 March 1957: 14.

News piece regarding Miller pleading not guilty in Federal District Court to an indictment of contempt of Congress. Miller's trial is set for 13 May 1957.

Cogley, John. "The Witnesses' Dilemma." *Commonweal* 15 March 1957: 612.

Full-page article written on the occasion of Miller's citation for contempt of Congress. Cogley reviews Lillian Hellman's testimony in which she pleaded the Fifth and Larry Parks's capitulation before the Committee on the threat of imprisonment in order to point out Miller's dilemma in choosing not to name names nor plead the Fifth Amendment.

"Miller Must Stand Trial." *New York Times* 13 April 1957: 9.

Short news piece announcing Federal District Judge Charles F. McLaughlin's refusal to dismiss the indictment accusing Miller of contempt of Congress.

McCarthy, Mary. "Naming Names: The Arthur Miller Case." *Encounter* 8 (May 1957): 23–25. Rpt. in *On the Contrary*. New York: Octagon, 1976. 147–54.

Important essay that details Miller's testimony before HUAC and offers pointed supportive commentary regarding the playwright's decision to refuse "to play the informer before a Congressional Committee." Says McCarthy, "The committee was not seeking information from Mr. Miller; it was applying a loyalty test. And for Mr. Miller it was not in reality a question of betraying specific people (who had already been denounced, so that his testimony could hardly have done them further harm), but of accepting the *principle* of betrayal as a norm of good citizenship. As a leading playwright with a wide audience, he was being asked to set an example of civic obedience; not Mr. Miller but the committee was to judge whether the disclosure of those names served any useful purpose."

"Miller Trial Delay Refused." *New York Times* 4 May 1957: 26.

Two-sentence news item announcing Federal District Judge Bolitha J. Laws's refusal to postpone the contempt trial of Miller, scheduled for 13 May.

Huston, Luther A. "Trial of Miller Attracts Crowds; Lawyers in Clash on Red Charge." *New York Times* 15 May 1957: 19.

News article detailing the first day of Miller's contempt of Congress trial, including details of the huge crowds of newspaper reporters, feature writers, and sketch artists that were present on the expectation that Marilyn Monroe would accompany Miller to his appearance. Large photo of Miller and his lawyer Joe Rauh Jr. accompanies text.

———. "Miller's Past Tie with Reds Retold." *New York Times* 16 May 1957: 17.

The second day of Miller's contempt trial is detailed. Judge McLaughlin limited the trial to the issue of pertinency.

"Reds 'Discipline' of Miller Argued." *New York Times* 17 May 1957: 10.

In the third day of Miller's contempt of Congress trial, lawyers argued over the how to determine when a person comes under Communist discipline. In an affidavit, Miller had denied that he had ever been under Communist discipline, but Richard Arens testified that it could be assumed that a person who attended meetings to which only known Communists were admitted was under party discipline.

"Judge Denies Point to Miller in Trial." *New York Times* 21 May 1957: 30.

In this short news piece, the *Times* reports that Federal Judge McLaughlin refused to strike government testimony from the record of Miller's trial for contempt, which was designed to show Miller was a Communist in the 1940s.

"Judge Bars Data on Miller Romance." *New York Times* 22 May 1957: 17.

A short news article detailing Miller's lawyer, Joe Rauh Jr.'s charge that HUAC had called Miller as a witness in order to "get some of the publicity he was receiving as Miss Monroe's suitor." Federal Judge McLaughlin ruled that Miller's romance with Monroe was "irrelevant and immaterial" to his trial.

"Miller Trial Ends; Verdict Postponed." *New York Times* 24 May 1957: 9.

Six-paragraph news piece announcing the ending of Miller's trial for contempt of Congress. The verdict is to be handed down at a later date.

Kalven, Harry, Jr. "A View from the Law." *New Republic* 27 May 1957: 8–13.

Kalven, a professor of law at the University of Chicago, in a lengthy essay, details Miller's appearance before HUAC with a focus on the legal implications and case law relating to his refusal to name names when asked to do so during his sworn testimony.

Steinbeck, John. "The Trial of Arthur Miller." *Esquire* June 1957: 86. Rpt. in *Contemporary Moral Issues*. Ed. Harry K. Girvetz. Belmont, Calif.: Wadsworth, 1969. 97–100. Rpt. in *Esquire* October 1973: 238, 446, 448,

Steinbeck offers a hypothetical situation of his standing trial for contempt of Congress, as is Miller, and what he would do and think were that the case.

"Playwright in Trouble." *New York Times* 1 June 1957: 8.

Long piece in the same issue of the *Times* as the article announcing Miller's conviction in his contempt of Congress case. In this article, Miller's life and literary career are profiled. A large photo of Miller and Monroe accompany the text.

Allsop, Kenneth. "Arthur Miller: Act II." *Economist* 1 June 1957: 790.

Article detailing the events and the legalities of Miller's trial for contempt of Congress for refusing to name names before HUAC.

Loftus, Joseph A. "Miller Convicted in Contempt Case." *New York Times* 1 June 1957: 1, 8.

Front page news article announcing Miller's conviction in his contempt of Congress trial. Sentence is to be announced at a later date. Maximum penalty is a year in jail and $1,000 fine. But, the article continues, "Judges seldom impose the maximum in these cases and no one has been imprisoned recently for refusing to talk about others when he has been frank about himself."

"Innocent and Guilty." *Newsweek* 10 June 1957: 32.

Half-page article detailing Miller's trial for contempt of Congress. A large photo of Miller and Monroe accompanies the text.

"Morality and Law." *Commonweal* 14 June 1957: 268–69.

Support piece that criticizes the Court's ruling of finding Miller guilty of contempt of Congress as an attack on the right of individuals to follow their conscience and a validation of those "Americans who fail to see that a defense of the democratic rights of American Communists is a defense, not of Communism, but of democracy."

Rovere, Richard H. "Arthur Miller's Conscience." *New Republic* 17 June 1957. 13–15. Rpt. as "The Conscience of Arthur Miller" in *The American Establishment and Other Reports, Opinions and Speculations*. New York: Harcourt, 1962. 276–84. Rpt. in *Contemporary Moral Issues*. Ed. Harry K. Girvetz. Belmont, Calif.: Wadsworth, 1963. 101–5. Rpt. in *The Crucible: Text and Criticism*. Ed. Gerald Weales. New York: Viking, 1971. New York: Penguin, 1996. 315–23.

Against the frame of Miller's testimony before HUAC, Rovere looks closely at "Miller's social ethic and at what he has been saying about the problems of conscience" in his plays and political life.

"Inquiry Reform Seen Inevitable." *New York Times* 19 June 1957: 16.

News item reporting that Miller is asking a federal court to throw out his conviction of contempt of Congress on the same grounds as those of John T. Watkins whose conviction was recently overturned.

"Testimony of Susan Warren (Susan Mildred Heiligman Frank), Accompanied by Counsel, Ira Gollobin." United States Congress, House, Committee on Un-American Activities. *Investigation of the Unauthorized Use of United States Passports, 85th Congress, 1st Session,* Part 5, June 26, 1957. Washington: United States Government Printing Office, 1957, pp. 1345–61.

Focuses on Susan Warren's alleged Communist affiliation, travel abroad without a passport, and recommendation of playwright Arthur Miller for membership in the Communist Party, U.S.A. Includes copy of infamous unsigned Communist Party application card submitted as evidence against Miller.

"Judge Reaffirms Guilt of Miller." *New York Times* 29 June 1957: 4.

Full column news article detailing Judge McLaughlin's reaffirmation of Miller's earlier conviction for contempt of Congress, but reversing himself on the second of two counts in which he had found Miller guilty a month before.

"One Round for Congress." *US News and World Report* 5 July 1957: 12.

News item reporting that Judge McLaughlin has refused to set aside Miller's contempt of Congress conviction.

"When Silence Is Contempt of Congress." *US News and World Report* 7 July 1957: 14.

Article reporting Miller's conviction of contempt of Congress for refusing to name names before HUAC.

Huston, Luther A. "Teacher Cleared in Contempt Case." *New York Times* 10 July 1957: 18.

News item reporting that Miller's lawyer, Joseph Rauh Jr. is going to make the case of Marcus Singer the basis of a new appeal for Miller. Singer's conviction for contempt has just been set aside.

"New Plea by Miller." *New York Times* 17 July 1957: 3.

Short news piece reporting that attorneys for Miller asked Judge McLaughlin to reverse himself and acquit him on his contempt of Congress conviction.

"Arthur Miller Fined; Plans an Appeal." *New York Times* 20 July 1957: 4.

Short news piece announcing Miller's penalty (fined $1,000 and given a suspended one-month jail sentence) for his conviction in his contempt of Congress conviction. Miller's decision to appeal this ruling is detailed. A large photo of a laughing Miller accompanies the text.

"Miller Asks Reversal." *New York Times* 26 July 1957: 8.
Short news piece that reports Miller's request for a reversal of his contempt of Congress conviction.

Lewis, Anthony. "A Red-Party Form Linked to Miller." *New York Times* 25 August 1957: 20.
Full-column news piece reporting that HUAC produced an application, dated 1943, for Communist Party membership in Miller's name. The card was not signed, making it a possibility that the card had been filled out by someone without Miller's knowledge.

"Curtain." *Newsweek* 29 July 1957: 26, 29.
Article detailing Miller's sentence for his conviction of contempt of Congress: a $500 fine, a one month suspended jail sentence, and three months of probation.

Hamilton, Jack. "Marilyn's New Life." *Look* 1 October 1957: 110–15.
Lengthy article full of blissful black-and-white photographs of the happy newlyweds at home in Connecticut.

1958

"Ten Are Elected to Arts Institute." *New York Times* 11 February 1958: 28.
News item reporting Miller's election as a member of the National Institute of Arts and Letters.

"Miller Files Appeal." *New York Times* 22 February 1958: 6.
Short news article detailing the filing of a brief by Miller's lawyer contending that HUAC had used his romance with Marilyn Monroe to seek publicity for itself.

Knox, Sanka. "Prizes Are Given in Arts, Letters." *New York Times* 22 May 1958: 31.
Item reporting Miller's induction into the American Academy and the National Institute of Arts and Letters, for "distinguished achievement in literature and the arts."

"Arthur Miller's Appeal Slated." *New York Times* 28 May 1958: 21.
Two-sentence news item reporting that the U.S. Court of Appeals had agreed to hear Miller's appeal of his contempt of Congress conviction.

"Miller in Court Plea." *New York Times* 12 June 1958: 26.
Short news piece reporting that Miller's attorneys asked the Federal Court of Appeals to throw out his contempt of Congress conviction.

Lewis, Anthony. "Miller Is Cleared of House Contempt." *New York Times* 8 August 1958: 1, 7.
Front page news report announcing the unanimous reversal of Miller's conviction of contempt of Congress. The U.S. Court of Appeals ruled that HUAC "had not sufficiently warned the playwright of the risk of contempt if he refused to answer its questions. The court ordered him acquitted." Large photo of a smiling Miller accompanies the text on page 7.

"Arthur Miller Cleared of Contempt of Congress." *Publisher's Weekly* 18 August 1958: 31–32.
Item reporting the reversal of Miller's conviction of contempt of Congress.

1959

"Gold Medal Winners." *New York Times* 28 January 1959: 21.
News item reporting that Miller is the recipient of the Gold Medal for drama from the National Institute of Arts and Letters for "distinguished achievement characterizing the entire work of the recipient."

Calta, Louis. "Phoenix Begins Subscriber Drive." *New York Times* 29 April 1959: 28.
In an article reporting a subscription drive for the Phoenix Theatre, Miller is quoted offering his praise of the six-year-old New York theatre organization as "a new element which has never been seen in this country, namely, a theatre which we hope will ultimately be comparable to the Old Vic and the Comédie Française."

"Arthur Miller to Be Honored." *New York Times* 9 September 1959: 50.
News item reporting that Miller is soon to be honored by the American Friends of Hebrew University in Philadelphia for his "distinguished achievement in dramatic arts."

1960

"Soviet to Print Arthur Miller." *New York Times* 11 August 1960: 6.

News item announcing that a Moscow publisher plans to publish a collection of Miller's plays, including *All My Sons, Death of a Salesman, The Crucible*, and *A View from the Bridge.*

Calta, Louis. "Marilyn Monroe to Divorce Miller." *New York Times* 12 November 1960: 1, 14.

Front page news article announcing Miller and Monroe's marital separation and decision to file for divorce. Unrelated, but eerily, there appears a large family photo of President Kennedy, Jackie, and Caroline adjacent to the divorce story.

"Tragic Beauty; Marilyn Monroe." *New York Times* 12 November 1960: 14.

Two-column profile of the life of Marilyn Monroe, including her three failed marriages. This article appears in the same issue, and next to the second page, of the announcement of Miller and Monroe's separation and divorce.

"Out of the Fish Bowl." *Newsweek* 21 November 1960: 37.

Describing Miller as a "tall, introspective egghead," this five-paragraph article announces the breakup of Miller and Monroe.

"End of a Famous Marriage." *Life* 21 November 1960: 88A–90.

Brief report of the separation of Miller and wife Marilyn Monroe, accompanied by five black-and-white photographs (some by Inge Morath) from the set of *The Misfits*. The article reports that the cause of the breakup is this: "Marilyn's work requires her to live amid crowds while Miller needs solitude."

"Popsie and Poopsie." *Time* 21 November 1960: 61.

Article that reports Miller and Monroe's plans to divorce.

1961

Zolotow, Maurice. *Marilyn Monroe*. New York: Bantam, 1961. 255–67.

Biography of Monroe that was written before her death and while she was still married to Miller. Zolotow sees *The Crucible* and *A View from the Bridge* as "triangle plays" that were written in an effort for Miller to work through his guilt at being attracted to Monroe while still married to first wife Mary Grace Slattery.

"Marilyn Monroe Sues." *New York Times* 22 January 1961: 86.
News item announcing that Marilyn Monroe has filed suit for divorce from Miller on the grounds of "incompatibility of character" in Juarez, Mexico. The couple have been separated since November and it is expected that the divorce will be final in a few days.

"Miss Monroe Divorced." *New York Times* 25 January 1961: 35.
Short news column announcing Monroe's trip to Juarez, Mexico, to get a divorce from Miller on the grounds of "incompatibility of character."

"Arthur Miller's Mother Dies." *New York Times* 7 March 1961: 35.
Single paragraph news report announcing the death of Miller's mother, Augusta, aged 70, of a heart ailment.

Archer, Eugene. "Pirated U.S. Play Filmed in Soviet." *New York Times* 10 March 1961: 24.
Archer reports that a Russian film company (Lenfilm) has made a movie of Miller's *Death of a Salesman* entitled *The Bridge Cannot Be Crossed*. Miller is reported as contemplating legal action against this possible copyright infringement.

"Church Upheld on Play." *New York Times* 10 November 1961: 11.
News item reporting that the Circuit Court in Milford, Connecticut, has ruled that the Sunday performance of Miller's *All My Sons* does not violate the state statute against works containing "objectionable content." The complaint was filed by the Citizens' Anti-Communist Committee, which cited Miller's HUAC testimony in their request.

1962

Alpert, Hollis. "An Afternoon with Marilyn Monroe, a Memory." *The Dreams and The Dreamers*. New York: Macmillan, 1962. Rpt. in *Marilyn Monroe: A Composite View*. Ed. Edward Wagenknecht. Philadelphia: Chilton, 1969. 39–44.
Alpert recounts an afternoon in August of 1959 when he was invited by his friend Joe Wohlhandler to assist him in helping Marilyn Monroe move her television set, which she was attempting to transport from her New York apartment to her home with Miller in Connecticut.

Calta, Louis. "Miller Donates Papers." *New York Times* 13 February 1962: 38.

News item reporting that Miller has donated his manuscripts —original drafts, revised and final versions—to the University of Texas Humanities Research Center in Austin, from his first play, *They Too Arise* to *The Crucible*.

"Arthur Miller Rewed." *New York Times* 22 February 1962: 19.

Short news article announcing Miller's marriage to Ingeborg Morath and details of their wedding.

Levy, Alan. "'A Good Long Look at Myself.'" *Redbook* August 1962. Rpt. in *Marilyn Monroe: A Composite View*. Ed. Edward Wagenknecht. Philadelphia: Chilton, 1969. 16–36.

Lengthy essay/interview in which Levy tries to discover the facts surrounding Marilyn Monroe's "state of mind" following her divorce from Arthur Miller, including quips by both Miller and Monroe's friends and associates.

Meryman, Richard. "Fame May Go By . . ." *Life* 3 August 1962. 31–38. Rpt. in *Marilyn Monroe: A Composite View*. Ed. Edward Wagenknecht. Philadelphia: Chilton, 1969. 3–15.

In this, her final interview, Marilyn Monroe discusses her views on fame and its effects on her life, her childhood in foster families, her struggle with shyness, and her continuing relationship with former husband Arthur Miller's father, Isadore.

Kirstein, Lincoln. "Marilyn Monroe: 1926–1962." *Nation* 25 August 1962. Rpt. in *Marilyn Monroe: A Composite View*. Ed. Edward Wagenknecht. Philadelphia: Chilton, 1969. 114–24.

In this essay memorializing Marilyn Monroe, Kirstein remarks that *The Misfits* "unlike her other films, is not essentially about her performance, or about an artist performing. It is about the almost pornographic horror of a famous man who is actually dying [Clark Gable] and a famous woman who is having a nervous breakdown."

"Arthur Millers Have Child." *New York Times* 29 September 1962: 15.

Brief blurb announcing the birth of Rebecca Augusta (named after Miller's mother) on 15 September Miller's daughter by Inge Morath.

1963

Schreiber, Flora Rheta. "Remembrance of Marilyn." *Good Housekeeping* January 1963. Rpt. in *Marilyn Monroe: A Composite View*. Ed. Edward Wagenknecht. Philadelphia: Chilton, 1969. 45–54.

Poignant profile and interview with Isadore Miller, Arthur's father, on the occasion of the death of his ex-daughter-in-law Marilyn Monroe. Says the elder Miller upon hearing of Monroe's death, "I chose to believe Marilyn was alive because I wanted so desperately to believe it."

"The Literary Wars." *New York Times* 8 October 1963: 37.

Brief news item from Roxbury, Connecticut, reporting that Miller lost an election to a post as a board of director of the Roxbury Library by four votes. Three posts were up for election, the winners being William Styron, John H. Humphrey, and Manfred Lee, the co-author of *Ellery Queen*.

Arnold, Martin. "Artists to Appeal for Space at Fair." *New York Times* 18 November 1963: 35.

Item reporting Miller's appeal, as a member of the Committee of Artists' Societies, for an art pavilion at the New York World's Fair.

1964

Avedon, Richard. *Nothing Personal*. New York: Atheneum, 1964. n.p.

Oversized book that contains an extreme black-and-white closeup photograph of Miller.

Wagenknecht, Edward. *Seven Daughters of the Theater*. Norman, Okla.: University of Oklahoma Press, 1964. 191–92, 202–9. Portion rpt. as "Rosemary for Remembrance" in *Marilyn Monroe: A Composite View*. Ed. Edward Wagenknecht. Philadelphia: Chilton, 1969. 162–200.

In this lengthy essay that surveys the life and career of Marilyn Monroe, Wagenknecht lambastes Miller for writing *After the Fall*, a play he calls "the most outrageous violation of privacy in the history of the drama. . . . To draw such a portrait of a person you have been married to (especially when she is no longer in a position to call you to account for it) would be unpardonable in my book even if everything stated were true and set forth in a straightforward factual account, but Mr. Miller has done something inconceivably worse than this by mixing his facts with obvious and demonstrable fictions and thus leaving his readers and his audiences without the necessary data to decide what, if anything, he wishes to affirm or to stand by."

"*Saturday Evening Post* to Print Miller's Plays." *New York Times* 11 January 1964: 15.

Item reporting that Miller's *After the Fall* will appear in the *Saturday Evening Post*. For the rights, the *Post* is playing in the "five figure range."

Calta, Louis. "*After the Fall* Is Sought Abroad." *New York Times* 8 February 1964: 15.

Calta reports that seventeen countries have acquired the rights to *After the Fall* while eleven are still in negotiation. Also noted is that Miller and his family are in Paris for a three-month stay.

Thompson, Howard. "*After the Fall* Bought for Film." *New York Times* 27 June 1964: 14.

Item announcing that Carlo Ponti and Ira Steiner have purchased the screen rights to *After the Fall* for 500,000. Miller will write the screenplay and Sophia Loren and Paul Newman will star.

"East Side Theater to Stage *View from the Bridge* in Fall." *New York Times* 25 July 1964: 11.

News item reporting that Miller is giving special permission for a new nonprofit theatre, the Fair World Theatre, to do three performances of *A View from the Bridge* without paying royalties. Miller is quoted as supporting the theatre for its desire to produce works that are socially meaningful. "The concept of getting people in the area engaged in cultural activity is a good one."

"Miller Reads New Play to Repertory Troupe." *New York Times* 27 August 1964: 28.

Brief news item reporting that Miller has read his new play, *Incident at Vichy*, to members of the Lincoln Center Repertory Company.

Esterow, Milton. "Lincoln Center Defied by Bliss." *New York Times* 7 December 1964: 45.

In a story reporting that the president of the Metropolitan Opera has refused to release assistant manager Herman Krawitz to become the managing director of the Lincoln Center for the Performing

Arts, Miller is briefly quoted regarding his relationship with the Repertory Theater. Says Miller, "My future relationship will depend upon conditions at the time I have another play."

Funke, Lewis. "Robert Whitehead Looks Forward." *New York Times* 27 December 1964: Sec. II: 1.

Funke reports that on the departure of producing director Robert Whitehead, Miller is expected to withdraw both *After the Fall* and *Incident at Vichy* from the Lincoln Center Repertory Theater Company.

1965

Hoyt, Edwin P. *Marilyn, the Tragic Venus*. New York: Duell, Sloan and Pearce, 1965. 182–235, 246–66, 257–58.

Often inaccurate account of the life of Marilyn Monroe that seems to rely heavily on gossip and innuendo for its "facts." Of note is the scathing psychological account of Miller, who Hoyt describes as "a woman's man" who "had been suckled by his first wife, smothered by his mother, cleansed by Marilyn, and now had found a mature woman [Inge Morath] to support his need."

Zolotow, Sam. "Lincoln Center Troupe to Drop Three Dramas from Repertory." *New York Times* 1 January 1965: 10.

Zolotow reports that Miller has withdrawn his *After the Fall* and *Incident at Vichy* from the repertoire of the Lincoln Center Repertory Theater Company in a dispute over operations.

Prideaux, Tom. "The Center That Set Off a Tempest." *Life* 22 January 1965: 42–43, 46.

Essay detailing the Lincoln Center controversy. Includes a large black-and-white photograph of Miller and Kazan sitting on a dock working on a script.

"Arthur Miller Declares *Pravda* 'Twisted' Play." *New York Times* 3 February 1965: 30.

News item reporting that Miller, in a Moscow interview, has denounced a review of *Incident at Vichy* that appeared in *Pravda*, which stated that the communist character had made the sacrifice for the Jew rather than the Austrian.

Halberstam, David. "Polish Students Question Miller." *New York Times* 17 February 1965: 36.

In Warsaw for rehearsals of a Polish production of *After the*

Fall, Miller gives a lecture and answers questions in an American literature class at the University of Warsaw. Halberstam reports that Miller's plays are popular in Poland because their themes are acceptable to the Polish government.

Nichols, Lewis. "In and Out of Books: Politics." *New York Times* 23 May 1965. 8.

In opposition to Miller's nomination as President of PEN International, the French have nominated Miguel-Angel Asturias.

"PEN Pals." *Newsweek* 26 July 1965. 92.

Article detailing the events at the PEN Annual Congress in Dubrovnik, Yugoslavia, at which Miller was named president of PEN International.

Fletcher, Adele Whitely. ". . . So That the Memory of Marilyn Will Linger On . . ." *Photoplay* September 1965. Rpt. in *Marilyn Monroe: A Composite View*. Ed. Edward Wagenknecht. Philadelphia: Chilton, 1969. 80–89.

In an essay recounting the author's memories of Marilyn Monroe three years after her death, Fletcher relates her experiences of visiting Miller and Monroe at their New York apartment with Elsa Maxwell, who was doing a piece on Monroe.

"Arthur Miller Spurns Invitation by Johnson." *New York Times* 28 September 1965: Sec. II: 2.

News item reporting that Miller has declined an invitation by President Johnson to attend the signing of the Arts and Humanities Act because of his opposition to the president's policy on Vietnam.

Cooke, Alistair. "Arthur Miller Tangles with LBJ." *Guardian* (London) 28 September 1965: 24.

News item reporting that Miller has declined an invitation by President Johnson to attend the signing of the Arts and Humanities Act because of his opposition to the president's policy on Vietnam.

1966

Gould, Jean. "Arthur Miller." *Modern American Playwrights*. New York: Dodd, Mead, 1966. 247–90.

Fairly accurate biographical essay covering Miller's life and career through *Incident at Vichy* (1964). Gould proclaims that Miller "is a popular playwright because he has the touch of common speech mingled with democratic idealism, poetic expression, and an ancient people's capacity for understanding the anguish of the soul."

"Arthur Miller, New York, 1966." *John Jonas Gruen, Facing the Artist.* Justin Spring. Munich: Pretel Verlag, 1999. 59.

Photograph of Miller in 1966 smoking a cigarette at a piano, looking left.

Walker, Alexander. *Celluloid Sacrifice.* New York: Hawthorn, 1966. Portion rpt. as "Body and Soul: Harlow and Monroe" in *Marilyn Monroe: A Composite View.* Ed. Edward Wagenknecht. Philadelphia: Chilton, 1969. 148–61.

In an essay comparing sex symbols Jean Harlow and Marilyn Monroe, Walker discusses Monroe's last film *The Misfits* (calling it "in hindsight" rather similar to *After the Fall*) and remarking that "the actress who made seriousness her aim has ended by making soulfulness her achievement."

"Arthur Miller Has Hepatitis." *New York Times* 20 January 1966: 29.

News item reporting that while in Brighton for the pre-production run of *Incident at Vichy*, Miller has been hospitalized with hepatitis.

"Miller Lauds PEN as Congress Closes." *New York Times* 19 June 1966: 84.

At the closing session of the International PEN Congress, Miller spoke about the organization's impact and called for writers to "emphasize that which is similar among us, isolate what separates us, resolve our differences and put aside those things that we cannot resolve."

Shepard, Richard. F. "*Times* Considers 2 Drama Reviews." *New York Times* 11 October 1966: 55.

At the urging of Miller, the *New York Times* is considering presenting two critical views on theatre, one as a daily and another in the Sunday drama section of the newspaper. Miller is quoted at a meeting of the Drama Desk association as being dissatisfied with the current state of theatre criticism in New York City. "We are slaves to published criticism in this country. People are being told what to think. I would like to see it broken up a little by a displacement of authority." When asked if he would like the job writing 1,000 words in fifty minutes, Miller responded with "I couldn't do it well, but I could do it as well as it is being done."

1967

Sorell, Walter. *The Story of the Human Hand*. New York: Bobbs-Merrill, 1967. 180–81, 184.

Analyzing the palm print of Arthur Miller (included on p. 184), Sorell concludes that "Miller's hand is one of inner conflict which accepts the outside challenge in order to react creatively to it. . . . The realistic brain line demands that there must be purpose to everything that is being done. But in spite of the dominating intellect, his is an intuitive approach to the creative process. . . . It could be a sculptor's or an architect's hand. It could be the hand of a farmer."

Raymont, Henry. "Harriet De Onis Gets Book Prize." *New York Times* 9 May 1967: 44.

Brief mention of Miller as being elected to an additional two-year term as president of PEN International.

"Writers Appeal on Soviet Jews." *New York Times* 21 May 1967: 12.

Miller is mentioned as among many writers who have signed a letter, written by Robert Penn Warren, that urges Russian writers to use their influence to help restore Jewish cultural institutions in their country.

"PEN Congress Urges Release of Writers." *New York Times* 1 August 1967: 33.

News item that mentions Miller as being reelected as president of PEN International at a Congress held in Abidjan.

Lask, Thomas. "18 Leading Poets and Writers Give Reading Stressing Peace." *New York Times* 13 November 1967: 60.

Miller is mentioned as participating in "Poets for Peace," an event held in New York City, sponsored by the Fellowship of Reconciliation. Miller read "prose comment" entitled "Why Kill a Nation No One Hates?"

1968

"Notes and Comments." *New Yorker* 13 January 1968: 19.

Opinion piece that attacks Miller for criticizing Americans who do not publicly stand either for or against the war in Vietnam, saying that such an act "is a step of limited value."

Borders, William. "Democrats Begin Hartford Battle." *New York Times* 22 June 1968: 19.

News item reporting that at a meeting of the resolutions committee of the Democratic Party in Connecticut, Miller offered a resolution calling for the immediate cessation of American bombing of North Vietnam and asking for peace negotiations to begin.

"Newman and Miller Named Delegates to Convention." *New York Times* 10 July 1968: 43.

News item reporting that Paul Newman and Miller have been named as Eugene McCarthy delegates from Connecticut to the Democratic National Convention, to be held in Chicago in August.

Gilroy, Harry. "Writers Life Voices at Cheetah Gala for McCarthy." *New York Times* 15 August 1968. 34.

Miller read sketch, "The Reason Why," to help raise money for the McCarthy campaign.

"Solzhenitsyn Plea Sent to Podgorny." *New York Times* 15 August 1968: 14.

Miller is mentioned as among the writers who have signed a letter, written by Rolf Hochhuth to Nikolai V. Podgorny (the Soviet head of state), that pleads for the elimination of the ban on the works of Solzhenitsyn.

Raymont, Henry. "Roundup of Writers in Prague Reported." *New York Times* 31 August 1968: 1, 2.

Miller is reported to be appealing to American writers to sign an appeal to the Soviet government to stop holding and beating Czech writers.

"Yevtushenko's Career." *New York Times* 8 December 1968: Sec. 4: 13.

Expatriate Polish writer Leopold Tyrmano strongly criticizes Miller and William Styron for their support for the Russian writer Yevgeny Yevtushenko. See interviews by Fosburgh and MacBeath for Miller's comments.

1969

Dekle, Bernard. "Arthur Miller: Spokesman of the 'Little Man.'" *Profiles of Modern American Authors*. Rutland, Vt.: Tuttle, 1969. 147–53.

Biographical essay that includes a brief analysis of *All My Sons*, *Death of a Salesman*, and *The Crucible*, the three plays that "have established him as one of this century's most important American dramatists."

Guiles, Fred Lawrence. *Norma Jean: The Life of Marilyn Monroe*. New York: McGraw Hill, 1969. Revised as *Legend: The Life and Death of Marilyn Monroe*. New York: Stein and Day, 1984.

Fairly accurate account of the life of Marilyn Monroe that includes a chapter entitled "Marilyn Miller" that details the couple's relationship from courtship through divorce.

"15 Americans Meet Soviet Group in Rye." *New York Times* 21 January 1969: 3.

Miller is mentioned as participating in the fifth Dartmouth Conference of U.S. and Russian citizens who support arms control.

Raymont, Henry. "Miller Refused Greek Book Plan." *New York Times* 3 July 1969: 29.

Raymont reports that Miller has refused to allow his books to be published in Greece until their "repressive" policies against writers ends.

———. "PEN Congress May Discuss Censorship of Soviet Writers." *New York Times* 12 August 1969: 36. Rpt. in *Times* (London) 13 August 1969: 1.

Miller is reported to be urging debate on the conditions in Russia that led to the defection of Soviet writer Anatoly Kuznetsov.

Shenker, Israel. "Arthur Miller Expresses Criticism of the Soviet Literary Scene." *New York Times* 17 August 1969: 26.

Shenker offers a summary of Miller's trip to the Soviet Union, which will be published in *Harper's* in September and then as a book entitled *In Russia*.

Brown, Frances. "Miller Opens PEN Congress in France." *New York Times* 16 September 1969. 43.

Brown offers details of the opening of the 36th International PEN Congress, including Miller's appeal to young writers to "make it apparent that the writer belongs to the street and not to the power."

"Sixteen Western Intellectuals Score Soviet Attacks on Solzhenitsyn." *New York Times* 5 December 1969. 47.

Miller is mentioned as among a group of writers who have signed a letter condemning the expulsion of Solzhenitsyn from his home country of Russia.

1970

Svendsen, Clara (text), and Frans Lasson (editor). *The Life and Destiny of Isak Dinesen.* New York: Random House, 1970: 198.

Large photograph of Miller, Marilyn Monroe, Carson McCullers, and Karen Blixen in McCuller's home in Nyack, January 1959.

"Teacher Backed in Stand on Pledge." *New York Times* 23 February 1970: 24.

Miller is mentioned as among a group of residents of Roxbury, Connecticut, who have signed a statement protesting the suspension of a teacher who refused to say the pledge of allegiance in her classroom.

"Brandeis Lands Two Generations in Arts Awards." *New York Times* 18 May 1970. 38.

News item reporting Miller as the recipient of the Creative Arts Award from Brandeis University for his "eloquent and stirring statements—in drama, story, and social action."

Gwertzman, Bernard. "Soviet Asks Tight Ideology Curb." *New York Times* 24 November 1970: 3.

Gwertzman reports that Miller's plays have been removed from the Soviet theatre repertoire because, he believes, of the book that Miller and wife Morath published on their journey there (*In Russia*).

Sidorsky, David. "Miller Disputed on Solzhenitsyn." *New York Times* 26 December 1970: 16.

Opinion piece in which Sidorsky expresses his disagreement

with Miller's essay "Banned in Russia" (*New York Times* 10 December 1970) that says that Solzhenitsyn had confined his attacks on the Russian system to Stalin. Says Sidorsky in *The First Circle*, Solzhenitsyn condemned many aspects of the current regime as well as Western fellow-travelers.

1971

Funke, Lewis. "By Arthur Miller." *New York Times* 7 February 1971: II: 1, 22.

News item announcing that Miller's new play will be based on *Hard Times* by Studs Terkel and center on the Great Depression.

Gwertzman, Bernard. "Jews in Soviet Are Warned against Espousing Zionism." *New York Times* 20 February 1971: 1–2.

Gwertzman reports that Miller is among those who are criticized in an article in *Isvestia* for their participation in a conference held in Brussels composed of Jewish organizations seeking to bring world attention to the Jewish situation in Russia.

Anderson, Robert, et al. "Repression in Brazil." *New York Times* 24 April 1971: 28.

Miller is among a group of writers who have signed a letter protesting the arrest and harassment of Augusto Boal after his return to Brazil from his U.S. visit.

"Notes on People." *New York Times* 9 December 1971: 59.

Brief news item reporting that Miller has been elected to the 50-member inner body of the National Institute of Arts and Letters called the American Academy of Arts and Letters.

1972

Bentley, Eric. *Theatre of War: Comments on 32 Occasions*. New York: Viking, 1972. 228.

In a chapter entitled "Thoughts on the Student Discontents," Bentley briefly mentions Miller as having brought up the issue that the United States government does not seem to want to stop the killing in Vietnam when President Johnson publicly declared that the Vietnamese have refused to negotiate, when, in fact, they have made such an offer. [See Miller's essay "Are We Interested in Stopping the Killing?" *New York Times* 8 June 1969: Sec. 2: 21.]

Carlisle, Olga, and Rose Styron. "Biographical Note." *Writers at Work: The Paris Review Interviews, Third Series*. Ed. George Plimpton. New York: Viking, 1972. 179.

Brief biographical note introducing a lengthy interview with the playwright at his home in Roxbury, Connecticut.

"Writers Seek to Bar Jailing of Ginzburg." *New York Times* 14 February 1972: 26.

News item reporting that forty writers, editors, and publishers, calling themselves the Committee for a Free Press, have issued a series of statements "deploring the imminent jailing of Ralph Ginzburg, who was convicted nine years ago of charges of mailing obscene materials." Miller is listed as among the group, and his letter, reprinted in the advertisement of 17 February, is quoted at length.

Janson, Donald. "Ginzburg Begins 3-Year Term for 1963 Obscenity Conviction." *New York Times* 18 February 1972: 16.

News item reporting the beginning of the prison sentence of publisher Ralph Ginzburg on an obscenity conviction for distributing a short-lived magazine called *Eros*. Miller's protest from the full-page advertisement printed 17 February is quoted at length.

McClean, Lydia. "A View from the Country: A Weekend with the Arthur Miller's." *Vogue* 15 March 1972: 102–9, 114.

Rare intimate photographic essay of Miller and family at his home in Roxbury, Connecticut, including relaxed laughing images of Miller, Morath, and daughter Rebecca, scenes from the interior of their almost two-hundred-year-old farmhouse, images from a picnic by the lake with poet Andrei Voznesensky and his wife, and various shots of Miller and Morath around their property.

Raymont, Henry. "U.S. Bars Cubans from Film Event." *New York Times* 24 March 1972: 8.

Miller is mentioned as among a group of writers protesting the U.S. State Department's refusal to issue temporary visas to four Cuban filmmakers so that they might participate in the First New York Festival of Cuban Films.

Corry, John. "Intellectuals in Bloom at Spring Gathering." *New York Times* 18 May 1972: 49.

Brief mention of Miller as present at the awards ceremony for the American Academy of Arts and Letters.

Clarity, James. "Notes on People." *New York Times* 31 May 1972: 37.

Brief news item reporting that Miller has donated a manuscript of a new, as yet unproduced, play to an auction hoping to raise funds for the Fellowship of Reconciliation, a group seeking a non-violent solution to the problems of keeping peace. The auction is to be held at the Vandam Theatre in Greenwich Village on 12 June 1972.

Ailey, Alvin, et al. "Dismissal of Kirov Dancer." *New York Times* 19 June 1972: 32.

Miller is mentioned as among a group of artists who have signed a letter protesting the dismissal of Jewish dancer Valery Panov from the Kirov State Dance Theatre, after he emigrated to Israel.

1973

Carpozi, George, Jr. *Marilyn Monroe: "Her Own Story."* New York: Universal-Award House, 1973.

Surprisingly accurate account of Miller and Monroe's romance and marriage with details of the wedding ceremony not seen before. Photos of the couple accompany the text.

Gross, Theodore L. "Arthur Miller." *The Literature of American Jews*. New York: Free Press, 1973. 239.

Brief biographical essay serving as an introduction to a reprint of Miller's short story "Monte Sant' Angelo," quoted as being the "only story" the playwright liked.

Mailer, Norman. *Marilyn*. New York: Grosset and Dunlap, 1973.

Biography of the life of Marilyn Monroe that presents a rather negative picture of Miller as Monroe's jealous and overbearing husband. Of note are the photographs by Inge Morath and Eve Arnold, among many others, of the couple's life and the filming of *The Misfits*.

Rosten, Norman. *Marilyn: An Untold Story*. New York: Signet, 1973. Portion rpt. as "Dear Marilyn" in *Marilyn Monroe: A Composite View*. Ed. Edward Wagenknecht. Philadelphia: Chilton, 1969. 90–106.

First-person account of Rosten's friendship with Marilyn Monroe. As a long-time friend and one-time collaborator of Miller's, Rosten offers his reading of Miller/Monroe relationship, including personal anecdotes and conversations. Of note is Rosten's memories regarding Miller's appearance before HUAC, which is somewhat at odds with the playwright's chronology of events. Rosten's own personal snapshots of Monroe and Miller accompany the text.

"5 in Various Fields Chosen for Awards." *New York Times* 4 May 1973: 27.

Brief news item reporting that Miller has been chosen to receive the Albert Einstein Commemorative Award from Yeshiva University for "extraordinary contributions to American letters and his devotion to cultural freedom."

Clarity, James. "Notes on People." *New York Times* 31 July 1973: 34.

Brief item reporting that Miller will soon take on the role of adjunct professor-in-residence at the University of Michigan where he will conduct informal seminars and advise the faculty on theatrical matters.

Calta, Louis. "News of the Stage." *New York Times* 4 November 1973: 83.

Short item reporting that Miller has given special permission to the Philadelphia Drama Guild, a community theatre that turned professional in 1971, to mount a production of *Death of a Salesman*, even though the Walnut Street Theatre is within 100 miles of Broadway. Previously, Miller had not allowed any productions of this play to be performed near New York for fear that the production would be reviewed as a professional work. Says Miller, "I think this group has the capacity to do the play." The Guild's production stars Martin Balsom and John Randolph and will run for three weeks.

1974

Ciment, Michael. "Working with Schulberg: *On the Waterfront* (1954), *A Face in the Crowd* (1957)." *Kazan on Kazan*. New York: Viking, 1974. 102.

In an interview on the subject of *On the Waterfront*, Kazan discusses working with Miller on a film about longshoremen ["The Hook"] in 1951, and his annoyance at Miller for calling off the project after Kazan had "spent a lot of time on it. It was an extremely abrupt and embarrassing decision."

Clurman, Harold. *All People Are Famous (instead of an autobiography)*. New York: Harcourt, 1974. 236, 247.

Two brief but significant mentions of Miller in Clurman's autobiography. In the first, Clurman relates a story of inviting Jacqueline Kennedy to see Miller's *Incident at Vichy* but she declined saying that Miller was "in her bad books because in *After the Fall* he had been so 'horrid to Marilyn.'" In the second, Clurman offers his assessment of Miller's character—"For all his unbending seriousness and a certain coldness of manner, there is more humor in him than is generally supposed. . . . Miller practices what he preaches."

"PEN Asks Amnesty for Jailed Writers." *New York Times* 6 January 1974: 2.

Miller is mentioned as among those members of PEN to propose that the UN create an amnesty year for 380 writers who have been imprisoned for "intellectual crimes."

1975

"Writers and Actors Criticize UNESCO for Curb on Israel." *New York Times* 7 February 1975: 3.

Miller is mentioned as among a group of writers and actors who have signed a letter to UNESCO criticizing its resolutions that cut off cultural aid to Israel and deny the country membership in regional groups.

Biskind, Peter. "The Politics of Power in *On The Waterfront*." *Film Quarterly* (Fall 1975): 25–38.

In an essay examining the ideological and historical context of Elia Kazan's *On the Waterfront*, Biskind offers the opinion that Kazan's film was essentially an answer to Miller's *The Crucible*, in which the main character would rather go to his death than inform against his friends. Of note is the footnote to this passage, which states that, according to Miller, the idea for *On the Waterfront* was originally his—"he had done a considerable amount of work on a script ["The Hook"] before [Bud] Schulberg came on the film."

"U.S. Urged to Guarantee Freedom to All Writers." *New York Times* 19 November 1975: 25.

News item reporting that Miller testified before the Permanent Subcommittee on Investigations on 18 November on the United

State's obligation to guarantee freedom of author's everywhere, "to insure their work without peril of suppression, harassment, torture, or death."

"25 Sign an Appeal to Ford in Spain." *New York Times* 21 November 1975: 17.

Miller is mentioned as among a group of writers who have signed a letter to President Ford urging a review of the U.S. policy toward Spain following the Franco regime.

"Colleagues Pay Tribute." *New York Times* 8 December 1975: 40.

On the death of Thornton Wilder, Miller is asked about his memories of the playwright. Says Miller, "He was magnanimous, wise, and worth listening to."

Corry, John. "Arthur Miller Turns Detective in Murder." *New York Times* 15 December 1975: 1, 46.

Lengthy front page news article detailing Miller's interest and involvement in Peter Reilly's murder case, whose conviction in the killing of his mother had "aroused his compassion."

———. "Arthur Miller and Others Contend Clock Absolves Youth Convicted of Matricide." *New York Times* 16 December 1975: 1, 47.

News item updating the case of Peter Reilly. Miller is mentioned as among those who are arguing that the conflicting accounts of time surrounding the death of Reilly's mother warrant a new trial for the youth.

1976

Barthel, Joan. *A Death in Canaan*. New York: Dutton, 1976.

Miller's involvement in securing the release of Peter Reilly, a teenager tried and convicted for the murder of his mother, is detailed in this book on the case.

Weatherby, W. J. *Conversations with Marilyn*. New York: Mason , 1976.

Fascinating collection of interviews with Monroe conducted over several years in which the actress discusses her life and career, her sex goddess image, her political beliefs, and her marriages.

Shenker, Israel. "Jewish Cultural Arts: The Big Debate." *New York Times* 13 January 1976: 42.

News item mentioning that Miller spoke on a panel on Jewish cultural arts, admitting that he has never been successful in determining where his Jewish identity "leaves off and [his] American nature begins."

Knight, Michael. "Hearing to Open on Bid for New Matricide Trial." *New York Times* 15 January 1976: 37.

On the occasion of a new hearing for Peter Reilly, Miller is reported to have set aside plans to write a new play in an effort to devote attention to proving that the teenager deserves a new trial.

———. "Reilly Freed in Miller's Murder as Suppressed Evidence Is Bared." *New York Times* 25 November 1976: Sec. 1: 1, 26.

Front page news story announcing the dropping of charges against Peter Reilly in the murder of his mother. Miller was instrumental in focusing nationwide attention on the case and funding a private investigator who discovered new evidence clearing Reilly of the crime. Photo of Miller and Reilly accompanies text.

Glueck, Grace. "Friends of Calder Honor Him." *New York Times* 8 December 1976: D22.

On the death of Alexander Calder, Miller, a close friend and neighbor of the sculptor, is quoted as praising Calder's commitment and simple decency.

1977

Browne, Malcolm. "Czech Police Hold a Dissident Writer." *New York Times* 11 January 1977: 15.

In a news story reporting the arrest of Czech dissident Pavel Kohout, Miller is quoted as urging President Carter to enforce the Helsinki accords. Says Miller, "The Czech regime is simply demonstrating to anyone who may have doubts that it is prepared to cut out a black hole in the cultural map of Europe."

Hoffman, Paul. "Czech Underground Literature Circulated Hand to Hand." *New York Times* 15 February 1977: 3.

Miller is mentioned as among fifty-four American writers who have sent a letter to Czech leader Gustav Husak protesting the recent arrests of dissidents and urging him to examine the charges as a contravention of the Helsinki accords.

1978

Arnold, Eve. *Flashback! The 50s*. New York: Knopf, 1978. 79.

Arnold's photographic essay on the 1950s in America. Included here for the shot of Miller dancing with Monroe on the set *The Misfits*.

Caute, David. "Arthur Miller and the Witches of Salem." *The Great Fear: The Anti-Communist Purge under Truman and Eisenhower*. New York: Simon and Schuster, 1978. 100, 247, 536–37.

In addition to excerpting Miller's testimony before Chairman Arens at his HUAC appearance in 1956, Caute details Miller's involvements that led to his being called before the Committee, and his past "blacklisting" by "film, television and radio companies."

Signoret, Simone. *Nostalgia Isn't What It Used to Be*. New York: Harper, 1978. 267, 276–96.

Signoret relates her memories of living next to Miller and Monroe at the Beverly Hills Hotel while her husband Yves Montand and Monroe were making *Let's Make Love*. She additionally offers her opinions as to Miller's play *After the Fall*—"I do think it's sad that the Kazan-Miller reassociation was celebrated across a box called a coffin. A coffin for a blonde. It seems to me that they disfigured her, at least in part; in any case, they betrayed what was best in her."

"Letter to Arthur Miller, 26 April 1978." *Kenneth Tynan Letters*. Ed. Kathleen Tynan. New York: Random House, 1994. 597-98.

Reprint of a letter from critic Kenneth Tynan addressed to Miller at 765 Kingman Avenue asking the playwright to write a statement of support for Tynan's "national or international recognition as a writer and journalist" in his efforts to obtain an immigrant visa. Footnote records that Miller supplied Tynan with a statement.

1979

Maslin, Janet. "Film: *On Home Ground*." *New York Times* 4 November 1979: 75.

Review of the ninety-minute CBC produced film by Harry Rasky interviewing Miller as the playwright walks around the streets of New York. Miller discusses his childhood, career, travels, and Marilyn Monroe and includes movie and television excerpts of Miller plays. Says Maslin, it is "interesting but not particularly insightful or informative" and "doesn't have the substance of an inquiry or an explanation. It's the work of a good listener."

Lask, Thomas. "Author Decries Casting of Miss Redgrave by CBS." *New York Times* 23 October 1979: C7.

News item reporting the immense dissatisfaction that Fania Fénelon has with the CBS production of her memoir *Playing for Time*. The French survivor of Auschwitz objects to both the casting of Vanessa Redgrave, a supporter of the PLO, to play her in the film and Miller's handling of the script. Says Fénelon, "The whole atmosphere is false."

1980

Navasky, Victor S. "Elia Kazan and the Case for Silence." *Naming Names*. New York: Penguin, 1980. 199–222.

Important study of the relationship between Miller and Elia Kazan before and after Kazan's friendly testimony before HUAC and Miller's own "ambiguous" testimony in 1956. Works examined include *The Crucible* and *A View from the Bridge*.

"Debut of Miller Play Planned." *Boston Globe* 18 January 1980: 17.

Short news item announcing Miller's first play in ten years, *The American Clock*, will have its world premiere at the Spoleto Festival USA.

Herman, Robin, and E. R. Shipp. "Notes on People." *New York Times* 13 March 1980: C21.

Brief item noting that Miller and Chinese playwright Cao Yu will make a joint public lecture in New York on 27 March at Columbia University on "Theatre in Modern China."

Shephard, Richard F. "A View from a Bridge between Two Cultures." *New York Times* 29 March 1980. 12.

Item that details Miller and Chinese playwright Cao Yu's lecture at Columbia University to a standing room only crowd. Miller spoke about his trip to China, compared the cultures of the United States and China, and discussed the Cultural Revolution.

Heilner, Sam. "Names and Faces." *Boston Globe* 3 April 1980:11.

Short news item reporting that sixty-five-year-old Miller rode his fifteen-year-old bicycle to Manhattan rehearsals of *The American Clock* due to a New York City transit strike.

———. "Names and Faces." *Boston Globe* 21 May 1980.

Brief news item regarding Joan Copeland's surprise at being asked by her brother, Arthur Miller, to play the lead in his new play *The American Clock.*

"Names and Faces." *Boston Globe* 18 August 1980.

Brief news item announcing the appearance of the Peking Opera in New York for the first time in fifty years. Miller is mentioned as present at the opening night reception at the Chinese mission to the UN.

Schonberg, Harold C. "Joan Copeland Remembers Mama: And so Does Her Brother Arthur." *New York Times* 16 November 1980: Sec. 2: 1, 5.

Details actress Joan Copeland's relationship with her brother Arthur Miller and her feelings about playing their mother in Miller's new work, *The American Clock.*

1981

Helterman, Jeffrey. "Arthur Miller." *Twentieth-Century American Dramatists, Part 2: K-Z*, vol. seven of *Dictionary of Literary Biography.* Ed. John MacNicholas. Detroit: Gale Research, 1981. 86–111.

Lengthy biographical statement that includes extensive plot synopsis and analysis of both major and minor works, up to *The American Clock.* Of special note are the illustrations, photographs, and reproductions that accompany the text, including playbills from *Salesman* and *After the Fall*, title page from the typescript for *Salesman* with Miller's notes, page from the revised typescript for *The Crucible*, page of handwritten notes from *After the Fall*, and sketch of the set design by Jo Mielziner for *After the Fall.*

Mailer, Norman. *Of Women and Their Elegance.* New York: Pinnacle, 1981.

Fictional first-person account of Marilyn Monroe's life written by a man who has never personally met his idol. As Monroe, Mailer discusses, at length, the Miller-Monroe attraction, marriage, and breakup.

Oppenheimer, Joel. *Marilyn Lives!* New York: Delilah Books, 1981.

In this photographic portrait of Monroe, framed by interviews with people "who loved her, cared about her, and who had been moved by her during the course of their own lives," Oppenheimer (poet and *Village Voice* columnist) includes several candid photographs of Miller and wife Monroe. Two photos of note: Miller and Monroe from behind as they walk their bikes; and a shot from above of a crowd with Miller and Monroe in the middle as the only two people looking up at the camera.

Barach, Malcolm J. "Names and Faces." *Boston Globe* 5 June 1981.

Short news item announcing Joan Copeland's (Miller's sister) winning the Drama Desk Award for her performance in her brother's semi-autobiographical play *The American Clock*, in which Copeland played their mother.

1982

Thurman, Judith. *Isak Dinesen: The Life of a Storyteller*. New York: St. Martin's, 1982. 467–68.

In this biography of the writer Dinesen, Miller and then wife Monroe are mentioned briefly as being invited by Carson McCullers to a luncheon with Isak Dinesen, who "longed to meet" Monroe. "Dinesen 'loved' Carson McCullers and enjoyed meeting Arthur Miller, but it was Marilyn who made the real impression. 'It is not that she is pretty,' she told Fluer Cowles, 'although of course she is almost incredibly pretty—but that she radiates at the same time unbounded vitality and a kind of unbelievable innocence. I have met the same in a lion cub that my native servants in Africa brought me. I would not keep her.'" A photograph of Miller, Monroe, McCullers, and Dinesen at the luncheon on 5 February 1959 is included in the text.

Fulman, Ricki. "Clayburgh Adds Her Voice to Nuclear Weapons Protest." *Boston Globe* (also *Daily News*) 10 June 1982.

In an expose of actress Jill Clayburgh's political life, Miller is mentioned as among the celebrities participating in a benefit for PAND, Performing Artists for Nuclear Disarmament, in Boston.

Bennetts, Leslie. "Broadway Producers and Dramatists Lock Horns over Antitrust Lawsuit." *New York Times* 21 August 1982: 17.

News article reporting on the antitrust lawsuit filed by the League of New York Theatres and Producers against the Dramatists Guild, protesting their royalty agreement. Miller is quoted as calling the suit "union-busting" and "absurd . . . they are attacking the main creators in the theater at the time when the theater is trying to clamber back from falling over the abyss."

1983

Barclay, Dolores. "Literary, Arts Figures Mourn the Theater's Tremendous Loss." *Boston Globe* 26 February 1983:17.

Miller is quoted in an article quoting various literary and theatrical artists regarding the late Tennessee Williams's impact on American theatre.

"Names and Faces." *Boston Globe* 21 March 1983.

Brief news item announcing Miller's arrival in Peking to direct a production of *Salesman*.

"Chinese Embrace *Salesman*." *Philadelphia Inquirer* 11 May 1983: E4.

Miller comments on his experience directing *Salesman* in China and the audience's reaction to this work's universal message.

Taylor, Maureen. "Names and Faces." *Boston Globe* 4 August 1983.

Brief news item that reveals that G. Gordon Liddy has auditioned for the role of Ben in Miller's Broadway revival of *Death of a Salesman* starring Dustin Hoffman. Liddy was invited to return for a second reading.

Rauh, Olie and Joe (as told to Harriet Lyons). "The Time Marilyn Hid Out at Our House." *Ms* 1 August 1983: 15–16.

Rauh and his wife recount the interesting story of when Miller and Monroe stayed at their Washington, D.C., home from 13–24 May 1957 during Miller's trial for contempt of Congress (Rauh was Miller's attorney). Calling it "unfair" and "wrong," both Olie and Joe express their displeasure with Miller for writing of his former wife in *After the Fall*. Of note is Miller's comment to Olie Rauh in response to her expressing how sorry she was upon hearing that the famous couple had divorced (in 1961): "I am too, and I know Marilyn is. But if I hadn't done this, I would be dead."

Barach, Malcolm J. "Names and Faces." *Boston Globe* 29 November 1983.

Brief news item that makes mention of nineteen-year-old Prince Edward's stage debut in Miller's *The Crucible*, playing the part of sixty-year-old Puritan judge.

Taylor, Maureen. "Names and Faces." *Boston Globe* 25 December 1983.

Short news item announcing Miller as the first recipient of the Alley Award, given by Houston's Alley Theatre in recognition of the playwright's contribution to the American theatre.

1984

"Brooks Atkinson, Was Drama Critic for N.Y. Times, Won Pulitzer, 89." *Boston Globe* 15 January 1984.

In an obituary for theatre critic Brooks Atkinson, Miller is quoted as praising him as "the only one who can be said to have presided over Broadway. . . . He lent the theatre a dignity and importance it did not usually merit. . . ."

Barach, Malcolm J. "Names and Faces." *Boston Globe* 26 January 1984.

News item detailing Miller's visit to Houston to receive the first Alley Theatre Award. Informal recitals of Miller's work by Arthur Kennedy, Mildred Dunnock, James Farentino, and Joan Copeland will be given during the $800 per plate dinner.

Johnson, Terry E. "Newsmakers." *Philadelphia Inquirer* 31 January 1984: E2.

Short item reporting Miller receiving the Alley Award in Houston, including the names of notables involved with the presentation and an excerpt of Miller's acceptance speech.

"Commencements." *Boston Globe* 14 May 1984.

Short news item announcing that Miller and wife Inge Morath both received honorary doctorate degrees from the University of Hartford. Miller is quoted as saying during his brief address to the graduating class, "I hope you begin your education now like we all have to do when we graduate."

Freedman, Samuel G. "*Salesman* Collaborators Part Ways." *New York Times* 15 August 1984: C17.

Lengthy news article reporting that producer Robert Whitehead has resigned from the revival of *Death of a Salesman*, starring Dustin Hoffman, just prior to the play's production for television. The source of the split with Miller is apparently due to both the financial arrangements and Mr. Whitehead's involvement with a production of *Medea* in Australia during the New York run of *Salesman* when Hoffman wanted to reduce the number of performances he played a week by two. Miller refused to comment on the disagreement saying, "I don't see a story there. I don't see anything of public interest."

Collins, William B. "Miller, in Renaissance, Is Honored by Penn." *Philadelphia Inquirer* 26 October 1984: C1.

Lengthy feature detailing Miller's attendance at the University of Pennsylvania to receive an honorary doctor of letters and star in a forum entitled "A Conversation with Arthur Miller." Miller's comments in response to audience questions are excerpted and include answers to questions regarding the threat of theatre critics on art and the declining state of the theatre in America.

"Olive Branch Awards." *Christian Century* 14 November 1984: 1058.

News item reporting that Miller spoke at the Olive Branch Awards, given for superior reporting on the nuclear arms race, on 29 October. The event was hosted by the Editors' Organizing Committee and the Writers' and Publishers' Alliance for Disarmament.

Freedman, Samuel G. "Miller Fighting Group's Use of Segment from *Crucible*." *New York Times* 17 November 1984: 14.

News item reporting that lawyers for Miller have demanded that the Wooster Group cease from using portions of *The Crucible* in his experimental work *L.S.D.*

Shewey, Don. "Miller's Tale." *Village Voice* 27 November 1984: 123.

Shewey writes of Miller's refusal to allow the Wooster Group to use portions of his *Crucible* in an avant-garde play entitled *L.S.D. (. . . Just the High Points . . .)*. While Miller denies that he had received the three requests for permission that Wooster Group director Elizabeth LeCompte has proof that she sent, he does admit that his legal move of a cease-and-desist letter, which prohibited the group from using his work in any way "lest it inhibit first-class productions in New York City," was "a dodge"—says Miller, "I'm not interested in the money. The aesthetics are involved. I don't want the play mangled that way. Period." Shewey argues that Miller should have given his consent because the Wooster Group is one of the few companies in New York "that has created an original, innovative body of work to rival legendary European troupes . . . [and] is [a] powerfully visionary theater."

Freedman, Samuel G. "Play Closes after *Crucible* Dispute." *New York Times* 28 November 1984: C21.

News item reporting that the Wooster Group has voluntarily shut down its production of *L.S.D.* in response to Miller's insistence that they cease using portions of *The Crucible* in their experimental work. Miller is quoted as saying that he would not pursue legal action because he doesn't want "to harm them. They were well-intentioned. It was just badly handled."

1985

Manso, Peter. *Mailer: His Life and Times*. New York: Penguin, 1985. 98–99, 538–40, 553, 557.

This oral biography of Norman Mailer's life includes recollections of Miller by Mailer, Norman Rosten, and John Leonard. Mailer recounts that while living in the same building as Miller in New York City in the late 1940s he had several encounters with the playwright as they both retrieved their mail. Mailer says he thought at the time that "this guy's never going anywhere." Rosten remembers how Mailer was eager to meet Monroe and asked him on many occasions to set it up. Rosten, being a close friend to Miller since college, didn't think it would be a good idea, saying, "Miller didn't want to set anything up with Mailer. He just didn't like the idea. Miller is a rabbi, and he didn't want this strange guy powering in. He wasn't a buddy of Mailer's, and they'd always had a vague sort of animosity toward each other. . . . Also, Marilyn and Arthur were already married, and at that time it made a difference, especially since Arthur was a very proper guy. I'm one of his oldest friends, but if I danced with Marilyn at a party and maybe held her a little too tight or whispered in her ear, he'd look at me and get a little nervous. It's his temperament. It wasn't just directed towards Mailer." Also discussed is Miller's reaction to the publication of Mailer's book *Marilyn*. A rare photo of Miller with Mailer and Soviet writers at the "Waldorf Conference" on 25 March 1949 appears on page 135.

Summers, Anthony. *Goddess: The Secret Lives of Marilyn Monroe*. New York: Macmillan, 1985.

Fairly accurate biography of Marilyn Monroe that includes details of her life with Miller.

Bush, Catherine. "Cease and Desist." *Performance Magazine* (June–July 1985): 34–36.

Bush details the controversy over the use of text from Miller's *The Crucible* in the Wooster Group's production of *L.S.D.*

"Miller Unveils New Play." *San Jose Mercury News* 9 October 1985: D7.

Filling in for an ailing Isaac Bashevis Singer at a PEN celebration evening of author readings, Miller read his new play *I Can't Remember Anything*. Also mentioned is Miller nearing completion of a major new work entitled *The Ride Down Mount Morgan* and his collaboration with writer Aaron Asher on his memoirs.

Seppy, Tom. "Writers Sue to Stop Colleague's Deportation." *Philadelphia Inquirer* 29 October 1985: A7. See also Paul Clancy, "She's Still without a Country." *USA Today* 20 June 1989: A2.

News item that mentions Miller as one of five prominent writers who have failed suit in federal court in an attempt to keep author Margaret J. Randall from being deported because of her writings on U.S. foreign and domestic policy.

Wright, Frank Lloyd. "Design for Living Room of a Connecticut House for Arthur Miller and Marilyn Monroe." *Architecture* (November 1985): 83.

Wright details his work for Miller and Marilyn Monroe in designing a house for them in Connecticut that was never built.

"Disputes Mar Writers Meeting in Moscow." *San Jose Mercury News* 30 November 1985: A16.

News item announcing Miller's involvement with a group of thirteen prominent American writers who attended the Soviet Writers Union meeting in Lithuania. The article reports that Miller had attempted to read a long list of names of imprisoned Soviet writers to the Soviets present, but was "stonewalled."

Pfeiffer, Bruce Brooks. "Marilyn Monroe Meets Frank Lloyd Wright." *House and Garden* December 1985: 62.

Essay detailing Frank Lloyd Wright's proposed design for Miller and Monroe's Connecticut home, which featured a circular living room with a projection booth and film vault, a second floor costume vault, an extensive baby nursery, and master bedroom.

1986

Steinem, Gloria. *Marilyn.* New York: MJF Books, 1986.

Psychological reading of the life of Marilyn Monroe with photographs by George Barris of the famous "last sitting." Steinem includes details of Monroe's relationship with Miller, describing him as a father-figure to the tormented orphan actress.

Salisbury, Stephen. "World Writers Address a Foe: Government." *Philadelphia Inquirer* 12 January 1986: A2.

Lengthy feature describing the excitement and controversy surrounding the 48th annual PEN Congress in New York City. Miller is quoted in relation to his visit to Vilnius, the capital of Lithuania, several months previously, when he startled the Soviets by reading a list of writers imprisoned in the Soviet Union. A breakthrough apparently occurred when Nikolai Federenko, secretary of the Soviet Writers Union, was willing to discuss the list with Miller privately.

Caldwell, Gail. "Shultz Opens PEN Congress." *Boston Globe* 13 January 1986: 21.

Article reporting events at the 48th International PEN Congress in New York City, which was expected to draw 700 authors from around the world. Miller is mentioned as one of eight participants in a $1000 a ticket famous-author evening, where he read from his works.

Beck, Marilyn. "Another Miller Play Going to Screen." *San Jose Mercury News* 6 March 1986: D10.

Gossip item announcing Warren Beatty's interest in co-producing and starring in a feature length film adaptation of Miller's *Some Kind of Love Story.* The one-act play will be filmed, the column continues, with the title *Almost Everybody Wins* [never produced film].

"Letters to the Editor: Don't Reconvene." *Philadelphia Inquirer* 5 August 1986: A12.

Response to Miller's op-ed piece of 13 July entitled "We, the People, Should Reconvene."

Connell, Joan. "Paying a Price for Dissent, Mexican Poet Fighting Order to Leave U.S." *San Jose Mercury News* 13 September 1986: F12.

News story reporting that poet Margaret Randall has been denied a green card to live and work in the United States and will soon be deported, despite a suit filed in federal court by Norman Mailer, Miller, Alice Walker, and Grace Paley challenging the constitutionality of the McCarran-Walter Act which empowers the federal government to bar aliens from the U.S. because of their political views.

Beck, Marilyn. "Streisand to Play Life Photographer." *San Jose Mercury News* 14 October 1986: D10.

Gossip item announcing (1) Miller's completion of a six-hour mini-series version of *The American Clock*, to star John Malkovich, (2) *Playing for Time* stage adaptation winning top prize at the Edinburgh Festival, and (3) Ed Harris being "paged to star" in *Almost Everybody Wins*, a film "based on Miller's one-act play," to be directed by Linda Yellen [film was not produced].

1987

Arnold, Eve. *Marilyn Monroe: An Appreciation*. New York: Alfred A. Knopf, 1987.

Above-average photographic essay of Marilyn Monroe by photographer Arnold, one of the assigned Magnum photographers signed to contribute to the documentation of the making of *The Misfits*. Arnold was with the production for two months and this book includes many of her color and black-and-white candid shots of the famous couple. The text is also notable for Arnold's conversations with Monroe and the latter's revelations regarding her feelings of abandonment by both her absent father and her soon-to-be ex-husband Miller.

Halliday, E. M. *John Berryman and the Thirties: A Memoir*. Amherst: U of Massachusetts P, 1987. 131–34.

Halliday, in a memoir of his years at Columbia and Ann Arbor and his friendship with poet John Berryman, mentions Miller as a fellow student at the University of Michigan, describing him as "tall, lean, dourly humorous, and thoroughly engrossed in becoming a successful playwright." Of note is the story of Mary Grace Slattery and Hedda Rowinski (later Rosten) arriving in the rain to Halliday and Bhain Campbell's house and asking them for instruction in love-making as both women were getting "serious" about their respective boyfriends (Arthur Miller and Norman Rosten). Both women were virgins and did not want their beaus to be disappointed that they did not have experience. As it turns out, the men declined. Rare candid shot of the Rostens and the Millers (all before marriage) appears on page 134.

Shaw, Sam, and Norman Rosten. *Marilyn among Friends*. New York: Henry Holt, 1987.

Rosten, a friend of Miller's since the University of Michigan, and, with his wife Hedda, close friends of Monroe and Miller, penned the text of this collection of two hundred photographs by Sam Shaw. Many color and black-and-white candid shots of the couple accompany the text.

Hanscom, Leslie. "Talks with Inge Morath, the Photographer Who Succeeded Marilyn Monroe." *Newsday* 1 February 1987: Ideas: 15.

Interview with Inge Morath on the occasion of the publication of an album of her work entitled *Portraits*. The photographer discusses her early career as a writer, her drift into photography, and her marriage to Miller.

Sheff, David. "When the Stars Came Out in Moscow under Gorbachev." *San Jose Mercury News* 21 June 1987: 14.

Miller and wife Inge Morath are mentioned in this lengthy article as a part of the troupe of celebrities invited to the Moscow International Forum for a Nuclear-Free World for the Survival of Mankind.

"'Beware the Sleeping Ogre,' American Playwright Says." *San Jose Mercury News* 16 November 1987: A4.

Short item quoting Miller as skeptical about how much Soviet writers would benefit from liberation under Gorbachev.

Collins, William B. "Arthur Miller: U.S. Stage Is What Needs a Revival." *Philadelphia Inquirer* 23 November 1987: E3.

Article that investigates Miller's bitterness at the negative attacks on his *The American Clock* and *The Archbishop's Ceiling* in the United States, while both plays were successful in London. While admitting that he had made some "bad revisions" to *Ceiling* while the original had been produced in London and that the lead in the U.S. production of *Clock* had been "terribly miscast," Miller mostly blames "that lethal New York combination of a single all-powerful newspaper and a visionless if not irresponsible theatre management" for both play's negative receptions.

Taylor, Robert. "Bookmaking." *Boston Globe* 29 November 1987: B40.

Brief news item announcing Miller's appearance and talk at the Boston Public Library's Rabb Lecture Hall, marking the playwright's only stop in the New England area on a limited promotional tour for his autobiography, *Timebends: A Life.*

"Stars Support Threatened Chileans." *San Jose Mercury News* 1 December 1987: A4.

News item that mentions Miller as one of 200 signers of a message of support for Chilean actors threatened with death for their opposition to the military government of President Augusto Pinochet.

"Book Critics Circle Nominations Announced." *Newsday* 8 December 1987: II: 16.

Miller's *Timebends* is listed as nominated in the biography category for a National Book Critics Circle Award for distinguished books.

Beck, Marilyn. "Andrews-Miller a Broadway Tandem?" *San Jose Mercury News* 17 December 1987: G10.

Two gossip items relating to Miller: (1) Julie Andrews is considering starring in the Broadway adaptation of Miller's *Playing For Time*, and (2) producer Linda Yellen has signed Peter Yates to direct Miller's *Almost Everybody Wins*, a feature version of his one act play [never produced].

1988

Kazan, Elia. *Elia Kazan: A Life*. New York: Knopf, 1988. 318–21, 358–59, 365–68, 410–16, 659–60, 666–68, 673–74, et passim.

Miller figures prominently in several portions of Elia Kazan's autobiography, most notably those involving their collaboration on several of Miller's projects, including *All My Sons*, "The Hook," *Death of a Salesman*, and *After the Fall.* As close friends ("like brothers") up to the time of Kazan's second appearance before HUAC (when he named names), and as a former lover of Marilyn Monroe's, Kazan offers an intimate assessment and eyewitness details regarding Miller's relationship and subsequent marriage to Monroe.

McCann, Graham. *Marilyn Monroe*. New Brunswich, N.J.: Rutgers UP, 1988.

Using critical theory, feminist perspectives, and film studies, McCann offers a portrait of the life and representations of Marilyn Monroe. Of note to Miller studies is the discussion of *After the Fall*, *The Misfits*, and the playwright's marriage to and divorce from Monroe in addition to his reactions regarding her death.

Taylor, Robert. "Bookmaking." *Boston Globe* 31 January 1988: Books: 102.

Literary news item announcing that Miller will be participating in a panel discussion during a three-day symposium on the freedoms of the teacher, artist, and writer to be held at Williams College.

Snider, Norman. "A Guy from the Neighbourhood." *Books in Canada* 17.2 (March 1988): 7.

Snider recounts an evening in the previous December when Miller, by invitation, read from his just-published autobiography, *Timebends*, at Massey Hall in Toronto. Says Snider, "Although Miller's performance was low-key and almost offhand, his reading had an impressive cumulative power, and was, in the end, a triumph."

Fetherston, Drew. "Papp to Host Benefit for Suppressed Czech Writers." *Newsday* 18 March 1988: Weekend: 2.

News item detailing the upcoming benefit at the New York Society for Ethical Culture by Sixty-Eight Publishers Corporation, "a Toronto-based company founded by Czech emigres and devoted to publishing Czech writers whose works have been suppressed." Miller is mentioned, among poet Galway Kinnell and authors Jane Smiley, Susan Sontag, and Kurt Vonnegut, as being among those who will read from the works of suppressed Czechoslovakian writers.

"Ask the Globe." *Boston Globe* 1 April 1988: 30.

In answer to a question by a reader regarding the disposition of Peter Reilly, the young man who was acquitted of the 1973 murder of his stepmother after Miller demanded a reinvestigation, *The Globe* reports that Reilly trained as an emergency technician and works for an ambulance service in Hartford.

Bernstein, Richard. "Long, Bitter Debate from the 50s: Views of Kazan and His Critics." *New York Times* 3 May 1988: C15.

On the occasion of the release of Elia Kazan's autobiography *Elia Kazan: A Life*, Bernstein examines several alternate readings of the director's appearance before HUAC in 1952 when he "named names," including Miller's and Lillian Hellman's take on the events both before and after Kazan's testimony.

Frymer, Murry. "How Success at First Made Arthur Miller Feel Boxed In." *San Jose Mercury News* 24 June 1988: E7.

Drawing heavily from Miller's work *Timebends: A Life*, this interesting biographical piece retells the events surrounding Miller's first successful Broadway show, *All My Sons*, including Miller's subsequent feelings of guilt over his success.

Ryan, Desmond. "Arthur Miller Is Set to Write a Screenplay." *Philadelphia Inquirer* 20 November 1988: H3.

Entertainment item reporting that producer Jeremy Thomas has persuaded Miller to write a screenplay, *Everybody Wins*, and that it will star Nick Nolte and Debra Winger.

James, Caryn. "Arthur Miller Embraces the Screen." *San Francisco Chronicle* 24 November 1988: E3.

Profile of Miller's screen writing ventures on the occasion of the start of shooting of his first original screenplay to reach the big screen (*Everybody Wins*). Miller discusses the development of the story, which he says is not based on real incidents.

1989

Cohen, Richard. "Like Sewer Alligator, Cowardly Intellectual Is a Myth." *San Jose Mercury News* 2 March 1989: D10.

In an article reporting that seven writers turned down a request to appear on *Good Morning America* to support Salman Rushdie, Miller is mentioned as being invited but having turned them down "with a quip about being fearful."

"Shamir Brings Plan for Arab Elections." *San Jose Mercury News* 5 April 1989: A2.

In a news article detailing Israeli Prime Minister Yitzhak Shamir's visit to Washington, D.C., in search of peace in the Middle East, Miller is mentioned as among 200 American Jews who signed a statement challenging the prime minister to open negotiation with the PLO.

Miller, Morton. "My Moments with Marilyn: P.S. Arthur Was There, Too." *Esquire* June 1989: 161–67.

Arthur Miller's first cousin, Morton, recalls his own experiences with Marilyn Monroe from 1955 to 1961, during her marriage to the playwright. Part of a special issue on the private lives of famous people.

Johnson, Kirk. "Arthur Miller's Vision of Love Becomes a Movie." *New York Times* 11 June 1989: H: 19, 22–23.

Feature article that details the genesis and production of Miller's first screenplay in twenty-eight years, *Everybody Wins*, starring Nick Nolte and Debra Winger, directed by Karel Reisz. The plot is loosely based on the real life story of Peter Reilly, a teenager accused of killing his mother but released, in part, due to Miller's involvement in the case. Photos of Miller and scenes from the film accompany the text.

"Censors Aim at Satanism, 'Dirty' Words." *Atlanta Constitution* 31 August 1989: A22.

News item reporting the results of People for the American Way's survey on censorship, which includes incidents in Wilkinson county where the censorship battle focused on Miller's *Death of a Salesman*.

Smith, Liz. "Peopletalk." *Philadelphia Inquirer* 26 December 1989: C2.

Gossipy item announcing Miller's new screenplay *Everybody Wins*. Miller is quoted as feeling "a terrific freedom" and "liberation in being able to depict the love story . . . as freely as I have. " Comparing this experience with his previous movie *The Misfits*, Miller says, "when Marilyn ran out of the house in despair and embraced a tree in the yard, the censors wanted to cut that scene out because they said it was masturbation."

1990

"Short Takes." *Los Angeles Times* 25 January 1990: P8.

Item reporting Miller's comments accusing the U.S. theatre of being superficial, made during a break in rehearsals for *The Price* at the Young Vic Theatre in England.

"Writers Unite in Plea for Worldwide Effort to Keep Rushdie Alive." *Atlanta Constitution* 12 February 1990: C6.

News item reporting Miller among more than 600 writers from

around the world signing a statement appealing to leaders to help stop the death threats against author Salman Rushdie.

"'He Is Such a Big Legend That I Didn't Believe He Physically Exists'" *San Jose Mercury News* 23 February 1990: A4.
In an article reporting Czechoslovakian President Vaclav Havel's schedule of events for his visit to New York City, Miller is mentioned as having spoken at a concert at the Cathedral of St. John the Divine where Havel received the Spirit of Freedom Award.

"Glimpses." *Los Angeles Times* 2 March 1990: P9.
Brief item announcing that Miller has been selected to receive the 1990 Sarah Josepha Hale Medal in a 29 September ceremony in Newport, New Hampshire.

Collins, Thomas. "What Next? All the President's Cellists?" *Newsday* 14 March 1990: Viewpoints: 57.
Whimsical opinion piece in which Collins nominates Miller as the perfect playwright-president because he is "a man not only of intellect, but of great insight and compassion."

"Arthur Miller Headed in Prague's Direction." *San Jose Mercury News* 26 March 1990: A4.
Brief news item filled with Miller details: (1) that the playwright has been invited to Prague for productions of *The Archbishop's Ceiling* and *The Crucible*; (2) that Lincoln Center Theater will mount the first New York production of *The American Clock* the following season; and (3) that Miller attended a preview of the The Roundabout Theatre's production of *The Crucible* with Vaclav Havel, who hopes to direct the play in Prague. Miller is quoted as being surprised by the effect his play had on the audience.

"Arthur Miller Honored for Works." *Los Angeles Times* 19 April 1990: P8.
Three-sentence item announcing that Miller has been selected to receive the 1991 Algur H. Meadows Award for Excellence in the Arts at Southern Methodist University. The award has a cash prize of $50,000.

"Prize Package." *American Theatre* June 1990: 53.
Brief mention of Miller winning the 1991 Algur H. Meadows Award for Excellence in the Arts, with a cash prize of $50,000.

The award will be presented at the Meadows School of the Arts at Southern Methodist University in Dallas in the spring of 1991.

Wolf, Matt. "Arthur Miller Generates Excitement in the Isles." *Orlando Sentinel* 24 June 1990: F4.

Discusses Miller's "status as a contemporary giant" in Great Britain while being viewed by some Americans as "passé."

Goldfarb, Michael. "Reverence Abroad as Arthur Miller's 75th Birthday Approaches." *Newsday* 29 July 1990: II: 3.

After a brief rundown of various productions of Miller plays being performed in Britain, Goldfarb investigates the reason for Miller's growing popularity abroad, including comments by Alan Ayckbourn, Michael Blakemore, and Chris Bigsby.

"Is the Pen Mightier than the Checkbook?" *San Jose Mercury News* 20 August 1990: B9.

In an article examining the controversy surrounding *New York Daily News* columnist Ken Auletta calling Saul Steinberg "sleazy," and the subsequent backlash, Miller is mentioned as one of fifty PEN board members who signed a letter of support to Steinberg, who the article describes as "a lavish contributor who encourages his wealthy friends to contribute lavishly" to PEN.

Kloer, Phil. "Voices behind the Faces of *War*." *Atlanta Constitution* 27 September 1990: D12.

Feature article detailing the various celebrity voices that make up *The Civil War* documentary by Ken Burns. Miller provided the voice for William T. Sherman.

Puig, Claudia. "Stage." *Los Angeles Times* 13 November 1990: F2.

Short news item quoting Miller as purporting that American artists are censoring their own works for the sake of government grants. His comments on self-censorship were made at a day-long humanities festival in Chicago called Expressions of Freedom, sponsored by the Illinois Humanities Council.

Wallach, Allan. "Tribute to a Playwright." *Newsday* 18 October 1990: B7. See also "Wonderful Town: Arthur Miller's Birthday Party." *Theater Week* 29 October 1990: 16.

Feature article detailing Miller's 75th birthday event held at Lincoln Center's Vivian Beaumont Theater in New York City. Fellow writers, actors, and family members paid tribute, excerpts of Miller's plays were performed, and a high school marching band accompanied a sparkler-holding audience to a rousing "Happy Birthday."

"Briefly Noted." *American Theatre* December 1990: 47.
Brief mention of Miller's 75th birthday at a performance of scenes from his plays directed by Gregory Mosher and presented at the Vivian Beaumont Theater in New York.

Wren, Christopher. "For Arthur Miller, Denial Is Key to Apartheid." *New York Times* 6 December 1990: A9.
News item announcing Miller's return from his first visit to South Africa where "he claimed to have found apartheid's birthplace suffused with the same frailties and follies that he has exposed in his plays."

"Arthur Miller's New Play Set for London." *New York Times* 21 December 1990: E16.
Brief news item reporting that Miller's new play, *The Ride Down Mount Morgan*, his first in five years, will be directed by Michael Blakemore and produced by Robert Fox. Explaining why the work will premiere in London instead of New York, Miller said, "The atmosphere is friendlier to plays there than it is here."

"Marilyn Monroe Ketubah Brings $13,700 at Sale." *Orlando Sentinel* 22 December 1990: A2.
Short news item announcing that the Jewish marriage certificate (printed and framed with a decorated border) of Marilyn Monroe and Arthur Miller sold in London at a Christie's auction for $13,700.

1991

Bloom, Ken. "Arthur Miller." *Broadway: An Encyclopedic Guide to the History, People and Places of Times Square*. New York: Facts on File, 1991. 246–47.
Two-column biographical note on Miller's career in theatre. Broad comments are typical, including: "Miller's humanity and compassion shine through his plays along with his profound sense of morality."

Haspeil, James. *Marilyn: The Ultimate Look at the Legend*. New York: Henry Hold, 1991.
Photographs, many of them candid, of Marilyn Monroe and

Miller on the set of *Some Like It Hot* and on the streets of New York City.

Rubin, Steven Joel. *Writing Our Lives: Autobiographies of American Jews, 1890–1990.* New York: Jewish Pub. Society, 1991. 209–10.
Brief biographical statement introducing an excerpt of Miller's autobiography dealing with the playwright's childhood and early "Jewish memories."

Yant, Martin. "Miranda Wrongs." *Presumed Guilty: When Innocent People Are Wrongly Convicted.* Buffalo: Prometheus. 82.
Miller is briefly mentioned for his active involvement in the Peter Reilly murder case—instrumental in rallying support from celebrities William Styron, Dustin Hoffman, Art Garfunkel, Candice Bergen, and Elizabeth Taylor.

Williams, Jeannie. "A Sober Note on a Starry Night." *USA Today* 17 January 1991: D2.
Celebrity column item that mentions Miller as among those present at the premiere of the film *Once Around*, directed by Lasse Hallstrom and starring Richard Dreyfuss as a terminally generous salesman of Lithuanian descent. With the Gulf Crisis on everyone's mind, Miller is quoted as saying that it was "beyond belief . . . God-awful. Too many young guys are going to pay for it."

Tomasson, Robert E. "Arthur Miller Reaches a New Group of Readers." *New York Times* 10 March 1991: 44.
Brief news item reporting Miller visiting an adult education group and having a literary discussion with them.

"Also Noted." *San Jose Mercury News* 8 July 1991: A4.
One sentence news item announcing that Miller will be attending the 300th anniversary of the witch trials in Salem, Massachusetts.

"Writers Pen Appeal for Death Row Inmate." *Orlando Sentinel* 15 July 1991: A2.
Brief news item reporting that Maya Angelou, Yevgeny Yevtushenko, and Miller have joined an appeal by the PEN American Center in New York for clemency for Harold Otey who is on death row in Nebraska for the 1977 murder of a woman during a burglary. While on death row, among other accomplishments, he has published three books on poetry. They urge clemency because of

Otey's model behavior in prison and their opposition to the death penalty.

English, Bella. "Salem's Plans Offend Witches." *Boston Globe* 18 September 1991: 21.

The year-long series of events commemorating the 300th anniversary of the Salem witch trials are discussed, including Miller's scheduled unveiling of a memorial sculpture and performance of *The Crucible*.

"Celebrities Sell Out for Environmentalists." *San Jose Mercury News* 12 November 1991: A4.

Short news item listing the various celebrity donations for an auction for the environmental group the Housatonic Valley Association in Litchfield, Connecticut. Miller is mentioned as giving a handwritten page from *The Ride Down Mount Morgan* and a page of notes for the screenplay of *The Crucible*.

1992

Karsh, Jousuf. *Karsh: American Legends*. Boston: Little, Brown, 1992: 24–25.

Large color portrait photograph of Miller seated on a piano bench with his left arm resting on the piano fills one page with a brief quote by Miller on opposite page—"Everyone has agonies. The difference is that I try to take my agonies home and teach them to sing."

Strasberg, Susan. *Marilyn and Me*. New York: Warner Books, 1992.

Strasberg's personal account of her relationship with Marilyn Monroe from the vantage point of being the daughter of Lee Strasberg, the founder of the Actors Studio, and Paula Strasberg, Monroe's acting coach for many years. She discusses Miller's intense dislike for her parents, which she saw as an issue about control, and her memories on the set of *The Prince and the Showgirl* and *The Misfits*.

Toperoff, Sam. *Queen of Desire*. New York: HarperCollins, 1992.

Fictional account of the life of Marilyn Monroe, including her relationship and marriage to Miller.

Wayne, Jane Ellen. *Marilyn's Men: The Private Life of Marilyn Monroe*. New York: St. Martin's, 1992.

Biography of Marilyn Monroe that traces the love interests in her life, which includes a chapter on her marriage to Miller entitled "Pa."

Jeffress, Jim. "Also Noted." *San Jose Mercury News* 17 January 1992: A4.

One sentence news item announcing that Miller will be traveling to Stockholm to direct *Death of a Salesman* at the Royal Dramatic Theatre.

Kelly, Kevin. "Edward Albee, Up Close and Personal." *Boston Globe* 3 April 1992: Arts and Film: 93.

In a short item about an interview with Miller on Bravo on 9 and 12 April, Kelly remarks that the playwright "glows in the fawningly protective attention, and makes some sweeping remarks about his plays, the theatre in general, Broadway in particular."

Hemmingway, Furney. "Miller Says of Monroe: Marilyn Was Pill Addict." *Atlanta Constitution* 4 August 1992: D2.

Short news item reporting that Miller said in an interview published in the Paris newspaper *Le Figaro* that Marilyn Monroe was "highly self-destructive," addicted to sleeping pills, and that he had put his career on the hold after his marriage in 1956 for her. Says Miller, "Marilyn was sick; the public knew nothing. She was totally dependent on sleeping pills, and they destroyed her bit by bit."

Dowd, Maureen, and Frank Rich. "Mrs. Bush and the Call of Author. Arthur." *New York Times* 20 August 1992: A17.

News item reporting events of the 1992 Republican National Convention included here for Barbara Bush's comparing herself to Arthur Miller, saying that they are both writers.

"Revealing Play." *Cincinnati Post* 24 August 1992: C2.

Short news item reporting Rebecca Miller's comments regarding her father's play *After the Fall*, which she is directing for the Ensemble Theatre of Cincinnati. Ms. Miller contends that the work is not necessarily autobiographical and that directing the play has taught her a lot about the relationship between Miller and Inge Morath, her parents.

Stein, Jerry. "Director Miller: *Fall* Transcends Marilyn Monroe." *Cincinnati Post* 2 September 1992: D1.

Feature reporting Rebecca Miller's views on directing her father's play *After the Fall* at the Ensemble Theatre of Cincinnati, including comments regarding the autobiographical nature of the play and her relationship with her father Arthur Miller.

———. "Arthur Miller's *Fall* Earns Highest Praise." *Cincinnati Post* 11 September 1992: C4.

Positive review of the Ensemble Theatre of Cincinnati's production of *After the Fall*, directed by Miller's daughter Rebecca. Of note is mention of the opening night curtain being held fifty minutes so that Miller and wife Inge Morath could see the beginning. The playwright and his wife were late due to a delayed flight.

"Arthur Miller in Israel." *San José Mercury News* 13 October 1992: A4.

Short news item discussing Miller's return to Israel, after a fifteen-year absence, to attend a performance of *Death of a Salesman*. Miller is quoted that he hadn't visited Israel since 1977 because he wasn't comfortable with the right-wing government, then added that only "negligence" kept him away.

1993

Spoto, Donald. *Marilyn Monroe: The Biography*. New York: HarperCollins, 1993. Excerpt as "Marilyn & Joe: The Dark Side of the Fairy Tale," in *Cosmopolitan* October 1993: 216+.

Well-researched and highly accurate biographical account of the life of Marilyn Monroe that includes her relationship with Miller.

Stuart, Sandra Lee, and John Prince. *The Pink Palace Revisited: Behind Closed Doors at the Beverly Hills Hotel*. Fort Lee, N.J.: Barricade, 1993. 100–103.

In this historical exposé of the Beverly Hills Hotel, brief mention is made of the time when Miller and then-wife Marilyn Monroe lived there in 1959 while Marilyn was making *Let's Make Love* at Twentieth Century-Fox. Based on interviews with former employees, the authors insinuate that Monroe and Montand moved in together when Miller and Montand's wife, Simone Signoret, had left town, that they had an affair, and at its end, Monroe was incessant in her attempts to rekindle the romance.

Tafel, Edgar. *About Wright: An Album of Recollections by Those Who Knew Frank Lloyd Wright*. New York: Wiley, 1993. 68–69, 82–84.

In a brief section on unbuilt commissions, Miller and Monroe are mentioned as inviting Wright to Connecticut to look at the land they had bought for a house. Miller is quoted as saying it was Monroe who had initiated the contact but it was the playwright who nixed the plans as "simply impossible. . . . He simply had us all wrong." Included in the text is a copy of Miller's typed letter to Tafel in response to a request for his recollections of Wright. Two sketches of the house designed by Wright accompany the text.

Bogard, Travis, and Jackson R. Byer. "'A Comradship-in-Arms': A Letter from Eugene O'Neill to Arthur Miller." *Eugene O'Neill Review* 17.1–2 (Spring/Fall 1993): 121–23.

Bogard and Byer trace the background of a piece of correspondence dated 29 April 1949 from Eugene O'Neill to Arthur Miller in which the former acknowledges receipt of a letter from Miller expressing his esteem of the older playwright and inviting him to see a performance of *Death of a Salesman*. Due to ill health, O'Neill declines but offers his hope that the two can meet in Boston.

Isaac, Dan. "Founding Father: O'Neill's Correspondence with Arthur Miller and Tennessee Williams." *Eugene O'Neill Review* 17.1–2 (Spring/Fall 1993): 124–33.

Isaac relates his discovery of a piece of correspondence from Miller to Eugene O'Neill while doing research on Williams and Miller at the University of Texas at Austin. The letter, dated 22 February 1949, apologizes to O'Neill for not responding sooner following O'Neill's wire of congratulations on Miller's win of the Drama Critics' Award for *All My Sons*, which was on Broadway opposite O'Neill's *The Iceman Cometh*, and inviting him to attend a performance of *Death of a Salesman*. See previous entry for O'Neill's reply.

Harris, John. "Decline and Fallacy." *Christopher Street* 199 (March 1993): 4–5.

Harris attacks what he sees as Miller's shortsightedness in blaming Broadway for the decline and fall of theatre in America when there are many nonprofit houses, regional theatres, and off-Broadway theatres in New York that "Miller barely recognizes."

Kleid, Beth. "Awards." *Los Angeles Times* 1 March 1993: F2.

News item announcing Miller as a winner of the film classic award for his 1961 film *The Misfits* at the Seventh Annual Genesis Awards in Century City, honoring those in the entertainment industry who spotlight animal issues.

Kilian, Michael. "Stage-Struck." *Chicago Tribune* 21 March 1993: Sec. 5: 3.

In this profile of actress Maryann Plunkett, Miller is mentioned as having praised her as the country's number one star.

"A Library's Friends Come to Its Aid." *New York Times* 23 May 1993: CN: 23.

News article detailing the efforts by Arthur Miller, Dustin Hoffman, Karen Valentine, and George Grizzard to raise $25,000 for an endowment to help operate the Minor Memorial Library in Roxbury, Connecticut, by performing a musical review to be held on 12 June 1993 called "Starry, Starry Night."

"Arthur Miller's Dramatic Solution." *San Jose Mercury News* 2 August 1993: A4.

Miller is quoted as suggesting to a group of students at the University of the South in Sewannee, Tennessee, that government subsidy for the arts as a solution to reverse the decline of theatre in America.

"Film Colony Protests China's *Concubine* Ban." *San Jose Mercury News* 4 September 1993: C3.

Gossip item that mentions Miller as among the celebrities who have signed a letter asking the International Olympic Committee to reject China's bid to host the 2000 Summer Olympics because of its suppression of the Cannes Film Festival-winning film *Farewell My Concubine*.

De Witt, Karen. "Clinton Confers Awards on 18 Cultural Figures." *New York Times* 8 October 1993: C3.

News item announcing Miller's National Medal of Arts Award by President Clinton on 7 October 1993.

Clinton, William Jefferson. "Remarks on Presenting Arts and Humanities Awards." *Weekly Compilation of Presidential Documents*. 29.40 (11 October 1993): 2018–22.

Miller is among seventeen National Medal of Arts recipients

honored in this speech of 7 October 1993 on the south lawn at the White House. Of Miller's career, President Clinton praises "the continuing energy he has brought to his work over such a long period of time, seeming forever young with something always new to say."

1994

Considine, Shaun. *Mad as Hell: The Life and Work of Paddy Chayefsky*. New York: Random House, 1994.xii, 118–36, 144, 209–10, 252.

In this book about the creative life of writer Paddy Chayefsky, Miller is discussed in relation to his involvement in the decision-making process of then wife Marilyn Monroe who turned down the role of Rita Shawn in Chayefsky's *The Goddess*, widely believed to be based on Monroe's life. Also examined are the early days of the couple's clandestine relationship that began while Miller was still married to his first wife Mary Grace Slattery.

Miracle, Berniece Baker, and Mona Rae. *My Sister Marilyn*. Chapel Hill, N.C.: Algonquin Books, 1994.

Miracle, the half sister to Marilyn Monroe, offers her memories of the actress and the playwright.

Koenenn, Joseph C. "Competitors for Oliviers." *Newsday* 8 March 1994: 50.

News item listing Miller's *The Last Yankee* as being among those nominated for Best Play in the 1994 Olivier Awards competition.

Stearns, David Patrick. "Miller Back in the Broadway Crucible." *USA Today* 22 April 1994: D8.

Profile of the playwright on the occasion of the opening of the Broadway production of *Broken Glass*. Miller discusses his current writing surge, the critical misunderstanding of his work, and former wife Marilyn Monroe, whom he calls a legitimately fascinating person but who has become "pure commercial exploitation."

Brozan, Nadine. "Chronicle." *New York Times* 28 October 1994: B2.

Announces the one-year appointment of Miller to professor of contemporary theatre at Oxford. Beginning January 1995, Miller will deliver a minimum of three lectures at the university.

"Inge Morath: Photographs, 1952–1992." *The Photographic Journal* 134 (October 1994): 382–84.

Article announcing a retrospective exhibit of Miller's wife, photographer Inge Morath, at the Royal Photographic Society at Bath, England, from 8 October to 27 November 1994. Of interest to Miller studies are Morath's photographs of her husband, Arthur, and his second wife, Marilyn Monroe.

"Literary Honors." *San Jose Mercury News* 9 November 1994: A4.

Miller is mentioned in this short news item as among the 400 delegates from eighty-seven nations attending the sixty-first World Congress of PEN International in Prague.

1995

Baty, S. Paige. *American Monroe: The Making of a Body Politic*. Berkeley, Calif.: U of California P, 1995.

Baty reads Marilyn Monroe as a mass-mediated image and icon. Miller is included not only for his marriage to Monroe but also for his contribution to the creation of the icon through *The Misfits*.

Lefkowitz, Frances. *Marilyn Monroe*. New York: Chelsea House, 1995.

Part of the "Pop Culture Legends" series, this slim biography of Marilyn Monroe contains two chapters covering her marriage to Miller. Four rarely printed photographs of the couple accompany the text.

Shapiro, Michael. "81—Arthur Miller." *The Jewish 100: A Ranking of the Most Influential Jews of All Time*. Secaucus, N.J.: Carol Publishing Group, 1995. 302–305.

Shapiro ranks Miller number eight-one on a list of the one-hundred most influential Jews of all time. The standard-fare biographical sketch relates no new insights into Miller's work nor does it discuss the role of religion in Miller's life or literature.

van Gelder, Lawrence. "Kay B. Barrett, Talent Scout and Entertainment Agent, 93." *New York Times* 19 January 1995: B11.

Obituary for talent scout and "powerful" agent who worked for Leland Hayward, MCA, and ICM. Barrett was Miller's representative for forty years.

Porterfield, Christopher. "West End Story." *Time* 27 March 1995: 73–75.

Lengthy essay on the lack of new plays on Broadway in which Porterfield ponders why London has a rich supply of fresh material. Miller is quoted as saying that the London theatre allows plays to survive while on Broadway, "it has to be the Second Coming or it's nothing."

Pike, Rebecca. "Five Oliviers for *She Loves Me*." *Daily Telegraph (*London) 3 April 1995.

Brief mention is made of Miller's *Broken Glass* winning the BBC's award for best play and actor Ken Stott winning for best actor in a supporting role.

"Hospitality Takes Center Stage at a Town's Festival for Its Native-son Playwright." *New York Times* 24 April 1995: 10.

Article that discusses the Independence, Kansas, yearly William Inge Festival and the awarding of the playwriting award to Miller.

Elsom, John. "The Pitfalls of Freedom." *World & I* 10.5 (May 1995): 104–12.

Article detailing the World Congress of the PEN Club, held in Prague in November 1994. Speaking to a packed audience of locals, Miller, Tom Stoppard, Vaclav Havel, and Ronald Harwood responded to questions regarding the political content of their dramas. Miller mentioned his process as a playwright and the unintentional political quality of his works. Photo of Miller with Havel and Harwood accompanies the text.

Brantley, Ben. "Wilder and Miller in One-Act Festival." *New York Times* 6 May 1995: 17.

Mixed review of a Miller play entitled *The Ryan Interview*, starring Mason Adams and Julie Lauren and directed by Curt Dempster. which premiered at the eigtheenth annual festival of one-act plays at the Ensemble Studio Theatre. The play depicts an old Connecticut Yankee being interviewed by a young female reporter on his 100th birthday.

"Benefits." *New York Times* 14 May 1995: Sec. 1: 46.

Short news item announcing that Miller will be among those honored for his contributions to the arts by the National Foundation for Jewish Culture. Amy Irving, Ron Rifkin, and Eli Wallach will perform at the Sylvia and Danny Kaye Playhouse at Hunter

College on 15 May. Tickets are $500 and the event is to raise money for arts grants.

Smolowe, Jill. "Justice: Untrue Confessions." *Time* 22 May 1995.
News article reporting the controversy surrounding the possibly coerced confession of Girvies Davis, a mentally retarded man who is awaiting death for killing an eighy-nine-year-old retired farmer. At article's end is mention of Miller's involvement in a similar case, that of Richard Lapointe, a brain-damaged dishwasher, who was convicted of raping and killing his wife's eighty-eight-year-old grandmother after a nine-hour interrogation in which he made several contradictory confessions.

Leon, Masha. "Masha Leon." *Forward* 16 June 1995: PG.
Details the events of the sixth annual National Foundation for Jewish Culture Achievement Awards on 15 May at the Sylvia and Danny Kaye Playhouse. Miller received the Literary Arts Award and Eli Wallach read two scenes from *The Price*.

Christiansen, Richard. "Arthur Miller, 80, American Playwright." *Chicago Tribune* 20 August 1995: Sec. 13: 2.
On the occasion of his 80th birthday, Christiansen discusses the literary career of Arthur Miller.

Rabinovitz, Jonathan. "For Many, Echoes of an Injustice in Connecticut; Convicted Slayer's Backers Say His Confession, Like One 20 Years Ago, Was Coerced." *New York Times* 15 September 1995: B1.
Lengthy news article detailing Miller's involvement in the case of Richard Lapointe, a brain-damaged man who was convicted of raping and killing his wife's eighty-nine-year-old grandmother. Says Miller, "It's the Peter Reilly case all over again. I thought we'd learned from that: that you cannot base a whole case on a confession, especially in the case of a person of mental capacity of this one."

Colford, Paul D. "Perpetual Arthur Miller Entering His 80th Year, He's as Productive as Ever." *Newsday* 28 September 1995: B2.
Brief essay/interview profiling Miller on the occasion of his being honored at the New York Public Library on his 80th birthday.

———. "Perpetual Arthur Miller Entering his 80th Year, He's as Productive as Ever." *Newsday* 28 September 1995: B2.

Article reporting the events of the preceding evening when friends and admirers gathered at the New York Public Library to celebrate Miller's 80th birthday. Also mentioned is the publication of three books: *Homely Girl, A Life, and Other Stories*, the reissue of *The Portable Arthur Miller*, and a new edition of *Timebends* with a new introduction. Mention is made of Miller traveling to Oxford University the next month to receive an honorary degree.

Lawson, Mark. "We Need You Arthur, Happy Birthday." *Guardian* (London) 2 October 1995: 11.

After noting the London celebrations marking Miller's 80th birthday, Lawson comments on the reasons why the American playwright is more appreciated in Great Britain than in his home country.

"Happy Birthday, Arthur." *Guardian* (London) 17 October 1995: Sec. 2: 12.

Tribute piece by authors Carlos Fuentes, Harold Pinter, and David Mamet published on the occasion of Miller's 80th birthday.

Rushdie, Salman. "Applause for the Playwright-as-Hero." *Los Angeles Times* 19 October 1995: M9.

Opinion essay praising Miller on the occasion of his 80th birthday—"His is a life dedicated as passionately to the remembrance, and the enlivening through art, of the small and the unconsidered, as it is to the articulation of the great moral issues of the day."

"80 Candles for a Theatrical Eminence." *New York Times* 29 October 1995: Sec. 2: 6.

Short news item detailing PEN American Center's plans to sponsor an evening of tribute and readings at Town Hall in Manhattan on 10 October to honor Miller on his 80th birthday.

Thurman, Judith. "Portrait: Arthur Miller, Master of the American Theater in Connecticut." *Architectural Digest* November 1995: 62–72.

Lengthy piece which discusses Miller's various country homes in Roxbury, Connecticut, including his first home in 1947 and his second farmhouse purchased when he married Marilyn Monroe. Also mentioned is his almost association with Frank Lloyd

Wright for a remodeling project on the second home, and his struggles to rebuild after a devastating 1984 fire that "gutted" the farmhouse and destroyed his personal archive and priceless library of books and drawings.

Marks, Peter. "Tribute to a Man Tried in the Crucible: Writers Ruminate on Arthur Miller's 80th Birthday." *New York Times* 1 November 1995: C15.

News article concerning the sold-out evening of readings and speeches in honor of Miller's 80th birthday at Town Hall in Manhattan. Organized by PEN American Center, the event was a reflection of Miller's influence on the American theatre.

"Arthur Miller's 80th Birthday Marked by Town Hall Gathering." *New York Times* 5 November 1995: L4.

Short news item recounting the events of Miller's 80th birthday celebration organized by the PEN American Center. Writers paid tribute to Miller's influence on American theatre as well as his political activism.

Kellman, Steven G. "Birthday of a Playwright." *The Nation* 13 November 1995: 579–80.

Reviews of three books published to commemorate Miller's 80th birthday: *Homely Girl, A Life*, *The Portable Arthur Miller* (new edition), and *Timebends, A Life* (new edition).

Capote, Susan. "Miller Time: When a Person's Life Becomes a Writers Property." *Village Voice* 14 November 1995: 102.

News article reporting the problems encountered by Chicago-based playwrights Carrie Betlyn and Peggy Dunne when they tried to stage their adaptation of Fania Fénelon's memoir, which they titled *The Musicians of Auschwitz*. Miller, who owns the "exclusive worldwide rights to this piece of history" refused to allow the work to be produced.

Greenberg, Brigitte. "Movement to Free Convicted Rapist-Killer Stirs Controversy." *Los Angeles Times* 10 December 1995: A1.

Lengthy article reporting the details of the controversy surrounding the arrest and conviction of Richard Lapointe for the rape and murder of his wife's grandmother. Miller is mentioned as contributing to an effort to help publicize the case, which he believes involves a violation of Lapointe's rights.

Schultz, Rick. "*J-PEGGED*: Arthur Miller." Mr. Showbiz. Starwave. 22 December 1995. http://showbiz.starwave.com/showbiz/audio/WAV/MILLER3. WAV.

Internet article profiling Miller on the occasion of his 80th birthday, prequel to Miller's on-line interview with "Mr. Showbiz" scheduled for 10 January 1996. Of note: little-known personal details such as his writing routine (every morning), his favorite bagel (sesame), how much sleep he needs at night (six hours, up by 5:30), and dream project (always the play he is currently working on).

1996

Clark, Colin. *The Prince, The Showgirl and Me*. New York: St. Martin's, 1996.

Diary account of events during making of *The Prince and the Showgirl*, starring Laurence Olivier and Marilyn Monroe, by the then twenty-three-year-old production assistant Colin Clark. Miller is portrayed unflatteringly throughout as jealous, selfish, over protective, meddling, and cruel.

Connery, Donald S., ed. "Chronology." *Convicting the Innocent: The Story of a Murder, a False Confession, and the Struggle to Free a 'Wrong Man.'*" Cambridge, Mass.: Brookline, 1996. 4.

In a chronology of the Richard Lapointe murder case, Miller is mentioned as speaking in mid-year 1994 at the Connecticut Bar Association's annual dinner regarding the Lapointe case as another miscarriage of justice.

Guilaroff, Sydney. "Marilyn." *Crowning Glory: Reflections of Hollywood's Favorite Confidant*. Los Angeles: General Pub. Group, 1996. 152, 157–58.

In a chapter about Marilyn Monroe, hairstylist to the stars Sydney Guilaroff relates his observations and Marilyn's comments regarding her marriage to Miller while working on *The Prince and the Showgirl*, *Some Like It Hot*, and *The Misfits*. Guilaroff says he sensed tension between the couple, which had "climbed to a fever pitch" during the filming of *The Misfits*. Of note is Guilaroff's claims that Miller was having an affair with photographer Inge Morath during the shoot, an allegation denied by Miller.

Kazin, Alfred. *A Lifetime Burning in Every Moment: from the Journals of Alfred Kazin.* New York: HarperCollins, 1996. 260–62.

Kazin briefly recollects that he and Miller "came upon each other in the Roxbury dump on Sunday morning" (some time between 1978–1993 according to the chapter title). At this impromptu meeting, Miller made mention of his bitterness at the *Times* "which has only one drama critic whom Arthur blames for his recent lack of acclaim on Broadway." Kazin continues by detailing his feelings regarding Miller: "Since I am the same age, another survivor of the terrible thirties and its radical dreams, I enjoy having Miller lecture me. Even in the dump. He brings a certain derision to it, like the blue workingman's shirt he wears to parties."

"Arthur Miller Gets Chatty on Web Site." *San Jose Mercury News* 9 January 1996: D3.

Short news item announcing Miller's decision to participate in a live on-line chat session from his New York City home on the Mr. Showbiz web site.

Dunham, Mike. "Playwright Miller to Attend Conference." *Anchorage Daily News* 7 February 1996: B2.

News item announcing Miller and Morath's intention to attend the Prince William Sound Community College's fourth annual theatre conference where he will make several public appearances in Valdez.

Lipton, Michael L. "Her Own Woman." *People Weekly* 16 February 1996: 81–83.

Short sketch of Miller's daughter Rebecca and her current directing work, a film entitled *Angela*, loosely based on her own childhood fears. Of note to Miller studies are his quoted comments regarding his daughter's talents and her interests. Photo of Rebecca at age two with her parents included.

Bickelhaupt, Susan, and Maureen Dezell. "Miller Makes the Play." *Boston Globe* 27 February 1996: Living: 74.

Brief news item reporting that Miller attended a matinee performance of *Death of a Salesman* starring Hal Holbrook, trying to decide whether to give this production his approval for a run on Broadway.

Goodnough, Abby. "A Master of Seduction Puts Hackensack on the Literary Map." *New York Times* 24 March 1996: Sec. 13NJ: 6.

Profiles Fairleigh Dickinson University professor Gene Barnett, who over the past twenty years has lured ninety different writers to his school to deliver lectures to his students. Miller agreed after a letter writing campaign that began in 1979.

"Turkish Writer Sentenced to Prison." *Christian Science Monitor* 1 May 1996: 13.

Profile of Turkish writer Yasar Kemal who was convicted for an article denouncing racism against minorities in his country. His sentence of twenty months in prison was suspended on the condition that he does not speak out again. Miller is mentioned as sending a letter of support to Kemal, calling the Turkish writer's sentence "a painful absurdity."

Taylor, Paul. "Theatre: *Misfits*, Royal Exchange, Manchester." *Independent* (London) 11 May 1996: 10.

Negative review of the stage play based on the making of *The Misfits*, that Taylor calls "bitty, unaccumulative, lacks either energy or bite and leaves you wondering what it was [Alex] Finlayson wanted to say through this famous story." Miller appears as a character in this play which focuses on the dissolution of his marriage to Marilyn Monroe.

Holloway, Lynette. "T. F. Gilroy Daly, 65, U. S. Judge, Is Dead." *New York Times* 12 July 1996: B7.

Lengthy news piece announcing the death of Judge Daly, who had gained prominence as the lawyer who had "won freedom for Peter A. Reilly. . . ." Miller's involvement with the Reilly case is summarized.

"Giving Voice to *The West*." *San Jose Mercury News* 15 September 1996: 8.

In this short news item listing the various celebrities doing voice over work for Ken Burns's and Stephen Ives's documentary *The West*, Miller is mentioned as among those participating.

Weber, Bruce. "Making Images of Jewish Icons." *New York Times* 19 September 1996: B1.

Lengthy essay detailing French photographer Frederic Brenner's life's project of photographing the faces of Jewish diaspora and his gathering of many famous American Jews, Miller included, on Ellis Island on 18 September 1996, for a group portrait. The photo taken that day accompanies the text.

Seligmann, Jean. "Jewish Roots: Back to Ellis Island." *Newsweek* 30 September 1996: 62.

Miller is mentioned as among eighteen eminent Jewish Americans who traveled to Ellis Island to be photographed by French photographer Frederic Brenner for his book *Jews/America/A Representation.* Photograph of Miller and others accompanies the text.

Brenner, Frederic. "Portraits of a People." *Life* September 1996: 60+.

Series of photographs of American Jews, including Miller, Walter Annenberg, Elie Wiesel, Kirk Douglas, Milton Berle, Neil Simon, Norman Mailer, Jerry Lewis, Lew Wasserman, Ruth Westheimer, Roy Lichtenstein, Ruth Bader Ginsburg, and Isaac Stern.

Grimes, William. "A Home for a Writer, but Not a Theatre." *New York Times* 25 October 1996: C2.

Short news item announcing the choice of Miller by the Signature Theatre Company as the focus of its 1997–98 mini-retrospective season. Underwritten by the Laura Pels Foundation, the season will include four production slots that will include a mix of full-length and one-act plays. Miller is quoted as being happy with their choice, "It's a nice idea, and I understand they do good work. It won't be all that different from what I usually do, but there are several plays involved, and that's what's attractive to me."

Dunham, Mike. "Unblinking Inge Morath Looks Death, Life in the Eye." *Anchorage Daily News* 25 August 1996: J1.

Lengthy biographical piece on Inge Morath, following her visit to Alaska to lecture on photography at the Prince William Sound Theatre Conference where her husband was the guest of honor.

Welch, Liz. "Choosing the Playwrights Who Can Go Home Again." *New York Times* 17 November 1996: Sec. 2: 8.

Interview with James Houghton in which he discusses the way in which the Signature Theatre Company chooses its writers in residence. Miller is mentioned as accepting the invitation, and the year-long commitment, to be produced by Signature in 1997–98.

Farber, Stephen. "Miller & Son." *New York Times Magazine* 17 November 1996: Sec. 6: 58–59.

Profile of the relationship between Miller and his son Robert, producer for Miller's film version of *The Crucible.*

Davies, Caroline. "Day-Lewis and Writer's Daughter Marry in Secret." *Daily Telegraph (*London) 18 November 1996.

Lengthy article detailing the private marriage of Daniel Day-Lewis and Miller's daughter Rebecca. Miller is quoted as describing the event as "a very happy occasion. A wonderful day." Asked if he thought that Day-Lewis would make a good son-in-law, Miller is quoted as responding, "I certainly hope so. No, I am sure he will."

Facter, Sue. "*Crucible* Couple Bows." *USA Today* 22 November 1996: D2.

Gossipy news item reporting the first "post-nuptial public appearance" of newlyweds Daniel Day-Lewis and Rebecca Miller at the premiere of the film version of *The Crucible.* When asked if he played matchmaker for his daughter, Miller is quoted as saying that they had known each other before he knew it.

"Keeping the Crowd on Its Toes." *New York Times* 1 December 1996: 61.

News article reporting the opening of *The Crucible* [film] and Miller's comments regarding the loving round of applause given him by the audience.

Jewel, Dan. "Day of Decision." *People* 2 December 1996: 57–58.

Article detailing the wedding of Daniel Day-Lewis and Miller's daughter Rebecca. Photo of father and daughter is also included. Of note is the mention that at the ceremony at the United Church of Strafford, Vermont, Arthur Miller read a poem that he had written for the occasion.

Gussow, Mel. "At 81, Playwright Finds His Work's as Hot as Ever." *Miami Herald* 3 December 1996: C1.

Brief overview of the resurgence of Miller works in production on stage, film, and television.

Berson, Misha. "Film Rediscovers Miller." *San Jose Mercury News* 22 December 1996: G9.

Profile of Miller's current popularity and his past unsatisfying relationship with the Hollywood movie industry.

"Arthur Miller Suddenly Hot in Hollywood." *Atlanta Constitution and Journal* 26 December 1996: F7.

Feature article describing Miller's current popular resurgence, including the making of the film version of *The Crucible*, starring Daniel Day-Lewis and Winona Ryder.

1997

Maerker, Christa. *Marilyn Monroe und Arthur Miller*. Berlin: Rowohlt, 1997.

In German, but included here for its previously unpublished photographs of Miller, wife Mary Grace Slattery, and their two children taken in 1953 and one of Miller (without glasses) and Elia Kazan taken in 1951.

Payne, Tom. *The A-Z of Great Writers*. London: Carlton, 1997. 247.

Brief literary biography accompanied by a photograph of Miller.

Chism, Olin. "Between the Lines of a Writer's Life." *Dallas Morning News* 23 January 1997: C1.

Miller is mentioned among the writers interviewed for the documentary film *William Styron: The Way of the Writer*, in which the playwright comments on Styron's controversial novel *The Confessions of Nat Turner*.

Rothstein, Edward. "On Naming the Names, in Life and Art." *New York Times* 27 January 1997: C13.

Critical commentary that discusses the links between Miller's film *The Crucible*, his relationship with Elia Kazan, and the anti-Communist era of the 1950s.

Bickelhaupt, Susan, and Maureen Dezell. "They Laughed When He Sat Down at the Typewriter." *Boston Globe* 1 April 1997: D2.

Miller is mentioned as one of a group of supporters who offered the Whitney Museum the rent money for Books & Co., a twenty-year-old bookstore scheduled to close because it can't afford a Whitney-imposed rent increase. Unfortunately, the Whitney said it had been approached by "other entities" interested in renting the space and will not allow Books & Co. to stay.

Carter, Bill. "Plays on 2000 and All That." *New York Times* 16 April 1997: C18.

ABC commissions a roster of famous playwrights in United

States, including Neil Simon, Miller, Mamet, Wasserstein, and August Wilson, to create original plays that will draw on the theme of the coming millennium; to be shown during one week in November 1999.

"Stars Denounce West." *Agence France Presse English Wire* 14 May 1997. *Dialog@Carl* (10 August 1999).

Newswire story reporting that Miller is among several hundred people who gathered at the New York Public Library to mark the publication of *The Courage to Stand Alone* by jailed Chinese dissident Wei Jingsheng.

Hertsgaard, Mark. "A Shining Moral Hero Abandoned in the Dark." *Los Angeles Times* 25 May 1997: M2.

In an article about Chinese author and political prisoner Wei Jingsheng, who, after eighteen years behind bars, is reportedly near death, Miller is mentioned as among important artists, writers, and musicians who helped honor Wei in absentia at the New York Public Library by reading and saluting Wei's writing.

Shogan, Robert. "A Time When the Business of Government Was Culture." *Los Angeles Times* 27 May 1997: F1.

News feature detailing the opening of a National Archives display featuring the works of artists funded by federal aid during FDR's administration. Miller is mentioned as one who received aid during that period of time.

Lyall, Sarah. "Literary Splendor among the Sheep." *New York Times* 31 May 1997: 11.

Article on the annual Hay Festival of Literature in Hay-on-Wye, Wales, and Miller's involvement, "lured perhaps by the chance to discuss the place of the writer in Eastern Europe."

"Those Who Knew Her." *American Photo* (May/June 1997): 71–72, 74, 100, 104.

Article presenting the encounter of twenty noted photographers with Marilyn Monroe. Miller is mentioned in the section about Milton Greene, which states that "by 1957 Monroe and Greene drifted apart under pressure from her jealous husband Arthur Miller."

Kempster, Norman. "Albright Sketches U.S. Vision of More United World." *Los Angeles Times* 6 June 1997: 4.

In an article reporting Secretary of State Madeleine Albright's commencement address at Harvard University, Miller is mentioned as one of eleven people honored at the ceremony.

"This Day, among Friends." *New York Times* 6 June 1997: 1

Short front page photograph with caption. Secretary of State Madeleine K. Albright speaking at Harvard's commencement and sitting next to Miller.

"Final Decisions on the Write Stuff." *Independent on Sunday* (London) 22 June 1997: 14–15.

The winner (Steve Timms) of the IoS/Panasonic writing competition for readers of the *Independent on Sunday* is printed—a theatre review of the *Misfits*, a stage play by Alex Finlayson at the Royal Exchange, Manchester, about the problems encountered during the making of the film of the same name (including the deterioration of Miller's marriage to Monroe). A "plodding, humour-impaired" Miller appears as a character in the play performed by Christian Burgess.

Greer, Herb. "Down and Out in London." *National Review* 30 June 1997: 52–53.

Feature article on playwright Harold Pinter that makes mention of Miller and Pinter's trip to Turkey and their subsequent publishing of a "bragging article about all this fun and games in a prominent London Sunday newspaper."

Brownrigg, Sylvia. "Books: I Wish I'd Written." *Guardian* (London) 10 July 1997: Sec. 2: 17.

In a commentary on writer Julio Cortazar, Miller is mentioned as having taken part in the memorial service for the author in New York in 1985.

Zimmer, William. "Cartier-Bresson at the Bruce: Taking a Look at America." *New York Times* 31 August 1997: Sec. 13CN: 14.

Review of the exhibit of the works of Henri Cartier-Bresson at the Bruce Museum in Greenwich, Connecticut. Miller is quoted from his introduction to the book based on the exhibition. (NOTE: Miller's wife, Inge Morath, worked with Cartier-Bresson at Magnum and together they were sent to the film set of *The Misfits* to photographically record the event.)

"Miller Time." *American Theatre* September 1997: 6.
Brief item announcing the Signature Theatre Company's move into a new 160 seat off-Broadway theatre and the various productions of Miller plays planned for the coming season at the Signature, the Roundabout, the Public, and the Papermill Playhouse.

Houghton, James. "Ever Earnest and Funny, Ever Relevant to Youth." *New York Times* 7 September 1997: Sec. 2: 8, 33.
Reports on the Signature Theatre Company's year-long retrospective of four Miller plays. Directors Scott Elliott, Barry Edelstein, and James Houghton discuss Miller's appeal with younger audiences.

Smith, Liz. "Di-Vesting Gown." *New York Post* 21 September 1997. http://206.15.118.165/092197/97.htm (4 April 1999).
Brief mention is made of Miller as one of the 1997 recipients of Amnesty International USA's Media Spotlight Award.

"Benefits." *New York Times* 21 September 1997: 58. See also John Carlin, "Luvvies Become Goodies—Seriously," *Independent on Sunday* (London) 28 September 1997: 13.
Brief mention of Amnesty International's Media Spotlight Awards to be held the following Tuesday. Miller, along with Mike Wallace, Jonathan Demme, and Charlayne Hunter-Gault will be among those honored for promoting human rights.

"Writers' Group Seeks to Free Iranian Editor." *Agence France Presse English Wire* 29 September 1997. *Dialog@Carl* (10 August 1999).
Newswire item reporting that Miller is a member of a committee of international writers and members of PEN who is protesting the jailing of Iranian writer and editor Faraj Sarkuhi in Iran.

Adamy, Janet. "Bollinger Proposes Miller Theater." *Michigan Daily* 29 October 1997. http://www.pub.umich.edu/daily/1997/oct/10-29-97/news/news2.html (11 April 1999).
News item announcing University of Michigan's President Lee Bollinger's decision to build a 500-seat theater in honor of Miller.

"The Write Stuff." *Miami Herald* 30 October 1997.
Brief blurb that mentions that Miller writes on a computer "but has doubts about it." Lamenting the way he once produced a script, Miller is quoted as saying, "A manuscript is really one of

the last of the man-made things. . . and now it isn't there anymore."

1998

Fearon, Peter. "Monroe, Miller, and a Secret Love Affair." *Hamptons Babylon: Life among the Super-Rich on America's Riviera*. Secaucus, N.J.: Birch Lane, 1998. 32–44.

Somewhat lurid chapter on Miller and Monroe's early relationship and subsequent marriage, against the backdrop of their summer home (Hill House) in Amagansett. Fearon repeats gossip-filled anecdotes regarding Marilyn's alleged promiscuity and numerous abortions, while attempting to offer support for his reading of their relationship by including quotes from Miller's autobiography, Amagansett locals, and several of the couple's friends. Not footnoted but Fearon does offer a general listing of sources consulted in rear of text.

Kotsilibas-Davies, James. *Milton's Marilyn: The Photographs of Milton H. Greene*. New York: Schirme, 1998.

Volume of photographs of Marilyn Monroe taken by her former partner Milton Greene, included here for the rich trove of candid wedding and reception pictures of Miller and Monroe.

Krementz, Jill. *The Jewish Writer*. New York: Henry Holt, 1998. 106–7.

In a book which samples 150 Jewish writers "who have enriched the culture of the world in the twentieth century," Miller is included with a quote from his *Paris Review* interview and a five-sentence biographical sketch, accompanied by a full-page black-and-white photograph of Miller reading at a table in his New York City apartment, 5 December 1997.

Leaming, Barbara. *Marilyn Monroe*. New York: Crown, 1998.

Well-researched biographical account of the life and career of Marilyn Monroe that includes details of her relationship with Arthur Miller, culled from letters, diaries, and interviews.

West, James L. W., III. *William Styron, A Life*. New York: Random House, 1998. 285–86, 401.

There are but two references of note in the biography of Styron. The first was a recollection from soon after Miller had married Marilyn Monroe and they had purchased property in Roxbury, Connecticut, where Styron also lived. The playwright and the author had not yet met, but Styron recalls that the locals were very excited by the attention their small community was getting, that property values skyrocketed, and that he caught one glimpse of Monroe one morning while he was driving by: she is a bathrobe putting out empty bottles of milk on the back stoop. Later in Styron's life, he and Miller became good friends, and after being urged to try his hand at writing for the stage, Styron would periodically visit Miller in his home and the two would discuss the difference between writing prose fiction and drama dialogue, which Miller felt was a freer form.

Wolfe, Donald H. *The Last Days of Marilyn Monroe*. New York: Morrow, 1998.

Biographical account of the life of Marilyn Monroe that includes substantial detail of her relationship with Miller.

Riggs, Doug. "Books Winter's Best Pulitzer-Prize Winners, Local Authors to Speak." *Providence Sunday Journal* 18 January 1998.

Short news article which announces Miller's appearance as the concluding speaker at the 1998 Brown University/*Providence Journal* Public Affairs Conference, "The New Agenda for the Arts," 23 February to 1 March.

"Authors to Give Lectures." *New York Amsterdam News* 5 February 1998: 22.

Short news item announcing Miller's decision to participate in Yeshiva University's "Author-in-Residence" program and present a public lecture.

"Peterborough: Arthur Miller Reconnects with Broadway." *Daily Telegraph* (London) 12 February 1998.

News item announcing Miller having completed a new play titled *Mr. Peters' Connections* and quoting Christopher Bigsby as saying he as intrigued after reading it—"It is in a non-realist style and very difficult."

Taitte, Lawson. "Productions Prove It's Miller's Time." *Dallas Morning News* 15 February 1998: C1.

Lengthy article detailing the Signature Theatre Company's season of Miller works. Comments of praise from Michael Mayer, James Fisher, James Houghton, Ed Bullins, and Sidney Berger are included.

Gale, William K. "'America's Greatest Living Playwright' Award, Applause Bestowed on Miller." *Providence Journal-Bulletin* 2 March 1998.

Short news article detailing the awarding of the Pell Award at the Rhode Island Convention Center to Arthur Miller as "America's Greatest Living Playwright."

Honan, William H. "Harlan Hatcher, 99, U. of Michigan President." *New York Times* 4 March 1998: B10.

Included for brief but significant mentioning of Miller. Says Miller wrote *The Crucible* in reaction to the anti-Communist paranoia he saw in 1953 on the campus of the University of Michigan.

Lyman, Rick. "Six Degrees of 'Footloose.'" *New York Times* 6 March 1998: E2.

On Stage and Off column that lists, among many other items, that Miller will be the first playwright to receive the Lucille Lortel Award for lifetime achievement in the theatre.

"Benefits." *New York Times* 8 March 1998: Sec. 9: 8.

Short blurb announcing a reading of Miller's 1941 radio comedy "The Pussycat and the Expert Plumber Who Was a Man" at the New Victory Theatre to benefit the theatre company's current season devoted to Miller's plays.

Bass, Cato. "Peggy Sherry, 66, Retired Teacher in DeKalb Schools." *Atlanta Constitution* 24 March 1998: B6.

Obituary for retired teacher Sherry, noted for arranging video conferences at DeKalb College with award-winning playwrights, Edward Albee, Alfred Uhry, and Arthur Miller.

Boxer, Sarah. "Close, but Keeping Her Distance." *New York Times* 27 March 1998: E39.

Profile of Inge Morath on the occasion of photographic retrospective at the Leica Gallery. Of note is Morath's feelings regarding one of her most famous subjects, Marilyn Monroe, who she met as a photographer for Magnum on the set of *The Misfits*.

Taylor, Robert. "Bookmaking." *Boston Globe* 29 March 1998: G3.

News item announcing Miller as the keynote speaker at the John F. Kennedy Library for an annual book event honoring authors.

"Front and Center." *American Theatre* April 1998: 8.
Brief mention of Miller winning the Pell Award from the state of Rhode Island for Lifetime Achievement.

Breslin, Meg McSherry. "Nora Smith, Host of Intellectual Gatherings." *Chicago Tribune* 4 April 1998: 19.
In this obituary for Nora Stone Smith, famous for hosting a salon for writers, artists, and activists in the 1960s and 1970s, Miller is mentioned as among her well-known guests.

Kenney, Michael. "Miller Draws PEN Awards Throng." *Boston Globe* 6 April 1998: C8. See also "Bacon Wins Fiction Award." *Patriot Ledger* (Quincy, Mass.) 6 April 1998.
With an overflow crowd of close to seven hundred at the John F. Kennedy Library, keynote speaker Miller talked about his years as president of PEN International and his goals to get Soviet writers to join.

Wadler, Joyce. "Portrait of a Photojournalist." *New York Times* 6 April 1998: A17.
Biographical feature of photographer Inge Morath on the occasion of her retrospective show at the Leica Gallery in New York. Morath comments on her marriage to Miller, including their first meeting, and her memories of Marilyn Monroe, who was the subject of a Magnum shoot on the set of *The Misfits*.

"Playwright Miller to Speak at Symposium Bearing His Name." *South Bend Tribune* 9 April 1998: D4.
Short news item detailing Miller's planned involvement with the Arthur Miller Symposium to be held at the University of Evansville, Indiana, 17–19 April 1998.

"People." *Star Tribune* 21 April 1998: B5.
Brief mention of Miller's appearance at the Arthur Miller Symposium at the University of Evansville in Indiana, prompted by Professor William Baer's decision in 1990 to send Miller a copy of the university's small poetry journal, *Formalist*. Miller liked the journal and eventually chose to become a member of the journal's advisory board.

"Newsmakers." *The Florida Times-Union* 21 April 1998.
Short news item offering details of Miller's appearance at the Arthur Miller Symposium at the University of Evansville in Indi-

ana from 17–19 April 1998. Of note is Miller's comment that many of the roles he has created are self-portraits.

van Gelder, Lawrence. "Footlights." *New York Times* 22 April 1998: E1.

Short news item announcing that Miller, along with author Ward Just, the poet C. K. Williams, and filmmaker Errol Morris are among sixteen American scholars, artists, and other professionals who have been named the first recipients of the Berlin Prize Fellowships. Miller has been designated the Distinguished Inaugural Senior Fellow. Miller will spend one or two academic semesters at the Hans Arnhold Center and work on a project that "could have significant impact on U.S.-German cultural and intellectual relations."

Butler, Charles. "And the Nominees Are. . ." *Sales & Marketing Management* May 1998: 6.

Item announcing the nominations for the "80 Most Influential Sales and Marketing People and Products of All Time" in honor of the eightieth anniversary of the journal. Miller is listed among the likes of Thomas Edison, Bill Gates, Henry Ford, and Martha Stewart. Readers are encouraged to cast their vote by 1 June 1998.

van Gelder, Lawrence. "Arthur Miller Gets Award from PEN" *New York Times* 9 May 1998: B10.

News item announcing Miller as the first ever recipient of the PEN/Laura Pels Foundation Award to a master American dramatist.

Kilborn, Robert, and Lance Carden. "Etceteras." *Christian Science Monitor* 18 May 1998: 2.

News item announcing Miller as the recipient of a lifetime achievement award from PEN at the 1998 book awards ceremony in New York.

Arenson, Karen W. "3 Playwrights Urge CUNY to Keep Taking Remedial Students." *New York Times* 19 May 1998: B8.

News item about playwrights Wendy Wasserstein, Tony Kushner, and David Henry Hwang urging the trustees of CUNY to continue accepting remedial students. Miller sent a statement, which Kushner read aloud, "describing himself as a slow starter who could not do chemistry" and making a case for giving all slow starters a chance.

Kornblut, Anne E. "Kohl, at Brandeis, Cites Ties with Israel." *Boston Globe* 25 May 1998: B3.

In an article reporting the commencement address of German Chancellor Helmut Kohl at Brandeis University, Miller is mentioned as receiving a doctor of humane letters for "his crusading spirit and fearless defense of freedom of expression."

Hentoff, Nat. "Safir Protects His Cops—Not You." *Village Voice* 26 May 1998: 22.

In an article denouncing police brutality in New York, Hentoff makes mention that on Wednesday, 27 May, he, Mike Wallace, Miller, William Styron, and Kelly Michaels will speak on this issue at a press conference at the New York Academy of Sciences.

Applebome, Peter. "In Reversal, Theatre Vows to Stage Play That Drew Threats." *New York Times* 29 May 1998: A1.

Lengthy article detailing the Manhattan Theatre Club's decision to stage Terrence McNally's new play, *Corpus Christi*, as planned, thus reversing its earlier decision to cancel the production because of objections, protests, and bomb threats. Miller, among thirty other playwrights, signed a statement of support praising the theater for its "brave and honorable decision."

"Brandeis 1998 Graduates Give Kohl Two Standing Ovations." *Jewish Advocate* 4 June 1998: 1.

News item that mentions Miller's acceptance of an honorary degree at Brandeis University.

Cockfield, Errol A. "Brookhaven Bidding on Estate." *Newsday* 4 June 1998: A35.

News item announcing that Brookhaven town officials have decided to try to buy the thirty-nine-acre Chandler Estate, once the home to Marilyn Monroe and Arthur Miller.

Hudson, Yvonne. "Arthur Miller Speaks to YU Students." *Yeshiva University Today Online* 11 June 1998. http://www.yu.edu/news/YUToday/6-11-98/Arthur%20Miller.html.

News item detailing Miller's audience discussion at Yeshiva University on the eve of the premiere of *Mr. Peters' Connections*.

Bianco, Robert. "Critic's Corner." *USA Today* 17 June 1998: D12.

Miller is listed as among those interviewed for PBS American Masters documentary on artist Alexander Calder.

Vellela, Tony. "*Beauty Queen* Director Puts Spotlight on Irish Stage." *Christian Science Monitor* 19 June 1998: B7.

Profile of Irish director Garry Hynes whose production of Martin McDonagh's *The Beauty Queen of Leenane* won her a Tony Award for Best Director. Miller is noted as attending a performance of *Lonesome West* and being so impressed with Ms. Hynes' work that he sent her a copy of his newest play, *Mr. Peters' Connections*, with an invitation to direct its premiere in New York.

Smith, Liz. "A New Day-Lewis." *New York Post* 18 June 1998. http://206.15.118.165061898/3418.htm (4 April 1999).

Gossip column announcement of the birth at New York's Beth Israel Hospital of Miller's grandson by daughter Rebecca and her husband Daniel Day-Lewis.

Maker, Elizabeth. "In Litchfield, a Benefit for Victims of Abuse." *New York Times* 21 June 1998: CN 14.

Article dealing with the fund-raising event, called the Magical Mystery Tour, at the Susan B. Anthony Project benefit, a nonprofit organization that helps victims of domestic violence and sexual abuse, for which Miller and Mia Farrow served as honorary co-chairpeople.

Johnson, Richard. "Page Six." *New York Post* 24 June 1998. http://206.15.118.165/062498/pagesix.htm (4 April 1999).

Gossip news item that mentions Miller's involvement in the plight of Michael Pardue, a forty-one-year-old man who has been in an Alabama prison for twenty-five years for three murders that he never committed. While the Alabama courts overturned the guilty verdict on the grounds that his confession was illegally obtained (coerced), the Mobile district attorney is fighting to keep him in prison for life for Pardue's attempted escape.

Gussow, Mel. "Artists See No Decency in Ruling on Grants." *New York Times* 2 July 1998: E1.

Lengthy article that includes reactions from artists on the Supreme Court's decision upholding a decency test for federal arts grants. Miller recalls his own experiences with facing two separate charges of indecency—once, in 1947, when *All My Sons* was condemned in Boston by the Catholic Church, and when the Legion of Decency demanded changes in *The Misfits*. Additionally, Miller comments on performance artist Karen Finley's controversial performance art. Says Miller, "Anyone who smears herself with chocolate needs all the support she can get. If she covered herself in vanilla, they might not have been so outraged."

Travis, Neal. "Gloria's Weekend for Jones." *New York Post* 10 August 1998. http://206.15.118.165/081098/travis.htm (4 April 1999).

Gossip news item that highlights Miller's attendance at a private screening and dinner at the SagPon Vineyard in East Hampton for the Merchant-Ivory film *A Soldier's Daughter Never Cries*, based on the book by Kaylie Jones, daughter of the late novelist James Jones.

Bozell, L. Brent, III. "What Invincible Political Ignorance Spews from Hollywood." *Human Events* 14 August 1998: 4.

Bozell awards Miller a silver medal for his comments regarding the Supreme Court's upholding of a decency test for federal arts grants, which Bozell calls "a commosensical no-brainer if ever there was one." Miller is reported in this article (without citation of source) to have said that "Certain kinds of art will always be called indecent, and they need support" and, referring to performance artist Karen Finley, "Anyone who smears herself with chocolate needs all the support she can get. If she covered herself in vanilla, they might not have been so outraged."

"New Faces of '98." *Entertainment Weekly* 14 August 1998: 71.

Short news article announcing the replacement of Anthony LaPaglia with Tony Danza in the acclaimed revival of *A View from the Bridge*, followed by the week's financial statistics for the top twenty-three Broadway shows. Of note is *Bridge*, which is in its 105th performance and has a 59.6% attendance ratio, with net weekly receipts totaling $171,116.

Bambarger, Bradley. "Keeping Score." *Billboard* 15 August 1998: 30.

Positive review of Decca/London's Penguin Music Series, which "pairs landmark classical works with personal essays on the music from renowned authors." Bambarger especially enjoyed Miller's notes for Beethoven's Symphonies Nos. 5 and 7 and his recollection of taking Lee J. Cobb to a Beethoven concert before the 1949 premiere of *Salesman* "in order to illustrate the ideals of timing and restraint in interpreting the character of Willy Loman."

"*Pack* Widow Gives Star an Earful." *New York Post* 18 August 1998. http://206.15.118.165/081898/pagesix.htm (4 April 1999). See also James Barron, "Public Lives." *New York Times* 18 August

1998: B2.

Gossip news item making mention of Miller's appearance, among other literary notables, at a party celebrating the release of *A Soldier's Daughter Never Cries* (a Merchant-Ivory film), hosted by Chris Meigher.

Krebs, Brenda. "New Awards for Old Stars." *Miami Herald* 21 August 1998.

News article announcing the 1998 recipients of the twenty-first annual Kennedy Center honors: Shirley Temple Black, Bill Cosby, Willie Nelson, John Kander and Fred Ebb, and Andre Previn. Of note, is the mention that the evening before the ceremony, Secretary of State Madeleine Albright will host a winners' dinner, chosen by 132 national committee members, of which Miller is one.

Preston Julia. "PEN Leader in Mexico Tells of Threats." *New York Times* 29 August 1998: B10.

New item in which Miller is mentioned as among twelve writers who have sent a letter to President Ernesto Zedillo of Mexico asking him to ensure the safety of writer Homero Aridjis, a leading opponent of the Mexican government who has been receiving death threats.

Morath, Inge. "About My Photographs." *Michigan Quarterly Review* 37.4 (Fall 1998): 695–712.

Essay on the enrichment of living with a writer by Miller's wife, photographer Inge Morath, followed by sixteen photographs (one taken by Jerzy Kosinski) showing Miller at work and relaxing on their farm in Roxbury, Connecticut.

Woodford, John. "In Honor of Arthur Miller '38." *Michigan Today* Fall 1998. http://www.umich.edu/~newsinfo/MT/98/Fal98/mt7f98.html (11 April 1999).

Interview with Professor Enoch Brater, an expert on modern drama, in which the University of Michigan professor talks about his decision to offer a course entitled "The Stages of Arthur Miller" devoted to the work of the famous UM alumnus.

"Worthwhile Theatrics: Arthur Miller Theatre Will Enhance Arts Community." *Michigan Daily* 10 September 1998. http://www.pub.umich.edu/daily/1998/09-10-98/edit/edit1.html (11 April 1999).

Editorial supporting University of Michigan President Lee Bollinger's decision to build a new theatre on the university campus in honor of famous alum Miller.

Sterngold, James. "For Artistic Freedom, It's Not the Worst of Times." *New York Times* 20 September 1998: Sec. 2: 1.

In this essay on the status of artistic freedom, Miller comments on the differences between the 1950s, when there was a "generalized organization commanding a black list," and today—"There's really no comparison to now in terms of the pressure that existed back then and the kinds of things that get done today."

Tkaczyk, Christopher. "Miller Began Rich Writing Career While Still at 'U'." *Michigan Daily* 24 September 1998. http://www.pub.umich.edu/daily/1998/sep/09-24-98/arts/arts2.html (11 April 1999)

Photo of Miller with a caption offering brief biographical information regarding his writing awards earned while a student at the University of Michigan.

Weissert, Will. "Miller Theatre Could Open in Less than Two Years." *Michigan Daily* 24 September 1998. http://www.pub.umich.edu/daily/1998/sep/09-24-98/arts/arts1.html (11 April 1999)

News item detailing University of Michigan President Lee Bollinger's decision to to build a mid-sized theater on campus and name it "in honor of one of the University's most famous graduates—Arthur Miller."

Siegel, Ed. "Art vs. Entertainment in America." *Boston Globe* 5 October 1998: B6.

In an article reporting the development of a new play by Robert Brustein at the ART entitled *Nobody Dies on Friday*, a play about the Strasbergs and Marilyn Monroe, Miller is mentioned for his own professed dislike of the Strasbergs (Paula and Lee) in his autobiography.

Kettle, Martin. "Arthur Miller Likens Pursuit of Clinton to Salem Witch-Hunts." *Guardian* (London) 16 October 1998: Sec. 1: 1.

News article detailing Miller's *New York Times* comments (reprinted in this issue of the *Guardian*) likening the "gut-wrenching hatred" of President Clinton's accusers to "the fury of the Salem ministers roaring down the Devil."

Letters. *New York Times* 16 October 1998: 26.

Four letters to the editor written in response to Miller's essay of 15 October, entitled "Salem Revisited," where the playwright likened the investigation of President Clinton to a witch hunt.

Bentham, Martin. "Arthur Miller Is Named as Playwright of the Century." *Daily Telegraph* (London) 18 October 1998.

Brief news item which announces Miller as the "best playwright of the 20th Century" in a survey by the Royal National Theatre of more than 800 playwrights, actors, directors, and art critics.

Dearth, Bill. *Daily News of Los Angeles* 18 October 1998: V2.

Letter to the editor written in support of Miller's essay of 15 October, entitled "Salem Revisited," where the playwright likened the investigation of President Clinton to a witch hunt.

Lister, David. "*Waiting for Godot* Voted Best Modern Play in English." *Independent on Sunday* (London) 18 October 1998: 3.

Short news item announcing the three most important plays of the 20th century in the English language, according to a survey by the Royal National Theatre. Samuel Beckett's *Waiting for Godot* was named as first, Miller's *Death of a Salesman* second, and Williams's *A Streetcar Named Desire* came in third.

Dirda, Michael. "Readings." *Washington Post* 18 October 1998: 15.

Lengthy commentary on the release of the new "Penguin Music Classics" series, which will include liner notes by Wendy Wasserstein, Garrison Keillor, and Arthur Miller.

Malpede, Karen. "A Role for Theatre in Fighting Terror." *New York Times* 18 October 1998: Sect. 2: 24.

In this feature article reporting on the events and surrounding controversy at the Cairo International Festival for Experimental Theatre, Miller is mentioned as providing a video greeting during the opening festivities.

van Gelder, Lawrence. "Footlights." *New York Times* 20 October 1998: E1.

News item announcing Miller's *Death of a Salesman* taking second place to Samuel Beckett's *Waiting for Godot* as the most significant plays of the twentieth century in a poll taken by the Royal National Theatre in London.

Wilcox, David. "Clintonite's Salem Scenario Misses Mark." *Daily News of Los Angeles* 20 October 1998: N12.

Calling Miller's attempt to draw an analogy between the witch-hunting activities of 300 years ago and the impeachment of President Clinton "preposterous," letter to the editor writer Wilcox argues that while Salem's goal was to execute the accused, Clinton's final punishment would only be to lose his job.

Kimball, Roger. "Literati Genuflect before St. Bill the Puritan-Slayer." *Wall Street Journal* 21 October 1998: A22.

Lengthy commentary on the recent deluge of public indictments of Kenneth Starr's tactics in the investigation of President Clinton by literary giants such as Toni Morrison, Jane Smiley, E. L. Doctorow, Cynthia Ozick, William Styron, and Arthur Miller. Miller is mentioned for his 15 October 1999 op-ed piece in the *New York Times* in which he "once again wheeled out the argument from his play *The Crucible*."

Smith, Liz. "The Greatest? Arthur Miller, British Say." *Philadelphia Inquirer* 21 October 1998: D2.

Incorrect news item announcing Miller's *The Crucible* being voted the second most important play of the twentieth century by more than 800 playwrights, actors, directors, and critics in a survey conducted by the British Royal National Theatre [the correct play was *Death of a Salesman*], and Miller being voted the playwright of the century.

Letters. *Daily News of Los Angeles* 22 October 1998: N14.

Two letters to the editor written in response to Miller's essay of 15 October, entitled "Salem Revisited," where the playwright likened the investigation of President Clinton to a witch hunt.

Letters. *New York Times* 22 October 1998: 26.

Two letters to the editor written in response to Miller's essay of 15 October, entitled "Salem Revisited," where the playwright likened the investigation of President Clinton to a witch hunt.

"Poll Says *Godot* Is Best Modern Play in English." *Christian Science Monitor* 22 October 1998: 2.

News item announcing the list of the top ten most important plays of the twentieth century, as voted in a survey by the British National Theatre of 800 playwrights, actors, directors, theatre professionals, and arts journalists. Miller's *Death of a Salesman* was voted number two, behind Beckett's *Waiting for Godot* and ahead of Williams's *A Streetcar Named Desire*. Miller's *The Crucible* placed number six.

Miller, Megan J. "Letter to the Editor." *Daily News of Los Angeles* 29 October 1998: N18.

Letter to the editor written in support of Miller's essay of 15 October, entitled "Salem Revisited," where the playwright likened the investigation of President Clinton to a witch hunt. Says Ms. Miller, the essay was "one of the most concise, rational, and important examples of critical thinking I've read concerning President Clinton's situation."

Chabot, Hillary. "Prejudice, Hate Crime on Agenda for ADL." *Boston Globe* 10 November 1998.

Brief news item announcing the eighty-fifth annual national meeting of the Anti-Defamation League in Boston and their honoring of both the *Boston Globe* and Arthur Miller with awards. Miller is to receive the Hubert H. Humphrey First Amendment Freedoms Prize.

Pacheco, Patrick. "Arthur Miller and the Life of a Playwright." *Newsday* 12 November 1998: B9.

Overview of Miller's current international popularity that includes comments by Patrick Stewart, star of the American premiere of *The Ride Down Mount Morgan* at the Public Theatre.

Johnson, Syrie. "The Writers' Circus Is Coming to Town." *Evening Standard* 11 December 1998: 30.

Interview with Hay-on-Wye festival chairman Peter Florence about his coup in bringing in the top literary talent and the current roster of notables who will be present at his new festival in London called The Word. Miller is mentioned as among those who have participated with enthusiasm in the past.

1999

Davidson, Bruce. *Portraits*. New York: Aperture, 1999. 54.

Black-and-white portrait photograph of Miller, wife Inge Morath, and daughter Rebecca, taken in New York City in 1987.

Dews, Carlos, ed. *Illumination and Night Glare: The Unfinished Autobiography of Carson McCullers*. U of Wisconsin P, 1999. 60-61.

McCullers briefly mentions Miller in reference to the time Isak Dinesen wanted to meet Marilyn Monroe and the couple was invited for lunch. Half-page black-and-white photograph of the luncheon accompanies the text.

Young, Jeff. *Kazan: The Master Director Discusses His Films: Interviews with Elia Kazan*. New York: Newmarket Press, 1999. 41, 120, 125.

Brief mention of Miller in three instances: in the first, Kazan says Miller is in the line-up scene in his 1947 *Boomerang*; in the second, that he knew he would lose Miller's plays when he named names before HUAC; and in the third, Kazan retells the story, previously published in his autobiography, of Miller backing out of "The Hook" with a phone call while Kazan was in a budget meeting for the production.

Jolley, H. Scott. "The Beat Goes On." *Elle* January 1999: 178.

Brief item announcing the release of a hand-bound book that costs $5,000 which pairs the text of authors such as Miller and Edward Albee with original art from Nan Goldin, Gus Van Sant, and others in a tribute to the late Allen Ginsberg. Profits from each signed edition will go toward student poetry scholarships.

"Writing through Reading Program Hosts a Reading by Playwright Arthur Miller." *New York Voice* (Harlem) 6 January 1999: 18.

News item announcing that Miller has agreed to be the first writer to participate in the sixth season of the Writing through Reading Program, hosted by the Union Settlement in collaboration with the 92nd Street Y Unterberg Poetry Center.

Kootnikoff, Lawrence. "Liberal Group Lobbies to Stop Clinton Impeachment Process." *Agence France Presse* 8 January 1999. *Lexis-Nexis* (9 January 1999).

Newswire article reporting that Miller was among fifty-three prominent Americans to take out a full-page ad in the *Washington Post* under the banner of People for the American Way, which called on the U.S. Congress to "listen to the people and stop the impeachment process."

"Britons Choose Plays of the Century." *New York Times* 24 January 1999: Sect. 5, p. 3.

Short news item which details London's Royal National Theatre's celebration of the twentieth century in a year-long program called NT2000. Each forty-five-minute program will be devoted to one of one hundred plays deemed the century's most significant. Miller is reported as the most frequently nominated author. While not reporting that Miller will personally attend, it is noted that, when possible, leading actors, authors, and original cast members will be invited to talk about the plays or read from them. *Death of a Salesman* is scheduled for a 23 March 1999 program.

Russo, Francine. "Classic Act: Barry Edelstein Takes Over CSC." *Village Voice* 26 January 1999: 122.

Lengthy feature reporting Barry Edelstein's new job as the head of the Classic Stage Company, his casting strategies, and plans for the theatre organization. Miller is mentioned as providing the "nod" that encouraged the board to interview Edelstein.

Samiljan, Tom. "Explaining the Classics." *Elle* February 1999: 72.

Short piece announcing Penguin Music Classics (London Records) decision to include CD booklets with their starter library of classical standards written by well-known authors. Miller's notes to Beethoven's Seventh Symphony includes the anecdote that Lee J. Cobb learned his dramatic climaxes for *Salesman* while listening to the work.

Paik, Felicia. "Private Properties." *Wall Street Journal* 5 February 1999: W8.

Short news item announcing that Frank McCourt, the author of the bestselling book *Angela's Ashes* has just purchased a twenty-five-acre piece of property as his "retreat" next door to Miller in Roxbury, Connecticut.

Lieberman, Paul. "Miller's Undying *Salesman*." *Los Angeles Times* 5 February 1999: A1.

Lengthy news article detailing the audience reactions to preview performances (they have "squirmed just like the ones in 1949") of the fiftieth anniversary production of *Salesman*, starring Brian Dennehy. Of biographical note, Lieberman reports that Miller is preparing to fly to Ireland to visit daughter Rebecca, her husband Daniel Day-Lewis, and their seven-month old son. "He's also eager to get away, at least for ten days, from everyone tugging at his sleeve, waiting for him to size up his *Salesman* once more."

"'It's All Right. I've Come Back.'" *New York Times* 11 February 1999: A1.

Photo of Miller at the opening of the fiftieth anniversary of *Death of a Salesman.*

"Dreams Fulfilled." *Chicago Sun-Times* 11 February 1999: 33.

Feature article that pays tribute to Miller on the occasion of his fiftieth anniversary production of *Salesman.* In it, Robin Rosenblate relates that while a junior at New Trier High School in 1983, she wrote a paper analyzing *All My Sons* and *Death of a Salesman* and was so moved by the plays that she wrote to Miller and sent him a copy of the paper. He wrote back telling her how much her letter had meant to him.

Fink, Mitchell. "Arthur Miller Ponders Death & His *Salesman.*" *Daily News* 12 February 1999.

News item regarding the opening of the fiftieth anniversary production of *Death of a Salesman*, including a list of celebrities present and Miller's comments about being the sole survivor of the original 1949 cast.

Wallis, David. "Antichrists among Us." *Nation* 15 February 1999: 6.

Editorial satirizing the Rev. Jerry Falwell's announcement that the Antichrist "is probably alive and a male Jew" by listing nine famous living Jewish men who might suit Falwell's bill, along with the Vegas odds. Miller is listed at 66–1 for his writing *The Crucible*, a play that "is interpreted as a parable of McCarthyism in which the ministers are the villains."

Tkaczyk, Christopher. "It's Miller Time." *Michigan Daily* 19 February 1999. http://www.pub.umich.edu/daily/1999/feb/02-19-99/news18.html (11 April 1999).

Lengthy profile of two works by Miller being produced at the University of Michigan (Miller's alma mater) the same semester—*The Crucible* and *All My Sons*.

Werts, Diane. "The TV Box." *Newsday* 18 February 1999: B31.

News article announcing a seminar on "Television and the Holocaust" to be held at the Museum of Television and Radio in New York City on 3 March 1999. Panelists include Miller and Ernest Kinoy.

"On Line." *Chronicle of Higher Education* 19 February 1999: A27.

News item announcing that Miller is among the authors who have agreed to participate in on-line chats with students who have purchased "bundled" books from Addison Wesley Longman and Penguin Putnam, publishers sponsoring the events.

Nemy, Enid. "Metropolitan Diary." *New York Times* 22 February 1999: B2.

Brief mention is made of one Roy Fox who attended a preview performance of the fiftieth anniversary production of *Death of a Salesman.* Mr. Fox noticed Miller sitting across the aisle taking notes. "Toward the end of the evening, there is a moment when the stage goes dark but there is more to come. One theatregoer, thinking the play had ended, began applauding. Mr. Fox then heard Mr. Miller's rather loud whisper: 'Not yet!'"

Oliphant, Thomas. "Honoring a Dishonorable Man." *Boston Globe* 2 March 1999: A15.

Op-ed piece that notes the very different political lives of thee men and one woman (Kazan, Cobb, Miller, and Mildred Dunnock), "united in an artistic triumph arguably without parallel in the American theater"—the original production of Miller's *Death of a Salesman*—on the occasion of Kazan's award for lifetime achievement by the Motion Picture Academy.

"High Broadway Ticket Prices Bar New Ideas, Miller Says." *Times Union* (Albany), 3 March 1999: A2.

While at the Carnegie Music Hall in Pittsburgh, this short news item quotes Miller as saying that "The fact is, and nobody listens to me, is that there are no new plays being written for Broadway today" because high ticket prices on Broadway are prohibiting unproven ideas from being produced.

Conlin, Bill. "Untitled." *Philadelphia Daily News* 9 March 1999.

In an essay about the late Joe DiMaggio, Conlin shares his memories of Miller, "a former neighbor of mine from Grace Court in Brooklyn Heights. . .[who] lived in a brownstone across the street from the six-story apartment complex where the Conlins dwelled in rent control Apartment 4-O."

"Letters to the Editor." *Los Angeles Times* 10 March 1999: 6.

Two letters to the editor written in response to Miller's commentary on the controversy surrounding Elia Kazan receiving an Academy Award for lifetime achievement.

Stearns, David Patrick. "Broadway in Bloom." *USA Today* 12 March 1999: E1.

In this lengthy feature article discussing the rich variety of choice of shows on Broadway this season, Stearns explores the "ruthless" business side of theatre that controls the art: "The minute a show's business drops, there's no slow fade into oblivion: It abruptly vanishes. . . ." Miller is mentioned, along with Brian Dennehy, as getting a rock-star's welcome at a recent book-signing at Barnes and Noble. Fans lined up at 6 a.m. to get a chance to meet the playwright and the star of *Death of a Salesman.*

Goldstein, Patrick. "A Fateful Decision, Damaging Fallout." *Los Angeles Times* 16 March 1999: F1.

Article detailing the events that brought director Elia Kazan before HUAC in 1952, including both his and Miller's differing accounts of their meeting at Kazan's house before the director's second appearance in which he named names.

Daly, Michael. "Kazan's Ghosts Haunt the Awards." *Daily News* 21 March 1999.

News and Views essay that offers a retelling of Elia Kazan's decision to name names before HUAC. Miller's relationship with Kazan and his own subsequent testimony in 1956 are also explored.

Davidson, Justin. "Met Making Plans for Bolcom's Opera." *Newsday* 29 March 1999: B13.

News item reporting the possibility (in negotiation) of William Bolcom's opera version of *A View from the Bridge* being produced at the Metropolitan Opera in New York in 2002.

Navasky, Victor. "The Forgotten Oscar." *Nation* 5 April 1999. 5–6.

Opinion piece in which Navasky (author of *Naming Names*) offers four possible responses to the Motion Picture Academy honoring Elia Kazan with a lifetime achievement Oscar: (1) to understand that Kazan's cooperation with the lesser-evil HUAC "to expose the greater-evil Stalinist Russia" was an act where the ends justify the means; (2) agree with Miller's position that, based on his own experiences, he is "sensitive to any attempts to, in effect, obliterate an artist's name because of his morals or political beliefs"; (3) agree with those who will protest the "honoring of a man who in their eyes dishonored the profession by failing to fight back when it counted"; or (4) to instead, give "an Oscar for the hundreds of blacklistees who never gave it back."

Druchniak, Jeff. "Miller Began Writing While at 'U'." *Michigan Daily* 9 April 1999. http://www.pub.umich.edu/ daily/1999/apr/04-09-99/news/news18.html (11 April 1999).

News item offering biographical information regarding Miller's days as a student at the University of Michigan. A rare photo of a twenty-three-year-old Miller in the role of Samson in *The Proud Pilgrimage* from 1938 accompanies the text.

"The Hopwood Program." http://www.umich.edu/~engldept/deptdocs/hopwood.htm (11 April 1999).

In a listing of awards and contests open to University of Michigan student writers, there is mention of "The Arthur Miller Award of the University of Michigan Club of New York Scholarship Fund," which is open to sophomores and juniors "who have demonstrated writing talent in the areas of drama, screenplay, fiction, or poetry." The prize is $1000.

de la Vina, Mark. "Arthur Miller–Attention Must Be Paid." *San Jose Mercury News* 18 April 1999: G1.

Lengthy feature article detailing Miller's appearance at San Jose State University to read from his latest play, *Mr. Peters' Connections.* Included are comments by Miller scholars Stephen Marino and Steven Centola, who offer their views on the continued success and social relevance of Miller and his works.

Pogrebin, Robin. "Playwrights of Old Flourish in Tony Nominations." *New York Times* 4 May 1999: B1. See also Ed Siegel, "*Parade* Leads Tony March on Broadway." *Boston Globe* 4 May 1999: D1.

News item announcing the 1999 Tony Award nominations, including six for the fiftieth anniversary production of *Death of a Salesman* starring Brian Dennehy and directed by Robert Falls. Miller will be awarded a special Tony for Lifetime Achievement at the ceremony on 6 June.

Dowling, Claudia Glenn. "Helmut Newton." *Life* Spring 1999: 134–45.

Profile of photographer Helmut Newton on the occasion of his award by *Life* magazine for "Lifetime Achievement in Magazine Photography." Miller, a recent Newton subject, is quoted in the article as saying "He lets you do what you want, until he lets you do what he wants."

McKinley, Jesse. "*Parade* Leads the Drama Desk Awards, Taking Six." *New York Times* 10 May 1999: E3.

Brian Dennehy was named as outstanding actor in a drama at the Drama Desk awards.

Fink, Mitchell. "Union Man Silver Crosses Picket Line." *Daily News* 14 May 1999.

News item which mentions those who did and did not choose to cross a union picketline in front of Ciprianis 42nd Street, where the 1999 PEN Literary Gala was being held. Miller attended the event and said, "It was more important for me to help PEN than worry about crossing a line. . . . PEN helps writers over five continents. They have one fund-raising event each year, and this was it."

van Gelder, Lawrence. "Footlights." *New York Times* 26 May 1999: A1.

In a brief news item announcing the various events scheduled at the 4th Lower East Side Festival of the Arts in New York City, Miller is mentioned as participating by making an appearance.

Goldstein, Laurence. "Untimeliness, after Arthur Miller." *TriQuarterly* (Spring/Summer 1999): 11–12.

Poem recounting incidents from Miller's short story "Please Don't Kill Any Thing."

"Mayor Giuliani Honors Arthur Miller, Eugene O'Neill, and Tennessee Williams at Annual Theatre Reception." Press Office of the Mayor of New York City 1 June 1999.

Press release announcing that Mayor Giuliani has proclaimed the week of May 31st through June 6th as Theatre Week in New York City and is honoring Miller at his annual Salute to the Theatre Reception at Gracie Mansion.

Brantley, Ben. "The Year Broadway Became the Boonies." *New York Times* 6 June 1999: Sec. 2: 1, 7.

Lengthy essay that examines the roster of Tony Award nominated plays and performers on the eve of the ceremony. Of note is the half-page comic illustration of noted playwrights, including Miller, by Hirschfeld.

Siegel, Ed. "*Salesman* Wins 4 Tonys." *Boston Globe* 7 June 1999: C6. See also Lloyd Rose, "Willy Loman, Winner." *Washington Post* 7 June 1999: C1. See also Robin Pogrebin, "This Year's Tonys Start Off with a Surprise." *New York Times* 7 June 1999: B1, 3. Color photograph of Miller and Inge Morath arriving the awards ceremony appears on page one. See also, Michael Ellison, "Dench Wins U.S. Stage Award." *Guardian* (London) 8 June 1999: 11.

Report of the 1999 Tony Awards proceedings, including details of Miller's acceptance speech for lifetime achievement in which he scolded Broadway producers for not taking chances on new American playwrights.

Sarkozy, Neshe. "Arthur Miller Swings into Town to Present Award." *Michigan Daily* 7 June 1999.

News item detailing the events surrounding Miller presenting the first Arthur Miller Award for Dramatic Writing at the University of Michigan.

Hentoff, Nat. "Look Who Crossed a Picket Line." *Village Voice* 8 June 1999: 28.

Hentoff reports on the various notables who chose to and chose not to cross a picket line by Local 6, Hotel, Restaurant, and Club Employees Union at Ciprianis the night of the PEN American Center's Awards gala at that restaurant. Miller is mentioned as one who crossed the line, along with Ron Silver, Dan Rather, Alan King, Oliver Stone, and Judy Blume. Those refusing to cross included Gay Talese, Spaulding Gray, George Stephanopoulos, and Paul Newman.

Weintraub, Bernard. "Top Agent Loses Role at I.C.M Talent Agency." *New York Times* 23 June 1999: E1.

News item announcing that Sam Cohn, agent to Miller, John Guare, E. L. Doctorow, Paul Newman, and Vanessa Redgrave, has been replaced as head of the New York office. Cohn, 70, will continue to represent his clients.

"The Fragile Bombshell." *Newsweek* 28 June 1999: 57.

Short article recounting the memories of Shelley Winters, John Springer, and Eli Wallach regarding Marilyn Monroe. Of note is Wallach's ruminations of the breakup of Miller and Monroe during the filming of *The Misfits*.

"American Playwright Arthur Miller Wins Gish Prize." *The Arts Report* 20 July 1999. www.infoculture.cbc.ca/archives/theatre/theatre_07201999_miller.html. (8 August 1999). See also Lawrence van Gelder, "Footlights." *New York Times* 20 July 1999: E1.

Short news item announcing Miller as the 1999 Dorothy and Lillian Gish Prize winner for his "lasting impact on the literary landscape of the United States." The Gish estate funds the award, which gives each recipient $200,000. The prize will be presented in New York on 14 October.

McShane, Larry. "Tough Week to Be an Artist in NYC." *AP Online* 1 October 1999.

Miller is reported as among the more than one hundred writers, artists, and actors who have signed a full-page advertisement supporting "Sensation," the controversial art exhibit at the Brooklyn Museum of Art that Mayor Giuliani has publicly opposed and threatened to revoke the funding for.

"Arthur Miller Honored in New York." *AP Online* 15 October 1999.

Article reporting Miller accepting the Dorothy and Lilian Gish Prize at a small gathering at the Hudson Theatre. Miller plans on distributing the prize money to various arts groups in New York.

Kinzer, Stephen. "Supporters Unconcerned About Possible Prosecution." *Dallas Morning News* 24 October 1999: A42.

Miller is listed as among forty-six world cultural figures endorsing a statement urging more rights for Kurds and ending the war that has been underway in the mostly Kurdish Southeast for fifteen years.

"The 100 Best Writers of the Century." *Writer's Digest* November 1999: 12+.

Miller is included on this list, compiled from 500 ballots cast on a web site and narrowed down by the editors from *Writer's Digest* to this list of one hundred due to his "better plays" that "typically have a strong sense of character or social awareness."

"Indelible Memories." *American Photo* November/December 1999: 56+.

American Photo asked forty-four "history makers" to name their photo of the century. Miller chose "Falling Soldier" (1936) by Robert Capa. "This picture, with its gallantry and pathos, helped inspire support in Europe and America for the Republic in a way that few images ever have for any cause."

Crowe, Cameron. "'Marilyn Monroe Had a Kind of Elegant Vulgarity About Her.'" *Daily Telegraph* (London) 8 November 1999: 16+.

In this extract of *Conversations with Billy Wilder*, director/author Cameron Crowe interviews director Billy Wilder about working with Marilyn Monroe on *The Seven Year Itch* and *Some Like It Hot*. In response to a question regarding Wilder's impression of Miller for accusing the director of "exploiting" his wife during the filming of *Some Like It Hot*, Wilder remarks, "He was an idiot." Additionally, Wilder tells a bawdy joke about Monroe meeting Miller's parents for the first time.

C.J. "Mum on Marilyn." *Star Tribune* (Minneapolis) 9 November 1999.

Gossipy item quoting an unnamed source that the Guthrie Theater was "advised to avoid 'the Marilyn subject' while interacting with" Miller during his visit to watch a production at the Guthrie Lab of his *Mr. Peters' Connections*, directed by James Houghton. When asked by actor Lawrence Hutera to autograph a photograph that showed Miller towel-drying Monroe's hair near a pool, Miller is reported to have said, "I'd rather not talk about her anymore."

Barron, James. "Public Lives: A $5,000 Apology." *New York Times* 10 November 1999: B2.

News item detailing the awarding of the Joseph Callaway Prize for protecting the right to privacy from the American Civil Liberties Union at a party at the Upper West Side apartment of producer Joseph Feury. Tony Randall, who introduced Miller, commented that the ACLU had declined to defend Miller when he was called before HUAC in the 1950s, to which Norman Siegel, the executive director of the New York group apologized, adding, "God forbid, if something like this should happen again, we would be there for you."

Levine, Susan. "White House Plans Starry Night." *Washington Post* 24 November 1999: B1.

Lengthy news item reporting Miller as among those celebrities and dignitaries who will be a guest of President and Mrs. Clinton for the Washington, D.C., New Year's Eve celebration.

2000

Stearns, David Patrick. “Timeless Arthur Miller.” *USA Today* 7 January 2000: E1.

Profile of the playwright that focuses on the plethora of important revivals of his plays either currently in production or in pre-production.

4. General Appraisals and Literary Criticism

Book-Length Studies

Bhatia, Santosh K. *Arthur Miller: Social Drama as Tragedy*. New Delhi: Arnold-Heinemann, 1985. Chapters on *The Crucible*, *A View from the Bridge*, and *The Price* have appeared in *Jodhpur Studies in English*, *Punjab Journal of English Studies*, and *Rajasthan University Studies in English*, respectively.

Bhatia offers a close reading of six of Miller's plays (*All My Sons*, *Death of a Salesman*, *The Crucible*, *A View from the Bridge*, *After the Fall*, and *The Price*) as tragedies with "a well pronounced social bias," and he concludes in stating that what Miller "attempts to dramatize is the failure of man and society to maintain a fruitful relationship with each other but he does so in such an adroit manner that the intensity and effectiveness of his plays as tragedies do not suffer."

Bigsby, C. W. E. (Christopher). *File on Miller*. London: Methuen, 1988.

Published as part of "Writers-Files" series, this small volume offers a Miller chronology, a section on Miller's plays (from *No Villain* to *Playing for Time*) that includes info on first performances, major revivals, publication, brief synopsis, and representative critical response, including Miller's own comments. It also provides a section on Miller's nondramatic works, a section entitled "The Writer on His Work," and a final bibliographical guide to other primary and secondary sources for further reading. Not annotated or comprehensive.

———, ed. *Cambridge Companion to Arthur Miller*. Cambridge: Cambridge UP, 1997.

A collection of fourteen critical essays on various periods of Miller's creative life. Contributors: Brenda Murphy, "The Tradtion of Social Drama: Miller and His Forebears"; Christopher Bigsby,

"The Early Plays"; Steven R. Centola, "*All My Sons*"; Matthew C. Roudané, "*Death of a Salesman* and the Poetics of Arthur Miller"; Thomas P. Adler, "Conscience and Community in *An Enemy of the People* and *The Crucible*"; Albert Wertheim, "*A View from the Bridge*"; Janet N. Balakian, "The Holocaust, the Depression, and McCarthyism: Miller in the Sixties"; William W. Demastes, "Miller's 1970s 'Power' Plays"; June Schlueter, "Miller in the Eighties"'; Christopher Bigsby, "Miller in the Nineties"; R. Barton Palmer, "Arthur Miller and the Cinema"; Malcolm Bradbury, "Arthur Miller's Fiction"; Stephen Barker, "Critic, Criticism, Critics"; and Susan Haedicke, "Arthur Miller: A Bibliographic Essay." See individual cites for annotation, source, and page numbers.

——— *The Portable Arthur Miller*. New York: Penguin, 1995.

Contains: "Biographical Notes" and "Introduction to the Original Edition" by Harold Clurman; "Introduction to the Revised Edition" by Bigsby; full texts of *Death of a Salesman*, *The Crucible*, *After the Fall*, *The American Clock*, *The Last Yankee*, and *Broken Glass*; excerpts from *Timebends* [autobiography, 1987] and *The Golden Years* [play, 1939]; and bibliography.

Bloom, Harold, ed. *Modern Critical Views: Arthur Miller*. New York: Chelsea, 1987.

A collection of ten critical essays, plus Bloom's introduction, on various Miller plays. Contributors: Raymond Williams, "Arthur Miller: An Overview"; Tom F. Driver, "Strength and Weakness in Arthur Miller"; Esther Merle Jackson, "*Death of a Salesman*: Tragic Myth in the Modern Theatre"; Clinton W. Trowbridge, "Arthur Miller: Between Pathos and Tragedy"; Orm Överland, "The Action and Its Significance: Arthur Miller's Struggle with Dramatic Form"; Dennis Welland, "The Drama of Forgiveness"; Leonard Moss, "The Perspective of a Playwright"; Neil Carson, "*A View from the Bridge* and the Expansion of Vision"; C. W. E. Bigsby, "Drama from a Living Center"; E. Miller Budick, "History and Other Spectres in *The Crucible*." Also included is a brief chronology and bibliography. See individual cites for annotation, source, and page numbers.

Brater, Enoch. *The Stages of Arthur Miller*. London: Thames and Hudson, 2000.

General overview that traces Miller's life and work for the general, well-informed reader.

Carson, Neil. *Arthur Miller*. New York: St. Martin's, 1982. Excerpt rpt. as "Miller's Nontheatrical Work" in *Readings on Arthur Miller*. Ed. Thomas Siebold. San Diego, Calif.: Greenhaven, 1997. 169–76.

Spanning Miller's literary career to *Playing for Time*, Carson's study offers a detailed analysis of individual works, including *The Misfits* and Miller's short stories, with discussion focusing on their political, social, and historical contexts.

Centola, Steven R., ed. *The Achievement of Arthur Miller: New Essays*. Dallas, Tex.: Contemporary Research, 1995.

Collection of fifteen new essays written specifically for this volume. Contributors are among the most prominent of today's Miller scholars, including: Christopher Bigsby, "A British View of an American Playwright"; Matthew C. Roudané, "From Page to Stage: Subtextual Dimensions in the Theater of Arthur Miller"; James A. Robinson, "Fathers and Sons in *They Too Arise*"; Brenda Murphy, "The Reformation of Biff Loman: A View from the Pre-Production Scripts"; Janet Balakian, "*Salesman*: Private Tensions Raised to a Poetic Social Level"; Charlotte Canning, "Is This a Play about Women? A Feminist Reading of *Death of a Salesman*"; Paula Langsteau, "Miller's *Salesman*: An Early Version of Absurdist Theatre"; Timothy Miller, "John Proctor: Christian Revolutionary"; Qun Wang, "The Tragedy of Ethical Bewilderment"; Jeanne Johnsey, "Meeting Dr. Mengele: Naming, Self (Re)Presentation and the Tragic Moment in Miller"; Terry Otten, "Arthur Miller and the Temptation of Innocence"; Robert A. Martin, "Arthur Miller's *After the Fall*: The Critical Context"; Gerald Weales, "Watching the *Clock*"; Steven R. Centola, "Temporality, Consciousness, and Transcendence in *Danger: Memory!*"; and June Schlueter, "Scripting the Closing Scene: Arthur Miller's *The Ride Down Mount Morgan*." See individual cites for annotation, source, and page numbers.

Clurman, Harold, ed. *The Portable Arthur Miller*. New York: Viking, 1971. Rpt. New York: Penguin, 1977.

Contains: "Biographical Notes" and "Editor's Introduction" by Clurman; full texts of *Death of a Salesman*, *The Crucible*, *Incident at Vichy*, and *The Price*; full texts of the short stories "The Misfits," "Fame," and "Fitter's Night"; excerpts from *In Russia*" and *The Misfits* [cinema novel]; "Lines from California" [poem]; and a bibliography of works by Arthur Miller.

Corrigan, Robert W., ed. *Arthur Miller: A Collection of Critical Essays*. Englewood Cliffs, N.J.: Prentice-Hall, 1969.

Contains: Robert W. Corrigan, "Introduction: The Achievement of Arthur Miller"; Eric Mottram, "Arthur Miller: The Development of a Political Dramatist in America"; Tom F. Driver, "Strength and Weakness in Arthur Miller"; Raymond Williams, "The Realism of Arthur Miller"; M. W. Steinberg, "Arthur Miller and the Idea of Modern Tragedy"; Brian Parker, "Point of View in Arthur Miller's *Death of a Salesman*"; Robert Warshow, "The Liberal Conscience in *The Crucible*"; Herbert Blau, "The Whole Man and the Real Witch"; Gerald Weales, "Arthur Miller's Shifting Image of Man"; and Harold Clurman, "Arthur Miller's Later Plays." See individual cites for annotation, source, and page numbers.

Glassman, Bruce. *Arthur Miller*. Englewood Cliff, N.J.: Silver Burdett, 1990.

Published as part of the "Genius! The Artist and the Process" juvenile series, *Arthur Miller* discusses the life of Miller and examines the common themes explored in his works. Forty-five photos (both color and black-and-white) from Miller's life and productions accompany the text. Includes short versions of a chronology, a bibliography, and a list of selected works.

Griffin, Alice. *Understanding Arthur Miller*. Columbia: U of South Carolina P, 1996.

Part of the "Understanding Contemporary American Literature" series and designed as an all-purpose introductory guide for students and nonacademics on how to read a certain contemporary writer, Griffin's work offers a play by play analysis of Miller's canon, beginning with *All My Sons* and ending with *Broken Glass*—identifying themes, point of view, structure, symbolism, and critical response.

Hayman, Ronald. *Arthur Miller*. New York: Ungar, 1972.

Hayman's study explores the tragic nature, father and son relationships, thematic concerns, structural format, language, and character of Miller's plays, up to and including *The Price*.

Hogan, Robert G. *Arthur Miller*. Minneapolis: U of Minnesota P, 1964. Excerpt rpt. as "A Comparison of *The Crucible* and *Death of a Salesman*" in *Readings on Arthur Miller*. Ed. Thomas Siebold. San Diego, Calif.: Greenhaven, 1997. 160–63.

Forty-five page literary biography (up to *After the Fall*) of Arthur Miller, who Hogan says writes in the tradition of Sophocles, Racine, and Ibsen. Of note is the analysis of some of Miller's published radio plays.

Huftel, Sheila. *Arthur Miller: The Burning Glass*. New York: Citadel, 1965. Portion rpt. as "Subjectivism and Self-Awareness." *Twentieth Century Interpretations of "The Crucible," a Collection of Critical Essays*. Ed. John H. Ferres. Englewood Cliffs, N.J.: Prentice-Hall, 1972. 104–106. Portion rpt. as "Miller, Ibsen, and Organic Drama." *Modern Critical Interpretations of Arthur Miller's "All My Sons."* Ed. Harold Bloom. New York: Chelsea, 1988. 33–45. Portion rpt. as *"The Crucible." Modern Critical Interpretations of "The Crucible."* Ed. Harold Bloom. New York: Chelsea, 1999. 3–18.

Analysis of Miller's literary output, including *Focus* and "A Bridge to the Savage World," up to and including *Incident at Vichy*. Of note is Huftel's examination of the critical reaction to both American and European productions and Miller's dramatic theory.

Martin, Robert A, ed. *Arthur Miller, New Perspectives*. Englewood Cliffs, N.J.: Prentice-Hall, 1982.

Contains: Robert A. Martin, "Introduction"; Kenneth Rowe, "Shadows Cast Before"; Orm Överland, "The Action and Its Significance: Arthur Miller's Struggle with Dramatic Form"; Paul Blumberg, "Work as Alienation in the Plays of Arthur Miller"; Ruby Cohn, "The Articulate Victims of Arthur Miller"; Thomas E. Porter, "The Mills of the Gods: Economics and Law in the Plays of Arthur Miller"; Gerald Weales, "Arthur Miller in the 1960s"; Leonard Moss, "Colloquial Language in *All My Sons*"; Enoch Brater, "Miller's Realism and *Death of a Salesman*"; Walter J. Meserve, "*The Crucible*: 'This Fool and I'"; J. L. Styan, "Why *A View from the Bridge* Went Down Well in London: The Story of a Revision"; Benjamin Nelson, "*A Memory of Two Mondays*: Remembrance and Reflection in Arthur Miller"; Stephen S. Stanton, "Pessimism in *After the Fall*"; Lawrence D. Lowenthal, "Arthur Miller's *Incident at Vichy*: A Sartrean Interpretation"; Gerald Weales, "All about Talk: Arthur Miller's *The Price*"; and Charles A. Carpenter, "Studies of Arthur Miller's Drama: A Selective International Bibliography, 1961–1979." See individual cites for annotation, source, and page numbers.

Martine, James J. *Critical Essays on Arthur Miller*. Boston: G. K. Hall and Co., 1979.

Collection of thirty critical essays, reviews, and interviews relating to ten Miller plays, from *The Man Who Had All the Luck* to *The Creation of the World and Other Business*. Includes a bibliographic essay as the introduction. Includes: Lewis Nichols, "The Philosophy of Work against Chance Makes Up *The Man Who Had All the Luck*"; John Chapman, "*The Man Who Had All the Luck* A Good Try, But Is Out of Luck"; Arvin Wells, "The Living and the Dead in *All My Sons*"; Barry Gross, "*All My Sons* and the Larger Context"; Brooks Atkinson, "*Death of a Salesman*, A New Drama by Arthur Miller, Has Premiere at the Morosco"; Frederick Morgan, "Review of *Death of a Salesman*"; Thomas E. Porter, "Acres of Diamonds: *Death of a Salesman*"; Irving Jacobson, "Family Dreams in *Death of a Salesman*"; Brooks Atkinson, "Fredric March in *An Enemy of the People*, Adapted by Arthur Miller"; David Bronson, "*An Enemy of the People*: A Key to Arthur Miller's Art and Ethics"; Richard Watts Jr., "Mr. Miller Looks at Witch-Hunting"; Thomas E. Porter, "The Long Shadow of the Law: *The Crucible*"; Robert A. Martin, "Arthur Miller's *The Crucible*: Background and Sources"; John Chapman, "Miller's *A View from the Bridge* Is Splendid, Stunning Theatre"; Arthur D. Epstein, "A Look at *A View from the Bridge*"; John Simon, "Review of *After the Fall*"; Walter Kerr, "The View from the Mirror"; Clinton W. Trowbridge, "Arthur Miller: Between Pathos and Tragedy"; Richard Watts Jr., "Arthur Miller Looks at the Nazis"; Martin Roth, "Sept-D'un-Coup"; Lawrence D. Lowenthal, "Arthur Miller's *Incident at Vichy*: A Sartrean Interpretation"; Alan S. Downer, "Review of *The Price*"; Walter Kerr, "The Other Arthur Millers"; C. W. E. Bigsby, "What Price Arthur Miller?: An Analysis of *The Price*"; Richard Watts, "Arthur Miller's *Creation* Opens at Shubert Theater"; Douglas Watt, "Miller's *Creation of the World* is a Plodding Comedy-Drama"; James J. Martine, "'All in a Boiling Soup': An Interview with Arthur Miller"; Daniel Walden, "Miller's Roots and His Moral Dilemma: or, Continuity from Brooklyn to *Salesman*"; Allen Shepherd, "'What Comes Easier—'The Short Stories of Arthur Miller"; and Irving Jacobson, "The Vestigal Jews on Mont Sant' Angelo." See individual cites for annotation, source, and page numbers.

Moss, Leonard. *Arthur Miller*. Boston: Twayne, 1967. Rpt. in revised form in *Arthur Miller, Revised ed*. Boston: Twayne, 1980. Portion rpt. as "Colloquial Language in *All My Sons*." Portion rpt. in *Arthur Miller: New Perspectives*. Ed. Robert A. Martin. Englewood Cliffs, N.J.: Prentice-Hall, 1982. 107–14.

Moss studies the life and literature of Miller, his style of dialogue, narrative conventions, symbolic devices, and structural principles in an effort to "judge the success with which progressions of personality, theme, and tension have been executed and interrelated." Includes a biographical chapter followed by chapters on *Death of a Salesman*, four social plays, *After the Fall* and *Incident at Vichy*, *The Price* and *The Crucible*, the perspective of Miller as a playwright, and an extensive bibliography.

Murray, Edward. *Arthur Miller: Dramatist*. New York: Ungar, 1967. Portion rpt. as "The Failure of Social Vision." *Modern Critical Interpretations of Arthur Miller's "All My Sons."* Ed. Harold Bloom. New York: Chelsea, 1988. 47–61.

Admittedly not interested in genre debates or the political or social influence on the Miller canon, Murray offers, instead, an inductive analysis of seven works by Miller, closely examining structure, character, language, and themes. Works examined include *All My Sons*, *Death of a Salesman*, *The Crucible*, *A Memory of Two Mondays*, *A View from the Bridge*, *After the Fall*, and *Incident at Vichy*.

Nelson, Benjamin. *Arthur Miller, Portrait of a Playwright*. New York: McKay, 1970.

Nelson explores Miller's "relationship to the world to which he addressed himself in a dozen plays" up to and including *The Price*, against the backdrop of the depression, Miller's struggles as a writer in the early 1940s, his success with *Death of a Salesman*, HUAC, and Marilyn Monroe.

Panikkar, N. Bhaskara. *Individual Morality and Social Happiness in Arthur Miller*. New Delhi: Milind, 1982. Atlantic Highlands, N.J.: Humanities, 1982.

Revision of author's Ph.D. thesis from the University of Kerala, 1978, that attempts to relate Miller's dramatic moral vision to the American ideal of social happiness.

Rajakrishnan, V. *"The Crucible" and the Misty Tower: Morality and Aesthetics of Commitment in the Theatre of Arthur Miller*. Madras: Emerald, 1988.

After a literary survey of the Miller canon, including his connection to and influence by Clifford Odets, Lillian Hellman, and Elmer Rice, Rajakrishnan offers a thematic and structural study of "4 social plays"—*All My Sons*, *Death of a Salesman*, *A View from the Bridge*, and *The Crucible*—followed by an evaluation of Miller's aesthetic theory as presented in *After the Fall*, *Incident at Vichy*, *The Price*, and *The Creation of the World and Other Business*. Rajakrishnan concludes that Miller's popularity in Europe is directly connected to the playwright's notion of commitment in his literary works.

Ram, Atma, ed. *Perspectives on Arthur Miller*. New Delhi: Abhinav, 1988.

A collection of ten papers presented at the Symposium on Arthur Miller held at Government Postgraduate College, Dharmsala, from 3–8 June 1985. They are grouped into three parts: Perspectives on Tragedy; A Critique of Society; and Tradition and Modernity. Dr. Atma Ram includes an introduction and bibliography. Includes: Som P. Ranchan, "Four Protagonists of Miller and Integral Consciousness"; Lalit M. Sharma, "Eddie Carbone and Willy Loman: A State of Stasis"; Gulshan R. Kataria, "King Lear and Willy Loman as Victims of Personal Identity"; O. P. Dogra, "Miller's *Death of a Salesman*: The Collapse of the Dream"; Dinkar Burathoki, "Father-Son Relationship in Miller's Plays"; Urmila Varma, "Modernity as a Theme and Technique in Arthur Miller's *Death of a Salesman*"; Kailash Chander, "Neurosis, Guilt and Jealousy in *A View from the Bridge*"; T. N. Dhar, "The Cognitive Rhythm in Arthur Miller: Theory and Practice"; Ramesh K. Srivastava, "The Manifest and the Hidden in Arthur Miller's *All My Sons*." See individual cites for annotation, source, and page numbers.

Schlueter, June, and James K. Flanagan. *Arthur Miller*. New York: Ungar, 1987. Portion rpt. in *Modern Critical Interpretations of "The Crucible."* Ed. Harold Bloom. New York: Chelsea, 1998. 113–21

Part of series entitled "Literature and Life: American Writers," this work contains twelve chapters (covering *All My Sons* through *The Archbishop's Ceiling*), a chronology through 1987, notes, and bibliography. With an introductory biographical chapter and a concluding chapter, each other chapter offers critical analysis of the plays. Partly relies on Flanagan's 1969 dissertation for chapters on *The Crucible*, *A View from the Bridge*, and *After the Fall*.

Siebold, Thomas, ed. *Readings on Arthur Miller*. San Diego, Calif.: Greenhaven, 1997.

Anthology of twenty-one essays on the Miller canon, published as part of the Greenhaven Press Literary Companion to "American Authors" series, organized in five chapters: articles on Miller as a writer; major themes; analysis of *Death of a Salesman*; analysis of *The Crucible*; analysis of other Miller works. Most are excerpts and all essays are reprinted from other sources with new titles. Includes in-depth biography, chronology, and short bibliography of primary and secondary sources. Includes: Christopher Bigsby, "An Interview with Arthur Miller"; Allan Seager, "Miller's Writing Process"; Arthur Miller, "Influences on Miller's Writing"; Sheila Huftel, "Miller's Questioning by the House Un-American Activities Committee"; Gerald M. Berkowitz, "The Domestic Realism of Arthur Miller"; Gerald Weales, "Understanding Miller's Heroes"; William B. Dillingham, "The Individual and Society in Miller's Plays"; William J. Newman, "The Role of the Family in Miller's Plays"; Oscar G. Brockett, "An Introduction to *Death of a Salesman*"; Richard J. Foster, "*Death of a Salesman* as Tragedy"; Edward Murray, "Characterization in *Death of a Salesman*"; Winifred L. Dusenbury, "Loneliness in *Death of a Salesman*"; C. W. E. Bigsby, "The Father/Son Relationship in *Death of a Salesman*"; Harold Clurman, "Willy Loman and the American Dream"; Henry Popkin, "The Historical Background of *The Crucible*"; Bernard F. Dukore, "Character Profiles in *The Crucible*"; Sidney Howard White, "Proctor, the Moral Hero in *The Crucible*"; C. J. Partridge, "Profiles of Elizabeth Proctor and Abigail Williams in *The Crucible*"; Robert Hogan, "A Comparison of *The Crucible* and *Death of a Salesman*"; Hersh Zeifman, "An Introduction to *All My Sons*"; and Neil Carson, "Miller's Nontheatrical Work."

Singh, Pramila. *Arthur Miller and His Plays: A Critical Study*. New Delhi: H.K., 1990.

Originally presented as the author's Ph.D. dissertation, U of Bihar, Muzaffarpur, Singh studies the Miller canon as a "theatre of ideas" and his plays as products of the liberal imagination whose purpose is to awaken the social conscience of the audience.

Welland, Dennis. *Arthur Miller*. New York: Grove, 1961.

Notable as the first book-length study of Miller to appear in print. Written for series entitled "Writers and Critics." Treats Miller as a man of letters and not exclusively as a dramatist.

———. *Miller: The Playwright*. London: Methuen, 1983.

Second, revised and expanded edition of *Miller: A Study of His Plays* published by Methuen in 1979. Introductory chapter followed by eleven others that offer critical analysis of Miller's dramas (film, theatre, and television) from *The Man Who Had All the Luck* to *The American Clock*. Includes chronology, notes, and listing of the American and British premieres of Miller's plays and films.

———. *Miller: A Study of His Plays*. London: Methuen, 1979. Portion rpt. as "Two Early Plays." *Modern Critical Interpretations of Arthur Miller's "All My Sons."* Ed. Harold Bloom. New York: Chelsea, 1988. 91–99.

Written for series entitled "Modern Theatre Profiles." Focuses on Miller as a dramatist and on the plays as pieces for theatrical representation. Studies Miller's work from *The Man Who Had All the Luck* to *The Archbishop's Ceiling*. Superseded by *Miller: The Playwright* in 1983.

White, Sidney Howard. *The Merrill Guide to Arthur Miller*. Columbus, Ohio: Merrill, 1970.

Lengthy essay discussing Miller's literary career (up to and including *The Price*) published as a forty-seven page pamphlet that offers an introduction to Miller "aimed at the beginning student." White concludes that there are but two words to describe Miller and his career—"intellectual" and "artist."

Critical Essays in Books

Abbott, Anthony S. "Arthur Miller and Tennessee Williams." *The Vital Lie: Reality and Illusion in Modern Drama*. Tuscaloosa: U of Alabama P, 1989. 129–47.

Abbott examines the protagonists of Miller's canon as "characters who desperately *need* the illusion of innocence to stay alive, to retain their dignity as human beings. At the same time [Miller depicts] the tragic results of that need, and the terrible things that those necessary lies do to the characters and the members of their families."

Adam, Julie. *Versions of Heroism in Modern American Drama: Redefinitions by Miller, Williams, O'Neill and Anderson*." London: Macmillan, 1994.

Adam considers the various ways in which the above playwrights "approach the issue of dramatic heroism and the related literary problem of modern tragedy." She examines selected plays in terms of what she labels four versions of heroism: "idealism, martyrdom, self-reflection, and survival." Miller plays studied: *After the Fall*, *All My Sons*, *The Crucible*, and *Death of a Salesman*.

Adler, Thomas P. "Arthur Miller: Fathers and Sons, Society and Self." *American Drama, 1940–1960: A Critical History*. New York: Twayne, 1994. 62–83, 223.

Adler explores the themes of individual dignity and self-worth in *All My Sons*, *Death of a Salesman*, *The Crucible*, and *A View from the Bridge*, and the tension that exists between self, image, and society.

———. "Conscience and Community in *An Enemy of the People* and *The Crucible*." *Cambridge Companion to Arthur Miller*. Ed. Christopher Bigsby. Cambridge: Cambridge UP, 1997. 86–100.

Framed against Miller's refusal to allow the Wooster Group to excerpt his play *The Crucible* in an experimental production entitled *L.S.D. (. . . Just the High Points . . .)*, Adler explores the playwright's own adaptation of Ibsen's *An Enemy of the People* and his integration of the transcripts of the actual Salem witch trials into *The Crucible* and his interpretation and misinterpretation of them by that act.

———. *Mirror on the Stage. The Pulitzer Plays as an Approach to American Drama*. West Lafayette, Ind.: Purdue UP, 1987. 100–11.

Adler explores the Pulitzer Prize winning *Salesman* as "a play about America, about the gradual deterioration of the dream into nightmare."

Alter, Iska. "Betrayal and Blessedness: Explorations of Feminine Power in *The Crucible*, *A View from the Bridge*, and *After the Fall*." *Feminist Rereadings of Modern American Drama*. Ed. June Schlueter. Cranbury, N.J.: Associated UP, 1989. 116–45. Rpt. in *Modern Critical Interpretations of "The Crucible."* Ed. Harold Bloom. New York: Chelsea, 1999. 123–51.

Alter investigates the extent to which Miller possesses a complex vision of female power determined by masculine authority in *The Crucible*, *A View from the Bridge*, and *After the Fall.*

Ariga, Fumiyasu. "The Experimental Spirit of the American Theatre in the Forties." *American Literature in the 1940s: Annual Report, 1975*. Tokyo: The Tokyo Chapter of the American Literature Society of Japan, 1976. 194–201.

With his use of experimental cinematic devices and expressionistic techniques, it would be a mistake, says Ariga, to think of Miller as a realistic playwright.

"Arthur Miller: A Biography." *Readings on Arthur Miller*. Ed. Thomas Siebold. San Diego, Calif.: Greenhaven, 1997. 14–30.

Lengthy overview of Miller's life and professional writing career, including his political activism, his life with Marilyn Monroe, and a decade-by-decade assessment of his dramatic successes.

Aughtry, Charles Edward. "Miller and Eclecticism." *Landmarks in Modern Drama: From Ibsen to Ionesco*. Boston: Houghton, 1963. 596–97.

Brief essay introducing an excerpt from Miller's "Introduction to the *Collected Plays*" and a reprint of the complete play of *Death of a Salesman*, in which Aughtry praises Miller as "not limited by any single convention but appropriates to his use the varied resources available to the modern dramatist: in a word, he is eclectic."

Aylen, Leo. "Miller." *Greek Tragedy and the Modern World*. London: Methuen, 1964. 248–57.

In an essay that discusses *Death of a Salesman*, *The Crucible*, and *A View from the Bridge* in relation to Greek tragedy, Aylen criticizes Miller's form as "not a satisfactory one, and that his example is not therefore one to be followed too closely. He has achieved his success in spite of, rather than because of, his medium."

Aziizumi, Norioki. "On the Conservative Mood of Broadway Plays." *American Literature in the 1950s: Annual Report, 1976*. Tokyo: The Tokyo Chapter of the American Literature Society of Japan, 1977. 132–39.

In an essay surveying American drama of the 1950s, Aziizumi argues that Miller's comparative Broadway failures of *The Cru-*

cible and *A View from the Bridge*, both "wildly successful in Europe," show "how deeply social climate can influence the success or failure of a play."

Balakian, Janet. "The Holocaust, the Depression, and McCarthyism: Miller in the Sixties." *Cambridge Companion to Arthur Miller*. Ed. Christopher Bigsby. Cambridge: Cambridge UP, 1997. 115–38.

Essay that examines Miller's personal life, political activism, and dramatic output in the 1960s. Points out Balakian, while his plays written during this period all look back on the Holocaust, McCarthyism, and the depression, they all "explore the problem of denial, and to Miller this was the central issue of the moment."

Banfield, Chris. "Arthur Miller." *American Drama*. Ed. Clive Bloom. New York: St. Martin's, 1995. 82–96.

Banfield defends Miller's less well-received one-act plays of the 1980s as a misperception by the public and his critics regarding Miller's moral convictions—his "single-minded morality had been devalued by a blurring of issues which for an earlier age must have seemed black and white." Also explored is Miller's critical acclaim in England, where he is heralded as a playwright of international significance. Plays studied include: *Elegy for a Lady*, *Some Kind of Love Story*, *I Can't Remember Anything*, and *Clara*.

Barker, Stephen. "Critic, Criticism, Critics." *Cambridge Companion to Arthur Miller*. Ed. Christopher Bigsby. Cambridge: Cambridge UP, 1997. 230–44.

Barker explores Miller's "complex relationship with the critical enterprise"—from the social, cultural, and ideological criticism inherent in his plays to his provocative relationship to critics of his works—in an effort to "examine how this complex set of themes has stimulated and interacted with his dramatic writing and production."

Barksdale, Richard K. "Social Background in the Plays of Miller and Williams." *College Language Association Journal* 6.3 (March 1963): 161–69.

After documenting the historical and literary comparisons between Arthur Miller, Ben Jonson, Tennessee Williams, and Shakespeare, Barksdale explores the "controlling social context" of *Death of a Salesman*, *A View from the Bridge*, *A Streetcar Named Desire*, *Cat on a Hot Tin Roof*, and *Orpheus Descending*.

Barnwell, Michael. "Arthur Miller Bends the Law." *American Theatre* October 1996: 12–14.

A discussion of the similarities between *All My Sons* and *The Ride Down Mount Morgan*, both staged in the summer of 1996 at the Williamstown Theatre Festival in Massachusetts. Both enforce Miller's interest in portraying an Everyman struggling with morality and his attitude toward the societal implications of guilt in men.

Ben-Zvi, Linda. "'Home Sweet Home': Deconstructing the Masculine Myth of the Frontier in Modern American Drama." *The Frontier Experience and the American Dream, Essays in American Literature*. Eds. David Mogen, Mark Busby, and Paul Bryant. College Station: Texas A & M UP, 1989. 217–25.

Ben-Zvi reads Miller's plays as "reenactments of the frontier story," particularly *Death of a Salesman*, which shows the gradual demise of the inscribed frontier myth. Additionally, she faults critics who "tend to replicate" Miller's indictment of women instead of "questioning this mythic pattern" and revealing Miller's appropriation of it.

Berkowitz, Gerald M. "1945–1960, The Zenith of the Broadway Theatre." *American Drama of the Twentieth Century*. New York: Longman, 1992. 75–86. Excerpt rpt. as "The Domestic Realism of Arthur Miller" in *Readings on Arthur Miller*. Ed. Thomas Siebold. San Diego, Calif.: Greenhaven, 1997. 64–72.

Berkowitz offers a thematic analysis of *All My Sons*, *Death of a Salesman*, *An Enemy of the People*, *The Crucible*, *A Memory of Two Mondays*, and *A View from the Bridge* as dramas of "domestic realism" that address private morality, public policy, tragic destiny, and the American Dream.

———. "1960–1975, The Post Broadway Era." *American Drama of the Twentieth Century*. New York: Longman, 1992. 156–60.

Berkowitz discusses Miller's shift in playwriting from domestic stories that explore larger social and political issues to focusing on individual experiences of guiltlessness—"the sense of having failed some abstract or specific moral obligation and thus of having proved oneself inadequate or unworthy" (*After the Fall*, *Incident at Vichy*, *The Price*, and *Creation of the World and Other Business*).

———. "1975–1990, A National Theatre." *American Drama of the Twentieth Century*. New York: Longman, 1992. 169–73.

Berkowitz examines Miller's later works, which offer an "even mix" of the social and thesis-driven dramas of his early years and the psychological and spiritual explorations of the 1960s (*Archbishop's Ceiling*, *American Clock*, *Some Kind of Love Story*, *Elegy for a Lady*, *I Can't Remember Anything*, and *Clara*).

Bigsby, Christopher. "Afterword to *Arthur Miller Plays: Four*. London: Methuen, 1994. 251–75.

Lengthy essay (written in 1989) offering analysis and background information on two early Miller works (*The Golden Years* and *The Man Who Had All the Luck*). Says Bigsby, "These were plays which expressed the vaguely held beliefs of a writer trying to make sense of the economic crisis which had come close to ruining his own family and which had challenged the most fundamental myths and basic political and social conventions of a nation."

———. "Afterword to *Arthur Miller Plays: Three*." London: Methuen, 1990. 253–56.

Bigsby discusses the plot and major themes of *Some Kind of Love Story* and *Elegy for a Lady* and asserts that the two one-act plays that comprise *Two Way Mirror* "mark a new phase in the career of America's leading dramatist."

———. "Arthur Miller." *Confrontation and Commitment: A Study of Contemporary American Drama, 1959–66*. Columbia: U of Missouri P, 1967. 26–49.

Bigsby principally examines *Death of a Salesman* and *After the Fall* as the two plays in the Miller canon that most clearly exemplify Miller's use of "theatre as a means of knowing" and whose "primary mood is one of affirmation built on confrontation." Concludes Bigsby, "Miller's triumph lies in his refusal to evade and his distrust of resolution. To him the core of action lies in integrity."

———. "Arthur Miller: The Moral Imperative." *Modern American Drama, 1945–1990*. Cambridge: Cambridge UP, 1992. 72–125.

Bigsby examines Miller's historical placement within and his influence on the development of the American social drama. He concludes that Miller's real achievement "is as a writer whose plays have proved so responsive to the shifting pressure of the social world and whose characters embody that desperate desire for dignity and meaning which is the source of their wayward energy, their affecting irony and their baffled humanity."

———. "A British View of an American Playwright." *The Achievement of Arthur Miller: New Essays*. Ed. Steven Centola. Dallas, Tex.: Contemporary Research, 1995. 17–29.

After disputing critic Robert Brustein and playwright Mac Wellman's notion that Miller's drama is "preplanned, therefore predictable" (Brustein) and "a collection of yammering skeletons" (Wellman), Bigsby defends Miller as an experimental playwright who has a "commitment to a morally accountable and socially responsible self," which "has not inhibited him from exploring the contingency alike of character and public myths."

———. *A Critical Introduction to Twentieth-Century American Drama, 2: Tennessee Williams, Arthur Miller, Edward Albee*. Cambridge: Cambridge UP, 1984. Portion rpt. as "Drama from a Living Center." *Modern Critical Views: Arthur Miller*. Ed. Harold Bloom. New York: Chelsea, 1987. 103–25. Portion rpt. as "*Death of a Salesman*: In Memoriam." *Modern Critical Interpretations: Arthur Miller's "Death of a Salesman."* Ed. Harold Bloom. New York: Chelsea, 1988. 113–28. Portion rpt. as "Arthur Miller." *Major Literary Characters: Willy Loman*. Ed. Harold Bloom. New York: Chelsea, 1991. 99–111. Excerpt rpt. as "The Father/Son Relationship in *Death of a Salesman*" in *Readings on Arthur Miller*. Ed. Thomas Siebold. San Diego, Calif.: Greenhaven, 1997. 125–31.

Important book-length chapter that examines the dominant themes, moods, and images, historical parallels, and issues relating to public versus private in the Miller canon. Of note is Bigsby's use of original manuscripts and notebooks, personal interviews, as well as the published versions of Miller's plays and non-dramatic works in this exhaustive study.

———. "The Early Plays." *Cambridge Companion to Arthur Miller*. Ed. Christopher Bigsby. Cambridge: Cambridge UP, 1997. 21–47.

Important essay that offers a close reading of all of Miller's Michigan plays—*No Villain*, *They Too Arise*, *The Grass Still Grows*, *Honors at Dawn*, *The Great Disobedience*, and *The Golden Years*—as works that address the themes and topics of the time.

———. "Introduction." *Cambridge Companion to Arthur Miller*. Ed. Christopher Bigsby. Cambridge: Cambridge UP, 1997. 1–9.

Standard-fare introductory literary biography of Miller that focuses on the playwright's inspirations and influences.

———. "Introduction." *Platform Papers 7: Arthur Miller*. London: Royal National Theatre, 1995. 3–5.

Essay that introduces the transcripts of three conversations between Miller and Christopher Bigsby conducted before audiences at the Lyttelton Theatre, 3 July 1984, and at the Olivier Theatre, 14 October 1991 and 3 August 1994. Bigsby discusses the "special relationship" that Miller has enjoyed with the British and the reasons for his immense popularity abroad.

———. "Introduction to the Revised Edition." *The Portable Arthur Miller*. Ed. Christopher Bigsby. New York: Penguin, 1995. xxv–xxxix.

Bigsby charts the thematic concerns, moral commitment, and dramatic strategy of Miller's plays to *Broken Glass*.

———. "Miller in the Nineties." *Cambridge Companion to Arthur Miller*. Ed. Christopher Bigsby. Cambridge: Cambridge UP, 1997. 168–83.

Bigsby details Millers's literary output of the 1990s (three new plays, a novella, essays, and film script for *The Crucible*) and reads them as commentaries on the "state of society and nature of human values."

Binder, Wolfgang. "Manners, Morals and Success in Modern American Drama." *From Rags to Riches: Le Mythe du Self-Made Man: actes du G.R.E.N.A. (Groupe de recherche et d'études nord-américaines): 6e colloque, 2-4 mars 1984*. Aix-en-Provence: Université de Provence, 1984. 121–35.

Binder examines American playwrights Clifford Odets, Lillian Hellman, and Miller "as examples of partial ideological critiques of individualism and family values in the context of an acquisitive, competitive society." Miller plays studied: *All My Sons*, *Death of a Salesman*, and *The Price*.

Bloom, Harold. "Introduction." *Modern Critical Views: Arthur Miller*. New York: Chelsea, 1987. 1–6.

Bloom's introduction to the book he edits centers on *All My Sons* and *Death of a Salesman* and "seeks to define how both plays, particularly the latter, achieve aesthetic dignity despite Miller's limitations as a writer."

Bradbury, Malcolm. "Arthur Miller's Fiction." *Cambridge Companion to Arthur Miller*. Ed. Christopher Bigsby. Cambridge: Cambridge UP, 1997. 211–29.

Bradbury examines Miller's fictional writings, discussing his choice of themes, use of dialogue, and literary technique, and compares his novel and short stories to his dramatic work.

Brater, Enoch. "Ethics and Ethnicity in the Plays of Arthur Miller." *From Hester Street to Hollywood: The Jewish-American Stage and Screen*. Ed. Sarah Blacher Cohen. Bloomington: Indiana UP, 1983. 123–36.

"Inspired rather than influenced" by the achievement of Clifford Odets to expose "with raw honesty what it was like to grow up as an urban American Jew in the thirties," Miller, according to Brater in his essay, turned away from his own immediate heritage to reveal an even older one "within the broader context of a pluralistic American culture," to "celebrate instead the universal in all its human potentiality." Brater discounts those critics who argue that Miller's characters are "crypto-Jewish heroes," and offers, instead, a theory of analysis that takes into account Biblical typology to reveal a canon concerned with a universal question pondered in universal terms—"How may a man make of the outside world a home?"

Broussard, Louis. "Everyman at Mid-Century." *American Drama: Contemporary Allegory from Eugene O'Neill to Tennessee Williams*. Norman: U of Oklahoma P, 1962. 116–21.

After comparing *Death of a Salesman* with Elmer Rice's *The Adding Machine*, Broussard examines Miller's work as a tragedy that places the blame for the main character's downfall between man and society.

Brustein, Robert. "The Theatre of Guilt." *Dumbocracy in America.: Studies in the Theatre of Guilt, 1987–1994*. Chicago: Elephant Paperbacks, 1994. 9–17.

Says Brustein, Miller's work centers on "guilt and expiation following a climactic confrontation that leads to catastrophe." Miller's characters "preserve their innocence through being victimized by others." Miller's popularity in England is because the British feel that the pleasures of nostalgia are preferable to the ardor of self-definition.

Burathoki, Dinkar. "Father-Son Relationship in Miller's Plays." *Perspectives on Arthur Miller*. Ed. Atma Ram. New Delhi: Abhinav, 1988. 75–85.

Burathoki examines Miller's "most recurrent motif—the conflicting father-son relationship" in *All My Sons*, *Death of a Salesman*, and *The Price*, and argues that the "constant tension" that Miller shows between family members in these plays is meant as a "social message to Americans" that "has to be seriously considered if we want to make the world a better place."

Burgoyne, Suzanne. "Belgian/American Theatre Exchanges: Reflections and Bridges." *New Theatre Vistas: Modern Movements in International Theatre*. Ed. Judy Lee Oliva. New York: Garland, 1996. 25–44.

Using Miller's book *Salesman in Beijing* as a model for intercultural theatrical work, Burgoyne directed her American students in a play by Belgian Paul Willems *It's Raining in My House*, and Belgian students in scenes from *Death of a Salesman* and *The Crucible*. Says Burgoyne, "I found Miller's search for a common humanity inspiring and his analogical method effective."

Centola, Steven R. "Introduction." *The Achievement of Arthur Miller: New Essays*. Dallas, Tex.: Contemporary Research, 1995. 11–16.

Introduction to a work of new essays that champion Miller's accomplishments as "America's greatest living playwright." Also discussed is what Centola terms the "disparity in the European and American reactions to Miller's drama in recent years." The essay ends with a brief detailing of each essay's contents and their importance in Miller studies.

———. "Introduction to the Expanded Edition." *The Theater Essays of Arthur Miller*. Revised ed. Eds. Robert A. Martin and Steven R. Centola. New York: Da Capo, 1996. xlv–liv.

Introduction to a collection of essays chosen because they comment on Miller's theater, chronicle developments in theatrical art, provide an insight into his dramatic methods, and offer a glimpse of the personal side of the playwright.

Chatterji, Ruby. "Existentialist Approach to Modern American Drama." *Existentialism in American Literature*. Ed. Ruby Chatterji. Atlantic Highlands, N.J.: Humanities, 1983. 80–98.

After a brief review of the development of existentialism, Chatterji offers an investigation into several plays by O'Neill, Albee, and Miller in an effort to chart the progression of existentialist thought in American drama. She concludes that "Even when appearing to be 'existentialist' the tendency of modern American drama is more towards social or psychological comment and explication than towards the exploration of man's metaphysical alienation." *After the Fall* fails as a true existential play on account of its hopeful resolution, which "seems somewhat more optimistic than the play's actual experience would allow for," while *Incident at Vichy* succeeds as an example of Sartre's 'drama of situation.'

Chiari, J. "Drama in the U.S.A." *The Landmarks of Contemporary Drama*. London: Herbert Jenkins, 1965. 146–57.

Chiari offers critical commentary on three Miller plays (*Death of a Salesman*, *A View from the Bridge*, and *After the Fall*). *Salesman* is not a tragedy because Loman's occupation and values for commercial success define him, which "can hardly be called a worthy, and least of all, a noble, idea. Willy Loman is a pathetic, sentimental, at times, laughable and even vulgar little man who has not grown up." While *Bridge* is Miller's "nearest and most successful approach to tragedy," the plight of its protagonist Eddie Carbone "is nowhere near the terror and pity inspired by the deaths of more archetypal figures." Chiari then dismisses *Fall* for its blatant and "straightforward autobiography" that undeniably depicts Miller's relationship with Marilyn Monroe. "And there lies the rub, for no amount of sophistry can transform this obviously lived relationship into an objective, dramatic structure." Says Chiari, "The reader or the listener is left bewildered and gnawed by self-disgust at the awareness that he may well have derived a certain amount of sadistic enjoyment at having been made to watch, as spectacle, the death-throes of an unfortunate human being who should have never been so used for a lesson in psychology and self-justification."

Clurman, Harold. "Arthur Miller: Theme and Variations." *Theater, The Annual of the Repertory Theater of Lincoln Center, Volume One*. Ed. Barry Hyams. New York: Repertory Theater Pub./ Playbill, 1964. 12–22. Rpt. in "Arthur Miller's Later Plays." *Arthur Miller: A Collection of Critical Essays*. Ed. Robert W. Corrigan. Englewood Cliffs, N.J.: Prentice-Hall, 1969. 143–68. Rpt. in *The Collected Works of Harold Clurman: Six Decades of Commentary on Theatre, Dance, Music, Film, Arts and Letters*. Eds. Marjorie

Loggia and Glenn Young. New York: Applause, 1994. 635–39.

After a brief biographical sketch, Clurman discusses Miller's moralism, his "strong family feeling," and use of language as exemplified through his stage work, up to and including *After the Fall*.

———. "Arthur Miller's Later Plays." *Arthur Miller: A Collection of Critical Essays*. Ed. Robert W. Corrigan. Englewood Cliffs, N.J.: Prentice-Hall, 1969. 143–68. A rpt. of three separate articles by Clurman combined into one: "Arthur Miller: Theme and Variations" from *Theater I*. New York: Hill and Wang, 1964; "Director's Notes: *Incident at Vichy* " from *Tulane Drama Review* 9.4 (1965): 77–90; and "The Merits of Arthur Miller" from *New York Times* 21 April 1968: II: 1, 7.

———. "Playwright's Symposium." *Playwrights Speak*. Ed. Walter Wager. New York: Delta, 1967. Rpt. in *The Collected Works of Harold Clurman: Six Decades of Commentary on Theatre, Dance, Music, Film, Arts and Letters*. Eds. Marjorie Loggia and Glenn Young. New York: Applause, 1994. 671–77.

In this introduction to interviews with playwrights, Clurman evaluates the Miller canon and concludes that "the austere intensity in Miller's work is that of the impassioned preacher. His passion leads him to the point of poetry. He arrives at it not through what is called the poetic sensibility or through a command of language but through his rigor in pursuit of wholeness."

———. "Biographical Notes and Editor's Introduction." *The Portable Arthur Miller*. New York: Viking, 1971. vii–xxv. Rpt. as "Introduction to the Original Edition" in *The Portable Arthur Miller*. Ed. Christopher Bigsby. New York: Penguin, 1995. xiii–xxiv.

Clurman offers a critical analysis of Miller's literary output through *The Price*. While there is "considerable variety in Miller's work," Clurman argues that viewed as a body of work, "we soon come to discern its essential unity. All his ideas are parts of one Idea."

———. "Reminiscences: An Oral History." *The Collected Works of Harold Clurman: Six Decades of Commentary on Theatre, Dance, Music, Film, Arts and Letters*. Eds. Marjorie Loggia and Glenn Young. New York: Applause, 1994. 982–83, 985–86.

In this edited and abridged interview, conducted for the Columbia University Oral History Research Office in 1979, Clurman discusses Miller's talent as a writer of "solid scripts" who, in his later works, failed to live up to this reputation. Of note are Clurman's comments regarding his resignation from the production of *Creation of the World and Other Business* ("for a number of reasons") and Miller's dependent relationships with his directors, particularly Clurman and Ulu Grosbard.

Cohn, Ruby. "The Articulate Victims of Arthur Miller." *Dialogue in American Drama*. Bloomington: Indiana UP, 1971. 68–96. Rpt. in *Arthur Miller: New Perspectives*. Ed. Robert A. Martin. Englewood Cliffs, N.J.: Prentice-Hall, 1982. 65–74. Rpt. *Modern Critical Interpretations: Arthur Miller's "Death of a Salesman."* Ed. Harold Bloom. New York: Chelsea, 1988. 39–46. Rpt. in *Major Literary Characters: Willy Loman*. Ed. Harold Bloom. New York: Chelsea, 1991. 50–57.

Cohn explores the use of language in the Miller canon, up to and including *The Price*, and concludes that Miller "forged his own distinctive dialogue" that "vibrates with questions, interruptions, oral inflections" by "dignified uneducated characters who articulate functionally in dramatic context."

———. "Which Is Witch?" *Public Issues, Private Tensions: Contemporary American Drama*. Ed. Matthew C. Roudané. New York: AMS, 1993. 77–87.

Cohn reads the personal and professional parallels between Miller and Lillian Hellman, as well as their uneasy personal and public relationships, as interesting commentary on the "witch hunt" milieu of the 1950s and 1960s. She further examines the civic and ethical considerations of censorship, both for both herself and for Miller, primarily through his refusal to allow the Wooster Group to use portions of *The Crucible* in an avant-garde production entitled *L.S.D. (. . . Just the High Points . . .)* in 1982–1984.

Cubeta, Paul M. "Biography." *Modern Drama for Analysis*, 3rd. ed. New York: Holt, 1966. 331–33.

In his "book on how to read drama," Cubeta offers a brief biography of Miller, and a selected descriptive bibliography, as an introductory note before the full-length version of *A View from the Bridge*. Following the play are various critical questions to "lead the student to consider the dimensions of modern dramatic literature not confined by the boundaries of nationalities, periods, or types."

de Bear Nichol, Bernard. "The American View—A Concrete Jungle." *Varieties of Dramatic Experience: Discussions on Dramatic Forms and Themes between Stanley Evernden, Roger Hubank, Thora Burnley Jones and Bernard de Bear Nichol*. London: U of London P, 1969. 221–48.

Lengthy conversation between Thora, Bernard, and Stanley that examines three plays by O'Neill (*Long Day's Journey into Night*, *Mourning Becomes Electra*, and *Desire Under the Elms*) and four by Miller (*All My Sons*, *Death of a Salesman*, *The Crucible*, and *After the Fall*). Stanley Evernden finds that while Miller in *Sons* creates "the illusion of real life," there is still "an overall effect of contrivance" and "one senses in the play something of the manipulated emotion of the comedy thriller." Of *Salesman*, he says, "Willy's story is absorbing, touching and relevant to man, but not archetypal. There are too many economic, sociological and psychological strings attaching it to a particular person, time and place." *The Crucible*, he continues, is Miller's statement that man "is free to make himself what he chooses to be." Finally, of *Fall*, Stanley finds that "Miller is a difficult dramatist to place and the indeterminate position of his thought in relation to social realism is reflected in the style of this play."

Demastes, William W. "Miller's 1970s 'Power' Plays." *Cambridge Companion to Arthur Miller*. Ed. Christopher Bigsby. Cambridge: Cambridge UP, 1997. 139–51.

Demastes reads Miller's 1970s plays (*Creation of the World and Other Business*, *The American Clock*, and *The Archbishop's Ceiling*) as "reflections on the issue of authenticating existence by assuming individual and collective responsibility for our various internal failures."

Dhar, T. N. "The Cognitive Rhythm in Arthur Miller: Theory and Practice." *Perspectives on Arthur Miller*. Ed. Atma Ram. New Delhi: Abhinav, 1988. 109–19.

Dhar argues that Miller's power and importance as a playwright rests on his ability to "look upon literature [as would the Greeks] as more public than private," and his "concern with the cognitive value of drama" as "intimately connected with his consciousness of the value and significance of the dramatic form." Plays examined: *All My Sons* and *The Crucible.*

Dillingham, William B. "Arthur Miller and the Loss of Consciousness." *Emory University Quarterly* 16 (Spring, 1960): 40–50. Rpt. in *"Death of a Salesman": Text and Criticism*. Ed. Gerald Weales. New York: Viking, 1967. Penguin, 1996. 339–49.

Dillingham studies *All My Sons*, *Death of a Salesman*, *The Crucible*, and *A View from the Bridge* as works in which the central focus is a character's "loss of conscience (and the efforts to regain it)." Tragedy occurs, says Dillingham, when Miller's characters choose to ignore their responsibility and their place in society.

Elsom, John. "The Trial of Arthur Miller." *Cold War Theatre*. London: Routledge, 1992. 13–24, 180.

Elsom explores Miller's political and personal life in the 1950s in an effort to highlight the climate surrounding and the influences on his plays and their reception in the United States.

Falb, Lewis W. *American Drama in Paris, 1945–1970: A Study of Its Critical Reception*. Chapel Hill: U of North Carolina P, 1973. 37–50, 122–24, 127, 132–35, 141–42, 146–47.

Falb examines productions of Miller's plays in Paris during the years 1945–1970 in an effort to document French critical and popular reaction. "Though Miller has earned repeated praise for some aspects of his craftsmanship, it is nonetheless clear that he is working in a mode which the French find old-fashioned." Text includes information regarding French translations of Miller's plays plus a chronology of American theatre in France.

Freedman, Morris. "Bertolt Brecht and the American Social Drama." *The Moral Impulse: Modern Drama from Ibsen to the Present*. Carbondale: Southern Illinois UP, 1967. 99–114.

Freedman argues that there is a comparison to be made between the social drama of Arthur Miller and the epic theatre of Bertold Brecht, mainly because Miller's works are "a plain attempt to transcend the particular and achieve the universal."

———. "The Jewishness of Arthur Miller: His Family Epic." *American Drama in Social Context*. Carbondale: Southern Illinois UP, 1971. 43–58.

Freedman surveys *All My Sons*, *Death of a Salesman*, *After the Fall*, and *The Price* as "an integrated saga in which there is a thematic progression" and reads these works as dramas "about the same family considered under changing circumstances and from different perspectives. The development from first play to fourth play provides a record of some of the changing values of American middle-class family life during the period in which they were written."

Frenz, Horst, ed. *American Playwrights on Drama*. New York: Hill and Wang, 1965.

Compilation of essays by American playwrights. Miller essays include: "Tragedy and the Common Man" on pp. 79–83, and "The Shadows of the Gods" on pp. 134–53.

Fuwa, Haruko. "Social Consciousness in American Theatre." *American Literature in the 1940s: Annual Report, 1975*. Tokyo: The Tokyo Chapter of the American Literature Society of Japan, 1976. 170–79.

Fuwa examines plays published during the 1940s, including *All My Sons* and *Death of a Salesman*, and concludes that while the plays of this period deal with family crises, "what characterizes Arthur Miller's plays is the consciousness of sins."

Gascoigne, Bamber. "Arthur Miller." *Twentieth-Century Drama*. London: Hutchinson University, 1962. 174–83.

Gascoigne traces Miller's development as an "intellectual and even didactic" dramatist whose "carefully planned characters spring into life and far outrun their author's intentions." While "ill-used by critics," Gascoigne praises Miller as "a dramatist of passion, conviction and intelligence. His prose, though less coloured than Williams', has a muscularity which enables it to be put to the most weighty purposes without seeming bombastic."

Gassner, John. "New American Playwrights: Williams, Miller, and Others." *Theatre in Our Times*. New York: Crown, 1954. 342–54. Rpt. in *On Contemporary Literature*. Ed. Richard Kostelanetz. New York: Avon, 1964. 48–63.

Gassner compares and contrasts the styles, language, and themes of Miller and Tennessee Williams as the two most significant post-war American playwrights. While Miller may never attain the level of the poet, says Gassner, his subject matter and theatricality point in the direction of a poetic drama. He finds Miller's strength in the tension he creates between moral passion and political idealism. Miller plays examined include *All My Sons* and *Death of a Salesman*.

Geisinger, Marion. *Plays, Players, and Playwrights: An Illustrated History of the Theatre*. New York: Hart, 1971. 590–651.

Lengthy overview of Miller's career and major works through *Incident at Vichy*. Impressive double page production shots from *The Crucible* (1952 original New York production) and *Death of a Salesman* (1949 original Broadway production) accompany the text.

Golden, Joseph. "The Modern Medievalists." *The Death of Tinker Bell: The American Theatre in the 20th Century*. Syracuse, N.Y.: Syracuse UP, 1967. 130–37.

Golden examines what he calls "the schizoid nature of human existence," where characters are torn between what they want as a human being and what is expected of them as a social integer.

Goodman, Charlotte. "The Fox's Cubs: Lillian Hellman, Arthur Miller, and Tennessee Williams." *Modern American Drama: The Female Canon*. Ed. June Schlueter. Rutherford, N.J.: Fairleigh Dickinson UP, 1990. 130–42.

Goodman studies the parallels between Hellman's *The Little Foxes*, Miller's *All My Sons*, and Williams's *The Glass Menagerie* and *A Streetcar Named Desire* to show Hellman's "significant impact during the decade when both Miller and Williams were coming of age."

Goodman, Walter. *The Committee: The Extraordinary Career of the House Committee on Un-American Activities*. New York: Farrar, Straus and Giroux, 1968. 391–94.

Overview of Miller's appearance before HUAC and his subsequent appeal of his conviction on contempt of Congress charges. Goodman opines that Miller's international celebrity status and prominence as a writer served to protect him, for it would have been an embarrassment to the court had he actually been sent to jail.

Gordon, Lois. "Biographical Statement." *Contemporary Dramatists* 5th ed. Ed. K. A. Berney. London: St. James, 1993. 448–52. Rpt. in *Contemporary American Dramatists*. Ed. K. A. Berney. London: St. James, 1994. 407–14.

Overview of Miller's literary accomplishments including an investigation into his central themes and dramatic styles, as well as his development as a playwright.

Gottfried, Martin. *A Theater Divided: The Postwar American Stage*. Boston: Little, Brown, 1967. 149–54, 241–48.

Gottfried's premise is that the American theatre, since World War II, has been split into two wings: a liberal left, moving toward change and interested in the new; and a conservative right, moving toward tradition and interested in the old. The conflict between these two natural forces has resulted in "a stultification of stage development." Miller is examined as a writer of the right, and "like all right-wing playwrights, assumes that man is capable of understanding his situation, and that the physical and social sciences, while unable to provide every answer to every question, *will* be able to provide those answers sooner or later." Miller plays examined include: *After the Fall*, *Death of a Salesman*, *The Crucible*, *A View from the Bridge*, and *Incident of Vichy*.

Greenfield, Thomas Allen. *Work and the Work Ethic in American Drama 1920–1970*. Columbia: U of Missouri P, 1982. 101–29.

Greenfield attempts to chart the history of the modern American dramatist's statements regarding his "time and his society" by examining work and the work ethic in selected plays. He finds in Miller's canon that it is "the relationship between a man and his work that provides perhaps the richest possible source for greater drama, for it is in the work place that the crises of great drama are acted out." Miller plays studied: *All My Sons*, and *Death of a Salesman*, and briefly *The Price*, and *A View from the Bridge*.

Gross, Theodore L. "Arthur Miller." *Representative Men: Cult Heroes of Our Time*. New York: Free Press, 1970. 276–77.

Brief biographical sketch used as preface to an excerpt reprinting of Miller's "Introduction to Collected *Plays*."

Harap, Louis. "The Jew in Drama." *Dramatic Encounters: The Jewish Presence in Twentieth-Century American Drama, Poetry, and Humor and the Black-Jewish Literary Relationship*. New York: Greenwood, 1987. 120–41. Excerpt rpt. in *Major Literary Characters: Willy Loman*. Ed. Harold Bloom. New York: Chelsea, 1991. 29–30.

Harap offers a close reading of the "Jewish elements," both overt and covert, in Miller's published and unpublished literary canon.

Harwood, Ronald. *All the World's a Stage*. Boston: Little, Brown, 1984. 275–80.

In this well-illustrated theatre history text, Harwood discusses Miller's contribution to postwar American drama and concludes that the playwright's "best work belongs to the decade that followed the war." A full-page photo of Miller and a color production still from the 1982 production of *A View from the Bridge*, starring Tony Lo Bianco, accompanies the text.

Heilman, Robert Bechtold. "Arthur Miller." *The Iceman, the Arsonist, and the Troubled Agent: Tragedy and Melodrama on the Modern Stage*. Seattle: U of Washington P, 1973. 142–64.

Heilman traces Miller's circular progression of themes in his canon, from "mere victim" in *The Crucible* to "private disaster" in *A View from the Bridge* to "reflective hero" in *After the Fall* to, finally, a return to older themes and forms in *The Price*.

Helterman, Jeffrey. "Biographical Statement." *The New Consciousness, 1941–1968, Concise Dictionary of American Literary Biography*. Detroit: Gale, 1987. 358–81. Rpt. from Helterman's essay in *DLB.7: Twentieth Century American Dramatists*.

Essay that discusses Miller's works published to 1984, including recent criticism and research of interest to the high school audience. Includes selected annotated bibliography.

Houghton, Norris. *The Exploding Stage: An Introduction to Twentieth Century Drama*. New York: Weybright and Talley, 1971. 59–67.

Prosaic examination of the major themes (social vs. personal, morality, fathers and sons) and dramatic techniques (retrospection, narrator who also serves as chorus) of Miller's plays from *All My Sons* to *After the Fall*.

Huftel, Sheila. "Miller, Ibsen, and Organic Drama." *Modern Critical Interpretations of Arthur Miller's "All My Sons."* Ed. Harold Bloom. New York: Chelsea, 1988. 33–45. [From Huftel's *Arthur Miller: The Burning Glass*. New York: Citadel, 1965. 84–102.]

Huftel explores Miller's thematic interest in evasion and commitment, the strength of his characters, and Ibsen's influence as seen in *All My Sons* and *An Enemy of the People*.

Hughes, Catharine. "Arthur Miller." *American Playwrights 1945–75*. London: Pitman, 1976. 32–43.

Hughes examines the Miller canon of full-length plays up to

The Creation of the World and Other Business in an effort to contextualize his work "in relation to the social, cultural, and political forces that have shaped his outlook."

Johnsey, Jeanne. "Meeting Dr. Mengele: Naming, Self (Re) presentation and the Tragic Moment in Miller." *The Achievement of Arthur Miller: New Essays*. Ed. Steven Centola. Dallas, Tex.: Contemporary Research, 1995. 101–107.

Johnsey argues that the "tragic moment" of *Death of a Salesman, The Crucible*, and *Playing for Time* occurs when the main characters insist upon self-nomination in response to overwhelming external pressures. These acts, says Johnsey, "are transformative for the characters in terms of self-realization."

Johnson, Kenneth E. "Memory Plays in American Drama." *Within the Dramatic Spectrum. The University of Florida Department of Classics, Comparative Drama Conference Papers*. Vol. VI. Ed. Karelisa V. Hartigan. Lanham, Md.: UP of America, 1986. 115–23.

Johnson argues that Ibsen is the most influential model for American dramatic style and explores the theme of memory in the plays of Miller and Tennessee Williams.

Kanamaru, Tosao. "McCarthyism and Arthur Miller." *American Literature in the 1950s: Annual Report, 1976*. Tokyo: The Tokyo Chapter of the American Literature Society of Japan, 1977. 140–46.

Kanamaru surveys the rise of McCarthyism in the United States and approaches Miller's writing, both essay and drama, as a response to the "irrational quality of hysteria" of the 1950s.

Kerr, Walter. "A Matter of Opinion." *How Not to Write a Play*. New York: Simon and Schuster, 1955. 51–67.

Kerr labels Miller a thesis playwright who "presents the political, social, or moral problem . . . and then argues a solution to that problem, or at least a defined interpretation of its meaning." Plays examined: *All My Sons* and *Death of a Salesman.*

Kitchin, Laurence. "The Potent Intruder: American Drama and Its Influence." *Mid-Century Drama*. London: Faber and Faber, 1960. 56–71, et passim.

Lauding *Salesman* as "a masterpiece of concentrated irony and controlled indignation," Kitchin praises Miller as a playwright who "goes in with a scalpel, dissects the morally diseased tissue at the roots of his theme and describes in human terms the damage it does to the body as a whole," but criticizes him for being mistaken in having one man forcibly kiss another in *A View from the Bridge* for its negative impact on an audience. Says Kitchin, "a person who reacts strongly to such will not appreciate what the play is trying to communicate," adding that he is not against the morality of such a dramatic action, but only responding to the right and wrong "ways of putting an audience on the alert."

Koon, Helene Wickham. "Introduction." *Twentieth Century Interpretations of "Death of a Salesman."* Ed. Helene Wickham Koon. Englewood Cliffs, N.J.: Prentice-Hall, 1983. 1–14.

Brief biographical sketch followed by overview of Miller's major thematic concerns, focusing on the debate over the tragic nature of *Salesman* and Loman's status as a modern Everyman.

Kurdi, Maria. "The Deceptive Nature of Reality in Arthur Miller's *Two Way Mirror*." *Cross Cultural Studies: American, Canadian, and European Literatures: 1945–1985*. Ed. Mirko Jurak. Ljubljana, Yugoslavia English Department: Edvard Kardelj University of Ljubljana, 1988. 267–71.

Kurdi examines *Two-Way Mirror*, a double bill of one-act plays first presented at the Long Wharf Theatre in 1982 under the title *2 by A. M.* (*Elegy for a Lady* and *Some Kind of Love Story*).

Lawson, John Howard. "The Dilemma of Arthur Miller." *Theory and Technique of Playwriting*. Revised ed. New York: Hill and Wang, 1960. xxvi–xxxii.

Lawson offers an overview of the Miller canon, from *All My Sons* to *A View from the Bridge*, in an effort to chart the progression of Miller's dramatic thought and thematic concerns.

Lumley, Frederick. "Broadway Cortege—Tennessee Williams and Arthur Miller." *Trends in 20th Century Drama: A Survey since Ibsen and Shaw*. New York: Essential Books, 1956: 184–93. Rpt. as "Broadway Cortege." *New Trends in 20th Century Drama: A Survey since Ibsen and Shaw*. New York: Oxford UP, 1972. 194–99.

Lumley separates the Miller canon into two sections—the tragedy of the common man and the nightmare of an intellectual guilt complex.

Maini, Darshan Singh. "The Moral Vision of Arthur Miller." *Indian Essays in American Literature*. Eds. Sujit Mukherjee and D. V. K. Raghavacharyulu. Bombay: Popular Prakashan, 1968. 85–96.

Maini highlights what he calls "the visionary quality" of Miller's plays and "the intensity of his moral passion," concluding that "whatever road he may elect to follow, it remains clear enough that his humanism will abide, that his moral vision will remain in constant attendance, and his integrity or courage will not falter."

Marcuson, Lewis R. *The Stage Immigrant: The Irish, Italians, and Jews in American Drama, 1920–1960*. New York: Garland, 1990.

Marcuson examines the portrayal of immigrants and first-generation Americans in the works of Eugene O'Neill, Clifford Odets, Tennessee Williams, Sidney Kingsley, Miller, and Paddy Chayefsky.

Martin, Robert A. "Introduction." *Arthur Miller, New Perspectives*. Englewood Cliffs, N.J.: Prentice-Hall, 1982. 1–12.

In the introduction to a collection of critical essays on Miller, Martin presents a lengthy biographical essay that explores the current state of Miller criticism and assesses his development as a playwright.

Martin, Robert A. "Editor's Introduction." *The Theater Essays of Arthur Miller*. Ed. Robert A. Martin. New York: Viking, 1978. xv–xxxix. Rpt. as "Introduction to the Original Edition" in *The Theater Essays of Arthur Miller*. Revised ed. Eds. Robert A. Martin and Steven R. Centola. New York: Da Capo, 1996. xix–xliii.

Calling Miller's essays on theatre and drama a collection that represents "a major contribution to the criticism and literature of our time," Martin offers a brief overview of the twenty-three essays and two interviews contained in the volume.

Maslon, Laurence, ed. *The Arena Adventure: The First 40 Years.* New York: Applause, 1990.

Oversized volume that chronicles the history of one of America's most influential regional theatres with over 200 photographs and twenty-one essays. Nine productions of Miller's works are included.

Mason, Jeffrey D. "Paper Dolls: Melodrama and Sexual Politics in Arthur Miller's Early Plays." *Feminist Rereadings of Modern American Drama*. Ed. June Schlueter. Cranbury, N.J.: Associated UP, 1989. 103–15.

Mason argues that Miller "borrows the methods and espouses the sexual politics of melodrama" in his first four major full-length plays (*All My Sons*, *Death of a Salesman*, *The Crucible*, and *A View from the Bridge*) by driving the action to a climactic moment of decision and then separating the protagonist from his family and pushing the women aside, requiring the male characters to choose in isolation.

Massa, Ann. "*Some Kind of Love Story:* Arthur Miller." *American Declarations of Love*. Ed. Ann Massa. New York: St. Martin's, 1990. 122–36.

Arguing that Miller's plays do not reflect what his theatre essays proclaim they do, Massa investigates the development of women, sex, love, and family relationships in the Miller canon. Concludes Massa, "There is still the tendency in Miller to describe his plays in the abstract terms which no longer seem relevant; perhaps because he find the pursuit of love unremittingly problematic."

McCarthy, Mary. "'Realism' in the American Theatre." *Harper's* July 1961: 45–52. Rpt. as "The American Realist Playwrights." *Encounter* July 1961: 24–31. Rpt. in *Discussions of Modern American Drama*. Ed. Walter J. Meserve. Boston: D. C. Heath, 1965. 114–27.

In a study of the characteristics of realist American playwrights, McCarthy finds that Miller has a "thirst for universality" and "not only a naive searching for another dimension but an evident hatred of and contempt for reality—as not good enough to make plays out of."

McDonough, Carla J. "Arthur Miller: Portrait of the Common Man." *Staging Masculinity: Male Identity in Contemporary American Drama*. Jefferson, N.C.: McFarland, 1997. 27–30.

This study examines issues of masculinity in plays by male playwrights and considers questions concerning the staging of male identity and how it reflects and affects male social interactions. McDonough includes a short essay on *Death of a Salesman* as the most significant example of a modern drama that "captures the instability and dilemma of traditional American masculinity."

McGilligan, Patrick, and Paul Buhle. *Tender Comrades: A Backstory of the Hollywood Blacklist*. New York: St. Martin's, 1997. 50–51.

Brief mention of Miller in an interview with Walter Bernstein. On the subject of Elia Kazan's political shift, Bernstein believes that Kazan made a deliberate choice to side with Spyros Skouras (head of Twentieth Century-Fox) under pressure from the William Morris Agency and his wife and move away from Miller politically for some "old slights" he had felt deeply.

Moss, Leonard. "The Perspective of a Playwright." *Modern Critical Views: Arthur Miller*. Ed. Harold Bloom. New York: Chelsea, 1987. 79–92. [From Moss, *Arthur Miller, Revised ed.* Boston: Twayne, 1980. 91–106.]

Moss examines Miller's canon in regard to his focus on characters who are "motivated by an obsession to justify themselves" and "fix their identities through radical acts of ego-assertion."

Mottram, Eric. "Arthur Miller: The Development of a Political Dramatist in America." *Stratford-upon-Avon Studies 10: American Theatre*. Eds. John Russell Brown and Bernard Harris. New York: St. Martin's, 1967. 127–62. Rpt. in *Arthur Miller: A Collection of Critical Essays*. Ed. Robert W. Corrigan. Englewood Cliffs, N.J.: Prentice-Hall, 1969. 23–57. Excerpted as "Jean-Paul Sartre's *Les Sorciéres de Salem*" in *Twentieth Century Interpretations of "The Crucible," a Collection of Critical Essays*. Ed. John H. Ferres. Englewood Cliffs, N.J.: Prentice-Hall, 1972. 93–94.

In this chapter-long critical survey of the Miller canon through *Incident at Vichy*, Mottram sees a logical progress "from the socialism of the 'thirties, through the confused liberalism of the 'forties, to the bewildered emptiness of the 'sixties. The plays are a barometer of his audience, measuring through his own sense of the pressures of the last quarter of a century."

Murphy, Brenda. "Arthur Miller: Previsioning Realism." *Realism and the American Dramatic Tradition*. Ed. William W. Demastes. Tuscaloosa: U of Alabama P, 1996. 189–202.

Essay investigating the development of realism throughout Miller's canon, revealing his interest in dramatizing the individual as experimental subject and world citizen.

———. "Informers: *The Hook, On the Waterfront, A View from the Bridge, After the Fall*." *Congressional Theatre: Dramatizing McCarthyism on Stage, Film, and Television*. Cambridge: Cambridge UP, 1999. 206–25, 281–83.

Murphy relates the details surrounding the genesis of Miller's "informer" dramas, the playwright's relationship with Elia Kazan, and both men's testimony before HUAC. Concludes Murphy, "In *After the Fall*, by ending his protestations of righteousness, Miller embraced the common guilt, and thus common humanity, of friendlies, unfriendlies, and bystanders, everyone involved in the HUAC hearings—except maybe the Committee."

———. "The Tradition of Social Drama: Miller and His Forebears." *Cambridge Companion to Arthur Miller*. Ed. Christopher Bigsby. Cambridge: Cambridge UP, 1997. 10–20.

Murphy charts the influences of classic Greek drama and Ibsen, discovered as a university student, on *All My Sons*, *A View from the Bridge*, and *The Man Who Had All the Luck*.

Murray, Edward. "Arthur Miller: *Death of a Salesman*, *The Misfits*, and *After the Fall*." *The Cinematic Imagination: Writers and the Motion Pictures*. New York: Ungar, 1972. 69–85.

Murray examines the expressionistic devices in *Death of a Salesman*, the cinema-novel "The Misfits," and *After the Fall* to show the cinematic techniques Miller employs in his plays and fiction.

Narumi, Hiroshi. "Theatrical Experiments in the Forties." *American Literature in the 1940s: Annual Report, 1975*. Tokyo: The Tokyo Chapter of the American Literature Society of Japan, 1976. 186–93.

Narumi surveys several experimental theatrical innovations from the 1940s, including theatre-in-the-round, the elimination of the curtain, the use of a narrator, flashback techniques, stage design and devices, and the departure from commercialism. Miller is highlighted for his use of a narrator character in *A View from the Bridge* and for his use of the flashback technique in *Death of a Salesman*. Says Narumi, "Miller succeeded very well in creating a world viewed from multiple angles in time and space, a kind of 'four-dimensional' theatre."

Nyren, Dorothy, ed. "Arthur Miller." *A Library of Literary Criticism; Modern American Literature* 4rd. ed. New York: Ungar, 1969. 338–45.

Excerpts of critical reviews of Miller's dramas and short stories.

Orr, John. "Williams and Miller: The Cold War and the Renewal of Tragedy." *Tragic Drama and Modern Society: Studies in the Social and Literary Theory of Drama from 1870 to the Present*. Totowa, N.J.: Barnes and Noble, 1981. 206–40.

Arguing that the predominant figural stress of the new drama produced in the Cold War era was psychosexual, with dramas portraying "the sexual bias of personal disaffection," Orr examines issues of betrayal, guilt, and the public versus the private in Miller's *A View from the Bridge* and *The Crucible*.

Otten, Terry. "Arthur Miller and the Temptation of Innocence." *The Achievement of Arthur Miller: New Essays*. Ed. Steven Centola. Dallas, Tex.: Contemporary Research, 1995. 109–17.

Arguing that Miller believes that ignorance disguised as innocence is the most morally destructive of all forces, Otten demonstrates that the false claim of innocence produces a self-ignorance that has tragic implications. Contrary to belief, it is guilt that restores the moral equilibrium of a world "after the fall" because it is "the very testimony of self-knowledge."

Palmer, R. Barton. "Arthur Miller and the Cinema." *Cambridge Companion to Arthur Miller*. Ed. Christopher Bigsby. Cambridge: Cambridge UP, 1997. 184–230.

Although critical and popular failures, Palmer examines the film versions of Miller's plays, including *All My Sons*, *Death of a Salesman*, *The Misfits*, *A View from the Bridge*, and *The Crucible* (French), and his uneasy relationship with Hollywood.

Parker, Dorothy, ed. *Essays on Modern American Drama: Williams, Miller, Albee, and Shepard*. Toronto: U of Toronto P, 1987.

Includes four essays about Miller's canon: Barry Gross, "*All My Sons* and the Larger Context"; C. W. E. Bigsby, "The Fall and After—Arthur Miller's Confession"; Robert A. Martin "Arthur Miller's *The Crucible*: Background and Sources"; and Lawrence D. Lowenthal "Arthur Miller's *Incident at Vichy*: A Sartrean Interpretation".

Porter, Thomas E. "The Mills of the Gods: Economics and Law in the Plays of Arthur Miller." *Arthur Miller: New Perspectives*. Ed. Robert A. Martin. Englewood Cliffs, N.J.: Prentice-Hall, 1982. 75–96.

Porter divides Miller's major works into two trilogies—three plays about business (*All My Sons*, *Death of a Salesman*, and *The Price*) and three about the judicial process (*The Crucible*, *A View from the Bridge*, and *After the Fall*)—in an effort to "describe these systems and to consider their function in the context of the dramatic action."

Pradhan, Narindar Singh. "Arthur Miller and the Pursuit of Guilt." *Studies in American Literature: Essays in Honour of William Mudler*. Delhi: Oxford UP, 1976. 28–42.

Pradhan traces the changing concerns of the theme of guilt in the works of Miller, concluding that it is Miller's position that neither man nor God is perfect and "a recognition of our common imperfections may lead to a sharing of our guilt and understanding."

———. *Modern American Drama: A Study in Myth and Tradition*. New Delhi: Arnold-Heinemann, 1978. 19–20, 65–76, 91–96, 119–21.

Pradhan outlines varying degrees of the Edenic theme in selected works of Eugene O'Neill, Thornton Wilder, Marc Connelly, Robert Sherwood, Clifford Odets, Lillian Hellman, Archibald MacLeish, Tennessee Williams, Edward Albee, and Arthur Miller. Miller dramas examined include: *All My Sons*, *Death of a Salesman*, *After the Fall*, *Incident at Vichy*, *The Creation of the World and Other Business*, and *The Misfits*. In Miller's plays, "the quest [for paradise] becomes a search for identity, which coupled with a sense of guilt results in the recognition that the dream of perfection is hopeless."

———. "Modern American Theories of Drama and Sociological Thought." *Twentieth Century American Criticism: Interdisciplinary Approaches*. Ed. Rajnath. New Delhi: Arnold-Heinemann, 1977.155–65.

Pradhan argues that while Miller "is perhaps the biggest Ibsenite," he is also "essentially an experimentalist, as is demonstrated by the variety of forms employed in his plays."

Ranchan, Som P. "Four Protagonists of Miller and Integral Consciousness." *Perspectives on Arthur Miller*. Ed. Atma Ram. New Delhi: Abhinav, 1988. 15–25.

Ranchan applies the notion of integral consciousness, as expressed by Sri Aurobindo in his *Future Poetry*, to four Miller protagonists—Joe Keller, Willy Loman, John Proctor, and Quentin—finding each character tragic by virtue of their unliberated, unintegrated development.

Robinson, James A. "Fathers and Sons in *They Too Arise*." *The Achievement of Arthur Miller: New Essays*. Ed. Steven Centola. Dallas, Tex.: Contemporary Research, 1995. 43–49.

Robinson examines Miller's first play, *They Too Arise* (written while a Michigan undergraduate), as a prototype of the "struggles between fatherhood and brotherhood in later plays," and to shed some light on "the issue of Miller's desired—but incomplete—assimilation into mainstream American culture."

Rollyson, Carl. "Arthur Miller." *Critical Survey of Drama, Vol. 4*. Revised ed. Ed. Frank N. Magill. Passadena, Calif.: Salem, 1994. 1673–90.

Listing of Miller's principal drama, including both production and publication dates, other literary forms, essay on Miller's achievements, biographical essay, play analysis through *Creation of the World and Other Business*, other major works, and a short five-item bibliography.

Rosefeldt, Paul. "Arthur Miller." *McGill's Survey of American Literature, Vol. 4*. Ed. Frank N. Magill. Passadena, Calif.: Salem, 1991. 1363–73.

Biographical essay, covering *All My Sons*, *Death of a Salesman*, *The Crucible*, and *After the Fall*, that traces Miller's literary career and important themes. Includes a brief bibliography.

Roth, John K., ed. "Arthur Miller." *American Diversity, American Identity: The Lives and Works of 145 Writers Who Define the American Experience*. New York: Holt, 1995. 168–71.

Sections of Miller essay include: biographical data, literary forms, achievements, biography, thematic analysis, and (brief) bibliography. Miller is a playwright whose works "concern primarily the individual's relation to society and the issues of personal identity and human dignity."

Roudané, Matthew C. "From Page to Stage: Subtextual Dimensions in the Theater of Arthur Miller." *The Achievement of Arthur Miller: New Essays*. Ed. Steven Centola. Dallas, Tex.: Contemporary Research, 1995. 31–41.

Roudané defines five primary forms of didascalia (stage directions) and examines the theoretical implications of didascalic discourse in Miller's plays.

———. "Myths of the American Dream." *American Drama since 1960: A Critical History*. New York: Twayne, 1996. 176–205.

After a detailed analysis of the myth of the American dream expressed throughout the Miller canon, Roudané concludes that the playwright deserves a centralized status in American theatre history for his ability to elevate "the civic function of serious drama in a way that defines the ethical landscape of the United States."

Rowe, Kenneth. "Shadows Cast Before." *Arthur Miller, New Perspectives*. Ed. Robert A. Martin. Englewood Cliffs, N.J.: Prentice-Hall, 1982. 13–32.

After sharing his memories of Miller as a student of playwriting at the University of Michigan, Rowe details the plot, structure, themes, and characters of five of Miller's student works—*No Villain*, *They Too Arise*, *The Grass Still Grows*, *The Great Disobedience*, and *Honors at Dawn*.

Sasahara, Takeshi. "Lyricism in the American Drama of the Forties." *American Literature in the 1940s: Annual Report, 1975*. Tokyo: The Tokyo Chapter of the American Literature Society of Japan, 1976. 202–207.

Essay that offers a cursory examination of lyricism in the works of Tennessee Williams, Miller, William Inge, and Eugene O'Neill.

Sata, Masunori. "American Realism and Arthur Miller's Struggle." *The Traditional and the Anti-Traditional: Studies in Contemporary American Literature*. Ed. Kenzaburo Ohashi. Tokyo: Tokyo Chapter of the American Literature Society of Japan, 1980. 174–90, et passim.

Sata investigates the label of "realist" playwright placed on Miller from critics such as Mary McCarthy and concludes that while "Miller is a legitimate American realist and moralist, having the urge to create plays seriously meant for people of common sense," he is also an "idealist and metaphysician having the urge to discuss man's fate. These two urges drive Miller at one time to write realistic and at other times to write unrealistic plays, always seeking after a new form."

———. "Antimony in Courtroom Drama and Old Testament Drama." *American Literature in the 1950s: Annual Report, 1976*. Tokyo: The Tokyo Chapter of the American Literature Society of Japan, 1977. 174–82.

Sata praises *The Crucible* as "one of the finest courtroom plays" of the 1950s, and *The Creation of the World and Other Business* as "a rather flawed play but which was still a stimulating and provocative one."

———. "Arthur Miller's Warning Concerning the American Dream." *American Literature in the 1940s: Annual Report, 1975*. Tokyo: The Tokyo Chapter of the American Literature Society of Japan, 1976. 219–25.

Sata studies the concept of the American dream as a dream of success and concludes from Miller's works (both dramatic and theoretical) that "Miller's warning is that one must know oneself rightly and deeply; one must throw away one's wrong dream and stick fast to the good dream" in order to attain a degree of self-knowledge.

Sato, Susumu. "The 'Awakening' Theme in Clifford Odets and Arthur Miller." *American Literature in the 1940s: Annual Report, 1975*. Tokyo: The Tokyo Chapter of the American Literature Society of Japan, 1976. 180–85.

Sato compares the plays of Clifford Odets from the 1930s to Arthur Miller in the 1940s and concludes that the differences in the personal and social awakenings represented in their works reflect not only the change in social climate from one decade to the next but also the differences in the artistic temperaments of the two playwrights.

Savran, David. *Communists Cowboys and Queers: The Politics of Masculinity in the Works of Arthur Miller and Tennessee Williams*. Minneapolis: U of Minnesota P, 1992.

Savran explores the politics of masculinity in Miller's plays, films, and short stories in an effort to expose issues of gender and sexuality inherent, but undisclosed, in the playwright's work.

Scanlan, Tom. "Reactions I: Family and Society in Arthur Miller." *Family, Drama, and American Dreams*. Conn.: Greenwood, 1978. 126–55.

Scanlan argues that despite Miller's attempts to "move his plays into a larger social context," he fails in his efforts to dramatize "subjects other than the individual consciousness concerned for its own integrity and adjustment to family."

Schlueter, June. "Miller in the Eighties." *Cambridge Companion to Arthur Miller*. Ed. Christopher Bigsby. Cambridge: Cambridge UP, 1997. 152–67.

Schlueter details Miller's personal life, political involvements, and literary output (essays, short plays, books of reportage, autobiography, teleplay, and full-length plays) for the decade of the 1980s.

———. "The Private and Public Lives of a Dramatic Text: Reading within the Dialogic Mode." *Public Issues, Private Tensions: Contemporary American Drama*. Ed. Matthew C. Roudané. New York: AMS, 1993. 281–93.

Schlueter examines dramatic dialogue as a distinct literary form, with examples from works by Tennessee Williams, Arthur Miller, and Sam Shepard.

———, ed. *Feminist Rereadings of Modern American Drama*. Cranbury, N.J.: Associated UP, 1989.

Contains essays on drama of Eugene O'Neill, Arthur Miller, Tennessee Williams, Edward Albee, and Sam Shepard. Miller essays include: Gayle Austin, "The Exchange of Women and Male Homosocial Desire in Arthur Miller's *Death of a Salesman* and Lillian Hellman's *Another Part of the Forest*"; Kay Stanton, "Women and the American Dream of *Death of a Salesman*"; Jeffrey D. Mason, "Paper Dolls: Melodrama and Sexual Politics in Arthur Miller's Early Plays"; and Iska Alter, "Betrayal and Blessedness: Explorations of Feminine Power in *The Crucible*, *A View from the Bridge*, and *After the Fall*."

Schneiderman, Leo. "Arthur Miller: Drama from the Standpoint of Self Psychology." *Motherless Children, Fatherless Waifs: Fictional Protagonists and the Artist's Search for the Real Self*. San Bernardino, Calif.: Borgo, 1996. 24–44.

Applying the theories of Heinz Kohut, Schneiderman attempts a psychological interpretation of Miller and his plays. Miller's dramatic characters represent "different kinds of 'idealism' based on unconscious self-destructive motives associated with unhealthy self-object experiences in childhood."

Schroeder, Patricia R. "Hearing Many Voices at Once: The Theatre of Emily Mann." *Public Issues, Private Tensions: Contemporary American Drama*. Ed. Matthew C. Roudané. New York: AMS, 1993. 249–65.

Schroeder discusses the thematic similarities between Miller and Emily Mann—both have "always been concerned with the complex ecological exchanges between the water and the fish"—and examines three of Mann's plays as examples of her well-deserved status as "heir apparent to Miller as America's foremost social playwright."

Schvey, Henry I. "Arthur Miller: Songs of Innocence and Experience." *New Essays on American Drama*. Eds. Gilbert Debusscher and Henry I. Schvey. Atlanta, Ga.: Rodopi, 1989. 75–97.

Schvey surveys Miller's full-length plays, up to and including *The American Clock* (1980), as expressions of Miller's pervading moral vision. "For although the recent plays have grown more complex intellectually, they often fail to convince on the stage; Arthur Miller's journey from innocence to experience has been a difficult birth, both for the dramatist and his audience."

Schwarz, Alfred. *From Büchner to Beckett: Dramatic Theory and the Modes of Tragic Drama*. Athens: Ohio UP, 1978. 21, 87–93, 117–22, 161–82, et passim.

Schwartz examines Miller's development as a tragic social dramatist, offering analysis of *The Crucible*, *A View from the Bridge*, *After the Fall*, and Miller's theatre essays. Concludes Schwarz, "Arthur Miller has remained true to his dictum of the mid-fifties that the fate of mankind is social. But his idea of society has changed."

Scott, William B, and Peter M. Rutkoff. "Life without Father: Postwar New York Drama." *New York Modern: The Arts and the City*. Baltimore: Johns Hopkins UP, 1999. 321–50.

In a book that documents the legacy of New York artists "in capturing the energy and emotions of the urban experience," the authors examine the genesis, themes, and social significance of five Miller works (*All My Sons*, *Death of a Salesman*, *The Crucible*, *A View from the Bridge*, and *After the Fall*). Also discussed is the mutual influences between Tennessee Williams and Miller, the collaborative relationship between Miller and director Elia Kazan, Miller's testimony before HUAC in 1956, and the controversy surrounding the playwright's political involvements.

Sharma, Lalit M. "Eddie Carbone and Willy Loman: A State of Stasis." *Perspectives on Arthur Miller*. Ed. Atma Ram. New Delhi: Abhinav, 1988. 26–34.

Sharma argues that the tragedy of *Death of a Salesman* and *A View from the Bridge* is that both plays have main characters who are caught in a state of stasis whereby they "cannot reconcile to the idea that there are things which are impossible, not impossible in themselves but beyond the terms of their existence."

Sharpe, Robert B. "Modern Trends in Tragedy." *Irony in the Drama: An Essay on Impersonation, Shock, and Catharsis*. Chapel Hill: U of North Carolina P, 1959. 180–203.

Sharpe traces the development of Miller's ironic dramatic sense, from *The Man Who Had All the Luck* to *A View from the Bridge*, as "the most important element in his themes and in his manipulation of his themes as he shapes them into plays." Sharpe hails Miller for contributing "two important things": the "rediscovery of the value of building tension by dramatic irony just before a play's turning point"; and the use of a "modified form of ironic self-expression through a memory variant of the flash-back . . . which does not sacrifice the chief actor's ironic impersonation while the flash-back is going on."

Sievers, W. David. *Freud on Broadway: A History of Psychoanalysis and the American Drama*. New York: Hermitage, 1955. 376–96. New York: Cooper Square, 1970. 388–99. Rpt. in *Two Modern American Tragedies: Reviews and Criticism of "Death of a Salesman" and "A Streetcar Named Desire."* Ed. John D. Hurrell. New York: Scribner's, 1961. 139–45.

Thirty-three American playwrights responded to Sievers's questionnaire, sent "to obtain evidence as to the actual extent of Freudian influence upon the drama." A brief review of Miller's dramaturgy to *The Crucible* is followed by the playwright's responses, which include his acceptance of the label but not admitting any prethought, methodology, or plan that it has occurred. " For good or ill, [I] am not conscious of using Freudian ideas, but am told that is what I do!" Says Sievers, "From his plays and the comments on his questionnaire it would seem that Miller, of all

American playwrights, comes the closest thus far to illustrating Freud's prediction that ultimately writers will assimilate psychoanalysis 'at so deep a level of knowing that they will not be aware that they are employing it: it will have to them the character of self-evidence.'"

Stambusky, Alan. A. "Arthur Miller: Aristotelian Canons in the Twentieth Century Drama." *Modern American Drama: Essays in Criticism*. Ed. William E. Taylor. Deland, Fla.: Everett/Edwards, 1968. 91–115.

Stambusky examines Miller's canon (up to *After the Fall*) as it relates to Aristotle's ancient tragic concepts in the *Poetics*, especially as it relates to the "noble man." He faults Miller for believing that the "little man" is an apt hero of modern tragedy, writing "He must be rather a 'great' man who somehow represents an intimation at least of the nobility of which human nature is capable." While deciding that Miller is "closer to the ancient tragic concept than any of his leading American contemporaries," the author still finds that "Miller may never reach the exalted heights of tragedy that the ancients did."

Stein, Rita, and Friedhelm Rickert, eds. "Arthur Miller." *Major Modern Dramatists*. New York: Ungar, 1984. 24–41.

Chronologically arranged excerpts presenting an overview of critical response to Miller.

Styan, J. L. "Realism in America.: Williams and Miller." *Modern Drama in Theory and Practice, Vol. 1: Realism and Naturalism*. Cambridge: Cambridge UP, 1981. 137–48, 118–20.

Styan considers Miller a social dramatist who has both "worked with, and departed from, the accepted mode of realism, but is wedded to the belief that the role of the playwright is to project ideas upon an audience." Plays discussed: *Death of a Salesman*, *The Crucible*, and *A View from the Bridge*.

Szondi, Peter. "Memory: Miller." *Theory of the Modern Drama*. Ed. and Translated by Michael Hayes. Minneapolis: U of Minnesota P, 1987. 91–95.

Szondi explores *All My Sons* and *Death of a Salesman* as examples of Miller's "evolution from imitator to innovator"—a change in style and dramatic form that mirrors the development of drama from the turn-of-the-century to the modern day.

Walden, Daniel. "Miller's Roots and His Moral Dilemma; or, Continuity from Brooklyn to Salesman." *Critical Essays on Arthur Miller*. Ed. James J. Martine. Boston: G. K. Hall, 1979. 189–96.

Biographical essay that traces the roots of Miller's characters, their moral dilemmas, and the themes present in his dramatic work.

Wang, Qun. "The Tragedy of Ethical Bewilderment." *The Achievement of Arthur Miller: New Essays*. Ed. Steven Centola. Dallas, Tex.: Contemporary Research, 1995. 95–100.

Wang examines *All My Sons*, *Death of a Salesman*, and *The Price* and argues that tragedy occurs when characters become entrapped in a state of moral confusion or "ethical bewilderment" that misleads them to embrace values contrary to their true selves.

Weales, Gerald. "Arthur Miller" *The American Theatre Today*. Ed. Alan Downer. New York: Basic, 1967. 85–95. Rpt. as "Arthur Miller's Shifting Image of Man" in *Arthur Miller: A Collection of Critical Essays*. Ed. Robert W. Corrigan. Englewood Cliffs, N.J.: Prentice-Hall, 1969. 131–42.

While Weales sees *After the Fall* and *Incident at Vichy* as inferior works that in no way diminish Miller's stature as a great American playwright, he examines the similarities in idea, technique, and language between them and Miller's earlier works.

———. "Arthur Miller: Man and His Image." *American Drama since World War II*. New York: Harcourt, 1962. Portion rpt. in *Tulane Drama Review* 7 (September, 1962): 165–80. Rpt. in "*Death of a Salesman": Text and Criticism*. Ed. Gerald Weales. New York: Viking, 1967. 350–66. Rpt. in *"The Crucible": Text and Criticism*. Ed. Gerald Weales. New York: Viking, 1971. 333–51. Excerpt rpt. as "Understanding Miller's Heroes" in *Readings on Arthur Miller*. Ed. Thomas Siebold. San Diego, Calif.: Greenhaven, 1997. 73–81.

Weales examines the heroes and their concerns with identity in the Miller canon.

———. "Biographical Statement." *Great Writers of the English Language*. Ed. James Vinson. New York: St.Martin's, 1979. 406–409.

Brief biographical essay that discusses Miller's literary career and prevalent themes in his major works.

———. "Theatre without Walls." *A Time of Harvest: American Literature 1910–1960*. Ed. Robert E. Spiller. New York: Hill and Wang, 1962. 130–43.

Brief mention is made of Miller's strength as a playwright: it "does not lie in his obvious ability to give his characters flesh; it lies in the central concern that informs his work. . . . the protagonist's need to separate himself from the wrong images and to find the right."

———. "Williams and Miller." *The Jumping Off Place: American Drama in the 1960's*. New York: Macmillan, 1969. 14–23. Portion rpt. as "Arthur Miller in the 1960s." *Arthur Miller: New Perspectives*. Ed. Robert A. Martin. Englewood Cliffs, N.J.: Prentice-Hall, 1982. 97–105.

In this revised essay [from "Arthur Miller: Man and His Image" in his *American Drama since World War II*. New York: Harcourt, 1962. 3–17], Weales compares the quest for identity in *After the Fall*, *Incident at Vichy*, and *The Price* with Miller's earlier plays.

Welland, Dennis. "Two Early Plays." *Modern Critical Interpretations of Arthur Miller's "All My Sons."* Ed. Harold Bloom. New York: Chelsea, 1988. 91–99. Originally entitled "Three Early Plays" from Welland's *Miller: A Study of His Plays*. London: Methuen, 1979. 20–35.

Welland compares *The Man Who Had All the Luck* and *All My Sons* as plays "cast in the same dramatic mold" and obvious antecedents to later Miller works.

Williams, Raymond. "Arthur Miller." *Drama: From Ibsen to Brecht*. New York: Oxford UP, 1969. 267–76. Rpt. as "Arthur Miller: An Overview.". *Modern Critical Views: Arthur Miller*. Ed. Harold Bloom. New York: Chelsea, 1987. 7–16.

Marxist critic Williams examines Miller's evolution, from his method of employing Ibsen's retrospective method in *All My Sons* to his reliance on "the alternative tradition of semi-articulate exposure" found in *After the Fall*. This progression of methodology, Williams argues, shows "both the difficulties of development of the form [Miller] had chosen and the intense disintegrating pressures of a powerful contemporary structure of feeling."

Zeifman, Hersh. "All My Sons After the Fall: Arthur Miller and the Rage for Order." *The Theatrical Gamut: Notes for a Post-Brechtian Stage.* Ed. Enoch Brater. Ann Arbor: U of Michigan P, 1995. 107–20.

Zeifman examines *All My Sons* as a play "so tightly constructed that it is practically straightjackeded" by Miller's impulse to create order out of his own inner chaos. Zeifman then reads *After the Fall* as a revision of *Sons*—"it would take Miller seventeen years to examine Chris's complicity and guilt, to expose the spuriousness of the apparent order in *All My Sons*, in effect to rewrite the play under a different title: *After the Fall*."

Zeineddine, Nada. *Because It Is My Name: Problems of Identity Experienced by Women, Artists, and Breadwinners in the Plays of Henrik Ibsen, Tennessee Williams, and Arthur Miller*. London: Merlin, 1991. 155–211.

Zeineddine explores the problems of identity and "intricate relations between conformity and the breadwinner's terms for his creativity" in three plays by Miller—*All My Sons*, *Death of a Salesman*, and *A View from the Bridge*.

Critical Essays in Journals and Magazines

Adler, Henry. "To Hell with Society." *Tulane Drama Review* 4 (May 1960): 53–76. Rpt. in *Theatre in the Twentieth Century*. Ed. Robert Corrigan. New York: Grove, 1963. 245–72.

Adler says Miller fails as a social dramatist because "his work includes just those qualities which, he seems to think, make him Ibsen's superior: his rationalism and his democratic social consciousness."

Adler, Thomas P. "The Embrace of Silence: Pinter, Miller and the Response to Power." *The Pinter Review* 5.1 (1991): 4–9.

Brief essay in which Adler discusses the political statements embodied in the plays of Miller and Harold Pinter.

Bigsby, Christopher. "Arthur Miller: Poet." *Michigan Quarterly Review* 37.4 (Fall 1998): 713–24.

Keynote address delivered at the Miller Symposium at the University of Evansville in Indiana on 17 April 1998. Bigsby praises Miller as "incontestably a poet, one who sees the private and public worlds as one, who is a chronicler of the age and a creator of metaphors."

Billman, Carol. "Women and the Family in American Drama." *Arizona Quarterly* 36 (1980): 35–48.

Billman discusses the study of "everyman" made in the family dramas of Eugene O'Neill, Tennessee Williams, and Arthur Miller, finding that in Miller, the women "necessarily occupy a central position, [but] little attention is paid to their subordination or suffering."

Blau, Herbert. "Spacing Out in the American Theater." *Kenyon Review* 15.2 (Spring 1993): 27–39.

Lengthy essay on space (physical and psychic) in American theatre history. Mention is made of Miller in regards to *Death of a Salesman* and Miller's dissatisfaction with the Broadway "marketplace"—"we have no real theatre. We have shows, which isn't really the same thing."

Blumberg, Paul. "Sociology and Social Literature: Work Alienation in the Plays of Arthur Miller." *American Quarterly* 21 (Summer 1969): 291–310. Rpt. as "Work as Alienation in the Plays of Arthur Miller," in *Arthur Miller: New Perspectives*. Ed. Robert A. Marin. Englewood Cliffs, N.J.: Prentice-Hall, 1982. 48–64.

Blumberg demonstrates how the dramatic form can be used to both illustrate and deepen an understanding of ideas commonly employed by sociologists. He specifically examines the concept of "alienation of labor" and how Miller has incorporated this theme in his work. Works discussed include *All My Sons*, *Death of a Salesman*, *The Misfits*, and *A Memory of Two Mondays*.

Boruch, Marianne. "Miller & Things." *Literary Review* 24.4 (Summer 1981): 548–61.

Boruch intelligently argues that Miller is a great playwright because he can use things or objects, in themselves, thematically —"not simply as properties to be touched then discarded on the way to discovery, but somehow as the discovery itself."

Brink, André. "Seminar in Salzburg." *Plays and Players* (London) 1996 December/1997 January: 21.

Account of theatre seminar in Salzburg that addressed issues of artistry, entertainment, and social commentary, concentrating on an opening day master class taught by Miller and David Thacker, where scenes from Miller's *I Can't Remember Anything* and *Death of a Salesman* were enacted.

Brooks, Charles. "The Multiple Set in American Drama." *Tulane Drama Review* 3 (December 1958): 30–41.

This essay looks closely at ways in which multiple set dramas achieve larger visions of life than single set or shifting scene plays of the past. Brooks details Miller's *Death of a Salesman*, calling it "the single play which best realizes the potentialities of the multiple set."

Brustein, Robert. "The Memory of Heroism." *Drama Review* 4 (March 1960): 5–7. Rpt. in *The Third Theatre*. New York: Knopf, 1969. 238–47.

Brustein examines the concept of Greek tragedy and determines, among other things, that Miller's works could not be termed tragic in the classic sense. The "essential difference that separates the Greeks from ourselves" is reduced to one point: "the tragic to us is an accident we seek to avoid because it makes our lives poorer; for the Greeks it is an inevitability they do not hesitate to confront because it ultimately gives dignity to life and enlarges the possibilities of man."

———. "Why American Plays Are Not Literature." *Harper's* October 1959: 167–173. Rpt. in *American Drama and Its Critics: A Collection of Critical Essays*. Ed. Alan S. Downer. Chicago: U of Chicago P, 1965. 245–55.

Brustein laments the lack of a firm literary tradition in the United States in terms of its playwrights. Few playwrights, besides Miller, write in other forms or even feel comfortable with the label "intellect." "Arthur Miller is one American playwright with the ambition to write mature drama which transcends the family crisis, the sexual conflict, and the individual psychosis." He ends with a call to novelists to write plays, and a call to professional theatres to produce them.

Cassell, Richard A. "Arthur Miller's 'Rage of Conscience.'" *Ball State Teachers College Forum* 1 (Winter 1960–61): 31–36.

Cassell surveys *All My Sons*, *Death of a Salesman*, *A View from the Bridge*, and *The Crucible* in an effort to reveal Miller's convictions and ideas about social drama and the tragic hero.

Centola, Steven R. "Confrontation with the Other: Alienation in the Works of Arthur Miller and Jean-Paul Sartre." *Journal of Evolutionary Psychology* 1–2 (March 1984): 1–11.

Centola discusses the "numerous correspondences" between

"the ideas implicit in Miller's plays" and Jean-Paul Sartre's philosophy of existentialism.

Clurman, Harold. "Main Streams of American Drama." *World Theatre* (1966). Rpt. in *The Collected Works of Harold Clurman: Six Decades of Commentary on Theatre, Dance, Music, Film, Arts and Letters*. Eds. Marjorie Loggia and Glenn Young. New York: Applause, 1994. 615–17.

After a brief summation of the negative critical reaction to *After the Fall* and *Incident at Vichy*, Clurman argues that three points regarding Miller need to be emphasized: "(a) that properly produced [Miller's plays] are extremely effective stage pieces, (b) that they develop Miller's basic preoccupation: what men owe one another, and (c) that Miller is still a force that can be counted on to provide us in the future with provocative drama."

Collins, Anthony R. "Arthur Miller and the Judgment of God." *South-Central Bulletin* (College Station, Tex.) 42 (Winter 1982): 120–24.

Collins examines *All My Sons*, *The Crucible*, *Death of a Salesman*, *A View from the Bridge*, and *After the Fall* to "illuminate the ways in which Miller has used the presence or absence of a moral stance and/or God for dramatic purposes and how this usage traces an evolution in Miller's concept of moral action."

Cook, Kimberly K. "Self-Preservation in Arthur Miller's Holocaust Dramas." *Journal of Evolutionary Psychology* 14.1–2 (March 1993): 99–108.

Cook reads *Incident at Vichy* and *Playing for Time* as works that explore "the male and female struggles to maintain an essential element of the human self." Cook argues that Miller offers a realistic portrait of "the separate, but parallel, crisis which arose for men and women, from the raging fires of the holocaust."

Corrigan, Robert W. "The Achievement of Arthur Miller." *Comparative Drama* 2 (1968): 141–60. Rpt. as "Introduction: The Achievement of Arthur Miller." *Arthur Miller: A Collection of Critical Essays*. Ed. Robert W. Corrigan. Englewood Cliffs, N.J.: Prentice-Hall, 1969. 1–22. Rpt. in *The Theatre in Search of a Fix*. Ed. Robert W. Corrigan. New York: Delacorte, 1973. 325–42. Edited version appears in *Contemporary Dramatists*. Ed. James Vinson. New York: St. Martin's, 1973. 542–44.

Using Erik Erikson's model, Corrigan divides Miller's canon

(to date) into two periods: the first includes all plays up to and including the two-act revision of *A View from the Bridge*, plays that exhibit a "crisis of identity;" the second period includes *The Misfits* to *The Price*, and those that exhibit a "crisis of gerativity"—the drama of characters who accept full responsibility for what they have or have not done.

———. "The Search for New Endings: The Theatre in Search of a Fix, Part III." *Theatre Journal* 36.2 (May 1984): 153–63.

Corrigan sees Miller's lifelong experimentation with dramatic form and his recent turn to writing travel books and directing *Salesman* in China as indicative of the breakdown of the modernist tradition.

Costello, Donald P. "Arthur Miller's Circles of Responsibility: *A View from the Bridge* and Beyond." *Modern Drama* 36.3 (September 1993): 443–53.

Costello investigates Miller's seeming preoccupation with self and society and concludes that his dramatic works investigate how humans can work out the interconnections between the self, society, and the universe, forming circles of responsibility that are the basis of morality.

Crandell, George W. "Arthur Miller's Unheard Plea for Jewish Refugees: 'Hitler's Quarry.'" *ANQ* 13.1 (Winter 2000): 33+.

Crandell reprints a neglected article from 1941 in which Miller "draws attention to the widespread persecution of the Jews and deplores the U.S. State Department's failure to assist the thousands of Jewish people" who are attempting to escape Nazism. Crandell prefaces it with an evaluation of the importance of the article's early insights and influence on Miller's later dramas.

Dillingham, William B. "Arthur Miller and the Loss of Conscience." *Emory University Quarterly* 16 (Spring 1960): 40–50. Excerpt rpt. as "The Individual and Society in Miller's Plays" in *Readings on Arthur Miller*. Ed. Thomas Siebold. San Diego, Calif.: Greenhaven, 1997. 82–89.

According to Dillingham, tragedy occurs in Miller's plays when his characters forfeit their responsibility for themselves and others either through ignorance or false values, consequently losing their sense of integrity and conscience.

Downer, Alan S. "Mr. Williams and Mr. Miller." *Furioso* 4 (Summer 1949): 66–70.

Downer compares the poetic elements in plays by Tennessee Williams and Arthur Miller.

Driver, Tom F. "Strength and Weakness in Arthur Miller." *Tulane Drama Review* 4.4 (May 1960): 45–52. Rpt. in *Discussions of Modern American Drama*. Ed. Walter J. Meserve. Boston: D. C. Heath, 1965. 105–13. Rpt. in *Arthur Miller: A Collection of Critical Essays*. Ed. Robert W. Corrigan. Englewood Cliffs, N.J.: Prentice-Hall, 1969. 59–67. Rpt. in *Modern Critical Views: Arthur Miller*. Ed. Harold Bloom. New York: Chelsea, 1987. 17–25. Excerpt rpt. in *Major Literary Characters: Willy Loman*. Ed. Harold Bloom. New York: Chelsea, 1991. 9–10.

Driver finds that Miller's dramatic weakness is his "unresolved contradictions" regarding a moralism that does not "speak of a good in the light of which morality would make sense," and that Miller's strength is his ability to speak directly to his audiences.

Farnsworth, T. A. "Arthur Miller: Moralist and Crusader." *Contrast* (Capetown, South Africa) I (Winter 1961): 84–87.

Essay that compares and contrasts the dramatic styles and techniques of Miller and Terence Rattigan and praises Miller for the "power and intensity" of his work.

Feldman, Robert Lee. "Arthur Miller's Neglected Article on Nazi War Criminals' Trials: A Vision of Evil." *Resources for American Literary Study* 15 (Autumn 1985): 187–96.

Felman reprints a neglected article by Miller from 1964 on the Nazi war crimes trials in Frankfurt, Germany, prefacing it with an evaluation of the importance of the article's insights and influence on Miller's later dramas.

Flaxman, Seymour L. "The Debt of Williams and Miller to Ibsen and Strindberg." *Comparative Studies*, Special Advance Issue (1963): 51–59.

Lengthy essay that charts the influence of Ibsen and Strindberg on the Miller canon. While indebted to them, Flaxman argues, Miller does little to add to their dramatic traditions.

Fruchter, Norm. "On the Frontier: The Development of Arthur Miller." *Encore* January 1962: 17–27.

Assessment of Dennis Welland's *Arthur Miller* included here for its lengthy argument against this book that Fruchter feels avoids making critical evaluations of Miller's work and ignores the process of Miller's development as a playwright.

Ganz, Arthur. "The Silence of Arthur Miller." *Drama Survey* 3.2 (October 1963): 224–37. Excerpted in *Twentieth Century Interpretations of "The Crucible", a Collection of Critical Essays*. Ed. John H. Ferres. Englewood Cliffs, N.J.: Prentice-Hall, 1972. 107–108. Revised rpt. as "Arthur Miller: Eden and After." *Realms of the Self: Variations on a Theme in Modern Drama*. N.Y.: New York UP, 1980. 122–44. Excerpt rpt. in *Major Literary Characters: Willy Loman*. Ed. Harold Bloom. New York: Chelsea, 1991. 22–25.

Ganz discusses Miller's eight-year silence between the premiere of *A View from the Bridge* and the screenplay for *The Misfits*, compares his writing from before and after the silence, and concludes that Miller "has perhaps recognized the inadequacy of a simplistic view of man as inherently virtuous."

Gianakaris, C. J. "Absurdism Altered: *Rosencrantz and Guildenstern Are Dead*." *Drama Survey* 7 (Winter 1968): 52–58.

Giankaris argues that Tom Stoppard's *Rosencrantz and Guildenstern Are Dead* is an example of an absurdist play that does not, as Miller had stated previously regarding the genre, present a negative and sophomoric view of life that deals only with superficial themes of existence.

Goldstein, Laurence. "The Fiction of Arthur Miller." *Michigan Quarterly Review* 37.4 (Fall 1998): 725–45.

Goldstein studies the thematic concerns of Miller's fiction—the "neglected corpus of a major writer"—highlighting its overall positivism.

———. "Introduction." *Michigan Quarterly Review* 37.4 (Fall 1998): 585–89.

Tribute piece serving as an introduction to a special issue commemorating the fiftieth anniversary of *Death of a Salesman*. Goldstein relates Miller's beginnings as a playwriting student at the University of Michigan to his role as a playwright who has "challenged and helped to define social and aesthetic currents in the last half-century."

Hallett, Charles A. "The Retrospective Technique and Its Implications for Tragedy." *Comparative Drama* 12 (1978): 3–21.

This study examines the types of experiences that can be rendered by the retrospective plot by explaining retrospective techniques in selected classical and modern dramas. There is a brief discussion of *Death of a Salesman*, which Hallett calls "objective" in its retrospection because Miller is asking the audience to play detective and learn that "society had taught Willy the wrong values and destroyed him for remaining faithful to those values."

Hayman, Ronald. "Arthur Miller: Between Sartre and Society." *Encounter* 37 (1971): 73–79.

Hayman critically examines the Miller canon, finding *Death of a Salesman* his most successful drama because it is a complete departure from the usual tight chronological sequence of his other works and thus its structure "protects him from any suggestion of one-to-one correlations between cause and effect." Miller should stay away from tight structures and return to loose ones to accommodate those plays that "ride a neurotic hobbyhorse."

Hynes, Joseph A. "Arthur Miller and the Impasse of Naturalism." *South Atlantic Quarterly* 62 (1963): 327–34.

Hynes argues that *All My Sons*, *Death of a Salesman*, and *A View from the Bridge* are essentially the same play, similar in character and concerned with an individual hero within the social scheme. Additionally, Miller uses naturalism as "a means of permitting confused thinking to look respectable and reflective of complexity. . . . Arthur Miller is a first-rate man of the theater, but he seems to me not yet a sufficiently mature dramatist."

Isser, Edward R. "Arthur Miller and the Holocaust." *Essays in Theatre* 10.2 (May 1992): 155–64." Rpt. in Isser's *Stages of Annihilation: Theatrical Representations of the Holocaust*." Rutherford, N.J.: Fairleigh Dickinson UP, 1997. 62–72.

Isser labels Miller's interpretation of the holocaust as universalistic and humanist (a horrific event that is also well within the continuum of Western tradition). Miller's dramaturgy is "concerned with the ethical issues confronting an individual in the face of monolithic power." Works studied include: *After the Fall, Incident at Vichy*, *Broken Glass*, *Playing for Time*, and *Focus*.

Jacobson, Irving. "The Child as Guilty Witness." *Literature and Psychology* 24.1 (1974): 12–23.

With its rare instance of a child as a main character, Jacobson offers a close reading of Miller's short story "I Don't Need You Any More" in an effort to more closely understand family themes in Miller's canon.

Kane, Leslie. "Dreamers and Drunks: Moral and Social Consciousness in Arthur Miller and Sam Shepard." *America Drama* 1 (Fall 1991): 27–45.

Kane compares and contrasts the plays of Miller and Sam Shepard and their similar disillusionment with the American Dream and mythical father-and-son relationships.

Kellman, Steven G. "Birthday of a Playwright." *Nation* 13 November 1995: 579–80.

Kellman offers an overview of three concurrent books that are being published to commemorate the 80th birthday of Arthur Miller—*Homely Girl, A Life, and Other Stories*, *The Portable Arthur Miller*, and *Timebends: A Life*.

Kliewer, Warren. "Schools of One." *Journal of American Drama and Theatre* 2.2 (Spring 1991): 5–23.

In this essay on early American theatrical innovators, emphasizing their influence on modern trends, Kliewer argues that Miller owes an unacknowledged debt to artists of the past, especially those who, before him, created artistically successful plays on the same subject as his *The Crucible*, including, James Nelson Barker, Mary Wilkins Freeman, Cornelius Mathews, and Henry Wadsworth Longfellow.

Kracht, Fritz Andre. "Rise and Decline of U.S. Theatre on German Stages." *American-German Review* 32 (June–July 1966): 13–15.

It is Kracht's belief that the success of *Death of a Salesman* and *The Crucible* in Germany following the war was due to the fact that these plays presented a startling view of America that had not been seen in the official "re-education" program conducted by the United States.

Kuchwara, Michael. "Miller Defines Drama." *English Journal* 83.7 (November 1994): 109.

Short piece about "America's oldest playwright" and his thoughts on America's "entertainment culture" where "serious theatre and its ideas are less than an afterthought."

Lannon, William. "The Rise and Rationale of Post World War II American Confessional Theater." *Connecticut Review* 8.2 (April 1975): 73–81.

Lannon studies *Death of a Salesman* as a powerful and sophisticated confessional play that indicts the American system, and *A View from the Bridge* as an example of "Miller's continuing concern with the plight of the inner man."

Lehman, David. "November 9." *Michigan Quarterly Review* 37.4 (Fall 1998): 654.

Poem inspired by a meeting with Miller.

Macey, Samuel L. "Nonheroic Tragedy: A Pedigree for American Tragic Drama." *Comparative Literary Studies* 6 (1969): 1–19.

In a general way, Macey traces the development of the nonheroic tragedy in an attempt to demonstrate the relationship between this form and the American tragic drama of Eugene O'Neill, Tennessee Williams, and Arthur Miller.

Martin, Robert A. "Arthur Miller: Public Issues, Private Tensions." *Studies in the Literary Imagination* 21.2 (Fall 1988): 97–106. Rpt. in *Public Issues, Private Tensions: Contemporary American Drama*. Ed. Matthew C. Roudané. New York: AMS, 1993. 65–75.

Martin addresses the silence in Miller's playwriting between *A View from the Bridge* in 1956 and *After the Fall* in 1964 with special attention to Miller's shift in philosophical stance.

Mathur, S. C. "Arthur Miller—A Realist." *Triveni: Journal of Indian Renaissance* 53 (1984): 38–40.

Mathur discusses the ways that Miller differs from traditional realists and, by enlarging and greatly modifying the traditional, has "given it a new shape, meaning and significance."

———. "The Plays of Arthur Miller." *Triveni: Journal of Indian Renaissance* 56.2 (1987): 64–67.

Brief essay in which Mathur investigates the recurrent themes of "unrelatedness and allientation" in the plays of Arthur Miller.

McAnany, Emile G. "The Tragic Commitment: Some Notes on Arthur Miller." *Modern Drama* 5 (May 1962): 11–20.

McAnany examines Miller's "significant body of dramatic theory and critical comment on contemporary serious drama" and, after summarizing his main points, concludes that these works distinguish the playwright for his "important contributions to the tradition of the American theater."

McKinney, Priscilla S. "Jung's Anima in Arthur Miller's Plays." *Studies in American Drama 1945–Present* 3 (1988): 41–63. Excerpt rpt. in *Major Literary Characters: Willy Loman*. Ed. Harold Bloom. New York: Chelsea, 1991. 30–31.

McKinney analyzes Miller using Jungian theory, concentrating on the interplay of male and female voices and the universal debate within individual minds, expressed in family confrontation.

McMahon, Helen. "Arthur Miller's Common Man: The Problem of the Realistic and the Mythic." *Drama and Theatre* 10 (Spring 1972): 128–33.

Lengthy essay in which McMahon examines three myths common to the work of Arthur Miller—the American Dream myth, the myth of the common man, and motifs and patterns of Judeo-Christian myths.

Meyer, Kinereth. "'A Jew Can Have a Jewish Face': Arthur Miller, Autobiography, and the Holocaust." *Prooftexts* 18.3 (1 September 1998): 239–58.

Meyer reads Miller's autobiography *Timebends* and his dramas for the stage as texts that relate directly and indirectly to his self-definition as "a second-generation American Jew."

Miller, Gabriel. "'Purpose Is But the Salve to Memory': Clifford Odets, Elia Kazan, Arthur Miller, and the American Stage." *American Drama* 1.1 (Fall 1991): 61–84.

An account of the careers of Odets, Kazan, and Miller and how they intertwine, both as public figures and as artists committed to their own personal visions.

Moss, Leonard. "Arthur Miller and the Common Man's Language." *Modern Drama* 7 (May, 1964): 52–59. Rpt. in *The Merrill Studies in "Death of a Salesman."* Ed. Walter Meserve. Ohio: Merrill, 1972. 85–92. Excerpt rpt. in *Major Literary Characters: Willy Loman*. Ed. Harold Bloom. New York: Chelsea, 1991. 14–15.

Moss examines Miller's "distinctive achievement" of colloquial speech in *All My Sons*, *Death of a Salesman*, *A View from the Bridge*, and *The Misfits*.

Myers, Paul. "Arthur Miller." *Dramatics* February 1948: 3–4.

Overview of Miller's short career to date, included here for the details presented of Miller's pre-Broadway days. Photographic still from original stage production accompanies the text.

Nelson, Benjamin. "Avant-Garde Dramatics from Ibsen to Ionesco." *Psychoanalytic Review* 55 (1968): 505–12.

Nelson argues that Miller, Tennessee Williams, and Edward Albee are Freudian playwrights who have introduced sexual abnormality and perversion as familiar elements in the drama. Additionally, Nelson labels Ibsen and Strindberg as proto-Freudians, and Samuel Beckett, Eugene Ionesco, and Jean Genet as post-Freudians.

Nilsen, Helge Normann. "From *Honors at Dawn* to *Death of a Salesman*: Marxism and the Early Plays of Arthur Miller." *English Studies* 75.2 (March 1994): 146–56.

Nilsen examines the influence of Marxism in Miller's first three published plays. He concludes that Miller's dramas offer a strong indictment of the American system of capitalism and suggests that Miller is perhaps proposing a new socialist world based upon love and mutual respect rather than cutthroat competition.

Överland, Orm. "The Action and Its Significance: Arthur Miller's Struggle with Dramatic Form." *University of Toronto Quarterly* 35 (1966): 144–57. Rpt. in *Modern Drama* 18.1 (March 1975): 1–14. Rpt. in *Modern Critical Views: Arthur Miller*. Ed. Harold Bloom. New York: Chelsea, 1987. 51–63. Rpt. in *Arthur Miller: New Perspectives*. Ed. Robert A. Martin. Englewood Cliffs, N.J.: Prentice-Hall, 1982. 33–47.

Överland charts Miller's struggle with dramatic form and argues that Miller's theories regarding "social drama and its relationship to the realistic and unrealistic modes of drama should be regarded as rationalizations of his own attempts to express himself clearly" and justify his work. Miller's greatest strength as a playwright lies in his use of the realistic mode, and Överland urges Miller "to return to the kind of work that has placed him in the front rank of contemporary dramatists."

Popkin, Henry. "Arthur Miller: The Strange Encounter." *Sewanee Review* 68 (1960): 34–60. Rpt. in *American Drama and Its Critics: A Collection of Critical Essays*. Ed. Alan S. Downer. Chicago: U of Chicago P, 1965. 218–39. Excerpt rpt. in *Major Literary Characters: Willy Loman*. Ed. Harold Bloom. New York: Chelsea, 1991. 10–13.

Popkin asserts that there exists a "strange encounter" in Miller's works manifesting as a confrontation between "the dead level of banality" and "the heights and depths of guilt" that produces "a liberal parable of hidden evil and social responsibility." He perceives a pattern in each of Miller's major dramatic works where ordinary, uncomprehending people are matched with extraordinary demands and accusations, producing a central tension "between little people and big issues" and confirming the audience's belief "that little people cannot live up to big standards."

Porter, Thomas E. "Strong Gods and Sexuality: Guilt and Responsibility in the Later Plays of Arthur Miller." *American Drama* 6.1 (Fall 1996): 89–112.

Porter examines the relationship of God and sexuality in *The Creation of the World and Other Business*, *After the Fall*, *The Ride Down Mount Morgan*, and *The Archbishop's Ceiling*.

Prudhoe, John. "Arthur Miller and the Tradition of Tragedy." *English Studies* 43 (October 1962): 430–39.

Prudhoe examines Miller's theory of tragedy and his experiments with the form and use of language in his plays.

Raymond, Gerard. "Miller-Time in London: An American Playwright in Exile." *Theater Week* 16 April 1990: 30–31.

Raymond investigates why Miller is more produced in London than New York, concluding that in addition to the country going through an "Ibsen phase," and despite the fact that Miller's plays are "specifically American," his plays do not lose their power or their contemporaneity when they cross the Atlantic."

Reno, Raymond H. "Arthur Miller and the Death of God." *Texas Studies in Language and Literature* 11 (1969): 1069–87.

Finding Miller's dramas a series of rewrites with similar themes and situations, Reno suggests that not only is Miller probing his own work, rediscovering his main concerns and giving "them greater prominence and clarity," but he is also producing "something of a corporate work" that constitutes "a vast work dealing with the death of God."

"The Responsible Man." *Economist* (London) 14 July 1990: 91.
Feature essay reporting on the career of Miller, his treatment of characters, and the themes in *The Crucible*, *An Enemy of the People*, and *After the Fall.*

Roudané, Matthew C. "Arthur Miller and His Influence on Contemporary American Drama." *American Drama* 6.1 (Fall 1996): 1–13.
Roudané explores Miller's continuing influence on modern American drama in the work of Albee, Shepard, and David Rabe.

Scanlan, Thomas M. "The Domestication of Rip Van Winkle: Joe Jefferson's Play as Prologue to Modern American Drama." *Virginia Quarterly Review* 50 (Winter 1974): 51–62.
An examination of Joe Jefferson's play *Rip Van Winkle* as precursor to family-themed plays of Eugene O'Neill, Arthur Miller, and Tennessee Williams.

Schraepen, Edmond. "Arthur Miller's Constancy: A Note on Miller as a Short Story Writer." *Revue des Langues Vivantes* 36 (1970): 62–71.
Schraepen examines two Miller short stories ("I Don't Need You Any More" and "The Prophecy") as to whether, and to what extent, they deal with similar themes found in the playwright's dramas.

Schroeder, Patricia R. "Arthur Miller: Illuminating Process." *REAL—The Yearbook of Research in English and American Literature* 3 (1985): 265–93. Rpt. in *The Presence of the Past in Modern American Drama.* Cranbury, N.J.: Associated UP, 1989. 76–104.
Schroeder examines Miller's handling of the relationship between past and present time on the stage and the problems he has encountered in portraying the past in his plays.

Seagar, Allan. "The Creative Agony of Arthur Miller." *Esquire* October 1959: 123–126. Rpt. in *"Death of a Salesman": Text and Criticism.* Ed. Gerald Weales. New York: Viking, 1967. 326–38. Rpt. in *Lilliput* 46 (January 1960): 30–33. Rpt. as "Miller's Writing Process" in *Readings on Arthur Miller*. Ed. Thomas Siebold. San Diego, Calif.: Greenhaven, 1997. 39–48.
Saeger explores Miller's creative struggle from initial insight to finished work as an agonizing artistic process.

Shepherd, Allen. "'What Comes Easier—': The Short Stories of Arthur Miller." *Illinois Quarterly* 34.3 (February 1972): 37–49. Rpt. in *Critical Essays on Arthur Miller*. Ed. James J. Martine. Boston: G. K. Hall, 1979. 197–205.

Shepherd examines nine short stories from Miller's first collection, entitled *I Don't Need You Any More*, and concludes that they are "notably uneven and collectively are not distinguished."

Simon, John. "The Tragedy of American Theatre." *Holiday* March 1966: 76–83, 169, 171, 173–74, 176–77.

Lengthy essay on the state of the American theatre, a condition that Simon sees as "a theatre with neither top nor bottom, only a spreading, sagging middle." Simon says of Miller's latest works, *After the Fall* and *Incident at Vichy*, that they "have confirmed what has become progressively more apparent; that he has the sort of mind that simplifies things out of their complex reality, without having the style, the poetry, that could turn simplification into an aesthetically authentic experience." Of note is the color photograph of Miller and small daughter Rebecca, not hitherto seen before.

Steinberg, M. W. "Arthur Miller and the Idea of Modern Tragedy." *Dalhousie Review* 40 (Autumn 1960): 329–40. Rpt. in *Arthur Miller: A Collection of Critical Essays*. Ed. Robert W. Corrigan. Englewood Cliffs, N.J.: Prentice-Hall, 1969. 81–93. Excerpted in *Twentieth Century Interpretations of "The Crucible," A Collection of Critical Essays*. Ed. John H. Ferres. Englewood Cliffs, N.J.: Prentice-Hall, 1972. 98–100.

Steinberg examines *All My Sons*, *Death of a Salesman*, and *The Crucible* as well as Miller's essays on tragedy to reveal "the terms of his definition," concluding that the playwright has "been giving his common man tragic stature, and the result has been a strengthening and an intensifying of the tragic quality in his plays."

Steppat, Michael P. "Self Choice and Aesthetic Despair in Arthur Miller and Tennessee Williams." *Literary Criterion* 20.3 (1985): 49–59.

Steppat asserts that Kierkegaard's philosophy of existentialist individualism has influenced both Tennessee Williams and Arthur Miller and can be seen in the tragic effect of *A Streetcar Named Desire* and *Death of a Salesman*—"the anatomy of despair as a result of refusing self-choice."

Stitt, Milan. "Gratitude Must Be Paid." *Horizon* 17 December 1984: 17.

Stitt traces Miller's influence on twentieth-century drama such as Mamet's *Glengarry Glen Ross* and Rabe's *Hurlyburly* and praises Miller's introduction of the flashback technique as the most important dramatic device innovation since the sixteenth century. He finds Mamet less hopeful but more comic than Miller and Rabe's characters similar to Miller's, but prone to give up instead of suffering gladly.

Trowbridge, Clinton W. "Arthur Miller: Between Pathos and Tragedy.." *Modern Drama* 10.3 (December 1967): 221–32. Rpt. in *Critical Essays on Arthur Miller*. Ed. James J. Martine. Boston: G. K. Hall, 1979. 125–35. Rpt. in *Modern Critical Views: Arthur Miller*. Ed. Harold Bloom. New York: Chelsea, 1987. 39–50.

Trowbridge examines Miller's drama, from *All My Sons* to *Incident at Vichy*, and concludes that, on the whole, it "hovers between pathos and tragedy," mostly never truly achieving "the exaltation of great tragedy." Interestingly, Trowbridge finds *After the Fall* "to be not only [Miller's] greatest triumph but one of the few genuinely tragic plays of our time."

Tuttle, Jon. "The Efficacy of Work: Arthur Miller and Albert Camus' 'The Myth of Sisyphus.'" *American Drama* 6.1 (Fall 1996): 61–72.

Tuttle applies Camus's belief that "the struggle itself . . . is enough to fill a man's heart" to Miller's *The Price*, *A View from the Bridge*, and *A Memory of Two Mondays.*

Tynan, Kenneth. "American Blues: The Plays of Arthur Miller and Tennessee Williams." *Encounter* 2.5 (1954): 13–19. Rpt. in *Curtains*. New York: Atheneum, 1961. 257–66. Rpt. in *The Modern American Theater: A Collection of Critical Essays*. Ed. Alvin B. Kernan. Englewood Cliffs, N.J.: Prentice-Hall, 1967. 34–51.

Tynan explores the commonalities between Tennessee Williams and Arthur Miller focusing on their shared theme of frustration. Miller plays examined: *The Man Who Had All the Luck*, *All My Sons*, *Death of a Salesman*, and *The Crucible*.

Vajda, Miklos. "Arthur Miller: Moralist as Playwright." *New Hungarian Quarterly* 16 (1975): 171–80.

Reprint of the text of the introduction to the third Hungarian edition of *Arthur Miller's Collected Plays*, published in 1975.

Concludes Vajda, it is "a reassuring and comforting thought that with incredible constancy Miller's art continues to develop and continuously enriches and renews itself with each new play; the basic principle of his work, the writer's deep moral ardor, will never be outmoded."

Vaughan, Peter. "Miller Time Began Early for Thacker." *Minneapolis Star Tribune* 9 February 1997: F16.

Interview with David Thacker in which the director discusses his working relationship with Miller, his admiration for the playwright's dramas, and his opinion as to the reason why Miller is more appreciated in England than in the United States. Of biographical note is the mention of Miller having recently undergone back surgery making him unable to make the transatlantic trip to see the *Death of a Salesman* revival at the Royal National Theatre.

Vos, Nelvin. "The American Dream Turned to Nightmare: Recent American Drama." *Christian Scholar's Review* 1 (Spring 1971): 200–202.

Vos explores the disillusionment that results from belief in the ideal of success represented by the American Dream and its resultant influences on the American theatre. Joe Keller (*All My Sons*) and Willy Loman (*Death of a Salesman*) are examined as two "money-seeking fathers" who are "repudiated by their sons which culminates in the father's self-destruction."

Weales, Gerald. "American Drama since the Second World War." *Tamarack Review* 13 (Autumn 1959): 86–99.

In this survey of American theatre since the end of World War II, Weales identifies Miller as one of the two dramatists [Tennessee Williams being the other] who can lay claim to being considered "major." His strength as a playwright "lies in his ability to give flesh to personal relationships without considering that that is the end of his job. The relationships become societal as well as personal and in doing so they become revelations and self-revelations."

———. "Arthur Miller and the 50s." *Michigan Quarterly Review* 37.4 (Fall 1998): 635–51.

Keynote address at the Third International Arthur Miller Conference at Utica College on 18 September 1996. Fascinating and informative, Weales offers his most significant recollections about the 1950s, politics, and theatre. Pulling together information from news stories, autobiographies, documentary evidence, and interview sources, Weales discusses Miller's career (political and literary) up to *After the Fall.*

———. "Arthur Miller Takes the Air." *American Drama* 5.1 (Fall 1995): 1–15.

Weales analyzes seventeen of Miller's radio plays, including a brief background of the works and several of the play's producers.

West, Paul. "Arthur Miller & the Human Mice." *Hibbert Journal* 61 (January 1963): 84–86.

Calling Miller's works "Christian plays," West's essay examines what he defines as Miller's dramatic philosophy—"a man must fulfil [sic] his obligations to his fellows without losing either his all to society or his sense of his own uniqueness."

Whitley, Alvin. "Arthur Miller: An Attempt at Modern Tragedy." *Transactions of the Wisconsin Academy of Sciences, Arts, and Letters* 42 (1953): 257–62.

Whitley argues that both *All My Sons* and *Death of a Salesman* are inconsistent with Miller's own theory of tragedy—"One may well ask if enlightenment on the part of the audience is an effective substitute for enlightenment on the part of the hero"—and that Miller's theory of tragedy is not feasible because of a fallacy in his logic.

Wiegand, William. "Arthur Miller and the Man Who Knows." *Western Review* 21 (Winter 1957): 85–103. Rpt. in *"Death of a Salesman": Text and Criticism*. Ed. Gerald Weales. New York: Viking, 1967. 290–312. Rpt. in *"The Crucible": Text and Criticism*. Ed. Gerald Weales. New York: Viking, 1971. 290–314.

Wiegand explores the themes of Miller early college and radio plays for their influence on Miller's later works. Includes a bibliography of unpublished plays and published radio dramas.

Willett, Ralph W. "The Ideas of Miller and Williams." *Theatre Annual* 22 (1965–66): 31–40.

Arguing that neither Tennessee Williams nor Miller are original in their dramas, Willett traces the influences of Emerson and other American writers of the nineteenth century in his belief that individuals can become great. Unfortunately, he continues, Miller's work leans toward incoherence because he presents too many sides of an issue and "defeats his end, the social theatre that will teach us how to live."

Williams, Raymond. "From Hero to Victim: The Making of Liberal Tragedy, to Ibsen and Miller." *Modern Tragedy*. Stanford: Stanford UP, 1966. 87–105. Excerpt rpt. in *Major Literary Characters: Willy Loman*. Ed. Harold Bloom. New York: Chelsea, 1991. 15.

Williams looks at the plays of Arthur Miller in an effort to trace the transformation of the tragic hero into the tragic victim.

———. "The Realism of Arthur Miller." *Critical Quarterly* 1 (Summer 1959): 140–49. Rpt. in *Universities and Left Review* 7 (Autumn 1959): 34–37. Rpt. in *"Death of a Salesman": Text and Criticism*. Ed. Gerald Weales. New York: Viking, 1967. 312–25. Rpt. in *Arthur Miller: A Collection of Critical Essays*. Ed. Robert W. Corrigan. Englewood Cliffs, N.J.: Prentice-Hall, 1969. 69–79.

Williams evaluates Miller as a social realist playwright and the "central figure in the drama and consciousness of our time." Plays studied include, *All My Sons*, *Death of a Salesman*, *The Crucible*, and *A View from the Bridge*.

Wooster, Gerald, and Mona Wilson. "Envy and Enviability Reflected in the American Dream: Two Plays by Arthur Miller." *British Journal of Psychotherapy*. 14.2 (1997): 182–88.

The authors read *The Man Who Had All the Luck* and *Broken Glass* as explorations of "manic-depressive envy dynamics as they occur in interpersonal relationships—in a small family and community group in the first play and in a marital relationship in the second."

Critical Essays in Newspapers

Atkinson, Brooks. "Art Takes Second Place." *New York Times* 11 November 1960: 28.

Atkinson comments on Miller's interview with Harry Brandon entitled "The State of the Theatre," stating that the lack of status by American artists is due to the fact that the United States does not have a tradition of regarding artists as important because "as a nation, we were overwhelmed with the problems of survival in the early days."

Beaufort, John. "Miller, Odets and Man's Dilemma." *Christian Science Monitor* 5 March 1949: 12.

Beaufort uses Miller's definition of tragedy from his preface to *Salesman*—"the consequence of a man's total compulsion to evaluate himself justly"—as an introduction to some observations regarding a production of Clifford Odet's *The Big Knife*.

Bermel, Albert. "Right, Wrong and Mr. Miller." *New York Times* 14 April 1968: Sec.2: 1, 7.

Bermel traces Miller's canon to *The Price* and concludes that while no one can say that the playwright lacks "high seriousness," one cannot also say that he has "discernibly grown as a playwright since *Salesman* and *The Crucible*. With *The Price* he has merely added some scrapings of domestic friction to his output and another humorless half-martyr to his *dramatis personae*."

Brustein, Robert. "Drama in the Age of Einstein." *New York Times* 7 August 1977: II: 1, 22. Rtp. as "The Crack in the Chimney: Reflections on Contemporary American Playwriting." *Images and Ideas in American Culture*. Ed. Arthur Edelstein. Mass.: Brandeis UP, 1979. 141–57. Rpt. as "Theatre in the Age of Einstein: The Crack in the Chimney." *Critical Moments: Reflections on Theatre & Society, 1973–1979*. New York: Random, 1980. 107–123. Rpt. and revised as "Reimagining the Drama." *Reimagining American Theatre*. New York: Hill and Wang, 1991. 19–32.

Contrary to established critical thought, Brustein postulates that Miller's themes and actions are "not Ibsenite in the least." Instead of "attempting to repeal the simple, fundamental law of cause-and-effect," which was Ibsen's dramatic trademark, Miller, in every play, reinforces the pattern that every action "has an equal and opposite reaction."

Clurman, Harold. "The Merits of Mr. Miller." *New York Times* 21 April 1968: II: 1, 7. Rpt. as "Arthur Miller's Later Plays." *Arthur Miller: A Collection of Critical Essays*. Ed. Robert Corrigan. Englewood Cliffs, N.J.: Prentice-Hall, 1969. 143–68. Rpt. in *The Collected Works of Harold Clurman: Six Decades of Commentary on Theatre, Dance, Music, Film, Arts and Letters*. Eds. Marjorie Loggia and Glenn Young. New York: Applause, 1994. 690–92.

In this reply to Albert Bermel's article (Bermel, Albert. "Right, Wrong and Mr. Miller." *New York Times* 14 April 1968: Sec. 2: 1, 7.), Clurman argues that Miller had significantly evolved as a playwright since *The Crucible*. His later plays reveal a "trait of self-doubt" and a new moralism that alters the form of his dramas.

Gussow, Mel. "In the Plays of Fledglings, Imitations of Immortality." *New York Times* 8 March 1999: E2.

In an article on two lost plays of Tennessee Williams (*Not about Nightingales*) and Harold Pinter (*The Hothouse*), Gussow details the genesis of Miller's early drama "The Great Disobedience," a prison play written while Miller was a student at the University of Michigan and, when rejected for the Hopwood Award, was placed in a trunk and forgotten.

———. "A Rock of the Modern Age, Arthur Miller Is Still Everywhere." *New York Times* 30 November 1996: A17.

A profile of Miller detailing one of the busier seasons in his sixty-year career. Also examines Miller's critical acclaim in England, anecdotal origins to play titles, and relevance of *The Crucible* [film] to current sensibilities.

Krutch, Joseph Wood. "Ten American Plays That Will Endure." *New York Times Magazine* 11 October 1959: 34, 69–70.

In a lengthy article, Krutch prognosticates what ten twentieth-century American plays which will continue to be produced and revived. Miller's *Death of a Salesman* is cited as choice number four. While Krutch originally thought the work "ploddingly prosy in a literal, Dreiserian way," he admits to realizing that it is ultimately the consensus of the audience that matters and not his own reservations.

Lawson, Mark. "Writers' Rot and the Queen Mum Syndrome." *Independent* (London) 16 August 1994: 16.

Overview of Miller's literary career that Lawson says goes against the standard shape of literary careers, the inverted V or pyramid. Miller's career can be drawn as a V, with "early high achievement and a mid-life decline compensated for by a set of brilliant pensioner miniatures."

"London-New York: A One-Way Street?" *New York Times* 21 February 1999: Sec. 2: 1.

Lengthy excerpts from a discussion between critics Vincent Canby, Ben Brantley, and Peter Marks regarding the surge of British productions on American stages. Miller is mentioned for his popularity in Britain. Says Peter Marks, "He's so cynical about American culture and American politics. The English love that."

Siegel, Ed. "Broadway Opens to Everyone." *Boston Globe* 12 March 1999: D1.

Focusing on the fiftieth anniversary production of Miller's *Death of a Salesman* and the playwright's views on what has kept serious new drama off of Broadway, Siegel explores the accessibility of Miller, Tennessee Williams, and Eugene O'Neill and their current popularity, despite their plays being "as safe as shaving with a switchblade and as comforting as a nightmare."

Sullivan, Dan. "Arthur Miller to Brits: Don't Blow It." *Los Angeles Times* 28 May 1989: C7.

Feature article that explores the reasons behind Miller's acclaim in Great Britain.

Tynan, Kenneth. *Observer* (London) 14 October 1956. Rpt. in *Kenneth Tynan Profiles*. New York: Random, 1995. 140–43.

Brief overview of Miller's career to date. Says Tynan, "Miller may not be the greatest playwright of his century, but the man who fills the role will have to own a large number of his attributes and ambitions."

Wolf, Matt. "Miller-Mania." *Chicago Tribune* 16 September 1990: Sec. 13: 22.

Wolf offers details concerning the two major productions of Miller's plays (*After the Fall* and *The Crucible*) that are slated to be mounted in the fall in London.

Brief Mentions in Books, Journals, Newspapers

Atkinson, Brooks. *Broadway*. New York: Macmillan, 1970. 397–400, 453–54. Rpt. in "Withdrawal Symptoms." *Broadway*. Rev. ed. New York: Limelight, 1985. 407–10.

Biographical essay that includes a comparison between Miller and Tennessee Williams as representative 1940s playwrights with a common point of view. Included are discussions of *Death of a Salesman* and *After the Fall*.

Beck, Carl. *Contempt of Congress: A Study of the Prosecutions Initiated by the Committee on Un-American Activities, 1945–1957*. New York: Da Capo, 1974 (unabridged replication of first edition published in New Orleans by T.D. Hauser in 1959). 148–52, 169, 170–71.

A brief review of Miller's testimony in his appearance before

HUAC in 1956 and his subsequent appeal based on pertinency.

Bonin, Jane F. *Major Themes in Prize-Winning American Drama*. Metuchen, N.J.: Scarecrow, 1975. 21, 43–46, 131–33.

In a book that explores Pulitzer Prize-winning plays "for the attitudes they contain," Bonin examines the themes of women and marriage, and work and material rewards as they relate to *Death of a Salesman*, and the theme of religion as a cloak for cruelty in *The Crucible*. Bonin is critical of Miller's treatment of Linda Loman as "a wife who conforms to the conventional notion that a woman should subordinate herself to her husband's judgment, even when that judgment is bad."

Bryer, Jackson, ed. *Conversations with Lillian Hellman*. Jackson: UP of Mississippi, 1986. 48, 59, et. passim.

Of note are Hellman's conversations with Thomas Meehan in 1962 when she discusses Miller's playwriting skills and with John Phillips and Anne Hollander in 1964 [from "The Art of the Theatre I: Lillian Hellman, an Interview." *Paris Review* 9 (Winter/Spring 1965): 73–74.] when she reveals her contempt for *After the Fall*—"So you put on a stage your ex-wife who is dead from suicide and you dress her up so nobody can mistake her. Her name is Marilyn Monroe, good at any box office, so you cash in on her, and cash in yourself, which is maybe even worse."

Carpozi, George, Jr. *Marilyn Monroe: Her Own Story*. New York: Belmont Books, 1961.

Surprisingly accurate account of the Miller/Monroe romance and marriage with details of their wedding not seen before. Many photos of the couple accompany the text.

Cleaver, James. *Theatre through the Ages*. New York: Hart, 1967. 387–98.

In this survey of western theatre from Greek to modern times, Cleaver includes brief plot synopses and play analyses of *All My Sons*, *Death of a Salesman*, *The Crucible*, *A View from the Bridge*, *After the Fall*, and *Incident at Vichy*.

Clum, John. *Acting Gay: Male Homosexuality in Modern Drama*. Revised ed. New York: Columbia UP, 1994. 13–16, 332–33.

Clum explores how theatre has been a vital force in gay culture through a series of close readings of the central works to chart the history of male homosexuality drama. Clum studies *A View from the Bridge* and *After the Fall* and finds that "much of Arthur Miller's writing exists to vindicate crass patriarchal brutality."

Cohen, Arthur A. *The American Imagination after the War: Notes on the Novel, Jews, and Hope. The B. G. Rudolph Lectures in Judaic Studies*[pamphlet]. Syracuse University, 25 March 1981.

In a pamphlet of a lecture that assesses the impact of World War II on the American imagination, Cohen argues that the new imagination (the paranoid style) has it epistemological roots in the moral and psychological phenomenology of Sartre and Kafka's notion of the density of the absurd. Miller works with the old myths of Americanism and Judaism and recasts them.

Conover, David. *Finding Marilyn: A Romance*. New York: Gosset and Dunlap, 1981.

Written by "the photographer who discovered Marilyn Monroe," and drawing heavily upon his personal journals, this reminiscence seeks to "add immeasurably to your view of the child-girl innocent erotic we all knew as Marilyn Monroe and how she lived and died." Of importance to Miller studies is Conover's analysis of the breakup of Marilyn Monroe Productions and supposed insider information regarding the early part of the Miller-Monroe marriage.

Connery, Donald S. *Guilty Until Proven Innocent*. New York: Putnam, 1977.

Nonfiction account of Peter Reilly murder case, including Miller's personal and financial involvement, which was instrumental in overturning Reilly's conviction of matricide.

Conrad, Christine. "The Unfinished Memoirs of Kermit Bloomgarden." *American Theatre* November 1988: 24–29, 52–56.

Fascinating anecdotal account of the pre- through post-production experiences producing both *Death of a Salesman* and *The Crucible*, including Bloomgarden's assessment of Lee J. Cobb ("a disturbed and unhappy man"), Miller's rehearsal worries for both plays, Kazan's directing technique, and Bloomgarden and Miller's strained working relationship with Jed Harris, the director of the premiere production of *The Crucible*.

Elsom, John. "Binky Beaumont's West End." *Cold War Theatre*. London: Routledge, 1992. 25–36, 181.

In a chapter on the Cold War atmosphere's effects on theatrical production in London in the 1950s, Elsom discusses Miller's trip there in 1956 to accompany wife Marilyn Monroe during her filming of *The Prince and the Showgirl* and to attend rehearsals of his play *A View from the Bridge*, directed by Peter Brook.

Faas, Ekbert. *Tragedy and After: Euripides, Shakespeare, Goethe*. Buffalo, New York: McGill-Queens UP, 1984.

Faas examines the death of tragedy and the redefinition of the tragic genre in the works of Euripides, Shakespeare, Pirandello, Goethe, and Miller.

Fried, Richard M. *Nightmare in Red: The McCarthy Era in Perspective*. Oxford: Oxford UP, 1990. 155–56.

Miller is briefly mentioned for his refusal to both name names or take the Fifth, as well as the ironic implications of his composing *The Crucible* while friend and namer of names Kazan directed *On the Waterfront*.

Frommer, Myrna Katz, and Harvey Frommer. *It Happened on Broadway: An Oral History of the Great White Way*. New York: HBJ, 1998. 36, 65, 70–78, 254, 278.

First-hand accounts and anecdotes from Philip Langner, Flora Roberts, Hal Holbrook, Clive Barnes, Douglas Watt, Howard Kissel, and Paul Libin regarding the Broadway productions of Miller's *Death of a Salesman*, *The Crucible*, and *Broken Glass*.

Guernsey, Otis L., Jr. *Curtain Times: The New York Theater: 1965–1987*. New York: Applause, 1987. et passim.

A collection of reprints of the annual critical surveys originally published in the *Best Plays* series of yearbooks, from 1964 to 1987. Each survey is a comprehensive overview of a whole New York theater season. Miller's plays mentioned include: *After the Fall*, *Incident at Vichy*, *A View from the Bridge*, *The Price*, *The Crucible*, *The Creation of the World and Other Business*, *Death of a Salesman*, and *The American Clock*.

———, ed. *Best Plays of 1997–1998*. New York: Limelight, 1998. 18–19, 284.

Overview of the Signature Theatre Company devoting its season of productions to Miller plays, including *A View from the Bridge*, *American Clock*, *Last Yankee*, *I Can't Remember Anything*, and *Mr. Peters' Connections*.

Kanfer, Stefan. *A Journal of the Plague Years: A Devastating Chronicle of the Era of the Blacklist*. New York: Atheneum, 1973. 109, 120–21, 218–24, 250–52.

Miller is discussed in four separate occurrences: (1) his involvements and recollections with the Waldorf Peace Conference in 1948; (2) the boycott placed on the road company of *Salesman* (that "Communist-dominated play") in Peoria by Vincent Harnett; (3) "the creative divorce of Arthur Miller and Elia Kazan"; and (4) Miller's participation with the New York City Youth Board in 1955, which resulted in his being blacklisted by the *Journal-American* and *World-Telegram* and his subsequent withdrawal from the film project about youth gang activity.

Kazacoff, George. *Dangerous Theatre: The Federal Theatre Project as a Forum for New Plays*. New York: Peter Lang, 1989. 238–45.

Miller content includes details of the production history of Miller's first play, *They Too Arise*, written while he was a student at the University of Michigan, and the winner of the Avery Hopwood Award in 1936 (from U of M), and the first prize in the FTP's Bureau of New Plays Contest in 1937. Of note are the reprints of portions of the playreader's reports for the drama. Kazacoff insinuates that one unsigned and exceptionally glowing report that recommends that the play be given an "immediate try-out" may have been penned by Miller himself, who was then "a writer in the Playwriting Department, and also a playreader at the time."

Kobal, John. *People Will Talk*. New York: Knopf, 1985.

Miller is mentioned (in reference to wife Marilyn Monroe) in three of the forty-one interviews with Hollywood personalities: Jack Cole, 593–607; Henry Hathaway, 612–613; and Kim Stanley, 698–699.

———, ed. *Marilyn Monroe: A Life on Film*. London: Hamlyn, 1974.

Mostly photographic study of the career of Marilyn Monroe. Of special note are photos from the production of *The Misfits* (color and black-and-white) and the candid shots of Miller and Monroe during the filming of *Some Like It Hot* and *Let's Make Love*.

Krutch, Joseph Wood. *American Drama since 1918: An Informal History*. Revised ed. New York: Braziller, 1957: 324–29.

Krutch provides a brief overview of Miller's theatrical career from *All My Sons* to *A View from the Bridge*. *Sons* "exhibited a talent sufficient to cause critics to overestimate somewhat its actual merits," and *Salesman* presented an atmosphere "of lives unrelievedly drab while the moral is again slightly ambiguous."

Leech, Clifford. *The Critical Idiom: Tragedy*. London: Methuen, 1969. 38, 74.

Extremely brief Miller commentary but worth noting. Leech disregards *Death of a Salesman* as a tragedy and Willy Loman as a tragic hero because, ultimately, "he is the victim of the American dream rather than of the human condition." Leech also contends that *A View from the Bridge* is not tragedy just because Miller uses Alfieri to "voice final words of lament," for the chorus is "not essential in modern tragedy. The tragic writer can let his figures' anguish speak for itself."

Mellen, Joan. *Marilyn Monroe*. New York: Pyramid, 1973. 49–57, 129–38.

Part of the "Pyramid Illustrated History of the Movies" series, this slim paperback biography of Monroe includes information on her marriage to Miller and the filming of *The Misfits*. Of interest to Miller studies is the large number of photographs that accompany the text.

Millstein, Gilbert. "The Playwright's Ordeal by Fire." *New York Times Magazine* 12 December 1954: 12, 26.

In an essay that explores the "opening night syndrome" as experienced by several prominent playwrights, Miller is mentioned for his habit of walking out of the theatre when scenes that he has doubts about are being played. Small black-and-white photograph of Miller accompanies the text.

Morehouse, Ward. *Matinee Tomorrow*. New York: Whittlesey House, 1949. 191–93.

Morehouse presents his own critical history, based on personal observation, of the New York stage from the 1870s to 1949. Miller content includes Morehouse's comments on Miller's first two plays: *The Man Who Had All the Luck*—"It had one of those three-or four-performance runs which have been known to drive young promising dramatists from the theater forever"; and *All My Sons*—by this time, Miller has developed "a sharp sense of dramatic situation, a feeling for character, and a talent for trenchant dialogue."

O'Connor, Peter. "The Wasteland of Thomas Pynchon's *V.*" *College Literature* 3 (1976): 49–55.

O'Connor begins this essay on Thomas Pinchon's *V* by quoting Miller's reflection that 1949 was the last year of "an unbreakable cultural unity." This statement is in opposition to Eliot's assertion that modern man was faced with alienation in 1922. O'Connor examines each author's claim and concludes that not only is the awareness of the past more coherent than the present, but that Eliot's vision was "prophetic of a condition which would not begin to become evident in a conscious, public way until after World War II."

Pauly, Thomas H. *An American Odyssey: Elia Kazan and American Culture*. Philadelphia, Pa.: Temple UP, 1983. 71–77, 118–24, 182–87, 236–38.

Pauly presents details regarding Kazan's involvement with Miller in the productions of *All My Sons*, *Death of a Salesman*, "The Hook," and *After the Fall*. Of note is the large degree to which Kazan influenced the young Miller, at one point spending three weeks working closely with Miller establishing [*All My Sons*'s] "core and defining how each character related to it." In addition to minor alterations, Kazan advised Miller to completely revise the third act, thus an angry resolution was "replaced by a circumspect compassion and a discomforting enlargement in self-understanding."

Rollyson, Carl. *A Life of the Actress: Marilyn Monroe*. New York: Da Capo, 1993.

Film professor Rollyson examines the life of Marilyn Monroe as an actress. Of interest to Miller studies are the analyses of "Please Don't Kill Any Thing" and *The Misfits*, which Rollyson calls the "Film of Her Life."

Rumbold, Judy. "EastEndorsement." *Guardian* (London) 26 April 1993: Sec. 2: 4.

Rumbold examines the U.S. popularity of the British soap opera "EastEnders," highlighting historian Dan Abramson's comparison of the program's scriptwriters to Chekhov and Miller.

Smith, Wendy. *Real Life Drama: The Group Theatre and America, 1931–1940*. New York: Knopf, 1990. 420–21.

Miller's involvement with the Lincoln Center Repertory Theater is briefly mentioned for the artistic failure but financial success of *After the Fall*, directed by Elia Kazan, and the "better notices" for *Incident at Vichy*, directed by Harold Clurman.

Taubman, Howard. *The Making of the American Theatre*. New York: Coward-McCann, 1965. 275, 291–92, 371–72, et passim.

Historical account of the development of the American theatre that naturally includes references to Miller and the importance of his drama to modern audiences.

Wertheim, Albert. "The McCarthy Era and the American Theatre." *Theatre Journal* 34.2 (May 1982): 211–22.

Wertheim discusses McCarthy era plays that attacked HUAC investigations or protested author's innocence of Communist sympathies in dramatic works, including Miller.

Wright, William. *Lillian Hellman: The Image, the Woman*. New York: Simon and Schuster, 1986. 267–68, 297, 349–50.

Mention is made of Miller in reference to three areas: Hellman's parody in 1964 of his *After the Fall*, entitled "Lillian Hellman Wants a Little Respect for Her Agony"; Hellman's alleged promiscuity and Miller's assertion that Hellman "came onto every man she met"; and Hellman's later antagonism for Miller.

5. Stage Plays

The Man Who Had All the Luck

Critical Essays in Journals and Magazines

Murphy, Brenda. "*The Man Who Had All the Luck*: Miller's Answer to *The Master Builder*." *American Drama* 6.1 (Fall 1996): 29–41.
Murphy compares and examines Ibsen's *The Master Builder* as the source for Miller's *The Man Who Had All the Luck*.

Production Reviews

Barnes, Howard. "P.S.—He Needed It." *New York Herald Tribune* 24 November 1944: 22. *New York Theatre Critics' Reviews* 5 (1944): 73.
Negative review of Miller's first Broadway play. Says Barnes, it "is incredibly turbid in its writing and stuttering in its execution. . . . the show writhes through an unpleasant, unexciting and downright mystifying maze."

Barry, Alan. "*The Man Who Had All the Luck*." *Tribune* (London) 17 August 1990. *London Theatre Record* 10.16 (1990): 998.
Negative review of the first revival of Miller's play, directed by Paul Unwin and playing at the Young Vic. Of the script, Barry remarks that *The Man Who Had All the Luck* "is not a play Miller would have written later in life."

Billington, Michael. "*The Man Who Had All the Luck*." *Guardian* (London) 1 August 1990. *London Theatre Record* 10.16 (1990): 999.
Positive review of the first revival since the short-lived Broadway production in 1944, directed by Paul Unwin and playing at the Young Vic. "Imperfectly structured it may be, but the play bears the unmistakable stigmata of talent."

Chapman, John. "A Good Try, But Is Out of Luck." *New York Daily News* 24 November 1944. *New York Theatre Critics' Reviews* 5 (1944): 73. Rpt. in *Critical Essays on Arthur Miller*. Ed. James J. Martine. Boston: G. K. Hall, 1979. 3–4.

While criticizing the play by saying that Miller's "first offering tries a lot of things—too many by far—and most of them flop," Chapman praises the young playwright for his "sense of theatre and a real if undeveloped way of making stage characters talk and act human."

Christopher, James. "*The Man Who Had All the Luck*." *Time Out* (London) 8 August 1990. *London Theatre Record* 10.16 (1990): 998.

Negative review of the play's first revival, performed at the Young Vic after a move from the Bristol Old Vic. Says Christopher, "After a disconcertingly inert beginning, Paul Unwin's production remains uncommitted until the chill twists of the second half prompt the cast to start plumbing the emotional potential."

Denford, Antonia. "*The Man Who Had All the Luck*." *City Limits* (London) 9 August 1990. *London Theatre Record* 10.16 (1990): 997.

While the play "remains centrally unsatisfactory," Denford praises this first full-scale revival since 1944, directed by Paul Unwin at the Young Vic, as "an enjoyable piece of theatre."

Gore-Langton, Robert. "*The Man Who Had All the Luck*." *Sunday Correspondent* (London) 12 August 1990. *London Theatre Record* 10.16 (1990): 1000.

Mixed review of the first revival since the play's initial Broadway premiere in 1944. Says Gore-Langton, "Paul Unwin's production seems decent enough—not one of the Young Vic's great shows but no less than competent."

Hirschhorn, Clive. "*The Man Who Had All the Luck*." *Sunday Express* (London) 5 August 1990. *London Theatre Record* 10.16 (1990): 1000.

Highly laudatory review of the first revival of Miller's 1944 play that Hirschhorn calls "an impressive piece of dramatic excavation."

Hoyle, Martin. "*The Man Who Had All the Luck.*" *Financial Times* (London) 1 August 1990. *London Theatre Record* 10.16 (1990): 997.

Negative review of the first revival and European premiere (at the Young Vic) of Miller's 1944 play. Hoyle blames the director and design team rather than the play itself—whose "elements of fable emphasized by Miller himself, is crushed by the realistic production style that makes the story look simplistic, the characters either exaggerated or incomplete."

Hurren, Kenneth. "*The Man Who Had All the Luck.*" *Mail on Sunday* (London) 5 August 1990. *London Theatre Record* 10.16 (1990): 998.

Negative review of the first revival since the play's premiere in 1944, directed by Paul Unwin. Says Hurren, "the play's chief interest is the glimpses it affords into Miller's questing approach to drama and his first tentative tangles with family themes."

Kemp, Peter. "*The Man Who Had All the Luck.*" *Independent* (London) 1 August 1990. *London Theatre Record* 10.16 (1990): 999–1000.

Respectful review of the play's first revival, performed at the Young Vic. Says Kemp, Paul Unwin's "excellently illuminating production shows how *The Man Who Had All the Luck*, though a theatrical flop, augured well for Miller's subsequent dramatic career."

Kronenberger, Louis. "A Big Problem, A Small Play." *PM* 24 November 1944. *New York Theatre Critics' Reviews* 5 (1944): 73.

Kronenberger decries Miller's work as a "far from satisfactory play" that is "neither compelling enough as theater, nor significant enough, by a long shot, as drama."

Morehouse, Ward. "*The Man Who Had All the Luck* Is Folksy, Philosophical and Tiresome." *New York Sun* 24 November 1944. *New York Theatre Critics' Reviews* 5 (1944): 74.

Ending on the hope that Miller's next play will prove a better drama, Morehouse criticizes *The Man Who Had All the Luck* as "an ambling piece, strangely confused at times and rather tiresome for a considerable portion of the evening."

Morley, Sheridan. "*The Man Who Had All the Luck*." *Herald Tribune* (London) 8 August 1990. *London Theatre Record* 10.16 (1990): 1000.

Positive review of the first revival of *The Man Who Had All the Luck*, directed by Paul Unwin and playing at the Young Vic. Morley praises this play for containing "the seeds of the later and infinitely greater Miller plays."

Nathan, David. "*The Man Who Had All the Luck*." *Jewish Chronicle* (London) 10 August 1990. *London Theatre Record* 10.16 (1990): 1000.

Nathan offers the comment that Miller's first Broadway play, now enjoying its first revival at the Young Vic, seems to have been written "under the influence of all those films [sic] in which a helpless James Stewart was protected by a guardian angel."

Nathan, George Jean. "*Man Who Had All the Luck*." *Theatre Book of the Year, 1944–45, A Record and an Interpretation*. New York: Knopf, 1945. 171–73.

Negative review in which Nathan chides the young Miller for his treatment of a theme that is "so diffuse, disorderly and opaque that it was often impossible to decipher just what he was driving at." Nathan attacks Miller's first Broadway play as "an amateurish paraphrase and extension of the kind of one-act vaudeville play written twenty-five years ago."

Nichols, Lewis. "The Philosophy of Work against Chance Makes Up *The Man Who Had All the Luck*." *New York Times* 24 November 1944: 18. *New York Theatre Critics' Reviews* 5 (1944): 73–74. Rpt. in *Critical Essays on Arthur Miller*. Ed. James J. Martine. Boston: G. K. Hall, 1979. 1–2.

Mostly negative review of Miller's drama that Nichols finds "lacks either the final care or the luck to make it a good play. But he has tried, and that is something."

Nightingale, Benedict. "*The Man Who Had All the Luck*." *Times* (London) 1 August 1990. *London Theatre Record* 10.16 (1990): 999.

Fairly positive review of the first revival, directed by Jack Unwin, and playing at the Young Vic after its transfer from the Bristol Old Vic. Nightingale feels it is "a pleasure to come across a major writer's apprentice attempts to define the cosmos for himself and us."

Onwordi, Sylvester. "*The Man Who Had All the Luck*." *What's On* (London) 8 August 1990. *London Theatre Record* 10.16 (1990): 1000.

Rave review of the first revival, playing at the Young Vic and directed by Paul Unwin, in which Onwordi calls Miller's play "first rate" and "a great show which satisfies on every level. It is definitely worth seeing."

Osborne, Charles. "*The Man Who Had All the Luck*." *Daily Telegraph* (London) 1 August 1990. *London Theatre Record* 10.16 (1990): 998–99.

In his review of the first revival of *The Man Who Had All the Luck*, directed by Paul Unwin at the Young Vic, Osborne disputes Miller's claim that the reason why his first Broadway production failed was because "it managed to baffle all but two of the critics," by suggesting that the script has some major problems, such as "a silly plot; tedious characters, the majority of whom appear to be brain-damaged; and poor construction."

Rascoe, Burton. "Good Luck at the Forrest." *New York World-Telegram* 24 November 1944. *New York Theatre Critics' Reviews* 5 (1944): 74.

Highly positive review in which Rascoe praises Miller's play as a "touching" and "intelligent" drama. "This is not a play to knock you out of your seat, roll you in the aisles, cause you to dance in the street or throw your hat in the air. It is a much finer drama than that. It is a unique event."

Schickel, Richard. "Good *Luck*." *Time* 22 May 2000.

Schickel lauds the first-ever U.S. revival of *The Man Who Had All the Luck*, at the Ivy Substation in Culver City, California, as "crude" but "you leave admiring the vigor of a compelling young talent on his way to becoming a major one."

Shulman, Milton. "*The Man Who Had All the Luck*." *Evening Standard* (London) 31 July 1990. *London Theatre Record* 10.16 (1990): 997–98.

While the play is obviously "a work of a young and inexperienced playwright," this revival at the Young Vic, Shulman feels that "Paul Unwin's production has the authentic feel of Miller angst."

Truss, Lynne. "*The Man Who Had All the Luck*." *Independent on Sunday* (London) 5 August 1990. *London Theatre Record* 10.16 (1990): 1000.

Mixed review of the first revival of Miller's 1944 play, directed by Paul Unwin and playing at the Young Vic after its move from the Bristol Old Vic. Says Truss, "the plot has more loose ends than the bins in Vidal Sassoon, and it is no coincidence that the best moments . . . come when [Unwin] deals with the much more promising sub-plot."

Waldorf, Wilella. "*The Man Who Had All the Luck*." *New York Post* 24 November 1944. *New York Theatre Critics' Reviews* 5 (1944): 74.

Waldorf criticizes the play for its lack of clarity and "muddled" message. "There are a lot of ideas knocking around the stage of the Forrest but they are frittered away."

All My Sons

Book-Length Studies

Bloom, Harold, ed. *Modern Critical Interpretations of Arthur Miller's "All My Sons."* New York: Chelsea, 1988.

Contains: Harold Bloom, "Introduction"; Arthur Miller, "The Question of Relatedness," Steven Centola, "Bad Faith and *All My Sons*"; Leonard Moss, "*All My Sons*"; Edward Murray, "The Failure of Social Vision"; June Schlueter, "The Dramatic Strategy of *All My Sons*"; Arvin R. Wells, "*All My Sons*"; Harold Clurman, "Thesis and Drama"; Barry Gross, "*All My Sons* and the Larger Context"; Orm Överland, "The Action and Its Significance: Miller's Struggle with Dramatic Form"; Dennis Welland, "Two Early Plays"; Sheila Huftel, "Miller, Ibsen, and Organic Drama"; Samuel A. Yorkes, "Joe Keller and His Sons"; Ruby Cohn, "Theatre and Drama"; and C. W. E. Bigsby, "Realism and Idealism."

Critical Essays in Books

Bigsby, C. W. E. "Drama from a Living Center." *A Critical Introduction to Twentieth-Century American Drama 2: Tennessee Williams, Arthur Miller, Edward Albee*. New York: Cambridge UP, 1984. Rpt. in *Modern Critical Views: Arthur Miller*. Ed. Harold Bloom. New York: Chelsea, 1987. 103–25. Rpt. as "Realism and Idealism" in *Modern Critical Interpretations of Arthur Miller's "All My Sons."* Ed. Harold Bloom. New York: Chelsea, 1991. 107–12.

Bigsby examines Miller's *All My Sons* as a well-made morality play which "rests very squarely on Ibsen's work, and in particular on *The Wild Duck*."

Bloom, Harold. "Introduction." *Modern Critical Interpretations of Arthur Miller's "All My Sons."* Ed. Harold Bloom. New York: Chelsea, 1988. 1–4.

After lamenting the lack of significant American dramatists compared to the plethora of important poets and novelists, Bloom introduces this work of essays by various scholars on Miller's *All My Sons* by discussing what he sees as the play's strengths and weaknesses and its representative themes of guilt and father-and-son relationships that would eventually haunt the Miller canon.

Centola, Steven R. "*All My Sons*." *Cambridge Companion to Arthur Miller*. Ed. Christopher Bigsby. Cambridge: Cambridge UP, 1997. 48–59.

Centola discusses the genesis, dramatic form, themes, social commentary, characters, and significance of *All My Sons*, stressing the universality of the play that "has a resonance that transcends its contemporary society and immediate situation."

———. "Bad Faith and *All My Sons*." *Modern Critical Interpretations of Arthur Miller's "All My Sons."* Ed. Harold Bloom. New York: Chelsea, 1988. 123–33.

Centola explores the "social implications of an individual's bad faith" in Miller's *All My Sons*, and concludes that the collapse of the Keller family is "emblematic of a deeper, broader disintegration of humanistic values that could spell disaster to a world trapped in its own bad faith."

Counts, Michael L. *Coming Home: The Soldier's Return in Twentieth-Century American Drama*. New York: Peter Lang, 1988. 85, 133, 199, 209.

Brief mention is made of Miller's *All My Sons* for the portrayal of Chris Keller as the "bitter disillusioned homecomer" who has harsh criticism for what he sees as uncaring civilians. Counts praises Miller for tackling the theme of individual responsibility.

Herron, Ima H. "Our Vanishing Towns." *The Small Town in American Drama*. Dallas: Southern Methodist UP, 1969. 466–67.

Brief discussion of *All My Sons* as a play that uses "the idea of immorality as a force affecting family life in manufacturing towns." Herron finds Miller's first successful Broadway play a realistic portrayal of a guilty man that "may be extended to symbolize an evil characteristic of our pragmatic society."

Lerner, Max. "Sons and Brothers." *Actions and Passions: Notes on the Multiple Revolution of Our Time*. New York: Simon and Schuster, 1949. 22–24.

Lerner praises Miller's drama, over the season's other important play, O'Neill's *The Iceman Cometh*, "because it grapples with the central moral problem of our world: the betrayal of men's brotherhood, the question of whether the fabric of brotherhood can be rebuilt."

Marino, Stephen A. "Religious Language in Arthur Miller's *All My Sons*." *Journal of Imagism* 3 (Fall 1998). 9–28.

Marino examines Miller's use of religious language, metaphors, images, and allusions in *All My Sons* to help solve the critical debate as to whether the play is a social drama or a family play, concluding that it is not exclusively either type, but instead a conflict between these two forces.

Moss, Leonard. "Colloquial Language in *All My Sons*." Rpt. in *Arthur Miller: New Perspectives*. Ed. Robert A. Martin. Engelwood Cliffs, N.J.: Prentice-Hall, 1982. 107–14. Rpt. as "*All My Sons*." *Modern Critical Interpretations of Arthur Miller's "All My Sons."* Ed. Harold Bloom. New York: Chelsea, 1988. 101–106. [From Moss' *Arthur Miller*. New York: Twayne, 1967. 37–43. Also Moss's *Arthur Miller*. Rev. ed. New York: G. K. Hall, 1980. 17–23.]

Moss finds that for two of its three acts *All My Sons* is "an extremely well constructed work." In its third act, however, the play proves a "letdown" because Miller directed the dramatic focus away from Joe Keller's loss to that of his son's, thereby undercutting the source of the play's emotional power that Miller had cultivated during most of his play—"His desire to formulate 'social' truths has restricted his talent for capturing inward urgencies in colloquial language."

Murray, Edward. "The Failure of Social Vision." *Modern Critical Interpretations of Arthur Miller's "All My Sons."* Ed. Harold Bloom. New York: Chelsea, 1988. 47–61. [From Murray's *Arthur Miller, Dramatist*. New York: Ungar, 1967. 1–21.]

Murray examines the structure of *All My Sons* and criticizes the "repetition and inconsequential byplay," the fortuitous nature of the "slip of the tongue" serving as the play's dramatic turning point, the arbitrary nature of the action, the improbability of George's visit, and the confusion regarding who is the protagonist of the play.

Schlueter, June. "The Dramatic Strategy of *All My Sons*." *Arthur Miller*. New York: Ungar, 1987. Rpt. in *Modern Critical Interpretations of Arthur Miller's "All My Sons."* Ed. Harold Bloom. New York: Chelsea, 1988. 113–22.

Schlueter studies the deftly crafted structure of *All My Sons*, which, she says, draws on the "retrospective technique that has come to be identified as 'Ibsenesque.'"

Srivastava, Ramesh K. "The Manifest and the Hidden in Arthur Miller's *All My Sons*." *Perspectives on Arthur Miller*. Ed. Atma Ram. New Delhi: Abhinav, 1988. 120–29.

Srivastava argues that "it is by the juxtaposition of both the visible and the submerged, the seen and the unseen, that Miller makes the play interesting and valuable both to the common reader and the serious literary critics." *Sons* is a suspenseful, realistic, message play—he who "closes his eyes to the stark realities of life or the consequences of his actions, as do Joe and Kate, is likely to end up tragically."

Wells, Arvin R. "*All My Sons*." *Insight I*. Frankfurt: Hirschgroben, 1962. 165–74. Rpt. in revised form as "The Living and the Dead in *All My Sons*." *Modern Drama* 7.1 (May 1964): 46–51. Rpt. in *Critical Essays on Arthur Miller*. Ed. James J. Martine. Boston: G. K. Hall, 1979. 5–9. Rpt. in *Modern Critical Interpretations of Arthur Miller's "All My Sons."* Ed. Harold Bloom. New York: Chelsea, 1988. 27–32.

Wells argues that *All My Sons* has "a density of texture so much greater than that of the typical thesis play" because Miller's characters "do not simply reflect the values and attitudes of a particular society; they use those values and attitudes in their attempts to realize themselves."

Zeifman, Hersh. "*All My Sons*." *International Dictionary of Theatre*, vol. 1, *Plays*. Eds. Mark Hawkins-Dady and Leanda Shrimpton. Chicago: St. James, 1992. 13–14. Rpt. as "An Introduction to *All My Sons*" in *Readings on Arthur Miller*. Ed. Thomas Siebold. San Diego, Calif.: Greenhaven, 1997. 165–68.

While Miller's first successful Broadway play has "some of the predictable elements of soap opera that disqualifies it as a great drama," Zeifman argues that *All My Sons* still stands as an important work because it explores some major themes that Miller will use throughout his canon, as well as an intricate plot structure resulting in a powerful emotional impact.

Critical Essays in Journals and Magazines

Boggs, W. Arthur. "*Oedipus* and *All My Sons*." *Personalist* 42 (Autumn 1961): 555–60.

Boggs compares *All My Sons* to Sophocles' *Oedipus* and suggests that Miller's play fails as a tragedy of recognition and is similar to *Oedipus* on only superficial levels.

Clurman, Harold. "The Meaning of Plays: *All My Sons*." *Tomorrow* June 1947. Rpt. as "Arthur Miller, 1947." *Lies Like Truth*. New York: Macmillan, 1958. 64–68. Rpt. as "Thesis and Drama" in *Modern Critical Interpretations of Arthur Miller's "All My Sons."* Ed. Harold Bloom. New York: Chelsea, 1988. 15–18. Rpt. in *The Collected Works of Harold Clurman: Six Decades of Commentary on Theatre, Dance, Music, Film, Arts and Letters*. Eds. Marjorie Loggia and Glenn Young. New York: Applause, 1994. 107–10.

Clurman counters critics who have (1) characterized Miller's play "as a war play or a play about the returned G.I. or as an attack on war profiteers," (2) suggested that Miller has exonerated Joe Keller "by making the 'system' responsible for his guilt," and (3) complained that the drama's plot is too complicated.

Coen, Frank. "Teaching the Drama." *English Journal* 56 (November 1967): 1136–39.

As an example of critical analysis for the student at the high school level, Coen compares *All My Sons* with Ibsen's *The Master Builder*.

Gorelik, Mordecai. "The Factor of Design." *Tulane Drama Review* 5 (March 1961): 85–94.

In a lengthy article that explains "that a stage setting is not mere background; that it is, instead, a dramatic image of environment," designer Mordecai Gorelik discusses his approach to the premiere production of *All My Sons* and his discovery of the proper metaphor for the stage setting.

Gross, Barry. "*All My Sons* and the Larger Context." *Modern Drama* 18.1 (March 1975): 15–27. Rpt. in *Essays on Modern American Drama: Williams, Miller, Albee, and Shepard*. Ed. Dorothy Parker. Toronto: U of Toronto P, 1987. 55–67. Rpt. in *Critical Essays on Arthur Miller*. Ed. James J. Martine. Boston: G. K. Hall, 1979. 10–20. Rpt. in *Modern Critical Interpretations of Arthur Miller's "All My Sons."* Ed. Harold Bloom. New York: Chelsea, 1988. 63–76.

Essay in which Gross examines the father-and-son conflict in *All My Sons* from Chris's side and comments on the implicit ironies in the son's loss of innocence.

Loughlin, Richard L. "Tradition and Tragedy in *All My Sons*." *English Record* 14 (February 1964): 23–27.

Loughlin compares Miller's *All My Sons* with the book of Genesis, Greek tragic epics, and medieval morality plays such as *Everyman* and concludes with a discussion of the nature of tragedy.

Överland, Orm. "The Action and Its Significance: Arthur Miller's Struggle with Dramatic Form." *Modern Drama* 18.1 (March 1975). 1–14. Rpt. as "The Action and Its Significance: Miller's Struggle with Dramatic Form" in *Modern Critical Interpretations of Arthur Miller's "All My Sons."* Ed. Harold Bloom. New York: Chelsea, 1988. 77–89.

Frequently quoted essay in which Överland considers the effects of Miller's distrust of the theatre as a means of communication and his theories of dramatic form on his career as a playwright. While Miller's theories of drama "should be regarded primarily as rationalizations of his own attempts to express himself clearly," Överland hopes that since Miller "has demonstrated that he has been extremely sensitive to [critical] responses [to his plays]," he may eventually "accept the common verdict of critics and audiences and return to the kind of work that has placed him in the front rank of contemporary dramatists."

Robinson, James A. "*All My Sons* and Paternal Authority." *Journal of American Drama and Theatre* 2.1 (Winter 1990): 38–54.

Robinson compares the father/son conflict in *All My Sons* to traditional Jewish themes, suggesting a connection with Miller's own Jewish struggle.

Yorkes, Samuel A. "Joe Keller and His Sons." *Western Humanities Review* 13.4 (Autumn 1959): 401–407. Rpt. in *Modern Critical Interpretations of Arthur Miller's "All My Sons."* Ed. Harold Bloom. New York: Chelsea, 1988. 19–26.

Yorkes argues that *All My Sons* is an "affirmation of private loyalty" that foreshadows Miller's stand before HUAC.

Critical Essays in Newspapers

Stuart, Jan. "Political Playwrights Get a Vote." *Newsday* 25 May 1997: C14.

Essay praising the political content of *All My Sons* and praising it for its "profoundly emotional level."

Production Reviews

"*All My Sons*." *Booklist* 15 March 1947: 220.

Brief review and plot summary that lauds *All My Sons* as a "serious but moving play about ordinary people and their family loyalty."

"*All My Sons* a Hit." *New York Times* 12 May 1948: 33.

News item reporting the favorable reception of the London production of *All My Sons*. Includes excerpts from reviews.

"Ancient Truths, Modern Spirit." *Jewish Week* 23 May 1997.

Negative review of the Roundabout Theatre revival—"the spirit is missing, perhaps never more so than now, in Barry Edelstein's blanched and dispirited production."

Atkinson, Brooks. "Arthur Miller: *All My Sons*." *The Lively Years: 1940–1950*. New York: AP, 1973. 188–91.

While effective in 1947, *All My Sons* ultimately suffers from a "craftsmanship" that "is too contrived for the modern theatre. It eliminates any feeling of spontaneity in the action of the play. It dramatizes what the characters do, and not what they think. It proves a point; it creates nothing."

———. "Arthur Miller's *All My Sons* Brings Genuine New Talent into the Coronet Theatre with Expert Cast of Actors." *New York Times* 30 January 1947: 21.

Atkinson lauds Miller's second Broadway play as "fresh," "exciting," "honest," "forceful," and "a piece of expert dramatic construction. . . . Mr. Miller's talent is many-sided. Writing pithy yet unselfconscious dialogue, he has created his characters vividly, plucking them out of the run of American society, but presenting them as individuals with hearts and minds of their own."

———. "Mare's Nest Inquiries." *New York Times* 7 September 1947: II: 1.

Atkinson responds to critics who have labeled *All My Sons* an "insurgent or Communist play" and unrepresentative of American life. Says Atkinson, "These small arms attacks . . . suggest that American tolerance and flexibility, over which we have been thumping our chests internationally for some time, are getting a little thin. Either a playwright has or has not the freedom to choose his own subjects without first making sure that he does not tread on touchy toes."

———. "Welcome Stranger." *New York Times* 9 February 1947: II 1. Rpt. in *Broadway Scrapbook*. New York: Theatre Arts, 1947. 277–79.

In this positive review of the premiere production, Atkinson praises the characters, plot, and Miller's use of language, concluding that the play is the "most talented work by a new author in some time."

"Audio Reviews: *All My Sons* by Arthur Miller." *Library Journal* 15 October 1999: 121.

Positive review of the L.A. Theatre Works audio production of Miller's play, starring Julie Harris, James Farentino, and Arye Gross. Recorded from a live performance, the tapes are a recommended purchase for those interested in or studying theatre.

Barnes, Clive. "Arthur Miller's *All My Sons*." *New York Times* 29 October 1974: 32.

Negative review of the Signature Theatre revival that Barnes calls "dated" and "a simplistic recruiting poster for black and white morality."

———. "Right and Wrong." *New York Post* 23 April 1987. *New York Theatre Critics' Reviews* 48 (1987): 274–75.

Barnes lauds the Long Wharf Theatre revival, starring Richard Kiley and directed by Arvin Brown, as "vigorous and richly enjoyable" and "a fine American play in a fine American staging—and a reminder of a Broadway now lost."

Barnes, Howard. "Too Many Duds." *New York Herald Tribune* 30 January 1947: 15. *New York Theatre Critics' Reviews* 8 (1947): 478.

Negative review that applauds Miller's obvious "acute feeling for the theater and a certain sense of form," but condemns *All My Sons* for his failure "to superimpose a classical tragic outline on subject matter which is, at best, confused."

Beaufort, John. "Miller Drama *All My Sons* Still Speaks to Today." *Christian Science Monitor* 23 April 1987. *New York Theatre Critics' Reviews* 48 (1987): 277.

Laudatory review of the Long Wharf revival, directed by Arvin Brown—"With a fine cast headed by Richard Kiley, the production honors the work that, notwithstanding mixed notices, established Miller as a major new American dramatist and brought him his first success."

Beyer, William. "The State of the Theatre: Midseason Highlights." *School and Society* 5 April 1947: 250–51.

Positive review of the premiere Broadway production that Beyer calls the "most moving and provocative new play of the season" by a "playwright to be watched and keenly anticipated."

Brantley, Ben. "Arthur Miller Visits the Sins of the Fathers upon the Children." *New York Times* 5 May 1997: C11.

Favorable review of the Roundabout Theatre's "attention-commanding" revival of *All My Sons* directed by Barry Edelstein and starring John Cullum and Linda Stephens.

Brown, John Mason. "New Talents and Arthur Miller." *Saturday Review of Literature* 1 March 1947: 22–24.

While the Broadway premiere of *All My Sons* is excellently staged by Elia Kazan, the play fails due to a "false and unresolved central theme."

Carr, Jay. "*All My Sons* Strong, Fresh at Long Wharf." *Boston Globe* 24 October 1986: Arts and Film: 51.

Highly positive review of the Long Wharf Theatre production of *All My Sons*, directed by Arvin Brown. Says Carr, Miller's play is "admirably crafted" with a "beautifully modulated staging that emphasizes the strength to be found in traditional craftsmanship and represents regional theater at its best."

Chapman, John. "A Lot Goes On but Little Happens in Backyard Drama, *All My Sons*." *New York Daily News* 30 January 1947. *New York Theatre Critics' Reviews* 8 (1947): 478.

Chapman feels that the same scant praise he felt for Miller's first play can also be said of *All My Sons*: "long before they got through talking and Mr. Begley had shot himself I was ready to go home."

Coleman, Robert. "*All My Sons* Not Very Convincing." *New York Daily Mirror* 30 January 1947. *New York Theatre Critics' Reviews* 8 (1947): 478.

Even though "first-nighters remained after the curtain" to give *All My Sons* a standing ovation, Coleman says he was left "cold" by Miller's "grim indictment of war profiteers and selfish mothers. . . . He has underwritten. He seldom succeeds in bringing his characters to life and their speech is stilted and choppy, failing to illuminate satisfactorily their actions."

Curry, Jack. "The Agony and the Ordinary in Miller's Powerful *Sons*." *USA Today* 23 April 1987. *New York Theatre Critics' Reviews* 48 (1987): 276.

Favorable review of the Long Wharf Theatre revival starring Richard Kiley, directed by Arvin Brown. Curry praises the production as "stunning," "supercharged," and "acted to the hilt."

Eaton, Walter. "In Too Many Directions." *New York Herald Tribune Weekly Book Review* 9 March 1947: 19.

Negative review of the published version of *All My Sons* that Eaton says "seems to start in one direction, then goes in another and never, even at the end, achieves that clarity and unity of effect a fine play ought to have, and which would make this one a very fine play indeed."

Feingold, Michael. "Antique Shows." *Village Voice* 13 May 1997: 91.

Negative review of the Roundabout Theatre revival of *All My Sons* starring John Cullum and Linda Stephens, directed by Barry Edelstein. Says Feingold, "the two-faced approach—jacking up the rhetorical heat while brushing aside the inner life—mostly produces the usual result of trying to walk in two directions at once."

Fleming, Peter. "The Theatre." *Spectator* (London) 21 May 1948: 612.

While finding the London premiere production of *All My Sons* a moralizing work, Fleming praises the play as "sincere, deft, [and] at times distinguished."

Franklin, Nancy. "The Cost of Success." *New Yorker* 2 June 1997: 93–94.

Franklin praises the Roundabout Theatre production of *All My Sons*, directed by Barry Edelstein and starring John Cullum, Linda Stephens, and Michael Hayden, as "strong" and having "just as much power, if not more," as *Death of a Salesman*.

Freedley, George. "*All My Sons*." *Library Journal* 15 March 1947: 466.

Brief review of the premiere production that names Miller as "Broadway's newest playwright of importance."

Garland, Robert. "*All My Sons* Bows at Coronet Theatre." *New York Journal American* 30 January 1947. *New York Theatre Critics' Reviews* 8 (1947): 476.

After reminding his readers that Miller's first play was out of luck, Garland praises *All My Sons* as "engrossing" and "impressive" and advises the public to put Miller's second drama on their "non-musical 'must list.'"

Gassner, John. "The Theatre Arts." *Forum* 107 (March 1947): 271–75.
While recognizing the social and political themes implicit in *All My Sons*, Gassner argues that it is the main characters' reluctance to face the truth that "catches up" with them.

Gilder, Rosamond. "Broadway in Review." *Theatre Arts* 31 (April 1947): 19.
Positive review of the premiere Broadway production that Gilder feels "demonstrates [Miller's] capacity to build character and to plot compelling action."

Green, E. M. "*All My Sons*." *Theatre World* 43 (April 1947): 32.
Positive review of the London production. Green praises the the play's dialogue, taut situations, and powerful moral impact.

Hawkins, William. "*All My Sons* a Tense Drama." *New York World-Telegram* 30 January 1947. *New York Theatre Critics' Reviews* 8 (1947): 475.
Positive review in which Hawkins praises Miller for his "forceful play" written "in simple, clean, human speech. . . . The strength of the play is its revelation that a wide horizon is becoming a necessity for intimate happiness."

Henry, William A., III. "Avenging Fury." *Time* 4 May 1987: 107. *New York Theatre Critics' Reviews* 48 (1987): 276.
Positive review of the Broadway revival starring Richard Kiley and directed by Arvin Brown. Henry lauds the production that opened at the Long Wharf and moved to Broadway as an "exceptional" work that shows "Miller at his best."

Hobson, Harold. "Hobson's Choice." *Drama* 143 (Spring 1982): 26.
Positive review of *All My Sons*, directed by Michael Blakemore and starring Colin Blakely, that Hobson says is "constructed with intricate mastery" and is "superior to the Shakespeare of *Othello*."

Hodgson, Moira. "*All My Sons*." *Nation* 23 May 1987: 695.
Hodgson believes that the Long Wharf revival of *All My Sons*, directed by Arvin Brown and starring Richard Kiley, is "marred by Joyce Ebert's overblown acting."

Hope-Wallace, Phillip. "Plays in Performance." *Drama* (Autumn 1948): 11.

Calling *All My Sons* an "inquest revelation," Hope-Wallace criticizes Miller for not making Joe Keller's fate more important to the play's structure and feels that the theme of family guilt demands the writing of a poet such as T. S. Eliot or Henrik Ibsen.

Kelly, Kevin. "*All My Sons* Hits Home." *Boston Globe* 26 March 1987: Arts and Film: 77.

Calling the Long Wharf revival of *All My Sons*, directed by Arvin Brown and starring Richard Kiley, "an engrossing and affecting play," Kelly feels the production of this "sturdy and compelling drama" goes far to reintroduce us to the "power and historic sweep of Arthur Miller's play."

Kissel, Howard. "*Sons* Moves into Overkill." *New York Daily News* 23 April 1987. *New York Theatre Critics' Reviews* 48 (1987): 273.

Negative review of the revival starring Richard Kiley and directed by Arvin Brown. Says Kissel, "Despite a largely sensitive production, *All My Sons* now seems like an overloaded circuit, throwing off electrical sparks, but is no longer capable of projecting current."

Kronenberger, Louis. "A Serious Theme Makes for Compelling Theater." *New York PM Exclusive* 31 January 1947. *New York Theatre Critics' Reviews* 8 (1947): 477.

Even though he admits that "matters sometimes get overheated," Kronenberger finds that on the whole, Miller's second Broadway show is "a compelling play" by a playwright who "has brought to it three things very vital to a serious stagework: he has a dramatic sense, he has a human sense, and he has a moral sense."

Krutch, Joseph Wood. "Drama." *Nation* 15 February 1947: 191, 193.

While Krutch criticizes Miller for his predictable plot, he praises *All My Sons* for possessing a "real dramatic force."

Lardner, John. "B for Effort." *New Yorker* 8 February 1947: 50.

Negative review of the premiere Broadway production, staged by Elia Kazan, that Lardner feels is a contrived drama by a praiseworthy author whose war-profiteering themes do not ring true.

Lida, David. "*All My Sons*—A Review." *Women's Wear Daily* 23 April 1987. *New York Theatre Critics' Reviews* 48 (1987): 273–74.

Unfavorable review of the Long Wharf Theatre revival, starring Richard Kiley and directed by Arvin Brown. Lida calls the play "tortuously melodramatic," a "diatribe against big business, capitalism and compromise, with superficial characters and a few speeches piously begging for humanism and brotherly love."

Mandell, Jonathan. "*All My Sons* Fails to Detonate." *Newsday* 5 May 1997: B5.

Mixed review of the Roundabout Theatre revival, starring John Cullum and directed by Barry Edelstein. Mandell criticizes the performances that "do not match the relentless power of the script" and feels that the "drama is undercut by an overemphasis on the symbolism, accomplished through the set and some added stage business."

McCalmon, George. "*All My Sons*." *Players Magazine* November 1948: 47–48.

Mixed review that criticizes the play's "contrived dramaturgy and strained coincidence" and praises the overall effect of the work's "unrelenting and awesome power."

Morehouse, Ward. "*All My Sons*, Intelligent and Thoughtful Drama, Superbly Played at Coronet." *New York Sun* 30 January 1947. *New York Theatre Critics' Reviews* 8 (1947): 477.

Finding no fault with *All My Sons*, Morehouse praises Miller's play as "intelligent," Kazan's direction as "knowingly staged," Arthur Kennedy and Ed Begley's performances as "fine" and "convincing," and Mordecai Gorelik's design as an "excellent setting." Concluding, Morehouse predicts, "the Broadway theater has a new playwright of enormous promise."

"Moscow Acclaims a Hellman Play." *New York Times* 18 October 1949: 34.

In an essay discussing the Moscow production of Lillian Hellman's *Another Part of the Forest*, *All My Sons* is mentioned as a previous production that had been "sharply criticized on the grounds that it presented an unsound philosophy."

Nathan, George Jean. "*All My Sons*." *Theatre Book of the Year, 1946–47*. New York: Knopf, 1947. 290–93.

While "honest" and "sincere," Nathan finds the premiere production of *All My Sons*, directed by Elia Kazan and starring Ed Begley, an "undistinguished" and predictable work.

"New Play in Manhattan," *Time* 10 February 1947: 68, 70.

Mixed review of the premiere Broadway production, staged by Elia Kazan, that criticizes *All My Sons* for being forceful but not effective and praises Miller as the "most interesting of Broadway's new serious playwrights."

Oliver, Edith. "Miller's *Sons*." *New Yorker* 4 May 1987: 127.

Oliver praises the Long Wharf revival, directed by Arvin Brown and starring Richard Kiley, as having "excellent" acting and a production that "succeeds in disguising some of the shortcomings of the play."

———. "Off Broadway." *New Yorker* 11 November 1974: 106–107.

Negative review of the Signature Theatre Company revival that Oliver attacks for its "verbal ineptitude and dumb-cluck moral fervor" that proved "such a nuisance in Miller's later work."

Phelan, Kappo. "The Stage and Screen: *All My Sons*." *Commonweal* 14 February 1947: 445–46.

Mixed review of the premiere production of *All My Sons* that Phelan calls a "grave, wholly absorbing, inevitable play" about "the big inescapable questions."

Rich, Frank. "Theater: Richard Kiley in Miller's *All My Sons*." *New York Times* 23 April 1987. *New York Theatre Critics' Reviews* 48 (1987): 272.

Generally positive review of the Richard Kiley revival, directed by Arvin Brown, in which Rich praises the production as "smart" and well acted, but, ultimately, "too topical for its own theatrical good." Says Rich of Miller's drama, "Mr. Brown's staging cannot camouflage Mr. Miller's creaky, waiting-for-the-other-shoe-to-drop exposition (supplied by phone, letter and prattling neighbors) or bald symbols (a fallen tree) or melodramatic plot twists."

Ridley, Clifford A. "Miller's First Success, *All My Sons*, in Anniversary Staging." *Philadelphia Inquirer* 7 May 1997: D4.

Negative review of the Roundabout Theatre Company's fiftieth anniversary production of *All My Sons*, directed by Barry Edelstein, that Ridley calls a "disappointment" whose "principal problem" is its casting.

Rogoff, Gordon. "All My Plots." *Village Voice* 5 May 1987: 90.
Rogoff praises Arvin Brown's revival at the Long Wharf Theatre, starring Richard Kiley and Joyce Ebert, as an "honest presentation of a dishonest life."

Sauvage, Leo. "All My Sons." *New Leader* 20 April 1987: 20–21.
Sauvage blames both the Long Wharf production and the performances of Richard Kiley and Joyce Ebert for *All My Sons* failing to "articulate the problem of justice, which lies at the heart of the play."

Siegel, Joel. "*All My Sons*." ABC. WABC, New York. 22 April 1987. *New York Theatre Critics' Reviews* 48 (1987): 227.
Glowing review of the Arvin Brown production of *All My Sons*, starring Richard Kiley, that Siegel calls "great theatre" with "exquisite direction," "fine acting," and a "brick solid play."

Simon, John. "*All My Sons*." *New York* 4 May 1987: 122.
In his favorable review of the Long Wharf revival, directed by Arvin Brown, Simon praises Richard Kiley's performance as Joe Keller as "superb" but the production "overwrought."

———. "Second Helping." *New York* 19 May 1997: 67–68.
Negative review of the Roundabout Theatre's revival, directed by Barry Edelstein. Simon calls the cast "poor," the story "improbable," and the production "ludicrous."

"Son and Father." *Newsweek* 10 February 1947: 85.
Negative review of the Broadway premiere that charges *All My Sons* with being crowded with "more plot and circumstance than the theme requires."

Stearns, David Patrick. "*All My Sons*, Timeless Tragedy." *USA Today* 7 May 1997: D8.
Favorable review of the Roundabout Theatre's revival, directed by Barry Edelstein. It emerges, says Stearns, "as a complex morality tale of cosmic retribution for crimes against humanity, and does so with the monumentality of Greek tragedy."

Taylor, John Russell. "Plays in Performance." *Drama* 144 (Summer 1982): 29–30.

Taylor spends the bulk of his review of *All My Sons*, directed by Michael Blakemore and starring Colin Blakely, explaining his dislike for Miller's playwriting. Says Taylor, "Miller comes over as a writer who has made himself into a dramatist entirely by taking pains, but without any natural, instinctive feeling for the theatre at all. . . . It is a perfectly decent evening in the theatre, and it is easier to catalogue its virtues than to explain precisely why, in the last analysis, they are not enough."

Terry, C. V. "Broadway Bookrack." *New York Times Book Review* 6 April 1947: 12.

Positive review of the printed version of Miller's play that Terry praises for having an emotion that "springs" from the printed page. Says Terry, "despite that tendency to speak in short pants, [Miller] has a great deal more than youth on his side."

Wallach, Allan. "*Sons* of Arthur Miller." *Newsday* 23 April 1987: II 7. *New York Theatre Critics' Reviews* 48 (1987): 275.

Wallach praises Richard Kiley's performance in the Long Wharf Theatre revival, directed by Arvin Brown, as a "thoughtful, well-conceived performance," but criticizes Miller's play as having "serious flaws that can't be concealed."

Watt, Douglas. "Miller's Paternity Pursuit." *New York Daily News* 1 May 1987. *New York Theatre Critics' Reviews* 48 (1987): 273.

Mixed review of the Long Wharf Theatre revival starring Richard Kiley, directed by Arvin Brown. Watt finds the first half "interminable," but concedes that "the evening comes powerfully alive in the second half, thanks to Miller's gathering storm and the strong performances of Richard Kiley as Joe Keller . . . and Jamie Sheridan as his loving but despairing son."

Watts, Richard, Jr. "A Striking But Uneven Drama About the Soldier's Return." *New York Post* 30 January 1947. *New York Theatre Critics' Reviews* 8 (1947): 476.

While complimenting Miller for a "drama of force and passion," Watts laments the "uneven" quality of the writing, which he describes as "overwrought, hysterical, overplotted, and unwieldy, as well as impassioned and impressive."

Wilson, Edwin. "*All My Sons*." *Wall Street Journal* 6 May 1987. *New York Theatre Critics' Reviews* 48 (1987): 276.

Very brief, but favorable, review of the Richard Kiley revival, directed by Arvin Brown. Wilson praises the direction, which played down "the faults of over-mechanized construction" and "emphasized the human concerns."

Worsley, T. C. "The Theatre." *New Statesman and Nation* (London) 22 May 1948: 412.

Brief positive review of the London production, staged by Elia Kazan. Worsley sees Ibsen's influence in Miller's strong central issue, which makes up for the play's artificial characters and themes.

Wyatt, Euphemia Van Rensselaer. "Theater." *Catholic World* 164 (March 1947): 552–53.

In this positive review, Wyatt lauds the sensitive direction of Elia Kazan in the Broadway premiere of *All My Sons*.

Young, Stark. "Theatre: Good Occasion." *New Republic* 10 February 1947: 42.

Highly positive review of the New York premiere that praises Miller's story, theme, and characters, as well as Elia Kazan's direction for working "wonders for the thematic and human values of the play."

Related Interviews and Profiles (not with Miller)

Kelly, Kevin. "*All My Sons* Kiley's Latest Quest." *Boston Globe* 22 March 1987: Arts and Film: 91.

Interview and biographical piece on Richard Kiley on the occasion of his tour as Joe Keller in Miller's *All My Sons*. Kiley discusses his approach to the role and his views on the importance of Miller's play in revealing "the distorted, peculiarly American idea we have of money, and what money is for."

Schumach, Murray. "A Director Named 'Gadge.'" *New York Times Magazine* 9 November 1947: 18, 54–56.

Lengthy profile of Elia Kazan published just prior to the opening of *A Streetcar Named Desire*. Miller is quoted as praising Kazan for his ability to "hit the audience in the belly because he knows all people are alike in the belly no matter what their social position or education."

News Reports, Letters to the Editor, and Related Matter

"*All My Sons*." *Life* 10 March 1947: 71–72.
Article announcing the Broadway premiere of *All My Sons*.

"*All My Sons*." *New York Times* 29 June 1947: II: 3.
Production photograph of John Forsythe at Chris Keller and Beth Merrill as his mother, captioned "one of the moving moments from *All My Sons*."

"*All My Sons*." *New York Times* 19 October 1947: II: 3.
Same photograph from 29 June 1947 newspaper, with the caption reporting that a special performance of the play will benefit the Stage Relief Fund.

"*All My Sons* Hit in Holland." *New York Times* 21 October 1947: 26.
News item reporting that the Dutch premiere of *All My Sons* in Rotterdam is playing to full houses.

"Death Merchants Again." *New York Times* 12 June 1947: 24.
Op-ed piece that opposes *All My Sons* as America's entry at the World Youth Festival in Prague.

Pacheco, Patrick. "Five Years of Progress: Blind Actors in Miller's *All My Sons*." *Newsday* 13 June 1989: II: 7.
Article detailing the fifth annual New York production of the Theatre by the Blind, who is opening *All My Sons* at the Samuel Beckett Theatre. Also noted is Miller's "delighted" reaction to tackling the play—"I hadn't thought of it in that way, but it could be fascinating. It's very possible that it would take on an added dimension."

Reed, Edward. "Portents in Books: A Year of Theatre Publishing." *Theatre Arts* 31 (April 1947): 47–50.
While in narrative form, this article is essentially a listing of theatre books published in the past year. Of note is the half-page photograph production still from *All My Sons*, depicting Ed Begley, Beth Merrill, and Arthur Kennedy in a dramatic pose.

Taylor, Harvey. "The Return of *All My Sons*." *New York Times* 18 January 1948: II: 2.
News item offering details of the "courage and enterprise on the part of the Dramatic Guild of Detroit and a love of good theatre on the part of the Guild's sole financial backer, Robert L. Stevens,"

who "resented" the short-term run of *All My Sons* outside of Broadway and offered to underwrite its Detroit booking. The Detroit production stars Sidney Blackmer and John Forsythe.

Death of a Salesman

Book-Length Studies

Bloom, Harold., ed. *Major Literary Characters: Willy Loman*. New York: Chelsea, 1991.

Contains: Harold Bloom, "Introduction"; critical extracts; Miller's "Introduction to *Collected Plays*"; "*Death of a Salesman*: A Symposium"; Ruby Cohn, "The Articulate Victims of Arthur Miller"; Dan Vogel, "Willy Tyrannos"; A. D. Choudhuri, "*Death of a Salesman*: A Salesman's Illusion"; Robert N. Wilson, "The Salesman and Society"; Jeremy Hawthorn, "Sales and Solidarity"; C. W. E. Bigsby, "Arthur Miller"; Leah Hadomi, "Dramatic Rhythm in *Death of a Salesman*"; and Kay Stanton, "Women and the American Dream of *Death of a Salesman*." See individual cites for annotation, source, and page numbers.

———. *Modern Critical Interpretations: Arthur Miller's "Death of a Salesman."* New York: Chelsea, 1988.

Includes the following essays: Esther Merle Jackson, "*Death of a Salesman*: Tragic Myth in the Modern Drama"; Peter Szondi, "Memory and Dramatic Form in *Death of a Salesman*"; Brian Parker, "Point of View in Arthur Miller's *Death of a Salesman*"; Ruby Cohn, "The Articulate Victims of Arthur Miller"; William Heyen, "Arthur Miller's *Death of a Salesman* and the American Dream"; Christopher Innes,"The Salesman on the Stage: A Study in the Social Influence of Drama"; D. L. Hoeveler, "*Death of a Salesman* as Psychomachia"; Richard T. Brucher, "Willy Loman and the Soul of a New Machine"; William Aarnes, "Tragic Form and Possibility of Meaning in *Death of a Salesman*"; and C. W. E. Bigsby, "*Death of a Salesman*: In Memoriam." See individual cites for annotation, source, and page numbers.

Dukore, Bernard F. *"Death of a Salesman" and "The Crucible": Text and Performance*. Atlantic Highlands, N.J.: Humanities, 1989.

Dukore explores, in a brief overview format, two of Miller's most famous works. "Part One: Text" discusses in six chapters per play, various critical commentary and literary concerns associated historically with each play (for instance, the question of the tragic nature of each drama, use of language, dramatic structure, character, and themes). "Part Two: Performance" examines aspects of selected productions (direction, scenery, lighting, and acting) to compare and contrast various interpretations of both plays.

Harshbarger, Karl. *The Burning Jungle: An Analysis of Arthur Miller's "Death of a Salesman."* Washington, D.C.: UP of America, 1979.

Harshbarger argues that previous critics have ignored several important considerations in regard to the characters in *Death of a Salesman*, including Linda's role as a central participant in the tragic action of the play, Biff as possibly repeating old patterns and resuming his loser life after Willy's death, Willy's inevitability to commit suicide regardless of Biff's return, and Happy's ability to reach out beyond himself, making him a character who is more concerned with Willy's suffering than Biff.

Hurrell, John D. ed. *Two Modern American Tragedies: Reviews and Criticism of "Death of a Salesman" and "A Streetcar Named Desire."* New York: Scribner's, 1961.

Anthology collection intended to aid students in their search for sources in the formulation of a research paper. Essays that apply to Miller include the following: John Gassner, "Tragic Perspectives: A Sequence of Queries"; Miller's "Tragedy and the Common Man" and "On Social Plays"; Brooks Atkinson, George Jean Nathan, Eleanor Clark, and Harold Clurman, "Review of *Death of a Salesman*"; William J. Newman, "Arthur Miller's *Collected Plays*"; "Our Colossal Dad"; "A Matter of Hopelessness in *Death of a Salesman*"; Richard J. Foster, "Confusion and Tragedy: The Failure of Miller's *Salesman*"; and W. David Sievers, "Tennessee Williams and Arthur Miller." See individual cites for annotation, source, and page numbers.

Koon, Helene Wickham. ed. *Twentieth Century Interpretations of "Death of a Salesman."* Engelwood Cliffs, N.J.: Prentice-Hall 1983.

Helene Wickham Koon, "Introduction"; Lois Gordon, "*Death of a Salesman*: An Appreciation"; B. S. Field Jr., "*Death of a Salesman*"; Sighle Kennedy, "Who Killed the Salesman?"; Stephen A. Lawrence, "The Right Dream in Miller's *Death of a Salesman*" ; Dennis Welland, "*Death of a Salesman*"; Barclay W. Bates, "The Lost Past in *Death of a Salesman*"; Arthur K. Oberg, "*Death of a Salesman* and Arthur Miller's Search for Style"; Charlotte F. Otten, "Who Am I? A Re-Investigation of Arthur Miller's *Death of a Salesman*"; Brian Parker, "Point of View in Arthur Miller's *Death of a Salesman*"; Paul N. Siegel, "Willy Loman and King Lear." See individual cites for annotation, source, and page numbers.

Meserve, Walter J., ed. *The Merrill Studies in "Death of a Salesman."* Columbus, Ohio: Merrill, 1972.

Contains: John Gassner, "The Theatre Arts"; Harold Clurman, "Theatre: Attention"; Dennis Welland, "*Death of a Salesman* in England"; Robert Abirached, "Allex à Aubervilliers," Friederich Luft, "Arthur Miller's *Death of a Salesman*"; Rajinder Paul, "*Death of a Salesman* in India"; Barry Edward Gross, "Peddler and Pioneer in *Death of a Salesman*"; John V. Hagopian, "Arthur Miller: The *Salesman*'s Two Cases"; Remy Saisselin, "Is Tragic Drama Possible in the Twentieth Century"; George de Schweinitz, "*Death of a Salesman*: A Note on Epic and Tragedy"; Esther Merle Jackson, "Tragic Myth in the Modern Theatre"; Gordon Couchman, "Arthur Miller's Tragedy of Babbitt"; Guerin Bliquez, "Linda's Role in *Death of a Salesman*"; Sister M. Bettina, SSND, "Willy Loman's Brother Ben: Tragic Insight in *Death of a Salesman*"; Leonard Moss, "Arthur Miller and the Common Man's Language"; and Arthur K. Oberg, "*Death of a Salesman* and Arthur Miller's Search for Style." See individual cites for annotation, source, and page numbers.

Murphy, Brenda. *Miller: "Death of a Salesman."* Cambridge: Cambridge UP, 1995.

Using Miller's notebooks, drafts of the script, and director's notes as source material, Murphy creates a critical history of *Death of a Salesman*, exploring the genesis of the premiere production and the role and value of subsequent productions worldwide in the development of the theatre in America.

Murphy, Brenda and Susan C.W. Abbotson. *Understanding "Death of a Salesman": A Student Casebook to Issues, Sources, and Historical Documents*. Westport, Conn.: Greenwood, 1999.

Part of the Greenwood Press "Literature in Context" series. Topics such as the play's significance and its impact on American culture are explored along with more than sixty excerpts from essays, advertisements, and articles on subjects such as cultural myths and values, economic interests and forces, American business culture, family and gender expectations, and sports and American life. Also included are study questions, topics for written or oral exploration, and lists of suggested reading.

Partridge, C. J. *Death of a Salesman.* Oxford: Blackwell, 1969.

Part of a series of introductions to the great classics of English literature ("Notes on English Literature"), this slim volume (58 pp.) offers three essays that provide a background to understanding Miller's text—discussions of the social reality reflected in the play, the values of the "image" of the salesman, and Miller's "unusual" dramatic technique. Includes a short biographical appendix and suggestions for future reading.

Roudané, Matthew C. *Approaches to Teaching Miller's "Death of a Salesman."* New York: MLA, 1995.

Part of the "Approaches to Teaching World Literature" series designed to present different points of view on teaching specific literary works that are widely taught at the undergraduate level, Roudané has gathered fourteen essays and arranged them into the following larger themes: Miller and the Modern Stage, Text and Performance, Critical Concerns, and American Myths. Part One by Roudané includes a bibliographic essay on materials, including readings for students and teachers, biographical and bibliographical sources, critical studies, collections, selected readings, and editions.

Weales, Gerald. ed. *"Death of a Salesman": Text and Criticism.* New York: Viking, 1967. New York: Penguin, 1996.

Prefatory matter includes an introduction by Weales and the text of the play. The volume includes the following critical essays, interviews, reviews, and articles, followed by some literary analogues: Jo Mielziner, "Designing a Play: *Death of a Salesman*"; Robert Garland, "Audience Spellbound by Prize Play of 1949"; William Hawkins, "*Death of a Salesman* Powerful Tragedy"; John Mason Brown, "Even as You and I"; Harold Clurman, "The Success Dream on the American Stage"; Eleanor Clark, "Old Glamour, New Gloom"; T. C. Worsley, "Poetry Without Words"; William Beyer, "The State of the Theatre: The Season Opens"; John Gassner, "*Death of a Salesman*: First Impressions, 1949"; A. Howard Fuller, "A Salesman Is Everybody"; Ivor Brown, "As London Sees Willy Loman"; Daniel E. Schneider, M.D., "Play of Dreams"; George Ross, "*Death of a Salesman* in the Original"; Judah Bierman, James Hart, and Stanley Johnson, "Arthur Miller, *Death of a Salesman*"; George de Schweinitz, "*Death of a Salesman*: A Note on Epic and Tragedy"; Joseph A. Hynes, "'Attention Must Be Paid'"; William Wiegand, "Arthur Miller and the Man Who Knows"; Raymond Williams, "The Realism of Arthur Miller"; Allan Seager, "The Creative Agony of Arthur Miller"; William B. Dillingham, "Arthur Miller and the Loss of Conscience"; and Gerald Weales, "Arthur Miller: Man and His

Image." See individual cites for annotation, source, and page numbers.

Critical Essays in Books

Adamczewski, Zygmunt. "The Tragic Loss—Loman the Salesman." *The Tragic Protest*. The Hague: Martinus Nijhoff, 1963. 172–92.

In an essay examining the tragedy of Willy Loman, Adamczewski finds the overall power of Miller's drama comes from Willy's ordinariness—the more ordinary he is the more the audience may feel it is happening to them and thus identify with his plight. "Loman can be seen tragically by you, because he exists for you, he stands out from the background of his world, even if his stance is staggering and stumbling, even if he sinks down, he sinks before your eyes which can appreciate what has been lost. . . . The loss which he senses and which you can witness is radical: the loss of his self."

Adler, Thomas P. "Miller's Mindscape: A Scenic Approach to *Death of a Salesman*." *Approaches to Teaching Miller's "Death of a Salesman."* Ed. Matthew C. Roudané. New York: MLA, 1995. 45–51.

In his essay, Adler details his teaching methodology of focusing on the scenic design elements of *Death of a Salesman* as a means of raising "questions about the textural authority of set descriptions; about the relation between the memory structure of the play and music cues; about the interplay of realism and expressionism; about the formal connections between certain dramaturgical devices and the limited point of view in fiction; about narrativity in drama; and about the play's coda, what Miller calls the Requiem, and how it effects closure."

Austin, Gayle. "Arthur Miller's *Death of a Salesman*." *Feminist Theories for Dramatic Criticism*. Ann Arbor: U of Michigan P, 1990. 47–51.

Austin examines *Salesman*'s female characters, finding the images presented "damaging" and "problematic." Says Austin, "The overpowering impression the play leaves is that, for men, sex with women in empty, mothers and wives are necessary but ineffectual, and the most important thing is to bond successfully with other men."

———. "The Exchange of Woman and Male Homosocial Desire in Arthur Miller's *Death of a Salesman* and Lillian Hellman's *Another Part of the Forest*." *Feminist Rereadings of Modern American Drama*. Ed. June Schlueter. Cranbury, N.J.: Associated UP, 1989. 59–66.

Applying feminist theories of Gale Rubin, Marx, Lévi-Strauss, Freud, and Eve Kosofky Sedgwick to *Death of a Salesman*, Austin attempts to show how the dual pattern of women being exchanged among men and their representation as objects to be exchanged "eliminates women as active subjects in the play."

Balakian, Janet. "Beyond the Male Locker Room: *Death of a Salesman* from a Feminist Perspective." *Approaches to Teaching Miller's "Death of a Salesman."* Ed. Matthew C. Roudané. New York: MLA, 1995. 115–24.

Balakian explains her feminist approach to *Death of a Salesman* as contrary to the common feminist argument that the play "paves the way for the displacement of women in contemporary plays." By examining ways in which the women in Miller's work are marginalized, she argues that they are consciously created to raise the question as to "whether the dichotomized image of woman as either mother or whore is a desirable cultural trait."

———. "*Salesman*: Private Tensions Raised to a Poetic Social Level." *The Achievement of Arthur Miller: New Essays*. Ed. Steven Centola. Dallas, Tex.: Contemporary Research, 1995. 59–67.

Balakian explores *Death of a Salesman* as an expressionistic rendering of the public and private conflict that is inside Willy Loman's consciousness. Miller uses Willy's breakdown as metaphor for the collapse of the American dream of success. Says Balakian, not only has "Miller raised the private to the social or poetic in *Salesman*, but he has also created a new form."

Barker, Stephen. "The Crisis of Authenticity: *Death of a Salesman* and the Tragic Muse." *Approaches to Teaching Miller's "Death of a Salesman."* Ed. Matthew C. Roudané. New York: MLA, 1995. 82–101.

In his essay, Barker details his teaching methodology of considering *Death of a Salesman* "within the context of traditional notions of the tragic," and treating the play "as an exemplum of the tragic vision in the twentieth century, quintessentially defining the crisis of authenticity that is the tragic."

Bentley, Eric. "Better than Europe?" *In Search of Theatre*. New York: Knopf, 1953. 84–88. Rpt. in *Two Modern American Tragedies: Reviews and Criticism of "Death of a Salesman" and "A Streetcar Named Desire."* New York: Scribner's, 1961. 131–34.

After praising *Death of a Salesman* as a "signal event in New York theatrical life" and Cobb's performance as "strong enough to hold up any play," Bentley chides Miller's "poetic" style and "murky" story. Says Bentley, "If it is too much to ask that Miller know which of two feasible plays he wanted to write, one can ask that he clear aside rhetorical and directional bric-a-brac and look more closely at his people."

Berlin, Normand. "Doom-Session: *The Master Builder*, *The Visit*, *Death of a Salesman*." *The Secret Cause: A Discussion of Tragedy*. Amherst: U of Massachusetts P, 1981. 125–51, 184–85..

Berlin attempts to examine "precisely why the label 'tragedy' does not adequately describe Miller's play" in order, he says, "to understand more clearly the importance of the secret cause" (mystery, primal urges, supernatural, terror of the unknown).

Bierman, Judah, James Hart, and Stanley Johnson, eds. "Arthur Miller's *Death of a Salesman*." *The Dramatic Experience*. Engelwood Cliffs, N.J.: Prentice-Hall, 1958. 490–93. Rpt. in *"Death of a Salesman": Text and Criticism*. Ed. Gerald Weales. New York: Viking, 1967. New York: Penguin, 1996. 265–71.

Essay that explores Miller's use of time to help tell the full story of Willy Loman's last forty-eight hours and investigates the tragic nature of the play, concluding that though Willy "has something of the heroic spirit, he only vaguely comprehends that his life is without meaning or substance. . . . we reject him because his life, the *unexamined* life, is not worth living."

Bigsby, C. W. E. (Christopher). "The Father/Son Relationship in *Death of a Salesman*" in *Readings on Arthur Miller*. Ed. Thomas Siebold. San Diego, Calif.: Greenhaven, 1997. 125–31. A rpt. portion of *A Critical Introduction to Twentieth-Century American Drama, 2: Tennessee Williams, Arthur Miller, Edward Albee*. Cambridge: Cambridge UP, 1984.

Bigsby effectively argues that the driving force in *Death of a Salesman* is the strained relationship between Willy and Biff, who must ultimately learn to accept his father while rejecting the corrupted values that he promotes.

———. "Introduction." Miller's *Death of a Salesman*. New York: Penguin, 1998. vii–xxvii. Rpt. as "Afterword." Miller's *Death of a Salesman*. New York: Penguin, 1999. 111–30.

Bigsby discusses the historical context and origins of Miller's play, Miller's use of time, the work's technical innovations and themes, the ethnicity of Willy Loman, critical interpretations, and the importance of a salesman as the central character in the play.

Bloom, Harold. "Introduction." *Major Literary Characters: Willy Loman*. New York: Chelsea, 1991. 1–4.

Introduction to a collection of critical essay on Willy Loman in which Bloom argues that *Death of a Salesman* is not tragic but full of pathos.

———. "Introduction." *Modern Critical Interpretations: Arthur Miller's "Death of a Salesman."* New York: Chelsea, 1988. 1–5.

Despite finding *Death of a Salesman*'s literary status somewhat questionable, Bloom admits that the play, when properly staged, is not only an effective drama, but one that "memorably achieves a pathos that none of us would be wise to dismiss."

Brater, Enoch. "Miller's Realism in *Death of a Salesman*." *Arthur Miller: New Perspectives*. Ed. Robert A. Martin. Engelwood Cliffs, N.J.: Prentice-Hall, 1982. 115–26.

Brater charts Miller's development as a realist playwright, examining the dramatic technique of *The Man Who Had All the Luck* (faulty), *All My Sons* (melodramatic), and *Death of a Salesman* (masterpiece).

Bredella, Lothar. "Literary Texts and Intercultural Understanding: Arthur Miller's Play *Death of a Salesman*." *Understanding the USA: A Cross-Cultural Perspective*. Ed. Peter Funke. Tübingen: Narr, 1989. 200–19.

Bredella uses *Death of a Salesman* as an example of a work of literature that encourages students to find its perspective and thus assists in the development of reasoning skills. Says Bredella, the meaning of Miller's play is not identical with one of the positions presented in the play but has to be created by the reader by comparing various positions.

Brockett, Oscar. *The Theatre: An Introduction*, 2nd ed. New York: Holt, Rinehart and Winston, 1969. Rpt. in excerpt form as "An Introduction to *Death of a Salesman*" in *Readings on Arthur Mill-*

er. Ed. Thomas Siebold. San Diego, Calif.: Greenhaven, 1997. 96–101.

Brockett examines the psychological action of *Salesman* and the effective use of nonrealistic staging and mood music to enhance the conflict and confused psychological state of its characters.

Brod, Harry. "The Case for Men's Studies." *Making of Masculinities: The New Men's Studies*. Ed. Harry Brod. Boston: Unwin, 1987. 39–62.

While attempting "to establish the validity of the emerging field of men's studies," Brod mentions *Death of a Salesman* as "the most eloquently profound single statement of mainstream contemporary American male dilemmas."

Brustein, Robert. "Show and Tell." *New Republic* 7 May 1984: 27–29. Rpt. in *Who Needs Theatre?* New York: Atlantic Monthly Press, 1987. 67–71.

In a comparative review of two plays about salesmen, *Death of a Salesman* and David Mamet's *Glengarry Glen Ross*, Brustein praises Mamet's play over Miller's for "unwittingly" accentuating a long-criticized "flaw in Miller's conception"— his failure to tell his audience just what Willy Loman sells.

Cameron, Kenneth M., and Theodore J. C. Hoffman. "Arthur Miller: *Death of a Salesman*." *The Theatrical Response*. New York: Macmillan, 1969. 170–78.

Cameron and Hoffman offer an analysis of *Death of a Salesman* by examining the play's plot, character, and idea.

Canning, Charlotte. "Is This a Play about Women?: A Feminist Reading of *Death of a Salesman*." *The Achievement of Arthur Miller: New Essays*. Ed. Steven Centola. Dallas, Tex.: Contemporary Research, 1995. 69–76.

Canning explores several possible feminist approaches to reading *Salesman* and observes, contrary to traditional analysis, that Miller's women characters play a crucial role in the dramas and are not, in fact, the marginalized figures that feminists have made them out to be.

Choudhuri, A. D. "*Death of a Salesman*: A Salesman's Illusion." *The Face of Illusion in American Drama*. Atlantic Highlands, N.J.: Humanities, 1979. 94–111. Rpt. in *Major Literary Characters:*

Willy Loman. Ed. Harold Bloom. New York: Chelsea, 1991. 66–78.

"Arthur Miller dramatises not only the longings and disappointments of the little man in America and the inhuman attitude of the business world towards a man not useful to the organisation, but what is more important, he focuses our attention on the credibility gap between the American drama and the American Reality."

Clurman, Harold. "Questions and Answers." *On Directing*. New York: Macmillan, 1972. 165–66.

In a chapter that contains some summary replies to questions most commonly asked regarding directing, Clurman relates several tricks that he has used through the years to "deal with the individual actor's hang-ups." Of note is his anecdote regarding directing Thomas Mitchell in the touring company of *Death of a Salesman* and Clurman's stratagem of directing Mitchell through his partners in the scene.

Cohen, Paula Marantz. "Why Willy Is Confused: The Effects of a Paradigm Shift in *Death of a Salesman*." *Approaches to Teaching Miller's "Death of a Salesman."* Ed. Matthew C. Roudané. New York: MLA, 1995. 125–33.

In this essay, Cohen discusses his reasons for shifting his teaching methodology from a conventional social reading that "conceives of Willy Loman as the alienated man" to one that locates *Death of a Salesman* "in respect to an important transition in Western society: the transition from industrialism to postindustrualism." In this way, Cohen says he has the advantage of focusing on the development of technology, "a focus that renders certain conventional ideological arguments less relevant."

Cohn, Ruby. "'Oh, God I Hate This Job.'" *Approaches to Teaching Miller's "Death of a Salesman."* Ed. Matthew C. Roudané. New York: MLA, 1995. 155–62.

In her essay, Cohn compares and contrasts the salesman character from three male dramatist's work: Miller's *Death of a Salesman*, O'Neill's *The Iceman Cometh*, and Mamet's *Glengarry Glen Ross* as a way in which to highlight each plays's distinctive idioms.

Cole, Susan Letzler. *The Absent One: Mourning Ritual, Tragedy, and the Performance of Ambivalence*. University Park: Pennsylvania State UP, 1985. 124–29.

Cole explores *Death of a Salesman* as "the most explicit modern dramatic rendering of sons' ambivalent mourning for the death of the father."

Corrigan, Robert W. *The World of the Theatre*. Glenview, Ill.: Scott, Foresman, and Company, 1979. 82–86.

In a chapter devoted to describing the nature and the world of the theatre and how that world is constructed, Corrigan offers an essay entitled "The Action of *Death of a Salesman*," which explores the reason why modern audiences are moved by the play and continue to identify with it. A production still from the 1949 production accompanies the text.

Crawford, Cheryl. *One Naked Individual: My Fifty Years in the Theatre*. New York: Bobbs-Merrill, 1977. 213.

Interesting anecdote in which Crawford relates the details of one of her "howling mistakes" when she was asked to read Miller's new play, *Death of a Salesman*, and decide overnight if she was interested in producing it. She admits that she "didn't care much for the title," that she was "bothered" by the play's flashbacks, and that Willy Loman struck her "as pathetic rather than tragic." She declined to produce the play—"The rest is history."

Davidson, Peter. "*Death of a Salesman*." *International Dictionary of Theatre*, vol. 1, *Plays*. Eds. Mark Hawkins-Dady and Leanda Shrimpton. Chicago: St. James, 1992. 176–78.

Brief essay that examines the themes, plot, and genesis of *Death of a Salesman*.

Davis, Walter A. *Get the Guests: Psychoanalysis, Modern American Drama, and the Audience*. Madison: U of Wisconsin P, 1994.

Davis pairs classic and frequently performed American dramas (including *Death of a Salesman*) with potential audience groupings for a psychoanalytic profile of why each play is effective.

Deer, Irving, and Harriet A. Deer, eds. *Selves: Drama in Perspective*. New York: HBJ, 1975. 334–414.

Short biographical essay of Miller, followed by the script of *Death of a Salesman*, followed by an analysis of the play as "the best-known literary expressions of disillusionment." Production still from the original Broadway production accompanies the text.

Demastes, William W. "Miller's Use and Modification of the Realist Tradition." *Approaches to Teaching Miller's "Death of a Salesman."* Ed. Matthew C. Roudané. New York: MLA, 1995. 74–81.

In this essay, Demastes discusses his teaching approach to *Death of a Salesman* as an examination of dramatic form, especially definitions of realism and the ways in which Miller "reinvents our traditional notions of the realistic image."

Dogra, O. P. "Miller's *Death of a Salesman*: The Collapse of the Dream." *Perspectives on Arthur Miller*. Ed. Atma Ram. New Delhi: Abhinav, 1988. 53–61.

Dogra argues that *Death of a Salesman* is concerned with public issues rather than personal dilemmas, offers "a bitter complaint about the American socio-moral system," and represents Miller's moral indictment against the American dream of success.

Dolan, Jill. "Feminism and the Canon: The Question of Universality." *The Feminist Spectator as Critic*. Ann Arbor: UMI Research, 1988. 5, 31–33. Rpt. as "Bending Gender to Fit the Canon: The Politics of Production." *Making a Spectacle: Feminist Essays on Contemporary Women's Theatre*. Ed. Lynda Hart. Ann Arbor: U of Michigan P, 1989. 318–44.

Dolan makes a brief comparison between *Death of a Salesman* and *'night Mother* as works of "kitchen-sink realism." While Miller's play is canonized as a tragic masterpiece, Marsha Norman's play, with similar themes and suicide-endings, is labeled a melodrama because the implications of the female character's death "do not resonate enough to be considered a tragedy by the generic male spectator."

Dusenbury, Winifred L. "Personal Failure." *The Theme of Loneliness in Modern American Drama*. Gainesville: U of Florida P, 1960. 8–37. Excerpt rpt. as "Loneliness in *Death of a Salesman*" in *Readings on Arthur Miller*. Ed. Thomas Siebold. San Diego, Calif.: Greenhaven, 1997. 116–24.

Lengthy essay that offers an analysis of *Salesman* "from the point of view of the function of the theme of loneliness which runs through it." Says Dusenbury, "The skill of Arthur Miller lies in the fact that he has taken this idea—a concept which is in itself not dramatic, not full of possible plot situations—and composed a drama in which that idea is made the main purpose of the action by the exemplification in plot, character, and speech of the situation of the misguided American salesman."

Eisinger, Chester E. "Focus on Arthur Miller's *Death of a Salesman*: The Wrong Dreams." *American Dreams, American Nightmares*. Ed. David Madden. Carbondale: Southern Illinois UP, 1970. 165–74.

Eisinger studies the competing dreams of urban idyll and business success as an identity crisis in *Death of a Salesman*, concluding that Miller "has written a confused play because he has been unwilling or unable to commit himself to a firm position with respect to American culture. . . . Willy is not a tragic hero; he is a foolish and ineffectual man for whom we feel pity. We cannot equate his failure with America's."

Evans, Gareth Lloyd. "American Connections—O'Neill, Miller, Williams and Albee." *The Language of Modern Drama*. Totowa, N.J.: Rowman and Littlefield, 1977. 177–204.

Evans examines the language of *Death of a Salesman*, and notes Miller's use of tense, banality, repetition, and rhythm.

Fisher, Walter R., and Richard A. Filloy. "Argument in Drama and Literature: An Exploration." *Advances in Argumentation Theory and Research*. Eds. J. Robert Cox and Charles Arthur Willard. Carbondale: Southern Illinois UP, 1982. 343–62.

In an essay that investigates fictive forms of communication, the authors examine the nature and use of argument in *Death of a Salesman*.

Foster, Richard J. "Confusion and Tragedy: The Failure of Miller's *Salesman*." *Two Modern American Tragedies: Reviews and Criticism of "Death of a Salesman" and "A Streetcar Named Desire."* Ed. John D. Hurrell. New York: Scribner's, 1961. 82–88. Excerpt rpt. as "*Death of a Salesman* as Tragedy" in *Readings on Arthur Miller*. Ed. Thomas Siebold. San Diego, Calif.: Greenhaven, 1997. 102–109.

Foster finds fault with both the critical commentary that protests that *Death of a Salesman* is not a tragedy and Miller's assertion that it is. Says Foster, "The play fails simply because it is sentimental . . . we discover that Miller is relying not on ideas but on a frequently self-contradictory and often quite arbitrary melange of social and moral clichés and the stock emotional responses attached to them."

Gardner, R. H. "Tragedy of the Lowest Man." *The Splintered Stage: The Decline of the American Theater*. New York: Macmillan, 1965. 122–34.

Death of a Salesman "falls short of qualifying" as a great play because it "lacks the clarity of *The Crucible* and *A View from the Bridge*." Gardner ponders and dismisses both often asserted theses that *Salesman* is an attack on the American Dream and that Willy was drawn to represent a Lear of the modern middle classes.

Gassner, John. *Form and Idea in Modern Theatre*. New York: Holt, 1956. 13, 43.

Two references to Miller of note. In the first, Gassner discusses the alternating styles of realism and expressionism found in *Death of a Salesman*, and in the second, praises *All My Sons* for Miller's "'discussion,' by means of both argument and dramatic action, of the fallacy of exclusive family loyalty."

Gonzalez, Alexander G. "Utilizing the Initial Stage Directions of *Death of a Salesman*." *Approaches to Teaching Miller's "Death of a Salesman."* Ed. Matthew C. Roudané. New York: MLA, 1995. 33-36.

Treating the play as "great literature" and a "superb drama," Gonzalez begins his section on *Death of a Salesman* by pursuing a minute analysis of the lengthy preliminary stage directions as "prose poetry, "rich in symbolism and deep in significance." This, he explains, is "useful in promoting an understanding of the more complex forms of those themes that arise later on."

Gordon, Lois. "*Death of a Salesman*: An Appreciation." *The Forties: Fiction, Poetry, and Drama*. Ed. Warren French. Deland, FL: Everett/Edwards, 1969. 273–83. Rpt. in *Twentieth Century Interpretations of Death of a Salesman.* Ed. Helene Wickham Koon. Engelwood Cliffs, N.J.: Prentice-Hall, 1983. 98–108.

Gordon praises *Death of a Salesman* as "unequaled in its brilliant and original fusion of realistic and poetic techniques, its richness of visual and verbal texture, and its wide range of emotional impact," and reads Willy's suicide as his "triumphant revenge upon the dream that has broken him."

Haedicke, Susan C. "Celebrating Stylistic Contradictions: *Death of a Salesman* from a Theatrical Perspective." *Approaches to Teaching Miller's "Death of a Salesman."* Ed. Matthew C. Roudané. New York: MLA, 1995. 37–44.

Appreciating the play's "theatrical viability," Haedicke details the importance of teaching her students to look for "producible interpretations" rather than for a single "correct" literary meaning. To this end, they must design their own sets, sketch the floor plans, and direct portions of the text, as well as have the option of viewing the video production (starring Dustin Hoffman). In this way, her students develop an "understanding that may ultimately grow into a coherent and theatrically exciting production or an insightful and complex analysis."

Hagopian, John V. "*Death of a Salesman.*" *Insight I, Analyses of American Literature*. 3nd rev. ed. Frankfurt: Hirschgraben, 1971. 174–86. Rpt. in shorter form as "Arthur Miller: The Salesman's Two Cases." *Modern Drama* 6.2 (September 1963): 117–25. Rpt. in *The Merrill Studies in "Death of a Salesman."* Ed. Walter Meserve. Columbus, Ohio: Merrill, 1972. 34–42.

Hagopian asserts that Miller has created in Willy Loman a schizophrenic character that represents two different genres: the "dazzlingly experimental social drama" and the "conventionally-made drama of a moral struggle toward insight and honest personal commitment."

Hallman, Ralph. "Alienation through Toil." *Psychology of Literature: A Study of Alienation and Tragedy*. New York: Philosophical Library, 1961. 114–22.

Hallman posits that the tragedy of *Death of a Salesman* is Willy Loman's complete alienation from himself and his family stemming from his misplaced belief "that man can only realize himself through work."

Harder, Harry. "*Death of a Salesman*: An American Classic." *Censored Books: Critical Viewpoints*. Eds. Nicholas Karolides, Lee Burress, John M. Kean. Metuchen, N.J.: Scarecrow, 1993. 209–19.

Harder proffers the argument that *Death of a Salesman* should be taught in high schools "both as a significant comment on society and human values and as an outstanding example of the art of drama."

Harris, Andrew. "*Death of a Salesman*." *Broadway Theatre*. New York: Routledge, 1994. 48–67.

Fascinating account of the premiere production of *Death of a Salesman*, including historical details, critical reaction, anecdotal commentary, interviews with principal artists (Miller, Dunnock, Kazan, Bloomgarden), design details, and audience response.

Hawthorn, Jeremy. "Sales and Solidarity: Arthur Miller's *Death of a Salesman*." *Multiple Personality and the Disintegration of Literary Character from Oliver Goldsmith to Sylvia Plath*. London: Arnold, 1983. 108–116. Rpt. in *Major Literary Characters: Willy Loman*. Ed. Harold Bloom. New York: Chelsea, 1991. 90–98.

Hawthorn reads Willy Loman as a character subjected to intolerable and contradictory pressures from society, family, and work, but insists on seeing these pressures as normal, uncontradictory, and manageable. This split forces Willy to blame himself for his failure, precipitating his self-destruction.

Heilman, Robert B. "Miller's *Death of a Salesman*." *Tragedy and Melodrama in American Drama*. Seattle: U of Washington P, 1968. 233–37.

Finding that *Death of a Salesman* is "difficult to judge because it is so deeply rooted in two emotions that almost define our way of life: the pathos of obsolescence and the wracking tensions of insecurity," Heilman concludes that despite the drama's "contemporary attractiveness, the play has a hero so limited that this is a limitation of the play itself."

Heyen, William. "Arthur Miller's *Death of a Salesman* and the American Dream." *Amerikanisches Drama und Theater im 20. Jahrhundert*. Eds. Alfred Weber and Siegfried Neuweiler. Göttingen: Vandenhoek and Ruprecht, 1975. 192–221. Rpt. in *Modern Critical Interpretations: Arthur Miller's "Death of a Salesman."* Ed. Harold Bloom. New York: Chelsea, 1988. 47–58.

Heyen presents an unusual "personal and impressionistic essay" on *Death of a Salesman*, a play he calls "simple and absurd and beautiful and true," focusing his commentary on "how the play feels and smells and looks."

Hobson, Harold. "The Involved Theatre." *The Theatre Now*. London: Longmans, 1953. 121–25.

Hobson disputes George Jean Nathan's assertion that Miller's play was "inadequately written" by extolling what he finds as tender, "exceedingly moving and true," and a play "beautifully and movingly written, eloquent, yet perfectly within the common American idiom."

Hurt, James. "Family and History in *Death of a Salesman*." *Approaches to Teaching Miller's "Death of a Salesman."* Ed. Matthew C. Roudané. New York: MLA, 1995. 134–41.

Hurt details in his essay the reasons for constructing a family history of the characters in *Death of a Salesman* as a way to "enter the lives of the Lomans and to start excavating the story behind the discourse of the actual text." Focusing his teaching methodology on the family tree of the Loman family provides the students in Hurt's classes "a concrete focus for analyzing the family as well as for placing it within the framework of history."

Ishizuka, Koji. "Two Memory Plays: Williams and Miller." *American Literature in the 1940s: Annual Report, 1975*. Tokyo: The Tokyo Chapter of the American Literature Society of Japan, 1976. 208–12.

Brief essay exploring Tennessee Williams's *The Glass Menagerie* and Miller's *Death of a Salesman* as memory plays, both "openly nostalgic or sentimental in their manner or style."

Jacobi, Martin J. "The Dramatist as Salesman: A Rhetorical Analysis of Miller's Intentions and Effects." *Approaches to Teaching Miller's "Death of a Salesman."* Ed. Matthew C. Roudané. New York: MLA, 1995. 62–73.

In his essay, Jacobi explains his methodology of teaching *Death of a Salesman* as a work of literature and applying the theories of Kenneth Burke and Wayne Booth to a rhetorical criticism approach to the play.

Kahn, Sy. "Through a Glass Menagerie Darkly: The World of Tennessee Williams." *Modern American Drama: Essays in Criticism*. Ed. William E. Taylor. Deland, Fla.: Everett, 1968. 71–89.

This essay includes a brief mention of Miller in regard to Kahn's assertion that part of the reason for Tennessee Williams's success is that his plays "touch at the center of American life." Kahn says that "*Salesman* succeeds magnificently because Willy Loman's dreams, defeat and death make manifest the unvoiced fears of so many who, like Willy, suspect they have the wrong dream, and suspect too that the American gospel of material success and of being well-liked is a swindle."

Kataria, Gulshan Rai. "King Lear and Willy Loman as Victims of Persona Identity." *Perspectives on Arthur Miller*. Ed. Atma Ram. New Delhi: Abhinav, 1988. 35–49.

Using Jungian terminology, Kataria argues that King Lear and Willy Loman are similar characters by virtue of their natures and psychic lives—both "are grave victims of persona identity which envelopes their private lives and spells disaster for all concerned."

Kazan, Elia. "Experiencing the Play: *Death of a Salesman*." *A Theater in Your Head*. Kenneth Thorpe Rowe. New York: Funk and Wagnalls, 1960: 44–51.

Excerpts from Kazan's notebooks for *Death of a Salesman*. Includes Kazan's general notes on the play's basic themes and through lines, notes on the character of Willy Loman and the characters in the past, directing and style notes, notes on directing Willy's actions, and physical descriptions of Kazan's notebook and playscript.

Kintz, Linda. "The Sociosymbolic Work of Family in *Death of a Salesman*." *Approaches to Teaching Miller's "Death of a Salesman."* Ed. Matthew C. Roudané. New York: MLA, 1995. 102–14.

Kintz details her teaching approach to *Death of a Salesman* as one which combines "aesthetics and history through a grammar of space by showing the relation between urban social space in the twentieth century and the different ways in which people live themselves as human subjects."

Koon, Helene Wickham, ed. "Introduction." *Twentieth Century Interpretations of "Death of a Salesman."* Engelwood Cliffs, N.J.: Prentice-Hall, 1983. 1–14.

Brief overview of Miller's life and literary career, followed by an examination of critical response to *Death of a Salesman,* the critical debate surrounding the play's themes, and Miller's "skilled use of tradition and originality."

Krutch, Joseph Wood. *'Modernism' in Modern Drama: A Definition and an Estimate*. Ithaca, New York: Cornell UP, 1953. 123–30.

Krutch considers Miller's *Death of a Salesman* and Tennessee Williams's *A Streetcar Named Desire* to determine whether they express a "positive confession of faith." He finds Miller a moralist and his play a "qualified reaffirmation of the individual's privilege of being, within certain limits, what he chooses to be."

Langsteau, Paula. "Miller's *Salesman*: An Early Version of Absurdist Theatre." *The Achievement of Arthur Miller: New Essays*. Ed. Steven Centola. Dallas, Tex.: Contemporary Research, 1995. 77–85.

Contrary to *Death of a Salesman*'s label as a work of social realism, Langsteau examines six theatrical techniques (symbolic set, violation of time sequence, dream quality, use of nonrational events, devaluation of language, and the cycle of the play) as evidence of Miller's absurdist tendencies.

Leaska, Mitchell. "20th Century Tragedy: British and American: Miller." *The Voice of Tragedy*. New York: Speller, 1963. 273–78.

Calling *Death of a Salesman* "one of the most intuitively wrought plays portraying American society," Leaska examines the tragic dimensions of Miller's work as a play that "bespeaks his conviction that life is comprised of acts committed by men in their struggle against mortality."

Lewis, Allan. "The American Scene: Williams and Miller." *The Contemporary Theatre*. New York: Crown, 1969. 286–88, 293–301. Revised and rpt. as "The American Theatre." *The Contemporary Theatre: The Significant Playwrights of Our Time*. New York: Crown, 1971. 341–56. Revised ed. New York: Crown, 1975. 341–56.

Lewis compares playwrights Miller and Tennessee Williams and says that *Death of a Salesman* has all the elements of a modern tragedy but only succeeds as a father-and-son conflict. While attempting to be a twentieth-century morality play about Everyman, Miller's work is but the "personal failure of one lost soul."

Lounsberry, Barbara. "'The Woods Are Burning': Expressionism in *Death of a Salesman*." *Approaches to Teaching Miller's "Death of a Salesman."* Ed. Matthew C. Roudané. New York: MLA, 1995. 52–61.

In this essay, Lounsberry laments the deliberate "tipping of the scales toward greater realism" that she has noticed in productions of *Death of a Salesman*. For this reason, she focuses her teaching of Miller's play on what she considers to be the work's highest achievement: the balance that exists between expressionism and realism (or "the intermingling of individual psychology and social forces"). After a brief historical introduction on the origin of expressionism, Lounsberry examines *Salesman*'s expressionistic elements, including the play's musical motifs, setting and set design, lighting, characters, and costumes.

Mabley, Edward. *Dramatic Construction: An Outline of Basic Principles*. New York: Chilton, 1972. 292–313.

Detailed synopsis and analysis of *Death of a Salesman*, including a discussion of such topics as protagonist and objective, obstacles, major crisis and climax, exposition, characterization, development, dramatic irony, preparation, effects, and plausibility.

Mander, John. "Arthur Miller's *Death of a Salesman*." *The Writer and Commitment*. Philadelphia: Dufour, 1962. 138–52.

Mander argues that Miller's *Death of a Salesman* suffers from a dual commitment to the ideologies of Marx and Freud, and concludes that "if an artist is, in this way, the servant of two masters, his work will suffer . . . [and] we are bound to say: a house divided against itself cannot stand."

Manocchio, Tony, and William Petitt. "The Loman Family." *Families under Stress: A Psychological Interpretation*. London: Routledge, 1975. 129–68.

Manocchio and Petitt examine the dynamics of the Loman family in *Death of a Salesman*, including issues relating to the work role, expectations, differentness, secrets, fantasy, and the model child. The authors conclude that with the proper therapy, "the salesman could have retained his integrity" and there "would have been no need for a destructive fantasy" or "for anyone to fall victim to an unfulfilled desire."

McCarthy, Mary. "Introduction." *Sights and Spectacles, 1937–1956*. New York: Farrar, Straus and Cudahy, 1956. ix–xvi.

McCarthy finds the popularity of *Death of a Salesman* "puzzling." "The public," she says, "seems to be, literally, a glutton for punishment. . . . The trouble with [*Salesman*] is that it strives to be a tragedy and becomes instead confused and hortatory."

McCollom, William G. *Tragedy*. New York: Macmillan, 1957: 16–17.

The author offers a brief discussion of Miller's views on the nature of tragedy, especially as it relates to *Death of a Salesman*. Says McCollom, "[*Salesman*] fails as a tragedy because Miller fails to see that the world of tragedy must be more than a temporary political and social climate if the hero is to have more than a transitory significance. . . . Even if Willy were a fully acceptable hero, his world would sharply limit the meaning of his action."

McElroy, Davis Dunbar. *Existentialism and Modern Literature*. Secaucus, N.J.: Citadel Press, 1972. 54–58.

McElroy examines *Death of a Salesman* as "an open attack upon the spiritual poverty of life in this country, as well as a bitter criticism of certain American ideals," and advises his readers to follow Miller's warning, dramatized by Willy Loman's tragic end: choose your own highest destiny and "become a real person; that is, the kind of significant being which is worthy of making a choice which will influence the future of mankind."

Meserve, Walter J. "Preface." *The Merrill Studies in "Death of a Salesman."* Ed. Walter J. Meserve. Columbus, Ohio: Merrill, 1972. v–ix.

Meserve uses a poem entitled "Who Killed Willy Loman?" as a framing device for this collection of essays that point out the appeal of *Salesman* as a work that inspires multifarious critical approaches and analyses.

Mielziner, Jo. "Designing a Play: *Death of a Salesman* (With Some Time Off for *South Pacific*)." *Designing for the Theatre: A Memoir and a Portfolio*. New York: Bramhall House, 1965. 23–64, 145–47. Rpt. in *"Death of a Salesman": Text and Criticism*. Ed. Gerald Weales. New York: Viking, 1967. New York: Penguin, 1996. 187–98.

Journal type account of Mielziner's design development for *Death of a Salesman*, from first reading to road show. Significant also for the inclusion of portfolio design drawings and sketches for premiere production.

Morse, Donald E. "The 'Life Lie' in Three Plays by O'Neill, Williams, and Miller." *Cross Cultural Studies: American, Canadian, and European Literatures: 1945–1985*. Ed. Mirko Jurak. Ljubljana, Yugoslavia, English Department: Edvard Kardelj University of Ljubljana, 1988. 273–77.

Morse examines *Death of a Salesman* as the portrayal of "the failure of a life lie of unearned success," and Willy Loman as living the wrong dream—"he lived a life lie of success that affected everyone he became involved with for the tissue of lies he wove had to be propped up by family and friends at great cost."

Muller, Herbert J. "Modern Tragedy." *The Spirit of Tragedy*. New York: Knopf, 1956. 316–17. Rpt. in *Major Literary Characters: Willy Loman*. Ed. Harold Bloom. New York: Chelsea, 1991. 5–6.

Muller finds *Death of a Salesman* deficient in its study of "a little man succumbing to his environment, rather than a great man destroyed by his greatness." Calling the play "pretentious" because Miller mixes the colloquial with the "supra-realistic effects," Muller concludes that "the excitement over Willy would seem to be more a social than a literary portent."

Murphy, Brenda. "The Reformation of Biff Loman: A View from the Pre-Production Scripts." *The Achievement of Arthur Miller: New Essays*. Ed. Steven Centola. Dallas, Tex.: Contemporary Research, 1995. 51–57.

Murphy examines Miller's early conception of Biff Loman from pre-production versions of *Death of a Salesman* in an attempt to explain the dramatic unevenness of Biff's self-realization against Willy's psychological downfall. She shows how Biff's character was not originally intended to be a moral counterforce to Willy and was, instead, designed "far less virtuous and a good deal more like Willy's [character] than in the published version."

Murray, Edward. "Characterization in *Death of a Salesman*." *Readings on Arthur Miller*. Ed. Thomas Siebold. San Diego, Calif.: Greenhaven, 1997. 110–15. [From Murray's *Arthur Miller: Dramatist*. New York: Ungar, 1967. 22–51.]

Murray contends that while the main characters in *Death of a Salesman* are well developed and complex, the minor characters are static and flat and not fully drawn.

Paul, Rajinder. "*Death of a Salesman* in India." *The Merrill Studies in "Death of a Salesman."* Ed. Walter Meserve. Ohio: Merrill, 1972. 23–27.

Paul praises Miller's *Death of a Salesman* as "the most popular play" in India citing that there is a "great identification available to the Indian milieu in Miller's plays."

Porter, Thomas E. "Acres of Diamonds: *Death of a Salesman*." *Myth and Modern American Drama*. Detroit: Wayne State UP, 1969. 127–52. Rpt. in *Critical Essays on Arthur Miller*. Ed. James J. Martine. Boston: G. K. Hall, 1979. 24–43.

Porter examines the myth of the American Dream of the success of the self-made man to *Death of a Salesman*.

———. "Introduction: The Dramatic Milieu and American Drama." *Myth and Modern American Drama.* Detroit: Wayne State UP, 1969. 11–25.

Introduction to a book that, among other works by American playwrights, examines Miller's *Death of a Salesman* as a representative American play, considering plot, structure, character, and setting to discover how these elements of drama relate to their cultural milieus.

Quasimodo, Salvatore. "American Theatre." *The Poet and the Politician and Other Essays*. Trans. Thomas G. Bergin and Sergio Pacifici. Carbondale: Southern Illinois UP, 1964. 148–51.

Nobel Prize-winning poet Quasimodo (1959) praises Miller for making "an important discovery for the contemporary theatre"—"He has taken a man by the shoulders, an ordinary man, and has pushed him on to the boards of the stage, forcing him to speak. To speak about himself, in the present and in the past, to undo the last knots of his definitive day. Miller has brought back 'the character' into the theatre."

Rama Murthy, V. *American Expressionistic Drama; Containing an Analyses of Three Outstanding American Plays: O'Neill, "The Hairy Ape"; Tennessee Williams, "The Glass Menagerie"; Miller, "Death of a Salesman."* Delhi: Doaba, 1970. 73–100.

Discussion centering on the background, themes, language, familial and social issues, playwriting technique, and tragic nature of *Death of a Salesman.*

Rosefeldt, Paul. "Escape of the Father and the Son's Hopeless Quest—1: Tennessee Williams' *The Glass Menagerie*, Arthur Miller's *Death of a Salesman*." *The Absent Father in Modern Drama*. New York: Peter Lang, 1995. 39–50.

Rosefeldt examines the symbolic shadow of the absent father in Miller's *Death of a Salesman* and concludes that the act of pursuing the absent father has lead Willy Loman, inevitably, to his tragic downfall and "into a frontier from which there is no return."

Roudané, Matthew C. "*Death of a Salesman* and the Poetics of Arthur Miller." *Cambridge Companion to Arthur Miller*. Ed. Christopher Bigsby. Cambridge: Cambridge UP, 1997. 60–85.

Considering *Death of a Salesman* as a "deceptively simple" play that "quickly dissolves into filial ambiguity, civic paradox, and philosophic complexity," Roudané studies the play's universality, set, imagery, family models, daring use of time, language, allusions, and contribution to the myth of the American Dream.

Rowe, Kenneth. *A Theater in Your Head.* New York: Funk and Wagnalls, 1960. 44–59, 60–61, 66–69..

Rowe, Miller's playwriting teacher at the University of Michigan, offers excerpts from Kazan's notebooks for *Death of a Salesman* and an analysis of Kazan and Mielziner's function in the original 1949 Pulitzer Prize-winning production of Miller's play.

Rusch, Frederick L. "Approaching Literature through the Social Psychology of Erich Fromm." *Psychological Perspectives on Literature: Freudian Dissidents and Non-Freudians: A Casebook*. Ed. Joseph Natoli. Hamden, Conn.: Archon, 1984. 79–99.

Rusch offers a Frommian interpretation of *Death of a Salesman* to help provide a social context to the characters and explain their behavior. Willy, says Rusch, is a product of a "marketing orientation" who lives "in a fantasy created by the hype of the new American marketplace." Willy is a character of "split allegiances" —to both the older matriarchal order in his desperate desire for love and to the patriarchal order in his need for authoritarian control.

Rutnin, M. M. "*Death of a Salesman*: A Myth or Reality in a Developing Country." *Asian Response to American Literature.* Ed. C. D. Narasimhaiah. New York: Barnes and Noble, 1972. 171–80.

Essay in four sections: a summary of the critical response and an analysis of the power of *Death of a Salesman,* which Rutnin cites at the American self-identification with the character of Willy Loman and his problems; an explanation as to why *Salesman* cannot be successful in Thailand; an explanation as to why *Salesman* cannot be appreciated as great literature in Thailand (because of the many cultural and religious differences); and the metaphoric relevance of the play to the peoples of Thailand (the striking parallel between the tragedy of a small American man and a small developing nation).

Schlueter, June. "Re-membering Willy's Past: Introducing Postmodern Concerns through *Death of a Salesman*." *Approaches to Teaching Miller's "Death of a Salesman."* Ed. Matthew C. Roudané. New York: MLA, 1995. 142–54.

In this essay, Schlueter admits her "continuing challenge" in finding new and important ways to approach *Death of a Salesman* since it has become so familiar. Her approach, however, is one based in the context of postmodernism that entails a questioning of the play's historicity. Schlueter assigns her students the task of constructing a detailed chronology or personal history of the Loman family in order to understand "the determining nature of history." In addition, her focus is on deconstructing Willy's memories as represented in Miller's play as a way to question "the historicity of knowledge, the nature of identity," and "the epistemological status of fictional discourse."

Scholes, Robert. "The Rise of English in Two American Colleges." *The Rise and Fall of English: Reconstructing English as a Discipline*. New Haven: Yale UP, 1998. 18.

In an essay that shows how English came to occupy its present place in the American educational system, Scholes recounts how, as an undergraduate, he had been sent to New York from Yale to see whether Miller's *Death of a Salesman* "could indeed meet the exacting academic standard for 'true tragedy.'" Says Scholes, "I cannot remember the verdict on that count, but the play shook me down to my shoes, because it represented a business and family life so close to my own experience that it drove me to face, however briefly, the actual conditions and possibilities of my own existence. More than any other single experience, it changed my life and started me on the path I have since followed."

Selden, Raman. "Text: Arthur Miller, *Death of a Salesman*. Theory: Binary Oppositions." *Practicing Theory and Reading Literature: An Introduction*. Lexington: UP of Kentucky, 1989. 55–60.

Brief essay that investigates significant binary opposites in *Death of a Salesman* in an attempt to discover the meaning inherent in binary patterns.

Sharma, Jaidev and V. P. "America, the Salesman, and the Artist: A Study of *The Glass Menagerie*, *The Iceman Cometh*, and *Death of a Salesman*." *Perspectives on Arthur Miller*. Ed. Atma Ram. New Delhi: Abhinav, 1988. 62–74.

This essay examines the similarities between three different playwrights' portrayal of postwar salesman characters. "Each play evaluates the American experience through the salesman figure and thus becomes a judgment on, and a demystification of, the success myth which the American experience promotes."

Smith, Susan Harris. "Contextualizing *Death of a Salesman* as an American Play." *Approaches to Teaching Miller's "Death of a Salesman."* Ed. Matthew C. Roudané. New York: MLA, 1995. 27–32.

Using the assertion that *Death of a Salesman* is the quintessential modern American drama as a point of entry, Smith instructs her students to examine the play's themes and structures as an inquiry into the problem of American essentialism. Issues include: "the dominance of the white male experience as the 'American' experience and of the white male playwright in the dramatic canon; the concomitant marginalization of women and of racial and ethnic minorities; the articulation and impact of the idea of the American dream on American culture and drama; the search for an individual identity as well as a place in the American landscape; and the dramaturgical strategies modern playwrights use to position the audience and to explore the issues."

Spears, Timothy B. "Conclusion: The Death of the Salesman." *100 Years on the Road: The Traveling Salesman in American Culture*. New Haven: Yale UP, 1995. 221–33.

In a book about the history of the traveling salesman in the United States, Spears offers a brief analysis of *Death of a Salesman* as a work that "signals Arthur Miller's recognition that the emergence of mass commercial culture augured the death of the salesman."

Spindler, Michael. "Consumer Man in Crisis: Arthur Miller's *Death of a Salesman*," *American Literature and Social Change: William Dean Howells to Arthur Miller*. Bloomington: Indiana UP, 1983. 202–13. Rpt. in extract form in *Major Literary Characters: Willy Loman*. Ed. Harold Bloom. New York: Chelsea, 1991. 25–27.

Spindler reads *Death of a Salesman* as "the capstone text" representing America's "transition from a production-oriented to a consumption-oriented economy and the ideological conflicts and literary responses generated by that transition."

Stanton, Kay. "Women and the American Dream of *Death of a Salesman*." *Feminist Rereadings of Modern American Drama*. Ed. June Schlueter. Cranbury, N.J.: Associated UP, 1989. 67–102. Rpt. in *Major Literary Characters: Willy Loman*. Ed. Harold Bloom. New York: Chelsea, 1991. 129–56.

Stanton reads Miller's depiction of the American Dream in *Death of a Salesman* as "male-oriented" and requiring "unacknowledged dependence upon women as well as women's subjugation and exploitation." The American Dream of *Death of a Salesman*, says Stanton, is "unbalanced, immature, illogical, lying, thieving, self-contradictory, and self-destructive. . . . It prefers to destroy itself rather than to acknowledge the female as equal or to submit to a realistic and balanced feminine value system."

Stephens, Judith Louise. "Women in Pulitzer Prize Plays, 1918–1949." *Women in American Theatre*. Eds. Helen Krich Chinoy and Linda Walsh Jenkins. New York: TCG, 1987. 149–51.

Stephens studied the female characters from Pulitzer Prize dramas from 1918–1949 in an effort to (1) "determine whether some of the criticisms pertaining to the women characters found in American fiction were valid when applied to female dramatic characters," and (2) analyze these characters, note their shared traits, and record "what, if any, changes occurred over each decade." Linda Loman was among those who were "primarily motivated by love of their husband and/or family," suffered "from the Eve-Mary Syndrome," was essentially a "selfless character" who exhibited "a brand of selflessness" on which she thrived. Linda lost her self-identity but also seemed to take on "an awesome and pervading power which becomes both a nurturing and destructive force."

Szondi, Peter. "Memory and Dramatic Form in *Death of a Salesman*." *Theory of Modern Drama*. Minneapolis: University of Minnesota Press, 987. Rpt. in *Modern Critical Interpretations: Arthur Miller's "Death of a Salesman."* Ed. Harold Bloom. New York: Chelsea, 1988. 19–23.

Szondi charts Miller's evolution from "imitator to innovator," looking at *All My Sons* as a preservation of Ibsen's analytical approach to social dramaturgy and *Death of a Salesman* as a surrender of dramatic form. Miller's development as a dramatist in these two plays shows that "instead of an interpersonal action that would call forth discussion of the past, the present generated by the thematic discloses the psychic state of the individual overpowered by memory."

Varma, Urmila. "Modernity as a Theme and Technique in Arthur Miller's *Death of a Salesman*." *Perspectives on Arthur Miller*. Ed. Atma Ram. New Delhi: Abhinav, 1988. 89–95.

Varma argues that Miller's experimentation with expressionistic overtones and his departure from the traditions of realism in *Death of a Salesman*, "in order to reveal the chaotic state of mind of Willy Loman," reveals "the introduction of the novel technique in drama."

Vogel, Dan. "Willy Tyrannos." *The Three Masks of American Tragedy*. Baton Rouge: Louisiana State UP, 1974. 91–102. Rpt. in *Major Literary Characters: Willy Loman*. Ed. Harold Bloom. New York: Chelsea, 1991. 58–65.

Vogel details the debate surrounding the tragic nature of *Death of a Salesman* and compares the play to Sophocles' *Oedipus Tyrrannos*, finding thematic, situational, and formal similarities between them.

von Szeliski, John. *Tragedy and Fear: Why Modern Tragic Drama Fails*. Chapel Hill: U of North Carolina P, 1971. 61, 86–87, 90–91, 106–109. Rpt. in *Major Literary Characters: Willy Loman*. Ed. Harold Bloom. New York: Chelsea, 1991. 15–19.

Investigation into the pessimistic vision that Miller "unconsciously" created with *Death of a Salesman* and a review of Miller's theory on the tragedy of the common man as it relates to the same play.

Vorlicky, Robert. *Act Like a Man: Challenging Masculinities in American Drama*. Ann Arbor: U of Michigan P, 1995. 8–9.

Brief mention of *Salesman* as it relates to Linda Loman's "verbal contributions to the progression of dialogue towards characters' self-disclosures." Contrary to those who criticize Linda as "a quintessential male-constructed object," Volricky stresses the importance of her character to the overall development of the action of her play. "Her voiced contributions, like those of most women characters in realist drama, have direct impact on ensuing verbal exchanges *and* dramatic actions—despite, or perhaps because of, her sex and gender."

Watson, G. J. "Ibsen and Miller: The Individual and Society." *Drama, an Introduction*. London: Macmillan, 1983. 125–31, 200–201.

Watson explores *Death of a Salesman* as social tragedy and concludes that Miller's "fundamental belief that society can be changed" is antithetical to Ibsen's idea of the "tragic impasse" and thus negates the tragic nature of the work.

Weales, Gerald.. "Introduction." *"Death of a Salesman": Text and Criticism*. New York: Viking, 1967. New York: Penguin, 1996. vii–xx.

In an introduction to a collection of critical reactions and a "wide variety of opinions" on Miller's *Death of a Salesman*, Weales offers a brief overview of the works contained within the volume whose purpose, he states, is to provide questions, not answers.

Welland, Dennis. "*Death of a Salesman*." *Twentieth Century Interpretations of "Death of a Salesman."* Ed. Helene Wickham Koon. Engelwood Cliffs, N.J.: Prentice-Hall, 1983. 15–32. [From *Miller: A Study of His Plays*. London: Eyre Methuen, 1979. 36–53.]

Welland examines differing critical attitudes towards *Death of a Salesman*, both British and American, and defends the play from those who have attacked it as Marxist (Eleanor Clark), conflicted (Eric Bentley), structurally confused, better off placed in a Jewish milieu (Mary McCarthy), and vague in its assignment of emotional identification (Bentley).

———. "*Death of a Salesman* in England." *The Merrill Studies in "Death of a Salesman."* Ed. Walter J. Meserve. Columbus, Ohio: Merrill, 1972. 8–17.

Welland examines the critical response that *Death of a Salesman* has received in England, concluding that "for all the differences of opinion, Miller has become a respected and honored dramatist in England, largely because of the impact of this play."

Wellwarth, George E. *Modern Drama and the Death of God*. Madison: U of Wisconsin P, 1986. 144–45. Rpt. in *Major Literary Characters: Willy Loman*. Ed. Harold Bloom. New York: Chelsea, 1991. 27–29.

Brief discussion of *Death of a Salesman* as an "unintentionally synthetic drama,' concluding that Miller's own definition of tragedy does not apply because Willy's self-image has been chosen for him.

Whitman, Robert. *The Play-Reader's Handbook*. New York: Bobbs-Merrill, 1966. 46–49, 208–209.

Whitman examines the setting of *Death of a Salesman* as "Miller's attempt to suggest rather than show, to represent inner as well as outer realities." Of note is Whitman's assertion that *Salesman* "falls short of tragedy" because the audience knows at the end of the play why Willy has done what he did. "Tragedy," says Whitman, "acknowledges the fact of incomprehensibility, of the limitation of human powers, while at the same time reassuring us that behind the apparent contradictions and incoherence there is both dignity and meaning to existence."

Wilson, Robert N. "The Salesman and Society." *The Writer as Social Seer*. Chapel Hill: U of North Carolina P, 1979. 56–71. Rpt. in *Major Literary Characters: Willy Loman*. Ed. Harold Bloom. New York: Chelsea, 1991. 79–89.

Wilson argues that the power of Miller's tragedy is rooted in the psychological depth of the family relationships in the play as well as a grasp of fundamental elements of life in the United States.

Critical Essays in Journals and Magazines

Aarnes, William. "Tragic Form and the Possibility of Meaning in *Death of a Salesman*." *Furman Studies* 29 (December 1983): 57–80. Rpt. in *Modern Critical Interpretations: Arthur Miller's "Death of a Salesman*." Ed. Harold Bloom. New York: Chelsea, 1988. 95–111.

Aarnes reads the character of Willy Loman as "a pathetic man caught in a tragic form" due to his lack of control over his faculties, his lack of moral strength, his victimization by society, his belief in a false definition of success, his incessant lying and self-delusion, and his lack of insight.

August, Eugene. "*Death of a Salesman*: A Men's Studies Approach." *Western Ohio Journal* 7.1 (1986): 53–71.

August argues that Willy's abandonment by his father, and thus his lack of a male role model in his youth, precipitated his own adult male role problems with his sons.

Babcock, Granger. "What's the Secret?: Willy Loman as Desiring Machine." *American Drama* 2.1 (Fall 1992): 59–83.

Babcock interprets the character of Willy Loman as a puppet or capital machine rather than as a tragic figure.

Barnett, Gene. "The Theatre of Robert Bolt." *Dalhousie Review* 48 (Spring 1968): 13–23.

Barnett compares Miller's *Death of a Salesman* with Robert Bolt's *The Flowering Cherry*, concluding Willy Loman is a more universal character than Jim.

Bateman, Mary B. "*Death of a Salesman*: A Clinical Look at the Willy Loman Family." *International Journal of Family Therapy* 7 (Summer 1985): 116–21.

Bateman uses a separation-individuation model to explore the dynamics of the Loman family in *Death of a Salesman.*

Bates, Barclay W. "The Lost Past in *Death of a Salesman.*" *Modern Drama* 11 (September 1968): 164–72. Rpt. in *Twentieth Century Interpretations of "Death of a Salesman."* Ed. Helene Wickham Koon. Engelwood Cliffs, N.J.: Prentice-Hall, 1983. 60–69.

Bates argues that modern society is ultimately responsible for the destruction of Willy because it could not tolerate his anachronistic four-sided nature: "the arche-typal cherisher of the pastoral world, the pre-industrial-revolution artisan, the ham-handed outlaw frontiersman, and the dutiful patriarchal male intent upon transmitting complex legacies from his forbears to his progeny."

Becker, Benjamin J. "*Death of a Salesman*: Arthur Miller's Play in the Light of Psychoanalysis." *American Journal of Psychoanalysis* 47.3 (Fall 1987): 195–209.

Becker investigates the psychological meaning of *Death of a Salesman* and attempts to "penetrate the innermost layers of Willy's personality" by tracing both the character's personality from birth on and how other characters in the play "stand for projections of Willy's own unconscious traits."

Bertin, Michael. "'Riding on a Smile and a Shoeshine': The Broadway Salesman." *Theater* 16.1 (Fall/Winter 1984): 75–79. Rpt. in *Essays in Honor of Stanley Kauffmann*. Ed. Bert Cardullo. Lanham, Md.: UP of America, 1986. 103–107.

While admitting that the play "is good enough to allow creative actors the chance of transcending" its flaws, Bertin finds fault with the text of Miller's *Death of a Salesman* saying that the playwright "fails to extend compassion into insight."

Bettina, Sister M. "Willy Loman's Brother Ben: Tragic Insight in *Death of a Salesman.*" *Modern Drama* 4 (February 1962): 409–12. Rpt. in *The Merrill Studies in "Death of a Salesman."* Ed. Walter J. Meserve. Columbus, Ohio: Merrill, 1972. 80–83.

Bettina offers a reading of the expressionistic character of Willy's brother Ben as the personification of Willy's dream and "a projection of his brother's personality rather than an individual human force."

Bigsby, Christopher. "The Dream of Tomorrow." Stagebill for *Death of a Salesman.* Royal National Theatre. 31 October 1996: n.p.

Essay in which Bigsby offers information on the origins of Miller's story, analysis of the importance of the past and its relationship to the present, a discussion of the play's central conflict, and an overview of the success of the play worldwide.

Bleich, David. "Psychological Bases of Learning from Literature." *College English* 33 (October 1971): 32–45.

Bleich discusses two cases of response to Miller's *Death of a Salesman* in an effort to "indicate how the need to derive instruction of the play is connected with an interjected sense of parental authority."

Bliquez, Guerin. "Linda's Role in *Death of a Salesman*." *Modern Drama* 10 (February 1968): 383–86. Rpt. in *The Merrill Studies in "Death of a Salesman."* Ed. Walter Meserve. Columbus, Ohio: Merrill, 1972. 77–79.

Bliquez reads the character of Linda Loman as a negative force who wrongfully supports her husband's hollow dreams instead of his life and reality and evaluates the part she plays in Willy's downfall.

Brooks, Charles. "The Multiple Set in American Drama." *Tulane Drama Review* 3 (December 1958): 30–41.

Brooks looks closely at the ways in which multiple set dramas achieve larger visions of life than the single set or shifting scene plays of the past. *Death of a Salesman* is praised as "the single play which best realizes the potentialities of the multiple set."

Brucher, Richard. "Pernicious Nostalgia in *Glengarry Glen Ross*." *David Mamet's "Glengarry Glen Ross": Text and Performance*. Ed. Leslie Kane. New York: Garland, 1996. 211–25.

Brucher examines the line of salesman plays in modern American drama, from O'Neill's *The Iceman Cometh*, to Miller's *Death of a Salesman*, to Mamet's *Glengarry Glen Ross*, and concludes that all three are "deeply interested in myth as a source of social dislocation." While Miller "extends and redirects O'Neill's dramatic use of nostalgia," Mamet "subverts the inherited line of nostalgia operating in Miller's play"—deploying it "to conjure fake communal feelings intended to deceive people."

———. "Willy Loman and *The Soul of a New Machine*: Technology and the Common Man." *Journal of American Studies* 13 (December 1983): 325–36. Rpt. in *Modern Critical Interpretations: Arthur Miller's "Death of a Salesman."* Ed. Harold Bloom. New York: Chelsea, 1988. 83–94.

This essay compares Miller's *Death of a Salesman* and Tracy Kidder's *The Soul of a New Machine*. "What is finally compelling about Willy Loman and Tom West is their compulsive need to dramatize their work, to redefine it with words that evoke the American past and its values of personality and individualism, and then through their work see substantial freedom."

Burgard, Peter J. "Two Parts Ibsen, One Part American Dream: On Derivation and Originality in Arthur Miller's *Death of a Salesman.*" *Orbis Litterarum*. 43.4 (1988): 336–53.

Burgard examines Miller's debt to Ibsen "in both thematic and formal composition" as implicitly undermining his supposed originality, concluding that *Death of a Salesman* "controverts the originality the author himself claims for it."

Calhoun, William A., II. "Arthur Miller's Death of a Doctrine or Will the Federal Courts Abstain from Abstaining? The Complex Litigation Recommendations' Impact on the Abstention Doctrines." *Brigham Young University Law Review* 1995.3 (1995): 961+.

Lengthy essay that compares the duality in Miller's *Death of a Salesman* with the duality that exists in the American Law Institute's Complex Litigation Recommendations.

Carlson, Harry G. "Salesman in Time Warp." *Western European Stages* 8.2 (Spring 1996): 63–66.

Account of the Stockholm, Sweden, production of *Death of a Salesman* at the experimental Plazateatern, directed by Thorsten Flinck.

Carpenter, Bruce. "The Little Man and Arthur Miller." *Theatre Time* (Summer 1949): 57–61.

Carpenter examines the drama of the "Little Man" and investigates whether it is an apt subject for tragedy, concluding that Willy Loman is "a completely tragic portrayal for he is torn in conflict between love for his sons and his selfish desire for social exoneration." Additionally, Willy is a universal character who is, ultimately, responsible for his own downfall. A full-page black-and-white production still from the original production of *Death of a Salesman* accompanies the text (requiem scene).

Carson, Herbert. "A Modern Everyman." *Central States Speech Journal* 12 (Winter 1961): 111–13.

Carson examines the similarity between *Death of a Salesman* and the English Morality drama *Everyman* and concludes that "While Willy is still the allegorical character found in morality drama, he is something more: as Arthur Miller admits, today's Everyman is a victim."

Centola, Steven R. "Family Values in *Death of a Salesman.*" *CLA Journal* 37 (September 1993): 29–41.

Centola identifies and analyzes Willy Loman's values in order to "appreciate the intensity of Willy's struggle" and to "help explain why *Death of a Salesman* is a tragedy."

———. "A Sartrean Reading of Arthur Miller's *Death of a Salesman.*" *Journal of Evolutionary Psychology* 9 (August 1988): 297–302.

Centola offers a Sartrean reading of *Death of a Salesman* to help reveal the "more metaphysical issues in the play" and explain the play's universal appeal.

Cook, Kimberly K. "Valentin and Biff: Each Unhappy in His Own Way?" *Journal of Evolutionary Psychology* 16.1–2 (March 1995): 47–52.

Cook compares the wasted lives of Henry James's Valentin de Bellegarde with Miller's Biff Loman "and the family dynamics which formed the personalities" of both characters, suggesting that despite their differences in social status, religion, occupation, and nationality, "these two families share the same kind of pain."

Cook, Larry W. "The Function of Ben and Dave Singleman in *Death of a Salesman.*" *Notes on Contemporary Literature* 5 (January 1975): 7–9.

Cook argues that the inconsistency of Willy Loman's treatment of his sons is not the result of Miller's "superficial thinking," but is derived from the conflict between the two views of life represented in the play by Willy's brother Ben ("ruthless competitor") and Dave Singleman ("well-liked individual").

Couchman, Gordon W. "Arthur Miller's Tragedy of Babbitt." *Educational Theatre Journal* 7 (October 1955): 206–11. Rpt. in *The Merrill Studies in "Death of a Salesman."* Ed. Walter Meserve.

Columbus, Ohio: Merrill, 1972. 68–75.

Couchman compares *Death of a Salesman* with Sinclair Lewis's *Babbitt*, concluding that "at its best, Arthur Miller's play shares with Sinclair Lewis's novel a rare gift for the poetic in the colloquial which redeems both works from being merely depressing."

de Schweinitz, George. "*Death of a Salesman*: A Note on Epic and Tragedy." *Western Humanities Review* 19 (Winter 1960): 91–96. Rpt. in *"Death of a Salesman": Text and Criticism*. Ed. Gerald Weales. New York: Viking, 1967. New York: Penguin, 1996. 272–79. Rpt. in *The Merrill Studies in "Death of a Salesman."* Ed. Walter Meserve. Columbus, Ohio: Merrill, 1972. 52–57.

In an effort to answer the question whether *Death of a Salesman* is a tragedy, de Schweinitz defines the tragic tradition of Western culture and applies them to Miller's play.

Diamond, Catherine. "*Death of a Salesman*." *Theatre Journal* 45 (March 1993): 108–10.

Diamond describes The Performance Workshop production at the National Theater in Taipei, Taiwan, of Miller's *Salesman*, including details of the initial requests and subsequent agreements for Yang Shipeng, director of the Hong Kong Repertory Theatre, to direct a translation of the play, Yang's attempt to present the play without concessions to its Chinese audiences, the impact of the production, and the challenges presented by the modern Chinese acting style.

Dillon, John. "*Salesman no shi*: A Director Discovers the Japanese Essence in an American Classic." *American Theatre* (November 1984): 12–15.

Director Dillon discusses his experiences staging and adapting *Death of a Salesman* in Japan.

Faux, Jeff. "What Now Willy Loman?" *Mother Jones* November 1983: 52–54. Excerpts rpt. in *Understanding "Death of a Salesman": A Student Casebook to Issues, Sources, and Historical Documents*. Ed. Brenda Murphy and Susan C. W. Abbotson. Westport, Conn.: Greenwood, 1999. 212–14.

Faux argues that even though *Death of a Salesman* was written in the 1940s, "Willy Loman could again symbolize a wide-spread middle-class tragedy—people trapped by expectations of status that no longer fit the cruel realities of the labor market."

Ferguson, Alfred R. "The Tragedy of the American Dream in *Death of a Salesman.*" *Thought* 53 (1978): 81–98.

Ferguson sketches a history of the American Dream and argues that Willy Loman is not a tragic hero, but the anti-hero of a failed mythology.

Fichandler, Zelda. "Casting for a Different Truth." *American Theatre* May 1988: 18–23.

In an essay that ruminates on the consequences of taking non-traditional casting as far as one could go, Fichandler posits the question (unanswered): "Can Willy Loman become Wanda Loman without destroying the fabric of the play" whose primary images and point of view are decidedly male?

Field, B. S., Jr. "Hamartia in *Death of a Salesman.*" *Twentieth Century Literature* 18 (1972): 19–24. Rpt. as "*Death of a Salesman*" in *Twentieth Century Interpretations of "Death of a Salesman."* Ed. Helene Wickham Koon. Engelwood Cliffs, N.J.: Prentice-Hall, 1983. 79–84.

Field argues that Willy Loman's "miserable life, miserable death, and that miserable funeral too, are appropriate and decorous" punishment for his "weakness," his "incompetence," his "isolation from nature," his "incapacity to explain his own situation to himself," his "feelings of a loss of identity," his "spiritual dryness," his "lack of love," his "erroneous worship at the alter of personality," and his criminality at making "moral eunuchs of his own sons."

Fuller, A. Howard. "A Salesman Is Everybody." *Fortune* 39 (May 1949): 78–80. Rpt. in *"Death of a Salesman": Text and Criticism.* Ed. Gerald Weales. New York: Viking, 1967. New York: Penguin, 1996. 240–43.

Fuller, president of the Fuller Brush Company from 1943 to 1959, offers his opinion on Miller's drama, saying that its appeal will extend beyond the salesman-audience to "any man whose illusions have made him incapable of dealing realistically with the problems of everyday life. . . . Nearly everyone who sees it can discover some quality displayed by Willy and his sons that exists in himself and in his friends and relatives." Included is a lengthy quote spoken by Miller to Fuller's sales department that points out the double significance of Willy's occupation—he sells products and sells himself. Says Miller, "He is Everyman."

Garebian, Keith. "*Death of a Salesman.*" *Journal of Canadian Studies* 18 (Fall 1983): 152–53.

Garebian faults Guy Sprung's Canadian production of *Death of a Salesman* (designed by Ming Cho Lee) for its miscasting of Nehemiah Persoff as "a most Jewish Willy" whose "wry geniality and complaint made Willy less massive than he could be."

Gassner, John. "Aspects of the Broadway Theatre." *Quarterly Journal of Speech* 35 (February 1949): 289–96.

Despite not being a masterpiece of dramatic literature, or being well written, and having as its hero a "loud-mouthed dolt and emotional babe-in-the-woods," *Death of a Salesman* is "often moving and even gripping" and "expresses a viewpoint of considerable importance" that holds its audience by "making experience of directly recognizable people and situations the paramount consideration."

———. "Tragic Perspectives: A Sequence of Queries." *Tulane Drama Review* 2 (May 1958): 7–22. Rpt. in *Two Modern American Tragedies: Reviews and Criticism of "Death of a Salesman" and "A Streetcar Named Desire."* Ed. John D. Hurrell. New York: Scribner's, 1961. 16–27. Excerpt rpt. in *Major Literary Characters: Willy Loman*. Ed. Harold Bloom. New York: Chelsea, 1991. 7–8.

While Gassner finds that Willy Loman is a tragic hero "by his fine resentment of slights, by his battle for self-respect, and by his refusal to surrender all expectations of triumph for, and through, his son," he also judges it to be a "low tragedy" because of Willy's limitation of language and intelligence.

Gomez, Andrea A. "Modern Tragedies." *St. Louis University Research Journal* 19.1 (June 1988): 35–84.

Summary and analysis of *Death of a Salesman* as a modern tragedy that dramatizes "the needs and aspirations of the representative modern man."

Gordon, Andrew. "Richard Brautigan's Parody of Arthur Miller." *Notes on Modern American Literature* 6:1 (Spring/Summer 1982): Item 8.

Gordon details the similarities between Richard Brautigan's sardonic black comedy takeoff on Miller's *Salesman* entitled *Willard and His Bowling Trophies: A Perverse Mystery* (1975), including their similar story lines, characters, and thematic concerns.

Graybill, Robert V. "Why Does Biff Boff Bimbos? Innocence as Evil in *Death of a Salesman*." *Publications of Arkansas Philological Association* 13 (Fall 1987): 46–53.

Graybill studies Biff's tragic flaw of innocence in an effort to show that *Death of a Salesman* is "as much a result of Biff's innocence as it is Willy's immorality."

Groff, Edward. "Point of View in Modern Drama." *Modern Drama* 2.3 (December 1959): 268–82.

Lengthy essay that briefly examines point of view in *Death of a Salesman* that Groff calls the "simplest and most effective dramatization of the mind's activities" with a psychological complexity that fuses past and present.

Gross, Barry. "Peddler and Pioneer in *Death of a Salesman*." *Modern Drama* 7 (February 1965): 405–10. Rpt. in *The Merrill Studies in "Death of a Salesman."* Ed. Walter Meserve. Columbus, Ohio: Merrill, 1972. 29–34.

Gross studies Miller's use of the American frontier tradition and the motifs of peddler and pioneer in *Death of a Salesman.*

Hadomi, Leah. "Fantasy and Reality: Dramatic Rhythm in *Death of a Salesman*." *Modern Drama* 31.2 (June 1988): 157–74. Rpt. as "Dramatic Rhythm in *Death of a Salesman*." *Major Literary Characters: Willy Loman*. Ed. Harold Bloom. New York: Chelsea, 1991. 112–28. Revised and rpt. as "Rhythm between Fathers and Sons: *Death of a Salesman*." *The Homecoming Theme in Modern Drama. The Return of the Prodigal*. New York: Edwin Mellen, 1992. 49–62, 149–50.

Hadomi explores the ways in which the rhythmic organization of *Death of a Salesman* is expressed in three structural elements: characterization, symbolism, and plotting.

Hark, I. R. "A Frontier Closes in Brooklyn: *Death of a Salesman* and the Turner Thesis." *Postscript* (1986): 1–6.

Essay in which Hark compares Turner's theory of the closing of the American frontier to *Death of a Salesman*, concluding that Willy Loman was doomed by its tragic limitation.

Hart, Jonathan. "The Promised End: The Conclusion of Hoffman's *Death of a Salesman*." *Literature/Film Quarterly* 19.1 (1991): 60–65.

Hart examines the ending of the Hoffman *Death of a Salesman* "to see whether it can illuminate the critical problem of the conclusion of Miller's plays and of its genre [tragedy]."

Hays, Peter L. "Arthur Miller and Tennessee Williams." *Essays in Literature* 4 (1977): 239–49.

Hays examines the similarities between Miller's *Death of a Salesman* and Williams's *The Glass Menagerie* and finds evidence that Williams's earlier work directly influenced Miller in form, theme, production elements, and characterization (over-protective mother figure, rebellious children, demanding parents, and male visitors).

Heilman, Robert B. "Salesmen's Deaths: Documentary and Myth." *Shenandoah* 20 (Spring 1969): 20–28. Rpt. in *Tragedy and Melodrama: Versions of Experience*. Seattle: Washington UP, 1968. 233–37.

This essay compares and contrasts Eudora Welty's short story "The Death of a Traveling Salesman" (1936) and Miller's play *Death of a Salesman* (1949), finding them quite dissimilar in character, location, feeling, and message.

Henian, Yuan. "*Death of a Salesman* in Beijing." *Chinese Literature* 10 (October 1983): 103–109. Rpt. in *The Chinese: Adapting the Past, Building the Future*. Eds. Robert F. Dernberger, et al. Ann Arbor: University of Michigan Center for Chinese Studies, 1986. 605–10.

First-hand account of Miller's visit to China in 1983 to direct his *Death of a Salesman* in Beijing, including his rehearsal process, working with translators and interpreters, and Chinese audience response to his American tragedy.

Hoeveler, D. L. "*Death of a Salesman* as Psychomachia." *Journal of American Culture* 1 (1978): 632–37. Rpt. in *Modern Critical Interpretations: Arthur Miller's "Death of a Salesman."* Ed. Harold Bloom. New York: Chelsea, 1988. 77–82.

Hoeveler argues that none of the characters in *Death of a Salesman* are real but are, instead, "filtered through Willy's perceptions" and represent "aspects of his splintered mind."

Hume, Beverly. "Linda Loman as 'The Woman' in Miller's *Death of a Salesman*." *NMAL: Notes on Modern American Literature* 9 (Winter 1985): Article 14, n.p.

Hume compares Linda Loman with The Woman as characters

who both contain "traces of intense materialism."

Hunter, Frederick J. "The Value of Time in Modern Drama." *Journal of Aesthetics and Art Criticism* 16 (1958): 194–201.

This essay examines the factor of time, "from a technical point of view, as a variable in the effects of a variety of plays." *Death of a Salesman* is studied for its effect of "double time": not only does the play take place during the last day of Willy's life, but he experiences the past and the world of his imagination. These lapses in time are motivated "by Willy's search for self-justification."

Hynes, Joseph. "Attention Must Be Paid." *College English* 23 (April 1962): 574–78. Rpt. in *"Death of a Salesman": Text and Criticism*. Ed. Gerald Weales. New York: Viking, 1967. New York: Penguin, 1996. 280–89.

Hynes finds Miller's work rife with "structural difficulties of varying importance" that, despite the force of the play, has a theme buried in its own confusion.

Innes, Christopher. "The Salesman on the Stage: A Study in the Social Influence of Drama." *English Studies in Canada* 3.3 (Fall 1977): 336–50. Rpt. in *Modern Critical Interpretations: Arthur Miller's "Death of a Salesman."* Ed. Harold Bloom. New York: Chelsea, 1988. 59–75.

Innes analyses Eugene O'Neill's *The Iceman Cometh*, Arthur Miller's *Death of a Salesman*, and Jack Gelber's *The Connection* as explorations of the business world on the American stage.

Inserillo, Charles R. "Wish and Desire: Two Poles of the Imagination in the Drama of Arthur Miller and T. S. Eliot." *Xavier University Studies* 1 (Summer–Fall 1962): 247–58.

Inserillo compares Miller with T. S. Eliot and finds Willy Loman to be a romantic hero who fails to find the "magic" of his life and must turn to suicide to make his dreams a reality.

Jackson, Esther Merle. "*Death of a Salesman*: Tragic Myth in the Modern Theatre." *CLA Journal* 7.1 (September 1963): 63–76. Rpt. in *The Merrill Studies in "Death of a Salesman."* Ed. Walter Meserve. Columbus, Ohio: Merrill, 1972. 57–68. Rpt. in *Modern Critical Views: Arthur Miller*. Ed. Harold Bloom. New York: Chelsea, 1987. 27–37. Rpt. *Modern Critical Interpretations: Arthur Miller's "Death of a Salesman."* Ed. Harold Bloom. New York: Chelsea, 1988. 7–18.

Jackson examines Miller's *Death of a Salesman* within the context of the classic tragic form and the play's impact as a "myth of contemporary life."

Jacobson, Irving. "Family Dreams in *Death of a Salesman*." *American Literature* 47 (1975): 247–58. Rpt. in *Critical Essays on Arthur Miller*. Ed. James J. Martine. Boston: G. K. Hall, 1979. 44–52.

Jacobson argues that while Willy yearns after the images of success projected by his brother Ben, Dave Singleman, and his son Biff, he fails to succeed because he is not, like them, a man who makes the world his home.

James, Stuart B. "Pastoral Dreamer in an Urban World." *University of Denver Quarterly* 1.3 (1966): 45–57.

James criticizes Miller's treatment of Willy Loman as a character who romanticizes "the role of the past in American history," making it impossible for him to have any sort of "accurate evaluation of the present."

Jones, Chris. "Attention Must Be Paid." *American Theatre* 1 January 1999: 12.

Short article in which Jones details the casting of Brian Dennehy, "a colossus of an actor with a stentorian voice" (in the fiftieth anniversary production of *Death of a Salesman*) in a part that Miller intended to be about "that archetypal Little Guy, Willy Loman."

Kanfer, Stefan. "Broadway Flashbacks." *New Leader* 8–22 March 1999: 22–23.

Kanfer examines the 1990s appeal for a 1940s play (*Death of a Salesman*), and concludes "as this most modern revival demonstrates, attention must be paid to Willy Loman. No matter who tells it, his story is permanent."

Kennedy, Sighle. "Who Killed the Salesman?" *Catholic World* 170 (May 1970): 110–16. Rpt. in *Twentieth Century Interpretations of "Death of a Salesman."* Ed. Helene Wickham Koon. Englewood Cliffs, N.J.: Prentice-Hall, 1983. 33–40.

After examining two popular notions regarding the cause of Willy's suicide (that Willy's irrational desire for success killed him or that he was a victim of economic forces beyond his control or design), Kennedy argues that "Willy's tragedy must not be set at the door of his particular type of work," rather, that Willy's death results from the sum of the "the very multiplicity of problems" that confronts him throughout his life.

Kernodle, George. R. "The Death of the Little Man." *Tulane Drama Review* I.2 (1955–56): 47–60.

Kernodle examines the "little man" in three decades (1920s, 1930s, 1940s) as dominant reactions to modern dilemmas. *Death of a Salesman* addresses "the central problem of the modern man in a city—a vision of himself and his place in the world."

Klapp, Orrin E. "Tragedy and the American Climate of Opinion." *Centennial Review of Arts and Science* 2 (Fall 1958): 396–413.

In a lengthy essay that studies the lack of tragic form in American culture, Klapp briefly examines Miller's assertion that the common man is an apt subject for tragedy and agrees with the playwright, as long as the hero "is allowed some loophole of noble choice" and whose victimization "becomes an *opportunity*" for "that burst of heroic determination in defeat which is the essence of tragedy."

Kopald, Meredith. "Arthur Miller Wins a Peace Prize: Teaching, Literature, and Therapy." *English Journal* 81.3 (March 1992): 57–60.

In discussing her teaching method of asking her students to write reaction essays in response to first readings of literature, Kopald recounts the story of Jason, as student whose life was changed in a positive manner after reading Miller's *Death of a Salesman.*

Kramer, Mimi. "The Greatest Salesman of Them All." *New Criterion* 2 (1984): 58–64.

Essay that examines the plethora of salesman plays currently appearing on Broadway, reviews the critical reaction to Miller's *Death of a Salesman*, and offers a reading of the work in light of current sensibilities. Kramer finds that "For thirty-five years Miller has managed to fool Broadway audiences into thinking that he sees the salesman as a dreamer, a man to whom attention must be paid. In this he demonstrates a closer kinship to the characters of David Mamet and Meredith Wilson than to the playwrights themselves. He may, in fact, turn out to be the greatest salesman of them all."

Krohn, Alan. "The Source of Manhood in *Death of a Salesman.*" *International Review of Psycho-Analysis* 15 (1988): 455–63.

Krohn studies the psychologies of Willy and Biff Loman and the play's ability to tap unconscious fantasies in its audiences. Krohn concludes that *Death of a Salesman*'s "universal appeal, and especially its appeal to men, may well be that it deals with the problem of transmission of full male genitality and generativity from one generation to the next, a problem that concerns fathers and sons in every culture."

Lahr, John. "Birth of a Salesman." *New Yorker* 25 December 1995 & 1 January 1996: 110–11. (includes "In Memoriam" by Arthur Miller). Rpt. in excerpt form in *Independent on Sunday* (London) 2 May 1999: 1+.

Lahr relates his discovery of a manuscript, written when Miller was seventeen, in the Harry Ransom library at the University of Texas at Austin "which foreshadows his masterpiece, *Death of a Salesman.*"

Lawrence, Stephen A. "The Right Dream in Miller's *Death of a Salesman.*" *College English* 25 (April 1964): 547–49. Rpt. in *Twentieth Century Interpretations of "Death of a Salesman."* Ed. Helene Wickham Koon. Engelwood Cliffs, N.J.: Prentice-Hall, 1983. 56–59.

In this brief essay, Lawrence posits that "both society and Willy are responsible for the death of a salesman," and reads Happy's graveside declaration that he is going to "take over where his father left off" as Willy's redemption.

Lenz, Harold. "At Sixes and Sevens—A Modern Theatre Structure." *Forum* (Houston) 11 (Summer–Fall 1973, Winter 1974): 73–79.

Lenz reads *Death of a Salesman* as a modern European morality play about a family "at sixes and sevens with itself and with the real world because its members have no separate identities, no independent imaginations, no creative impulse that would free them from the mechanistic dream of a mechanistic success."

Leyburn, Ellen. "Comedy and Tragedy Transposed." *Yale Review* 53 (Summer 1964): 555–57.

Leyburn argues that not only is Willy Loman not a tragic figure, but that he is more like a "long line of aging comic butts who have tried to convince an unbelieving world and themselves that they are 'well-liked.'"

Miles, Thomas O. "Three Authors in Search of a Character." *Personalist* 46 (Winter 1965): 65–72.

Miles compares the male characters in Albert Camus's *Exile and the Kingdom*, Aldous Huxley's *Brave New World*, and Miller's *Death of a Salesman*, concluding that Willy cannot evolve as a character at the same rate as his environment because he "senses himself contradicted by the nature of the culture around him."

Miller, E. S. "Perceiving and Imagining at Plays." *Annli Instituto Universitario Orientale* (Naples) 6.18 (1963): 5–11.

Miller argues that Miller manipulates the audience through flashbacks and shortened elapsed time to create ambiguity in our awareness of Willy Loman.

Miller, Jordan. "Myth and the American Dream: O'Neill to Albee." *Modern Drama* 7 (September 1964): 190–98.

Jordan Miller examines five significant plays by Eugene O'Neill (*The Great God Brown* and *Marco Millions)*, Arthur Miller (*Death of a Salesman*), Tennessee Williams (*Camino Real*), and Edward Albee (*The American Dream*) as warnings of "the fatal possibility of losing everything in the process of trying to achieve the goals of the Myth of the American Dream."

Mitchell, Giles. "Living and Dying for the Ideal: A Study of Willy Loman's Narcissism." *Psychoanalytic Review* 77.3 (Fall 1990): 391–407.

Mitchell argues that the primary cause of Willy Loman's failure and final suicide is "his ego-ideal, which is pathologocially narcissistic."

Murphy, Brenda. "Willy Loman: Icon of Business Culture." *Michigan Quarterly Review* 37.4 (Fall 1998): 754–66.

Murphy examines the public, critical, and business world reaction to *Death of a Salesman*. Initially, the business world attempted to divorce itself from Miller's image of the loser-salesman, but later came to use the play and the image of Willy Loman in advertising and marketing reports, until at last the work became part of the popular culture.

"New Breed of Salesman, Not Like Willy." *Newsweek* 1964: 94–97. Rpt. in *Understanding "Death of a Salesman": A Student Casebook to Issues, Sources, and Historical Documents*. Ed. Brenda Murphy and Susan C. W. Abbotson. Westport, Conn.: Greenwood, 1999. 203–207.

After exploring the "distasteful" aspects of the American salesman, this essay points out the shift from the Willy Loman style of sales with its emphasis on the sales pitch and personal relationships with buyers to the modern breed of better educated salesmen who emphasize service to their customers.

Oberg, Arthur K. "*Death of a Salesman* and Arthur Miller's Search for Style." *Criticism* 9 (Fall 1967): 303–11. Rpt. in *The Merrill Studies in "Death of a Salesman."* Ed. Walter Meserve. Columbus, Ohio: Merrill, 1972. 92–99. Rpt. in *Twentieth Century Interpretations of "Death of a Salesman."* Ed. Helene Wickham Koon. Engelwood Cliffs, N.J.: Prentice-Hall, 1983. 70–78.

Oberg praises what he calls Miller's "stylistically clichéd language, based on the inflection of a New York Jewish speech and rising to a peculiarly American idiom" as the play's most misunderstood and distinctive quality.

Otten, Charlotte F. "Who Am I? A Re-Investigation of Arthur Miller's *Death of a Salesman*." *Cresset* 26 (February 1963): 11–13. Rpt. in *Twentieth Century Interpretations of "Death of a Salesman."* Ed. Helene Wickham Koon. Engelwood Cliffs, N.J.: Prentice-Hall, 1983. 85–91.

Otten examines *Death of a Salesman* as a "profound" and "universal" play that "could speak to every person of every country of every age," much the same way as Sophocles' *Oedipus Rex*.

Otten, Terry. "*Death of a Salesman* at Fifty—Still 'Coming Home to Roost.'" *Texas Studies in Literature and Language* 41.3 (Fall 1999): 280–310.

Extremely thorough essay that examines the issues raised in the critical debates regarding the tragic nature of *Death of a Salesman*, concluding that "what we are left with is perhaps a tragedy despite itself. . . . the play completes the tragic pattern of the past becoming the present, and it affirms the tragic dictum that there are inevitable consequences to choices . . . not 'high tragedy' in Aristotelian terms," but "something more than melodrama or 'low tragedy' in its revelation of tragic vision, choice, awareness, and consequence."

Parker, Brian. "Point of View in Arthur Miller's *Death of a Salesman*." *University of Toronto Quarterly* 35 (January 1966): 144–57. Rpt. in *Modern Critical Interpretations: Arthur Miller's "Death of a Salesman."* Ed. Harold Bloom. New York: Chelsea,

1988. 19–23. Rpt. in *Arthur Miller: A Collection of Critical Essays*. Ed. Robert W. Corrigan. Engelwood Cliffs, N.J.: Prentice-Hall, 1969. 95–109. Rpt. in *Twentieth Century Interpretations of "Death of a Salesman."* Ed. Helene Wickham Koon. Engelwood Cliffs, N.J.: Prentice-Hall, 1983. 41–55.

Contrary to those critics who attack *Death of a Salesman* for its "blurred line between realism and expressionism," Parker defends Miller's structural technique of "apparent uncertainty in apportioning realism and expressionism" as "one of the play's most subtle successes."

Phelps, H. C. "The Fat and the Lean Years of Biff and Bernard: An Overlooked Parallelism in *Death of a Salesman*." *Notes on Contemporary Literature* 25.4 (September 1995): 9–11.

In his brief essay, Phelps argues that Bernard's success, which runs parallel to Biff's failure, should be read as a "sign of the values of hard work, self-discipline, and realistic ambition that no one in the Loman family seems able to recognize, much less act upon." Bernard's function in *Death of a Salesman* is to highlight Miller's bias toward the hard-working life rather than Biff's aimless searching existence.

———. "Miller's *Death of a Salesman*." *Explicator* 1 June 1995: 239–40.

Short essay that examines the conclusion and requiem of *Death of a Salesman* to "reveal a far greater degree of ambiguity than has been acknowledged" (i.e., Loman's determination to commit suicide because Biff has at last declared his "love" for his father).

Pinsker, Sanford. "'The End of the Tether': Joseph Conrad's Death of a Salesman." *Conradiana* 3 (1971): 74–76.

Short essay in which Pinsker compares the characters of Henry Whalley in Conrad's "The End of the Tether" and Willy Loman in *Death of a Salesman*, finding similarities in their predicaments.

Pruiksma, Thomas H. "Stranger at Home." *The Ecologist* 28.6 (November/December 1998): 343–48.

Taking the form of a meditation on *Death of a Salesman*, Pruiksma's lengthy essay "is about what it means to be an American in an age of ecological crisis—how we relate with each other, how we relate to the land, and how these relations are related."

Ranald, Margaret Loftus. "*Death of a Salesman*: Fifteen Years After." *Comment* (New Zealand) 6 (August 1965): 28–35.

Ranald finds the Miller's play dated after the passage of time and rejects Willy Loman as a tragic character, asking if any play of the current era "can fully express the pity, the terror, and the resultant purgative joy, of the human condition."

Riche, Martha Farnsworth. "Willy Loman Rides Again." *American Demographics* 10 (March 1988): 8. Rpt. in *Understanding "Death of a Salesman": A Student Casebook to Issues, Sources, and Historical Documents*. Ed. Brenda Murphy and Susan C.W. Abbotson. Westport, Conn.: Greenwood, 1999. 208–209.

Essay that explores the "old-fashioned" but still-employed method of organizing sales territories by county, a method that Edward Spar, president of Market Statistics, calls "simply a matter of convenience and geographic logic."

Robson, John M. "Tragedy and Society." *Queen's Quarterly* 71(Autumn 1964): 419–33.

Robson's argument concerning tragedy is that while the mask makes if possible for man to be a hero, it also separates the hero from society. Willy Loman in *Death of a Salesman* ends in failure when the demands for success made upon the mask of the salesman becomes too great for the man beneath the mask. "So complete is [Willy's] acceptance of his *persona* that his rage approaches madness when others comment on his ever more obvious failures."

Saisselin, Remy G. "Is Tragic Drama Possible in the Twentieth Century." *Theatre Annual* 17 (1960). 12–21. Rpt. in *The Merrill Studies in "Death of a Salesman."* Ed. Walter J. Meserve. Ohio: Merrill, 1972. 44–51.

In an essay examining the nature of tragic drama, Saisselin briefly mentions *Death of a Salesman* as a work that does not qualify as a tragedy because Willy Loman is a pathetic character who "dies having learned nothing . . . he is not of universal interest and he is not noble."

Sastre, Alfonso. "Drama and Society." *Tulane Drama Review* 5 (December 1960): 102–10.

An open letter on *Death of a Salesman*, addressed to those critics who center their commentary "not on the work itself, but on the reality to which the work bears witness."

Schaars, M. J. "Arthur Miller, Willy Loman and Jason: Responses to Meredith Kopald." *English Journal* 81.3 (March 1992): 61–62.

Two essays by teachers in response to Meredith Kopald's article "Arthur Miller Wins Peace Prize: Teaching, Literature, and Therapy." Both find fault with Kopald's ambivalence at Jason's first reader-response to *Death of a Salesman* and marvel that the situation turned out as well as it did considering its context.

Schneider, Daniel E. M.D. "Play of Dreams." *Theatre Arts* 33 (October 1949): 18–21. Rpt. in *"Death of a Salesman": Text and Criticism*. Ed. Gerald Weales. New York: Viking, 1967. New York: Penguin, 1996. 250–58. Rpt. as "A Modern Playwright—Study of Two Plays by Arthur Miller" in *The Psychoanalyst and the Artist*. New York: Farrar, 1950.

Psychiatrist Schneider evaluates *Death of a Salesman* for its powerful effect as "a dream turned inside out; a brilliant perception and portrayal of the impossible and impermissible ways in which we hurl ourselves against reality and failing, dream out action and consequence as we sleep in our own inner universe of wishes."

Sharma, P. P. "Search for Self-Identity in *Death of a Salesman*." *Literary Criterion* 11 (Summer 1974): 74–79.

Sharma examines the father-son conflict in *Death of a Salesman* and investigates the unenlightened death of Willy Loman, concluding that son Biff's enlightenment at the end of the play makes him a strong candidate for the true protagonist of the play.

Shatzky, Joel. "Arthur Miller's 'Jewish' Salesman." *Studies in American Jewish Literature* 2 (Winter 1976): 1–9.

Shatzky considers how *Death of a Salesman* reflects the development of Miller's artistic and societal sensibility as a Jewish American and notes that this play, unique among American plays, does not suffer in a Yiddish translation.

———. "The 'Reactive Image' and Miller's *Death of a Salesman*." *Players* 48 (February–March 1973): 104–10.

Shatzky argues that Miller's narrow and helpless view of Willy "precludes his success on any level" making "the validity of the American dream in *Death of a Salesman* " never fully realized.

Shaw, Patrick W. "The Ironic Characterization of Bernard in *Death of a Salesman*." *Notes on Contemporary Literature* 11 (May 1981): 12.

In this brief essay, Shaw questions the flattering portrait of Bernard, "a character who clearly succeeds within the capitalist system that Miller otherwise discredits," and concludes that through this positive portrayal Miller is cautioning against an intolerant system that hypocritically offers the promise of success.

Shipley, Joseph T. "Miller's *Salesman*: A Second Look." *New Leader* 10 June 1950: 27.

Shipley gives *Death of a Salesman* a "second look," attending a performance of the play with Albert Dekker in the role of Willy Loman. Shipley applauds Dekker for giving the work "a new and more valid significance." Shipley notes that "the role of Linda Loman and her contribution to the downfall of the male Lomans must not be overlooked. . . . She coddled him, allowing him to find a refuge in his dreams and fancies, instead of gently recalling him to reality."

Shockley, John S. "*Death of a Salesman* and American Leadership: Life Imitates Art." *Journal of American Culture* 17.2 (Summer 1994): 49–56.

Shockley compares Willy Loman with Ronald Reagan and suggests that both the play and Reagan's presidency are dramas about the strength of the American Dream and the level of self-deception involved in that belief.

Siegel, Lee. "Cultural Misconceptions." *New Republic* 2 August 1999: 18–22.

In a lengthy report on the changes that have taken place within the *New York Times* organization and the effects of those changes on the paper and for the public, Siegel looks at the *Times*' obsessive coverage of *Death of a Salesman* to highlight his argument that "Cultural subjects increasingly appear in just about every section of the paper, from the business pages to the editorial page."

Siegel, Paul N. "The Drama and the Thwarted American Dream." *Lock Haven Review* 7 (1965): 52–62.

Siegel traces the motif of the thwarted American Dream in American plays written since World War I as a record of the growing frustration of man in modern society. *Death of a Salesman* is examined for its "unusually powerful effect upon its audiences, an effect which came, whether they realized it or not, from its presentation of the blind alley into which Willy Loman had been led by the American dream."

———. "Willy Loman and King Lear." *College English* 17 (March 1956): 341–45. Rpt. in *Twentieth Century Interpretations of "Death of a Salesman."* Ed. Helene Wickham Koon. Engelwood Cliffs, N.J.: Prentice-Hall, 1983. 92–97.

Siegel compares *Death of a Salesman* with *King Lear* in an effort to show that Miller's work "is a viable representative of the same rare species" of drama whose "tragically mistaken" main character's "capacity to dream and to struggle commands [our] respect."

Smith, Harry W. "An Air of the Dream: Jo Mielziner, Innovation, and Influence, 1935–1955." *Journal of American Drama and Theatre* 5 (Fall 1993): 42–54.

Smith traces the development of designer Jo Mielziner between 1935 and 1955 in an effort to reveal three significant developments that are now standard practices in theatre production: the designer as a "forceful" element in the production team; a streamlining of the pace of the performance through new styles and approaches to scenography; and the renaissance of the open or thrust stage. *Death of a Salesman* is examined as the "dominant icon" of American scenography with its significant influence on the evolution of set design.

Stavney, Anne. "Reverence and Repugnance: Willy Loman's Sentiments toward His Son Biff." *Journal of American Drama and Theatre* 4.2 (Spring 1992): 54–62.

Stavney examines Willy Loman's conflicting feelings of attraction and repulsion toward his son Biff in light of René Girard's framework of triangular desire. Says Stavney, Willy Loman has "lived his life in response to others. . . . Willy's desires are borrowed from those around him. He is caught up in the American Dream of success."

Steene, Birgitta. "The Critical Reception of American Drama in Sweden." *Modern Drama* 5 (May 1962): 71–82.

Article that includes details regarding the critical impact of *Death of a Salesman* in Sweden. Says Steene, few critics "would agree that its tragic impact was universal." It was not until director Alf Sjöberg toned down the "American atmosphere" and stressed the expressionism that the play became "not the tragedy of an American salesman, but the Tragedy of Fatherhood."

Steyn, Mark. "The Revenge of Art" *New Criterion* March 1999: 46–50.

Lengthy essay detailing the fiftieth anniversary production of *Death of a Salesman* directed by Robert Falls, in which Steyn explores the work's thematic relevance, critical response to the original production, Miller's political involvements, and the "inanity" of Miller's "rage" against Broadway "shows" versus London "plays." "Listen to Miller's critique and you understand the glibness of much of his later work: is a man who sees the form he's worked in all his life in such facile cartoon terms likely to have much to tell us about the rest of the world?"

Tyson, Lois. "The Psychological Politics of the American Dream: *Death of a Salesman* and the Case for an Existential Dialectics." *Essays in Literature* 19.2 (Fall 1992): 260–78.

Tyson offers a close reading of *Death of a Salesman* using existential dialectics as a framework in an attempt to answer the question, "How do psychology and ideology intersect in this drama to make the traditional Americanist separation of psyche and socius an untenable theoretical construct?"

Vogel, Dan. "From Milkman to Salesman: Glimpses of the Galut." *Studies in American Jewish Literature* 10.2 (Fall 1991): 172–78.

Vogel surveys critical commentary that reads *Death of a Salesman* as having a "Jewish tone and consciousness," and asserts that "Miller's supreme creation, Willy Loman," is "bound by an unconscious continuity to Sholom Aleichem's supreme creation, Tevye the milkman of Kasrilivke."

Waterstradt, Jean Anne. "Making the World a Home: The Family Portrait in Drama." *Brigham Young University Studies* 19 (1979): 201–21.

Waterstradt examines the treatment of the family in literature in the context of "Mormonism's overriding commitment to the family." Investigating why the family tragedy of *Death of a Salesman* affects its readers in such a personal way, she concludes that this negative example of family life is "too easily recognizable for us to scoff at; their plight is too familiar for us to feel superior to them."

Wattenberg, Richard. "Staging William James's *World of Pure Experience*: Arthur Miller's *Death of a Salesman*." *Theatre Annual: A Journal of Performance Studies* 38 (1983): 49–64.

Wattenberg compares the dramatic form of *Salesman* with the notion of a "world of pure experience" as conceived by William James.

Weales, Gerald. "Plays and Analysis." *Commonweal* 12 July 1957: 382–83. Rpt. in *Major Literary Characters: Willy Loman*. Ed. Harold Bloom. New York: Chelsea, 1991. 6.

Finding Willy Loman Miller's "most completely realized character," Weales laments that *Death of a Salesman* has a confused conflict (love as the opposite of success)—"Willy is so carefully conceived as a victim of self-delusion . . . that it is impossible to conceive of him as ever having the right dream. The theme of the play is swallowed by the excellence of the character who should embody it."

Wellek, Judith S. "Kohut's Tragic Man: An Example from *Death of a Salesman*." *Clinical Social Work Journal* 21.2 (Summer 1993): 213–25.

Wellek applies Heinz Kohut's self-psychology framework and Andrew Morrison's definition of shame to an examination of Willy Loman's sense of self, his awareness of shame, and his decision to commit suicide.

"Why Willy Loman Lives." *Economist* (London) 19 June 1999: 28.

Essay that investigates the modern relevance of *Death of a Salesman*, currently enjoying a popular resurgence, despite a positive economy and low unemployment rate.

Witt, Jonathan. "Song of the Unsung Antihero: How Arthur Miller's *Death of a Salesman* Flatters Us." *Literature and Theology* 12.2 (June 1998): 205–16.

Witt argues that Willy Loman, the "unheroic protagonist" in *Death of a Salesman*, flatters the audience by virtue of our alienation from his downfall. Further, that Miller romanticizes Loman through what Witt calls "the audience's paradox"—the tension that is created when a work employs "an obscure and lowly character as protagonist and so makes him the center of our attention," thus becoming "famous."

Zoglin, Richard. "The Kindness of Foreigners." *Time* 3 February 1997: 72–73.

Zoglin explores the reasons behind the current influx of successful American revivals to the British stage (including the National Theatre's production of *Death of a Salesman*, starring Alun Armstrong, directed by David Thacker), and finds the Thacker production "elegant."

Zorn, Theodore E. "Willy Loman's Lesson: Teaching Identity Management with *Death of a Salesman*." *Communication Education* 40 (April 1991): 219–24.

Zorn, an assistant professor of Speech Communication at the University of North Carolina at Chapel Hill, explains his methodology in using *Death of a Salesman* to "illustrate the reciprocal relationship between self-concept and communication in the negotiation of identities."

Critical Essays in Newspapers

"Attention Must Still Be Paid." *Minneapolis Star Tribune* 28 June 1999: A6.

Essay arguing for the cultural relevancy of a fifty-year-old play about a man who "became a symbol of the dark side of the American Dream that he so firmly believed in."

Carroll, Luke P. "Birth of a Legend: First Year of *Salesman*." *New York Herald Tribune* 5 February 1950: Sec. 5: 1.

Carroll relates the phenomenon of Miller's *Death of a Salesman* becoming "a legend in many parts of the world" after only one year in production, including details of the play's impact on theatre audiences and other ordianry people who have written Miller 1,087 letters from those who have both seen the play and only heard about it.

Freedman, Samuel G. "Parent's Worst Sin Is Betraying a Child's Admiration." *USA Today* 9 February 1999: A17.

After detailing the flashback scene between Willy and Biff in the Boston hotel room, Freedman praises the timing of the fiftieth anniversary production of *Death of a Salesman*, starring Brian Dennehy, for "in Biff's discovery of his father's true self, Miller has given contemporary audiences a piercing commentary on President Clinton's hypocrisy." Freedman finds parallels between Biff's discovery of Willy's adultery with Chelsea Clinton's assumed reaction to her father's indiscretion with Monica Lewinsky.

Hansberry, Lorraine. "An Author's Reflections: Willy Loman, Walter Younger, and He Who Must Live." *Village Voice* 12 August 1959: 7. Excerpt rpt. in *Major Literary Characters: Willy Loman*. Ed. Harold Bloom. New York: Chelsea, 1991. 8–9.

Hansberry discusses the universal relevancy of *Death of a Salesman*, concluding that "the potency of the great tale of a salesman's death was in our familiar recognition of his entrapment which, suicide or no, is *deathly*."

Goodman, Walter. "Miller's *Salesman*, Created in 1949, May Mean More to 1975." *New York Times* 15 June 1975: II: 1, 5.

After surveying the critical praise that the original postwar production of *Death of a Salesman* received in 1949 at a time when America was moving toward prosperity, Goodman investigates the continued power of Miller's drama in a time when "things are not going well," when "many who played by the rules and thought they were secure are for the first time experiencing insecurity; salesmen are in trouble and the country is not in a giving mood."

Gurewitsch, Matthew. "Rediscovering an American Classic by Way of Britain; a Country of Lesser Giants." *New York Times* 4 April 1999: Sect. 2: 1.

Gurewitsch investigates what makes a classic drama and finds that America has yet to produce a drama "worthy to set beside the Greek tragedians, Shakespeare, Calderon, Schiller, Ibsen, [or] Chekhov"—all of "our masterpieces of serious drama are dramas of failure," including Miller's *Death of a Salesman*.

Kakutani, Michiko. "A *Salesman* Who Transcends Time." *New York Times* 7 February 1999: Sec. 2: 1.

Lengthy commentary in which Kakutani relates various debates surrounding the literary and theatrical value of *Death of a Salesman*—its status as a tragedy, the ethnicity of the play's hero, and the reputation of the playwright as "an epigone of Ibsenism, a preachy, pompous and, yes, portentous writer who belongs, like Clifford Odets and Lillian Hellman, to the middlebrow, premodernist past."

Lyons, Donald. "*Salesman* Turns 50." *New York Post Online* (4 April 1999).

Lyons examines the theme of family in *Death of a Salesman*, concluding that "it is the family that wants to determine and the individual that wants to break free. In the charged polarity between these forces lies the source of much American drama."

Mamet, David. "The Jew for Export." *Guardian* (London) 30 April 1994. Rpt. in *Make-Believe Town: Essays and Remembrances*. Boston: Little, Brown, 1996. 137–43.

In an essay discussing the position of the Jew as a minority in film and theatre, Mamet says he feels that "a great contribution to Jewish and to Jewish American history is lost" because Miller never avowed *Death of a Salesman* as a Jewish story.

Mason, M. S. "The Guthrie's Shows Tap Many Cultures." *Christian Science Monitor* 27 August 1991: Arts: 10.

In an article on nontraditional casting, mention is made of the Guthrie Theater's casting black actors as the Loman family and critical reaction, including comments by the actors themselves, is examined.

Miller, Matthew. "Hail Arthur Miller's Gift to Culture as the Antidote to Lewinsky's." *Minneapolis Star Tribune* 17 February 1999: A15.

Essay encouraging a reexamination of Miller's *Death of a Salesman* at a "moment when our culture itself seems to have been impeached."

Rose, Lloyd. "The Many Faces of the Salesman; Onstage, an Enduring American Archetype." *Washington Post* 25 April 1999: G1.

Essay examining the emblematic figure of the salesman on the American stage, who, according to Rose, "without precisely defining it, contains within himself the darker contradictions of his society."

Roth, Morry. "Un-Do *Death of a Salesman*: Vince Lombardi vs. Willy Loman." *Variety* 16 April 1969: 7. Excerpt rpt. in *Understanding "Death of a Salesman": A Student Casebook to Issues, Sources, and Historical Documents*. Ed. Brenda Murphy and Susan C. W. Abbotson. Westport, Conn.: Greenwood, 1999. 207–208.

Roth explores the attempts by American business to offset Miller's "sales-derogating drama" *Death of a Salesman* by showing "Second Chance," a sales motivational film by Vince Lombardi.

Sandomir, Richard. "Lingerie or Hardware, It's a Heavy Burden." *New York Times* 30 March 1999: E1.

Sandomir ruminates on the specific nature of Willy Loman's

line of sales, pulling clues from Miller's script as well as consulting Gerald Weales, a Miller scholar. Ultimately lamenting his inability to pin down the facts, Sandomir feels that "perhaps knowing the products would help us understand [Willy's] spiral into emotional destruction."

Schvey, Henry. "Willy Loman in the White House." *St. Louis Post-Dispatch* 8 October 1998: B7.

Interesting essay in which Schvey compares the character of Willy Loman in *Death of a Salesman* to President Bill Clinton.

Swanson, Stevenson. "*Death* Alive at 50, Arthur Miller's Sobering Play Is a Half-Century Old, but its Message Still Churns Up Americans' Fear of Failure." *Chicago Tribune* 10 February 1999: 1.

After brief note of the forthcoming Broadway opening of the Goodman Theatre's critically acclaimed production of *Death of a Salesman* starring Brian Dennehy, Swanson discusses possible reasons why the play continues to affect its audiences—because "the issues it addresses, such as the lure of money and the brutal way American business punishes failure, are as alive in 1999 as they were in 1949."

Tierney, John. "Willy Loman: Revenge of a Nephew." *New York Times* 8 February 1999: B1.

Article detailing Miller's model for Willy Loman (his uncle Manny Newman) and the play's relevance to modern society. Says Tierney, "Willy Loman is not a representative figure—most Brooklyn salesmen did quite nicely over the last half century, and few of them were ever as pathetic as Willy. But to certain Manhattanites, it may be comforting to imagine the vulgarians like him and Manny Newman are hopelessly stuck across the river."

Williams, Tennessee. "Concerning the Timeless World of the Play." *New York Times* 14 January 1951: 13. Rpt. as "The Timeless World of a Play" in *Two Modern American Tragedies: Reviews and Criticism of "Death of a Salesman" and "A Streetcar Named Desire."* Ed. John D. Hurrell. New York: Scribner's, 1961. 49–52. Rpt. in *Perspectives on Drama*. Eds. James L. Calderwood, and Harold E. Toliver. New York: Oxford UP, 1968. Rpt. as "Introduction to *The Rose Tattoo*." *Three by Tennessee*. New York: New American Library, 1976. 129–33.

Williams defends Miller's *Death of a Salesman* against criticism by Ivor Brown who "reveals a strikingly false conception of what plays are." Brown had written that the character of Willy Loman was the sort of man that any audience member would have kicked out of an office had he applied for a job or started a conversation about his troubles. Says Williams, because of the conventions of drama of showing us what we miss, "we would receive [Willy] with concern and kindness and even respect."

Production Reviews

Abirached, Robert. "Allez à Aubervilliers." *Le Nouvel Observateur* 27 (20 May 1965): 32–33. Rpt. in *The Merrill Studies in "Death of a Salesman."* Ed. Walter J. Meserve. Columbus, Ohio: Merrill Pub., 1972. 17–19.

Positive review of the French production of *Death of a Salesman* that Abirached calls "a modern tragedy" that "shows the unbearable tension that is created between a human being and the society that molds him."

Atkinson, Brooks. "*Death of a Salesman*: Arthur Miller's Tragedy of an Ordinary Man." *New York Times* 20 February 1949: II: 1. Rpt. in *Two Modern American Tragedies: Reviews and Criticism of "Death of a Salesman" and "A Streetcar Named Desire."* Ed. John D. Hurrell. New York: Scribner's, 1961. 54–56.

Atkinson lauds Miller's play as "one of the finest dramas in the whole range of the American theatre. Humane in its point of view, it has stature and insight, awareness of life, respect for people and knowledge of American manners and modern folkways. From the technical point of view, it is virtuoso theatre."

———. "*Death of a Salesman* a New Drama by Arthur Miller, Has Premiere at the Morosco." *New York Times* 11 February 1949: 27. *New York Theatre Critics' Reviews* 10 (1949): 361. Rpt. as "Arthur Miller: *Death of a Salesman*" in *The Lively Years 1940–1950*. New York: AP, 1973. 203–207. Rpt. in *Critical Essays on Arthur Miller*. Ed. James J. Martine. Boston: G. K. Hall, 1979. 21–22.

Atkinson praises *Death of a Salesman* for its "superb" writing and "deeply moving" performances. . . . Miller has looked with compassion into the hearts of some ordinary Americans and quietly transferred their hopes and anguish to the theatre."

———. "Much Prized Play." *New York Times* 15 May 1949: II: 1.
Atkinson applauds the public for recognizing the play's integrity, noting that *Death of a Salesman* ranks as one of the great works of the American theatre.

———. "Portrait of Willy." *New York Times* 12 March 1950: II: 1.
In addition to reporting on the casting change of Gene Lockhart replacing Lee J. Cobb after thirteen exceptional months of playing Willy Loman, Atkinson notes the universality and insightful themes of the play.

———. "Thomas Mitchell Brings His Portrait of Willy Loman to the Morosco." *New York Times* 21 September 1950: 20.
Atkinson feels that the casting of Thomas Mitchell, replacing Gene Lockhart (who replaced Lee J. Cobb), in the role of Willy Loman has weakened the production, making it less serious and pathetic instead of tragic.

Bagar, Robert. "*Death of a Salesman* an Unsung Opera." *New York World Telegram* 26 March 1949: 5.
Bagar lauds the music for *Death of a Salesman*, composed by Alex North, noting the five main themes that constitute the symphonic work. Of note is Bagar's comment that, all told, the music runs just under twenty-four minutes. "If it went over 24 and a half," he continues, "it would be considered a score for a musical show, requiring, as you may well imagine, additional weekly expenditures by the sponsors. It would be in a higher union-regulation bracket."

Barnes, Clive. "*Death of a Salesman* Comes Alive." *New York Post* 30 March 1984. *New York Theatre Critics' Reviews* 45 (1984): 326–27.
Calling the Dustin Hoffman, John Malkovich revival "magnificent, muted and moving," Barnes extols Michael Rudman's direction as "definitive," Hoffman's Willy as "a performance of genius," and Miller's play "one of the triumphs of 20th-Century drama."

———. "*Salesman* Is Still a Seller." *New York Post* 14 February 1999. http://www.deathofasalesman.com/rev-99-nypost-barnes.htm (11 May 1999).
Barnes surveys some seven different Willy Loman's since Lee J. Cobb's original in 1949 and finds that Brian Dennehy's perfor-

mance in the fiftieth anniversary production "magnificent" and that the Robert Falls production "defines our world."

———. "Scott Puts Acting Magic in *Salesman*." *New York Times* 27 June 1975: 26. *New York Theatre Critics' Reviews* 36 (1975): 225.

Rave review of the Circle in the Square revival directed by and starring George C. Scott. Barnes lauds Scott's performance as "exciting beyond words, and almost literally leaving criticism speechless," Scott's staging as "bold and vivid," and Miller's tragedy as "gratifyingly as magnificent, as dense and as meaningful a play as it was first produced soon after World War II."

Barnes, Howard. "A Great Play Is Born." *New York Herald Tribune* 11 February 1949: 14. *New York Theatre Critics' Reviews* 10 (1949): 358.

Barnes lauds the premiere production, stating that "A great play of our day has opened at the Morosco. *Death of a Salesman*, by Arthur Miller, has majesty, sweep and shattering dramatic impact."

Beaufort, John. "Miller's *Death of a Salesman* Is Reborn on Broadway." *Christian Science Monitor* 30 March 1984. *New York Theatre Critics' Reviews* 45 (1984): 331.

Beaufort lauds the Dustin Hoffman, John Malkovich production as "a renaissance rather than merely a worthy revival," and praises Hoffman's Willy Loman as "an extraordinary performance. It is a revelation."

———. "Visions of America's Past—Recent." *Christian Science Monitor* 27 June 1975: 26. *New York Theatre Critics' Reviews* 36 (1975): 224.

In an otherwise positive review, Beaufort faults the Circle in the Square revival directed by and starring George C. Scott for its "intimate actor-to-spectator relationship of the arena auditorium, the unsparing drabness of Marjorie Kellogg's scenery, and a certain heavy-handed naturalism in which the literal predominates over illusion."

Bemrose, John. "Dreams and Despair." *Maclean's* 16 June 1997: 62–63.

Generally favorable review of the Stratford Festival's production of *Death of a Salesman*, directed by Diana Leblanc. On a negative note, Bemrose criticizes Al Waxman's Willy Loman as "too opaque, too earthbound, too far from desperation. He never really catches the tragic fever that would light the stage."

Bentley, Eric. "Back to Broadway." *Theatre Arts* 33 (November 1949): 12–15.

Bentley argues that *Death of a Salesman* is not a true tragedy for it only arouses pity—the "'tragedy' destroys the social drama" and the "social drama keeps the 'tragedy' from having fully dramatic stature."

Beyer, William. "The State of the Theatre: The Season Opens." *School and Society* 3 December 1949: 363–64. Rpt. in *"Death of a Salesman": Text and Criticism*. Ed. Gerald Weales. New York: Viking, 1967. New York: Penguin, 1996. 228–30.

Positive review of the premiere production, starring Lee J. Cobb and Mildred Dunnock, that Beyer calls "provocative, moving, and occasionally eloquent." Of note is Beyer's opinion that the play "is essentially the mother's tragedy . . . Willy's plight is sad, true, but he is unimportant and too petty, commonplace, and immature to arouse more than pity, and the sons are of a piece with their father."

Billington, Michael. "*Death of a Salesman.*" *Guardian* (London) 2 November 1996. *Theatre Record* 16.22 (1996): 1366.

Billington calls the Royal National Theatre production, directed by David Thacker, "a well-staged revival that understands how Miller's social realism melts into the framework of a dream."

Blumenthal, Eileen. "Liked, but Not Well Liked." *Village Voice* 10 April 1984: 77.

Negative review of the Michael Rudman production, starring Dustin Hoffman. Blumenthal finds the play rife with "lapses in craft" and a "clumsy, misguided attempt at tragic stature. . . . Willy Loman played by a movie star, in a production surrounded by movie star PR, like Willy Loman with Mythic Significance, is no longer the little man for whom the play pretends to plead for attention."

Brantley, Ben. "A Dark New Production Illuminates *Salesman.*" *New York Times* 3 November 1998: E1.

Lengthy favorable review of the Goodman Theatre's production of *Death of a Salesman*, directed by Robert Falls and starring

Brian Dennehy. Brantley praises the direction, the performances, the play, and Miller—"Mr. Fall's production comes closer than any I have witnessed in taking us" to the original title of the work, "Inside His Head."

———. "So Attention Must Be Paid. Again." *New York Times* 11 February 1999: B1.

With "powerhouse staging" and "majestic" acting by Brian Dennehy, Brantley commends the fiftieth anniversary production, directed by Robert Falls, as a "harrowing revival" and "almost operatic emotional sweep in examining one unhappy family and the desperate, mortally wounded father at its center."

"Bringing Miller Back into Favour." *Financial Times* (London) 12 February 1999: Arts: 12.

Positive review of the fiftieth anniversary production, starring Brian Dennehy and directed by Robert Falls, in which the critic calls the show "solid and simple."

Brooks-Dillard, Sandra. "*Salesman* Filled with Sadness." *Denver Post* 7 March 1996: E8.

While praising Hal Holbrook as having "almost unbelievable virtuosity," Brooks-Dillard dislikes this production of *Death of a Salesman*, directed by Gerald Freedman, for not being "able to overcome Miller's talky first act or the theater's notoriously bad sound system."

Brown, Georgina. "*Death of a Salesman.*" *Mail on Sunday* (London) 10 November 1996. *Theatre Record* 16.22 (1996): 1365.

"Disappointing" production by the Royal National Theatre Company, directed by David Thacker, that suffers because of Alun Armstrong's "distinctly underwhelming performance" as Loman.

Brown, Ivor. "Loman over Jordan." *Observer* (London) 31 July 1949: 6.

In a now famous review of the London production of *Death of a Salesman*, starring Paul Muni, Brown remarks on the differing reactions of New York and London audiences to the play. While Britons know themselves to be less vulgar in belief in material goods and popularity as a measure of success, and thus less inclined to identify with the play, New Yorkers applaud Willy as a "form of penitence, since most of them would kick him out as a pestilent nuisance if he came badgering them for help."

———. "As London Sees Willy Loman." *New York Times Magazine* 28 August 1949: 11, 59. Rpt. in *The Play*. Ed. Eric Bentley. Engelwood Cliffs, N.J.: Prentice-Hall, 1951. 732–36. Rpt. in *"Death of a Salesman": Text and Criticism*. Ed. Gerald Weales. New York: Viking, 1967. New York: Penguin, 1996. 244–49.

Brown complains that *Death of a Salesman* is too provincial for British tastes and too specifically American. Additionally, Brown argues that there is no tragedy because the protagonist is not worth bothering about.

Brown, John Mason. "American Tragedy." *Saturday Review of Literature* 6 August 1949. Rpt. in *Still Seeing Things*. J. M. Brown. New York: McGraw-Hill, 1950. 185–95. Rpt. in *Dramatis Personae: A Retrospective Show*. John Mason Brown. New York: Viking, 1963. 23–30.

Brief mention of *Death of a Salesman* as the "story of a 'little man' who is sentenced to discover his smallness rather than a big man undone by his greatness." Brown agrees with Miller that the common man is as apt a subject for tragedy in its highest sense as kings were.

———. "Seeing Things: Even as You and I." *Saturday Review of Literature* 26 February 1949: 30–32. Rpt. in *Still Seeing Things*. J. M. Brown. New York: McGraw-Hill, 1950. 196–204. Rpt. in *Dramatis Personae: A Retrospective Show*. John Mason Brown. New York: Viking, 1963. 94–100. Rpt. in *"Death of a Salesman": Text and Criticism*. Ed. Gerald Weales. New York: Viking, 1967. New York: Penguin, 1996. 205–11.

Brown praises *Death of a Salesman* as "the most poignant statement of man as he must face himself to have come out of our theatre. It finds the stuffs of life so mixed with the stuffs of the stage that they become one and indivisible."

Brustein, Robert. "The Artifact Museum." *New Republic* 5 April 1999: 29.

Brustein lauds the 1999 revival, starring Brian Dennehy and Elizabeth Franz, as a "powerfully acted" production that "still has a wrenching power, much of it derived (despite occasional archaisms such as 'Nobody dast blame this man') from the perfect pitch of the dialogue."

Cagle, Jess. "Revival Meeting." *Entertainment Weekly* 12 March 1999: 58.

Brief item praising the fiftieth anniversary production, starring Brian Dennehy and Elizabeth Franz, as a work that has "taken its rightful place in the pantheon of Great World Literature." Cagle additionally praises Franz's Linda for becoming "the play's unlikely spine."

Canby, Vincent. "For This *Salesman*, a Soft Sell Is the Way." *New York Times* 21 February 1999: Sec. 2: 14.

Mixed review of the fiftieth anniversary production of *Death of a Salesman* starring Brian Dennehy and directed by Robert Falls. Says Canby, "The production doesn't do damage to this seminal work, but the play isn't fully there. . . . Mr. Dennehy can play the superficial Willy, the hail-fellow-well-met drummer, but the anguished soul within never emerges with conviction."

Cassidy, Claudia. "Claudia Cassidy Reviews *Death of a Salesman*." *Chicago Daily Tribune* 21 October 1949. Rpt. in *The Passionate Playgoer: A Personal Scrapbook*. Ed. George Oppenheimer. New York: Viking, 1963. 600–601.

Highly positive review of the Chicago production staged by Harold Clurman and starring Thomas Mitchell. Says Cassidy, "This is a somber, compassionate, penetrating, and powerful play that grips you by the throat before it has finished."

———. "Looking Back to Richer Plays." *Chicago* (March 1984): 20–24.

In a review of three revivals (Tennessee Willliams's *The Glass Menagerie*, Miller's *Death of a Salesman*, and William Saroyan's *The Time of Your Life*), Cassidy feels that Dustin Hoffman "lacks the statue, physical and theatrical" to play the part of Willy Loman. "He is a good actor—we all know that. But here he is dwarfed and unimportant, a fatal blow to a play whose death knell sounds like the lift of the curtain."

Chapman, John. "*Death of a Salesman* a Fine Play, Beautifully Produced and Acted." *New York Daily News* 11 February 1949. *New York Theatre Critics' Reviews* 10 (1949): 361.

Praising *Death of a Salesman*'s writing, acting, directing, and design, Chapman urges his readers to attend a performance: "To see it is to have one of those unforgettable times in which all is right and nothing is wrong."

Christiansen, Richard. "Brilliant Revival Proves a Golden Anniversary, for *Salesman*." *Chicago Tribune* 29 September 1998. http://www.deathofasalesman.com/rev-98-chictribune.htm (27 February 1999).

Highly laudatory review of the fiftieth anniversary production directed by Robert Falls and starring Brian Dennehy. Says Christiansen, "It's a mind-opening production, in a staging so inventive and a performance so powerful that it creates a new standard of excellence for an ageless drama."

———. "Hoffman, *Salesman* Deliver a Powerful Product." *Chicago Tribune* 20 January 1984: Sec. 2: 8.

Christiansen says that the Michael Rudman production of *Death of a Salesman*, starring Dustin Hoffman and John Malkovich, "sometimes drags and sometimes limps. . . . But when the drama connects, when the agony within Willy cries out, or when his errant son Biff finallly tries to show him the truth of his life, the emotional powerof the 35 year old play rips through the years and staggers its audience with its force."

———. "*Salesman* Hits Road with Better Wares." *Chicago Tribune* 17 February 1984: Sec. 5: 2.

Christiansen reports of the ending of the five week run of *Death of a Salesman*, starring Dustin Hoffman, that has "settled down technically and noticeably improved esthetically."

Clark, Eleanor. "Old Glamour, New Gloom. " *Partisan Review* 16.6 (June 1949): 631–35. Rpt. in *Two Modern American Tragedies: Reviews and Criticism of "Death of a Salesman" and "A Streetcar Named Desire."* Ed. John D. Hurrell. New York: Scribner's, 1961. 61–64. Rpt. in *"Death of a Salesman": Text and Criticism*. Ed. Gerald Weales. New York: Viking, 1967. New York: Penguin, 1996. 217–23.

Rare negative review of the premiere production of *Death of a Salesman* that Clark calls "flat," "unpleasantly pompous," and "a very dull business." Clark continues: "Everything is stated, two or three times over, all with a great air of something like poetry about it but actually with no remove, no moment of departure from the literal whatever; through scene after snappy scene the action ploughs along on a level of naturalism that has not even the virtue of being natural."

Clurman, Harold. "Attention!" *New Republic* 28 February 1949: 26–28. Rpt. in Clurman's *Lies Like Truth*. New York: Macmillan, 1949. Rpt. in *The Merrill Studies in "Death of a Salesman."* Ed. Walter J. Meserve. Columbus, Ohio: Merrill Pub., 1972. 6–8. Rpt. in *The Collected Works of Harold Clurman: Six Decades of Commentary on Theatre, Dance, Music, Film, Arts and Letters*. Eds. Marjorie Loggia and Glenn Young. New York: Applause, 1994. 188–90.

While faulting *Death of a Salesman* for its lack of "genuine pathos" and its "tone of histrionic bravura," Clurman rates the overall production as "a high point of significant expression in the American theatre of our time."

———. "*Death of a Salesman*." *Nation* 19 July 1975: 59–60. Rpt. in *The Collected Works of Harold Clurman: Six Decades of Commentary on Theatre, Dance, Music, Film, Arts and Letters*. Eds. Marjorie Loggia and Glenn Young. New York: Applause, 1994. 848–49.

In a mixed review of the Circle in the Square revival of *Death of a Salesman*, starring George C. Scott, Clurman praises the text of the play as "one of the signal best in the entire American repertory" and Scott's acting as "vivid" and "arresting," but faults the production for suffering "from a certain dryness, overcome only by the intrinsic spirit of the text."

———. "The Success Dream on the American Stage." *Tomorrow* 8 (May 1949): 48–51. Rpt. in "Arthur Miller, 1949." *Lies Like Truth*. New York: Macmillan, 1958. 68–72. Rpt. in *"Death of a Salesman": Text and Criticism*. Ed. Gerald Weales. New York: Viking, 1967. New York: Penguin, 1996. 212–16. Rpt. in *Two Modern American Tragedies: Reviews and Criticism of "Death of a Salesman" and "A Streetcar Named Desire."* Ed. John D. Hurrell. New York: Scribner's, 1961. 65–67 Rpt. in *The Collected Works of Harold Clurman: Six Decades of Commentary on Theatre, Dance, Music, Film, Arts and Letters*. Eds. Marjorie Loggia and Glenn Young. New York: Applause, 1994. 199–202. Rpt. as "Willy Loman and the American Dream" in *Readings on Arthur Miller*. Ed. Thomas Siebold. San Diego, Calif.: Greenhaven, 1997. 132–36.

While admitting to some minor flaws in the premiere production of the play, starring Lee J. Cobb and Mildred Dunnock and directed by Elia Kazan, Clurman dismisses other critics' objections and lauds Miller's work as "one of the outstanding plays in the repertory of the American theatre." It is Willy's belief in the false ideology of American dream that finally destroys him.

Coe, Richard L. "Arena's *Death*: Alive and Well." *Washington Post* 24 October 1974: B1, 11.

Coe lauds the Arena Stage production, starring Robert Prosky and Dorothea Hammond, as "one of the finest in its history" and containing "a cast without a weak link."

Coleman, Robert. "*Death of a Salesman* Is Emotional Dynamite." *Daily Mirror* 11 February 1949. *New York Theatre Critics' Reviews* 10 (1949): 360.

Reporting that opening night audiences were stirred "so deeply that sobs were heard throughout the auditorium," Coleman praises the production of *Death of a Salesman* as an "exciting and devastating a theatrical blast as the nerves of modern playgoers can stand" and urges his readers to "rush to the Morosco early this morning to purchased tickets" and not to "forget to take along a plentiful supply of handkerchiefs."

Coveney, Michael. "*Death of a Salesman*." *Observer* (London) 3 November 1996. *Theatre Record* 16.22 (1996): 1363–64.

Lukewarm review of the Royal National Theatre Company revival, directed by David Thacker, that Coveney finds "decent" and "respectful."

Cunningham, Dennis. "*Death of a Salesman*." CBS. WCBS, New York. 29 March 1984. *New York Theatre Critics' Reviews* 45 (1984): 332.

Mixed review of the Dustin Hoffman *Death of a Salesman* that Cunningham likes for its "intelligence" and "professionalism," but criticizes for Hoffman's "mechanical" performance.

Darlington, W. A. "London Sees Miller's *Death of a Salesman*." *New York Times* 7 August 1949: II: 1.

Darlington argues that the London production of *Death of a Salesman* succeeds despite the American themes and characters due to the universal nature of the work as an indictment of materialism in every country.

de Jongh, Nicholas. "*Death of a Salesman*." *Evening Standard* (London) 1 November 1996. *Theatre Record* 16.22 (1996): 1364–65.

After calling the Royal National Theatre Company revival "sumptuous," de Jongh questions the continued accolades afforded Miller's work—"The play still exerts its dramatic hold, but its truths do not strike me as arranged in arresting or profound theatrical form."

"*Death of a Salesman.*" *Booklist* 1 May 1949: 289.

Brief positive review of the printed version of Miller's play. "All the Lomans, even the disillusioned but loving wife, are weak in one way or another, but each merits some degree of the reader's sympathy."

"*Death of a Salesman.*" *New Yorker* 21 May 1949: 117.

Positive review of the published version of *Death of a Salesman* that the author calls "a deeply affecting tragedy."

"*Death of a Salesman.*" *Times* (London) 29 July 1949: 9, 12.

Positive review of the London premiere of *Death of a Salesman*, starring Paul Muni and Kevin McCarthy—it is "beautifully produced and meticulously well-acted."

"*Death of a Salesman* Acclaimed in Vienna." *New York Times* 4 March 1950: 10.

Excerpts from positive review of the Austrian production of *Death of a Salesman.*

"*Death of a Salesman* at the Phoenix." *Theatre World* (October 1949): 11–18.

Positive review of the London production, starring Paul Muni, that lauds the direction of Elia Kazan and the sets and lighting of Jo Mielziner. Photographs of the London production accompany the text.

"*Death of a Salesman* Moves Londoners." *New York Times* 29 July 1949: 12.

News article announcing the successful opening of *Death of a Salesman* at the Phoenix Theatre in London in which "there were fifteen curtain calls and a big hand for Paul Muni as Willy Loman." The article summarizes the London critics' reaction to the production and predicts a long run for the play.

Eaton, Walter P. "The *Salesman* in Cold Type." *New York Herald Tribune Weekly Book Review* 22 May 1949: 6.

Negative review of the printed release of *Salesman* that Eaton feels "lacks literary merit." "The script will prove difficult," he continues, and "certainly far less rewarding emotionally, than its stage performance" with a main character whose "fatal flaw is lack of character."

Fanger, Iris. "American Dramas Take to Broadway." *Christian Science Monitor* 23 April 1999: 19.

Overview of three American plays of World War II vintage which are all appearing in the 1999 Broadway season: *The Iceman Cometh*, *Death of a Salesman*, and a newly discovered play by Tennessee Williams entitled *Not About Nightingales*. Of *Salesman*, Fanger praises the performances of Brian Dennehy and Elizabeth Franz, the staging of Robert Falls, and the set design of Mark Wendland. Says Fanger, "On the evening I attended, the audience sat stunned throughout the three hours, broken only by one intermission, as if seeing the play for the first time."

Feingold, Michael. "Durable Goods." *Village Voice* 23 February 1999: 131.

Mostly negative review of the fiftieth anniversary production of *Death of a Salesman* directed by Robert Falls and starring Brian Dennehy. Feigold criticizes Dennehy's performance as "limited" and having "no patience with Willy's weakness," faults the design of the production as "pointlessly moving," decries Miller's "mannerist posturing of the final scene," and makes note of the lack of women in the play, besides the wife Linda, who "aren't whores." On a positive note, Feingold praises Elizabeth Franz' Linda as a "strong, ferociously affectionate performance."

Feldberg, Robert. "An American Tragedy Rises to the Occasion Again." *The Record* (Bergen County, N.J.) 11 February 1999: Y1.

Favorable review of the fiftieth anniversary production starring Brian Dennehy, directed by Robert Falls, that Feldberg calls "exciting," "remarkable," "memorable," and "timeless."

Fleming, Peter. "The Theatre." *Spectator* (London) 5 August 1949: 173.

Negative review of the London production at the Phoenix Theatre, starring Paul Muni. Says Fleming, Miller should have used "satire rather than sentiment" to depict a story that is "really a matter for laughter rather than for tears."

Foss, Roger. "*Death of a Salesman*." *What's On* (London) 6 November 1996. *Theatre Record* 16.22 (1996): 1367–68.

Positive review of the Royal National Theatre Company revival, directed by David Thacker. Says Foss, "*Death of a Salesman* undoubtedly jangled post-war American nerves, and this important new production makes you wonder why we have learned so little since then."

Gabriel, Gilbert W. "Honor Thy Father." *Theatre Arts* 33 (April 1949): 14–16.

Positive review of the Broadway premiere that Gabriel finds a "fine thing, finely done" with "a compelling, surging quasi-poetry."

Garland, Robert. "Audience Spellbound by Prize Play of 1949." *New York Journal American* 11 February 1949: 24. *New York Theatre Critics' Reviews* 10 (1949): 358. Rpt. in *"Death of a Salesman": Text and Criticism*. Ed. Gerald Weales. New York: Viking, 1967. New York: Penguin, 1996. 199–201.

In what would later become a legendary opening night story, Garland reports of the opening night audience's unusual reaction to *Death of a Salesman*: they "made no effort to leave the theatre at the final curtain-fall . . . that first-night congregation remained in its seats . . . an expectant silence hung over the crowded auditorium. Then, believe me, tumultuous appreciation shattered the hushed expectancy."

Gassner, John. "The Theatre Arts." *Forum* April 1949: 219–21. Rpt. as "*Death of a Salesman*: First Impressions, 1949." *The Theatre in Our Times: A Survey of the Men, Materials and Movements in the Modern Theatre*. New York: Crown, 1954. 364–73. Rpt. as "Home-Grown Tragedy" in *Theatre U.S.A, 1665–1957*. Ed. Bernard Hewitt. New York: McGraw-Hill, 1959. 444–48. Rpt. in *"Death of a Salesman": Text and Criticism*. Ed. Gerald Weales. New York: Viking, 1967. New York: Penguin, 1996. 231–39. Rpt. as "The Theatre Arts." *The Merrill Studies in "Death of a Salesman."* Ed. Walter J. Meserve. Columbus, Ohio: Merrill, 1972. 2–6.

Positive review of the premiere production of *Salesman*, starring Lee J. Cobb and directed by Elia Kazan, that Gassner rates as "one of the triumphs of the mundane American stage."

Gibbs, Wolcott. "*Death of a Salesman.*" *New Yorker* 19 February 1949: 58, 60.

Gibbs praises *Death of a Salesman* for its focus on Loman as a victim of a society that has no more use for him and a martyr to his dreams.

Girson, Rochelle. "*Death of a Salesman.*" *Saturday Review of Literature* 13 August 1949: 31.

Positive review of the printed release of *Death of a Salesman* that Girson feels, in some respects, "comes off even better [than the live stage production] . . . words don't sound false as they did on stage."

Gore-Langton, Robert. "*Death of a Salesman.*" *Daily Express* (London) 8 November 1996. *Theatre Record* 16.22 (1996): 1368.

In this negative review of the Royal National Theatre Company revival, Gore-Langton criticizes Miller's play as having "a fat vein of boredom running through it," and David Thacker's direction as "too referential to become a classic."

Gottfried, Martin. "Rebirth of the *Salesman.*" *New York Post* 27 June 1975. *New York Theatre Critics' Reviews* 36 (1975): 222.

Gottfried criticizes the Circle in the Square revival, directed by and starring George C. Scott, for "doomed from the start" staging ("the play was born to a proscenium stage") and the uneven direction which makes the play seem as if it was "directed by the actors themselves." Hearty praise goes to Miller, however, for the production's "unmistakable proof, for so many who have forgotten, that is one of the greatest plays ever written by an American; a major tragedy; a classic."

Grant, Steve. "*Death of a Salesman.*" *Time Out* (London) 6 November 1996. *Theatre Record* 16.22 (1996): 1364.

Positive review of the Royal National Theatre Company revival, directed by David Thacker. "This is a great production of one of the few genuinely immortal works of post-war theatre."

Gross, John. "*Death of a Salesman.*" *Sunday Telegraph* (London) 3 November 1996. *Theatre Record* 16.22 (1996): 1367.

Mixed review of the Royal National Theatre Company revival, directed by David Thacker. Gross says he was "moved and impressed by a number of individual scenes" and "taken aback by its over-all pumped-up portentousness."

Grove, Lloyd. "Hoffman's High-Powered *Salesman.*" *Washington Post* 2 March 1984: Weekend, p. 9.

Grove praises the "exceptionally well cast" drama, starring Dustin Hoffman, Kate Reid, and John Malkovich, appearing at the Eisenhower Theater in Washington, D.C., and reports of a woman in the audience crying out "Oh, no! Don't" at the moment in the play when Willy Loman "blows all his money to overtip a waiter."

Gussow, Mel. "Black *Salesman.*" *New York Times* 9 April 1972: 69.

Positive review of the all-black production of *Death of a Salesman* at the Center Stage in Baltimore, directed by Lee D. Sankowich and starring Richard Ward, that Gussow says has become "an insightful drama about the superimposition of white standards of repressed black people."

Hagerty, Bill. "*Death of a Salesman.*" *News of the World* (London) 10 November 1996. *Theatre Record* 16.22 (1996): 1365.

Mixed review of the Royal National Theatre Company revival, directed by David Thacker. Says Hagerty, "Miller's play makes superb theatre but says little for mankind's progress in getting its priorities right."

Hanks, Robert. "*Death of a Salesman.*" *Independent on Sunday* (London) 3 November 1996. *Theatre Record* 16.22 (1996): 1362–63.

Hankes criticizes David Thacker's direction of the Royal National Theatre Company production as having a "slightly plodding sincerity [that] leaves you wondering whether this is quite the great play you thought."

Hawkins, William. "*Death of a Salesman*: Powerful Tragedy." *New York World-Telegram* 11 February 1949: 16. *New York Theatre Critics' Reviews* 10 (1949): 359. Rpt. in *"Death of a Salesman": Text and Criticism*. Ed. Gerald Weales. New York: Viking, 1967. New York: Penguin, 1996. 202–204.

Hawkins praises *Death of a Salesman* as a play "written along the lines of finest classical tragedy," that "skillfully transcend[s] the limits of real time and space."

Helbig, Jack. "Rebirth of *Salesman.*" *Daily Herald* 2 October 1998. http://www.deathofasalesman.com/rev-98-dailyherald.htm (27 February 1999).

Highly positive review of the fiftieth anniversary production starring Brian Dennehy at the Goodman Theatre in Chicago. Helbig says that he thought he "knew" the play but admits that this production "revealed textures in *Salesman* that I'd never seen before, layers of meaning no previous production had revealed so poignantly—or as pointedly—before."

Henning, Joel. "*Salesman* Revived." *Wall Street Journal* 5 October 1998: A28.

Favorable review of the Goodman Theatre's revival of *Death of a Salesman*, starring Brian Dennehy, in which Henning praises Elizabeth Franz's Linda Loman as transcending "Mr. Miller's limitations" and sustaining "a measured performance throughout, flawlessly alternating between displays of feral strength in defending the declining Willy against their sons and blank submissiveness in the face of Willy's bloated ego."

Hewes, Henry. "Opening Up the Open Stage." *Saturday Review of Literature* 24 August 1963: 34.

Negative review of the Tyrone Guthrie production of *Death of a Salesman*, starring Hume Cronyn and Jessica Tandy, that Hewes finds "funny" because of the small size of Cronyn as Willy and the refined nature of Tandy as Linda. Hewes believes that the success of the 1949 production may be due to Miller's decision to revise his script and change the language of the play to cast a much larger man (Lee J. Cobb) than originally envisioned.

Hobson, Harold. "From America." *Sunday Times* (London) 31 July 1949: 2.

Negative review of the London production, starring Paul Muni, that Hobson finds inferior to the New York premiere with Lee J. Cobb. Says Hobson, Cobb is a "dynamo of energy" and his "speed and certainty are missing in London."

"Hoffman Unconvincing as 60-Year-Old Loman." *San Jose Mercury News* 13 September 1985: F5.

Negative review of the video version of *Death of a Salesman* starring Dustin Hoffman. The unnamed critic finds that Hoffman's "self-conscious" performance "looked like a turtle with a scrawny neck stretching out of a baggy shell."

Hope-Wallace, Philip. "*Death of a Salesman.*" *Guardian* (London) 30 July 1949: 5.

Negative review of the London production, staged by Kazan and starring Paul Muni, that Hope-Wallace finds inferior to the New York premiere.

Hulbert, Dan. "Broadway Is Buying *Salesman.*" *Atlanta Journal and Constitution* 14 March 1999: L5.

Positive review of the fiftieth anniversary revival, starring Brian Dennehy and directed by Robert Falls, that Hulbert calls a "shatteringly sad story so thrillingly told. . . . There hasn't been a more moving theatrical experience in many years."

Isherwood, Charles. "Rebirth of a *Salesman.*" *Variety* 11 February 1999. http://www.deathofasalesman.com/rev-99-variety.htm (27 February 1999).

Isherwood applauds the fiftieth anniversary production of *Death of a Salesman*, starring Brian Dennehy and directed by Robert Falls, for its treatment of the "great classic as a new play" with a "lyrical dignity and fierce urgency."

Jenkins, Peter. "The Ugly Spectacle of Failure." *Spectator* (London) 29 September 1979: 25–26.

Positive review of the Lyttelton revival. Says Jenkins, "The glory of this production is that it unleashes all of that theatricality while avoiding the sentimental pitfall. By this means it loyally exposes the greatness of the play."

Jones, Chris. "Legit Reviews: *Death of a Salesman.*" *Variety* 5 October 1998: 78.

Jones praises the fiftieth anniversary production, directed by Robert Falls and starring Brian Dennehy, as "sufficiently radical and provocative. . . . It gives one of the great works in the American canon a theatrical kick back out on the road."

Kalem, T. E. "A *Défi* to Fate." *Time* 7 July 1975: 43. *New York Theatre Critics' Reviews* 36 (1975): 222.

Rave review of the Circle in the Square revival that calls the production "redoubtable," George C. Scott's performance as Willy Loman "staggering," and Scott's direction "extraordinary."

Kauffmann, Stanley. "*Death of a Salesman*." *New Republic* 19 July 1975: 20, 33. Rpt. in *Persons of the Drama*. New York: Harper and Row, 1976. 142–45. Rpt. in *Major Literary Characters: Willy Loman*. Ed. Harold Bloom. New York: Chelsea, 1991. 19–21.

In his review of the Circle in the Square revival, starring and directed by George C. Scott, Kauffmann feels that *Death of a Salesman* falters because of poor dialogue, that "slips into a fanciness that is slightly ludicrous," cloudy themes, and a confused critique of the business world.

Kelly, Kevin. "Hoffman Perfect as Willy Loman." *Boston Globe* 24 February 1984.

Lengthy positive review of "first-rate" revival of *Death of a Salesman*, starring Dustin Hoffman and John Malkovich, directed by Michael Rudman. Kelly praises both the acting as "memorable" and the play as a "solid masterwork."

Keown, Eric. "At the Play." *Punch* (London) 10 August 1949: 163.

Positive review of the London production of *Death of a Salesman*, starring Paul Muni and Kevin McCarthy. Says Keown, "This is a play of outstanding quality, on a theme vital to the times."

Kerr, Walter. "This *Salesman* Is More Man than Myth." *New York Times* 29 June 1975: II: 1, 5.

Positive review of the Circle in the Square revival, directed by and starring George C. Scott, that Kerr finds superior to other productions in Scott's decision to play the role of Willy Loman, not as a once successful man destroyed by the American Dream, but as a man who has "*always* had to compensate, to inflate his indeterminate place in the scheme of things." This production places the work as a play about people and not a social indictment on the "failed American myth."

Kirkley, Donald. "If You Have Tears." *Baltimore Sun* 23 January 1951: 10.

Positive review of the touring company production of *Death of a Salesman*, appearing at Ford's Theatre in Baltimore, starring Thomas Mitchell, Peggy Allenby, Paul Langton, Darren McGavin, and Howard Smith. Says Kirkley, Miller has written "with insight and compassion, imagination and dramatic power, and the audience is soon deeply absorbed in the unfolding of the pitiful story."

Kissel, Howard. "*Death of a Salesman*." *Women's Wear Daily* 30 March 1984. *New York Theatre Critics' Reviews* 45 (1984): 329.

Kissel praises the revival of *Salesman* (starring Dustin Hoffman and John Malkovich) as "strong," but criticizes Hoffman's performance as "a collection of mannerisms" that "often suggest a maladroit child trying to amuse his elders. . . . One admires Hoffman's ingenuity and energy, but one wonders if the performance would be more touching if it were less effortful."

Klinghoffer, David. "Undying *Salesman*." *National Review* 8 March 1999: 54–55.

Favorable review of the fiftieth anniversary production directed by Robert Falls and starring Brian Dennehy. Klinghoffer admits a certain amount of surprise that such an old play "can speak with fresh power to contemporary audiences. . . . The play works amazingly well. Not as any type of socialist harangue, but rather as a meditation on manhood."

Kroll, Jack. "Hoffman's Blazing Salesman." *Newsweek* 9 April 1984: 107. *New York Theatre Critics' Reviews* 45 (1984): 327.

Kroll's positive review focuses on Dustin Hoffman's performance, which he calls "brave and uncompromising" and one that gives "a unique force to his portrayal of the most deeply divided character in American drama."

———. "Triumph." *Newsweek* 7 July 1975: 61. *New York Theatre Critics' Reviews* 36 (1975): 223.

Kroll lauds the Circle in the Square revival starring and directed by George C. Scott as "a great public ritualizing of some of our deepest and deadliest contradictions," and Scott's performance as Willy Loman as "perhaps the most devastating burnt-out case ever seen on the stage" and "a signal event in the life of the American theater."

Krutch, Joseph Wood. "Drama." *Nation* 5 March 1949: 283–84.

Rare negative review of *Death of a Salesman*, directed by Elia Kazan and starring Lee J. Cobb and Mildred Dunnock. Krutch says the play fails to extend itself beyond its precise message and commonplace dialogue that shows Miller, unlike Tennessee Williams, to have a lack of ability with language and ingenuity.

Kuchwara, Michael. "A Weak *Salesman*." *Washington Times* 21 February 1999: D5.

Mixed review of the fiftieth anniversary production starring Brian Dennehy and Elizabeth Franz, directed by Robert Falls, that Kuchwara calls "an imperfect revival" that "still packs a punch."

Lahr, John. "Fugitive Mind." *New Yorker* 8 March 1999: 92–93.

While lamenting that the casting of the fiftieth anniversary production of *Death of a Salesman* is "generally uneven," and that the play "has to contend with an ugly revolving set, designed by Mark Wendland, which robs it of a sense of place and hobbles its pace," Lahr lauds it for still packing "a wallop" and concludes that "Miller's reading of the nation's collective unconscious is so accurate that the flaws in this somewhat overpraised production hardly matter . . . its revival is not to be missed."

Lask, Thomas. "How Do You Like Willy Loman?" *New York Times* 30 January 1966: II: 23.

Positive review of the album recordings of *Death of a Salesman*, which brought back Lee J. Cobb and Mildred Dunnock to reprise their roles, and *A View from the Bridge*. Lask believes that the audience's reaction to *Death of a Salesman* depends on their "reaction" to the character of Willy Loman—"If the playgoer finds him without stature, without those qualities that catch and hold the sympathies, he will find the play worthless too."

Luft, Friedrich. "Arthur Miller's *Death of a Salesman*, Hebbel-Theater [Berlin]" *Stimme der Kritik-Berliner Theater seit 1945*. Velber bei Hannover: Friedrich Verlag, 1965. 82–85. Rpt. in *The Merrill Studies in "Death of a Salesman."* Ed. Walter J. Meserve. Columbus, Ohio: Merrill, 1972. 19–22.

Positive review of the Berlin production of *Death of a Salesman* that Luft calls "almost better than the one in New York . . . because here it takes greater pains to get acquainted with what is familiar over there."

Lyons, Donald. "Miller's *Death* Gets New Life." *New York Post* 11 February 1999. http://www.deathofasalesman.com/rev-98-nypost.htm (27 February 1999).

Highly positive review of the fiftieth anniversary production, starring Brian Dennehy and Elizabeth Franz, that Lyons calls "no humdrum revival, but a re-energizing and re-imagining of this emotional tidal wave of a play."

Lyons, Jeffrey. "Review: *Death of a Salesman.*" *WNBC-TV, Channel 4* 11 February 1999. http://www.deathofasalesman.com/rev-99-wnbc-tv.htm (27 February 1999).

Positive review of the fiftieth anniversary production of *Death of a Salesman* starring Brian Dennehy and Elizabeth Franz, directed by Robert Falls, that Lyons calls "magnificent," "deeply moving," and "a play for the ages," adding, "watching Brian Dennehy act is a privilege."

"Magnificent Death." *Newsweek* 21 February 1949: 78.

Highly laudatory review of the New York premiere that praises the directing of Elia Kazan, the acting of both Cobb and Dunnock, and Miller for writing such "a vivid, emotion-shattering, and deeply moving play."

Malloy, Darina. "Dennehy's Masterful *Salesman.*" *Irish Voice* 2 March 1999: 22.

Positive review of the fiftieth anniversary production of *Death of a Salesman*, directed by Robert Falls, that especially notes Brian Dennehy's performance. Says Malloy, "he roars like a lion and whimpers like a broken man in all the right places."

McCulloh, T. H. "The Tragedy of Willie [sic] Loman Still Rings True." *Los Angeles Times* 2 November 1995: Calendar: 1.

Favorable review of the Studio City revival of Miller's *Death of a Salesman* directed by Jules Aaron and starring "soap opera stars" Jason Brooks and Peter Barton.

McIlroy, Randal. "Willy Loman Lives." *Maclean's* 27 January 1997: 63.

Favorable review of the Manitoba Theatre Centre's production of *Death of a Salesman* directed by Gloria Muzio. Calling the play "as fresh and disturbing as today's employment statistics [Canada]" that "speaks to the uncertainty of the contemporary world."

Morehouse, Ward. "Triumph at the Morosco." *New York Sun* 11 February 1949. *New York Theatre Critics' Reviews* 10 (1949): 360.

Positive review in which Morehouse calls *Death of a Salesman* a "poignant, shattering and devastating drama" and "a triumph of writing, in acting and in stagecraft."

Morgan, Frederick. "Notes on the Theater." *Hudson Review* 2 (Summer 1949): 272–73. Rpt. in *The Play*. Ed. Eric Bentley. Engelwood Cliffs, N.J.: Prentice-Hall, 1951. 746–47. Excerpt rpt. in *Critical Essays on Arthur Miller*. Ed. James J. Martine. Boston: G. K. Hall, 1979. 23.

In an essay that examines the "tawdriness and stupidity" of American theatre, Morgan blasts *Death of a Salesman* as "miserable"—"Miller has the makings of some sort of play; but he was unfortunately unable to bring a single spark of dramatic intelligence to bear on his material. The terms in which he conceived of his theme are so trite and clumsy as to invalidate the entire play and render offensive its continual demand for the sympathy and indulgence of the audience . . . the tone of the play can best be described as a sustained snivel."

Morley, Sheridan. "*Death of a Salesman*." *Spectator* (London) 9 November 1996. *Theatre Record* 16.22 (1996): 1365.

While stating that the revival by the Royal National Theatre Company is "not bad," Morley attacks David Thacker's production as "woefully undercast and unwisely set as a a kind of surrealist dream sequence," and Alun Armstrong's Willy Loman as "so wildly out of place, walking and looking and sounding like a defeated Scots trade-union secretary rather than the man with the case of samples forever in his trunk and on his mind."

Nathan, David. "*Death of a Salesman*." *Jewish Chronicle* (London) 8 November 1996. *Theatre Record* 16.22 (1996): 1365.

Brief positive review of the Royal National Theatre Company revival, directed by David Thacker, that Nathan calls an "excellent" production "which honours this great American play."

Nathan, George Jean. "The Theatre." *American Mercury* June 1949: 679–80.

Nathan argues against the tragic nature of *Death of a Salesman* because in the character of Willy Loman we do not see a man whose mind is in "strong conflict with the stronger fates," but rather a "mindless man already beaten by them."

———. "Tragedy." *American Mercury* (June 1949): 679–80. Rpt. in *Theatre Book of the Year, 1948–1949*. New York: Knopf, 1949. 279–85. Rpt. in *Two Modern American Tragedies*. Ed. John D. Hurrell. 57–60. Rpt. as "Arthur Miller" in *The Magic Mirror: Selected Writings on the Theatre*. George Jean Nathan. New York:

Knopf, 1960. 243–50.

Despite what he sees as Kazan's "obvious" direction and Lee J. Cobb's "bullish" Willy Loman, Nathan lauds Miller's play for (1) its ability to evoke compassion, not only for the life lost but for the life that might have been, (2) for Miller's simple writing "without pretentiousness," and (3) for the "uncompromising honesty of its emotion."

"New Plays in Manhattan." *Time* 21 February 1949: 74–76.

Generally favorable review of the Broadway premiere, directed by Elia Kazan and starring Lee J. Cobb, that praises Miller for having the daring to write a work revealing "a tragedy of a typical American who loses out by trying too hard to win out," and his work for its "solid, sometimes stolid prose."

Nightingale, Benedict. "*Death of a Salesman*." *The Times* (London) 2 November 1996. *Theatre Record* 16.22 (1996): 1364.

Nightingale praises this revival by the Royal National Theatre Company for the "crisp" and "lucid" direction of David Thacker and the "marvelous" acting of Alun Armstrong as Willy Loman—"his performance embraces kindliness and desperation, weariness of soul and intensity of paternal devotion. His is as complete a salesman as I've seen."

———. "Hard Slog." *New Statesman* (London) 28 September 1979: 478–79.

While the revival at the Lyttelton is "technically flawed and even dated," the themes of the play are so great as to compensate for a weak production. Says Nightingale, "The play is about being old, frightened, aghast at failures behind the emptiness ahead. It's about the parent who seeks vicarious fulfillment in his children, and the child painfully trying to cohere his brainwashed remnants into a personality truly his own. Above all, it's about the life lies in which most of us sometimes find sanity and cause for survival."

———. "*Salesman* Demonstrates Its Enduring Strengths." *New York Times* 8 April 1984: H: 3, 11.

Lengthy positive review of the Michael Rudman production of *Death of a Salesman* starring Dustin Hoffman. Nightingale calls Loman "a protagonist who will continue to move and fascinate audiences as long as American drama exists."

O'Toole, Fintan. "Rebirth of a *Salesman*." *Daily News* 11 February 1999. http://www.deathofasalesman.com/rev-99-nydaily-news.htm (27 February 1999).

Glowing review of the fiftieth anniversary production of *Death of a Salesman* in which O'Toole praises all aspects, from performance to set design. Says O'Toole, "It pays Miller the ultimate compliment of treating his great classic as a new play."

Peter, John. "*Death of a Salesman*." *Sunday Times* (London) 10 November 1996. *Theatre Record* 16.22 (1996): 1366–67.

Positive review that likens the Royal National Theatre Company revival, directed by David Thacker, to the original Broadway production starring Lee J. Cobb—"lyrical but hard, compassionate but unforgiving, a private tragedy and a requiem for a nation."

Phelan, Kappo. "*Death of a Salesman*." *Commonweal* 4 March 1949: 520–21.

In this positive review of the New York premiere, directed by Elia Kazan and starring Lee J. Cobb and Mildred Dunnock, Phelan praises Miller's handling of memory in the play, helping to make *Death of a Salesman* one of the most important plays in America.

Probst, Leonard. "*Death of a Salesman*." NBC, New York. 26 June 1975. *New York Theatre Critics' Reviews* 36 (1975): 225.

While Probst praises the New York revival, directed by and starring George C. Scott, as "tremendous" and "memorable," he criticizes Scott's choice to "cast blacks as Willy's friends," adding "that doesn't work. Willy Loman wasn't that type."

"The Return of Paul Muni." *Sphere* (London) 13 August 1949: 247.

Brief negative review of the London production of *Death of a Salesman*, that calls Muni "a pathetic figure of a salesman," accompanied by photographs of the set and cast.

Rich, Frank. "Theater: Hoffman, *Death of a Salesman*." *New York Times* 30 March 1984: C3. *New York Theatre Critics' Reviews* 45 (1984): 324–25.

Lengthy review of the *Death of a Salesman* revival starring Dustin Hoffman and John Malkovich, directed by Michael Rudman. Rich acclaims the acting performances as ones that "demand that our attention be paid anew," Rudman's direction as "balanced," and the Miller play as a "masterwork."

Richards, David. "Rebirth of a *Salesman*." *Washington Post* 27 February 1984: B: 1, 6.

Highly laudatory review of the Broadway-bound revival (playing at the Kennedy Center's Eisenhower Theater in Washington, D.C.), starring Dustin Hoffman, John Malkovich, Stephen Lang, and Kate Reid, directed by Michael Rudman, that Richards calls "accomplished and forceful."

Ridley, Clifford A. "*Death of a Salesman* Again Shows Sturdiness." *Philadelphia Inquirer* 11 February 1999. http://www.deathofasalesman.com/ rev-99-phil-inquirer.htm (27 February 1999).

Ridley praises the fiftieth anniversary production of *Death of a Salesman*, starring Brian Dennehy and Elizabeth Franz, as "mostly terrific, though not without a few flaws. Every new *Salesman* generates its own revelations, and it's perhaps indicative of our changing perceptions of women that, despite Dennehy's huge open sore of a performance, much of this show belongs to Willy's wife, Linda."

Rose, Lloyd. "Hoffman's High Powered *Salesman*." *Washington Post* 2 March 1984: N9.

Rose praises the Michael Rudman production of *Death of a Salesman*, starring Dustin Hoffman, playing at the Eisenhower Theater in Washington, D.C., as an "exceptionally well-cast" show that "packs enough wallop to turn an audience into a Greek chorus."

———. "Lost in America." *Atlantic* April 1984: 130, 132.

Highly positive review of the Michael Rudman production of *Death of a Salesman*, starring Dustin Hoffman, that Rose calls " a production of tremendous, inspired intelligence."

———. "New Life for a *Salesman*." *Washington Post* 11 February 1999. http://www.deathofasalesman.com/rev-99-washington-post.htm (27 February 1999).

Favorable review of the fiftieth anniversary production starring Brian Dennehy and Elizabeth Franz, directed by Robert Falls. Rose finds the play's strength to be in the tortured relationship between Willy and son Biff—"This is a play about hating your father and loving your father and owing your father and, above all, never being good enough for your father. About letting the old man down."

Ross, George. "*Death of a Salesman* in the Original" *Commentary* 11.2 (February 1951): 184–86. Rpt. in *"Death of a Salesman": Text and Criticism*. Ed. Gerald Weales. New York: Viking, 1967. New York: Penguin, 1996. 259–64.

Highly laudatory review of the Yiddish Theatre Production in Brooklyn that Ross praises for its "moods of irony and pathos so familiar to Jews." Of note is Ross's opinion that "what one feels most strikingly is that this Yiddish play is really the original, and the Broadway production was merely—Arthur Miller's translation into English."

Schickel, Richard. "Rebirth of an American Dream." *Time* 9 April 1984: 104–105.

Lengthy review in which Schickel praises director Michael Rudman for his "fluid, driving production" (it "is not just a revival and a restaging, nor even a reinterpretation of the play, but a virtual reinvention of it"), Dustin Hoffman's performance of Willy Loman as "nothing short of a revelation," and Miller's play "a classic of the modern theater."

Schloff, Aaron Mack. "*Salesman* Lives, but Only Fitfully." *Jewish Week* 19 February 1999: 37.

Schloff says he felt "almost nothing" at the Robert Falls production of *Death of a Salesman*, starring Brian Dennehy, and criticizes Miller for creating "a Jewish-inspired everyman who has no God."

Sharp, Christopher. "*Death of a Salesman*." *Women's Wear Daily* 27 June 1975. *New York Theatre Critics' Reviews* 36 (1975): 221.

Sharp acclaims Scott's performance as Willy Loman in the Circle in the Square production as "a masterful acting job," but criticizes his overall interpretation for its aggrandizement of the role—"the evening might have had more effect if he had subordinated Willy for the sake of the play. As it is, Willy stands out, but the production falls down."

Shea, Robert A. "*Death of a Salesman*." *Canadian Forum* 29 (July 1949): 86–87.

Positive review of the premiere production, starring Lee J. Cobb and Mildred Dunnock. Says Shea, "It is a probing social study, and a moral plea stronger than is heard from any pulpit in the land."

Siegel, Ed. "Not Enough Attention Paid to This *Salesman*." *Boston Globe* 21 February 1996: L27.

Siegel blames the failure of *Death of a Salesman*, directed by Gerald Freedman and starring Hal Holbrook, on the fact that while Holbrook's Loman is a sympathetic character, he "is never a tragic one. He is a beaten, doddering, downtrodden man from the first scene to the last and therefore has nowhere to fall. He's spiritually dead on arrival."

Siegel, Joel. "*Death of a Salesman*." ABC. WABC, New York. 29 March 1984. *New York Theatre Critics' Reviews* 44 (1984): 332.

Siegel praises the Dustin Hoffman revival of *Death of Salesman* as "a once in a lifetime theatrical experience" in which Hoffman gives an "awesome, numbing, breath-taking performance."

Simon, John. "The Salesman Dies Again." *New York* 7 July 1975: 74.

Negative review of the Circle in the Square revival, directed by and starring George C. Scott, that Simon faults for Scott pulling out the play's "Jewishness" and eliminating the potential for tragedy.

Spencer, Charles. "*Death of a Salesman*." *Daily Telegraph* (London) 1 November 1996. *Theatre Record* 16.22 (1996): 1363.

Spencer praises David Thacker's direction of this revival by the Royal National Theatre Company as "outstanding" and "evocative," and apologizes for the "hard things" he has said about Miller's drama in the past—"There is no mistaking the tremendous compassion at its heart and I left the theatre feeling ashamed of my past denigration of Arthur Miller. He *can* be an irritating playwright. On this occasion he is also a great one."

———. "Rebirth of a Legend." *Daily Telegraph* (London) 2 November 1999.

While "expecting to be both bored and irritated by Miller's preachiness and clumsy stagecraft," Spencer admits to being moved to tears by David Thacker's "outstanding" production at the National Theatre, starring Alun Armstrong and Marjorie Yates.

Spillane, Margaret. "Life of a Salesman." *Nation* 8 March 1999: 7.

Spillane lauds the fiftieth anniversary production of *Death of a Salesman*, starring Brian Dennehy, as "stunning proof that theater, at this moment, may be doing its most radical work in memory. . . . This latest production of *Salesman* rescues Miller's play from the safe shelf of syllabus drama and reinstates it in its visceral power."

Stearns, David Patrick. "Miller's *Salesman* More Alive than Ever." *USA Today* 11 February 1999: D1.

Favorable review of the fiftieth anniversary production, directed by Robert Falls and starring Brian Dennehy, that Stearns calls "King Lear, American style."

———. "Sterling *Salesman* and Other Shining Shows in Chicago." *USA Today* 30 October 1998: E6.

In an article detailing the variety of excellent theatre productions in Chicago, critic Stearns lauds the Goodman production of *Salesman*, directed by Robert Falls and starring Brian Dennehy, as "definitive." Also explored are the subtle revisions made to this production.

Taubman, Howard. "Plays with Music between the Lines." *New York Times* 27 March 1949: II: 1, 3.

Taubman praises the musical score to *Death of a Salesman* a superb and a great aid to the drama's power.

———. "Willy Revisited." *New York Times* 20 July 1963: 11.

Positive review of the Tyrone Guthrie revival, starring Jessica Tandy and Hume Cronyn. Taubman feels the play's universal themes make this production "significant" and "compelling."

Taylor, John Russell. "*Death of a Salesman*." *Drama* 135 (January 1980): 38–40.

After admitting his dislike for Miller because he lacks an instinct for the sound of language and his plays contain "insufficiently examined, pseudo-humanistic messages which are ceremoniously shoved down our throats," Taylor blasts the National Theatre production of *Death of a Salesman*, starring Warren Mitchell, for the character of Willy Loman who "is never presented as anything but a self-deceiving, self-destructive fool who does not deserve a moment of anyone's time or attention."

Taylor, Paul. "*Death of a Salesman*." *Independent* (London) 2 November 1996. *Theatre Record* 16.22 (1996): 1366.

Scathing review of the Royal National Theatre Company revival. Taylor likens Thacker's direction with those instances when playwrights direct their own work and the only thing they can bring to the production is reverence—"David Thacker's Lyttelton revival of *Death of a Salesman* suggests that the same thing can occur when a director's close relation to a writer becomes that of embarrassingly uxorious spouse."

Thomas, Rob. "Masterful Revival." *Northwest Herald* 2 October 1998. http://www.deathofasalesman.com/rev-98-northwest.htm (27 February 1999).

Thomas praises the Goodman Theatre production, directed by Robert Falls, calling Brian Dennehy "a force of nature" as Willy Loman, and Elizabeth Franz "magnificent as the thin, reedy pillar that props him up."

Took, Barry. "Hello, Willy." *Punch* (London) 277 (1979): 581.

Took praises the Michael Rudman production, staged at the Lyttelton Theatre, for Warren Mitchell's outstanding "interpretation and understanding of Willy Loman . . . the whole production is a proud affirmation of what the British Theatre at its best can do."

Torre, Roma. "Review: *Death of a Salesman.*" *New York 1-TV* 11 February 1999. http://www.deathofasalesman.com/rev-99-new-york-1.htm (27 February 1999).

Positive review of the fiftieth anniversary production of *Death of a Salesman* starring Brian Dennehy and Elizabeth Franz, directed by Robert Falls, that Torre calls "masterful," "explosive," "heart-breaking," and a "transcendental production."

Trewin, J. C. "Good King Bernard." *Illustrated London News* (London) 27 August 1949: 320.

Negative review of the London premiere of *Death of a Salesman*, starring Paul Muni. While praising Muni's acting, Trewin did not feel that the play "had anything very exciting to say or that the characters were realized with imagination."

———. "Plays in Performance." *Drama* 15 (Winter 1949): 8.

Trewin credits the performance of Paul Muni as Willy Loman in the London production of *Death of a Salesman* from saving "an evening that is otherwise tangled, pretentious, and dull."

Trussell, Robert. "Monumental Theatre; Attention Must Be Paid to Those Who Defined American Drama." *Kansas City Star* 25 April 1999: J1.

Feature article detailing works by Miller, O'Neill, and Williams currently enjoying success on Broadway. Of note is Trussell's positive review of the fiftieth anniversary production of *Death of a Salesman* starring Brian Dennehy, who presents "a performance of epic proportions detailed with fine shadings."

Usher, Shaun. "*Death of a Salesman.*" *Daily Mail* (London) 1 November 1996. *Theatre Record* 16.22 (1996): 1365–66.

Brief positive review of the Royal National Theatre Company revival, directed by David Thacker and starring Alun Armstrong—"It may not be the definitive production . . . but it is a memorable one."

Watt, Douglas. "*Death of a Salesman*: Hoffman Shines in a Glorious Rebirth of Miller's Drama." *New York Daily News* 30 March 1984. *New York Theatre Critics' Reviews* 45 (1984): 328–29.

Glowing review of the Dustin Hoffman, John Malkovich revival, which Watt praises as "a work of consummate honesty and fervor."

———. "Scott in Miller's *Salesman.*" *New York Daily News* 27 June 1975. *New York Theatre Critics' Reviews* 36 (1975): 221.

Mixed review of the Circle in the Square revival starring George C. Scott, James Farentino, Harvey Keitel, and Teresa Wright, directed by Scott. Watt applauds the play's "shattering emotional experience," but laments Scott's direction, which he calls "uneven" and the theatre space itself, which he found inappropriate—"the play belongs behind a proscenium instead of sprawled out before us within the horseshoe-shaped seating area."

Watts, Richard, Jr. "*Death of a Salesman*: A Powerful Drama." *New York Post* 11 February 1949. *New York Theatre Critics' Reviews* 10 (1949): 359.

Praising Miller's growth as a playwright since *All My Sons*, Watts writes that *Death of a Salesman* has "a kind of cold intellectual clarity mixed with simple and unashamed emotional force" and "something to make strong men weep and think."

West, Hollie I. "*Death of a Salesman.*" *Washington Post* 14 April 1972: D1, 7.

West reviews the all-black production of *Death of a Salesman* at the Center Stage in Baltimore. While noting that Miller himself had "voiced his pleasure that his play was being presented with a black cast," West questions whether the play's dialogue and situations support the cultural shift.

Wilcocks, Dick. "*Death of a Salesman*." *Plays and Players* (London) February 1986: 28.

Mostly positive review of the Royal Exchange's (Manchester) revival of *Death of a Salesman*, directed by Gregory Hersov and starring Trevor Peacock and Avril Elgar, that lauds Peacock's Willy as "quite riveting from the very beginning."

Williamson, Audrey. *Theatre of Two Decades*. London: Rockliff, 1951. 181–82.

Brief review and plot synopsis of the London production of *Death of a Salesman*, starring Paul Muni, in 1949. Williamson admires Miller's "playing about with chronology," but laments that the drama "lacks perhaps the highest distinction of writing."

Wilson, Edwin. "Contrasting Views of American Life." *Wall Street Journal* 27 June 1975. *New York Theatre Critics' Reviews* 36 (1975): 223.

Part of a review round-up that offers criticism for the revivals of both *Death of a Salesman* and *Our Town*, Wilson comments that "neither is inspired but both prove rewarding."

———. "*Death of a Salesman*." *Wall Street Journal* 4 April 1984. *New York Theatre Critics' Reviews* 45 (1984): 325–26.

Calling the Dustin Hoffman, John Malkovich production "a major revival of a major play," Wilson spends the bulk of his review praising Hoffman's Willy as "a character that is true, whole and ultimately very moving."

Winer, Laurie. "*Salesman* Emphasizes the Despair." *Los Angeles Times* 28 March 1996: Calendar: 1.

Review of the 1996 Los Angeles production of *Death of a Salesman* starring Hal Holbrook and directed by Gerald Freedman. Calling it "one damned depressing play," Winer finds the production "plodding" and "downbeat," prompting one man at intermission to remark, "I think I'll just go home now and slit my wrists."

Winer, Linda. "Everyman Revisited, Dennehy Is Larger than Life in a Splendid *Salesman*." *Newsday* 11 February 1999: B2. http://www.deathofasalesman.com/rev-99-newsday.htm (27 February 1999).

Favorable review of the fiftieth anniversary production directed by Robert Falls, starring Brian Dennehy. Says Winer, this Willy Loman "does not just drag himself home . . . he crashes open the huge, eerily disconnected door with one last big kick, then stands looming in the doorway—for a heartbeat—like a man-mountain action hero on a final mission."

Worsley, T. C. "Poetry without Words." *New Statesman and Nation* (London) 6 August 1949: 146–47. Rpt. in *"Death of a Salesman": Text and Criticism*. Ed. Gerald Weales. New York: Viking, 1967. New York: Penguin, 1996. 224–27.

Mostly negative review of the London production, starring Paul Muni, that Worsley says is "an attempt to make a poetic approach to every day life without using poetry." Instead, the poetry is supplied by the symbols, lighting, and set. While the play "has a certain power," it is "heavily scented with self-importance. . . . The little theme is made to take itself much too seriously."

Wyatt, Euphemia Van Rensselaer. "The Drama." *Catholic World* (April 1949): 62–63.

Favorable review of the premiere production of *Death of a Salesman*, starring Lee J. Cobb and directed by Elia Kazan. Says Wyatt, "Written with relentless truth, with no eye on curtain lines or sure-fire scenes, Miller's play hits at the heart of the audience with the dull pain of a sledge hammer."

Zoglin, Richard. "American Tragedy." *Time* 15 February 1999: 77.

Positive review of the fiftieth anniversary production of *Death of a Salesman*, directed by Robert Falls and starring Brian Dennehy. Says Zoglin, "That [*Salesman*] continues to fascinate us is testimony to Miller's ability to pack so much—heartbreaking family drama, an Ibsenian tragedy of illusions shattered, and indictment of American capitalism—into one beaten-down figure with a simple case."

Related Interviews and Profiles (not with Miller)

"AOL Chat with Brian Dennehy." 21 February 1999. http://www.deathofasalesman.com/aol-chat-dennehy.htm (27 February 1999).

Dennehy answers questions regarding his approach to the role of Willy Loman in the fiftieth anniversary production directed by Robert Falls, the part's physical challenges, audience reaction to *Death of a Salesman*, critical influence (if any) on his acting choices, and his thoughts on working as an actor.

Beale, Lewis. "The Birth of an Actor." *Daily News* 7 February 1999.
Profile of the career of actor Brian Dennehy and his approach to the portraying Willy Loman in the fiftieth anniversary production of *Death of a Salesman*, directed by Robert Falls.

Bell, Karen. "Al Waxman on Stage." *Performing Arts and Entertainment in Canada* 31.1 (Summer 1997): 7.
Brief overview of actor Al Waxman's theatre career and love of television work, on the occasion of his playing Willy Loman in the 1997 Stratford Festival, in which Waxman calls the part "the greatest role of the century."

Bilderback, Walter. "Judd Hirsch." *American Theatre* May/June 1994: 38–39.
Interview with Judd Hirsch, starring in the Playmakers Repertory Theatre production of *Death of a Salesman*, directed by Jeffrey Hayden.

Blowen, Michael. "Hal Holbrook Tonight." *Boston Globe* 18 February 1996: B23.
Interview and biographical piece on actor Hal Holbrook as he tours in a production of *Death of a Salesman*, also starring Elizabeth Franz. Holbrook discusses his approach to the role of Willy Loman and his views on the modern relevancy of Miller's classic drama.

Breslauer, Jan. "Jack Klugman Enjoying This Stage of His Career." *Los Angeles Times* 18 September 1998: F2. See also Don Shirley, "Klugman's Prowess, Not Patter, Makes *Salesman* Work." *Los Angeles Times* 21 September 1998: F3.
Lengthy profile of Jack Klugman and his portrayal of Willy Loman in the Falcon Theatre's inaugural production of Miller's play.

"Brian Dennehy." *World of Hibernia* 5.1 (Summer 1999): 12.
Profile of Brian Dennehy and his role as Willy Loman in the fiftieth anniversary production of *Death of a Salesman*. Dennehy is quoted as being pleased with his return to Broadway in this part—"I will always be grateful for this experience. Not because it has been a success, but because it has given me back something I had lost along the way."

Brooks-Dillard, Sandra. "*Salesman* Prescient for Its Birth in the 1940s." *Denver Post* 3 March 1996: F1.

Interview with Gerald Freedman, director of the national touring company production of *Death of a Salesman*, starring Hal Holbrook and Elizabeth Franz. Freedman discusses his directorial approach, the relevance of the 1949 play to modern audiences, and Freedman's sense of pleasure with the cast of this production.

Dekker, Albert. "*Salesman*'s Traveling Understudy." *New York Times* 30 April 1950: II: 2.

Fascinating essay by the understudy of the part of Willy Loman. Dekker details his experiences of jumping into the role "on very short notice" in both New York and Chicago, how he learned and rehearsed the part, his agreement to be available at one of two telephone numbers twenty minutes away from the theatre until 8:15 p.m. every evening, and several incidences of his having to take over the role for Gene Lockhart. Says Dekker of the difficulty of the role, "Willy is ninety-six sides long and the continuity of thought is held by a thread, and that thread is very often broken."

Evans, Everett. "Requiem for a Dreamer." *Houston Chronicle* 5 October 1997: Z8.

Interview with Ralph Waite who is performing the role of Willy Loman in the Alley Theatre production directed by David Wheeler. Waite discusses his approach to the role.

Feldberg, Robert. "Director of *Salesman* Throws Out the Kitchen Sink." *The Record* (Bergen County, N.J.) 14 February 1999: 103.

Brief interview with Robert Falls in which the director of the acclaimed fiftieth anniversary production of *Death of a Salesman* comments on past interpretations of the work, which labeled it as "a piece of kitchen-sink realism." On the contrary says Falls, "It is a very dense, poetic work. It has a dreamlike quality."

———. "Director, Star Talk about 50th Anniversary Production of *Death of a Salesman*." *The Record* (Bergen County, N.J.) 9 February 1999.

Interview with director Robert Falls and actor Brian Dennehy in which Falls details his decision to restage *Death of a Salesman* in a new way and notes Miller's enthusiasm over his approach. Also mentioned is Miller's involvement with the transfer of the Chicago production to Broadway.

Frymer, Murry. "The Willy Loman's of Today's Layoffs Are No Less Tragic." *San Jose Mercury News* 25 February 1999: E1.

Opinion essay in which Frymer discusses the social and psychological aspects of *Death of a Salesman* and the current corporate downsizing trends and its consequences on the "Willy Lomans" of the world.

Givens, Ron. "*Salesman* Wife Finds Fame." *Daily News* 4 March 1999.

Profile of Elizabeth Franz and her approach to the role of Linda Loman in the fiftieth anniversary production of *Death of a Salesman*. She notes the similarities between Miller's play and her salesman father and his relationship with his sons. Her performance, she says, is fired by her father's rage.

Gussow, Mel. "Duston Hoffman's *Salesman*." *New York Times* 18 March 1984: Sec. 6: 36–38, 40, 46, 48, 86.

Lengthy profile and interview of Dustin Hoffman on the occasion of his performing the role of Willy Loman in *Death of a Salesman*. Hoffman discusses his career, approach to the role of Loman, his relationship with Miller, and his now-famous obsessive personality. Miller is quoted on Hoffman's approach—"He has that kind of feisty quickness that I always associated with Willy, changing directions like a sailboat in the middle of a lake with the wind blowing in all directions. He's a cocky little guy overwhelmed by the size of the world and trying to climb up to the top of the mountain. Dustin will create a new Willy. It ain't going to be the other one. It'll be his Willy."

Haun, Harry. "Requiem for a Heavyweight." *Playbill* February 1999: 8-9, 11.

Dennehy discusses the differences between playing Hickey in O'Neill's *The Iceman Cometh* and Willy in Miller's *Death of a Salesman*, his approach to the role of Loman, audience reaction to the play, and his feeling regarding performing "if not the greatest part ever written in America, certainly one of the two or three greatest."

Herman, Jan. "A New *Salesman* Pitch by Old Actor-Director Team." *Los Angeles Times* 25 March 1996: F6.

Interview/feature article with Hal Holbrook and director Gerald Freedman of the touring company of Miller's *Death of a Salesman*. Both talk of their approaches to this production and Miller is mentioned as taking a personal interest in it by attending two performances [Miami and Boston], talking with the cast, taking notes, and offering suggestions for improvements.

"Higher Call." *New Yorker* 26 March 1949: 21.
Interview with Lee J. Cobb in which the actor discusses his career, the role of Willy Loman, and the "amazing . . . identification the play gives to so many slices of society."

Jones, Chris. "The Man and the Challenge." *American Theatre* 16.6 (July/August 1999): 16–21.
Profile of Chicago theatrical director Robert Falls, including his development of the Goodman Theatre production of *Death of a Salesman*, starring Brian Dennehy, that later moved to Broadway and received rave reviews. Also mentioned are Miller's positive reactions to the Chicago production.

Kelly, Kevin. "'It All Sort of Seems Too Much.'" *Boston Globe* 30 September 1984.
Biographical piece on actor John Malkovich. Of note are his comments regarding his unconventional approach to the role of Biff Loman in *Death of a Salesman*, starring Dustin Hoffman.

Kolin, Philip C. "*Death of a Salesman*: A Playwright's Forum." *Michigan Quarterly Review* 37.4 (Fall 1998): 591–623.
Collection of short essays by American playwrights who were asked to reveal how *Death of a Salesman* influenced them, the American theatre, and American audiences, and why the play continues to "enlighten, disturb, and inspire." Playwrights include: Edward Albee, Kenneth Bernard, John Guare, Emily Mann, Robert Anderson, Horton Foote, A. R. Gurney, Mark Medoff, David Henry Hwang, Adrienne Kennedy, Jason Milligan, Tony Kushner, Karen Malpede, Joyce Carol Oates, Oyamo, Ari Roth, Neil Simon, Joan M. Schenkar, Jean-Claude Van Itallie, and Lanford Wilson.

Mesic, Penelope. "Free Willy." *Chicago Magazine* 47.9 (1 September 1998): 39. http://www.chicagomag.com/chicagomag/text/enter/stage/0998a.htm (4 April 1999).
Interview with Brian Dennehy and Robert Falls in which the actor discusses his preparation for the role of Willy Loman (Goodman Theatre revival) and the director explains his approach to Miller's classic drama.

Neill, Heather. "Direct Lines from Author." *Times Educational Supplement* (London) 25 October 1996: Sec. 2: 9.

Interview with David Thacker, the director of the National Theatre revival of *Death of a Salesman*, starring Alun Armstrong. Thacker discusses his approach to the play and his collaboration with Miller during the rehearsal period.

Poling, James. "Handy 'Gadget.'" *Colliers* 31 May 1952: 56–61.

Lengthy profile of Elia Kazan published in the month following his "friendly" testimony before HUAC, which details the director's career to date and offers insight on his style and methods through commentary by creative artists who have worked with him. Of note is Mildred Dunnock's tale of Kazan using a foil to stab at her and scream in the last scene of the first act in order to get her to give more emotion to the "attention must be paid" speech. Also of note is the paraphrase of Miller's assessment of Kazan as "a moralist to whom the theater is an ethical medium, to be used in bringing out the truths of the human tradition, and in unmasking the truths. Responds Kazan on being told of the comment, "I suppose he's right, but what a way of saying it."

Smith, Dinitia. "'I Have a Lot of Willy Lomans in My Life.'" *New York Times* 9 May 1999: Sec. 7.

Profile of Elizabeth Franz and her Tony award-winning performance as Linda Loman in the fiftieth anniversary production of *Death of a Salesman* starring Brian Dennehy and directed by Robert Falls. Franz discusses what she sees as Linda and Willy's sexual bond, her memories of her father that helped shape her role as a salesman's wife, and reviews her acting career to date.

Watt, Douglass. "He Couldn't Have a Pleasanter Name." *Daily News* 21 July 1949: 63.

Profile of composer Alex North that includes details of his efforts to score the opera version of *Death of a Salesman*. To date, he had only composed one song and Miller had contributed an idea for a lyric, but he has plans to continue on the project.

Weber, Bruce. "Opposites Attracted to Heat Onstage." *New York Times* 22 February 1999: E1.

Interview with Robert Falls and Brian Dennehy significant for its in-depth discussion of the genesis of the fiftieth anniversary production of *Death of a Salesman*. Of special note is Falls's recollection of Miller suggesting British actor Warren Mitchell for the role of Willy Loman, but when the director detailed his commitment to casting Brian Dennehy, Miller wholeheartedly agreed with his choice.

Wood, Daniel B. "West Meets East." *Christian Science Monitor* 27 March 1989: 14.

Interview with Ying Ruocheng, vice minister for culture in the performing arts and arts education in China. Of note is Ying's connection to *Death of a Salesman*—he translated Miller's play into Chinese and played Willy Loman in the acclaimed production in Beijing that Miller directed.

News Reports, Letters to the Editor, and Related Matter

Adams, Val. "Willy Loman Irks Fellow Salesman." *New York Times* 27 March 1966. Sec. 2: 25.

News item detailing the protests that have been launched over the upcoming airing of *Death of a Salesman* on CBS. The Sales Executive Club of New York proposed changes in the script "in order to improve the image of the salesman depicted in the drama," including the addition of a prologue called "Life of a Salesman," which would point out "that with modern, customer-oriented selling methods, Willy Lomans are ghosts of the past," and the elimination of certain lines that are "needless anti-selling, anti-business comments that run through the play and add nothing to either plot, mood or characterization."

Breit, Harvey. "A Brief Visit and Some Talk with Thomas Mann." *New York Times Book Review* 29 May 1949: Sec. VII: 12.

Interview with Thomas Mann in which the author mentions that he had recently seen *Death of a Salesman* and was "very much impressed. It is a real work of art. . . . It is interesting to see an American play that is full of American self-criticism, that deals with the cruelties of American life."

Brozan, Nadine. "Chronicle." *New York Times* 18 December 1995: B10.

Brief news item detailing the discovery by John Lahr, the drama critic for the *New Yorker*, of an early manuscript at the Arthur Miller Archive at the University of Texas at Austin that foreshadows *Death of a Salesman.*

Calta, Louis. "A New Willy Loman." *New York Times* 10 November 1949: 40. See also Leslie Midgley, "New *Salesman*—Gene Lockhart Returns to Broadway." *New York Herald Tribune* 6 November 1949.

Black-and-white studio photograph of Gene Lockhart with the title, "A New Willy Loman."

Castillo, Rafael. "Immigrant's Tale." *New York Times* 21 February 1999: Sec. 2: 7.

Letter to the editor in which Castillo praises *Death of a Salesman* as "an immigrant story" with main character Willy Loman "as the archetype of any common Joe working hard to achieve a dream. . . . *Salesman* has been appropriated by so many cultures because it viscerally addresses failure and the universal reality that not everybody becomes a success."

Chase, Tony. "Letters from Minneapolis." *Theater Week* 5 August 1991: 16–17.

A brief item regarding two Minneapolis theatre companies, the Guthrie Theater, which is presenting an African-American *Death of a Salesman*, and Theatre de la Jeune Lune, which is moving into a new space.

Cronston, E. B. "Bounder or Cad." *New York Times* 11 September 1949: Sec. VI: 6.

Letter to the editor in agreement with Ivor Brown's comments regarding London's reception to *Death of a Salesman.* Cronston expresses his view that Britons "recognized that this Willy Loman was a cad and mental bounder, apart from his business life. Seeing his character in this truer light, they could not—like myself—find him worth the tears."

Dawson, Kevin. "*Salesman* Revival." *Los Angeles Times* 9 February 1999: 6.

Letter to the editor written in response to "Miller's Undying *Salesman*" of 5 February. Dawson notes that after Noel Coward attended a performance in 1949 that he called *Death of a Salesman* "a glorification of mediocrity."

"*Death of a Salesman.*" *Life* 21 February 1949: 115, 117–18, 121.

Following a brief positive review of the New York premiere production, the article reports that *Death of a Salesman* pulled in a $250,000 in advance sales for a play that "pursues its cause with firm purpose and a minimum of sex."

Epstein, Charlotte. "Was Linda Loman Willy's Downfall?" *New York Times* 20 July 1975: Sec. 2: 5.

In response to Walter Goodman's article of 15 June 1975 in the *New York Times* in which he describes the character of Linda Loman as the loving little woman behind her salesman-husband, Epstein asserts that this "myopic view" is not supported in the text. Rather, Linda Loman, "for all her love, devotion, and unflagging loyalty," is "counter-productive and figures passively in the destruction of her family," making her a rather complex character.

Freedman, Samuel G. "*Salesman* Extended Run Imperiled." *New York Times* 20 April 1984: C3.

News item reporting that the planned extended run of *Death of a Salesman* is in question because the play's star, Dustin Hoffman, wants a contract that will stipulate he does seven performances a week instead of eight to accommodate such a demanding role. Shubert Organization president Bernard Jacobs is quoted as being in opposition to this arrangement. Not only will the show lose 12.5% in revenues but this contract will set a precedent that will influence other productions. *Death of a Salesman* is currently pulling in $100,000 a week above its $145,000 a week break-even point.

Getlin, Josh. "Leaving an Imprint on American Culture." *Los Angeles Times* 23 April 1998: A1.

In the fourth part in a series of articles on Jews in America, Getlin quotes Rabbi Arthur Hertzberg, historian, philosopher, and Talmudic scholar, as calling Miller's *Death of a Salesman* a "sanitized Yiddish play" that "makes as much sense in Yiddish as it does in English."

Henderson, James W. "Willy Loman." *New York Times* 11 September 1949: Sec. 6: 6.

Letter to editor written in response to Ivor Brown's article on London's response to Willy Loman. Says Henderson, "If the British and Mr. Brown have no tears for Willy Loman, it cannot be because this is simply an American tragedy. As a fact, I do not recall even so much as a sniffle after the New York performance."

Holden, Stephen. "On Stage and Off." *New York Times* 13 November 1998: E2.

Item about the moving of the Goodman Theatre's fiftieth anniversary revival from Chicago to Broadway. Miller had denied the rights to a Broadway run to the Hal Holbrook production in 1996 because "it just wasn't new."

Kolin, Philip C. "Willy's Birthday." *Michigan Quarterly Review* 37.4 (Fall 1998): 652–53.

Five stanza poem inspired by the character of Willy Loman.

Kristol, Irving, et al. "Controversy in the Drama Mailbag." *New York Times* 17 August 1952: II: 1, 3.

Six different letters to the editor (three for, two against, and one neutral) regarding Miller's article in the *New York Times* titled "Many Writers, Few Plays." The first, written by Kristol, executive secretary for the American Committee for Cultural Freedom, denounces the Miller essay for its "art of expressing absurdities with such an earnest solemnity that they then pass for plausible discourse."

Lebenberg, Bernard, et al. "Opinions from Theatregoers on Merits of New Drama by Arthur Miller." *New York Times* 15 February 1953: II: 3.

Five letters to the editor, each supporting *The Crucible* as a play of immense power and impact in opposition to those critics who have found it wanting when compared to Miller's masterpiece *Death of a Salesman.*

Marx, Bill. "*Loman Family Picnic* Is a Jewish Feast." *Boston Globe* 23 April 1998: D4.

Positive review of Donald Margulies's *The Loman Family Picnic* at the Portland Stage Company, which includes a character named Mitchell, a Jewish son who imagines his family's life as a musical version of *Death of a Salesman* entitled "Willy!"

"May Offer *Salesman* in Berlin." *New York Times* 9 June 1949: 35.

News item reporting that *Death of a Salesman* will soon be staged by Fritz Kortner in Berlin.

McDonald, George B. M.D. "Doctor's Diagnosis." *New York Times* 28 February 1999: Sec. 2: 4.

In a short letter to the editor, Dr. McDonald, head of the

gastro-enterology/hepatology section of the Fred Hutchinson Cancer Research Center in Seattle, writes that Willy Loman has "all the signs" and "all the symptoms" of Alzheimer's Disease.

McKinley, Jesse. "Big Sales for *Salesman*." *New York Times* 12 February 1999: E2.

Brief news item announcing the strong box office sales of the fiftieth anniversary production of *Death of a Salesman* (more than $240,000 by mid day) which McKinley called "a terrific start for a stage play."

———. "If the Dramatic Tension Is All in His Head." *New York Times* 28 February 1999: Sec. 4: 5.

News item detailing the psychological aspects of *Death of a Salesman*, including an evaluation by two psychiatrists who were sent the script by director Robert Falls. Both doctors diagnosed the character of Willy Loman as manic-depressive, with hallucinatory aspects. Miller disagrees with their findings and is quoted as saying, "Willy Loman is not depressive. He is weighed down by life. There are social reasons for why he is where he is."

"Muni to Quit *Salesman*." *New York Times* 11 December 1949: 84.

News item announcing that, due to ill health, Paul Muni will be forced to quit the role of Willy Loman in the London production that has been playing to "packed houses."

Newmark, Judith. "Miller and the Bard Come to the Rep." *St. Louis Post-Dispatch* 22 March 1998: D3.

Lengthy feature detailing the 1998–99 season of the Repertory Theatre of St. Louis, which will include its first ever production of *Death of a Salesman*, "a play of incalculable influence on American culture and a work of haunting sadness and beauty in its own right."

O'Toole, Fintan. "Broadway Crystal Ball." *Daily News* 2 May 1999.

Critic O'Toole offers his predictions for 1999 Tony Award nominations and winners. Of note is his credulity over the Tony Committee's decision that Elizabeth Franz (Linda Loman in *Death of a Salesman*) be considered for the Featured Actress award instead of the Leading Actress category, where, he says, "she clearly belongs."

"On Stage and Off." *New York Times* 17 September 1999: E2.

News item announcing the close of *Death of a Salesman* and the opening of *The Price*. All told, *Salesman* earned two million dollars for its investors. David Richenthal, lead producer for both productions, said the inability to find a replacement for Brian Dennehy was the main reason for the close.

"On Their Night Tables." *Sales & Marketing Management* 149.4 (April 1997): 80.

Listing of what three sales and marketing executives are currently reading. One executive, Dennis Lunder of American Greetings, recommends *Death of a Salesman* as "required reading before anyone terminates or demotes someone. The tragic truth is that the story has as much meaning today as it did when Miller wrote the play."

"Play Group Ignores *Salesman* Protest." *New York Times* 12 November 1954: 23.

News item reporting that Thomas E. Parradine, the vice president of Coca Cola and former vice-commissioner of the American Legion, has quit his role as Willy Loman in the Glen Players, Glenwood Landing, Long Island production because of Miller's political views.

"Protested Play Given." *New York Times* 10 December 1954: 42.

News item reporting that a replacement has been found for Thomas E. Parradine in the role of Willy Loman in the Glen Players, Glenwood Landing, Long Island production of *Death of a Salesman* after Parradine, the vice-president of Coca Cola, quit the role in a protest over Miller's "alleged association with un-American activities."

Rosenberg, Joyce M. "The Lighter Side of Business: Willy Loman, the Next Generation." *AP Online* 14 July 1999.

Brief news item noting that a print ad for Pixion software depicts Willy Loman's grandson selling his wares on the internet without having to leave his office. Says Rosenberg, "Grandpa's sample case sits over in the corner of his office, a reminder of what life was like before telecommuting."

"*Salesman* in Denmark." *New York Times* 16 March 1950: 41.

News item reporting the great critical success of the eagerly awaited production of *Death of a Salesman* in Copenhagen.

"*Salesman* Opens in Two German Cities." *New York Times* 28 April 1950: 25.

News item reporting the critical reaction in Dusseldorf (opened 27 April) and Munich (opened 28 April) to a production of *Death of a Salesman* as one of happy surprise that a capitalist country like the United States could produce a play in which the main character "goes to the dogs."

Smith, Sid. "Goodman Introduces New *Salesman* Character: The Set." *Chicago Tribune* 27 September 1998: Sec. 7: 1.

Lengthy feature article detailing the new design of Robert Falls's revival of *Death of a Salesman* at the Goodman Theatre and its break with Jo Mielziner's legendary original 1949 set.

Stearns, David Patrick. "Honest Is Relative." *USA Today* 2 December 1993: D8.

Positive review of the Manhattan Theater Club production of Donald Margulies's "wonderful loopy" *The Loman Family Picnic*. To escape the unraveling of their middle-class family, several characters make up a Broadway musical version of *Death of a Salesman* entitled "Willy!"

Weiss, Hedy. "Second Fiddle to None: Chicago Shows Are Hits on Broadway." *Chicago Sun-Times* 21 February 1999. http://www.deathofasalesman.com/weiss-chicago-sun-times.htm (9 May 1999).

News article detailing the recent influx of Chicago-originated plays to New York, including *Death of a Salesman*. Of note are the financial figures for post-opening day box office receipts and advance sales, suggesting that this revival has set a record for a straight play on Broadway. Miller is quoted as hopeful that "this production will shake people in New York out of their slumber and force them to ask why it can't happen here anymore. But I doubt it. Their sleep is deep."

Wren, Christopher S. "Willy Loman Gets China Territory." *New York Times* 7 May 1983: 13.

Lengthy feature detailing the unlimited-run revival of *Death of a Salesman* in China, translated into Chinese, directed by Miller, and cast from the Peking People's Art Theater. Of note is difficulty encountered in getting the "actors to drop the stylized gestures characteristic of Chinese Socialist drama and to behave naturally." Photo of Miller accompanies the text.

An Enemy of the People

Critical Essays in Journals and Magazines

Bronson, David. "*An Enemy of the People*: A Key to Arthur Miller's Art and Ethics." *Comparative Drama* 2 (Winter 1968–69): 229–47. Rpt. in *Critical Essays on Arthur Miller*. Ed. James J. Martine. Boston: G. K. Hall, 1979. 55–71.

This essays compares the work of Ibsen with that of Miller "who in handling the same characters, plot material, and construction, the measure of the latter as a playwright will be taken."

Dworkin, Martin S. "Miller and Ibsen." *Humanist* 3 (May/June 1951): 111–15.

Dworkin traces how Miller adapted Ibsen's original play of *An Enemy of the People*, "how he somewhat changed its intentions," and the play's new thematic implications to modern audiences.

Haugen, Einar. "Ibsen as Fellow Traveler: Arthur Miller's Adaptation of *Enemy of the People*." *Scandinavian Studies* 51 (1979): 343–53.

Haugen examines in detail the changes in Ibsen's play made by Miller for his adaptation of *An Enemy of the People*. While he agrees that Miller's adaptation (which includes trimmings and rewrites) is, ultimately, inferior to Ibsen's, Haugen commends Miller for "his sincere effort to restore Ibsen's relevancy at time when Americans needed to be reminded that majority rule can stifle truth by silencing its minorities."

Critical Essays in Newspapers

Melloan, George. "The Theater." *Wall Street Journal* 15 March 1971. *New York Theatre Critics' Reviews* 32 (1971): 336.

Not really a review, Melloan examines the Repertory Theater of Lincoln Center's revival of Miller's adaptation from the point of view of its topicality to a "generation when pollution and ecology have suddenly become important issues."

Production Reviews

"*An Enemy of the People*." *Theatre Arts* 35 (March 1951): 15.

Mixed review of Miller's adaptation of *An Enemy of the*

People, directed by Robert Lewis and starring Fredric March and Florence Eldridge. While Miller has retained Stockmann's story, he has lost the mood of Ibsen's original, gaining only melodrama.

"*An Enemy of the People*." *Time* 8 January 1951: 31.

Mixed review of Miller's adaptation of *An Enemy of the People*, directed by Robert Lewis and starring Fredric March and Florence Eldridge. While Miller's version "replaces the old flaccid translator's English with new blood," it seems more measured and "agitated" than Ibsen's original play.

Atkinson, Brooks. "First Night at the Theater." *New York Times* 29 December 1950: 14. *New York Theatre Critics' Reviews* 11 (1950): 154. Rpt. in *Critical Essays on Arthur Miller*. Ed. James J. Martine. Boston: G. K. Hall, 1979. 53–54.

Favorable review of Miller's adaptation of Ibsen's work. Atkinson praises the production and Miller's "vast improvement over the lugubrious Archer translation," which releases "the anger and scorn of the father of realism." Production photograph accompanies the text.

———. "Ibsen in a Rage." *New York Times* 7 January 1951: II: 1.

Atkinson discusses the historical context of Ibsen's original play and comments that, although Miller has made various changes to the script, he has still retained the central thesis of the play. Miller is praised for his "fresh, literal translation" that is "compact, idiomatic and eminently actable." Atkinson also retracts his earlier comment that William Archer's translation was "lugubrious," because Acher did not write the English translation to which he had previously referred.

———. "Miller's Ibsen: *An Enemy of the People*." *New York Times* 5 February 1959: 24.

Positive review of an off-Broadway production of *An Enemy of the People*, directed by Gene Frankel, that Atkinson calls a "rabble-rousing performance."

Barnes, Clive. "Miller Version of *An Enemy of the People*." *New York Times* 12 March 1971. 26.

Positive review of the Lincoln Center revival that Barnes says lacks the "essence of Ibsen's original" but contains interesting character confrontations that makes this one of Miller's best.

Barnes, Howard. "Ibsen Plus Miller." *New York Herald Tribune* 29 December 1950: 12. *New York Theatre Critics' Reviews* 11 (1950): 156.

Negative review in which Barnes finds the original Ibsen work "far better than they are in the present reworking." He finds the "broadened" focus that takes "in present day events" to be "an interesting idea, but not particularly successful."

Beyer, William H. "The State of the Theatre: Revivals 'Front and Center.'" *School and Society* 17 February 1951: 105.

Positive review of the premiere production of *An Enemy of the People*, directed by Robert Lewis and starring Fredric March and Florence Eldridge, that Beyer says retains its relevance because of its reliance on human psychology to propel the story.

Billington, Michael. "*An Enemy of the People.*" *Guardian* (London) 15 October 1988. *London Theatre Record* 8.21 (1988): 1441–42.

While finding the Young Vic production, directed by David Thacker, "magnificent," Billington laments the use of Miller's translation because "it softens and subtly distorts Ibsen's purpose."

Chapman, John. "Arthur Miller and Fredric March Put New Anger in Ibsen's *Enemy*." *New York Daily News* 29 December 1950. *New York Theatre Critics' Reviews* 11 (1950): 155.

Highly positive review of *An Enemy of the People* in which Chapman praises the production as "intensely alive and intensely angry" as well as Miller's playwriting "skill at making characters talk like people."

Clurman, Harold. "Coward and Feydeau." *Nation* 21 March 1959. Rpt. in *The Collected Works of Harold Clurman: Six Decades of Commentary on Theatre, Dance, Music, Film, Arts and Letters*. Eds. Marjorie Loggia and Glenn Young. New York: Applause, 1994. 382–83.

Clurman compares the 1953 Broadway production of *An Enemy of the People* to the 1959 Actors Playhouse revival. He praises the revival as a production that "comes to a raw and explosive life as a social melodrama."

———. "*An Enemy of the People.*" *Nation* 29 March 1971: 411–13.

Mixed review of the Lincoln Center revival in which Clurman protests that the play is considered Miller's work instead of Ibsen's.

———. "Lear and Stockmann." *New Republic* 22 January 1951: 21–22. Rpt. in *The Collected Works of Harold Clurman: Six Decades of Commentary on Theatre, Dance, Music, Film, Arts and Letters*. Eds. Marjorie Loggia and Glenn Young. New York: Applause, 1994. 254–56.

While admitting that the Broadway premiere of Miller's adaptation of *An Enemy of the People*, directed by Robert Lewis and starring Fredric March, "has made something of a poster of Ibsen's scrupulous realism," Clurman praises "Miller's Americanized version" as "something very rare and special."

Coleman, Robert. "*Enemy of People* Muddled in Version by Miller." *New York Daily Mirror* 29 December 1950. *New York Theatre Critics' Reviews* 11 (1950): 156.

Negative review in which Coleman finds Miller's adaptation "a rip-roaring, muddle-mooded melodrama" that Ibsen would "shudder" at. While finding Fredric March's performance "eloquent and stirring," Coleman dislikes the staging and direction by Robert Lewis. "We trust that Miller won't apply this technique to 'Oedipus Rex' at some future date."

Coveney, Michael. "*An Enemy of the People*." *Financial Times* (London) 14 October 1988. *London Theatre Record* 8.21 (1988): 1441.

Coveney praises the Young Vic production, directed by David Thacker as "electrifying" and "a complex, entirely pertinent dramatization."

———. "*An Enemy of the People*." *Financial Times* (London) 30 November 1988. *London Theatre Record* 8.24 (1988): 1665.

Calling the Young Vic production, directed by David Thacker and recently moved to the Playhouse, "magnificent," Coveney praises the European premiere as a "superbly acted production [that] crackles with humour, tension and robust argument."

Edwards, Christopher. "*An Enemy of the People*." *Spectator* (London) 29 October 1988. *London Theatre Record* 8.21 (1988): 1439.

Edwards praises the Young Vic production, directed by David Thacker and starring Tom Wilkinson, as "exuberant" and "theatrically effective."

Gardner, Lyn. "*An Enemy of the People*." *City Limits* (London) 20 October 1988. *London Theatre Record* 8.21 (1988): 1442.

Garner praises the Young Vic European premiere, directed by

David Thacker, as a "sparkling production" that "illuminates the play for our own time with all the panache and excitement of a grand firework display."

———. "*An Enemy of the People*." *Mail on Sunday* (London) 16 October 1988. *London Theatre Record* 8.21 (1988): 1442.
Four sentence review of the Young Vic production, directed by David Thacker, that Gardner calls "stirring."

Gibbs, Wolcott. "The Theatre." *New Yorker* 13 January 1951: 44.
Negative review of the premiere production of Miller's *An Enemy of the People*, directed by Robert Lewis and starring Fredric March and Florence Eldridge. Gibbs dislikes Miller's "modernized" adaptation that has been laced with "astonishing anachronisms," which makes the audience doubt the crisis of Ibsen's central character John Stockmann.

Gill, Brendan. "Bad Old Days." *New Yorker* 20 March 1971: 93–94.
Negative review of the Lincoln Center revival, directed by Jules Irving, that praises the acting of Philip Bosco and Stephen Elliott but condemns Miller's adaptation as "ugly and inaccurate."

Gillett, Roger. "*An Enemy of the People*." *What's On* (London) 19 October 1988. *London Theatre Record* 8.21 (1988): 1442–43.
Gillett lauds the Young Vic production, directed by David Thacker, and especially commends Tom Wilkinson's Dr. Stockmann as "little short of magnificent. . . . The production is lifted by his performance in it to the realms of the triumphant."

Gottfried, Martin. "Theatre: *An Enemy of the People* . . .'dubious importance.'" *Women's Wear Daily* 15 March 1971. *New York Theatre Critics' Reviews* 32 (1971): 335.
Gottfried condemns the Repertory Theater at Lincoln Center revival as a "mistaken" choice that is "drab" and a "dull and pointless use of a repertory theatre's possibilities. . . . The play does not belong in a museum. It belongs in a mausoleum." Miller's version, he writes, is wordy; "we can no longer sit still for pat speeches that have neither the energy nor the grandeur of true heroism but merely lie flat, so many cliches out of a reformer's handbook."

Harper, Mary. "*An Enemy of the People*." *What's On* (London) 14 December 1988. *London Theatre Record* 8.24 (1988): 1665.

Harper lauds the Young Vic production, directed by David Thacker and moved to the Playhouse, as "a first class performance in a first class production. . . . Replete with pertinence to our own times, from making money out of water to insider dealing, this play is a banquet for thought and passion—as the many standing ovations will testify."

Harris, Leonard. "*An Enemy of the People*." CBS. WCBS, New York. 11 March 1971. *New York Theatre Critics' Reviews* 32 (1971): 337.

Harris praises the Jules Irving production at Lincoln Center, starring Stephen Elliott and Philip Bosco, as "exciting and a real cathartic," a play that "cleanses us of our indignation and lets us go out to our daily rounds of compromise."

Hawkins, William. "Ibsen Play Turns Stage into Soapbox." *New York World-Telegram* 29 December 1950. *New York Theatre Critics' Reviews* 11 (1950): 154.

Mixed review in which Hawkins finds two serious faults: "there is an air of soapbox about the proceedings which never for a moment let me feel emotionally involved in the troubles of these people," and "the physical depiction of the principal antagonist . . . a chronic status quo man" of which Ibsen would have disapproved.

Hay, Malcolm. "*An Enemy of the People*." *Time Out* (London) 19 October 1988. *London Theatre Record* 8.21 (1988): 1441.

While finding the Young Vic production, directed by David Thacker, "a little way short of the excellence some reviewers have claimed for it," Hay says it is "perfectly pitched and controlled."

Hewes, Henry. "Conscience Makes Valiants of Us All." *Saturday Review of Literature* 21 February 1959: 34.

Mixed review of an off-Broadway production of *An Enemy of the People*, directed by Gene Frankel, that Hewes calls, "never boring, [but] its speed and explicit quality leave little margin for the human responses that would make this off-Broadway production more memorable and moving."

Hiley, Jim. "*An Enemy of the People*." *Listener* (London) 15 December 1988. *London Theatre Record* 8.24 (1988): 1664.

Hiley calls the David Thacker production "a humdrum affair," after its move from the "open-stage intimacy" of the Young Vic to the "skimpy sets behind the Playhouse's ornate proscenium."

Kalem, T. E. "Moral Pollution." *Time* 22 March 1971: 41. *New York Theatre Critics' Reviews* 32 (1971): 335.

Generally favorable review of the Repertory Theater of Lincoln Center's revival, starring Stephen Elliott and Philip Bosco, that, writes Kalem, "begins slowly but develops cumulative power."

Kalson, Albert E. "*An Enemy of the People*." *Theatre Journal* 32.3 (October 1980): 396–97.

Negative review of the Goodman Theatre production of *An Enemy of the Public*, directed by Gregory Mosher, that Kalson calls "plodding and tedious" with a "one-dimensional protagonist."

Kerr, Walter. "*An Enemy of the People*." *Commonweal* 19 January 1951: 374.

Mixed review of the premiere production of Miller's *An Enemy of the People*, directed by Robert Lewis and starring Fredric March and Florence Eldridge, that Kerr praises for its accessible translation but faults for its thematic ambiguity.

———. "How to Discover Corruption in Honest Men." *New York Times* 21 March 1971: Sec. 2: 3.

In his negative review of the Jules Irving revival at the Vivian Beaumont, starring Stephen Elliott and Philip Bosco, Kerr laments that "here neither realism nor rhetoric asserts itself enough to keep the play from seeming silly."

King, Francis. "*An Enemy of the People*." *Sunday Telegraph* (London) 16 October 1988. *London Theatre Record* 8.21 (1988): 1442.

Calling the Young Vic production, directed by David Thacker, "thrilling" and "tremendous" with "some half-dozen magnificent performances."

Kroll, Jack. "The People No." *Newsweek* 22 March 1971: 114–15. *New York Theatre Critics' Reviews* 32 (1971): 336.

Mixed review of the revival by the Repertory Theater of Lincoln Center, directed by Jules Irving and starring Philip Bosco and

Stephen Elliott. "Miller's version seems somehow like a vague and all-purpose polemic to be trotted out at any ideological crisis."

Krutch, Joseph Wood. "Arthur Miller Bowdlerizes Ibsen." *Nation* 5 May 1951: 423–24.

Negative review of the premiere production of Miller's *An Enemy of the People*, directed by Robert Lewis and starring Fredric March and Florence Eldridge, in which Krutch faults Miller for a bad adaptation and recommends that the playwright "cultivate a certain tough-mindedness in the face of the heresies of which he does not approve."

Malcolm, Donald. "The Theatre." *New Yorker* 14 February 1959: 68, 70.

Negative review of an off-Broadway production of *An Enemy of the People*, directed by Gene Frankel, that Malcolm feels lacks a meaningful translation.

Marshall, Margaret. "Drama." *Nation* 6 January 1951: 18.

Brief negative review of the premiere production of Miller's *An Enemy of the People*, directed by Robert Lewis and starring Fredric March and Florence Eldridge, that Marshall says highlights the "weaknesses of the original."

McAfee, Annalena. "*An Enemy of the People*." *Evening Standard* (London) 14 October 1988. *London Theatre Record* 8.21 (1988): 1442.

McAfee lauds the Young Vic production, directed by David Thacker, as "an inspiring and affecting evening."

McClain, John. "Everything Is Fine but Ibsen's Idea." *New York Journal American* 29 December 1950. *New York Theatre Critics' Reviews* 11 (1950): 156.

Mixed review in which McClain admits to finding the premise "implausible" as well as disliking its moral ("I happen to be personally prejudiced against a show which slyly makes a bum of our accepted way of life, especially at a time like this"). McClain praises the production for Fredric March's performance and Miller's "excellent job of adapting and modernizing the play."

Morley, Sheridan. "Two by Ibsen." *Playbill* 31 December 1988: 64.

Morley praises the David Thacker production at the Young Vic as "magnificent" for its "in-the-round intensity and the power of

Tom Wilkinson in the title role."

Nathan, George Jean. "*Enemy of the People*." *Theatre Book of the Year, 1950–51*. New York: Knopf, 1951. 167–70.

Negative review of Miller's revision of Ibsen's drama that Nathan says becomes an "over-accentuated melodrama frequently couched in language indistinguishable from that employed in gunmen motion pictures or novels of the Chicago underworld."

Newman, Edwin. "*An Enemy of the People*." NBC. NBC, New York. 11 March 1971. *New York Theatre Critics' Reviews* 32 (1971): 337.

Newman laments that "misfortune" of the New York revival, starring Stephen Elliott and Conrad Bain, is that it stresses "the melodrama rather than tone it down. It reached a point where some members of the audience were laughing where no laughs were intended, and applauding sentiments with which they agreed. These people were silly and ill-mannered, but the play clearly did not grip as it should."

Paton, Maureen. "*An Enemy of the People*." *Daily Express* (London) 17 October 1988. *London Theatre Record* 8.21 (1988): 1439.

Mixed review of the Young Vic production, directed by David Thacker, that Paton feels is initially stiff and would be a better play if the ending were better clarified.

Pollock, Arthur. "There's Truth for Everybody in *An Enemy of the People*." *Daily Compass* 10 January 1951: 12.

Highly lauditory review of the New York premiere of Miller's adaptation, starring Fredric March and Florence Eldridge. Says Pollock, "The actors at the Broadhurst play this old drama as earnestly as if what takes place in it were taking place today, with a wonderful freshness and vividness and lucidity that cause Ibsen's ideas to stir New York audiences as those of no Ibsen play have stirred listeners in as long as the oldest admirers of Ibsen revivals can remember."

Ratcliffe, Michael. "*An Enemy of the People*." *Observer* (London) 16 October 1988. *London Theatre Record* 8.21 (1988): 1440.

Ratcliffe praises Tom Wilkinson's Dr. Stockmann as "magnificent" in David Thacker's "stirring production" of Miller's "thrilling version" of Ibsen's play at the Young Vic.

Renton, Alex. "*An Enemy of the People*." *Independent* (London) 17 October 1988. *London Theatre Record* 8.21 (1988): 1439–40.

Calling the Young Vic European premiere, directed by David Thacker, an "exuberant, expressionistic production," Renton also praises Tom Wilkinson's Dr. Stockmann as "a glorious creation: a vain, chippy, but immensely likable *naif*, fatally flawed by his passion for truth."

Rose, Helen. "*An Enemy of the People*." *Time Out* (London) 7 December 1988. *London Theatre Record* 8.24 (1988): 1665.

Rose praises the Young Vic production, recently moved to the Playhouse Theatre, as a "fiercely compassionate translation, which here is given a stirring production by David Thacker."

Spencer, Charles. "*An Enemy of the People*." *Daily Telegraph* (London) 15 October 1988. *London Theatre Record* 8.21 (1988): 1440–41.

Positive review of the Young Vic production, directed by David Thacker. "The evening is as moving as it is thought-provoking with superb ensemble acting and a towering performance from Tom Wilkinson in the central role."

"Theatre." *Newsweek* 8 January 1951: 67.

Positive review of the premiere production of Miller's *An Enemy of the People*, directed by Robert Lewis and starring Fredric March and Florence Eldridge, that the critic praises as an invigorating adaptation producing an "electrifying dramatic effect."

Thompson, Alan. "Professor's Debauch." *Theatre Arts* (March 1951): 25–27.

Negative review of the premiere production of Miller's *An Enemy of the People*, directed by Robert Lewis and starring Fredric March and Florence Eldridge, that Thompson faults for an adaptation that changes Ibsen's work into an "appeal to contemporary fears of tyranny and sentiment for individual freedom," making it a work of "agitational propaganda."

Tinker, Jack. "*An Enemy of the People*." *Daily Mail* (London) 27 October 1988. *London Theatre Record* 8.21 (1988): 1443.

Tinker praises the Young Vic production, directed by David Thacker, for its seeming relevancy and fine performances.

———. "*An Enemy of the People*." *Daily Mail* (London) 6 December 1988. *London Theatre Record* 8.24 (1988): 1665.

Highly laudatory review of Young Vic production, directed by David Thacker and recently moved to the Playhouse, that Tinker calls an "impeccably detailed" revival of "Arthur Miller's wonderfully crafted version from the early Fifties."

Watt, Douglas. "*Enemy of the People* Given Vibrant Revival." *New York Daily News* 12 March 1971. *New York Theatre Critics' Reviews* 32 (1971): 334.

After praising the Repertory Theater of Lincoln Center's revival of *An Enemy of the People* as "distinguished," Watt acclaims Millers adaptation as "fluent and forceful."

Watts, Richard, Jr. "Henrik Ibsen and Arthur Miller." *New York Post* 29 December 1950. 25. *New York Theatre Critics' Reviews* 11 (1950): 155.

Mixed review in which Watts examines Miller's adaptation of Ibsen's work as applicable to the current day but of insufficient importance to warrant a production. "It is interesting to note the timelessness of Ibsen, but, on the whole, I would rather see Mr. Miller writing his own plays."

———. "Ibsen's Strong Man Alone." *New York Post* 12 March 1971. *New York Theatre Critics' Reviews* 32 (1971): 334.

While admitting that he doesn't "know the drama well enough to be sure about the extent of [Miller's] contribution to it," Watts praises the Repertory Theater of Lincoln Center's revival of Miller's adaptation: "But the important matter is that his version contains all the force and moral fury that Ibsen originally put into it and that it remains a dramatic work of great interest and distinguished stature."

Wyatt, Euphemia Van Rensselaer. "Theater." *Catholic World* February 1951: 387.

Wyatt believes that *An Enemy of the People* owes its success to "an excellent script" and the "rousing performance" of Fredric March as Stockmann.

Related Interviews and Profiles (not with Miller)

Dunham, Mike. "Arthur Miller Remills Ibsen's Sermon in Play." *Anchorage Daily News* 6 April 1997: E6.

Article examining University of Alaska Anchorage theatre professor David Edgecomb's views regarding Miller's adaptation of Ibsen's *An Enemy of the People*, including his feelings that the character of Stockmann was a study for John Proctor.

News Reports, Letters to the Editor, and Related Matter

"Miller Adaptation Borrows from Bush." *Atlanta Constitution* 13 March 1992: C3.

Short news item recounting the details of Miller's revision of *An Enemy of the People* to include some memorable lines by President Bush. "The line changes, thought up by an actor at the Long Wharf Theatre in New Haven, Connecticut, will be delivered mimicking Mr. Bush's mannerisms."

The Crucible

Book-Length Studies

Bloom, Harold, ed. *Modern Critical Interpretations of The Crucible*. New York: Chelsea, 1999.

Collection of thirteen previously printed essays on the history and criticism of Miller's work. Sheila Huftel, "*The Crucible*"; Stephen Fender, "Precision and Pseudo Precision in *The Crucible*"; Thomas E. Porter, "The Long Shadow of the Law: *The Crucible*"; Robert A. Martin, "Arthur Miller's *The Crucible*: Background and Sources"; William T. Liston, "John Proctor's Playing in *The Crucible*"; William J. McGill Jr., "The Crucible of History: Arthur Miller's John Proctor"; Michael J. O'Neal, "History, Myth, and Name Magic in Arthur Miller's *The Crucible*"; E. Miller Budick, "History and Other Spectres in Arthur Miller's *The Crucible*"; June Schlueter and James K. Flanagan, "*The Crucible*"; Iska Alter, "Betrayal and Blessedness: Explorations of Feminine Power in *The Crucible*, *A View from the Bridge*, and *After the Fall*"; Michelle I. Pearson, "John Proctor and the Crucible of Individuation in Arthur Miller's *The Crucible*"; Wendy Schissel, "Re(dis)covering the Witches in Arthur Miller's *The Crucible*: A Feminist Reading"; and Stephen Marino, "Arthur Miller's 'Weight of Truth' in *The Crucible*."

Dukore, Bernard F. *"Death of a Salesman" and "The Crucible": Text and Performance*. Atlantic Highlands, N.J.: Humanities, 1989. Excerpt rpt. as "Character Profiles in *The Crucible*" in *Readings on Arthur Miller*. Ed. Thomas Siebold. San Diego, Calif.: Greenhaven, 1997. 143–47.

Dukore explores, in a brief overview format, two of Miller's most famous works. "Part One: Text" discusses in six chapters per play, various critical commentary and literary concerns associated historically with each play (for instance, the question of the tragic nature of each drama, use of language, dramatic structure, character, and themes). "Part Two: Performance" examines aspects of selected productions (direction, scenery and lighting, and acting) to compare and contrast various interpretations of both plays.

Ferres, John H., ed. *Twentieth Century Interpretations of "The Crucible," a Collection of Critical Essays*. Engelwood Cliffs, N.J.: Prentice-Hall, 1972.

Includes the following essays: John H. Ferres, "Introduction"; G. L. Kittredge, "Witchcraft and the Puritans"; E. Latham, "The Meaning of McCarthyism"; John Gassner, "Miller's *The Crucible* as Event and Play"; R. Hayes, "Hysteria and Ideology in *The Crucible*"; Leonard Moss, "A Problem Playwright" by W. Kerr; "A 'Social Play'"; Dennis Welland, "The Devil in Salem"; Herbert Blau, "No Play Is Deeper than Its Witches"; Penelope Curtis, "Setting, Language, and the Force of Evil in *The Crucible*"; Henry Popkin, "Historical Analogy and *The Crucible*"; P. G. Hill, "*The Crucible*: A Structural View"; Eric Mottram, "Jean-Paul Sartre's *Les Sorcières de Salem*"; Robert Hogan, "Action and Theme in *The Crucible*"; M.W. Steinberg, "Arthur Miller and the Idea of Modern Tragedy"; J.W. Douglass, "Which Witch Is Which?"; Sheila Huftel, "Subjectivism and Self-Awareness"; Arthur Ganz, "The Silence of Arthur Miller"; and "A Private Meeting of John and Abigail" extra scene to the play by Arthur Miller; plus a selected bibliography.

Martine, James J. *"The Crucible": Politics, Property and Pretense*. New York: Macmillan, 1993.

Martine investigates the key themes, concepts, historical context, critical reception, character, dramatic structure, tragic nature, and literary and artistic analogues of *The Crucible.*

Partridge, C. J. *The Crucible*. Oxford: Blackwell, 1971. Excerpt rpt. as "Profiles of Elizabeth Proctor and Abigail Williams in *The Crucible*" in *Readings on Arthur Miller*. Ed. Thomas Siebold. San Diego, Calif.: Greenhaven, 1997. 152–59.

Part of a series of introductions to the great classics of English literature ("Notes on English Literature"). Says Partridge, "While the strained relationships between John Proctor, his wife Elizabeth, and Abigail Williams turns Abigail into a destructive force, it leads Elizabeth to greater self-awareness."

Ward, Robert. *The Crucible: An Opera in 4 Acts, Based on the Play by Arthur Miller*. Libretto by Bernard Stambler. New York: Highgate, 1961.

Weales, Gerald, ed. *"The Crucible": Text and Criticism*. New York: Viking, 1971. New York: Penguin, 1996.

Following a the text of *The Crucible*, this volume contains the following critical essays, reviews, and interviews: Henry Hewes, "Arthur Miller and How He Went to the Devil"; Walter Kerr, "*The Crucible*"; Brooks Atkinson, "At the Theatre"; Brooks Atkinson, "Arthur Miller's *The Crucible*"; "Witchcraft and Stagecraft"; Joseph T. Shipley, "Arthur Miller's New Melodrama Is Not What It Seems to Be"; Eric Bentley, "The Innocence of Arthur Miller"; Robert Warshow, "The Liberal Conscience in *The Crucible*"; Harold Hobson, "Fair Play"; Herbert Blau, "Counterforce I: The Social Drama"; Marcel Aymé, "I Want to Be Hanged Like a Witch"; Jean Selz, "Raymond Rouleau among the Witches"; David Levin, "Salem Witchcraft in Recent Fiction and Drama"; Penelope Curtis, "*The Crucible*"; Stephen Fender, "Precision and Pseudo Precision in *The Crucible*"; William Wiegand, "Arthur Miller and the Man Who Knows"; Richard H. Rovere, "Arthur Miller's Conscience"; Albert Hunt, "Realism and Intelligence: Some Notes on Arthur Miller"; Gerald Weales, "Arthur Miller: Man and His Image"; and Lee Baxandall, "Arthur Miller: Still the Innocent." See individual cites for annotation, source, and page numbers.

Critical Essays in Books

Aswad, Betsy B. "*The Crucible*." *Insight IV: Analyses of Modern British and American Drama*. Ed. Hermann J. Weiand. Frankfurt: Hirschgraben-Verlag, 1979. 230–38.

Intended for educators and students, this guide for the classroom offers a detailed plot description, a summary of critical response, an evaluation and analysis of the play, questions for consideration, and a short list for further reading for *The Crucible*.

Atkinson, Brooks. "Arthur Miller: *The Crucible*." *The Lively Years 1940–1950*. New York: Associated Press, 1973. 221–24.

With the passage of time, Atkinson finds that *The Crucible* has become a less powerful play than it was in 1953 at the height of the McCarthy era.

Ballet, Arthur. "*The Crucible*." *International Dictionary of Theatre*, vol. 1, *Plays*. Ed. Mark Hawkins-Dady and Leanda Shrimpton. Chicago: St. James, 1992. 162–63.

Essay that examines the plot, structure, theme, historical parallels, and genesis of *The Crucible*.

Bentley, Eric. "The American Drama, 1944–1954." *The Dramatic Event*. New York: Horizon, 1954. 244–62. Rpt. in *American Drama and Its Critics*. Ed. Alan S. Downer. Chicago: U of Chicago P, 1965. 188–202. Rpt. in Bentley's *The Theatre of Commitment and Other Essays on Drama in Our Society*. New York: Atheneum, 1967. 34–40.

Bentley believes that part of Miller's popularity stems from the ambiguity of his dramas (which has "a strong emotional resonance among our fellows")—"*The Crucible* is a play for people who think that pleading the Fifth Amendment is not only a white badge of purity but also a red badge of courage."

Bigsby, Christopher. "Introduction to *The Crucible*." *The Crucible*. New York: Penguin, 1995. vii–xxv.

Bigsby discusses the genesis, historical background, and sources of *The Crucible*, as well as the play's universal themes, Proctor's fatal flaw, and critical success.

Blau, Herbert. "Counterforce I: The Social Drama." *The Impossible Theatre, A Manifesto*. New York: Macmillan, 1964. 186–227. Portion rpt. as "The Whole Man and the Real Witch." *Arthur Miller: A Collection of Critical Essays*. Ed. Robert Corrigan. Engelwood Cliffs, N.J.: Prentice-Hall, 1969. 122–30. Excerpt in *"The Crucible": Text and Criticism*. Ed. Gerald Weales. New York: Viking, 1971. New York: Penguin, 1996. 231–38. Excerpt as "No Play Is Deeper than Its Witches" in *Twentieth Century Interpretations of "The Crucible," a Collection of Critical Essays*. Ed. John H. Ferres. Engelwood Cliffs, N.J.: Prentice-Hall, 1972. 61–66.

In an essay that argues that theatre is "the public art of crisis," Blau criticizes *The Crucible* as a limited social drama and for not being the "tough" play that Miller had claimed it was—"our principles are neither jeopardized nor extended, however much we may fail to live by them anyhow."

Bloom, Harold. "Introduction." *Modern Critical Interpretations of "The Crucible."* New York: Chelsea, 1999. 1–2.

Despite its inherent flaws, *The Crucible* has a "proven theatrical effectiveness" and "continues to benefit" American society. "We would have to be mature beyond our national tendency to moral and religious self-righteousness for *The Crucible* to dwindle into another period-piece, and that maturation is nowhere in sight."

Bredella, Lothar. "Understanding a Foreign Culture through Assimilation and Accommodation: Arthur Miller's *The Crucible* and Its Dual Historical Context." *Text-Culture-Reception: Cross-Cultural Aspects of English Studies*. Eds. Rüdiger Ahrens and Heinz Antor. Heidelberg: Carl Winter Universitätsverlag, 1992. 475–521.

Lengthy "teaching unit" that examines the function of a literary text in understanding American culture. In this endeavor, Bredella analyzes critical commentary to gain insight into how the play challenged political views of the 1950s, offers an interpretation of Miller's work to illustrate two forms of understanding (assimilation and accommodation), and studies the two historical contexts to which the play refers—Salem in 1692 and the McCarthy era of the 1950s.

Brustein, Robert. "The Theatre in London: The National Theatre at the Old Vic." *The Third Theatre*. New York: Knopf, 1969. 107–13.

After admitting that he was not enthusiastic about seeing *The Crucible*, "having endured it many times and never with much pleasure," Brustein praises the National Theatre's production, directed by Laurence Olivier, for taking "on some of the proportions of Shakespearian tragedy. . . . Most impressive of all was the transfiguration of Miller's dialogue. Spoken by the cast in English country accents, it developed such vigor and authority that I had to admit I had been underestimating the eloquence of the author's language in this work."

Cohn, Ruby, and Bernard F. Dukore. *Twentieth Century Drama: England, Ireland, the United States*. New York: Random House, 1966. 535–39.

Brief biographical sketch followed by even briefer "editorial material" on *The Crucible*, which discusses the work's major themes and motifs.

DelFattore, Joan. "Fueling the Fire of Hell: A Reply to Censors of *The Crucible*." *Censored Books: Critical Viewpoints*. Eds. Nicholas Karolides, Lee Burress, John M. Kean. Metuchen, N.J.: Scarecrow, 1993. 201–8.

Essay that summarizes the form and content of attacks on *The Crucible* while providing a rationale for countering the complaints.

Drama for Students: Presenting Analysis, Context and Criticism on Commonly Studied Dramas. Detroit: Gale, 1998.

Includes an introduction to Miller and the play, plot summary, descriptions of important characters and their relationships within the drama, analysis of important themes, and explanation of Miller's literary technique.

Ferres, John H. "Still in the Present Tense: *The Crucible* Today." *University College Quarterly* 17 (May 1972): 8–18. Rpt. as "Introduction." *Twentieth Century Interpretations of "The Crucible," a Collection of Critical Essays*. Ed. John H. Ferres. Engelwood Cliffs, N.J.: Prentice-Hall, 1972. 1–19.

After a brief biographical essay, Ferres focuses on the critical response, themes, historical relevancy, and literary value of *The Crucible*.

Foulkes, Peter A. "Demystifying the Witch Hunt (Arthur Miller)." *Literature and Propaganda*. London: Methuen, 1983. 83–104.

Foulkes investigates the historical processes of communication with which Miller's *The Crucible* was involved and which it attempted to challenge. Says Foulkes, "I have proceeded from the assumption that the play should properly be regarded not as propagandist but as attempted demystification of propaganda."

Gottfried, Martin. *Jed Harris: The Curse of Genius*. Boston: Little, Brown, 1984. 220–27.

Fascinating behind-the-scenes look at the pre-production of *The Crucible*, including details of Harris courting Miller to direct the premiere production after Miller's breakup with Kazan over Kazan's testimony before HUAC, his instability during the rehearsal process, and Miller's salvaging of the production late in the process.

Graubard, Mark. *Witchcraft and Witchhunts Past and Present: The Blame Complex in Action*. Rockville, Md.: Kabel, 1989.

After a thoughtful retelling of the events surrounding the Salem witchcraft trials of 1692, Graubard offers a lengthy commentary criticizing *The Crucible* as "deplorable" and a "misrepresentation" of the actual events and people of the times. Says Graubard, by way of analogy, "Had a Nazi writer composed anything in a similar vein about Jews in the Middle Ages killing Christian children to extract their blood for use in the Passover ritual and followed word for word Miller's manner of presenting history in true conformity, as he says, with the 'essential nature' of the theme and the 'dramatic purposes' of the playwright, the critical and literary world of our times would view such an apologia in an entirely different perspective." An additional chapter offers a comparison of *The Crucible* with primary records of the Puritan era, arguing that Miller's work presents a "falsification of history."

Greene, Alexis. "Elizabeth LeCompte and the Wooster Group." *Contemporary American Theatre*. Ed. Bruce King. New York: St. Martin's, 1991. 117–34.

In a chapter devoted to exploring the origins and impact of the avant-garde theatre company the Wooster Group, Greene offers details surrounding the controversy of the group's use of *The Crucible* in their experimental production *L.S.D.*

Herron, Ima H. "The Puritan Village." *The Small Town in American Drama*. Dallas: Southern Methodist UP, 1969. 30–35.

Calling *The Crucible* the "ultimate treatment" of superstition and injustice, Herron examines the differences between Miller's interpretation of motive in the Salem witch trials of 1692 and other authors' treatment of the same subject, including the manner in which Miller has chosen to characterize the real citizens of Salem and his altering of historical facts to make his play work.

Heuvel, Michael Vanden. "The Fractal Dimensions of a Fractious Culture: The Wooster Group and the Politics of Performance." *Performing Drama/Dramatizing Performance: Alternative Theater and the Dramatic Text*. Ann Arbor: U of Michigan Press, 1991. 97–155.

Huevel traces the development and legal conflicts surrounding the Wooster Group's use of Miller's play in *L.S.D.* as a deconstruction of the text, and raises questions regarding the nature and ownership of text as a construct.

Hogan, Robert. "Action and Theme in *The Crucible*." *Twentieth Century Interpretations of "The Crucible," a Collection of Critical Essays*. Ed. John H. Ferres. Engelwood Cliffs, N.J.: Prentice-Hall, 1972. 95–97. [From *Arthur Miller*. Minneapolis: U of Minnesota P, 1964. 27–29.]

Hogan finds *The Crucible* a more dramatic play than *Death of a Salesman*. Its strength lies in the "clarity with which the theme . . . emerges from the plot."

Huftel, Sheila. "*The Crucible*." *Modern Critical Interpretations of The Crucible*. Ed. Harold Bloom. New York: Chelsea, 1999. 3–18. [From Huftel, *Arthur Miller: The Burning Glass*. New York: Citadel, 1965. 124–48. Excerpted as "Subjectivism and Self-Awareness." *Twentieth Century Interpretations of "The Crucible," a Collection of Critical Essays*. Ed. John H. Ferres. Englewood Cliffs, N.J.: Prentice-Hall, 1972. 104–106.]

After a lengthy plot description, Huftel spends the bulk of her essay refuting certain aspects of Eric Bentley's criticism of the play, detailing Miller's own writing on the subject, and relating audience responses to various productions of the play.

Hughes, Catharine. "*The Crucible*." *Plays, Politics, and Polemics*. New York: Drama Book, 1973. 15–25.

While acknowledging the play's flaws (in its exposition, in its careless or deliberate oversimplifications of character, and in its obvious attempt to draw the analogy with the 1950s), Hughes offers a reading of the play that praises Miller's drama for "its vitality, power, and sense of moral outrage" that communicates "with an intensity that transcends these failings."

Johnson, Claudia Durst, and Vernon E. Johnson. "Literary Analysis." *Understanding "The Crucible": A Student Casebook to Issues, Sources, and Historical Documents*. Westport, Conn.: Greenwood, 1998. 1–26.

Part of the Greenwood Press "Literature in Context" series. Topics such as the play's theme, plot, characterization, the subject of the tragic hero, and Miller as a social playwright are explored.

Levin, David. "Historical Fact in Fiction and Drama: The Salem Witchcraft Trials." *In Defense of Historical Literature: Essays on American History, Autobiography, Drama, and Fiction*. New York: Hill and Wang, 1967. 77–97.

Levin examines Hawthorne's "Young Goodman Brown" and Miller's *The Crucible* for their use of the historical facts of the Salem witch trials of 1692. According to Levin, Miller presents an oversimplification of history and his fault lies in his misunderstanding of the period, its consequences, and his own "pedagogical intention" that leads him into historical and "aesthetic error."

Luere, Jeane. "A Director's Distortion of a Modern Classic: Arthur Miller's Shift in Stance." *Playwright versus Director: Authorial Intentions and Performance Interpretations*. Westport, Conn.:

Greenwood, 1994. 95–106.

Luere explores the "adversarial" working relationship between Miller and director Elizabeth LeCompte during her attempt to incorporate portions of *The Crucible* in her experimental production of *L.S.D. (. . . Just the High Points . . .)*. After citing Miller's assumption that LeCompte was "parodying his work, mocking his purpose, thus posing for him the risk of forestalling more conventional productions in the future," Luere agues that it was the lack of a collaborative and trusting relationship between them coupled with Miller's "increased professional status in the 1980s theatre world" that fueled the playwright's reluctance to grant authority for the free directorial interpretation of his script.

Malhotra, M. L. "Triumph and Tragedy: An Examination of Arthur Miller's *The Crucible*." *Bridges of Literature, 23 Critical Essays in Literature*. Ajmer: Sunanda, 1971. 63–77.

Malhotra examines John Proctor's position as the dramatic and moral center of the play and concludes that the play is a "panoramic" masterpiece and true tragedy because it has a sweep "wider than that of a play which concentrates on a single action."

Meserve, Walter. "*The Crucible*: 'This Fool and I.'" *Arthur Miller: New Perspectives*. Ed. Robert A. Martin. Engelwood Cliffs, N.J.: Prentice-Hall, 1982. 127–38.

Meserve examines the seeming foolish nature of John Proctor—his attitude, beliefs, judgment, and the "honest naivete that will be his undoing"—in an effort to show how he becomes "a wiser man than he realizes, one who can be mistaken for a heroic figure."

Miller, Timothy. "John Proctor: Christian Revolutionary." *The Achievement of Arthur Miller: New Essays*. Ed. Steven Centola. Dallas, Tex.: Contemporary Research, 1995. 87–93.

Milton scholar Timothy Miller offers a reading of John Proctor as a Christian revolutionary, an advocate of faith and conscience, and an adversary of institutionalized religion.

Morgan, Edmund S. "Arthur Miller's *The Crucible* and the Salem Witch Trials: A Historian's View." *Golden and Brazen World: Papers in Literature and History, 1650–1800*. Ed. John M. Wallace. Berkeley: U of California P, 1985. 171–86.

Morgan, a self-admitted "historian who plays the critic," examines *The Crucible*'s depiction of history and questions "how

[Miller's] assumptions about history have affected his understanding of his characters." While condoning Miller's simplification of the trials of 1692 as well as his transformation of character age and relationships to one another, Morgan protests what he calls Miller's "faulty image of Puritanism."

Moss, Leonard. "A 'Social Play.'" *Twentieth Century Interpretations of "The Crucible," a Collection of Critical Essays*. Ed. John H. Ferres. Engelwood Cliffs, N.J.: Prentice-Hall, 1972. 37–45. [From *Arthur Miller*. New York: Twayne, 1967. 59–66.]

Moss interprets *The Crucible* as a social play that focuses on the subjective reality of a public phenomenon with historical precedent and current actuality.

Murphy, Brenda. "Witch Hunt: *The Crucible*, *The First Salem Witch Trial*, *The Witchfinders*." *Congressional Theatre: Dramatizing McCarthyism on Stage, Film, and Television*. Cambridge: Cambridge UP, 1999. 133–61, 276–78.

Murphy traces the development of Miller's witch hunt drama *The Crucible*, from his discovery of Marion Starkey's *The Devil in Massachusetts* to his own research in Salem with the witch trial papers. Murphy additionally surveys the play's critical response, concluding that "the soical drama being enacted on the public stages of America's public buildings had found its most potent metaphor in the most horrific social drama of its colonial past."

Murray, Edward. "Dramatic Technique in *The Crucible*." *Twentieth Century Interpretations of "The Crucible," a Collection of Critical Essays*. Ed. John H. Ferres. Engelwood Cliffs, N.J.: Prentice-Hall, 1972. 46–53 [From *Arthur Miller: Dramatist*. New York: Ungar, 1967. 52–75.]

Murray examines the major and minor characters in *The Crucible* and concludes that Miller's dramatic technique succeeds in fusing the personal and the social, producing "an extremely effective drama."

Nannes, Caspar H. *Politics in the American Drama*. Washington, D. C.: Catholic UP, 1960. 184–86.

Brief examination of *The Crucible* as a play which deals with communism and loyalty oaths, written and produced at the time "when the controversy was at its height."

Nathan, George Jean. "American Playwrights, Old and New: Arthur Miller." *The Theatre in the Fifties*. New York: Knopf, 1953. 105–109.

While admitting that Miller's play about the Salem witch trials is "very far beneath the merit" of *Death of a Salesman*, Nathan admires the work's "powerful theme"—"it provides us with the encouragement in respect to our theatre and we badly stand in need of it." Nathan faults the play for its "editorial tincture," "didactic chill," and "superficial tremors."

Porter, Thomas E. "The Long Shadow of the Law: *The Crucible*." *Myth and Modern American Drama*. Detroit: Wayne State UP, 1969. 177–99. Rpt. in *Critical Essays on Arthur Miller*. Ed. James J. Martine. Boston: G. K. Hall, 1979. 75–92. Rpt. in *Modern Critical Interpretations of "The Crucible."* Ed. Harold Bloom. New York: Chelsea, 1999. 33–53.

Lengthy essay in which Porter reads Miller's *The Crucible* as "one of the most instructive attempts by a contemporary playwright to make use of the trial ritual and the attitudes that surround it."

Quasimodo, Salvatore. "Arthur Miller's *The Crucible*." *The Poet and the Politician and Other Essays*. Trans. Thomas G. Bergin and Sergio Pacifici. Carbondale: Southern Illinois UP, 1964. 160–61.

Quasimodo, Nobel Prize winner for poetry in 1959, finds that Miller's play suffers from "a defective poetic identity" because of deference to historical truth over "theatrical time." John Proctor and his wife "come late to the center of the stage and seem portrayed through approximations and attitudes rather than poetically considered. Here Miller's creative instinct has lost touch with the real and strays into melodrama."

Rama Rao, P. G. "Reflections of Twentieth Century America in a Seventeenth Century Witches' Cauldron." *Literature and Politics in Twentieth Century America*. Eds. J. L. Plakkoottami and Prashant K. Sinka. Hyderabad: American Studies Research Centre, 1993. 71–78.

Essay that revisits *The Crucible* as a reflection on both contemporary Russia and America, focusing on HUAC's investigation of Miller's political life.

Raphael, D. D. "The Dramatist as Philosopher." *The Paradox of Tragedy: The Mahlon Powell Lectures, 1959*. Bloomington: Indiana UP, 1961. 103–105.

Raphael briefly examines Miller's *Crucible* as a modern play that has a "claim to greatness" for its "exploration of the complex relations between moral good and moral evil."

Rouse, John. "Textuality and Authority in Theatre and Drama: Some Contemporary Possibilities." *Critical Theory and Performance*. Ed. Janelle G. Reinelt and Joseph R. Roach. Ann Arbor: U of Michigan P, 1992. 146–57.

In a chapter that investigates the relationship between dramatic text and theatrical performance, Rouse offers an analysis of the controversy surrounding the Wooster Group's efforts to include an adaptation of the final section of *The Crucible*'s four scenes within their production *L.S.D.* in 1984.

Savran, David. "*L.S.D. (. . . Just the High Points. . .)*: History as Hallucination." *The Wooster Group, 1975–1985: Breaking the Rules*. Ann Arbor: UMI Research, 1986. 170–220. Rpt. as *Breaking the Rules: The Wooster Group*. New York: TCG, 1988.

This chapter details the Wooster Group's production of *L.S.D.* in 1983 and their attempt to secure permission from Miller to include portions of *The Crucible* within the text of their piece. Included are the specifics surrounding Miller's refusal to allow them the rights to excerpt, including the several "cease and desist" orders from Miller's attorneys and Miller's statements to the press regarding his feelings about the production.—"The issue here is very simple. I don't want my play produced except in total agreement with the way I wrote it."

Scharine, Richard G. "*The Crucible*." *From Class to Caste in American Drama, Political and Social Themes since the 1930's*. New York: Greenwood, 1991. 83–87, 236.

Scharine examines the similarities between the Salem witch trials and the Cold War, highlighting the ironic implications of both historical periods in American political and social history. "The inability to separate the state from the voice of Heaven and the automatic consignment of those who disagree with it in any form or at any time to the Devil is the real crime of both *The Crucible* and the Cold War."

Schlueter, June, and James K. Flanagan. "*The Crucible*." *Modern Critical Interpretations of "The Crucible."* Ed. Harold Bloom. New York: Chelsea, 1999. 113–21. [From *Arthur Miller*. New York: Ungar, 1987.]

Essay that examines the theme of guilt in *The Crucible* and evaluates John Proctor as a hero "of extraordinary moral courage."

Strout, Cushing. "Analogical History: *The Crucible*." *The Veracious Imagination: Essays on American History, Literature, and Biography*. Middletown, Conn.: Wesleyan UP, 1981. 139–56.

Lengthy essay in which Strout examines historical commentary concerning the social origins of witchcraft to "find an illuminating way to appraise *The Crucible*, Miller's defense of it, and [Robert] Warshow's objections for Miller's strategy." Strout finds that Miller not only did not adequately grasp historical reality, but his work is "historically misleading" and ultimately flawed because "Miller could not move beyond the modern idea of the need (which Elizabeth expresses) for John Proctor to forgive himself. What is unimaginable from *The Crucible* is a John Proctor who finally forgave his enemies," which the real Proctor historically did.

Trócsányi, Miklós. "Two Views of American Puritanism: Hawthorne's *The Scarlet Letter* and Miller's *The Crucible*." *The Origins and Originality of American Culture*. Ed. Tibor Frank. Budapest: Akadémiai Kiadó, 1984. 63–71.

In a paper presented at the International Conference in American Studies, 9–11 April 1980, Trócsányi finds Nathaniel Hawthorne's *The Scarlet Letter* a more detailed and fuller description of New England Puritanism than Miller's *The Crucible*, which he says is "highly concentrated, a sharp, cruel and merciless play" that shows the "nature and *origins* of Puritanism in America."

Visweswara Rao, C. R. "Society and Contemporary Realism in Arthur Miller's *The Crucible*." *Literature and Politics in Twentieth Century America*. Eds. J. L. Plakkoottami and Prashant K. Sinka. Hyderabad: American Studies Research Centre, 1993. 65–70.

Essay that examines the "heightened naturalism" and theme of alienation of both social action and personality in *The Crucible*, concluding that Miller's play is "more than a mechanism of honesty and right dealing," but possesses a "deeper conception of relationships."

Weales, Gerald. "Introduction." *The Crucible: Text and Criticism*. New York: Viking, 1971. New York: Penguin, 1996. ix–xvii.

In this introduction to a collection of critical essays and reviews on *The Crucible*, Weales praises Miller for constructing a play with scenes that have "such vitality that they cannot be killed onstage."

Welland, Dennis. "The Devil in Salem." *Twentieth Century Interpretations of "The Crucible," a Collection of Critical Essays*. Ed. John H. Ferres. Engelwood Cliffs, N.J.: Prentice-Hall, 1972. 54–60. [From *Arthur Miller*. New York: Grove, 1961. 74–91.]

Welland praises Miller's drama for its historical accuracy, Shavian moral, literary depiction of evil, and technical achievement.

White, Sidney Howard. "Proctor, the Moral Hero in *The Crucible*" in *Readings on Arthur Miller*. Ed. Thomas Siebold. San Diego, Calif.: Greenhaven, 1997. 148–51. Rpt. from *The Merrill Guide to Arthur Miller*. Columbus, Ohio: Merrill, 1970.

John Proctor is the first true heroic figure, says White, because he not only realizes his moral responsibility to himself and his community, but he acts upon it and dies to maintain his integrity.

Whitman, Robert. *The Play-Reader's Handbook*. New York: Bobbs-Merrill, 1966. 61–62, 208–209.

Whitman finds arguments that insist that Miller was "using drama as a political weapon and making a thinly veiled attack on McCarthyism" irrelevant to *The Crucible*'s power and importance. Says Whitman, it is "the tragedy of John Proctor, the forces he defies, and the values he defends [that] are relevant to all men who exist as both individuals and social beings."

Critical Essays in Journals and Magazines

Aronson, Arnold. "The Wooster Group's *L.S.D. (. . . Just the High Points . . .)*. *The Drama Review* 29.2 (Summer 1985): 65–77.

Without going into the controversy surrounding Miller's refusal to allow the Wooster Group from using portions of his *The Crucible* in their play *L.S.D.*, Aronson details the original vision of Elizabeth LeCompte's work and her reasons for including pieces of the Miller text in the experimental play.

Auslander, Philip. "Toward a Concept of the Political in Postmodern Theatre." *Theatre Journal* 39 (March 1987): 20–34. Rpt. in *Presence and Resistance: Postmodernism and Cultural Politics in Contemporary American Performance*. Ann Arbor: U of Michigan P, 1992. 83–104.

Auslander examines the Wooster Group's production of *L.S.D (. . . Just the High Points . . .)* as "an investigation of the suppression of difference within cultural and political representations, the deconstruction of presence which enables that investigation to avoid merely restating the images and structure it evokes and finally, the Group's appropriation of Arthur Miller's *The Crucible* in its own performance text."

Aymé, Marcel. "I Want to Be Hanged Like a Witch." Trans. Gerald Weales. *Arts* (15–21 December 1954): 1, 3. Rpt. in *"The Crucible": Text and Criticism*. Ed. Gerald Weales. New York: Viking, 1971. New York: Penguin, 1996. 239–41.

Aymé discusses his frustrating work as translator/adaptor for Miller's play into French for a production at the Théâtre Sarah Bernhardt in 1954, directed by Raymond Rouleau, with Simone Signoret and Yves Montand. He speaks of his difficulty translating the story for a French audience who will naturally sympathize with the seduced orphan and whose main character, an "American petticoat-rumpler," won't evoke the feeling Miller intended.

Barlow, Dudley. "Seeking the Spheres to Connect Them." *Education Digest* 61 (February 1996): 32–35.

Barlow, a high school English teacher, writes of his discovery of contemporary parallels between the Miller drama, Jewish extremism, and the police investigation into an alleged child molestation ring in Wenatchee, Washington.

Bentley, Eric. "Do We Believe in Discussion." *New Republic* 2 July 1956: 22.

In an essay on controversial plays, Bentley notes that *The Crucible* is perhaps one of the most controversial plays of the past ten years but somehow aroused very little discussion in the press at the time of its premiere.

Bergeron, David M. "Arthur Miller's *The Crucible* and Nathaniel Hawthorne: Some Parallels." *English Journal* 58 (January 1969): 47–55.

Bergeron explores the similarities in setting, themes, and character in *The Crucible* and Nathaniel Hawthorne's *The Scarlet Letter*.

Bergman, Herbert. "'The Interior of the Heart': *The Crucible* and *The Scarlet Letter*." *University College Quarterly* 15.4 (1970): 27–32.

Bergman studies the similarities and differences between Miller's *The Crucible* and Hawthorne's *The Scarlet Letter* in order to reveal that Miller's work "goes beyond the interior psychological question of the effect of fraud" to "the exterior question of public hysteria."

Bonnet, Jean-Marie. "Society vs. the Individual in Arthur Miller's *The Crucible*." *English Studies* 63 (1982): 32–36.

Bonnet examines the "fundamental duality" of society and the individual in *The Crucible* and concludes that while the play is "not easily classified within the traditional categories of drama," it is, nonetheless, "highly successful."

Budick, E. Miller. "History and Other Spectres in Arthur Miller's *The Crucible*." *Modern Drama* 28.4 (December 1985): 535–52. Rpt. as "History and Other Spectres in *The Crucible*" in *Modern Critical Views: Arthur Miller*. Ed. Harold Bloom. New York: Chelsea, 1987. 127–44. Rpt. in *Modern Critical Interpretations of "The Crucible."* Ed. Harold Bloom. New York: Chelsea, 1999. 95–112.

Budick argues that with *The Crucible*, Miller searched "deep into American history, not to discover a convenient analogy to a contemporary problem, but to indicate the importance of registering the relativity and subjectivity of moral justice with the *absolute* moral principles of charity and humility and forgiveness."

Bush, Catherine. "Cease and Desist." *Performance Magazine* (June–July 1985): 34–36.

Bush details the controversy over the use of text from Miller's *The Crucible* in the Wooster Group's production of *L.S.D.*

Calarco, N. Joseph. "Production as Criticism: Miller's *The Crucible*." *Educational Theatre Journal* 29 (1977): 354–61.

Calarco describes, from a director's viewpoint, the critical process of a production—from initial script study through performance— of *The Crucible* at Wayne State University.

Callahan, Elizabeth. "The Tragic Hero in Contemporary Secular and Religious Drama." *Literary Half-Yearly* 8 (January–July 1967): 42–49.

Callahan compares Miller's *The Crucible* and T.S. Eliot's *Murder in the Cathedral* as Aristotelian tragedies.

Caruso, Cristina C. "'One Finds What One Seeks': Arthur Miller's *The Crucible* as a Regeneration of the American Myth of Violence." *Journal of American Drama and Theatre* 7.3 (Fall 1995): 30–42.

Caruso examines *The Crucible* as Miller's determined effort "to keep the patriarchal myth breathing, to edit out the marginal female characters who might interfere with this myth," thereby killing "the historical 'life' of the Salem Witch Trials by having the last word on them."

Cerjak, Judith A. "Beware the Loss of Conscience: *The Crucible* as Warning for Today." *English Journal* 76 (September 1987): 55–7.

Cerjak reexamines Miller's *The Crucible* "within the context of the witch hunts rampant in current society," concluding that the Salem witch trials are both a symbol and a warning for modern America to "question the sources of power controlling us."

Cox, Brian. "Twelve Days at Mow-Hat." *Drama* (1988): 5–6.

Part one of an excerpt of a journal kept by Cox during his stay in Russia to direct the students of the Moscow Art Theatre School in a diploma production of Miller's *The Crucible.*

Curtis, Penelope. "*The Crucible*." *Critical Review* (Sydney) 8 (1965): 45–58. Excerpted as "Setting, Language, and the Force of Evil in *The Crucible*." *Twentieth Century Interpretations of "The Crucible," a Collection of Critical Essays*. Ed. John H. Ferres. Englewood Cliffs, N.J.: Prentice-Hall, 1972. 67–76. Excerpted in *"The Crucible": Text and Criticism.* Ed. Gerald Weales. New York: Viking, 1971. New York: Penguin, 1996. 255–71.

Curtis sees *The Crucible* as "a work of some subtlety and range" that is unusual among Miller's plays in both setting and language.

Davis, Rick. "Digital Lit." *American Theatre* April 1995: 50–52.

Davis reviews the CD-ROM version of *The Crucible*. While its "glitzy features" will no doubt entice students to spend more time with the text than they might with a paper copy, the product is not useful to the professional or theatre scholar.

Ditsky, John M. "Stone, Fire and Light: Approaches to *The Crucible*." *North Dakota Quarterly* 46 (Spring 1978): 65–72.

Ditsky analyzes the various dualities of image patterns in *The Crucible*.

Douglass, James W. "Miller's *The Crucible*: Which Witch Is Which?" *Renascence* 15 (Spring 1963): 145–51. Rpt. as "Which Witch Is Which?" in excerpted form in *Twentieth Century Interpretations of "The Crucible," a Collection of Critical Essays*. Ed. John H. Ferres. Engelwood Cliffs, N.J.: Prentice-Hall, 1972. 101–103.

Douglass finds that in a drama filled with ironies, "the biggest irony is that its author seems wholly unconscious of the fact that a Devil, even a Devil of his own creation, is actually present in *The Crucible*" in the form of a malevolent government.

Erickson, Jon. "Appropriation and Transgression in Contemporary American Performance: The Wooster Group, Holly Hughes, and Karen Finley." *Theatre Journal* (May 1990): 225–36.

In a lengthy essay on "how appropriation and transgression have worked together in recent American theater and performance art," Erickson examines the controversy surrounding the Wooster Group's use of Miller's words from *The Crucible* in their performance piece *L.S.D.* in relation to the laws "designed to protect the property of the artist." While Miller saw their interpretation as "ridicule," director Elizabeth LeCompte chose the text "to examine ideological presuppositions but not to ridicule."

Fender, Stephen. "Precision and Pseudo Precision in *The Crucible*." *Journal of American Studies* 1.1 (April 1967): 87–98. Rpt. in *"The Crucible": Text and Criticism.* Ed. Gerald Weales. New York: Viking, 1971. New York: Penguin, 1996. 272–89. Rpt. in *Modern Critical Interpretations of "The Crucible."* Ed. Harold Bloom. New York: Chelsea, 1999. 19–31.

Fender supports a reading of *The Crucible* as "a dramatic contest of language," but questions the assumption that the Puritans in his play have some sort of a consistent moral outlook. He argues that the speech that Miller creates shows a society without moral referents. "Proctor serves himself by recovering his 'name'; he serves Salem by giving it a viable language."

Goldberg, Jonah. "Sexual Addiction." *National Review* 23 November 1998: 20–21.

In an article analyzing the cultural, social, and moral effects of

President Clinton's relationship with Monica Lewinsky, Goldberg compares the Clinton-Lewinsky sex scandal with Miller's *The Crucible*.

Hansen, Chadwick. "The Metamorphosis of Tituba, or Why American Intellectuals Can't Tell an Indian Witch from a Negro." *New England Quarterly* 47.1 (March 1974): 3–12.

Engrossing study by historian Hansen that details the life of the real Tituba, a Carib woman, who over the years has been changed by historians and dramatists to a black African practicing voodoo. Of note is Hansen's discussion of Miller's remaking of Tituba into a "Negro practicing voodoo" for *The Crucible*.

Hendrickson, Gary P. "The Last Analogy: Arthur Miller's Witches and America's Domestic Communists." *Midwest Quarterly* 33 (Summer 1992): 447–55.

Hendrickson examines *The Crucible*'s relevance to the McCarthy era and, in particular, studies the obvious analogies between the two witch hunts and Miller's "tactical" shifting reaction to criticism that accepted "a very clear contemporary parallel."

Hill, Philip G. "*The Crucible*: A Structural View." *Modern Drama* 10 (December 1967): 312–17. Rpt. in *Twentieth Century Interpretations of "The Crucible," a Collection of Critical Essays*. Ed. John H. Ferres. Engelwood Cliffs, N.J.: Prentice-Hall, 1972. 86–92.

Hill compares *The Crucible* to the well-made play and defends Miller's work against critic George Jean Nathan's pronouncement that the work was badly structured.

Hunt, Albert. "Realism and Intelligence: Some Notes on Arthur Miller." *Encore* 7 (May–June 1960). 12–17, 41. Rpt. in *'The Crucible": Text and Criticism*. Ed. Gerald Weales. New York: Viking, 1971. 324–32.

Hunt examines *The Crucible* as a realistic play and compares it to modern British realist dramas.

Levin, David. "Salem Witchcraft in Recent Fiction and Drama." *New England Quarterly* 28.4 (December 1955): 537–46. Rpt. in *"The Crucible": Text and Criticism*. Ed. Gerald Weales. New York: Viking, 1967. New York: Penguin, 1996. 248–54.

In this "essay review," Levin examines four literary works that focus on the Salem witchcraft trials in an effort to evaluate their historical validity and contemporary parallels. Of Miller's *The*

Crucible, Levin applauds the work for its brilliant dramatization of "the dilemma of an innocent man who must confess falsely if he wants to live," but ultimately faults Miller for his oversimplification of historical fact.

Liston, William T. "John Proctor's Playing in *The Crucible*." *Midwest Quarterly* 20 (Summer 1979): 394–403. Rpt. in *Modern Critical Interpretations of "The Crucible."* Ed. Harold Bloom. New York: Chelsea, 1999. 69–75.

Liston studies the character of John Proctor as different from all others in *The Crucible*: in his linguistic habits; his use of "metaphor to a greater extent than anyone else in the play"; and his habit of playfulness that "makes him a revolutionary, a threat to the community."

Lowe, Valerie. "'Unsafe Convictions': 'Unhappy' Confessions in *The Crucible*." *Language and Literature: Journal of the Poetics and Linguistics Association* 3.3 (1994): 175–95.

Lowe offers a close reading of the speech act of confession in *The Crucible* and argues that "the social status of the individuals involved affects the constitutive rules governing the act of confession itself."

Marino, Stephen. "Arthur Miller's 'Weight of Truth' in *The Crucible*." *Modern Drama* 38.4 (Winter 1995): 488–95. Rpt. in *Modern Critical Interpretations of "The Crucible."* Ed. Harold Bloom. New York: Chelsea, 1999. 177–85.

Lengthy study tracing the repetition of the word "weight" to "reveal how the word supports one of the play's crucial themes: how an individual's struggle for truth often conflicts with society."

Martin, Robert A. "Arthur Miller's *The Crucible*: Background and Sources." *Modern Drama* 20 (1977): 279–92. Rpt. in *Essays on Modern American Drama: Williams, Miller, Albee, and Shepard*. Ed. by Dorothy Parker. Toronto: U of Toronto P, 1987. 80–93. Rpt. in *Critical Essays on Arthur Miller*. Ed. James J. Martine. Boston: G. K. Hall, 1979. 93–104. Rpt. in *Modern Critical Interpretations of "The Crucible."* Ed. Harold Bloom. New York: Chelsea, 1999. 55–67.

In an effort to evaluate Miller's abilities in dramatizing real people and events into "a dramatically coherent rendition of the most terrifying chapters in American history," Martin compares

Miller's *The Crucible* with historical reality, citing background sources Miller worked with in fashioning his drama and other documents of the times.

McGill, William J., Jr. "The Crucible of History: Arthur Miller's John Proctor." *New England Quarterly* 54.2 (June 1981): 258–64. Rpt. in *Modern Critical Interpretations of "The Crucible."* Ed. Harold Bloom. New York: Chelsea, 1999. 77–81.

After a general review of the historical accuracy of *The Crucible*, McGill argues that while Miller did in fact alter historical truth in his writing of the play, those changes were made to support the drama of his making, thus capturing some "fundamental realities of the Salem events" and making Proctor's death as "all too real."

Miller, Jeanne-Marie A. "Odets, Miller and Communism." *College Language Association Journal* 19 (June 1976): 484–93.

Essay that studies Clifford Odets's *Till the Day I Die* as an anti-Nazi play and Miller's *The Crucible* as a veiled allegory to the McCarthy era. Both playwrights, says Jeanne-Marie Miller, "dared to dramatize current events and deliver a warning to the American people."

Mukerji, Nirmal. "John Proctor's Tragic Predicament." *Panjab University Research Bulletin: Arts* 4.2 (April 1973): 75–79.

Mukerji argues that, unlike Willy Loman, John Proctor is a true tragic figure because he has a self-awareness and self-realization that raises him to a noble level.

Navasky, Victor. "Starrism." *Nation* 19 October 1998: 5.

Lengthy editorial in which Navasky reiterates his stance (which first appeared in *Naming Names*) that the purpose of the HUAC hearings was a sort of degradation ceremony, which, sadly, closely resembles the "sexual McCarthyism" of the Kenneth Starr investigation of President Clinton. Concludes Navasky, "In the long run history has decided that it was not HUAC's or McCarthy's targets that were degraded. It was the country itself. Let us not let it happen again."

Oder, Norman. "Multimedia *Crucible* from Penguin and Voyager." *Publisher's Weekly* 5 September 1994: 25.

A pre-pub alert to the imminent publication of the CD-ROM version of Miller's play, which will include a multimedia disk with a Miller interview, the text of the play, articles, interviews with actors, and background material on both the Puritan and McCarthy eras. The book-and-disk package will be targeted at high school and college teachers.

O'Neal, Michael J. "History, Myth, and Name Magic in Arthur Miller's *The Crucible*." *CLIO* 12.2 (Winter 1983): 111–22. Rpt. in *Modern Critical Interpretations of "The Crucible."* Ed. Harold Bloom. New York: Chelsea, 1999. 83–93.

O'Neal offers a close reading of the final jail scene as it determines "Proctor's cry for his name as integral not only to the play's theme, but to its dramatic and historical method as well."

Otten, Terry. "Historical Drama and the Dimensions of Tragedy: *A Man For All Seasons* and *The Crucible*." *American Drama* 6.1 (Fall 1996): 42–60.

Otten compares Robert Bolt's *A Man for All Seasons* and Miller's *The Crucible* in the context of both historical determinism and individual choice.

Payne, Darwin R. "Unit Scenery." *Players Magazine* 33 (December 1956): 59, 62.

Detail regarding the scenery of a Southern Illinois University production of *The Crucible* that "was designed with the idea of matching visually and forceful simplicity of [Miller's] poetic drama, not merely presenting a succession of historically accurate, architecturally feasible rooms and locales."

Pearson, Michelle I. "John Proctor and The Crucible of Individuation in Arthur Miller's *The Crucible*." *Studies in American Drama, 1945–Present* 6.1 (1991): 15–27. Rpt. in *Modern Critical Interpretations of "The Crucible."* Ed. Harold Bloom. New York: Chelsea, 1999. 153–64.

Pearson charts the development of the character of John Proctor as a search for the essential self and examines Proctor's confrontation with and assimilation of his personality, which are represented by other characters in the play.

Pether, Penelope. "Jangling the Keys to the Kingdom: Some Reflections on *The Crucible*, on an American Constitutional Paradox, and on Australian Judicial Review." *Cardozo Studies in Law and Literature* 8.2 (Fall–Winter 1996): 317–37.

Lengthy essay offering a close law and literature analysis of *The Crucible*, whose absence from the law and literature canon, says Pether, "is due to its subversive feminist potential."

Popkin, Henry. "Arthur Miller's *The Crucible*." *College English* 26 (November 1964): 139–46. Rpt. in *Scholarly Appraisals in Literary Works Taught in High Schools*. Ed. Stephen Dunning, et al. Ill: National Council of Teachers of English, 1965, 110–17. Excerpted as "Historical Analogy and *The Crucible*" in *Twentieth Century Interpretations of "The Crucible," a Collection of Critical Essays*. Ed. John H. Ferres. Engelwood Cliffs, N.J.: Prentice-Hall, 1972. 77–85. Excerpt rpt. as "The Historical Background of *The Crucible*" in *Readings on Arthur Miller*. Ed. Thomas Siebold. San Diego, Calif.: Greenhaven, 1997. 138–42.

After summarizing the events in the 1950s that led to Miller's creation of *The Crucible*, Popkin offers a close reading of the play as a work "that keeps our attention by furnishing exciting crises, each one proceeding logically from its predecessor, in the lives of people in whom we have been made to take an interest." Also discussed is the importance of Miller's technique, borrowed from *The Poetics*, of constructing a character in John Proctor who is fatally flawed but who, ultimately, rises above his humanness in an effort to "have his goodness."

Sarver, Linda. "Seeing America Clearly." *Theatre Design and Technology* 32.5 (Fall 1995): 49–52.

Sarver surveys American plays designed by non-American designers at the Prague Quadrennial, including Zsolt Khell's design for the Cziky Gergely Színház production of *The Crucible*.

Savran, David. "The Wooster Group, Arthur Miller and *The Crucible*." *The Drama Review* 29.2 (Summer 1985): 99–109.

Savran details attempts by the Wooster Group to secure performance rights to *The Crucible* for use in their *L.S.D.* and other controversies surrounding the group's practices.

Schissel, Wendy. "Re(dis)covering the Witches in Arthur Miller's *The Crucible*: A Feminist Reading." *Modern Drama* 37.3 (Fall 1994): 461–73. Rpt. in *Modern Critical Interpretations of "The Crucible."* Ed. Harold Bloom. New York: Chelsea, 1999. 165–75.

Schissel offers a feminist critique of *The Crucible*, noting how the drama reinforces negative female stereotypes of femme fatales and cold, unforgiving wives in order to raise more masculine issues (i.e., universal virtues) to the level of catharsis. She argues that gynecophobia (fear and distrust of women) is not only implicit in Puritan mythology and Miller's version of events, but in the society that has produced most of Miller's critics.

Smith, Iris. "Authors in AmeriCalif.: Tony Kushner, Arthur Miller, and Anna Deveare Smith." *Centennial Review* 40.1 (1996): 125–42.

Smith investigates two different models of authorship that have dominated modern theatre, the lone author and the theatre collective. Miller is examined in relation to the paradox presented by his refusal to allow the Wooster Group to use portions of *The Crucible* in their *L.S.D.* in ways Miller's deemed inappropriate and a threat to his "good name," and the implications for theatre collectives of his public assertion of his rights as a legal author.

Standley, Fred L. "An Echo of Milton in *The Crucible*." *Notes & Queries* 15 (1968): 303. Rejoinder by Oliver H. P. Ferris. *Notes & Queries* 16 (1969): 268.

Standley argues that Miller's *Crucible* contains an almost identical passage as Milton's poem, "Another on the Same." Its only difference being a change of tone and intent "from humorous banter to tragic seriousness."

Walker, Philip. "Arthur Miller's *The Crucible*: Tragedy or Allegory?" *Western Speech* 20 (Fall 1956): 222–24.

Walker argues that the weakness of *The Crucible* is its conflicted intention. While the play could be read as a personal tragedy or political allegory, it does not focus on either one exclusively. To make the play work in the theatre, Miller should attempt to establish "an emphatic relationship between Proctor and the audience," eliminating the contemporary political and social parallels.

Warshow, Robert. "The Liberal Conscience in *The Crucible*." *Commentary* 15 (1953): 265–71. Rpt. in *The Scene Before You: A New Approach to American Culture.* Ed. Chandler Brossard. New York: Rinehart, 1955. 191–203. Rpt. in *The Immediate Experience*. Ed. Robert Warshow. New York: Doubleday, 1969. 189–203. Rpt. in *Arthur Miller: A Collection of Critical Essays*. Ed. Robert W. Corrigan. Engelwood Cliffs, N.J.: Prentice-Hall, 1969. 111–21. Rpt. in *"The Crucible": Text and Criticism*. Ed. Gerald Weales. New York: Viking, 1971. New York: Penguin, 1996. 210–26.

Warshow explores the universality of Miller's *The Crucible* and attempts to discern what Miller was trying to say through this play, concluding that its liberal message is lifeless because of the historical disguise that covers it.

Willis, Robert. "Arthur Miller's *The Crucible*: Relevant for All Times." *Faculty Journal* (East Stroudsburg) 1 (1970): 5–14.

Willis argues that *The Crucible* succeeds because of its universal themes, especially those regarding the conflict between public and private responsibility and the idea that there are evil individuals in the world who "under the guise of doing good, knowingly condemn their fellow men."

Woliver, C. Patrick. "Robert Ward's *The Crucible*: A Critical Commentary." *Opera Journal* 26.1 (March 1993): 3–31.

Woliver discusses Ward's adaptation of Miller's play, the opera's performance history, its musicology, and use of Miller's structure and plot.

Critical Essays in Newspapers

Billington, Michael. "After Its First Performance, *The Crucible* Was Rubbished. So Why Is It Now Regarded as One of the Century's Greatest Plays?" *Guardian* (London) 28 February 1997: 3.

Billington discusses the "enduring respect" for Miller's *The Crucible* and the adaptation of the play into an American film starring Daniel Day-Lewis.

Caplan, Betty. "Mr. Miller, the Misogynist?" *Guardian* (London) 11 December 1990: 33.

Caplan offers an analysis of *The Crucible* that concludes that Miller exploited the historical facts of the Salem witch trials "for its sensationalist value at the expense of accurate character development."

Melloan, George. "The Theater." *Wall Street Journal* 15 March 1971. *New York Theatre Critics' Reviews* 32 (1971): 336.

Not really a review, Melloan examines the Repertory Theater of Lincoln Center's revival of Miller's adaptation from the point of view of its topicality to a "generation when pollution and ecology have suddenly become important issues."

Burns, Margo. "Arthur Miller's *The Crucible*: Fact & Fiction." http://www.ogram.org/17thc/crucible.shtml (22 May 1998).

A student of the Salem witch trials (1692), Burns lists what she calls a "wide variety of minor historical inaccuracies" with Miller's telling of the tale in his play and film of *The Crucible*.

Production Reviews

Anderson, Paul. "*The Crucible.*" *Tribune* (London) 8 June 1990. *London Theatre Record* 10.11 (1990): 728.

Brief review in which Anderson calls the Royal National Theatre production, directed by Howard Davies, "a delight."

Asquith, Ros. "*The Crucible.*" *City Limits* (London) 7 June 1990. *London Theatre Record* 10.11 (1990): 729.

While lauding Miller's drama as "great," Asquith finds fault with the Royal National Theatre production, directed by Howard Davies, for being "a touch plodding—not helped by frocks straight out of the junior-paint-by-numbers-Quakers-manual."

Atkinson, Brooks. "At the Theatre." *New York Times* 23 January 1953: 15. *New York Theatre Critics' Reviews* 14 (1953): 386. Rpt. in *"The Crucible": Text and Criticism*. Ed. Gerald Weales. New York: Viking, 1971. New York: Penguin, 1996. 192–94.

While praising *The Crucible* as a "powerful play," Atkinson concludes that Miller's work contains "too much excitement and not enough emotion" and lacks the stature and universality of a masterpiece.

———. "At the Theatre." *New York Times* 2 July 1953: 20. Rpt. as "Arthur Miller's *The Crucible* in a New Edition with Several New Actors and One New Scene." in *"The Crucible": Text and Criticism*. Ed. Gerald Weales. New York: Viking, 1971. New York: Penguin, 1996. 194–96.

Atkinson praises the new edition of *The Crucible* appearing at the Martin Beck Theatre, starring E. G. Marshall and Maureen Stapleton, for acquiring "a certain human warmth that it lacked amid the shrill excitements of the original version." With changes including the addition of a brief scene between Proctor and Abigail, new actors in the lead roles, and a new "fluid" design, "this new edition of *The Crucible* considerably freshens the most genuine parts of the original production. The excitement is less metallic. The emotion is more profound."

———. "*The Crucible.*" *New York Times* 1 February 1953: II: 1.

While recognizing the over-indulgent direction of Jed Harris, Atkinson praises the premiere production of *The Crucible* for its important themes.

———. "*Crucible* Restaged." *New York Times* 1 June 1958: II: 1.
Atkinson praises the Arena Stage revival for "the scope and principle of Mr. Miller's accomplishment" and a staging that "adds excitement."

Barber, John. "*The Crucible*." *Daily Telegraph* (London) 9 December 1985. *London Theatre Record* 5.25/26 (1985): 1218.
Barber praises the David Thacker revival at the Young Vic as "a simple, fervent production which counts among the best things they have done in recent years."

Barnes, Clive. "*Crucible* Gives Hope." *New York Post* 11 December 1991. *New York Theatre Critics' Reviews* 52 (1991): 141.
Positive review of the National Actors Theatre's "first-rate" revival (their first production) starring Martin Sheen, Martha Scott, and Michael York, directed by Yossi Yzraely. Barnes considers Miller's work "an odd but great play" and "conceivably his finest."

———. "Miller's *Crucible*." *New York Times* 28 April 1972: 36.
Positive review of the Repertory Theater of Lincoln Center revival of *The Crucible*, starring Robert Foxworth, directed by John Berry and designed by Jo Mielziner, that Barnes praises for its "moral force" and "great dramatic impact."

———. "New York Notebook." *Times* (London) 13 May 1972: 10.
In a second positive review of Repertory Theater of Lincoln Center revival of *The Crucible*, starring Robert Foxworth, directed by John Berry and designed by Jo Mielziner, Barnes lauds Miller for a voice that is "always crisp, cold, and effective," that shows the playwright "at his best."

Bayley, Clare. "*The Crucible*." *What's On* (London) 6 June 1990. *London Theatre Record* 10.11 (1990): 729.
Bayley praises the Royal National Theatre revival, directed by Howard Davies, as "a fine production of a compelling and infinitely sage play."

Beaufort, John. "Actors Theatre Opens *Crucible*." *Christian Science Monitor* 18 December 1991: 14. *New York Theatre Critics' Reviews* 52 (1991): 142–43.
Beaufort lauds the National Actors Theatre revival as an "impressive" play that "has lost none of its power since Broadway first welcomed the work in 1953."

———. "Roundabout Theatre Offers a Stark *Crucible*." *Christian Science Monitor* 26 April 1990: Arts: 11.

Positive review of the Roundabout Theatre revival of *The Crucible* directed by Gerald Freedman, starring Randell Mell and Justine Bateman, that Beaufort calls "stark and powerful."

Bentley, Eric. "Miller's Innocence." *New Republic* 16 February 1953: 22–23. Rpt. as "The Innocence of Arthur Miller," *The Dramatic Event*. New York: Horizon, 1954. 90–94. Rpt. in *"The Crucible": Text and Criticism*. Ed. Gerald Weales. New York: Viking, 1971. New York: Penguin, 1996. 204–9. Rpt. in *What Is Theatre? Incorporating "The Dramatic Event" and Other Reviews, 1944–1967*. New York: Atheneum, 1968. 62–65, 461–62.

While praising Miller for saying something in *The Crucible* "that *has* to be discussed," and admitting that "the appearance of one such play by an author, like Mr. Miller, who is neither an infant, a fool, nor a swindler, is enough to bring tears to the eyes," Bentley criticizes the work for not being true enough to include a protagonist who has faults. Says Bentley, "[Proctor's] innocence is unreal because it is total. . . . *The Crucible* is *about* guilt yet nowhere in it is any *sense* of guilt because the author and director have joined forces to disassociate themselves and their hero from evil."

Beyer, William H. "The State of the Theatre: The Devil at Large." *School and Society* 21 March 1953: 185–86.

Beyer feels that *The Crucible* fails as "pure tragedy" because the melodramatic elements, such as are found in the frenzied, teeming scenes, desensitize its audience.

Brown, Georgina. "*The Crucible*." *Independent* (London) 1 September 1989. *London Theatre Record* 9.17 (1989): 1156.

Laudatory review of the Moscow Art Theatre student production (in Russian), directed by Brian Cox. Says Brown, Cox's "illuminating direction licks it with flames; it looks superb, glowing in halflight and formally blocked like a Dutch old master."

Brown, John Mason. "Seeing Things: Witch-Hunting." *Saturday Review of Literature* 14 February 1953: 41–42.

Mixed review of the premiere production of *The Crucible* that Brown faults for its reliance on themes instead of people to carry the story and its overabundance of characters. While it is not as good as Miller's previous dramas, says Brown, the work's "one indisputable virtue is that it is about something that matters."

Chapman, John. "Miller's *The Crucible* Terrifying Tragedy about Puritan Bigotry." *New York Daily News* 23 January 1953. *New York Theatre Critics' Reviews* 14 (1953): 383.

Chapman praises Miller's drama as "a stunning production, splendidly acted and strongly written."

———. "Arthur Miller Is No Chekhov in NRT Revival of *The Crucible*." *New York Daily News* 7 April 1964. *New York Theatre Critics' Reviews* 25 (1964): 395.

Chapman lauds the original 1953 production of *The Crucible* but criticizes the National Repertory Theatre production as a "rather juvenile and stereotyped exercise in dramatics."

Christopher, James. "*The Crucible.*" *Time Out* (London) 13 September 1989. *London Theatre Record* 9.17 (1989): 1155.

Christopher praises director Brian Cox for choosing Miller's play as the first production of the Moscow Art Theatre School and lauds the acting talents of the young students.

Clurman, Harold. "*The Crucible.*" *Nation* 15 May 1972: 636–37. Rpt. in *The Collected Works of Harold Clurman: Six Decades of Commentary on Theatre, Dance, Music, Film, Arts and Letters*. Eds. Marjorie Loggia and Glenn Young. New York: Applause, 1994. 813–15.

Positive review of the Repertory Theater of Lincoln Center revival of *The Crucible*, starring Robert Foxworth, directed by John Berry and designed by Jo Mielziner, that Clurman says "has unity." Of note is Clurman's lengthy lament over what he sees as younger actors who "seem unable to convey the expression of heightened emotion in clear speech."

Coleman, Robert. "*The Crucible* A Stirring, Well-Acted Melodrama." *New York Daily Mirror* 23 January 1953. *New York Theatre Critics' Reviews* 14 (1953): 385.

Coleman lauds Miller's work as "an arresting evening of theatre. A harrowing, suspenseful, intensely dramatic evening. In fact, it holds the spectator so well forward in his seat as to wear him down toward the end."

Coveney, Michael. "*The Crucible*." *Financial Times* (London) 8 September 1989. *London Theatre Record* 9.17 (1989): 1157.

Coveney praises the Moscow Art Theatre revival, directed by Brian Cox, for its fine acting and staging. Of note is this description: "Instead of the usually fraught farmer in Puritan black, we have a bearded ladykiller in well-worn jeans, a man who knows the sensual value of everything from a bowl of soup to his wife's bosom. The minute he is in the same room as Abigail, their past affair shoots through their limbs like an electric current, legs surreptitiously entwined, hands busy."

———. "*The Crucible*." *Observer* (London) 3 June 1990. *London Theatre Record* 10.11 (1990): 732.

Coveney criticizes the Howard Davies revival for being "humdrum" but lauds Miller's play as "one of the greatest," noting, "the further the play travels from the root analogy in the McCarthy show trials of the 1950s, the more powerful it becomes; the terror can and will rear up and swallow us at any moment."

Crist, Judith. "*The Crucible* More Fiery than Ever." *New York Herald Tribune* 7 April 1964: 14. *New York Theatre Critics' Reviews* 25 (1964): 296.

Crist hails the NRT's *Crucible* (directed by Jack Sydow) as a "brilliant revival" that "is undoubtedly the finest production of the Arthur Miller play that we have had here to date."

"*The Crucible*." *Booklist* 15 May 1953: 299.

Brief positive review of the printed version of *The Crucible* that the critic praises for Miller's ability to intensify "the dramatic values of the play without any sacrifice of historical accuracy."

"*The Crucible*." *Newsweek* 2 February 1953: 68.

Positive review of the premiere New York production, directed by Jed Harris. The play does not force a modern parallel and has "eloquence, force and a sense of theatre given to few practicing playwrights."

"*The Crucible*." *Theatre World* 61 (March 1965): 8.

Positive review of the Old Vic production of *The Crucible*, directed by Laurence Olivier and starring Colin Blakely and Sarah Miles.

"*The Crucible*." *Time* 2 February 1953: 48.

Mixed review of the premiere New York production, directed by Jed Harris. While Miller's play has "many scenes of real theatrical power," it ultimately misses the point of historical repression that originally caused the hysteria in 1692 Salem.

"*Crucible* Hailed in Argentina." *New York Times* 29 July 1955: 8.

Brief news item reporting the positive critical response of the Argentina production of *The Crucible* in Buenos Aires.

de Jongh, Nicholas. "*The Crucible*." *Guardian* (London) 2 June 1990. *London Theatre Record* 10.11 (1990): 730–31.

Positive review of the Howard Davies revival at the Olivier which de Jongh calls "the best by this otherwise overrated playwright" that "works through an apt forceful analogy between the America of the 1692s and the 1950s, in a kind of double focus and with double effect. It is also one of the modern theatre's most powerful examples of humanism triumphant."

Disch, Thomas M. "*The Crucible*." *Nation* 21 May 1990: 719.

Positive review of the Roundabout Theatre revival of *The Crucible* directed by Gerald Freedman, starring Randell Mell, Harriet Harris, and Justine Bateman, that Disch calls a "triumphant reminder of the power of the 1953 play."

Edwardes, Jane. "*The Crucible*." *Time Out* (London) 6 June 1990. *London Theatre Record* 10.11 (1990): 728.

Edwardes calls the Royal National Theatre production, directed by Howard Davies, "momentous" but with a "tendency to slip into melodrama."

Edwards, Christopher. "*The Crucible*." *Spectator* (London) 9 June 1990. *London Theatre Record* 10.11 (1990): 728.

While "Miller's characters are very rigidly conceived," Edwards lauds the Royal National Theatre production, directed by Howard Davies, for being "engrossing" and a "powerful and moving drama."

Esslin, Martin. "Team Work." *Plays and Players* (London) March 1965: 32–33.

Esslin praises this "highly successful production" of the National Theatre, starring Colin Blakely, Joyce Redman, and Sarah Miles, for "triumphantly" demonstrating "the value of genuine ensemble acting," without which "the lines of Miller's last scene must appear as cheap melodrama."

Farrell, Isolde. "From the Seine." *New York Times* 27 February 1955: II: 3.

Brief positive review of the French production of *The Crucible*, known as *Les Sorcières de Salem*, that Farrell calls "outstanding" and quotes a review from *Figaro* as stating that this is an "original, vigorous and significant play; one of the finest shows ever presented in Paris."

Feldberg, Robert. "Despite Flaws, Still a Classic." *The Record* (Bergen County, N.J.) 11 December 1991: D16.

Mixed review of the National Actors Theatre revival, starring Martin Sheen, Michael York, Fritz Weaver, and Martha Scott, directed by Yossi Yzraely. Says Feldberg, "Even with dramatic flaws, *The Crucible* remains strong theater, and the National Actors production, uneven though it is, gets much of it across."

Ferris, Oliver H. P. "An Echo of Milton in *The Crucible*." *Notes and Queries* 16 July 1969: 268.

Brief essay in response to Fred Standley's argument in *Notes and Queries* in August 1968 that there is a similarity between *The Crucible* and Milton's "Another on the Same," especially as it relates to Giles Corey's plea for "more weight." Ferris debunks this view as "ridiculous" and points out that the Corey phrase is based on Miller's historical research not the influence of Milton.

Fetherston, Drew. "Power Remains in *The Crucible*." *Newsday* 30 March 1990: Weekend: 13.

Fetherston gives much of the credit for the success of the show to the play itself rather than the Roundabout Theatre production, starring Justine Bateman and directed by Gerald Freedman, which he calls "earnest but uneven."

Funke, Lewis. "Theatre: *The Crucible*." *New York Times* 12 March 1958: 36.

After admitting only minor structural faults, Funke praises the Arena Stage revival as "provocative, stimulating, and inspiring."

Gardner, Lyn. "*The Crucible*." *City Limits* (London) 14 September 1989. *London Theatre Record* 9.17 (1989): 1155.

In this review of the Moscow Art Theatre School revival, directed by Brian Cox, Gardner laments that "in the closing moments the sheer passion of the play sweeps all before it but overall this is, for all its good intentions, just another good student production of a brilliant play."

Gassner, John. "Affirmations?" *Theatre at the Crossroads*. New York: Rinehart, 1960. 274–78. Rpt. as "Miller's *The Crucible* as Event and Play" in *Twentieth Century Interpretations of "The Crucible," a Collection of Critical Essays*. Ed. John H. Ferres. Englewood Cliffs, N.J.: Prentice-Hall, 1972. 27–31.

Gassner prefaces his negative review of the premiere production of *The Crucible*, directed by Jed Harris, with commentary regarding the "momentous, if imperfect" drama that "has importance in the career of a writer whose laudable ambition is to make contemporary American theatre aim high and who also has wishes to express the tensions of his own time and place."

Gibbs, Wolcott. "The Devil to Pay." *New Yorker* 31 January 1953: 39–40.

While noting that *The Crucible* is not as great a play as *Death of a Salesman*, Gibbs praises the premiere production, directed by Jed Harris, as "powerful" and the "most interesting" play of the New York season.

Gill, Brendan. "For the Prosecution." *New Yorker* 6 May 1972: 54–56.

Gill believes that the reason why the Lincoln Center revival of *The Crucible* succeeds is because it is "a well-told story about sexual rivalry and vengeance; these are great themes and nothing else matters a straw."

Goodman, Peter. "*Crucible* as Opera: A Classic Witch-Hunt." *Newsday* 9 December 1988: Weekend: 15.

Goodman praises the Julliard School production of the Robert Ward opera, based on Miller's play, as "strong" and "intelligent."

Gottfried, Martin. "*The Crucible*." *Women's Wear Daily* 1 May 1972. *New York Theatre Critics' Reviews* 33 (1972): 297.

After extolling the Repertory at Lincoln Center's revival as "powerful and heroic" and "the best work yet done at the Vivian Beaumont Theater," Gottfried praises Miller's drama as a "strong, sculptural, assertive play."

Gray, Dominic. "*The Crucible*." *What's On* (London) 13 September 1989. *London Theatre Record* 9.17 (1989): 1155.

Gray insists that "young writers and young actors cannot afford to miss this production," staged by the Moscow Art Theatre School and directed by Brian Cox, adding, "Others who remember a time when eight actors could be on stage together, and each could retain distinction and articulation, will not be disappointed."

Gross, John. "*The Crucible*." *Sunday Telegraph* (London) 3 June 1990. *London Theatre Record* 10.11 (1990): 732.

Gross condemns *The Crucible* for being a political parable that "rests on a false analogy" and possessing a "faint yet pervasive flavor of propaganda: everyone acts a little too much in character, the whole thing is rather too obviously a lesson in virtue."

Harris, Leonard. "*The Crucible*." CBS. WCBS, New York. 27 April 1972. *New York Theatre Critics' Reviews* 33 (1972): 298.

Mixed review of the Lincoln Center revival, starring Stephen Elliott and Robert Foxworth, in which Harris praises the play's "strength and anger" but dismisses the production as "pompous."

Hartley, Anthony. "Good Melodrama." *Spectator* (London) April 1956: 547.

Positive review of the London production that Hartley calls a play that is "fundamentally poetic without the self-conscious striving after artificiality which is the bore of the West End stage."

Hawkins, William. "Witchcraft Boiled in *The Crucible*." *New York World-Telegram* 23 January 1953. *New York Theatre Critics' Reviews* 14 (1953): 384.

Hawkins praises Miller's work as "big and bold and very theatrical." Of note is his documentation of the play's premiere night, which he says "was greeted with 19 curtain calls by a vociferous audience."

Hayes, Richard. "The Stage: *The Crucible*." *Commonweal* 20 February 1953: 498. Rpt as "Hysteria and Ideology in *The Crucible*." in *Twentieth Century Interpretations of "The Crucible," a Collection of Critical Essays*. Ed. John H. Ferres. Engelwood Cliffs, N.J.: Prentice-Hall, 1972. 32–34.

A mostly favorable review of the premiere production at the Martin Beck Theatre, Hayes finds *The Crucible* a "product of theatrical dexterity and a young man's moral passion, rather than of a fruitful and reverberating imagination."

Hemming, Sarah. "*The Crucible*." *Independent* (London) 6 September 1989. *London Theatre Record* 9.17 (1989): 1156.

Hemming calls the Moscow Art Theatre revival, directed by Brian Cox, "sexy, physical and impassioned" with "strong" individual performances that gives "tremendous power to Miller's final question about the possibility of goodness in a slippery world."

Hewes, Henry. "Distal and Proximal Bite." *Saturday Review* 20 May 1972: 62.

Hewes lauds this Lincoln Center revival for its timeliness, noting that the Vietnam era applies to the themes of authority and truth just as much as the McCarthy period.

Hiley, Jim. "*The Crucible*." *Listener* (London) 14 June 1990. *London Theatre Record* 10.11 (1990): 732–33.

Hiley calls *The Crucible* "one of the great plays of the century" and praises the Howard Davies revival at the Olivier as "beautifully pared-down" and packing "an emotional punch."

Hirschhorn, Clive. "*The Crucible*." *Sunday Express* (London) 3 June 1990. *London Theatre Record* 10.11 (1990): 729.

Calling the Royal National Theatre production, directed by Howard Davies, "a towering evening of theatre," Hirschhorn also praises the acting of Tom Wilkinson and Zoe Wanamaker as "impeccable."

Hobson, Harold. "Fair Play." *The Sunday Times* (London) 14 November 1954: 11. Rpt. in *"The Crucible": Text and Criticism*. Ed. Gerald Weales. New York: Viking, 1971. New York: Penguin, 1996. 227–30.

Positive review of the London premiere of *The Crucible*, starring Rosemary Harris and Edgar Werford, that Hobson praises for Miller's ability to not allow "his personal convictions to interfere with the dramatist's responsibility for presenting every one of his characters with understanding and sympathy."

Hope-Wallace, P. "Theatre." *Time and Tide* (London) 20 November 1954: 1544.

Negative review of the Bristol Old Vic production. Says Hope-Wallace, "Arthur Miller of course is preaching a topical sermon—about McCarthyism; the impact of the play must have been great in New York. But there are plenty of other pogroms—nearer home. No, if it makes less impact than it should, it is because all witch hunt plays are the same in the long run . . . This was only melodramatically 'moving'."

Hornby, Richard. "*The Crucible*." *Hudson Review* 65.1 (Spring 92): 111–13.

Mixed review of the National Actors Theatre production, starring Martin Sheen and Michael York, that Hornby calls "promising" and "encouraging beginning for this new, serious American theatre company."

Hoyle, Martin. "*The Crucible*." *Financial Times* (London) 9 December 1985. *London Theatre Record* 5.25/26 (1985): 1219.

Hoyle praises the David Thacker revival at the Young Vic, starring Matthew Marsh and Margot Leicester, as "solid, durable and still nail-bitingly vital theatre."

———. "*The Crucible*." *Financial Times* (London) 2 June 1990. *London Theatre Record* 10.11 (1990): 727.

Hoyle criticizes the Royal National Theatre production of *The Crucible*, directed by Howard Davies, as a "messy, ungripping and phonily excitable production" that possesses "the extraordinary combination of melodrama and dullness."

Hurren, Kenneth. "*The Crucible*." *Mail on Sunday* (London) 3 June 1990. *London Theatre Record* 10.11 (1990): 730.

Brief positive review of the Howard Davies revival at the Olivier, in which Hurren praises the work as written with "compassion" and a survivor not only of "the loss of the once-topical frame of reference, but some troubling flaws as well."

Kalem, T. E. "The Ethos of Courage." *Time* 15 May 1972: 59. *New York Theatre Critics' Reviews* 33 (1972): 298.

Positive review of the Repertory Theater at Lincoln Center's revival in which Kalem commends Miller's "courage," "personal integrity" and "ethical fervor."

Kauffmann, Stanley. "Right Down the Middle." *New Republic* 27 May 1972: 22, 34.

Kauffmann praises the Lincoln Center revival of *The Crucible* as a fine production of Miller's best play, even though the work is "thematically schizoid" and possesses a final act that is a "moral-metaphysical drama."

Kellow, Brian. "On the Beat." *Opera News* 64.1 (July 1999): 12.

Positive review of the Dicapo Opera Theatre's production of Robert Ward's adaptation of *The Crucible* that Kellow calls "strong. and appealing," and "one of the best productions of twentieth-century opera I've seen in some time."

Kerr, Walter. "*The Crucible*." *New York Herald Tribune* 23 January 1953: 12. *New York Theatre Critics' Reviews* 14 (1953): 385. Rpt. in *"The Crucible": Text and Criticism*. Ed. Gerald Weales. New York: Viking, 1971. New York: Penguin, 1996. 189–91. Rpt. in excerpted form. as "A Problem Playwright" in *Twentieth Century Interpretations of "The Crucible", a Collection of Critical Essays*. Ed. John H. Ferres. Engelwood Cliffs, N.J.: Prentice-Hall, 1972. 35–36.

After praising Miller's ability as an artist and a man who is "profoundly, angrily concerned with the immediate issues of our society" and recognizing the play's "very clear contemporary parallel," Kerr decries *The Crucible* as "taking a step backward into mechanical parable, into the sort of play which lives not in the warmth of humbly observed human souls but in the ideological heat of polemic."

———. "*The Crucible* Retells Salem's Violent Story." *New York Herald Tribune* 1 February 1953: Sec. 4: 1.

Kerr dislikes the premiere production of *The Crucible*, directed by Jed Harris, because its characters are mere abstractions, the work feels half-completed, and the outcome is more a social inquisition than a true drama.

———. "Good Causes Make Bad Dramaturgy." *New York Times* 27 June 1976: II: 5, 22.

Kerr blames both Miller and the American Shakespeare Theatre for the "botched" production of *The Crucible*, stating that while director Michael Kahn did not believe in the work, neither did Miller, who constructed his play so as to allow no sympathy with the dishonest characters. If we had been given the opportunity, Kerr continues, to grasp their "superstitions as lethal but devoutly bold convictions, we might really have been terrified of them. And we'd have given assent, not smug dismissal, to the unfolding events."

———. "Staged without Care or Kindness." *New York Times* 7 May 1972: II: 3.

Negative review of the Lincoln Center revival of *The Crucible*, directed by John Berry that Kerr criticizes for magnifying the play's inherent defects.

Kirchwey, Freda. "*The Crucible*." *Nation* 7 February 1953: 131–32.

Brief positive review of the premiere production, directed by Jed Harris, in which Kirchwey praises the final scene before the hanging as "immensely moving" and summarizes the play "with an eloquence that carries the audience . . . out of the theatre in a mood of resolve rather than despair."

Kissel, Howard. "*Crucible* Isn't That Bewitching." *New York Daily News* 11 December 1991. *New York Theatre Critics' Reviews* 52 (1991): 140.

Mostly negative review of the National Actors Theatre's revival directed by Yossi Yzraely and starring Michael York, Martha Scott, and Martin Sheen. Conceding that "it took great courage to write" during the height of the McCarthy witch hunt hysteria, Kissel laments that forty years later the play seems "rhetorical" and "contrived."

Koenig, Rhoda. "*The Crucible*." *Punch* (London) 15 June 1990. *London Theatre Record* 10.11 (1990): 729–30.

While admitting that she is "not keen on Miller," Koenig praises *The Crucible* as the playwright's "best" and praises the "chastity of language enforced by the period," which "gives Miller's dialogue a consistent sternness and sinew that produces a number of striking effects."

Kramer, Mimi. "More Weight: *The Crucible*." *New Yorker* 23 December 1991: 94–95.

Negative review of the National Actors Theatre revival of *The Crucible* that Kramer calls "a plodding production—not exactly what Mr. Miller and his play deserve."

"London Critics Hail Miller's *Crucible*." *New York Times* 11 April 1956: 28.

News item offering excerpts of the various London reviews of the English Stage Company production of *The Crucible* at the Royal Court Theatre.

Mackenzie, Suzie. "*The Crucible*." *Time Out* (London) 12 December 1985. *London Theatre Record* 5.25/26 (1985): 1216.

Calling Miller's play "a bona fide tearjerker," Mackenzie praises the David Thacker revival at the Young Vic for "masterfully" evoking "the community through finely detailed portraits of individuals."

McClain, John. "Play of Enormous Strength and Depth." *New York Journal American* 23 January 1953. *New York Theatre Critics' Reviews* 14 (1953): 383.

While wishing that Miller had written *The Crucible* "around people more presently understandable," McClain praises it as "a play of enormous strength, written with depth and intelligence . . . performed by a large and uniformly expert cast."

———. "Superb Repertory." *New York Journal American* 7 April 1964. *New York Theatre Critics' Reviews* 25 (1964): 297.

McClain acclaims the NRT's production ("incredibly simple and effective sets, plus the superior performances of a fine cast") as having "an impact and importance beyond the range of the original."

McMillan, Joyce. "*The Crucible*." *Guardian* (London) 1 September 1989. *London Theatre Record* 9.17 (1989): 1156–57.

McMillan praises the revival by the Moscow Art Theatre, directed by Brian Cox, for possessing a "wave of erotic energy powerful enough to shatter a few comfortable assumptions, both about the play itself, and about the way we use—or fail to use—sex in the theatre."

Morley, Sheridan. "*The Crucible*." *Herald Tribune* (London) 6 June 1990. *London Theatre Record* 10.11 (1990): 728. Rpt. as "Onstage London News: *The Crucible*." *Playbill* 31 July 1990: 64.

Mixed review of the Howard Davies revival at the Royal National Theatre in London that Morley says "gets off to a dangerously slow start" but "gathers all its traditional strength for the courtroom climax."

Nadel, Norman. "Miller's *Crucible* Re-enacted Recalls Sickness of the Land." *New York World-Telegram and Sun* 7 April 1964. *New York Theatre Critics' Reviews* 25 (1964): 297.

Nadel praises Miller's play for its "timelessness" and importance as "a warning, a goad and as a rock-ribbed, durable drama."

Nathan, George Jean. "Henrik Miller." *Theatre Arts* 37 (April 1953): 24–26.

Negative review of the premiere production of *The Crucible*, directed by Jed Harris, in which Nathan accuses Miller of having an indifference to the box office "accompanied by an unconscious indifference to any kind of theatrical audience, even one of the higher grade." "*The Crucible*, in sum, is an honorable sermon on a vital theme that misses because the sting implicit in it has been disinfected with an editorial tincture and because, though it contains the potential deep vibrations of life, it reduces them to mere superficial tremors."

Nightingale, Benedict. "*The Crucible*." *The Times* (London) 1 June 1990. *London Theatre Record* 10.11 (1990): 731–32.

Mixed review in which Nightingale says that the Howard Davies' revival at the Olivier "burned slowly, at times too slowly, but undeniably left the vitals scorched and seared."

Page, Tim. "*The Crucible*: Best Witch Hunt in Town." *Washington Post* 4 January 1999: C1.

Positive review of the Washington Opera's production of Robert Ward's *The Crucible*, directed by Bruce Beresford, that Page calls "engrossing," "haunting," and a "carefully plotted and deftly realized production."

Pascal, Julia. "*The Crucible*." *Jewish Chronicle* (London) 20 December 1985. *London Theatre Record* 5.25/26 (1985): 1218.

Calling David Thacker's revival at the Young Vic a "strong production," Pascal notes that she "saw the production at a schools matinee and the London adolescents were holding their breath."

Paton, Maureen. "*The Crucible*." *Daily Express* (London) 4 June 1990. *London Theatre Record* 10.11 (1990): 728.

Highly laudatory review of the Royal National Theatre production, directed by Howard Davies, that Paton calls "brilliantly emotional theatre."

Ponick, T. L. "*Crucible* Fuses Theme, Passion into Compelling Opera." *Washington Times* 17 January 1999: D1.

Ponick praises the Washington Opera production of Robert Ward's opera version of Miller's *The Crucible* as "brilliantly conceived and flawlessly performed, this is contemporary opera—and drama—at its best."

Randor, Alan. "*The Crucible*." *Jewish Chronicle* (London) 15 September 1989. *London Theatre Record* 9.17 (1989): 1156.

Brief review in which Randor calls the revival by the Moscow Art Theatre directed by Brian Cox "impressive" but occasionally "a little enthusiastic."

Ratcliffe, Michael. "*The Crucible*." *Observer* (London) 10 September 1989. *London Theatre Record* 9.17 (1989): 1155.

Ratcliffe praises this student production of *The Crucible* by the Moscow Art Theatre as "a Russian-language performance notable for the warmth of its erotic charge."

Raymond, Harry. "*The Crucible*, Arthur Miller's Best Play." *Daily Worker* 28 January 1953: 7.

Raymond, writing for a Communist newspaper, notes the similarities between the story of the Salem witch trials of 1692 and the current situation in the United States in which Communists and "other progressives" are being persecuted for their beliefs. Additionally Raymond dislikes the "Aunt Jemima black stereotype" of the character of Tituba.

Rich, Frank. "Miller's *Crucible*, Starring Sheen." *New York Times* 11 December 1991. *New York Theatre Critics' Reviews* 52 (1991): 142.

Mixed review of the National Actors Theatre inaugural revival starring Martin Sheen, Martha Scott, and Michael York, which praises Miller's play as "evergreen" and criticizes the production as "a stiff high-school edition" that is "doled out as something that is good for you, sour medicine that must be swallowed slowly."

Sanders, Kevin. "*The Crucible*." ABC. WABC, New York. 27 April 1972. *New York Theatre Critics' Reviews* 33 (1972): 298.

Calling the Lincoln Center revival, starring Stephen Elliott and Robert Foxworth, "handsomely staged and impressively acted," Sanders laments that "for all its dramatic and ethical worth, *The Crucible* is still a sermon."

Sargeant, Winthrop. "*The Crucible*." *American Record Guide* 29 (March 1963): 508–509, 588.

Positive review of the recording of the Robert Ward opera *The Crucible* that Sargeant calls "a profound work" and "a true music-drama—a rare thing in contemporary writing for the musical stage."

"Satan Comes to Salem." *Life* 9 February 1953: 87–88, 90.

Brief favorable review of the premier production of Miller's *The Crucible*, directed by Jed Harris. Black-and-white production photographs accompany the text.

Selz, Jean. "Raymond Rouleau among the Witches." *Les Lettres Nouvelles* 3 (March 1955): 422–26. Trans. by Gerald Weales an rpt. in *"The Crucible": Text and Criticism.* Ed. Gerald Weales. New York: Viking, 1971. New York: Penguin, 1996. 242–47.

Positive review of the French production of *The Crucible*, directed by Raymond Rouleau and starring Simone Signoret. Finding it a "magical" play about truth, Selz notes the play eliciting a response from one audience member who shouted out his feelings during the courtroom scene.

Shipley, Joseph T. "Arthur Miller's New Melodrama Is Not What It Seems to Be." *New Leader* 9 February 1953: 25–26. Rpt. in *"The Crucible": Text and Criticism.* Ed. Gerald Weales. New York: Viking, 1971. New York: Penguin, 1996. 201–203.

Negative review of the premiere production, directed by Jed Harris, that Shipley says is "not so much a creation of dramatic art as a concoction of the author's contriving mind" that is "a better analogy for iron-curtain than American justice."

Shulman, Milton. "*The Crucible*." *Evening Standard* (London) 1 June 1990. *London Theatre Record* 10.11 (1990): 727.

Mixed review of the Royal National Theatre production, directed by Howard Davies, that Shulman criticizes for the over-the-top hysterical antics of the girls in an "otherwise exemplary" and "durable masterpiece."

Simon, John. "*The Crucible*." *New York* 6 January 1992: 59–60.

Negative review of the National Actors Theatre revival, directed by Tony Randall and starring Martin Sheen, Martha Scott, and Michael York. Simon says the production's problems stem from "too many superficially and crudely conceived characters."

———. "Eloquence in Spite of Words." *New York Magazine* 15 May 1972: 70.

Simon praises the Lincoln Center revival, directed by John Berry, as a play that "holds the stage with tooth and nail as good plays must," but faults Miller's "pidgin-Colonial" language for being the work's main flaw.

———. "Maggie and Margaret." *New York* 9 April 1990: 103–104.
Negative review of the Roundabout Theatre revival of *The Crucible* directed by Gerald Freedman, starring Randell Mell, Harriet Harris, and Justine Bateman, that Simon calls "mediocre" and "awkwardly written and unbearably smug."

Small, Christopher. "Theatre." *Spectator* (London) 19 November 1954: 608.
Small praises the Bristol Old Vic production of *The Crucible* as "good, strong, rugged stuff" that abandons the historical parallels before they have been completed.

Spencer, Charles. "*The Crucible*." *Daily Telegraph* (London) 2 June 1990. *London Theatre Record* 10.11 (1990): 730.
Mixed review of the Howard Davies revival at the Olivier in which Spencer calls the play "flawed" and a work "that shows its age" but "noble" with performances that "grow in strength as the evening wears on and, by the end, attention is held in a vice-like grip."

Stearns, David Patrick. "*Crucible* a Searing Success." *USA Today* 12 December 1991. *New York Theatre Critics' Reviews* 52 (1991): 140–41.
Highly positive review of the National Actors Theatre revival starring Martin Sheen, Martha Scott, and Michael York. Writes Stearns, "A dense, talky play, the work has rarely seemed so concise or suspenseful than in this production."

———. "D.C.'s *Crucible* a Scalding Show." *USA Today* 11 January 1999: D5.
Mixed review of the Robert Ward opera *The Crucible*, directed by Bruce Beresford at the Washington Opera.

Tallmer, Jerry. "He Who Says No." *New York Post* 7 April 1964. *New York Theatre Critics' Reviews* 25 (1964): 298.
Tallmer acclaims the NRT's production as "clean" and "strong," especially Jack Sydow's direction, which has "given the Arthur Miller drama a trajectory and cumulative force I did not know it could command."

Taubman, Howard. "Theater: Return of *The Crucible*." *New York Times* 7 April 1964: 30. *New York Theatre Critics' Reviews* 25 (1964): 296.

Taubman declares that the NRT's revival of *The Crucible* "retains the fury of its intensity and its pride in the inviolability of man's dignity and honor" and is "a stirring dramatization of an idea and a commitment that bear continual reaffirmation."

Taylor, John Russell. "Plays in Performance." *Drama* 140 (2nd Quarter 1981): 25–26.

After admitting to not being a great admirer of Miller's plays, Taylor praises the Cottesloe production of *The Crucible*, directed by Bill Bryden, as a "superbly professional job."

Taylor, Paul. "*The Crucible*." *Independent* (London) 2 June 1990. *London Theatre Record* 10.11 (1990): 730.

Taylor says that the Howard Davies revival at the Olivier is lacking "any distinctive atmosphere, or sense of community destroying itself through paranoia. Major contributors to this absence are the nondescript set and the dull, uniform lighting."

Tinker, Jack. "*The Crucible*." *Daily Mail* (London) 1 June 1990. *London Theatre Record* 10.11 (1990): 731.

Tinker lauds *The Crucible*, revived by Howard Davies at the Olivier, as "immeasurably moving" and an "epic work delivered in epic style. What distinguishes it is that even in the full majestic sweep of its staging, nothing of the smaller nuances is lost."

Trewin, J. C. "Blanket of the Dark." *Illustrated London News* (London) 27 November 1954: 964.

While chiding the London premiere of *The Crucible*, starring Edgar Werford and Rosemary Harris, for its "singlemindedness," Trewin praises the play as powerfully affecting historical melodrama— "it is the kind of play found rarely, in which suspense can choke."

Tynan, Kathleen, ed. *Kenneth Tynan Letters*. New York: Random House, 1994. 193.

In the reprint of a letter to Christopher Fry in New York City, dated 29 January 1953, critic Kenneth Tynan relates that he saw *The Crucible* and felt it to be surprisingly like Lillian Hellman's *The Children's Hour* in shape, "but it is a failure dramatically, because Miller (unlike Hellman) doesn't give the other side its due."

Tynan, Kenneth. "*The Crucible* by Arthur Miller, at the Bristol Old Vic [1954]." *Curtains*. New York: Atheneum, 1961. 253–54.

Tynan criticizes *The Crucible* for the strength of its convictions—in taking sides that "all oppression is vile"—which Tynan finds "the ultimate weakness" of Miller's play.

Valdes, Lesley. "Strong Music for Dour Puritans." *Philadelphia Inquirer* 13 January 1999: D1.

Valdes praises the Washington Opera production of Robert Ward's *The Crucible* as "an opera worth attending not only for its aesthetic values but its recounting of the quest for morals in American history."

Wardle, Irving. "*The Crucible*." *Independent on Sunday* (London) 3 June 1990. *London Theatre Record* 10.11 (1990): 731.

Wardle praises Howard Davies' revival at the Olivier as "cooler and more spacious" than previous productions, "drawing you into the scenes of group hysteria and domestic intensity, and then allowing you to take a distanced view of the separate forces of bigoted idealism and masked self-interest that consigned the Salem martyrs to the gallows."

Watt, Douglas. "Arthur Miller's *Crucible* Returns." *New York Daily News* 28 April 1972. *New York Theatre Critics' Reviews* 33 (1972): 296.

Negative review of the Repertory Theater of Lincoln Center production directed by John Berry in which Watt calls the play "shoddy" and "so contrived and filled with bombast that pushing it beyond its limits, as is here attempted, just doesn't work."

Watts, Richard, Jr. "Mr. Miller Looks at Witch Hunting." *New York Post* 23 January 1953. *New York Theatre Critics' Reviews* 14 (1953): 384. Rpt. in *Critical Essays on Arthur Miller*. Ed. James J. Martine. Boston: G. K. Hall, 1979. 73–74.

Despite some "frailties," which includes Miller's inability to combine emotionality with intellectual insight and the play's "unfortunate superficiality," Watts concludes that *The Crucible* is "a hard-hitting and effective play that demands and deserves audience attention."

———. "The Witch Hunt in Old Salem." *New York Post* 28 April 1972. *New York Theatre Critics' Reviews* 33 (1972): 296.

Positive review of the Repertory Theater of Lincoln Center's revival directed by John Berry and starring Robert Foxworth. Watts acclaims the work as "an important American play" that is "powerful and effective in its own rights, but it is also striking because of the memories it brings back of the days of the McCarthy search for Communists and for the dramatist's statement on that monstrous period in the national annals."

Williams, Hugo. "*The Crucible*." *Sunday Correspondent* (London) 10 June 1990. *London Theatre Record* 10.11 (1990): 729.

Williams says that while the revival of *The Crucible*, directed by Howard Davies at the Olivier, "is handicapped" by the incoherence of William Dudley's design, the production "moves like a bush fire through the bewitched village, perfectly catching these lifelong acquaintances 'breaking of charity' with one another."

Wilson, Edwin. "Bewitched and Beguiled." *Wall Street Journal* 20 December 1991. *New York Theatre Critics' Reviews* 52 (1991): 144.

Mixed review of the National Actors Theatre revival starring Martin Sheen, Martha Scott, and Michael York. Wilson praises Miller's drama but finds the overall production "a disappointment" that "veers strongly toward melodrama and runs the risk of making the authority figures seem like simple villains rather than three-dimensional characters."

Winer, Linda. "Fine Cast Fires This *Crucible*." *New York Newsday* 6 December 1991. *New York Theatre Critics' Reviews* 52 (1991): 143–44.

Positive review of the National Actors Theatre revival starring Martin Sheen, Martha Scott, and Michael York. Writes Winer, "*The Crucible* is ablaze with first-rate actors making powerful theater."

"Witchcraft and Stagecraft." *New York Post* 1 February 1953: M9. Rpt. in *"The Crucible": Text and Criticism*. Ed. Gerald Weales. New York: Viking, 1971. New York: Penguin, 1996. 197–200.

Negative review of the premiere production that criticizes Miller for his "deceptive" inferences that are "invalid, whatever his original intention, Miller has pushed the people of Salem around in a loaded allegory which may shed some light on their time but ultimately succeeds in muddying our own."

Wolf, Matt. "*The Crucible.*" *City Limits* (London) 13 December 1985. *London Theatre Record* 5.25/26 (1985): 1218.

Wolf lauds the David Thacker revival at the Young Vic for passing "the superficial crucible of giving pace to a long evening and the more difficult one of bringing this drama's contemporary reverberations thrillingly, ringingly alive."

Worsley, T. C. "A Play of Our Time." *New Statesman and Nation* (London) 20 November 1954: 642.

Worsely praises *The Crucible*, playing at the Bristol Old Vic, for its use of language that is neither false nor awkward and Miller's handling of complicated material. On the other hand, he criticizes the play for forcing the Communist parallel and simplistic characterizations.

———. "Producers at Play." *New Statesman and Nation* (London) 14 April 1956: 370–71.

Worsely reiterates his objections to the play as expressed on 20 November 1954, and adds that the revival at the Royal Court Theatre "could have bitten much deeper."

Wyatt, Euphemia Van Rensselaer. "Theater." *Catholic World* (March 1953): 465–66.

Positive review of the premiere New York production, directed by Jed Harris and starring Arthur Kennedy and Beatrice Straight, that Wyatt calls "forthright and unrelenting."

Young, B. A. "*Crucible* Staged by Olivier." *New York Times* 20 January 1965: 35.

Young praises the National Theatre production, directed by Laurence Olivier, as a extraordinary revival of a powerful play.

Related Interviews and Profiles (not with Miller)

Arnold, Monty. "Just Plain Justine." *Playbill* 30 April 1990: 45–47.

Profile of *Family Ties* star Justine Bateman, now opening in *The Crucible* at the Roundabout Theatre. Bateman discusses her research and approach to the role of Abigail and her career.

Kelly, Kevin. "Experimental Wooster Group Survived." *Boston Globe* 15 April 1984.

Lengthy profile of Elizabeth LeCompte and her work with the Wooster Group, including her views on the Miller controversy surrounding her production of *L.S.D.*

Milward, John. "Like, Mallory Goes Legit." *Newsday* 29 March 1990: II: 8.

Profile and interview with Justine Batemen, opening as Abigail in *The Crucible* in the Roundabout Theatre revival. Bateman discusses her career and her excitement over her being cast in Miller's play.

Peck, Seymour. "Growth—and Growing Pains—of an Actor." *New York Times Magazine* 15 February 1953: 20, 34, 36.

Interview and profile of actor Arthur Kennedy printed during his run in *The Crucible* that offers insight into the rehearsal process, production issues, and controversy surrounding the premiere New York production directed by Jed Harris.

Trussell, Robert. "Tony Randall Tries to Create National Theater Company." *San Jose Mercury News* 26 December 1991: C6. See also Tony Vellela, "Tony Randall Unveils National Actors Theatre." *Christian Science Monitor* 5 December 1991: Arts: 14.

Profile of Tony Randall and his dream of a National Actors Theatre. Of note is an anecdote regarding the company's first production, Miller's *The Crucible*, in which Randall, at the last minute, had to take over the part of Danforth (script in hand) from actor Fritz Weaver, who lost his voice and could not perform.

Waters, Bob. "*The Crucible*: Robert Ward's Topic A Opera." *Washington Post* 3 January 1999: G5.

Profile of Robert Ward and the details of his efforts to adapt Miller's *The Crucible* into an opera.

News Reports, Letters to the Editor, and Related Matter

Ames, Lynne. "Student Find Parallels to Life in *The Crucible*." *New York Times* 1 November 1998: 14WC: 2.

Article that examines student reaction at Ardsley High School to their production of Miller's *The Crucible* as "relevant to things political and personal."

Atkinson, Brooks. "Return of a Classic." *New York Times* 15 March 1953: II: 1.

Atkinson expresses his disapproval of the American Bar Association's request that Miller change those lines from *The Crucible* that discuss the legal profession in a negative light.

Calta, Louis. "Patricia Neal Set to Co-Star in Play." *New York Times* 27 May 1959: 30.

Brief news item in the theatre section announcing that the off-Broadway production of *The Crucible* at the Martinique Theatre is set to close on 14 June 1959 after 533 performances.

"*Crucible* Will Continue Run." *New York Times* 16 June 1959: 39.

Brief news item announcing that the run of the off-Broadway production of *The Crucible* that was set to close on 14 June will continue its run.

"Into *The Crucible*." *School Librarian's Workshop* (May 1998): 3–4.

Article that offers "strategies for success" in teaching *The Crucible* in high school. The unnamed authors base their recommendations on the supposition that "Arthur Miller's *The Crucible* is not readily understood by students unless they know the socio-political forces that inspired it."

Kelly, Kevin. "*LSD* as Mind-Bending as Its Title." *Boston Globe* 19 April 1984: N11.

Highly positive review of the Wooster Group's *L.S.D., Just the High Points*, directed by Elizabeth LeCompte, and presented by the Boston Shakespeare Company in Boston, that Kelly calls a "stunning abbreviation of Arthur Miller's *The Crucible*" that "demands to be seen."

Lopez, Manny. "Dearborn Woman Is Working to Right Slight to Her Ancestors." *Detroit News* 17 January 1997: C5.

Feature news article detailing Trudy Charron (a distant relative of John Proctor) and her fight to correct what she perceives as an unjust portrayal of her ancestor in Miller's work.

"Memo." *New York Times* 17 May 1959: II: 1.

News item announcing that *The Crucible* has reached a landmark total of 500 performances, exceeded only by O'Neill's *The Iceman Cometh* at 565.

Raskin, A. H. "Maids and Lawyers Assail Stage 'Slurs.'" *New York Times* 9 March 1953: 1, 23.

News item reporting that Miller has declined the request by the American Bar Association to remove lines from *The Crucible* that put lawyers and the legal profession in a bad light.

Rothman, Stanley, Bernard Marcus, and Robert Warshow. "*The Crucible*." *Commentary* July 1953: 83–84.

Series of letters to the editor arguing that Warshow's previously published analysis of *The Crucible* (March 1953, *Commentary*), is an example of "confused and unsubstantial liberalism."

Signoret, Simone. *Nostalgia Isn't What It Used to Be*. New York: Harper and Row, 1978. 119–20.

Signoret discusses her involvement with the French film version of *The Crucible* (*Les Sorcières de Salem*), including her recollection of Miller giving his permission for the film with one stipulation: "He wanted it to be adapted by Jean-Paul Sartre or Marcel Aymé—no one else," that Miller and Sartre had "long correspondence" during the whole production, and that she "knew that the real Mrs. Proctor had been named Mary and that Miller had given her the name Elizabeth so that the couple's initials would be J and E, for Julius and Ethel [Rosenberg]."

"Trial Set to Begin for Woman Accused of Killing Husband." *New York Times* 5 January 1997: 21.

Lengthy news report detailing the case of Rita Gluzman, who is the first woman charged under the new Federal domestic violence law that was intended to protect women from abuse. Her charge is that she and Vladimir Zelenin attacked and killed her husband with axes. Of note to Miller studies is the mention in this article that Mrs. Gluzman's lawyer thought that "the new movie, *The Crucible*, . . . made him think of Mrs. Gluzman and her accuser," who has implicated her in return for a lighter sentence.

A View from the Bridge and *A Memory of Two Mondays*

Critical Essays in Books

Nelson, Benjamin. "*A Memory of Two Mondays*: Remembrance and Reflection in Arthur Miller." [From Nelson's *Arthur Miller: Portrait of a Playwright* . New York: David McKay, 1970. 199–208.] Rpt. in *Arthur Miller: New Perspectives*. Ed. Robert A. Martin. Engelwood Cliffs, N.J.: Prentice-Hall, 1982. 149–58.

Nelson offers a close reading of both plays making up the double bill of one-act plays.

Critical Essays Journals and Magazines

Ditsky, John M. "All Irish Here: The 'Irishman' in Modern Drama." *Dalhousie Review* 54 (Spring 1974): 94–102.

Ditsky argues that *A Memory of Two Mondays* reads as an Irish play, loaded with themes of "shared sorrows and hurts."

Production Reviews

Atkinson, Brooks. "Theatre: *A View from the Bridge*." *New York Times* 30 September 1955: 21. *New York Theatre Critics' Reviews* 16 (1955): 273.

Dismissing *Memory* as "pedestrian," Atkinson focuses his review of the double bill of one-acts on *Bridge*, which he finds a "disappointment." While the play contains "material for a forceful drama . . . Mr. Miller's blunt, spare characterizations . . . are not big enough for big tragedy."

———. "*A View from the Bridge*." *New York Times* 9 October 1955: II: 1.

Atkinson dislikes both plays, directed by Martin Ritt, calling them "flat and diffuse." While *A View from the Bridge* does reach its potential, Miller does not reveal enough about Eddie Carbone for the audience to give him their sympathy.

Barnes, Clive. "Plays by Williams and Miller Staged." *New York Times* 27 January 1976: 26. *New York Theatre Critics' Reviews* 37 (1976): 382.

Barnes calls the production "brilliantly staged" and the acting "splendid," but feels that Miller's work is "less impressive" than the first play on the double bill revival, *27 Wagons Full of Cotton* by Tennessee Williams, but "it does give a lot of very fine actors a chance to show off their very fine wares."

Beaufort, John. "Williams and Miller Revivals." *Christian Science Monitor* 4 February 1976. *New York Theatre Critics' Reviews* 37 (1976): 384.

Generally favorable review of a double bill of one-acts (Tennessee Williams's *27 Wagons Full of Cotton* and Arthur Miller's *A Memory of Two Mondays*), starring Tony Musante and Meryl Streep. "Though the text seems at times overwordy and too sentimental, the author's affection registers strongly in these vignettes."

Bentley, Eric. "Theatre." *New Republic* 19 December 1955: 21–22.

Bentley notes that Miller's *A View from the Bridge*, unlike his good friend Kazan's *On the Waterfront*, condemns the informer but seems "isolated from the great debates of our time." *A Memory of Two Mondays* needs tightening in order for it to succeed.

Chapman, John. "Arthur Miller's *View from the Bridge* Is Splendid, Stunning Theatre." *New York Daily News* 30 September 1955. *New York Theatre Critics' Reviews* 16 (1955): 273. Rpt. in *Critical Essays on Arthur Miller*. Ed. James J. Martine. Boston: G. K. Hall, 1979. 105-106.

Highly positive review in which Chapman praises Miller's double bill as "two superlatively fine plays" that "were given a superlatively fine production." "Miller, whose work has already commanded great respect, shows further development in his human insight, his theatrical skill and his quality as a poet."

Coleman, Robert. "Twin Bill at Coronet Fine for Box Office." *New York Daily Mirror* 30 September 1955. *New York Theatre Critics' Reviews* 16 (1955): 272.

Generally favorable review of both *Memory of Two Mondays* and *A View from the Bridge*: while *Memory* "is a lot of talk, accurate and salty talk, an little action," *Bridge* "will make the Coronet's turnstiles click for quite a spell."

Freedley, George. "*A View from the Bridge*." *Booklist* 15 January 1956: 205–206.

Brief review of the publication of the two one-act plays that Freedley praises for the "pared-to-the-bone style and skillful use of common speech" that heightens the pair's dramatic impact.

Gibbs, Wolcott. "The Theatre." *New Yorker* 8 October 1955: 92, 94–95.

After remarking that Miller's "command of the idiom is nearly perfect and his treatment of dramatic incident is beyond criticism," Gibbs chides the character of Alfieri as "distractingly literary" and "served merely to bring a superfluous and rather pretentious air of classroom erudition to an otherwise admirably forthright play."

Gottfried, Martin. "An Old Pair Gets New Shine." *New York Post* 27 January 1976. *New York Theatre Critics' Reviews* 37 (1976): 382.

Fairly positive review of the revival production of Tennessee Williams's *27 Wagons Full of Cotton* and Miller's *A Memory of Two Mondays* staged at The Playhouse by the Phoenix Theatre, starring John Lithgow, Meryl Streep, and Thomas Hulce, directed by Arvin Brown. Says Gottfried, "There is none of the maudlin in it, as one might expect, but a great deal of honest feeling and both its construction and writing are excellent."

Hawkins, William. "2-in-1 Bill Staged at Coronet." *New York World-Telegram* 30 September 1955. *New York Theatre Critics' Reviews* 16 (1955): 274.

Calling the double bill an "unusual evening of theater, made of material which is not very original," Hawkins dismisses *Memory* as "plotless" and *Bridge* as "bombastic."

Hayes, Richard. "I Want My Catharsis." *Commonweal* 4 November 1955: 117–18.

Extremely negative review of *A View from the Bridge* and *A Memory of Two Mondays*, which played as a double bill of one-act plays at the Coronet Theatre. "Everything that is specious and fraudulent in the American theater of serious intent seems to me concentrated in these two dramas of working-class life."

Hewes, Henry. "Broadway Postscript: Death of a Longshoreman." *Saturday Review of Literature* 15 October 1955: 25–26.

Hewes praises *A Memory of Two Mondays* as "real" and "important" but faults the direction by Martin Ritt for the production's rapid pace that emphasizes its comedy, resulting "in a feeling of inconsequentiality." Of *A View from the Bridge*, Hewes lauds Miller's character study of Eddie Carbone as "gripping, unflinchingly real as well as poetic."

Kerr, Walter. "Theater: *A View from the Bridge*." *New York Herald Tribune* 30 September 1955: 8. *New York Theatre Critics' Reviews* 16 (1955): 275.

Mixed review of Miller's double bill. While Kerr finds *A Memory of Two Mondays* "an interesting and sometimes affecting mood piece" and *A View from the Bridge* "a dramatic bonfire," he calls Miller's plays "a must for anyone who is at all interested in what the contemporary American theater is thinking about."

McClain, John. "Hail Heflin in Two Plays: Arthur Miller Dramas Show Fine Acting, but the People Are Dreary." *New York Journal American* 30 September 1955. *New York Theatre Critics' Reviews* 16 (1955): 274.

While praising Miller's "unqualified ear" and "legitimate understanding of the people he writes about," McClain concludes: "Maybe it's my fault, but I'm getting bored by these terribly significant plays about dreary people."

O'Connor, Frank. "The Most American Playwright." *Holiday* 19 February 1956: 65, 68, 70.

Mixed review of the double bill of one-acts. O'Connor finds *A Memory of Two Mondays* "a beautiful play," while *A View from the Bridge* is a play without scale that has at its center an inarticulate character—and "inarticulate character cannot be either classical or tragic. Even when played by as brilliant an actor as Van Heflin, he can only be dumb."

Probst, Leonard. "*27 Wagons Full of Cotton & A Memory of Two Mondays*." NBC, New York. 27 January 1976. *New York Theatre Critics' Reviews* 37 (1976): 385.

Negative review of the Phoenix Theatre production of Miller's one-act play, *A Memory of Two Mondays*, that Probst calls a "sometimes funny, sometimes forced social document about workers in a warehouse."

Sharp, Christopher. "Miller and Williams at the Phoenix." *Women's Wear Daily* 28 January 1976. *New York Theatre Critics' Reviews* 37 (1976): 385.

Finding the evening of two short plays "interesting, if not invigorating," Sharp applauds both Tennessee Williams's *27 Wagons Full of Cotton* and Miller's *A Memory of Two Mondays*, starring Meryl Streep and John Lithgow, directed by Arvin Brown.

Trauber, Shepard. "Drama." *The Nation* 22 October 1955: 348–49.
In this brief positive review of the New York premiere of one-acts, Trauber praises Miller as a playwright "whose thinking about human beings is always profound."

"*A View from the Bridge.*" *Theatre Arts* 39 (December 1955): 18–19.
Positive review of the double bill of one-acts. Praising the acting in both pieces, the critic lauds *A View from the Bridge* as a "lean, taught narrative," and says that *A Memory of Two Mondays* works because of the "gamy language" and natural situations.

"*A View from the Bridge.*" *Time* 10 October 1955: 53.
While *A Memory of Two Mondays* is "shapeless," *A View from the Bridge* is "better than good theatre at its best."

Watt, Douglas. "Depression Duet." *New York Daily News* 27 January 1976. *New York Theatre Critics' Reviews* 37 (1976): 383.
Highly positive review of the revival of *A Memory of Two Mondays*, which appeared on a double bill with Williams's *27 Wagons Full of Cotton*, starring Meryl Streep and John Lithgow, directed by Arvin Brown.

Watts, Richard, Jr. "Those New Plays by Arthur Miller." *New York Post* 30 September 1955. *New York Theatre Critics' Reviews* 16 (1955): 272.
Negative review in which Watts's expectations for a fine night of theatre written by "one of America's most important dramatists" were dashed after his attendance opening night: "it caused me not only disappointment but acute unhappiness." *A Memory of Two Mondays*, he calls "a mood piece," which was "admirably acted" but filled with "a kind of dramatic aimlessness about it that keeps it from being more than moderately interesting." *A View from the Bridge*, while "tense and almost steadily interesting," was "curiously commonplace and lacking in any particular freshness of viewpoint or insight."

Wilson, Edwin. "Revival Nights on Broadway." *Wall Street Journal* 2 February 1976. *New York Theatre Critics' Reviews* 37 (1976): 384.
Positive review of the revival of *Memory of Two Mondays* staged by the Phoenix Theatre, starring Meryl Streep and John Lithgow, directed by Arvin Brown. Says Wilson, "it vividly depicts a time and place which are very much a part of the American scene."

Wyatt, Euphemia Van Rensselaer. "Theater." *Catholic World* (November 1955): 144–45.

Negative review of both halves of the double bill. Wyatt dislikes *A Memory of Two Mondays* for its "very lewd interlude—supposedly comic—which is not only offensive but blasphemous," and criticizes *A View from the Bridge* for its "unrelenting" outcome that "never reaches the climax of classic tragedy because Eddie lacks nobility of motive."

News Reports, Letters to the Editor, and Related Matter

"*A Memory of Two Mondays* and *A View from the Bridge*." *New York Times Magazine* 18 September 1955: 78.

Brief text announcing the opening of the double bill of one-acts on 29 September accompanied by four production stills from both shows.

"Miller Work Hailed." *New York Times* 31 August 1955: 16.

Brief news item reporting that the pre-Broadway production of the double bill of one-acts, playing at the Fallmouth Playhouse, was well received by critics.

"Nostalgia and Passion by the River." *Life* 17 October 1955: 166–67.

Production photographs from the New York premiere of one-acts.

A View from the Bridge

Critical Essays in Books

Carson, Neil. "*A View from the Bridge* and the Expansion of Vision." *Modern Critical Views: Arthur Miller*. Ed. Harold Bloom. New York: Chelsea House, 1987. 93–102. Originally titled "*A View from the Bridge*" from Carson's *Arthur Miller*. New York: St. Martin's, 1982.

Carson examines Miller's development as a playwright as witnessed by his revision of the one-act *A View from the Bridge* into a full-length play.

Chander, Kailash. "Neurosis, Guild and Jealousy in *A View from the Bridge*." *Perspectives on Arthur Miller*. Ed. Atma Ram. New Delhi: Abhinav Publications, 1988. 96–108.

Contrary to those critics who label Miller's *A View from the Bridge* as melodrama, Chander strongly argues that the play "is undoubtedly a deep and disturbing tragedy" about a "neurotic character" who "was trying to resolve his dilemma but perished in the process."

Huerta, Jorge. "Looking for the Magic: Chicanos in the Mainstream." *Negotiating Performance: Gender, Sexuality, and Theatricality in Latin/o America*. Durham, N.C.: Duke UP, 1994. 37–48.

Brief mention is made of the Chicano adaptation of *A View from the Bridge*, which was transferred from Brooklyn to San Diego's Logan Heights, under the Coronado Bridge. According to Huerta, the move "made obvious sense and proved the universality of the immigrant experience in this country."

Rothenberg, Albert, and Eugene D. Shapiro. "The Defense of Psychoanalysis in Literature: *Long Day's Journey into Night* and *A View from the Bridge*." *Comparative Drama* 7.1 (Spring 1973): 51–67. Rpt. in *Critical Approaches to O'Neill*. Ed. John H. Stroupe. New York: AMS, 1988, 169–85.

Stating that *A View from the Bridge* has a defensive structure quite different than *A Long Day's Journey into Night* by O'Neill, the authors investigate the play's "simple bi-phasic quality" and conclude that there is a "lack of psychological development in the content of the tragedy." The relief that the audience feels at the death of Eddie is "rather shallow because it is produced by sudden action and a sense of moral retribution . . . rather than a gradual reaction of defensive tension and a slow movement."

Styan, J. L. "Why *A View from the Bridge* Went Down Well in London: The Story of a Revision." *Arthur Miller: New Perspective*. Ed. Robert A. Martin. Engelwood Cliffs, N.J.: Prentice-Hall, 1982. 139–48.

Styan explores the critical reaction to the one-act and two-act revision of *A View from the Bridge*, the changes that Miller effected from one script to the other, and Miller's own commentary regarding his revision.

Tynan, Kenneth. "Social Drama." *Curtains*. New York: Atheneum, 1961. 123–24.

Tynan's essay begins with praising Miller's essay "On Social Plays," which prefaces the American edition of *A View from the Bridge*, as "an artistic credo as stimulating as any of our time," then decries all tragedy that sets up "personal fulfillment as a tragic ideal," ending with a note that Miller's *View* was banned in England because one character accuses another of homosexuality, even though the accusation is false.

Wertheim, Albert. "*A View from the Bridge*." *Cambridge Companion to Arthur Miller*. Ed. Christopher Bigsby. Cambridge: Cambridge UP, 1997. 101–14.

Wertheim traces Miller's experiences working on the waterfront to his two waterfront works, the unpublished screenplay of "The Hook" and the play *A View from the Bridge.*

Critical Essays in Journals and Magazines

Ambrosetti, Ronald. "Next Door to the Earthly Paradise: Mythic Pattern in Italian-American Drama." *Journal of Popular Culture* 19.3 (Winter 1985): 109–18.

Ambrosetti reads *A View from the Bridge* as a modern version of "one of the oldest and most influential stories in the history of the world" with origins in Hellenistic Greece.

Centola, Steven R. "Compromise as Bad Faith: Arthur Miller's *A View from the Bridge* and William Inge's *Come Back, Little Sheba*." *Midwest Quarterly* 28.1 (Autumn 1986): 100–13.

Centola examines the negative effects of compromise on the lives of the characters in Miller's *A View from the Bridge* and Inge's *Come Back, Little Sheba*.

Edwards, John. "Arthur Miller: An Appraisal." *Time & Tide* 4 May 1961: 740–41.

Assessment of Miller as a social playwright who seeks a "tragic formula to accommodate the experience of ordinary man." Miller's most forceful attempt at tragedy, *A View from the Bridge*, fails because the playwright over-fashions his formula and under-nourishes his materials. Yet, says Edwards, "A Miller play stands out from its contemporaries for its craftsmanship, seriousness and daring. Anything from him is an event." Black-and-white photograph of Miller and wife Monroe accompanies the text.

Epstein, Arthur D. "A Look at *A View from the Bridge*." *Texas Studies in Literature and Language* 7 (Spring 1965): 109–22. Rpt. in *Critical Essays on Arthur Miller*. Ed. James J. Martine. Boston: G. K. Hall, 1979. 107–18.

Epstein examines the uneasy conflict between the mythic setting of *A View from the Bridge* and its realistic foreground.

Hurd, Myles R. "Angels and Anxieties in Miller's *A View from the Bridge*." *Notes on Contemporary Literature* 13 (September 1983): 4–6.

According to Hurd, critics have identified one of the illegal "submarines" as a homosexual, but readers have overlooked evidence that points to the latent gay leanings of the play's protagonist, Eddie Carbone. "Miller signposts these references to Eddie's homosexuality through his inclusion of allusions to angels to highlight the character's psychosexual anxieties."

Mattimoe, Edward J. "*A View from the Bridge*." *America* 14 February 1998: 28–29.

Mattimoe mostly relates the plot of the play and its genesis from idea to full-length production. He praises the Roundabout Theatre's 1998 production, starring Anthony LaPaglia and Allison Janney and directed by Michael Mayer, as "a story that would rivet the attention of any and all of them who could get to see it and of an even wider audience," and hopes it finds "a well-deserved spot on Broadway."

Merino, Raquel. "Arthur Miller's *A View from the Bridge* in Spanish." *Intin* 39 (1994): 231–38.

After discovering a 1980 Spanish translation of *A View from the Bridge*, Merino realized that what he had was not an acting edition of the play but "a rewrite, an entirely different play written by the target author having the source text as inspiration or excuse," thus revealing "striking facts about the history of the translation (may be translations) of this play into Spanish."

Critical Essays in Newspapers

Collins, William B. "Playwright Bedeviled by His Play." *Philadelphia Inquirer* 6 March 1989: E3.

Feature article offering background information on the genesis of Miller's play *A View from the Bridge.*

von Rhein, John. "Untried but True to Lyric Opera's Vision." *Chicago Tribune* 3 October 1999: Sec. 7: 1.

Feature article on the opera version of *A View from the Bridge*, commissioned by the Lyric Opera of Chicago, in which von Rhein questions whether it will stand the test of time.

Winer, Linda. "A New View of *View*." *Newsday* 21 April 1998: B2.

After noting the transfer of *A View from the Bridge* from off-Broadway to the commercial venue of the Neil Simon Theatre as well as "some useful recasting," Winer criticizes the play for Miller's use of the lawyer Alfieri as Greek chorus—"Each time Miller hauls out [Alfieri] . . . who intones to us about the vast meaning of this obvious culture-clash plot, we wince a little more and wish he would just let the characters get on with the show."

Production Reviews

Asquith, Ros. "*A View from the Bridge*." *City Limits* (London) 12 November 1987. *London Theatre Record* 7.22 (1987): 1414.

Asquith praises the Alan Ayckbourn revival of *A View from the Bridge*, starring Michael Gambon, playing at the Aldwych, as "one of those masterpieces of psychological and moral intensity that makes you think you really are in the presence of greatness."

"*A View from the Bridge*." *Playboy* September 1965: 50–51.

Positive review of the off-Broadway (Sheridan Square Playhouse) production of the two-act version of *A View from the Bridge*, directed by Ulu Grosbard. The critic concludes, "One additional surprise in this production is that it reveals, in Miller, a feeling for the rhythms of working-class speech."

Barkley, Richard. "*A View from the Bridge*." *Sunday Express* (London) 15 February 1987. *London Theatre Record* 7.4 (1987): 175.

Brief positive review that praises Alan Ayckbourn's revival as possessing "a driving compulsion" that "holds you petrified in an atmosphere of mounting doom."

Barnes, Clive. "Miller's Powerful *Bridge* Finally Makes It to B'way." *New York Post* 4 February 1983. *New York Theatre Critics' Reviews* 44 (1983): 378–79.

While admitting his "notorious" reputation for "giving Miller two-faced notices," Barnes praises the New York production, starring Tony Lo Bianco and Robert Prosky and directed by Arvin Brown, as a "fiercely competent work that suffers from nothing other than the pretensions of its author and the overpraise of its thinning number of admirers. I enjoyed it more than almost anything else during the scant season."

———. "*A View from the Bridge*." *New York Post* 15 December 1997. http://206.15.118.165/121597/1703.htm (4 April 1999).

Highly laudatory review of the Roundabout Theatre Company's revival of *A View from the Bridge*, directed by Michael Mayer. Says Barnes, "If you want gut-wrenching, mind-twisting drama, fantastically well played and staged, go no further than to the Roundabout Theatre, where Arthur Miller's powerfully envisaged, carefully wrought tragedy *A View from the Bridge* is finally getting its just American deserts in a landmark production worthy of its power."

Barnes, Stephanie. "*A View from the Bridge*." *Jewish Chronicle* (London) 20 February 1987. *London Theatre Record* 7.4 (1987): 171.

Barnes praises the Alan Ayckbourn revival and applauds Michael Gambon for his "bull-in-a-china shop presence" that "mesmerises throughout *A View from the Bridge*."

Beaufort, John. "Gripping Revival of Miller's *View from the Bridge*." *Christian Science Monitor* 10 February 1983. *New York Theatre Critics' Reviews* 44 (1983): 381.

Beaufort admires the New York production, starring Tony Lo Bianco and Robert Prosky, as an "intense personal and psychological drama."

Benedictus, David. "*A View from the Bridge*." *Evening Standard* (London) 13 February 1987. *London Theatre Record* 7.4 (1987): 173.

Benedictus praises the Alan Ayckbourn revival as "hugely passionate," and "beautifully directed," and possessing a performance by Michael Gambon that "chills the blood."

Billington, Michael. "Burnt Bridges." *Guardian* (London) 10 April 1995: Sec. 2, p. 10. *Theatre Record* 15.7 (1995): 421.

Mixed review of David Thacker's production of *A View from the Bridge*, starring Bernard Hill, at London's Strand Theatre, that Billington calls "no more than a routine revival."

———. "*A View from the Bridge*." *Guardian* (London) 14 February 1987. *London Theatre Record* 7.4 (1987): 171.

Billington praises Michael Gambon's Eddie Carbone as a "towering performance," and Alan Ayckbourn's direction as "superb." Says Billington, "Tragic heroes, we used to be told, have to fall from a great height. What this production proves is that it's the intensity of the despair rather than the depth of the descent that makes for true drama."

———. "*A View from the Bridge*." *Guardian* (London) 5 November 1987. *London Theatre Record* 7.22 (1987): 1411–12.

Billington lauds the Alan Ayckbourn production at the Aldwych. "It remains one of the great productions of our time not only because of Michael Gambon's towering central performance but because Alan Ayckbourn establishes the vital Miller connection between the tragic hero and the moral laws of the tribal community."

Brantley, Ben. "Incestuous Longings on the Waterfront." *New York Times* 15 December 1997: E1.

Favorable review of the Roundabout Theatre's production of *View from the Bridge*, directed by Michael Mayer. "With a cast that approaches perfection, the evening is etched throughout with precise, unobtrusive physical details that find the seeds of destruction in the seemingly insignificant."

Canby, Vincent. "A Classically Riveting *View from the Bridge*." *New York Times* 4 January 1998: Sec. 2: 6–7.

Favorable review of the Roundabout Theatre's production of *View from the Bridge*, directed by Michael Mayer. "Mr. Miller again shows us that contemporary plays can still move, disturb, provoke and even shock. *A View from the Bridge* demonstrates how pleasurable that can be."

Couling, Delia. "*A View from the Bridge*." *Tablet* (London) 28 February 1987. *London Theatre Record* 7.4 (1987): 169.

While praising Michael Gambon as "magnificent as the obsessed Eddie . . . emanating a frightening underlying mood of violence," Couling chastises the Alan Ayckbourn revival at the Cottesloe as "a story of Italian immigrants in New York" that "is as murky and forbidding as its waterfront setting."

Coveney, Michael. "*A View from the Bridge*." *Financial Times* (London) 4 November 1987. *London Theatre Record* 7.22 (1987): 1411.

Positive review of the Alan Ayckbourn production, moved to the Aldwych from the Cottesloe, that mainly focuses on the "great acting" of Michael Gambon as Eddie Carbone. "Gambon rolls and swaggers like a caged animal, his grunts and growls, boot shedding and cigar lighting all part of a perpetual motion that is overtaken in the fast lane by a passion he does not understand and cannot handle."

———. "*A View from the Bridge*." *Observer* (London) 16 April 1995. *Theatre Record* 15.7 (1995): 421

Negative review of the Bristol Old Vic revival, recently moved to the Strand, directed by David Thacker and starring Bernard Hill. Says Coveney, "it's a decent piece, but desperately scrappy and underwritten."

Cunningham, Dennis. "*A View from the Bridge*." CBS. WCBS, New York. 3 February 1983. *New York Theatre Critics' Reviews* 43 (1983): 381.

While praising Miller's work as "truly fine," Cunningham chides the Long Wharf production of *A View from the Bridge*, starring Tony Lo Bianco, as both "financially cut rate and emotionally cut rate. A small domestic squabble where a sweeping domestic tragedy should be."

Davidson, Justin. "A Trifecta in Chicago." *Newsday* 7 November 1999: D25.

Negative review of the William Bolcom opera version of *A View from the Bridge*, commissioned by the Lyric Opera of

Chicago. Says Davidson, "there is not an original note in *A View from the Bridge*, though Bolcom does juggle clichés with dexterity. . . . I found myself staying just ahead of the score in my head, so unimaginative were the transformations."

de Jongh, Nicholas. "*A View from the Bridge*." *Evening Standard* (London) 10 April 1995. *Theatre Record* 15.7 (1995): 422.

Positive review of the Bristol Old Vic revival, recently moved to the Strand, starring Bernard Hill. Says de Jongh, "David Thacker's production, which is as taut as a violin string, helps explain why *A View from the Bridge* speaks to us today with such dramatic urgency and relevance."

"The Directors." *Newsweek* 15 March 1965: 93.

Mixed review that praises Ulu Grosbard's direction for creating an "almost wholly satisfying theatrical experience, if not a revelatory one," but castigates Miller for his "basic failure of vision" and "a muddled grasp of how psychic action relates to existential truth."

Donoghue, Denis. "The Human Image in Modern Drama." *Lugano Review* 1 (Summer 1965): 167–68.

Donoghue argues that *A View from the Bridge* presents the image of a man who is "fully known through human relationships, time, place and the reality of passion," not like the rest of us who "settle for a safe half."

"Drama by Miller Opens in London." *New York Times* 12 October 1956: 35.

News item reporting on the London opening of the full-length version of *A View from the Bridge*, including excerpts from reviews for the premiere production.

Edwardes, Jane. "*A View from the Bridge*." *Time Out* (London) 18 February 1987. *London Theatre Record* 7.4 (1987): 175.

Positive review of the Alan Ayckbourn revival at the Cottesloe in which Edwardes praises both actor Michael Gambon and Miller for managing "to wrench one's own heart for the sake of an informer, a heel who provides protection to two illegal immigrants only to stitch them up."

Edwards, Christopher. "*A View from the Bridge*." *Spectator* (London) 21 February 1987. *London Theatre Record* 7.4 (1987): 174.

Edwards praises Michael Gambon's performance as Eddie Carbone as "both ignoble and dignified," and Alan Ayckbourn's revival at the Cottesloe "passionate" and "powerful."

———. "*A View from the Bridge*." *Spectator* (London) 14 November 1987. *London Theatre Record* 7.22 (1987): 1410.

Edwards reiterates both his praise for the performances and his reservations about the structure of the work for the Alan Ayckbourn production, starring Michael Gambon, which has recently transferred to the Aldwych from the Cottesloe for a limited run.

Feingold, Michael. "Past Motives." *Village Voice* 13 January 1998: 85.

Mixed review of the Roundabout Theatre's revival of *A View from the Bridge* starring Anthony LaPaglia and directed by Michael Mayer, in which Feingold praises the acting of LaPaglia but finds Miller's work pretentious in his "drive to inflate a small, scathing, domestic drama into earth-shattering high tragedy."

Findlater, Richard. "No Time for Tragedy?" *Twentieth Century* 161 (January 1957): 56–62.

Positive review of the London premiere of *A View from the Bridge* that Findlater calls "a powerful and important play" that he "nearly ruins" by the inclusion of the Chorus. Says Findlater, "No interpreter should be needed to invest a drama with the tragic spirit."

Grant, Steve. "*A View from the Bridge*." *Time Out* (London) 11 November 1987. *London Theatre Record* 7.22 (1987): 1410.

After praising both Alan Ayckbourn's production, recently transferred to the Aldwych from the Cottesloe, as "superb" and Michael Gambon's acting as bursting "with caged rage and cowardly-lion self pity," Grant commends Miller's play "which seems so honest, so pure in heart, so real, depicting as it does a time, a place, a story and a belief that to settle for half in life is both to survive and to die inside."

Gross, John. "*A View from the Bridge*." *Sunday Telegraph* (London) 16 April 1995. *Theatre Record* 15.7 (1995): 423.

Highly laudatory review of the Bristol Old Vic revival, recently moved to the Strand, directed by David Thacker and starring

Bernard Hill. Says Gross, this play is "Miller at his best—an honest, strongly constructed melodrama, with no trace of the dubious political agenda that weighs down so much of Miller's work."

Gussow, Mel. "Miller's *A View from the Bridge* Revived." *New York Times* 28 December 1981: C16.

Highly laudatory review of the Long Wharf Theatre production, directed by Arvin Brown and starring Tony Lo Bianco and William Swetland, that Gussow says certifies the play's "position as a modern American classic."

Hagerty, Bill. "*A View from the Bridge*." *Today* (London) 10 April 1995. *Theatre Record* 15.7 (1995): 424.

Recognizing the operatic qualities of Miller's play, Hagerty praises the Bristol Old Vic production, recently moved to the Strand, directed by David Thacker and starring Bernard Hill, as "a revival that soars like an aria."

Hartley, Anthony. "Waterfront." *Spectator* (London) 19 October 1956: 538–40.

Hartley praises the London premiere, directed by Peter Brook, as a play that is powerful enough "to overcome its defects."

Hasell, Graham. "*A View from the Bridge*." *What's On* (London) 19 April 1995. *Theatre Record* 15.7 (1995): 424.

Mixed review of the Bristol Old Vic revival, recently moved to the Strand, starring Bernard Hill. Says Hasell, "If David Thacker's new production doesn't quite pull it off, firstly by attempting an expressionistic style which contradicts Miller's realist intentions, and secondly by missing the required sexual emphasis in both the overt heterosexuality and the latent homosexual spheres, it still manages to enthrall on its own terms and offers some solid performances."

Hiley, Jim. "*A View from the Bridge*." *Listener* (London) 19 February 1987. *London Theatre Record* 7.4 (1987): 170–71.

Calling *A View from the Bridge* "monumental, sweeping, irrefutable," Hiley praises the Alan Ayckbourn revival as "a discreetly designed production that's grand without being pretentious, and a vast star performance that never overshadows the ensemble."

———. "*A View from the Bridge*." *Listener* (London) 12 November 1987. *London Theatre Record* 7.22 (1987): 1413.

Positive review of the Alan Ayckbourn revival, moved to the Aldwych from the Cottesloe, starring Michael Gambon, that praises the "astutely crafted drama" and the "meticulously tuned production" for combining into "a consummately fluent ensemble."

Hope-Wallace, Philip. "Theatre: *A View from the Bridge*." *Time and Tide* (London) 37 (1956): 1267.

Positive review of the London premiere at the Watergate Club that Hope-Wallace calls a work that is "relentless and the feeling in it is unusually strong and deep, with slowly built, unvarying and intense acting-situations which in Peter Brook's superb production pack a tremendous punch at you before the end."

Horner, Rosalie. "*A View from the Bridge*." *Daily Express* (London) 14 February 1987. *London Theatre Record* 7.4 (1987): 172.

Praising Michael Gambon's performance as Eddie Carbone as "towering," Horner lauds Miller's play for containing "elements of tragedy" of "such a strong force that once set in motion they move to their conclusion with an inevitability nothing can halt."

Hoyle, Martin. "*A View from the Bridge*." *Financial Times* (London) 13 February 1987. *London Theatre Record* 7.4 (1987): 172–73.

Hoyle praises the Alan Ayckbourn revival, starring Michael Gambon and Elizabeth Bell, as "a good, compact production."

Hughes, Allen. "Opera from Play by Miller Is Given." *New York Times* 19 October 1967: 56.

Hughes criticizes the Renzo Rossellini opera *Uno Sguardo del Ponte*, based on Miller's *A View from the Bridge*, for having a dated score and lacking the power and impact of the original play.

Hurren, Kenneth. "*A View from the Bridge*." *Mail on Sunday* (London) 8 November 1987. *London Theatre Record* 7.22 (1987): 1410.

Hurren advises that "nobody should miss this brilliant Alan Ayckbourn production in which Michael Gambon turns in the performance of the year" in this positive review of the revival newly transferred to the Aldwych from the Cottesloe.

Jameson, Sue. "*A View from the Bridge*." *London Broadcasting* (London) 4 November 1987. *London Theatre Record* 7.22 (1987): 1412.

Jameson praises the Alan Ayckbourn production, starring Michael Gambon and playing at the Aldwych after its move from the Cottesloe, as a "stunning performance" that "leaves an imprint almost impossible to erase. There are so few really remarkable evenings in the theatre, but this is one of them."

Kalem, T. E. "Blind Passion." *Time* 14 February 1983. 87. *New York Theatre Critics' Reviews* 44 (1983): 380.

Negative review of the New York production starring Tony Lo Bianco and Robert Prosky in which Kalem complains that "though Miller strove for Greek myth, his play is more of a tabloid melodrama."

Kemp, Peter. "*A View from the Bridge*." *Independent* (London) 14 February 1987. *London Theatre Record* 7.4 (1987): 172.

Kemp finds the Alan Ayckbourn revival impressive and "for all all its hankerings to seem august and classical, *A View from the Bridge* is usually robust and realistic: fierce and sometimes funny social drama, loud with lively everyday speech, strong on place and period."

Kennicott, Philip. "Bolcom's Genre-Spanning *Bridge*." *Washington Post* 11 October 1999: C1.

Positive review of the opera version of *A View from the Bridge*, commissioned by the Lyric Opera of Chicago, in which Kennicott concludes "Had this opera been written while Bernstein was at his peak, reviewers would have proclaimed a new genius to rival the master."

King, Francis. "*A View from the Bridge*." *Sunday Telegraph* (London) 15 February 1987. *London Theatre Record* 7.4 (1987): 173–74.

Calling Michael Gambon's Eddie Carbone as a "superb" performance "of the twisted, throttled passion of a man terrified of looking into his own heart and acknowledging what he finds there," King praises the Alan Ayckbourn revival as "an evening of theatre to appeal in equally abundant measure to the mind and the heart."

———. "*A View from the Bridge*." *Sunday Telegraph* (London) 8 November 1987. *London Theatre Record* 7.22 (1987): 1410.

King urges readers to see this production, directed by Alan Ayckbourn and starring Michael Gambon, recently transferred to the Aldwych from the Cottesloe, where they "can look forward to being both exalted by a tragic story and excited by Miller's total mastery of the dramatist's art."

Kingston, Jeremy. "*A View from the Bridge*." *The Times* (London) 11 April 1995. *Theatre Record* 15.7 (1995): 424.

Positive review of the Bristol Old Vic revival, recently moved to the Strand, starring Bernard Hill. While commenting that Alfieri protests his impotence too much, Kingston says "this is a quibble to set beside the blistering intensity of Miller's dialogue, played by David Thacker's great cast with such fidelity and passion."

Kissel, Howard. "*A View from the Bridge*." *Women's Wear Daily* 7 February 1983. *New York Theatre Critics' Reviews* 44 (1983): 380.

While dismissing Miller's drama for its "humdrum" theme, which is "less immediate for today's audiences," Kissel praises the production starring Tony Lo Bianco and Robert Prosky as "a rich evening of theater" and admits to finding himself surrendering to the play "largely because the performances are so highly charged."

Lahr, John. "Treachery Grows in Brooklyn: A Family Tragedy Echoes the Betrayals of McCarthyism." *New Yorker* 5 January 1998: 78–79.

Positive review of the Roundabout Theatre's highly acclaimed production of *A View from the Bridge*, which, says Lahr, "despite its cool Broadway reception in 1955, has proved to be a potent and durable American fable."

Lyons, Donald. "Arthur Miller Done Right." *Wall Street Journal* 17 December 1997: A20.

Favorable review of the Roundabout Theatre's revival of *A View from the Bridge*, directed by Michael Mayer. Says Lyons, "they've found the heart of the play and made it the most gripping theater in town."

Miller, Sarah Bryan. "Chicago Lyric Transforms Miller Play into a Memorable Opera." *St. Louis Post-Dispatch* 24 October 1999: F5.

Miller praises the William Bolcom opera version of *A View from the Bridge*, commissioned by the Lyric Opera of Chicago, and recommends that it "deserves to enter the repertory."

Morley, Sheridan. "*A View from the Bridge*." *Punch* (London) 18 November 1987. *London Theatre Record* 7.22 (1987): 1414.

Morley praises the Alan Ayckbourn revival, starring Michael Gambon, playing at the Aldwych, as "the definitive staging" of one of Miller's "tightest scripts."

———. "*A View from the Bridge*." *Spectator* (London) 15 April 1995. *Theatre Record* 15.7 (1995): 421.

Mixed review of the Bristol Old Vic revival, recently moved to the Strand, directed by David Thacker and starring Bernard Hill. Calling it "uncharacteristically creaky around the edges," Morley admits that the play has "mythic and epic" qualities, that is "only now for the first time beginning to show its age."

Morris, Tom. "*A View from the Bridge*." *Time Out* (London) 12 April 1995. *Theatre Record* 15.7 (1995): 423–24.

Negative review of the Bristol Old Vic revival, recently moved to the Strand, directed by David Thacker, that Morris calls "a less than terrifying production" containing a "subtle" performance of Bernard Hill as Eddie Carbone, who "lacks the irresistible monstrosity needed to pull the audience with him on his destructive course."

Murray, David. "*A View from the Bridge*." *Financial Times* (London) 12 April 1994. *Theatre Record* 15.7 (1995): 422.

Murray praises both David Thacker's direction as "stark" and Bernard Hill's Eddie Carbone as "superbly played" in this positive review of the Bristol Old Vic revival, recently moved to the Strand.

Nathan, David. "*A View from the Bridge*." *Jewish Chronicle* (London) 13 November 1987. *London Theatre Record* 7.22 (1987): 1413–14.

Positive review of the Alan Ayckbourn revival starring Michael Gambon, playing at the Aldwych after its move from the National, in which Nathan praises the direction for bringing together "Arthur Miller's spare, muscular writing with the inarticulate emotions it releases through a set of superb performances."

Newmark, Judith. "A View from the Theater Critic." *St. Louis Post-Dispatch* 24 October 1999: F5.

Mixed review of William Bolcom opera of *A View from the Bridge*, commissioned by the Lyric Opera of Chicago. Says Newmark, Miller's play "moves like a locomotive, relentlessly hurtling toward its inevitable destination. The new opera adapted from his play has the same unstoppable drive—and ends in the same wreck. . . Better? Worse? It's neither—it's just different."

Oliver, Edith. "The Theatre: Off-Broadway." *New Yorker* 6 February 1965: 94.

Oliver praises *A View from the Bridge*, directed by Ulu Grosbard, as Miller's "most forthright and least annoying play," and "an effective and exciting melodrama."

Osborne, Charles. "*A View from the Bridge.*" *Daily Telegraph* (London) 14 February 1987. *London Theatre Record* 7.4 (1987): 175.

Positive review of the Alan Ayckbourn revival at the Cottesloe, starring Michael Gambon. Osborne praises the directing as "impeccable," with a cast that "is vastly superior to the first English production at the Comedy Theatre in 1956 (which I remember clearly despite having sat through it only a few feet away from the disturbing presence of the playwright's wife Marilyn Monroe)."

———. "*A View from the Bridge.*" *Daily Telegraph* (London) 5 November 1987. *London Theatre Record* 7.22 (1987): 1412–13.

Osborne praises Alan Ayckbourn's revival, starring Michael Gambon, playing at the Aldwych, as "a production of which the National Theatre can be proud."

Paton, Maureen. "*A View from the Bridge*." *Daily Express* (London) 5 November 1987. *London Theatre Record* 7.22 (1987): 1413.

Rare negative review of the Alan Ayckbourn revival starring Michael Gambon, transferred to the Aldwych from the Cottesloe, in which Paton blames the production not the script, in which the actors were "dwarfed by a spectacular but over-ambitious set" and the actors "seemed dreadfully rattled."

———. "*A View from the Bridge.*" *Daily Express* (London) 8 April 1995. *Theatre Record* 15.7 (1995): 421–22.

Highly laudatory review of the Bristol Old Vic revival, recently moved to the Strand, starring Bernard Hill. Says Paton, "The stark staging of David Thacker's superlative production emphasizes all the tragic inevitability and classical simplicities of Arthur Miller's great play. The showdown is played out like a scene from a Western against a blood-red sky."

Purnell, Tony. "*A View from the Bridge*." *Daily Mirror* (London) 5 November 1987. *London Theatre Record* 7.22 (1987): 1410.

Says Purnell, in this positive review of the Alan Ayckbourn production starring Michael Gambon at the Aldwych, "Beg, borrow or steal a ticket to this classic tragedy. To miss it would be an even greater one."

Radin, Victoria. "*A View from the Bridge*." *New Statesman* (London) 20 February 1987. *London Theatre Record* 7.4 (1987): 170.

Radin calls the Alan Ayckbourn revival "fluent, authentic and nearly unbearably moving. . . . When he wrote *A View from the Bridge*, Miller was formulating his ideas for modern tragedy; in this production this passionate play achieves that status."

Ratcliffe, Michael. "*A View from the Bridge*." *Observer* (London) 15 February 1987. *London Theatre Record* 7.4 (1987): 175–76.

Favorable review of *A View from the Bridge* that Ratcliffe says "comes horribly close to the timeless comedy of age, youth and forbidden lust, but Ayckbourn heads this ambivalence off for as long as possible by the warmth, humour and familial affection of the opening scenes."

Ray, Robin. "*A View from the Bridge*." *Punch* (London) 25 February 1987. *London Theatre Record* 7.4 (1987): 169.

Highly laudatory review of *A View from the Bridge*. Says Ray, "It is not enough even to declare that there is not an English actor alive who could do it as well, let alone better. To Gambon belongs the ultimate accolade . . . he *is* Eddie Carbone."

"Revised *Bridge* Given in Capital." *New York Times* 9 November 1956: 34.

Review that praises the revised full-length version of *A View from the Bridge* as having a clearer story and theme, but faults the production for a bothersome narrator character.

Rich, Frank. "Arthur Miller's *View from the Bridge*: Tale of Horror." *New York Times* 4 February 1983: C3. *New York Theatre Critics' Reviews* 44 (1983): 377–78.

Calling this revival starring Tony Lo Bianco and Robert Prosky "stunning" and "a much-needed evening of electric American drama," Rich admits to his previous strong reservations about the work when it first appeared in 1955. He admires what he calls "Mr. Miller's ear for his characters' working-class vernacular" and his "strategically placed theatrical eruptions."

Ridley, Clifford A. "Arthur Miller's *A View from the Bridge* in Powerful Revival." *Philadelphia Inquirer* 15 December 1997: C6.

Favorable review of the Roundabout Theatre Company revival, directed by Michael Mayer and starring Anthony LaPaglia, in which critic Ridley praises David Gallo's evocative set, applauds the acting, with one exception, as "exceptional" and Miller's script as "a great play."

"Rome Sees Opera of Miller Play." *New York Times* 13 March 1961: 36.

News item reporting the opening of the Renzo Rossellini opera *Uno Sguardo del Ponte*, based on Miller's *A View from the Bridge*, that includes excerpts from critical response to the work.

Ross, Alex. "Brooklyn Bridges." *New Yorker* 1 November 1999: 120–22.

Positive review of the Lyric Opera of Chicago's production of *A View from the Bridge*. Says Ross, "*A View from the Bridge* falls short of greatness, but it does not aim for greatness, either. It wears the ruddy complexion of a work that has achieved exactly what it set out to do."

Scholem, Richard. "Our Man on Broadway." *Long Island Business News* 12 January 1998: 45.

Favorable review of the Roundabout Theatre revival, starring Anthony LaPaglia, in which Scholem praises Miller as "a master story teller" who "holds our rapt attention even though we know his tale's tragic conclusion at its outset."

Shannon, David. "*A View from the Bridge*." *Today* (London) 18 February 1987. *London Theatre Record* 7.4 (1987): 174.

While praising the Alan Ayckbourn revival as "excellently directed," Shannon laments that the production, "full of pace and pathos," is "let down only by slight sogginess of the play. Great tragic heroes are traditionally let down by having a single, major character flaw. Eddie's flaw is, unfortunately, that he is terribly stupid—at times this invites more irritation than compassion."

Sheed, Wilfrid. "Revival of a Salesman" [Review of revival]. *Commonweal* 19 February 1965: 670. Rpt. as "*A View from the Bridge*." *The Morning After: Selected Essays and Reviews*. New York: Farrar, Straus and Giroux, 1971. 168–71.

Sheed decries what she calls Miller's recent "uncompromisingly bad" writing, which makes one "tempted to say that he never was any good." While she dislikes his "Brooklyn Plays" (as she labels them), Sheed finds that they, and especially *A View from the Bridge*, "still work." Writes Sheed, "The intensity of Miller's plays comes from the fact that a family must find among its own members the whole range of human encounter. A rich man has friends in Quogue and a girl in the East eighties; a Miller man can only fall in love with his niece."

Shewey, Don. "Denial and Homophobia." *Advocate* 17 February 1998: 57–58.

Positive review of the Roundabout Theatre's "superb" revival, directed by Michael Mayer, in which Shewey praises Miller's play for being partly about homophobia, partly about sexual guilt, and partly about betrayal—it is both "topical" and "psychologically complex."

Shulman, Milton. "*A View from the Bridge*." *Evening Standard* (London) 4 November 1987. *London Theatre Record* 7.22 (1987): 1410–11.

Shulman praises the Alan Ayckbourn production starring Michael Gambon, which recently moved to the Aldwych from the Cottesloe for a limited run, as "a work always about to topple into melodrama, but saved from such a fate by the transparent integrity and impressive craftsmanship of Arthur Miller. With its background of seething Italian passion, its characters pushed to feverish extremities they can barely articulate, its plot rushing to inevitable tragedy, it is surprising that it has not by now been adapted into a modern opera."

Siegel, Ed. "In New York, Miller's Mastery Is in *View*." *Boston Globe* 17 February 1998: C1.

Review of several plays, including the Roundabout Theatre Company's production of *A View from the Bridge*, which Siegel praises as "a spectacular production" that "not only confirms Miller's power as a playwright but also establishes Anthony LaPaglia as one of the country's best actors."

Siegel, Joel. "*A View from the Bridge*." ABC. WABC, New York. 3 February 1983. *New York Theatre Critics' Reviews* 43 (1983): 381.

Siegel praises the New York production, directed by Arvin Brown and starring Tony Lo Bianco, as "an excellent production of a fine, fine play."

Silverman, Mike. "Great *View* for the Lyric Opera." *Washington Times* 6 November 1999: D3.

Silverman lauds William Bolcom's opera version of *A View from the Bridge*, commissioned by the Lyric Opera of Chicago, as "an evening of powerful theatre" that improves on Miller's original work by "adding a chorus of Eddie's neighbors and fellow workers in the Red Hook neighborhood of Brooklyn who function like the speaking chorus in a Greek tragedy."

Simon, John. "Death of a Stevedore." *New York* 12 January 1998: 49.

Negative review of the Roundabout Theatre revival, starring Anthony LaPaglia, in which Simon praises the "fine performances," but feels the production is "marred by same poetic pomposity that has afflicted most of [Miller's] work."

Sommers, Pamela. "A *Bridge* Worth Crossing." *Washington Post* 22 November 1995: B10.

Positive review of the Source Theatre production of *A View from the Bridge*, directed by Darryl V. Jones, that updated the story "from just after World War II to 1964 and recast longshoreman Eddie Carbone, his friends and family as Dominican rather than Italian extraction"—all with Miller's approval.

Spencer, Charles. "*A View from the Bridge*." *Daily Telegraph* (London) 10 April 1995. *Theatre Record* 15.7 (1995): 423.

Mixed review of the Bristol Old Vic revival, recently moved to the Strand, directed by David Thacker and starring Bernard Hill. Says Spencer, "This is a solid, well-crafted production of a solid, well-crafted play. But like so much of Miller, it is also ever so slightly dull."

Stearns, David Patrick. "Langella's Lyrical *Cyrano* and LaPaglia's Narrow *View*." *USA Today* 18 December 1997: D3.

Negative review of the Roundabout Theatre production of *A View from the Bridge* starring Anthony LaPaglia, that critic Stearns feels "would be better without him." LaPaglia, he continues, "misses the character's visionary intelligence, making his fall less compelling than it could be."

———. "Rebuilt *Bridge* Takes Direct Route." *USA Today* 12 October 1999: D5.

Positive review of William Bolcom's opera adaptation of *A View from the Bridge*, commissioned by the Lyric Opera of Chicago, that places the success of the production on "Bolcom's keen sense of working-class diction and Miller's willingness to rethink (with co-librettist Arnold Weinstein) his work."

Swed, Mark. "A Fine Musical Bridge to *View*." *Los Angeles Times* 11 October 1999: F1.

Mixed review of the opera version of *A View from the Bridge*, commissioned by the Lyric Opera of Chicago, that Swed says "beautifully evokes the lyricism of the original's words. But some drama is lost in the translation."

Taubman, Howard. "Theatre: Miller Revival." *New York Times* 29 January 1965: 24.

Taubman praises *A View from the Bridge* as an "agonized story of a man on an emotional rack . . . naked and unashamed."

Teachout, Terry. "Doo-Wop and Knife Fights." *Time* 25 October 1999: 123.

Highly laudatory review of the opera version of Miller's *A View from the Bridge*, commissioned by the Lyric Opera of Chicago that Teachout says "packs the theatrical punch of a double boilermaker."

Tinker, Jack. "*A View from the Bridge*." *Daily Mail* (London) 13 February 1987. *London Theatre Record* 7.4 (1987): 174.

Tinker lauds the Alan Ayckbourn revival at the Cottesloe, starring Michael Gambon, as "a master class in theatrical wizardry and commitment."

———. "*A View from the Bridge*." *Daily Mail* (London) 4 November 1987. *London Theatre Record* 7.22 (1987): 1412.

Tinker says that "no praise can be too high or fulsome for the wonders Alan Ayckbourn's subtle and spare direction brings to Arthur Miller's deeply disturbing family tragedy" in this revival playing at the Aldwych.

———. "*A View from the Bridge*." *Daily Mail* (London) 8 April 1995. *Theatre Record* 15.7 (1995): 423.

Positive review of the Bristol Old Vic production, recently moved to the Strand, directed by David Thacker and starring Bernard Hill, that Tinker calls a "splendid new revival" with "superbly defined performances."

Tommasini, Anthony. "Music Unlock's a Play's Secrets." *New York Times* 11 October 1999: E1.

Highly laudatory review of the opera version of *A View from the Bridge*, commissioned by the Lyric Opera of Chicago, that Tommasini says is "a strikingly designed, musically accomplished production with an excellent cast."

Trewin, J. C. "Quick Change." *Illustrated London News* (London) 27 October 1956: 720.

Positive review of the two-act London premiere of *A View from the Bridge*, directed by Peter Brook and starring Anthony Quayle, Ian Bannen, and Mary Ure, that Trewin calls "an economically-wrought play that drives straight at its point." Of note is the information provided that to see the play, one had to become a member of the New Watergate Theatre Club, for Miller's play was unlicensed for public performance by the Lord Chamberlain.

von Rhein, John. "Retro Fit." *Chicago Tribune* 11 October 1999. See also John von Rhein, "Bolcom Hits a Homer." *American Record Guide* 63.1 (January/February 2000): 14+.

Calling William Bolcom's opera version of *A View from the Bridge*, commissioned by the Lyric Opera of Chicago, "a stunning production" and "an impressive achievement."

Waleson, Heidi. "*A View from the Bridge*." *Wall Street Journal* 13 October 1999: A28.

Positive review of the premiere of the William Bolcom opera adaptation of *A View from the Bridge*, commissioned by the Lyric Opera of Chicago, that Waleson calls "an unusually gripping piece of theater. For its dramatic power alone, the opera deserves to be seen everywhere."

Watt, Douglas. "A *Bridge* under Troubled Waters." *New York Daily News* 4 February 1983. *New York Theatre Critics' Reviews* 44 (1983): 379–80.

Negative review of the New York premiere, starring Tony Lo Bianco and Robert Prosky and directed by Arvin Brown, in which Watt laments the production's "drabness" as "a play that seems to have had its day."

Webster, Margaret. "A Look at the London Season." *Theatre Arts* 41 (May 1957): 28–29.

Webster faults the London premiere production, directed by

Peter Brook, for losing the one-act play's "sense of a people of ancient lineage, reborn on the Brooklyn waterfront, yet still the prey of those smoldering, buried passions which wrought the classic tragedies."

White, Jim. "*A View from the Bridge*." *Independent* (London) 18 November 1987. *London Theatre Record* 7.22 (1987): 1414.

Brief positive review of the Alan Ayckbourn revival, playing at the Aldwych after its move from the National, that focuses on the talents of Michael Gambon's portrayal of Eddie Carbone. Says White, "Gambon hauls his audience through the apocalyptic climax, leaving them exhausted, certain that there is no theatre experience like melodrama, played as sure-footedly as this."

Wilson, Edwin. "M. Moliere and Mr. Miller Return." *Wall Street Journal* 25 February 1983. *New York Theatre Critics' Reviews* 44 (1983): 382.

Wilson praises the New York production, starring Tony Lo Bianco and Robert Prosky, for its "bristling scenes of confrontation and tense plot twists . . . the kind of drama we have sorely lacked in recent years."

Winer, Linda. "A Different *View* Point." *Newsday* 10 August 1998: B2.

Winer praises Tony Danza's performance in *A View from the Bridge* (replacement for Anthony LaPaglia) as having "presence" and "passions" and the knowledge of "how to be an ensemble player while still holding the stage."

———. "An Obstructed *View*." *Newsday* 15 December 1997: B2.

While praising the acting of Anthony LaPaglia and Allison Janney, Winer criticizes the Roundabout Theatre Company's revival of *A View from the Bridge*, directed by Michael Mayer, for its claim of "mythic qualities" and the character Alfieri as "an impossible contrivance that reappears periodically to try to convince us of the tale's great resonant significance."

Wolf, Matt. "*A View from the Bridge*." *City Limits* (London) 19 February 1987. *London Theatre Record* 7.4 (1987): 173.

Mixed review of the Alan Ayckbourn revival at the Cottesloe. While criticizing Miller for nearly stopping "the play in its tracks to congratulate himself on its pedigree," Wolf argues that "if you can't ignore the author's high-handedness, there is an occasion to be had here: the sight of an actor [Michael Gambon] scaling Olympian heights of which the play can only dream."

Worsley, T. C. "Realistic Melodrama." *New Statesman and Nation* (London) 20 October 1956: 482.

Worsley praises the premiere London production, directed by Peter Brook, as "tense, vivid" and "atmospheric," but faults Miller for attempting to "establish from the outside of the play some sort of universality."

Wren, Celia. " Miller Time." *Commonweal* 13 February 1998: 21.

The second part of this review is devoted to the Roundabout Theatre's 1998 production of *View* starring Anthony LaPaglia and directed by Michael Mayer. Wren questions Miller's use of Alfieri as a dramatic devise and Stephen Spinella's "unnerving performance" which "may still leave audiences wondering why Miller created such an ostensibly superfluous character."

Related Interviews and Profiles (not with Miller)

Chand, Paul. "Profile: David Thacker." *Drama* (1989): 18–19.

Interview with David Thacker, the artistic director of the Young Vic, in which he discusses working with Miller on *A View from the Bridge*.

Drukman, Steven. "A Two-Career Man: Theater Director and Jewish Mother." *New York Times* 3 January 1999: Sec. 2: 5.

Profile of prolific Broadway director Michael Mayer. Miller's comments on Mayer's critically acclaimed revival of *A View from the Bridge*, starring Anthony LaPaglia, are included. Says Miller, "Mayer achieved more of my original intention—evoking a community and finding the tragic size of this play. I'd trust him with any of my plays."

Gold, Sylviane. "Almost Nothing to Lean on but Onstage Chemistry." *New York Times* 18 January 1998: Sec. 2: 4.

Interview with actors Anthony LaPaglia and Allison Janney, and director Michael Mayer from the Roundabout Theatre Company's production of *A View from the Bridge*. They discuss how they worked together to find an acting style "that would best serve Arthur Miller's play."

Pacheco, Patrick. "LaPaglia on His Views from the *Bridge*." *Newsday* 14 May 1998: B11.

Short interview with Anthony LaPaglia in which the actor discusses the "noble honesty" of Eddie Carbone. Of note is the background information on the project, including LaPaglia's hiring of Michael Mayer to direct.

Robelot, Jane, and Mark McEwen. "Tony Danza's Role in Arthur Miller's Classics on Broadway." *CBS This Morning* 20 August 1998. Broadcast transcript.

Danza discusses his first learning he was cast as Anthony LaPaglia's replacement in the revival of *A View from the Bridge* and his trips to the Times Square ticket booth to hand out flyers on the show.

Shewey, Don. "Michael Mayer." *Advocate* 17 February 1998: 59.

Short biographical sketch of Michael Mayer, director of the highly acclaimed revival of *View from the Bridge*.

Tkaczyk, Christopher. "U Prof, Miller Play Build Operatic *Bridge*." *Michigan Daily* 7 October 1999.

Interview with William Bolcom, head of the School of Music Department of Composition, on the occasion of his completion of the opera version of Miller's *A View from the Bridge*. Bolcom discusses the development of the project and his feelings regarding the operatic nature of the original work.

News Reports, Letters to the Editor, and Related Matter

Barnes, Clive. "A Great *Bridge* Built on Powerful Cast." *New York Post* 17 April 1998. http://206.15.118.165/041798/1885.htm (4 April 1999).

Brief article announcing the move (a "major event") of *View* to a commercial theatre from the non-profit Roundabout Theatre. Barnes praises the production as "unequivocally the most powerful ensemble performance to be found in New York."

"*Bridge* to Close." *New York Times* 25 August 1998: E8.

Short news item announcing that the Roundabout Theatre Company's revival of Miller's *A View from the Bridge*, directed by Michael Mayer and currently starring Tony Danza, is to close, having had a run of 251 regular performances and 23 previews.

Ericson, Raymond. "Arthur Miller, Italian Style." *New York Times* 15 October 1967: II: 19.

Ericson announces that a production of Renzo Rossellini's opera *Uno Sguardo del Ponte* will open in Philadelphia soon. The Italian opera is based on Miller's *A View from the Bridge.*

Evans, Everett. "Going Back to *Bridge.*" *Houston Chronicle* 26 September, 1999: Z10.

Lengthy feature article that offers an overview of the production history and critical response to Miller's *A View from the Bridge* and reports of the Alley Theatre's intention to mount a revival for their new season, directed by Stephen Rayne.

Gates, David. "Doo-Wop Hits the Opera." *Newsweek* 18 October 1999: 76.

William Bolcom attends to last minute details of the opera version of *A View from the Bridge* before its opening night at the Lyric Opera of Chicago.

Hughes, Bob. "Overture to a Season." *Wall Street Journal* 10 September 1999: W2.

News item reporting the particulars of Miller's play *A View from the Bridge* being adapted into a full-scale opera, commissioned by the Lyric Opera of Chicago.

Kaufman, Sarah. "Rebuilding a *Bridge* with Miller." *Washington Post* 24 November 1995: N45.

Article that details director Darryl Jones's initial approach to Miller to seek permission to update *A View from the Bridge* to 1964 and make the family from the Dominican Republic. Miller granted permission, but insisted that the concept be historically plausible and that he retain rights to edit any rewrites.

Kerner, Leighton. "The Great American Opera." *Village Voice* 6 April 1999: 116–17.

Lamenting the lack of a great American opera, Kerner offers a brief history of opera in the United States, culminating in a listing of various opera schedules to come. Mention is made of the Lyric Opera of Chicago's intention to stage (in October 1999) *View from the Bridge*, with libretto by Arnold Weinstein and Arthur Miller. The work, he says, will arrive at the Met in a few years.

Lyman, Rick. "A Question of Perception." *New York Times* 12 December 1997: E2.

News item reporting actor Anthony LaPaglia's request for Miller's permission to stage a revival of *View* and the extent to which Miller became actively involved in the production (giving notes, attending rehearsals, offering advice).

———. "*View* to Close Briefly, Then Open at Neil Simon." *New York Times* 17 February 1998: E3.

News piece announcing the closing of the Roundabout Theatre Company's acclaimed revival production of Miller's play and its reopening April 3 at the Neil Simon Theatre for a commercial run. Production photograph of Anthony LaPaglia as Eddie Carbone accompanies the text.

"Miller's *View* Extended in NY." *Boston Globe* 18 February 1998: Arts and Film.

Short news item announcing the Roundabout's acclaimed production of *A View from the Bridge* will be moved to the Neil Simon Theatre.

Paller, Rebecca. "Hot Tickets." *Opera News* 64.3 (September 1999): 18+.

Lengthy feature article that provides information on various operas for the 1999–2000 season in the United States, including William Bolcom's adaptation of Miller's *A View from the Bridge*, commissioned by the Lyric Opera of Chicago.

van Gelder, Lawrence. "Footlights." *New York Times* 8 July 1998: E1.

Brief news item announcing that Tony Danza will be taking over the role of Eddie Carbone from Anthony LaPaglia on 31 July.

"*View from the Bridge* to Close." *New York Times* 3 December 1966: 45.

Brief news item reporting that the Sheridan Square Playhouse production of *A View from the Bridge*, directed by Ulu Grosbard, will close on 11 December 1966 after 780 performances.

Weber, Bruce. "Accommodating Cadences of Drama, *View from the Bridge* Nears Completion." *New York Times* 9 September 1999: E1.

Fourth in a series of nine articles concerning the adaptation of

A View from the Bridge into an opera, commissioned by the Lyric Opera of Chicago, this essay offers details on the first rehearsal of the production.

———. "Its Initial Run over, *View* Hopes to Join List of Operas That Endure." *New York Times* 11 November 1999: E1.

Final essay in a series of nine articles concerning the adaptation of *A View from the Bridge* into an opera, commissioned by the Lyric Opera of Chicago, this piece reports on the closing night events, including various principal's opinions as to the lasting power of this new work.

———. "A Long Day of Talking and a Big Night of Singing." *New York Times* 11 October 1999: E1.

Eighth in a series of nine articles on the creation of the opera version of *A View from the Bridge*, this piece reports the details of opening day events of the opera, including a public symposium on the creation of the work, held in the morning, with panelists Miller, Davies, Bolcom, Weinstein, and Galati, and the opening night festivities.

———. "The Maestro as Midwife: As Conductor, Dennis Russell Davies Brings Life to a New Opera." *New York Times* 29 September 1999: E1.

Sixth in a series of nine articles on the adaptation of *A View from the Bridge* into an opera, commissioned by the Lyric Opera of Chicago, this piece focuses on conductor Davies' artistic contribution to the production.

———. "The Opera's Director, Yes, but Not a Dictator: Path Can Be Tricky When Others Pick the Cast." *New York Times* 19 August 1999: E1.

Third in a series of nine articles on the adaptation of *A View from the Bridge* into an opera, commissioned by the Lyric Opera of Chicago, this feature offers a profile of director Frank Galati, including his directorial approach and design for the production.

———. "The Premiere Is Sometimes the Easy Part." *New York Times* 20 September 1999: E1.

Fifth in a series of feature articles on the transformation of Miller's *A View from the Bridge* into an opera, commissioned by the Lyric Opera of Chicago, this piece discusses the tenuous nature of new American operas and the financial and creative risks involved in mounting a new work of this nature.

———. "Reality Hits Singers in the Home Stretch: On a Real Stage, Bracing for an Audience." *New York Times* 7 October 1999: E1.

Seventh in a series of nine feature articles on the transformation of Miller's *A View from the Bridge* into an opera, commissioned by the Lyric Opera of Chicago, this piece interviews the singers who discuss their concerns, obstacles, rehearsal process, and approach to their roles for a new work.

———. "A Traditional Backer Changes His Traditional Ways." *New York Times* 11 August 1999: E1.

Second in a series of nine articles on the creation of the opera version of *A View from the Bridge*, this essay profiles investor Sidney L. Port and his $125,000 donation to the production of *View* at the Lyric Opera of Chicago.

———. "*A View from the Bridge* Is a Fresh American Contender." *New York Times* 4 August 1999: E1.

First in a series of nine articles on the making of *A View from the Bridge* into an opera, this piece focuses on composer William Bolcom's experiences in bringing his vision to life. Of special note is the mention of Miller as contributing an aria for Marco entitled "An Immigrant's Land." The opera will premiere on October 9 at Chicago Lyric Opera and run nine performances in four weeks.

"Word of Mouth." *Conde Naste* October 1999: 54.

Brief news item announcing the operatic world premiere of *A View from the Bridge* at the Chicago Lyric Opera and including details for purchasing tickets. Of note is the black-and-white photo of Miller walking on a bridge with his first two children in 1961 that accompanies the text.

After the Fall

Critical Essays in Books

Clausen, Robert Howard. "The Cry of Failure." *The Cross and the Cries of Human Need; Messages for Lent and Every Season.* Minneapolis, Minn.: Augsburg, 1973. 15–31.

In an effort to incorporate the messages of writers and artists who expose "in a powerful way, the problems and sicknesses of this world and its people," Clausen offers a selection from Miller's *After the Fall* from Act II (to be presented before the congregation) followed by a Christian mediation entitled "The Cross Means Hope."

Gunther, Max. *Virility 8: A Celebration of the American Male.* Chicago: Playboy, 1975. 74–76.

In a section on the "aggressive thinker" type of man, Miller's relationship with Marilyn Monroe is discussed and analyzed, particularly in the context of Miller's play *After the Fall.*

Lewis, Allan. "Arthur Miller—Return to the Self." *American Plays and Playwrights of the Contemporary Theatre.* New York: Crown, 1965. 35–52. Revised ed. New York: Crown, 1970. 35–52.

Calling *After the Fall* as "a brooding, sensitive, compelling, and incomplete play," Lewis recounts the critical response that the play inspired and asserts that with its "unduly harsh" critical reaction, the play would not have survived had it been a commercial Broadway production. "A repertory system saved the play, and public response has rebuked the critics."

Martin, Robert A. "Arthur Miller's *After the Fall*: The Critical Context." *The Achievement of Arthur Miller: New Essays.* Ed. Steven Centola. Dallas, Tex.: Contemporary Research, 1995. 119–26.

Martin defends *After the Fall* as a play with universal themes and significant theatrical innovations, and attacks those critics who fail to grasp the play's most important aspect: its message that "within us we have a common humanity."

Meyer, Nancy and Richard. "*After the Fall*: A View from the Director's Notebook." *Theater: An Annual of the Repertory Theater of Lincoln Center, Volume Two*. Ed. Barry Hyams. New York: Hill and Wang, 1965. 43–73.

Major excerpts from Kazan's production notebook for *After the Fall*, including a physical description of the notebook, as well as an analysis, overview, and evaluation of the work by the Meyers.

Otten, Terry. "The Fall and After." *After Innocence: Visions of the Fall in Modern Literature*. Pittsburgh: U of Pittsburgh P, 1982. 113–48.

Otten offers a close reading of *After the Fall* as a drama about "a man who must unequivocally face his own complicity in the evil of his age and in the suffering of those whose lives he has directly touched." Otten defends Miller's drama against those who view it as a "whitewashing" of both Quentin's guilt ("by acknowledging the guilt of all"), and, by parable, of Miller's own culpability in his three failed marriages, including the death of former wife Marilyn Monroe.

Stanton, Stephen S. "Pessimism in *After the Fall*." *Arthur Miller: New Perspectives*. Ed. Robert A. Martin. Engelwood Cliffs, N.J.: Prentice-Hall, 1982. 159–72.

Lengthy essay that reviews *After the Fall*'s critical record and summarizes "some of more provocative and more limited or erroneous assessments to date" of Miller's most controversial play.

Welland, Dennis. "The Drama of Forgiveness." *Modern Critical Views: Arthur Miller*. Ed. Harold Bloom. New York: Chelsea House, 1987. 65–77. [Originally titled "*After the Fall*" from Welland's *Arthur Miller: A Study of His Plays*. London: Methuen, 1979. 90–104.]

Welland examines the negative critical reaction to Miller's controversial play and offers a close reading of *After the Fall* as a drama of self-forgiveness. Concludes Welland, "*After the Fall*, for all its faults, merits respect greater than is sometimes accorded it and closer critical attention than is possible in the theatre."

Wertheim, Albert. "Arthur Miller: *After the Fall* and After." *Essays on Contemporary American Drama*. Ed. Hedwig Block and Albert Wertheim. Munich: M. Hueber, 1981. 19–32.

Wertheim analyzes Miller's canon following the eight year hiatus from Broadway before *After the Fall*, including *Incident at*

Vichy, *The Price*, *The Archbishop's Ceiling*, and *The American Clock*, and finds that the events in Miller's personal life in those eight years had "a profound impact on the subject matter and themes of what one could label the second flowering of Arthur Miller's playwriting career."

Whitehead, Robert. "Preface." *Psychology and Arthur Miller* by Richard I. Evans. New York: Dutton, 1969. xi–xvii.

Essay praising Miller's talent and abilities, significant for Whitehead's revelation that Miller was aware, some two months prior to rehearsal for *After the Fall*, that his play might "be construed as a play about Marilyn," contradicting Miller's public and written assertions to the contrary.

Critical Essays in Journals and Magazines

Bigsby, C. W. E. "The Fall and After: Arthur Miller's Confession." *Modern Drama* 10 (September 1967): 124–36. Rpt. in *Essays on Modern American Drama: Williams, Miller, Albee, and Shepard*. Ed. Dorothy Parker. Toronto: U of Toronto P, 1987. 68–79.

Bigsby discusses *After the Fall* as "not merely the confession of an individual anxious to resolve the paradox of his life but also man's attempt to catalogue the sins of a generation in a search for comprehension." Also discussed is the play's obvious derivation from Camus's *The Fall* (La Chute), first published in 1956.

Brashear, William R. "The Empty Bench: Morality, Tragedy, and Arthur Miller." *Michigan Quarterly Review* 5 (1966): 270–78. Rpt. in *The Gorgon's Head: A Study in Tragedy and Despair*. Athens: U of Georgia P, 1977. 134–49.

Brashear defends Miller's *After the Fall* as "unfairly received" and a play that "dispels any doubt that [Miller] is not only the heir to Ibsen but is himself a more exclusive example of the social dramatist *par excellence*." Further, he makes the bold point that Miller's work is "awkward" and "embarrassingly personal" because of its "*objectivity*, because it is the work of an *objective* artist. The tragedian, if we care to believe Nietzsche, is the supreme *subjective* artist (poet), not because he deals with what is personal to himself as an individual or proclaims his own arbitrary convictions about 'things,' but because he does not commit the epistemological fallacy of positing a reassuring objective world of 'things': *i.e.*, of matter, of ideas, of societies, of values, of morals, of language itself."

Buitenhuis, Peter. "Arthur Miller: The Fall from the Bridge." *Canadian Association for American Studies Bulletin* 3 (Spring-Summer 1967): 55–71.

Buitenhuis reads *After the Fall* as Miller's *King Lear*, in which he breaks away from standard theories of dramatic behavior to give us the "poor forked animal facing the elements of his own psychology." Miller "stripped away" the innocence of the American dream "to reveal the nightmare of unrelatedness and guilt at its centre."

Burhans, Clinton S., Jr. "Eden and the Idiot Child: Arthur Miller's *After the Fall*." *Ball State University Forum* 20.2 (Spring 1979): 3–16.

After examining the structure, themes, and recurring symbols in *After the Fall*, Burhans concludes that the play is "a serious and underestimated achievement in modern tragedy. It is seldom produced; but now that time is cushioning the personal torments it once too obviously reflected, the play deserves reconsideration."

Carter, Steven R. "Images of Men in Lorraine Hansberry's Writing." *Black American Literature Forum* 19.4 (Winter 1985): 160–62.

Carter examines the victimization of male characters through their own oppression of women in three plays by Hansberry (*A Raisin in the Sun*, *The Sign in Sidney Brustein's Window*, and *Les Blancs*) as compared to Miller's *After the Fall*.

Casty, Alan. "Post-Loverly Love: A Comparative Report." *Antioch Review* 26 (Fall 1966): 399–411.

Casty compares Saul Bellow's *Herzog*, Fellini's *81/2*, and Miller's *After the Fall* as works of intellectual and emotional destruction and a quest for love.

Centola, Steven R. "The Monomyth and Arthur Miller's *After the Fall*." *Studies in American Drama 1945 to the Present* 1 (1986): 49–60.

Centola examines the similarities between the dramatic structure of *After the Fall* and the structural organization of the monomyth as presented in Joseph Campbell's *The Hero with a Thousand Faces*.

———. "Unblessed Rage for Order: Arthur Miller's *After the Fall*." *Arizona Quarterly* 39.1 (Spring 1983): 62–70.

Centola offers a psychoanalytic reading of *After the Fall* as expressed through Miller's use of expressionistic techniques in the play's setting, scenery, lighting, and distorted time-sequence.

"Charting the Course: Inge Morath's Photographs of Arthur Miller's *After the Fall*." *New Theatre Review* 15 (Fall/Winter 1996): 32–35.

Important photographic essay of the rehearsal process for *After the Fall*, the premiere production at the new Lincoln Center Repertory Theater. Some never before published, these seven photographs are from Inge Morath's *After the Fall* collection.

Cismaru, Alfred. "Before and *After the Fall*." *Forum* (University of Houston) 11.2 (1973): 67–71.

Essay comparing Miller's *After the Fall* with Albert Camus's novel *The Fall* (1956)—"For the similarity does not bear on the title only: resemblances of situation, of tone, of mood, often of vocabulary and setting recall the work of the 1957 Nobel Prize winner, and throb closer to the interests of the literary historian."

Engle, John D. "The Metaphor of Law in *After the Fall*." *Notes on Contemporary Literature* (1979): 11–12.

Four-paragraph essay that offers a brief overview of Miller's use of the metaphor of law to help present Quentin's transformation into a man who understands his guilt.

Ganz, Arthur. "Arthur Miller: After the Silence." *Drama Survey* 3.4 (Spring–Fall 1964): 520–53.

Ganz examines the controversy surrounding Miller's "intimate depiction of the playwright's relations with the late Marilyn Monroe" in *After the Fall* as relevant commentary—"If the very presentation of a play is a breach of bad taste, that fact inevitably influences our estimate of it"—and further explores the play's structure as "striking and unconventional" but "not consistently maintained" and therefore "weakened."

Gianakaris, C. J. "Theatre of the Mind in Miller, Osborne and Shaffer." *Renascence* 30 (1977): 33–42.

Gianakaris compares *After the Fall* with John Osborne's *Inadmissible Evidence* and Peter Shaffer's *Equus*, concluding that these works coincide on many thematic and technical points.

Gilman, Richard. "Getting It Off His Chest, but Is It Art?" *Bookweek* 8 March 1964: 6, 13. Rpt. in *Common and Uncommon Masks: Writings on Theatre 1961–1970*. New York: Random House, 1971. 156–59.

On the occasion of the play's publication, Gilman laments that "*After the Fall* is a disastrous failure but its public life is a triumph of propaganda and publicity, more deeply still of the bombastic and adolescent over the very notion of what is mature."

Goyen, William. "*After the Fall* of a Dream." *Show* September 1964: 44–47, 86–87.

First-hand account of the activities of the Repertory Theater of Lincoln Center during the early months of its existence. Goyen, as writer-in-residence on a grant from the Ford Foundation, had daily contact with the organization, including attending rehearsals and meetings of *After the Fall* and being privy to private conversations. Of note is Goyen's assertion, contrary to Miller's published account, that the Maggie character was overtly modeled after Marilyn Monroe and that Miller discussed this fact at length with Barbara Loden, the actress who played the Maggie role.

Hellman, Lillian. "Lillian Hellman Asks a Little Respect for Her Agony: An Eminent Playwright Hallucinates after a Fall Brought on by a Current Dramatic Hit." *Show* May 1964.

Scathing parody of Miller's current work *After the Fall* in which Hellman conceives of six replies to letters of complaint and complement stirred up by her denial as to the autobiographical nature of her "current hit" *Buy My Guilt*, being performed in a converted tiger cage at the Bronx Zoo.

Jacobson, Irving. "Christ, Pygmalion, and Hitler in *After the Fall*." *Essays in Literature* 2 (August 1974): 12–27.

Jacobson explores the mythic dimensions of the Christ, Pygmalion, and Hitler motifs as "convenient labels for conflicting patterns in Quentin's personality" in *After the Fall* in order to examine the nature of the self that lies at the core of the play.

Kennedy, Carroll E. "*After the Fall*: One Man's Look at His Human Nature." *Journal of Counseling Psychology* 12 (Summer 1965): 215–17.

Kennedy says he brings *After the Fall* "to the pages of a professional journal of counseling" because of a self-admitted personal connection to "some of the players' emotions and was moved to introspection and inquiry by the concepts being considered." Kennedy feels that the play provides a meaningful forum for student discussion—"The hero, on the verge of re-entry into the world, is not unlike the college student on the edge of entry into the world of the post-AB."

Kilbourn, William. "Theatre Review: *After the Fall*." *Canadian Forum* 44 (March 1965): 275–76. Earlier version of this review was broadcast by CBC on "Viewing the Shows," 6 December 1964.

Dismissing the autobiographical question as "interesting but secondary," Kilbourn praises *After the Fall* for speaking "of our time and our condition" with "vividly alive" characters.

Koppenhaver, Allen J. "*The Fall* and after: Albert Camus and Arthur Miller." *Modern Drama* 9 (September 1966): 206–9.

Essay that examines the marked similarities of vision between Miller's drama *After the Fall* and Camus's novel *The Fall*. Of note is Koppenaver's argument against an autobiographical reading of the play since "no one protested Camus' use of autobiographical material" in a novel that dealt with the same subject and materials.

Martin, Robert A. "Arthur Miller's *After the Fall*: 'A Play about a Theme.'" *American Drama* 6.1 (Fall 1996): 73–88.

Martin defends *After the Fall* as a play that "attempts to show the universality of man's struggle within himself as to how we are able and unable to live and communicate with ourselves and others in society."

Meyer, Nancy and Richard. "Setting the Stage for Lincoln Center." *Theatre Arts* 48 (January 1964): 12–16, 69.

Essay that details the first read-through and rehearsal process of *After the Fall*, the genesis of the script, its details, and its development, and the workings of the Lincoln Repertory Theater. Six photographs of importance accompany this text.

Mielziner, Jo. "Designing a Play: *Death of a Salesman* (With Some Time Off for *South Pacific*)." *Designing for the Theatre: A Memoir and a Portfolio*. New York: Bramhall, 1965. 218–19.

Design rendering for second production of *After the Fall*, a national tour for a proscenium stage.

Moss, Leonard. "Biographical and Literary Allusion in *After the Fall*." *Education Theatre Journal* 18 (March 1966): 34–40.

Moss feels that "Miller's purpose in referring to his personal experience" in *After the Fall* "has been widely misunderstood." After detailing the biographical similarities between Miller's life and the characters and situations presented in his play, Moss then examines Miller's use of "autoplagiarism" as "a form of allusion less obvious than autobiography" in which he duplicates "analogous lines and situations in his previous writing," forming "his principal motif."

Murray, Edward. "Point of View in *After the Fall*." *CLA Journal* 10 (1966): 135–42.

Murray, disagreeing with critics who value the "objective worth" of *After the Fall*, finds that the play "suffers from a serious defect in dramatic construction—namely, a faulty and ill-chosen point of view that renders the structure of the play static and repetitious, destroys any effective tension and irony the material of the play might inherently possess, underlines the inadequacy of Miller's verbal gifts, makes his leading character, Quentin, suspect because the cards are stacked too obviously in his favor, and, finally, reduces the theme nearly to thesis, thus destroying what is in itself a serious and important statement, because the point of view leads Miller into over-simplification and over-conceptualization of content."

Nolan, Paul T. "Two Memory Plays: *The Glass Menagerie* and *After the Fall*." *McNeese Review* 17 (1966): 27–38.

Nolan compares Miller's *After the Fall* with Tennessee Williams's *The Glass Menagerie* as memory plays, chiefly concerned with "that action that is understood and retained in the mind of the protagonist."

Sontag, Susan. "Theater." *Vogue* 15 August 1965: 51–52.

Sontag compares Miller's *After the Fall* with John Osborne's *Inadmissible Evidence*, finding "striking" similarities in theme, structure, and circumstance.

Steene, Birgitta. "Arthur Miller's *After the Fall*: A Strindbergian Failure." *Modern Sprak* 58 (December 1964): 446–52.

Steene compares Miller's *After the Fall* with August Strindberg's *To Damascus*, finding both similar in form, idea, and character, with each play's hero experiencing a "private catharsis."

Stinson, John J. "Structure in *After the Fall*: The Relevance of the Maggie Episodes to the Main Themes and Christian Symbolism." *Modern Drama* 10 (1967): 233–40.

Stinson offers a reading of the characters of Quentin and Maggie in *After the Fall* as Christlike redeemers and examines the structural integrity of the second act to determine whether negative critical reactions to the autobiographical nature of the play can be supported.

Critical Essays in Newspapers

Hanscom, Leslie. "*After the Fall*: Arthur Miller's Return." *Newsweek* 3 February 1964: 49–52.

Lengthy article detailing the "disappointment" following the "spectacular premiere" of Miller's *After the Fall*, the "eagerly awaited" first offering of the new Lincoln Center Repertory Theater. After reviewing the historical opening of three classical repertory theaters in one year, Hanscom compares the details of Miller's life with situations and characters in his new play. Various photos of Miller and scenes from the production accompany the text.

Production Reviews

Armitstead, Claire. "*After the Fall*." *Financial Times* (London) 21 June 1990. *London Theatre Record* 10.13 (1990): 823.

Favorable review of the Michael Blakemore revival at the Cottesloe, starring Josette Simon. Says Armistead, *After the Fall* is a play "which, self-indulgent though it is, unfolds like a journey to the center of the century."

Asquith, Ros. "*After the Fall*." *City Limits* (London) 28 June 1990. *London Theatre Record* 10.13 (1990): 821.

While calling the Michael Blakemore revival "painstaking and imaginative," Asquith laments that the production is still "a too-confessional portrait of the author's marriage to Monroe (thinly disguised as Maggie, a singer). This is because that relationship dominates the entire second half of the play, and it is overlong and overdetailed."

Barnes, Clive. "That Other Arthur Miller Play." *New York Post* 5 October 1984. *New York Theatre Critics' Reviews* 45 (1984): 212–13.

While finding the play "badly constructed," Barnes praises the

Playhouse 91 revival starring Frank Langella as "a fine production that may leave doubts as to the play's enduring merits, but at least erases suspicions as to the author's motives."

Baxandall, Lee. "Arthur Miller: Still the Innocent." *Encore* (May–June 1964): 16–19. Rpt. in *"The Crucible": Text and Criticism*. Ed. Gerald Weales. New York: Viking, 1971. Penguin, 1996. 352–58.

Baxandall condemns Miller's play as a "spectacular failure" that is "rhetorical as language, insufficiently imagined as characters in action, and defective in its basic aesthetic and moral structure."

Bayley, Claire. "*After the Fall*." *What's On* (London) 27 June 1990. *London Theatre Record* 10.13 (1990): 824–25.

While admitting that *After the Fall* is "undoubtedly a treacherous play to stage," Bayley applauds Michael Blakemore's production as "accessible and enjoyable" and a work that "expertly involves us in the grand scheme and for me Miller's formal experiment, with its constant interruptions and surprises, avoids some of the longeurs of his more obviously realistic plays."

Beaufort, John. "Though Time Has Tempered It, *After the Fall* Is Still Unsettling." *Christian Science Monitor* 9 October 1984. *New York Theatre Critics' Reviews* 45 (1984): 213.

Beaufort finds the Playhouse 91 revival starring Frank Langella a "long and complex play," and remarks that the confessional process of the play is, even after twenty years, still making "the listener feel uncomfortable even while it is absorbing him."

Billington, Michael. "*After the Fall*." *Guardian* (London) 22 June 1990. *London Theatre Record* 10.13 (1990): 823.

Negative review of the Michael Blakemore revival, starring Josette Simon, in which Billington laments that, although *After the Fall* "is about big themes and imbued with Miller's own racking honesty, it is more psychiatric confession than satisfactory play."

Brahms, Caryl. "Marilyn, Dolly, and Dylan." *The Spectator* (London) 14 February 1964. 213.

While condemning Miller for his "hideously bad and bitter taste" in dramatizing Marilyn Monroe in *After the Fall* so soon after her death, Brahms praises his dramatic portrait of his late wife—"To recreate a figure as innocent, as truthful, as human, as trusting, as generous, as intellectually inadequate, as striving, as shrill, as sensual, as hurt, as ruined, as disintegrating, as Marilyn, is to fulfill the function of a playwright."

Brustein, Robert. "Arthur Miller's Mea Culpa," *New Republic* 8 February 1964: 26–30. Rpt. in *Seasons of Discontent: Dramatic Opinions, 1959–1965*. New York: Simon and Schuster, 1965. 243–47.

Highly negative and lengthy review of *After the Fall* in which Brustein calls Miller's play "a three-and-one-half-hour breach of bad taste, a confessional autobiography of embarrassing explicitness, during which the author does not stop talking about himself for an instant while making only the most perfunctory gestures toward concealing his identity."

Chapman, John. "*After the Fall* Overpowering." *New York Daily News* 24 January 1964. In *New York Theatre Critics' Reviews* 25 (1964): 374.

Highly positive review of the premiere production at the Lincoln Center Repertory Theater. Chapman commends Miller's play for its "clarity" and Robard's "dramatic marathon" performance as "monumental."

Christopher, James. "*After the Fall*." *Time Out* (London) 27 June 1990. *London Theatre Record* 10.13 (1990): 821.

Brief negative review of the Michael Blakemore revival, starring Josette Simon and James Laurenson. Christopher calls the production "disappointing" and a failure in its efforts to "accommodate the text's indulgent ambitions."

Cohen, Nathan. "Hollow Heart of a Hollow Drama." *National Review* 7 April 1964: 289–90.

Dismissing the "aggressively autobiographical" nature of *After the Fall* as of "no consequence critically," Cohen reports his dislike for the play on the grounds that it is merely "a dramatized monologue" whose greatest flaw is his main character, Quentin, who "is too shallow and illogical in his reasoning to be an intellectual . . . he is in fact vain and cold, disdainful of the human race, incapable of giving of himself to others, far more a cannibal than those he accuses of eating him alive. Certainly he is incapable of being the heroic center of any play."

Corliss, Richard. "Wounds That Will Not Heal." *Time* 15 October 1984: 113. *New York Theatre Critics' Reviews* 45 (1984): 214.

Negative review of the 1984 Playhouse 91 off-Broadway revival of *After the Fall*, directed by John Tillinger and starring Frank Langella and Diane Wiest. "Fiction is revealed as self-pitying psychodrama, and Miller's descent into himself risks being taken as a wallow in metaphysical sleaze."

Coveney, Michael. "*After the Fall*." *Observer* (London) 24 June 1990. *London Theatre Record* 10.13 (1990): 824.

Coveney feels that "in spite of the off-putting pomposity" of Miller's play, the Michael Blakemore revival at the Cottesloe, starring Josette Simon, "was worth doing."

Driver, Tom F. "Arthur Miller's Pilgrimage." *Reporter* 27 February 1964: 46, 48.

Mixed review of the premiere production of *After the Fall*, directed by Elia Kazan and starring Jason Robards and Barbara Loden, that Driver says lacks "aesthetic distance" and "seems soft, if not vacant, at the center," but delivers strong performances by Robards and Loden.

Edwards, Christopher. "After Monroe." *Spectator* (London) 30 June 1990: 46–47. *London Theatre Record* 10.13 (1990): 821.

Edwards calls the Michael Blakemore production at the Cottesloe, starring Josette Simon and James Laurenson, "a fine revival of Miller's uneven work." Says Edwards, "The production outflanks our prurient interests by casting the lithe black actress" in a "powerful performance."

Epstein, Leslie. "The Unhappiness of Arthur Miller." *Tri-Quarterly* (Spring 1965): 165–73.

Negative review of both *After the Fall* and *Incident at Vichy* in which Epstein compares the character of Quentin with Hamlet and Miller with Ibsen. Of *After the Fall*, Epstein concludes that "it is precisely because it too often blurs, dissolves into compulsive ratiocination and a sea of second thoughts that the play is so complete a failure."

"Facsimile of Marilyn Monroe in Miller's Play." *Times* (London) 24 January 1964: 8.

Mostly negative review of premiere production of *After the Fall* at New York's Lincoln Center for the Performing Arts that questions Miller's disavowal of autobiographical intentions and his shaping of the play "as to give the impression that he is defending himself."

Gassner, John. "Broadway in Review." *Educational Theatre Journal* 16 (May 1964): 177–179. Rpt. as "The Lincoln Center Repertory Company: *After the Fall*." *Dramatic Soundings*. New York: Crown, 1968. 547–50.

Ambivalent review of *After the Fall* that praises Miller's effort "to restore to playwriting some of the elbow-room it lost with the advent of realism" while condemning the play for failing to "live up to either the author's or his producers' expectations. It may be defined as a little private drama inflated into a large public one or extended into a panorama of little agonies."

Gilman, Richard. "Still Falling." *Commonweal* 14 February 1964: 600–601. Rpt. in *Common and Uncommon Masks: Writings on Theatre 1961–1970*. New York: Random House, 1971. 152–55.

Mostly negative review of *After the Fall* in which Gilman states that Miller "is more to be pitied than condemned" for writing a play in which "everything inadequate, pretentious and self-serving in the life of our theater, and indeed in that of our wider culture, has converged to raise up a monument to the false and the self-deluding."

Gold, Sylviane. "Phoenix or Still Turkey?" *Wall Street Journal* 9 October 1984. *New York Theatre Critics' Reviews* 45 (1984): 213–14.

Gold praises the performances of Frank Langella and Dianne Wiest in this Playhouse 91 revival, but concludes that "Ms. Wiest and Mr. Langella can't remove the play's fatal strain of bombastic self-pity, or its hopelessly pedestrian conclusion: We are all guilty, so life must go on."

Gross, John. "*After the Fall*." *Sunday Telegraph* (London) 24 June 1990. *London Theatre Record* 10.13 (1990): 823–24.

While praising the acting of both Josette Simon and James Laurenson and the "great skill" of director Michael Blakemore, Gross admits that "in the end you are left with a few fine scenes floating around in a thick soup of unrealised rhetoric."

Herman, Jan. "*After the Fall*: Mind over Miller." *Los Angeles Times* 19 May 1995: Calendar:. 28.

Positive review of the Vanguard Theatre's revival of Miller's *After the Fall*, directed by Dan Rosenblatt.

Hewes, Henry. "Quentin's Quest." *Saturday Review* 15 February 1964: 35.

While finding the play's method "intriguing," Hewes faults Miller's play for its obvious biographical content, which has the effect of making the audience "less interested in Maggie as a part of Quentin's experience and more interested in understanding what seems to be the real-life story of Marilyn." Hewes concludes his review by suggesting that the play might reach its full potential if it was "either rewritten to suit this style of performance, or be performed in a different style in another kind of theatre."

Hiley, Jim. "*After the Fall*." *Listener* (London) 5 July 1990. *London Theatre Record* 10.13 (1990): 826–27.

Calling Josette Simon's performance as Maggie "hypnotically convincing," Hiley praises *After the Fall* "as impressive as *The Crucible*—wise, sorrowful, heart-rending."

Hirschhorn, Clive. "*After the Fall*." *Sunday Express* (London) 24 June 1990. *London Theatre Record* 10.13 (1990): 822.

Hirschhorn praises *After the Fall*, seen here at the Cottesloe directed by Michael Blakemore, for the creation of the character of Maggie—"In the light of everything that has been written and diagnosed about Monroe, Miller's first-hand account of her impossible demands and childish insecurities is directly plugged into the heart and the soul. It is the play's greatest achievement."

Hobson, Harold. "*After the Fall* Has Charm in Milan." *Christian Science Monitor* 22 November 1965: 10.

Positive review of the Milan, Italy, production of *Fall* in which Hobson praises Georgio-Albertazzi for giving "the narrator an impulsive and unconscientious charm which draws the attention away from the self-justificatory aspects of the character, and concentrates on the play's genuine merit."

Hurren, Kenneth. "*After the Fall*." *Mail on Sunday* (London) 24 June 1990. *London Theatre Record* 10.13 (1990): 826.

Calling the Michael Blakemore revival at the Cottesloe "an exorcism," Hurren praises the production from freeing the audience from making "the Monroe connection" to "ponder what else is in the head of Miller's mouthpiece, the lawyer Quentin."

Kerr, Walter. "Miller's *After the Fall*—As Walter Kerr Sees It." *New York Herald Tribune* 24 January 1964: 1, 11. *New York Theatre Critics' Reviews* 25 (1964): 376.

Negative review of the premiere production at the Lincoln Center Repertory Theater. Kerr faults what he sees as the "confessional" nature of the play, which "constitutes neither an especially attractive nor especially persuasive performance" because it seems to "be about its playwright, not at all about the shadowy alter ego he calls Quentin."

———. "The View from the Mirror." *Thirty Plays Hath November*. New York: Simon and Schuster, 1969. 214–17. Rpt. in *Critical Essays on Arthur Miller*. Ed. James J. Martine. Boston: G. K. Hall, 1979. 122–24.

Kerr criticizes Miller for not having a degree of detachment from the main character, and instead of creating a work of theatrical power, the playwright "ended up seeming to discuss himself, to justify himself."

Kissel, Howard. "*After the Fall.*" *Women's Wear Daily* 8 October 1984. *New York Theatre Critics' Reviews* 45 (1984): 211–12.

Negative review of the Playhouse 91 revival starring Frank Langella and directed by John Tillinger. "*After the Fall* is still an alienating, unsatisfying play. . . . Only the Marilyn material is still potent and [Miller's] handling of it still seems shabby."

Koenig, Rhoda. "Monroe Doctrine." *Punch* (London) 6 July 1990: 44. *London Theatre Record* 10.13 (1990): 825.

Positive review of the London production of *After the Fall* in which Koenig praises Michael Blakemore's "sharp, emphatic production" but accuses the "script's basic inertia" of fighting "him and his excellent cast at every turn."

Lenoir, Jean-Pierre. "Paris Critics Cold to *After the Fall.*" *New York Times* 25 January 1965: 21.

News article reporting on the critical reaction of the French production of *After the Fall* that includes excerpts from reviews, mostly negative.

McCarten, John. "Miller on Miller." *New Yorker* 1 February 1964: 59.

Calling Miller's first drama in nine years "transparently autobiographical," McCarten questions the ethics of "bringing one's very recent marital life into public view in infinite detail," but says that during the scenes with Maggie that Miller "builds up a real head of dramatic steam" that "makes Maggie a figure well worth our pity."

McClain, John. "Arthur Miller's *After the Fall* Tour de Force by Robards." *New York Journal American* 24 January 1964. *New York Theatre Critics' Reviews* 25 (1964): 376.

While finding the cast of the Lincoln Center Repertory Company "overwhelming," Jason Robard's performance "magnificent and ceaseless," and Elia Kazan's direction "consistently authoritative," McClain condemns Miller's play for being "pretentious and intolerably long," and admits that he was "offended by its lack of taste. . . . I never got the message."

Miller, Jonathan. "Broken Blossoms." *New York Review of Books* 5 March 1964: 4–5.

Miller rebukes *After the Fall* as an "uneasy yet intimate alliance between the Thirties Left and the slick commercial liberalism of Broadway and television drama."

"Miller's Tale." *Time* 31 January 1964: 54.

Negative review of *After the Fall* that faults the play for lacking "all tragic sense" and requesting that the audience share the immense guilt of the main character.

Morley, Sheridan. "*After the Fall*." *Herald Tribune* (London) 27 June 1990. *London Theatre Record* 10.13 (1990): 824. Rpt. in *Playbill* 31 August 1990: 48.

Morley praises the Michael Blakemore production at the National Theatre for laying "that unquiet spirit to rest forever by having the character of the doomed singer played by a black actress, Josette Simon," but criticizes Miller's play for rating "far below such classics as *Death of a Salesman* or *All My Sons* or *The Crucible* . . . for the closer he gets to his own home, the more unable Miller is to write real drama or confrontation or to deal with structure."

Munk, Erika. "Men's Business." *Village Voice* 16 October 1984: 113–14.

Lengthy mixed review of the Playhouse 91 revival, directed by John Tillinger and starring Frank Langella. Says Munk, "In the long run, *After the Fall* has no more cultural significance—*and no less*—than a thought-stopping late-night talk show."

Murray, William. “The Production’s the Thing.” *New West* 12 September 1977. SC–20.

Negative review of the Company of Angels production of *After the Fall*, directed by Harris Yulin and starring Yulin, Julie Cobb, and Mimi Cozzins. Says Murray, “Overall, a strong cast for a flawed play much in need of help to maximize its not inconsiderable virtues.”

Nadel, Norman. “Miller Play One of Inward Vision.” *New York World-Telegram* 24 January 1964. *New York Theatre Critics’ Reviews* 25 (1964): 375.

Positive review complimenting the premiere production at the Lincoln Center Repertory Theater as “a powerful and portentous drama—one to arouse an audience and enrich a season,” “a somber, funny, tragic and terrifying triumph of purposeful introspection,” and “a beautiful, remarkable play.”

Nathan, David. “*After the Fall.*” *Jewish Chronicle* (London) 29 June 1990. *London Theatre Record* 10.13 (1990): 824.

While admiring Michael Blakemore’s “finely tuned, skillfully directed production,” Nathan chides Miller for creating a “theatre of self-laceration, a public confessional for a dramatist who cannot write a dull line and who cannot stop picking over his past.”

Nightingale, Benedict. “*After the Fall.*” *The Times* (London) 21 June 1990. *London Theatre Record* 10.13 (1990): 827.

Nightingale feels that the reason why *After the Fall* “flopped in America in 1964, has never been seen in London, and remains hard to stage” is because it is “a long, personal monologue into which supporting characters wander, often defying chronology or logic, as if free-associated in a dream.”

O’Connor, John J. “TV: Miller’s *After the Fall* on NBC.” *New York Times* 10 December 1974: 91.

Calling the play “an egotistical abomination,” O’Connor admits that this TV adaptation directed by Gilbert Cates is, “it must be noted, better than the original stage production,” with reworked scenes, a change of emphasis, and a tightening of the overall structure.

Osborne, Charles. “*After the Fall.*” *Daily Telegraph* (London) 22 June 1990. *London Theatre Record* 10.13 (1990): 822–23.

Mixed review in which Osborne praises Michael Blakemore’s

direction as "impressively staged" version of a play that reveals "Miller at his most pretentiously self-absorbed."

Paton, Maureen. "*After the Fall*." *Daily Express* (London) 21 June 1990. *London Theatre Record* 10.13 (1990): 825.

Brief favorable review of the Michael Blakemore revival at the Cottesloe that Paton calls a "splendid evocation of the frightened Fifties," and a production that "finally laid to rest the ghost of Marilyn Monroe" in the casting of black actress Josette Simon in the role of Maggie.

"Poetry and Drama." *Virginia Quarterly Review* 40 (Summer 1964): cxii.

Negative review of the published version of *After the Fall* [Viking, 1964] in which the unnamed reviewer concedes that while the play is not as bad as the critics have said, and is, in fact, "moving," "interesting," and "acute," Miller's drama "is still a real corker: awkward, humorless, pretentious, tedious, and repetitious."

Popkin, Henry. "*After the Fall*, 'The Real Shocker.'" *Vogue* 15 March 1964: 66.

Popkin argues that Miller's depiction of ex-wife Monroe is a diversion from "the real shocker': "the whole purpose of the play is to absolve Quentin of any responsibility for anything that happens to others. The others are guilty; only Quentin is innocent."

Price, Jonathan R. "Arthur Miller: Fall or Rise?" *Drama* 73 (Summer 1964): 39–40.

In this positive review of premiere production of *After the Fall* that Price feels "will outlive the clamor caused by its success." Price defends Miller's work and insists that "honesty impelled him to deal with materials from his private life, but he has managed to see them as public issues."

Prideaux, Tom. "A Desperate Search by a Troubled Hero," *Life* 7 February 1964: 64B–65.

Prideaux argues that Miller uses ex-wife Marilyn Monroe in *After the Fall* as a tragic example of the human condition and defends Miller against charges of bad taste leveled at him by critics.

Rich, Frank. "*After the Fall* Is Revived." *New York Times* 5 October 1984: C3. *New York Theatre Critics' Reviews* 45 (1984): 210–11.

While applauding the Playhouse 91 revival of *After the Fall* for its staging, revised and edited text, and Frank Langella's "driving performance," Rich admits still feeling that the play "is never as moving or profound as it wants to be" and "remains a collection of sporadically arresting autobiographical fragments—all floating in a glutinous interior monologue that substitutes tortuous rhetoric for psychological or metaphysical insight."

Rogoff, Gordon. "Theatre." *Nation* 10 February 1964: 153–54.

Mostly negative review of *After the Fall*, in which Rogoff calls the play "more a young author's autobiographical first novel than a mature artist's play, it is a dispiriting, unhappy, often infuriating beginning for the new company."

Shulman, Milton. "*After the Fall.*" *Evening Standard* (London) 21 June 1990. *London Theatre Record* 10.13 (1990): 825.

Shulman criticizes the Michael Blakemore revival at the Cottesloe for casting a black actress, Josette Simon, in the role of Maggie, saying that "while it was understandable that an austere intellectual like Miller should be flattered into a union with America's sex goddess, the likelihood of a prominent, ambitious Jewish lawyer marrying a black singer with a shady past does put considerable strain on one's credulity."

Simon, John. "*After the Fall.*" *New York* 15 October 1984: 84–85.

Despite some revisions by Miller, Simon finds the revival of *After the Fall*, directed by John Tillinger, "insufferable . . . the play is poorly cast and badly acted" and "a moral and artistic embarrassment."

———. "Theatre Chronicle." *Hudson Review* 17 (Summer 1964): 234–236. Rpt. as "Review of *After the Fall.*" in *Critical Essays on Arthur Miller*. Ed. James J. Martine. Boston: G. K. Hall, 1979. 119–21.

Highly negative review of the premiere production of *After the Fall* that Simon calls "megalomania combined with hypocrisy."

Sontag, Susan. "Going to the Theater." *Partisan Review* 31 (Spring 1964): 284–87. Rpt. as "Going to Theater, etc." *Against Interpretation and Other Essays*. New York: Dell, 1966. 146–51.

Negative review of *Fall* in which Sontag criticizes Miller's play as "mere self-indulgence" that "elevates personal tragedies, and demeans public ones—to the same dead level." Sontag also delves into what she calls the "appalling combination" of Miller and Kazan as the play's primary creators and their previous history of "turbulent relations."

Taubman, Howard. "A Cheer for Controversy." *New York Times* 2 February 1964: II: 1.

Taubman praises *After the Fall* as a mature work in which its hero, unlike Willy Loman, accepts responsibility for his actions.

———. "Theater: *After the Fall*." *New York Times* 24 January 1964: 18. *New York Theatre Critics' Reviews* 25 (1964): 377.

Highly positive review of the premiere production at the Lincoln Center Repertory Theater. Taubman praises the work as "a pain-wracked drama" that "is also Mr. Miller's maturest. . . . For to sit in Mr. Miller's theater is to be in an adult world concerned with a search that cuts to the bone."

Taylor, Paul. "*After the Fall*." *Independent* (London) 27 June 1990. *London Theatre Record* 10.13 (1990): 827.

Taylor praises the Michael Blakemore revival as "fine" and a production that "resembles less a striptease than a spiritual consciousness-raising session, an illustrated sermon on survival."

Tinker, Jack. "*After the Fall*." *Daily Mail* (London) 26 June 1990. *London Theatre Record* 10.13 (1990): 821.

Brief review of the Michael Blakemore revival that focuses on the "rare and potent presence" of Josette Simon in the role of Maggie, who "has all the mercurial, nerve-ended vulnerability demanded" for the part.

Wardle, Irving. "*After the Fall*." *Independent on Sunday* (London) 24 June 1990. *London Theatre Record* 10.13 (1990): 825–26.

Wardle lauds the Michael Blakemore revival for disassociating the character of Maggie from Marilyn Monroe by casting black actress Josette Simon in the role he chastises this production for a set that "reflects what is most wrong with the play."

Watt, Douglas. "*After the Fall* Goes Boom!" *New York Daily News* 5 October 1984. *New York Theatre Critics' Reviews* 45 (1984): 211.

Negative review of Playhouse 91 revival, starring Frank Langella and directed by John Tillinger. Says Watt, "The result is an amorphous mass of a play, briefer than before and with fewer people slipping in and out, but still adding up to nothing."

Watts, Richard, Jr. "The New Drama by Arthur Miller." *New York Post* 24 January 1964: 38. *New York Theatre Critics' Reviews* 25 (1964): 374.

Positive review of the premiere production at the Lincoln Center Repertory Theater that praises Miller's play as "impressive" and lauds Jason Robards for "one of his finest performances" that deserves "high praise." Watts laments that Miller's "lengthy, undeniably autobiographical drama is also a disappointing and self-indulgent kind of personal apologia, often strong, moving and perceptive, and yet frequently lost in its own waywardness."

Williams, Hugo. "*After the Fall*." *Sunday Correspondent* (London) 24 June 1990. *London Theatre Record* 10.13 (1990): 822.

Mixed review of the Michael Blakemore revival, in which Williams writes, "if the play's weakness is somehow built into the play's subject matter, it is also that which permits the central character of Maggy [sic] to shine amid the dust. Perhaps that is why Josette Simon looks so like a star, in the part which makes it all worthwhile."

Related Interviews and Profiles (not with Miller)

Fergusson, Francis. "A Conversation with Digby R. Diehl." *Transatlantic Review* 18 (Spring 1965): 115–20.

Fergusson comments on *After the Fall* as "a sensational but pretentious play" and criticizes Miller for asking his audience to identify or "take seriously as a universal specimen of a human creature of our time, the hero of this play. What I feel is lacking is something of the attitude of the author towards his material which would relate it to a more general human vision—and that's my notion of the willful myopia."

Hyams, Barry. "A Theater: Heart and Mind." *Theater, The Annual of the Repertory Theater of Lincoln Center, Volume One*. Ed. Barry Hyams. New York, 1964. 49–78.

Interviews with individuals important to the early development of The Repertory Theater of Lincoln Center, including Robert Whitehead, Jo Mielziner, Arthur Miller, Jose Quintero, S. N. Behrman, and David Hays. The final portion is devoted to the last segment of Elia Kazan's speech to the acting company on their first day (23 October 1963).

Lustig, Vera. "Sympathy for the Devil." *Plays and Players* (London) July 1991: 22–23.

Josette Simon discusses acting in traditionally white roles, specifically *After the Fall* and John Webster's *The White Devil.*

Mann, Paul. "Theory and Practice: An Interview with Paul Mann." *Tulane Drama Review* 9 (Winter 1961): 84–96.

In an interview with the director of actor training at the Repertory Theater of Lincoln Center, Paul Mann discusses his approach to the role of the Father in *After the Fall* and some of his specific acting choices for the part.

Schechner, Richard, and Theodore Hoffman. "'Look, There's the American Theatre': An Interview with Elia Kazan." *Tulane Drama Review* 9 (Winter 1964): 61–83.

Important interview in which Kazan candidly discusses his thoughts on Miller's *After the Fall*, including the play's critical reaction, his rehearsal process, his directing style, Miller's relationship with Lincoln Center, casting issues, and the experimental qualities of the play.

News Reports, Letters to the Editor, and Related Matter

Calta, Louis. "Arthur Miller Conducts Reading for His Lincoln Repertory Play: Rehearsal Is Held above a Restaurant for Company's Initial Production—Playwright Calls Work 'Happy.'" *New York Times* 25 October 1963: 39.

News article announcing the first rehearsal of *After the Fall*, a first reading by its author, held in private following the departure of the press. Admitting that it took him two years to write, Miller is quoted as saying, "It's the happiest work I have ever performed." Of note is the following: "Mr. Miller said that his play was partly biographical. 'All of my plays are, but this one less than the others,' he remarked."

Esterow, Milton. "Arthur Miller's Play Generates Strong Controversy." *New York Times* 31 January 1964: 14.

News piece detailing the controversy surrounding the autobiographical nature of *After the Fall*, including Miller's response to the mostly negative critical response that his play has received.

———. "Miller Is Writing Play for Center." *New York Times* 26 October 1962: 25.

Full column article announcing Miller's plans to give his first play in seven years to the Lincoln Center for the Performing Arts in "the hope of creating a new atmosphere in the theatre." Kazan is announced as the director of the yet unnamed play [*After the Fall*].

Gent, George. "NBC Arranges Program Exchange with BBC." *New York Times* 27 June 1973: 111.

News item reporting that Miller has adapted *After the Fall* for television.

"Marilyn's Ghost Takes the Stage," *Life* 7 February 1964: 64A.

Article that notes the premiere of *After the Fall*, accompanied by production photographs.

Thompson, Alan. "*After the Fall* Brought to Film." *New York Times* 27 June 1964: 14.

Announces the purchase of the screen rights to *After the Fall* by Carlo Ponti and Ira Steiner for a reported $500,000. Set to star Ponti's wife Sophia Loren and Paul Newman, the film was to be released by MGM and directed by Fred Zinnermann.

Wallach, Allan. "Casting Color Aside." *Newsday* 1 July 1990: II: 4.

In an article detailing the practice of nontraditional casting, Miller is quoted as saying that, in the instance of *After the Fall* at the National Theatre in London when Josette Simon was cast as Maggie, he didn't think "that [race] should quite be the issue. I think the issue is who's the best actor for the part, if it's at all conceivable for a black person to be in the part."

Incident at Vichy

Critical Essays in Books

Bouchard, Larry D. "Rolf Hochhuth: Vocation and Silence." *Tragic Method and Tragic Theology: Evil in Contemporary Drama and Religious Thought*. University Park: The Pennsylvania State UP, 1989. 101.

Brief mention of *Incident at Vichy* in the context of narrative dramas that "create dramatic encounters at the boundaries of silence, where to speak or not to speak is the choice at stake."

Clurman, Harold. "Director's Notes: *Incident at Vichy*." *Tulane Drama Review* 9.4 (Summer 1965): 77–90. Rpt. in *On Directing*. New York: Macmillan, 1972. 242–53.

Diary-type entries of Clurman's approach to directing the premiere production of *Incident at Vichy* at the Repertory Theater of Lincoln Center in 1964, including first impressions, conversations, early notes, and character breakdowns.

———. "Rehearsals Continue." *On Directing*. New York: Macmillan, 1972. 114.

Clurman relates an anecdote regarding his directing of Hal Holbrook in *Incident at Vichy* in which the actor was cast against his type and struggled to understand his character's vindictiveness. A photograph of Miller and Clurman during rehearsals for *Vichy* appears opposite the text.

Issacharoff, Michael. "Comic Space." *The Theatrical Space*. Ed. James Redmond. Cambridge: Cambridge UP, 1987. 187–98.

Essay for the "Themes in Drama" series that investigates the use of space in relation to comic traditions. Issacharoff briefly discusses *Incident at Vichy* as a representation of "perhaps the most extreme point of tragic closeness. . . . There is no escape possible."

Langer, Lawrence L. "The Americanization of the Holocaust on Stage and Screen." *From Hester Street to Hollywood: The Jewish-American Stage and Screen*. Ed. Sarah Blacher Cohen. Bloomington: Indiana UP, 1983. 213–30.

Langer compares four attempts "to bring the Holocaust theme to the American stage"—Goodrich and Hackett's *The Diary of*

Anne Frank, Millard Lampell's *The Wall*, Miller's *Incident at Vichy*, the film *Judgment at Nuremberg*, and the TV epic *Holocaust*. While finding that most writing of the Holocaust suffers from a "moral oversimplification," Langer praises Miller's work for shifting "the center of moral responsibility for the situation of the Jews from the victims to the the well-intentioned spectator. . . . *Incident at Vichy* illuminates the difficulty, perhaps the impossibility, of affirming the tragic dignity of the individual man, when it has been soiled by the ashes of anonymous millions."

Murphy, Brenda. "Forensics: The Self and Others: *Darkness at Noon*, *Montserrat*, *Incident at Vichy*." *Congressional Theatre: Dramatizing McCarthyism on Stage, Film, and Television*. Cambridge: Cambridge UP, 1999. 226–40, 283–85.

Murphy reads Miller's *Incident at Vichy* as a work that "uses Nazism as a touchstone for all dehumanizing governmental oppression in the 20th century."

Rahv, Philip. "Arthur Miller and the Fallacy of Profundity." *The Myth and the Powerhouse*. New York: Farrar, Straus and Giroux, 1965. 225–33. Rpt. in *Literature and the Sixth Sense*. Boston: Houghton, 1970. 385–91.

Rahv finds the ending of *Incident at Vichy* "surprising" and "objectionable. . . . It is an ending dramatically unearned, so to speak, because on the symbolic plane at least it contradicts the entire emphasis of the ideas that preceded it. It is a melodramatic contrivance pure and simple."

Schiff, Ellen. "The Jew as Metaphor." *From Stereotype to Metaphor: The Jew in Contemporary Drama*. Albany: State U of NY Press, 1982. 211–17.

Framing this chapter around the question of "to what extent does the Jew retain his Jewish identity as he represents people generally," Schiff studies Miller's *Incident at Vichy* and concludes that the play "shows how man's recognition of himself vis-à-vis his fellows leads him to a new understanding of who he is and, equally noteworthy, what a Jew is."

Wertham, Frederic. *A Sign for Cain: An Exploration of Human Violence*. New York: Macmillan, 1966. 351.

Brief mention is made of Miller's depiction of an Austrian nobleman "who sacrifices his life to save a Nazi victim." Says Wertham, "we have no comprehensive sociology of National

Socialism, but among the well-established sociological facts is the devoted participation of German and Austrian aristocrats in all the departments and activities of the Nazi movement, especially the most ruthless ones. As a group they were more involved than any other section of the population. . . . Making a nobleman the hero in a play about Nazi genocide is historically misleading. Art may give us personal dreams, but it should not give us social illusions."

Critical Essays in Journals and Magazines

Baxandall, Lee. "Arthur Miller's Latest." *Encore* 12 (March–April 1965): 19–23.

Baxandall argues that *Incident at Vichy* represents "an advance in the author's moral thought," relevant to many contemporary events, and "his best ethically to date."

Lowenthal, Lawrence D. "Arthur Miller's *Incident at Vichy*: A Sartrean Interpretation." *Modern Drama* 18 (March 1975): 29–41. Rpt. in *Essays on Modern American Drama: Williams, Miller, Albee, and Shepard.* Ed. Dorothy Parker. Toronto: U of Toronto P, 1989. 94–106. Rpt. in *Critical Essays on Arthur Miller*. Ed. James J. Martine. Boston: G. K. Hall, 1979. 143–54. Rpt. in *Arthur Miller: New Perspectives*. Ed. Robert A. Martin. Engelwood Cliffs, N.J.: Prentice-Hall, 1982. 173–87.

Lowenthal offers a Sartrean reading of *Incident at Vichy*, which, he says, is "a clear structural example of Sartre's definition of the existential 'theatre of situation.'"

Roth, Martin. "Sept-D'un-Coup." *Chicago Review* 19.1 (1966): 108–11. Rpt. in *Critical Essays on Arthur Miller*. Ed. James J. Martine. Boston: G. K. Hall, 1979. 139–42.

In this negative review of *Incident at Vichy*, Roth blasts Miller for having a literary sensibility that is "essentially undramatic—he is a man in the wrong profession."

Production Reviews

Brustein, Robert. "Muddy Track at Lincoln Center." *New Republic* 26 December 1964: 26–27. Rpt. in *Seasons of Discontent: Dramatic Opinions, 1959–1965*. New York: Simon and Schuster, 1965. 259–63.

Very negative review of *Incident at Vichy* that Brustein says suffers greatly from only partly understood ideas and possesses a "noisy virtue and moral flatulence."

Bryden, Ronald. "Dead Ernest." *New Statesman* (London) 4 February 1966: 170.

Bryden faults *Incident at Vichy*, appearing in London, as possessing the Miller "curse" that "prevents his plays from rising to their themes."

Epstein, Leslie. "The Unhappiness of Arthur Miller." *Tri-Quarterly* (Spring 1965): 165–73.

Negative review of both *After the Fall* and *Incident at Vichy* in which Epstein compares the character of Quentin with Hamlet and Miller with Ibsen. Of *Incident at Vichy*, Epstein attacks it as a "heavy-handed production" that "suffers" because "Miller is again unable to locate and assign guilt."

"Guilt Unlimited." *Time* 11 December 1964: 84.

Negative review of the Lincoln Center premiere that criticizes *Incident at Vichy* for faulty logic and a story that makes characters responsible for acts that they are powerless to prevent.

Hewes, Henry. "Waiting Periods." *Saturday Review of Literature* 19 December 1964: 24.

Hewes faults *Incident at Vichy*, directed by Harold Clurman at the Lincoln Center, for being more a thesis than a play and much better suited to the "precisely controlled close-up medium of the motion picture."

"*Incident at Vichy*." *Booklist* 15 April 1965: 779.

Brief positive review of *Incident at Vichy* that praises the work as an "effective succinct commentary on the Nazi treatment of Jews."

"*Incident at Vichy*." *Choice* 2 (May 1965): 166.

Lauding the play for its honesty, this anonymous critic concludes that with the writing of *Incident at Vichy* "Miller has returned as one of the theater's finest practitioners."

"*Incident at Vichy* in London Premiere." *New York Times* 27 January 1966: 28.

News article reporting and summarizing the mostly negative reviews of *Incident at Vichy* in its London production.

Kerr, Walter. "Kerr on New Miller Play, *Incident at Vichy*." *New York Herald Tribune* 4 December 1964: 14. *New York Theatre Critics' Reviews* 25 (1964): 117.

Negative review of premiere production at the Lincoln Center Repertory Theater directed by Harold Clurman and starring Hal Holbrook and David Wayne. Kerr condemns what he sees as a play "constructed in such a way—deliberately, repetitively, as penitentially as a thrice-struck breast—that the author seems to wish us to feel oppressed rather than freshly informed."

Lambert, J. W. "Plays in Performance: *Incident at Vichy*." *Drama* 80 (Spring 1966): 20–21.

Lambert criticizes *Incident at Vichy* for containing character "types" instead of real people and of having dialogue that lacks "resonances" of passion.

Lewis, Theophilus. "*Incident at Vichy*." *America* 23 January 1965: 147–49.

Lewis discusses the themes and "timeless universal values" of *Incident at Vichy*.

McCarten, John. "Easy Doesn't Do It." *New Yorker* 12 December 1964: 152.

McCarten argues that while the thesis of *Incident at Vichy* is incontrovertible, the play lacked "dramatic flair" and was filled with dialogue that "sounded to me so stilted as a bad interpretation of a language the interpreter is not entirely familiar with."

McClain, John. "Lincoln Center's 'Wish Fulfillment.'" *New York Journal American* 4 December 1964: 23. *New York Theatre Critics' Reviews* 25 (1964): 119.

While conceding that the premiere production at the Lincoln Center Repertory Theater (directed by Harold Clurman) is "not very theatrical and it takes quite a time to get going," McClain praises the play for its "first-class" writing and "exceptional" performances.

Nadel, Norman. "Miller Calls World as Witness." *New York World-Telegram* 4 December 1964. *New York Theatre Critics' Reviews* 25 (1964): 118.

Nadel praises the premiere production at the Lincoln Center Repertory Theater as a "brief, pungent drama" with an "outstanding" cast, and lauds Miller for "his craftsmanship as a playwright.

. . . He doesn't pretend to tell us where to look, in order to see ourselves. And whether we like it or not, we see ourselves in that detention room at Vichy."

Novick, Julius. "*Incident at Vichy.*" *Nation* 21 December 1964: 504.

Novick faults *Incident at Vichy* for emphasizing idea over drama and Miller for neglecting "his greatest gift," which is "creating meaning through *action.*"

Popkin, Henry. "*Incident at Vichy.*" *Vogue* 15 January 1965: 27.

Popkin faults *Incident at Vichy* for being nothing more than a "ritualized discovery of evil in a haze of facile small talk."

Spurling, Hilary. "Miller's Phoenix." *Spectator* (London) 4 February 1966: 137, 139.

While praising the performance of the premiere production of *Incident at Vichy* as "superb," Spurling criticizes Miller's play for containing arguments that "are often banal, shallow, even stupid."

Taubman, Howard. "Inquiry into Roots of Evil." *New York Times* 20 December 1964: II: 3.

Taubman compares *Incident at Vichy* to Robert Lowell's *Benito Cereno* and Hannah Arendt's *Eichmann in Jerusalem* as works that use an incident as a "point of departure for a moral inquest."

———. "Theatre: *Incident at Vichy* Opens." *New York Times* 4 December 1964: 44. *New York Theatre Critics' Reviews* 25 (1964): 116.

Highly positive review of the premiere production at the Lincoln Center Repertory Theater. Taubman enthusiastically writes, "Arthur Miller has written a moving play, a searching play, one of the most important plays of our times. . . . *Incident at Vichy* returns the theater to greatness."

Watt, Douglas. "Arthur Miller's *Incident at Vichy* Joins Lincoln Center Repertory." *New York Daily News* 4 December 1964: 64. *New York Theatre Critics' Reviews* 25 (1964): 119.

Negative review of the Lincoln Center Repertory Theater production. Watt laments that "there are flurries of strong language and bits of contrived theatrics . . . but mostly there is an indulgence in philosophical claptrap."

Watts, Richard, Jr. "Arthur Miller Looks at the Nazis." *New York Post* 4 December 1964: 72. *New York Theatre Critics' Reviews* 25 (1964): 116. Rpt. in *Critical Essays on Arthur Miller*. Ed. James J. Martine. Boston: G. K. Hall, 1979. 137–38.

Fairly positive review of the second offering at the Lincoln Center Repertory Company in which Watts laments that the play "is hardly one of [Miller's] major works," but concedes that "it is continuously absorbing and indicates that he is getting back into his stride as a playwright of ideas."

"We Are All Scum." *Newsweek* 14 December 1964: 86.

With "hoarsely delivered sermons" and a story filled with "philosophical confusion," *Incident at Vichy* resembles a "second-rate but superficially engrossing movie about the Nazis."

News Reports, Letters to the Editor, and Related Matter

"Waiting to Be Exterminated." *Life* 22 January 1965: 39–40.

Brief note on the premiere of *Incident at Vichy* notable for the inclusion of six black-and-white photographs from the production.

The Price

Critical Essays in Books

Bigsby, C. W. E. "What Price Arthur Miller? An Analysis of *The Price*." *Twentieth Century Literature* 16.1 (1970): 16–25. Rpt. in *Critical Essays on Arthur Miller*. Ed. James J. Martine. Boston: G. K. Hall, 1979. 161–71.

Bigsby sees *The Price* as a great improvement over Miller's previous two dramas, avoiding their "pretentious dialogue" and "simple-minded manipulation," proving that Miller has "at last emerged from the personal and artistic difficulties which he has experienced since the mid-fifties."

Clausen, Robert Howard. "The Cry of Futility." *The Cross and the Cries of Human Need; Messages for Lent and Every Season.* Minneapolis, Minn.: Augsburg, 1973. 72–87.

In an effort to incorporate the messages of writers and artists who expose "in a powerful way, the problems and sicknesses of this world and its people," Clausen offers a selection from Miller's *The Price* from Act II (to be presented before the congregation) and a Christian meditation entitled "The Cross Means Dedication."

Gruber, Christian P. "*The Price.*" *Insight IV: Analyses of Modern British and American Drama*. Ed. Hermann J. Weiand. Frankfurt: Hirschgraben-Verlag, 1979. 224–30.

Intended for educators and students, this guide for classroom work offers a detailed plot description, a summary of critical response, an evaluation and analysis of the play, questions for consideration, and a short list for further reading for Miller's *The Price*.

Robinson, James A. "Both His Sons: Arthur Miller's *The Price* and Jewish Assimilation." *Staging Difference: Cultural Pluralism in American Theatre and Drama*. Ed. Marc Maufort. New York: Peter Lang, 1995. 121–39.

Robinson argues that unlike *All My Sons* and *Death of a Salesman*, Miller sees the father in *The Price* "in a more complicated fashion, a fashion which makes apparent Miller's Judaism and the ethical questions it raised in his mind about his assimilation into modern American capitalistic culture."

Schiff, Ellen. "Myths and Stock Types." *From Stereotype to Metaphor: The Jew in Contemporary Drama*. Albany: State U of NY Press, 1982. 68–73.

Schiff investigates the myth of "the Jew whose identity derives from money" as he appears in Miller's *The Price*, and applauds the character of Gregory Solomon as "a thoroughly delightful character whose wit and wisdom provide the most successful port of Miller's play."

Critical Essays in Journals and Magazines

Chaikin, Milton. "The Ending of Arthur Miller's *The Price*." *Studies in the Humanities* 8.2 (1981): 40–44.

Chaikin offers a reading of the ending of *The Price* in which Victor retires from the police force and with his inheritance finally pursues his dream deferred because of his father's greedy need.

Czimer, Jozsef. "Price and Value." *Hungarian Quarterly* 10 (Winter 1969): 169–74.

Czimer discusses the details of the Hungarian translation of *The Price* and its production in Budapest on 25 April 1969, including specifics relating to the play's critical reaction, Miller's significant reputation in Hungary, and a comparison of the Hungarian version with the original New York production.

Massa, Ann. "*The Price*." *Journal of Dramatic Theory and Criticism* (Spring 1990): 210–11.

Interesting essay in which Massa compares the original production, including the appearance and contents of the program, with the Young Vic revival in London. She finds that "a good deal was initially lost" in changing the staging to a theatre-in-the-round, placing an intermission between the acts, enlarging the program and featuring a large photograph of Miller—illustrating "the cult of personalities prevailed over the action"—and a program note by Christopher Bigsby that "tended toward cult and cliche."

Weales, Gerald. "All about Talk: Arthur Miller's *The Price*." *Ohio Review* 13.2 (Winter 1972): 74–84. Rpt. in *Arthur Miller: New Perspectives* Ed. Robert A. Martin. Engelwood Cliffs, N.J.: Prentice-Hall, 1982. 188–99.

Weales examines the language in *The Price* and how Miller uses it to inhibit, rather than further, the communication between the brothers.

Willett, Ralph W. "A Note on Arthur Miller's *The Price*." *Journal of American Studies* 5 (December 1971): 307–10.

Willett studies *The Price* with this question in mind: "how far do its characters penetrate beyond the insights of those in previous plays, beyond the recognition of a future that can be no more than a repetition of the present."

Winegarten, Renee. "The World of Arthur Miller." *Jewish Quarterly* 17 (Summer 1969): 48–53.

Essay that summarizes Miller's career and reputation in England and extols *The Price* for containing the character of Gregory Solomon, the "first positive symbol of that dignity and self-respect which his earlier characters found only in death."

Production Reviews

Armitstead, Claire. "*The Price*." *Financial Times* (London) 8 February 1990. *London Theatre Record* 10.3 (1990): 167–68.

Armistead praises the David Thacker revival at the Young Vic and Miller for this "powerful piece which keeps its engines in its second act, roaring out of a surprisingly low-geared first half on an all-too-familiar jet of long suppressed sibling resentments."

Barnes, Clive. "Even Today *The Price* Is Right." *New York Post* 11 June 1992. *New York Theatre Critics' Reviews* 53 (1992): 231.

Positive review of the Roundabout Theatre revival starring Eli Wallach and Hector Elizondo, directed by John Tillinger, that Barnes calls "glistening bright."

———. "The *Price* Is Right." *New York Post* 21 April 1979. *New York Theatre Critics' Reviews* 40 (1979): 204.

Highly favorable review of the off-Broadway revival directed by John Stix, which Barnes considers "better than the original Broadway version back in 1968. It has more fluency and juice." Of Miller's work, Barnes feels that "the play itself is one of Miller's better works . . . it probably represents his best writing to date."

———. "Reappraisal of *The Price*." *New York Times* 30 October 1968: 39.

Barnes reiterates his praise of *The Price*, after his second viewing, as "engrossing" and "one of Miller's two or three best plays."

———. "Theater: Arthur Miller's *The Price*." *New York Times* 8 February 1968: 37. *New York Theatre Critics' Reviews* 29 (1968): 352.

After reporting that the opening night audience had been "deeply moved" by the premiere production, Barnes lauds Miller's work as "one of the most engrossing and entertaining plays that Miller has ever written. It is superbly, even flamboyantly, theatrical. . . . Go expecting a great evening in the theater, and it does, I think, emphatically deliver the goods."

Beaufort, John. "Miller's Memory Bank of a Play." *Christian Science Monitor* 19 June 1992: Arts: 12. *New York Theatre Critics' Reviews* 53 (1992): 232.

Positive review of the Roundabout Theatre Company's revival of *The Price*, directed by John Tillinger, starring Hector Elizondo, Jo Spano, and Eli Wallach. Says Beaufort, Miller's drama "retains its theatrical potency" with a "meticulously balanced cast" and "sympathetic direction."

———. "*The Price*." *Christian Science Monitor* 20 April 1979. *New York Theatre Critics' Reviews* 40 (1979): 203.

Favorable review of the off-Broadway revival, directed by John Stix, especially the character of Gregory Solomon, whom Beaufort calls "the richest and most humanly appealing figure" in the play.

Billington, Michael. "*The Price*." *Guardian* (London) 9 February 1990. *London Theatre Record* 10.3 (1990): 166–67.

Positive review of the David Thacker revival at the Young Vic, which Billington lauds as "a fine production of a fine, penetrating play that treats the stage as a moral combat-zone in which, suggests Miller, the only victory belongs to harsh and pitiless truth."

Borak, Jeffrey. "WTF Season Ends with Dramatic Impact." *Berkshire Eagle* 21 August 1999.

Borak calls the Williamstown Theatre Festival revival, directed by James Naughton, "a riveting, richly textured production."

Brantley, Ben. "Heirlooms as a Playing Field for Conflict." *New York Times* 16 November 1999: B: 1, 3.

Negative review of the Broadway revival, directed by James Naughton and starring Jeffrey DeMunn, Harris Yulin, and Bob Dishy. Brantley calls the production "seriously imbalanced" that lacks both spontaneity and a "revivifying new perspective."

Brown, Georgina. "*The Price*." *Independent* (London) 9 February 1990. *London Theatre Record* 10.3 (1990): 168.

Brown praises David Thacker's "blistering" revival of Miller's play—"Crammed with pithy aphorisms, it adds up to something both richer and more ragged which considers the price paid for our carefully crafted versions of truth."

Brustein, Robert. "The Unseriousness of Arthur Miller." *New Republic* 24 February 1968: 38–41. Rpt. in *The Third Theatre*. New York: Knopf, 1969. 103–106.

Negative essay that attacks Miller's play as "an empty grave" that "is virtually divorced from concerns that any modern audience can recognize as its own." Brustein decries what he sees as Miller's poor writing— "Everything is signaled, climaxes are superimposed, and exits are timed for applause rather than as natural departures. . . . The play as a whole gives us merely the appearance of significance, behind which nothing meaningful is happening."

Bunce, Alan. "*The Price* and *Joe Egg* Arrive on Broadway." *Christian Science Monitor* 12 February 1968.

Bunce praises *The Price* as a compelling play and "a stunning example of a difficult and often unproductive form of theatre. A little less adroitness on Miller's part, a slight shift in emphasis, a small let down in the sustained excellence of the performances, and this might easily have been a dramatically sterile talk session."

Campbell, Karen. "Williamstown *Price* Tears at Heart." *Boston Globe* 24 August 1999. C3.

Campbell praises the Williamstown Theatre revival, directed by James Naughton, as "riveting . . . both wickedly funny and painfully tragic, sometimes veering between the tow with breathtaking shifts of dynamics, a caustic one-liner leading to a sharp-edged barb that tears at the heart with its blistering familiarity."

Canby, Vincent. "For Arthur Miller, a Past Recollected Gives Life Its Form." *New York Times* 21 November 1999: Sec. 2: 8.

Lengthy essay lauding the revival of *The Price*, directed by James Naughton and starring Bob Dishy, Jeffrey DeMunn, and Harris Yulin, that Canby calls "an astonishing piece of work" that is superior to *Death of a Salesman*. "We discover, as if for the first time, that [Miller] is not only a master of the complex mechanics of the theatrical idiom, but also a writer of spontaneous grace, compassion, humor and delicacy."

Chapman, John. "*The Price*, Miller's New Play, Absorbing, Splendidly Acted." *New York Daily News* 8 February 1968. *New York Theatre Critics' Reviews* 29 (1968): 353.

Praising the premiere production, directed by Ulu Grosbard, as "an absorbing play" and Miller's writing for its "great vigor and exceptional clarity," Chapman finds *The Price* "spell binding in its intensity as it moves headlong, without interruption, from a lightly amusing beginning to an emotion-stirring finish."

Clurman, Harold. "Theatre." *Nation* 26 February 1968: 281–83.

Negative review of the premiere production in which Clurman faults *The Price* for not living up to its intentions and being a play that is merely a dialogue between two brothers who represent the idealist versus the pragmatist.

Cohen, Marshall. "The Sins of the Sons." *Atlantic* June 1968: 120–22.

Mixed review of the premiere production of *The Price* that Cohen finds contains an incomplete ethical investigation.

Cooke, Richard P. "Restoration of Miller." *Wall Street Journal* 9 February 1968. *New York Theatre Critics' Reviews* 29 (1968): 353.

Positive review of the premiere production starring Pat Hingle and Arthur Kennedy. Writes Cooke, "*The Price* is a first-rate evening of theater and an appropriate one in which to welcome Mr. Miller back to the full exercise of his talents."

Coveney, Michael. "*The Price*." *Observer* (London) 11 February 1990. *London Theatre Record* 10.3 (1990): 173.

Mixed review of the David Thacker revival at the Young Vic that Coveney feels "sags dangerously" in the second act but is "both quicker and closer than the 1969 London premiere."

Downer, Alan S. "Old, New, Borrowed and (a Trifle) Blue: Notes on the New York Theatre, 1967–1968." *Quarterly Journal of Speech* 54 (October 1968): 203–206. Rpt. as "Review of *The Price*" in *Critical Essays on Arthur Miller*. Ed. James J. Martine. Boston: G. K. Hall, 1979. 155–57.

Positive review of the premiere production that Downer praises for the "economy" of its writing, set, and character."

Duberman, Martin. *Partisan Review* (Summer 1968).

Duberman admits being "impressed by Miller's intermittent insights . . . and moved by the play's central dilemma" in this favorable review for the premiere production of *The Price.*

Eck, Michael. "WTF Reveals Power in Miller's *Price*." *Times Union* (Albany) 21 August 1999.

While Eck calls the script "as wordy, depressing and pretentious as Miller gets," he praises the "excellent" Williamstown Theatre Festival revival, directed by James Naughton, for revealing "all the power of the play."

Eder, Richard. "Miller's *Price* Moves to Broadway." *New York Times* 20 June 1979: Sec. III, p. 17. *New York Theatre Critics' Reviews* 40 (1979): 202.

Mostly negative review of the revival moved to Broadway after two months off-Broadway, directed by John Stix. Comments Elder, "despite its appealing moments, it fails to rise to the position and purpose of its attempts."

Edwardes, Jane. "*The Price*." *Time Out* (London) 14 February 1990. *London Theatre Record* 10.3 (1990): 167.

Edwardes praises the David Thacker revival at the Young Vic as a "marvelously played and totally absorbing" production.

"Embers of Resentment." *Time* 22 June 1992. *New York Theatre Critics' Reviews* 53 (1992): 236.

Brief positive review of the Roundabout Theatre revival of *The Price*, starring Eli Wallach and Hector Elizondo, directed by John Tillinger, that finds the play "rich and intriguingly complex."

"Faulty Family Feud." *Financial Times* (London) 31 March 1999: Arts: 15.

Mixed review of the Bristol Old Vic revival, directed by Jan Sargent, that succeeds as a play but fails as a production that "does not take us under the cultural skin to appreciate the full collective burden of such memories."

Feingold, Michael. "Hesterectomy." *Village Voice* 30 November 1999: 77.

Mixed review of the revival starring Jeffrey DeMunn, Harris Yulin, and Bob Dishy that Feingold says "would all be dismissible trivia" were it not for the "remarkable comic role" of the "pesky, philosophic used-furniture dealer older and grander than the antiques he peddles."

Feldberg, Robert. "Family Turmoil, A La Arthur Miller." *The Record* (Bergen County, N.J.) 11 June 1992: C13.

In this negative review, Feldberg attacks Miller's play as "a static, awkwardly symmetrical work" that has not "gained anything from the uninspired production, staged by John Tillinger" at the Roundabout Theatre, starring Hector Elizondo and Eli Wallach.

———. "Revisiting and Acknowledging the Past with Miller." *The Record* (Bergen County, N.J.) 16 November 1999: Y3.

Mixed review of the Broadway revival, directed by James Naughton and starring Harris Yulin, Bob Dishy, and Jeffrey DeMunn, that Feldberg calls a "first-rate production of a second-rank Arthur Miller play."

Gardner, Lyn. "*The Price*." *City Limits* (London) 15 February 1990. *London Theatre Record* 10.3 (1990): 165.

While expressing the feeling that "Miller's 1968 play is too formulaic and contrived to qualify as really great drama," Gardner admits that in "David Thacker's cleverly restrained and truthful production [at the Young Vic] it has moments of such astonishing and painful insight that one can hardly bear to watch."

Gerard, Jeremy. "*The Price*." *Variety* 15 June 1992. *New York Theatre Critics' Reviews* 53 (1992): 235.

Gerard praises the Roundabout Theatre revival, starring Eli Wallach and Hector Elizondo, directed by John Tillinger, as "a very well cast and thoughtfully staged" production.

Gill, Brendan. "The Theatre: In the Wilderness." *New Yorker* 17 February 1968: 99.

Gill faults *The Price* for its message that we are defined by our self-deceptions.

Gilliatt, Penelope. *Observer* (New York) 11 February 1968.

Calling *The Price* a "beautifully intelligent new play," Gilliatt favorably notes that the work is "obdurately at odds with anything else in the New York theatre."

Gottfried, Martin. "Theatre: *The Price*." *Women's Wear Daily* 8 February 1968. *New York Theatre Critics' Reviews* 29 (1968): 354.

Extremely negative review of the premiere production directed by Ulu Grosbard. Gottfried condemns the play as "an old fashioned drama, and a carelessly written one, displaying Mr. Miller as a slackening artist. . . . The author has taken a fairly obvious problem in living . . . and talked it to death while missing its essence. In a real way, *The Price* is a failure in logic. . . . The play has its moments but it may very well be, sadly, that the playwright has had his day."

Gross, John. "*The Price*." *Sunday Telegraph* (London) 11 February 1990. *London Theatre Record* 10.3 (1990): 174.

Positive review of the David Thacker revival at the Young Vic in which Gross praises the acting as "excellent" and the play as "Miller at his best."

Gussow, Mel. "Miller's *Price* Revived." *New York Times* 20 April 1979: C5.

Gussow praises the revival of *The Price*, directed by John Stix and starring Fritz Weaver and Joseph Buloff, as "at least the equal of the 1968 Broadway version." A black-and-white photograph from the production accompanies the text.

———. "With Such Furniture, the Shopping Is over." *New York Times* 11 June 1992. *New York Theatre Critics' Reviews* 53 (1992): 234.

Positive review of the Roundabout Theatre revival, directed by John Tillinger, that Gussow calls "scrupulous."

Hewes, Henry. "Used People." *Saturday Review* 24 February 1968: 38.

Hews praises the premiere production of *The Price* as good theatre despite the play's nebulous ending and the interminable confrontation between the two brothers.

Hiley, Jim. "*The Price*." *Listener* (London) 22 February 1990. *London Theatre Record* 10.3 (1990): 174.

Hiley lauds the David Thacker revival as "mesmerizing" and praises Miller for creating characters with "robust compassion. No British dramatist writes with such effortless conviction about ordinary people. Yet he also goes against the feverish, self-regarding grain of much American drama. Miller remains incorruptibly measured."

Hornby, Richard. "*The Price*." *Hudson Review* 65.3 (Autumn 1992): 456–57.

Hornby praises the revival of *The Price* by the Roundabout Theatre Company, starring Hector Elizondo, Joe Spano, and Eli Wallach, as "just about perfect."

Hurren, Kenneth. "*The Price*." *Mail on Sunday* (London) 11 February 1990. *London Theatre Record* 10.3 (1990): 173.

Brief review in which Huren lauds the David Thacker revival at the Young Vic as "superbly acted" and an example of "Miller at his most passionate and compassionate."

Javed, Khalid Omar. "*The Price*." *What's On* (London) 14 February 1990. *London Theatre Record* 10.3 (1990): 173-74.

Positive review of the David Thacker revival at the Young Vic. Says Javed, "The play touches something in all of us. Miller takes a hammer and nails your conscience leaving you teased and dazed, picking your brains asking what are the rights and wrongs, who are the guilty and innocent, the weak and strong, the gullible, the fallible, the forgivable."

Kalem, T. E. "Cry for Justice." *Time* 2 July 1979: 65. *New York Theatre Critics' Reviews* 40 (1979): 203.

Mixed review of the Broadway revival directed by John Stix. Kalem dislikes the play's "tirades that tend to drone when they should crackle," but admires the character of Gregory Solomon who "saves the evening" and "is a marvelous comic invention . . . rich in juice and joy."

Kanfer, Stefan. "Miller Plays Variations on *Salesman*." *Life* 8 March 1968: 18.

Negative review of the premiere Broadway production of the half-Ibsen, half-Yiddish *The Price*, that Kanfer says cannot be saved by the comic character of Solomon.

Kerr, Walter. "Mr. Miller's Two New Faces." *New York Times* 18 February 1968: Sec. 2: 1, 3. Rpt. as "The Other Arthur Millers." *Thirty Plays Hath November*. New York: Simon and Schuster, 1969. 217–20. Rpt. in *Critical Essays on Arthur Miller*. Ed. James J. Martine. Boston: G. K. Hall, 1979. 158–60.

Kerr praises *The Price* as a more relaxed and natural play than Miller's earlier works and contends that the work's lack of a definite resolution is not a weakness but rather a sign of Miller's maturity as a dramatist.

Kissel, Howard. "*The Price*." *Women's Wear Daily* 23 April 1979. *New York Theatre Critics' Reviews* 40 (1979): 204.

Glowing review of the off-Broadway revival directed by John Stix. Kissel is mistaken, however, when he states that the play's premiere in 1968 "received largely condescending reviews."

Klein, Alvin. "Taking to the Stage for Sustenance." *New York Times* 29 August 1999.

Positive review of the Williamstown Theatre Festival revival, directed by James Naughton, that Klein calls "the most gripping realization of *The Price* in this theatregoers's memory, which goes back to the play's opening night at the Morosco Theatre."

Koenig, Richard. "Arthur Miller's *The Price*." *Catholic World* May 1968: 74–75.

Koenig praises *The Price* as an absorbing piece of theatre that is really a "modern morality play thinly disguised as drama."

Kroll, Jack. "*The Price*." *Newsweek* 19 February 1968: 104.

While Kroll lauds *The Price* for its "insight into the dynamics and dialects of guilt," he criticizes Miller for not "driving straight for the breaking point" and leaving his own life out of the debate.

Kuchwara, Michael. "*Price* Looks at Bruising Brotherly Love." *Kansas City Star* 21 November 1999: J9.

Positive review of the Broadway revival, directed by James Naughton, starring Jeffrey DeMunn and Harris Yulin. Kuchwara praises Miller for demonstrating "his craftsmanship at creating character and building dramatic tension."

Lewis, Theophilus. "*The Price*." *America* 30 March 1968: 422–23.

Lewis applauds *The Price* as an exhilarating drama while admitting that the play leaves many questions unanswered.

Lyons, Donald. "*The Price* Is Right." *New York Post* 15 November 1999.

Highly laudatory review of the James Naughton revival that originated at the Williamstown Theatre Festival, starring Jeffrey DeMunn, Bob Dishy, and Harris Yulin, that Lyons calls "beyond praise."

Monaghan, Charles. "Arthur Miller as Gnostic." *National Review* 21 May 1968: 511–12.

Monaghan praises *The Price* as Miller's best play since *Death of a Salesman* because of the character of Gregory Solomon. Of note are Monaghan's summary of the New York theatre critics' reviews for the premiere production.

Morley, Sheridan. "*The Price*." *Herald Tribune* (London) 14 February 1990. *London Theatre Record* 10.3 (1990): 167.

Despite the play's "handicaps," says Morley of the David Thacker revival, "the quartet comes together on that powerhouse cockpit stage at the Young Vic to give a chamber concert of intense intellectual and familial agony. In the end, this is a play about the impossibility of knowing what is going to be of value either in furniture or in often vainly sacrificed lives."

Nathan, David. "*The Price*." *Jewish Chronicle* (London) 16 February 1990. *London Theatre Record* 10.3 (1990): 165.

Calling it a "great play," Nathan praises both the acting of Marjorie Yates and Bob Peck, in the David Thacker production at the Young Vic, and the Miller's script that "bares the brothers' lives, stripping away all the subterfuges of re-written family history."

Nightingale, Benedict. "Family Sores." *New Statesman* (London) 14 March 1969: 384–85.

Negative review of the London production that Nightingale finds implausible in its depiction of the "spiritual transformation" of characters who lie and fail in a "dreary world of negatives."

———. "*The Price*." *The Times* (London) 8 February 1990. *London Theatre Record* 10.3 (1990): 165–66.

Nightingale praises the Young Vic revival as full of "expert performers" and argues that "David Thacker's sensitive yet robust production may well establish it, at any rate in British eyes, among [Miller's] masterpieces."

"Old Scores." *Times Literary Supplement* (London) 10 October 1968: 1154.

Positive review of the published version of *The Price* that is compared to *Death of a Salesman* in its reliance on the past as informing the present. The Franz brothers and their uninteresting conflict sidetracks the play.

Oliver, Edith. "*The Price* Is Half Right." *New Yorker* 22 June 1992: 84. *New York Theatre Critics' Reviews* 53 (1992): 234.

Oliver praises the first act of the Roundabout Theatre revival, starring Hector Elizondo and Eli Wallach, directed by John Tillinger, as "rollicking," but laments that the second act is "an all-time joy killer. . . It wouldn't be a bad idea to see the first act of *The Price* and then call it quits."

Osborne, Charles. "*The Price*." *Daily Telegraph* (London) 9 February 1990. *London Theatre Record* 10.3 (1990): 168.

While confessing his dislike for theatre presented in the round, Osborne praises the David Thacker revival at the Young Vic for maintaining the intensity that Miller has built up in the script and delicately charting the "shifting moods of his characters."

Peter, John. "Rest of the Week's Theatre." *Sunday Times* (London) 28 March 1999.

Brief positive review of the Bristol Old Vic revival, directed by Jan Sargent and starring Clive Mantle and Malcolm Tierney, that Peter calls "a thrillingly powerful production."

"*The Price*." *Time* 16 February 1968: 76–77.

Calling *The Price* "a museum piece of a play," the unnamed critic remarks that this work resembles earlier Miller successes.

"*The Price* Acclaimed by Critics in London." *New York Times* 6 March 1969: 36.

News item reporting the overwhelming positive response of London theatre critics to *The Price*. Includes excerpts of reviews.

"*The Price* Is Right and Perfect for Broadway." *Daily News* 16 November 1999. http://www.theatre.com! (18 November 1999).

Positive review that lauds *The Price* revival directed by James Naughton as a "brilliantly bracing production" that "delivers tough comedy and an unflinching vision of the toll that life demands from us."

Raines, Mary B. "*The Price*." *Library Journal* 15 April 1968: 1649–50.

Raines acclaims *The Price* as a "powerful, compassionate play" that dissects "the frailties of man with consummate artistry."

Richardson, Jack. "Theater Chronicle." *Commentary* April 1968: 74–76.

Negative review of the premiere New York production. Richardson faults the work merely providing "a dilemma and some epitaphs for his characters in a language that is never precise or startling."

Rose, Lloyd. "Arthur Miller: In the Shame of the Father." *Washington Post* 13 February 1994: G4.

Positive review of the Arena production, directed by Joe Dowling and starring Robert Prosky and James B. Sikking. Rose calls it "terrific—a passionate, full-blooded show."

Rutherford, Malcolm. "Romeo and Arthur Miller: Of Inspiration and Effort." *Encounter* (London) 74.3 (April 1990): 74–75.

Calling the Young Vic revival, directed by David Thacker, "a revelation," Rutherford questions why a play so good has "so seldom been seen in London before?"

Shulman, Milton. "*The Price.*" *Evening Standard* (London) 8 February 1990. *London Theatre Record* 10.3 (1990): 173.

Shulman praises the David Thacker revival for proving "that when it comes to recording the angst of the American male there is no more perceptive observer than Arthur Miller."

Siegel, Joel. "*The Price.*" ABC. WABC, New York. 19 June 1979. *New York Theatre Critics' Reviews* 40 (1979): 205.

Positive review of the New York revival of *The Price*, starring Fritz Weaver and Joseph Buloff, that Siegel calls "one wonderful evening in the theatre."

Simon, John. "*The Price.*" *New York* 13 June 1992: 66. *New York Theatre Critics' Reviews* 53 (1992): 237.

Negative review of the Roundabout Theatre revival, starring Eli Wallach and Hector Elizondo, directed by John Tillinger, that Simon calls "a sweaty effort to recycle shopworn ingredients."

———. "Settling the Account." *Commonweal* 1 March 1968: 655–56.

Negative review in which Simon criticizes *The Price* for being "improbable, uncompelling, old-fashioned, humorless for all its jokes, and undramatic. It is a well-meaning, respectable, middlebrow anachronism, and, I am afraid, a bore."

———. "Theatre Chronicle." *Hudson Review* 21 (Summer 1968): 322.
Negative review of the New York premiere production in which Simon blames Miller for his "obsessive dredging up of the same family trauma" that is found in most of his plays.

Stearns, David Patrick. "Revival of *Price* Is Right on Target." *USA Today* 16 November 1999: D5.
Stearns praises the revival of *The Price*, starring Bob Dishy, Jeffrey DeMunn, and Harris Yulin, as "loaded with enough ideas to keep your brain busy for weeks—sometimes at the expense of theatricality."

Streiker, Lowell. "Sons and Brothers." *Christian Century* 27 March 1968: 405–406.
In this positive review of the New York premiere production, Streiker lauds *The Price* as Miller's best play in recent years. It is a work about how each of us "chooses his role" and plays "it until the destroying end."

Stuart, Jan. "A Gift from Miller That's Worth *The Price*." *New York Newsday* 11 June 1992. *New York Theatre Critics' Reviews* 53 (1992): 233.
Positive review of the Roundabout Theatre revival, starring Hector Elizondo and Eli Wallach, that Stuart lauds for its "sturdy, leak-proof staging" and praises as "the strongest revival the Roundabout has enjoyed in a long spell."

Taitte, Lawson. "Balance Due." *Dallas Morning News* 26 November 1999: A45.
Mixed review of the Broadway revival, starring Jeffrey DeMunn, Harris Yulin, and Bob Dishy, that blames director James Naughton for not guiding the actors "with a sure hand."

Taubman, Howard. "*The Price* in Tel Aviv." *New York Times* 19 October 1968: II: 29.
Taubman examines the Tel Aviv production of *The Price* and the shift that occurs when all the characters, not just Solomon, are made Jewish.

Tinker, Jack. "*The Price.*" *Daily Mail* (London) 22 February 1990. *London Theatre Record* 10.3 (1990): 166.
Tinker praises the David Thacker revival at the Young Vic for proving in this play about "the personal struggles of everyday life,

that [Miller] is a dramatist of undeniable power, insight, intellect and no mean wit."

Vaughan, Peter. "Guthrie Offers Memorable *Price.*" *Minneapolis Star Tribune* 14 February 1997: E6.

Positive review of the Guthrie Theater production of *The Price,* directed by David Thacker, that Vaughan calls "exquisite."

Wardle, Irving. "*The Price.*" *Independent on Sunday* (London) 18 February 1990. *London Theatre Record* 10.3 (1990): 166.

Wardle praises the David Thacker production at the Young Vic, saying that "with memories of Pat Hingle and Arthur Kennedy slogging out the fraternal duel in the original Broadway production," he had been "unprepared for the delicacy" of this revival. Thacker's "strategy is to delay the brothers' confrontation until the last possible moment."

Watt, Douglas. "Actors in Miller Play Give *Price* Their Best." *New York Daily News* 20 June 1979. *New York Theatre Critics' Reviews* 40 (1979): 202.

Mixed review of revival directed by John Stix that opened off-off-Broadway in April 1979 and moved to Broadway in June of the same year. Watt advises his readers to visit this production, assuring them it will be "very much worth your while," but faults the play's characters whom he finds "a tiresome lot" with "problems of such minimal interest that an evening spent with them begins to feel like a lifetime."

———. "*The Price.*" *Daily News* 19 June 1992. *New York Theatre Critics' Reviews* 53 (1992): 232.

Positive review of the Roundabout Theatre revival starring Hector Elizondo and Eli Wallach, directed by John Tillinger, that Watt calls a "fine production" of a "solidly written play" with "dialogue ringing true at every turn."

Watts, Richard, Jr. "Conflict between Two Brothers." *New York Post* 8 February 1968. *New York Theatre Critics' Reviews* 29 (1968): 354.

Negative review of the premiere production starring Pat Hingle and Arthur Kennedy that Watts says is "disappointingly lacking in effective resolution and steady interest" and "lacks dramatic power."

Weales, Gerald. "The Song of Solomon." *Reporter* 21 March 1968: 42, 44.

Weales comments that *The Price* is similar in theme to Miller's earlier works in its "examination of guilt and the attempt to escape it," and acclaims the work for Miller's creation of Gregory Solomon, a character both funny and dramatic.

Weatherby, W. J. "Messengers or Actors." *Guardian* (London) 17 February 1968: 7.

With its peculiarly forced ending, *The Price* "strains to be reasonable at the expense of the wildness of the spirit."

Wilson, Edwin. "Eli Wallach Back on Stage." *Wall Street Journal* 30 June 1992. *New York Theatre Critics' Reviews* 53 (1992): 236.

Positive review of the Roundabout Theatre revival, directed by John Tillinger. Wilson lauds the play as "rich material" and Eli Wallach for "delivering Solomon's one-liners and sage advice with impeccable timing."

Winer, Linda. "Little People, Big Drama." *Newsday* 16 November 1999: B2.

Winer calls the James Naughton production, starring Harris Yulin and Jeffrey DeMunn, a "soul-stirring revival" that "seems fired with a sense of urgency now."

Related Interviews and Profiles (not with Miller)

Green, Blake. "*Price* of Success." *Newsday* 15 November 1999: B3.

Interview with James Naughton, director of the acclaimed revival of *The Price*, starring Bob Dishy, Harris Yulin, and Jeffrey DeMunn. Naughton discusses the "classic conflict" of *The Price* and his interest in directing the play, both for the Williamstown Theatre Festival in 1998 and the Broadway revival.

Kerr, Walter. "Inverted Miller Works Perfectly." *New York Times* 8 July 1979: D: 5, 18.

Lengthy profile of actor Joseph Buloff who plays Solomon in the revival of *The Price* directed by John Stix.

Wallach, Allan. "A Two-Act Summer." *Newsday* 18 June 1992: B66.

Profile of actors Eli Wallach and wife Anne Jackson. Wallach discusses his approach to the role of Solomon in The Roundabout Theatre production of Miller's *The Price.*

News Reports, Letters to the Editor, and Related Matter

"Letters on *The Price*." *New York Times* 12 May 1968: II 5.

Nine letters to the editor written in response to the Harold Clurman-Albert Bermel debate regarding both *The Price* and Miller's merits as a playwright. See Clurman "The Merits of Mr. Miller" and Bermel "Right, Wrong, and Mr. Miller."

"*The Price* Will Close." *New York Times* 14 January 1969: 36.

News item announcing the closing of *The Price* in New York after 425 performances and the imminent opening of the play in London in February.

McKinley, Jesse. "More from Miller." *New York Times* 19 November 1999: E2.

News item reporting that producer David Richenthal is doubling his advertising budget to ensure the revival's success. Says Richenthal, "I'll spend any amount of money to advertise this play to help find it an audience. Whatever it takes. Because audiences love it, and I love it."

Shenker, Israel. "Arthur Miller Adjusting *The Price* for London." *New York Times* 15 February 1969: 20.

News item reporting that Miller has attended some rehearsals of the London production of *The Price* and offered some ideas to the cast and director prior to the play's opening.

The Creation of the World and Other Business

Critical Essays in Books

Clurman, Harold. "Letter to Boris Aronson Apropos of *Creation of the World and Other Business*." *On Directing*. New York: Macmillan, 1972. 292–99.

In a letter written to designer Aronson, Clurman details his concept of Miller's "philosophical comedy" *The Creation of the World and Other Business*, including his ideas regarding character, theme, setting, lighting, make-up, and costumes.

Critical Essays in Journals and Magazines

Centola, Steven R. "What Price Freedom? The Fall Revisited: Arthur Miller's *The Creation of the World and Other Business*." *Studies in the Humanities* 12 (June 1985): 3–10.

Despite its negative critical response, Centola contends that *The Creation of the World and Other Business* deserves attention "not only because it represents Miller's first experiment with comedy, but also because it contributes to our understanding of his enduring vision of the human condition and gives us valuable insight into his interpretation of the process involved in the fall into that condition."

Production Reviews

Barnes, Clive. "Arthur Miller's *Creation of the World*." *New York Times* 1 December 1972. 28.

Negative review of the New York premiere production in which Barnes chides the play as a "victory of craft over artistry and mind over matter" with "the air of a comic strip version of Genesis."

Gill, Brendan. "Here Comes the Clowns." *New Yorker* 9 December 1972: 109.

In this negative review of the premiere New York production of *The Creation of the World and Other Business*, Gill laments that while the first two acts work well, the third act is merely an "incoherent assortment of debates."

Gottfried, Martin. "*Creation of the World and Other Business*." *Women's Wear Daily* 4 December 1972. *New York Theatre Critics' Reviews* 33 (1972): 153.

Gottfried decries Miller's re-telling of the Old Testament's as "coy, fake, fatuous biblicism laced with night school wisdom. . . . Perhaps I am wrong in this respect, but not as wrong as Miller in choosing this foolish project for his tremendous talent (a talent that we and he must respect)."

Harris, Leonard. "*The Creation of the World and Other Business*." CBS. WCBS, New York. 30 November 1972. *New York Theatre Critics' Reviews* 33 (1972): 154.

Fairly positive review of the New York production, directed by Gerald Freedman and starring Zoe Caldwell and George Grizzard, that Harris calls "an amusing minor play" that is "played by all the cast with wit and clarity."

Hewes, Henry. "Arthur Miller's Cosmic Chuckles." *Saturday Review* January 1973: 57.

Calling the premiere production of *The Creation of the World and Other Business* "unfunny," Hewes offers his hope that Miller will not "retreat from developing what seems to some of us the most down-to-earth aspect of his talent," namely his comic writing ability as expressed with the creation of Solomon in *The Price*.

Hughes, Catharine. "Picking Up the Pieces." *America* 30 December 1972: 570.

Negative review of *The Creation of the World and Other Business* in which Hughes writes that the play is "more interesting in its aspirations than successful in their realizations."

Kalem, T. E. "Adam and Evil." *Time* 11 December 1972: 122. *New York Theatre Critics' Reviews* 33 (1972): 152.

Kalem castigates Miller for composing a "feeble, pointless play" that he wishes someone had stopped him from writing.

Kauffmann, Stanley. "*Creation of the World and Other Business*." *New Republic* 23 December 1972: 26, 35.

Kauffmann believes that when Miller wrote *The Creation of the World and Other Business* he must have been "starving for subject matter" and "anxious to keep busy." Miller fails profoundly in his treatment of the father-and-son conflict in the beginning of the play.

Kerr, Walter. "Arthur Miller, Stuck with *The* Book." *New York Times* 10 December 1972: Sec. 2: 3, 5.

Negative review of *The Creation of the World and Other Business*. Kerr finds the play "casually imagined" and lacking control.

Kroll, Jack. "Theater." *Newsweek* 11 December 1972: 80. *New York Theatre Critics' Reviews* 33 (1972): 151.

Negative review notable for its brevity (two sentences). Says Kroll, Miller's play "deserves no comment or any attempt to unravel its stupefyingly boring muddleheadedness and I hereby order my fingers to stop typing about it."

Probst, Leonard. "*The Creation of the World and Other Business*." NBC, New York. 30 November 1972. *New York Theatre Critics' Reviews* 36 (1975): 154.

Negative review of the New York production, starring Zoe Caldwell and George Grizzard, that Probst says "has the feeling of a metaphysical problem that's been bothering Miller for a long time. . . . but he fails to make it clear, interesting, or believable on stage."

Richardson, Jack. "Arthur Miller's Eden." *Commentary* February 1973: 83–85.

Richardson says that Miller's *The Creation of the World and Other Business* points up other faults in his earlier plays and his tendency to cheapen "life through his readiness to understand it too quickly and to festoon it with gaudy pronouncements."

Sanders, Kevin. "*The Creation of the World and Other Business*." ABC. WABC, New York. 30 November 1972. *New York Theatre Critics' Reviews* 33 (1972): 153.

Negative review of the New York production, starring Zoe Caldwell, Bob Dishy, and Stephen Elliott, that Sanders says is "well acted and imaginatively staged, but this production really doesn't have much to say, or wittily. Humour is obviously not Miller's forte."

Watt, Douglas. "Miller's *Creation of the World* Is a Plodding Comedy-Drama." *New York Daily News* 1 December 1972. *New York Theatre Critics' Reviews* 33 (1972): 151. Rpt. in *Critical Essays on Arthur Miller*. Ed. James J. Martine. Boston: G. K. Hall, 1979. 175–76.

Negative review of the premiere production that Watt decries as "a play devoid of wonder, mystery or even the satisfying caress of fancy. . . . In fact, [Miller's] world gives the impression of having taken longer to create than God's."

Watts, Richard, Jr. "Arthur Miller's *Creation* Opens at Shubert Theater." *New York Post* 1 December 1972. *New York Theatre Critics' Reviews* 33 (1972): 150. Rpt. in *Critical Essays on Arthur Miller*. Ed. James J. Martine. Boston: G. K. Hall, 1979. 173–74.

After conceding that "Miller has tackled quite an ambitious subject for himself," Watts concludes that even though "it starts out with a good first act. . . . By the end it seems to me to have become both confused and confusing."

Weales, Gerald. "Cliches in the Garden." *Commonweal* 22 December 1972: 276.

Weales find *The Creation of the World and Other Business* to be Miller's worst play and the "most pretentious and most vulgar reworking of the Bible" in memory.

Wilson, Edwin. "Adam and Eve in the Garden." *Wall Street Journal* 4 December 1972. *New York Theatre Critics' Reviews* 33 (1972): 152.

Mixed review that praises the play's telling of the story of Creation in which Miller "frequently fleshes out the narrative with great charm and insight," and laments the fact that the "other business mentioned in the title is where the trouble begins, for this is not one play but three."

News Reports, Letters to the Editor, and Related Matter

"Arthur Miller, the Great American Playwright, Writes on God and Man, Good and Evil." *Vogue* January 1973: 132–33, 166.

Excerpts from *The Creation of the World and Other Business*.

Calta, Louis. "Clurman Quits *Creation*." *New York Times* 17 October 1972: 35.

News item announcing that the director of *The Creation of the World and Other Business* has quit the show at the opening in Washington, D.C., citing "differences of opinion over its interpretation."

———. "Miller Has a New Play for Broadway." *New York Times* 9 September 1971: 50.

Item announcing the opening in January or February of 1972 of Miller's new "catastrophic comedy" *The Creation of the World and Other Business*.

———. "Play by Miller Due on Broadway." *New York Times* 19 May 1972: 19.

News item reporting that *The Creation of the World and Other Business* will open 16 November on Broadway.

Hellman, Lillian. "Baby Cries." *New York Times* 21 January 1973: II: 18.

Letter to the editor in which Hellman speaks out against an essay by Tom Buckley that previously appeared in the *Times*. Buckley had written a piece on the rehearsal history of *The Creation of the World and Other Business* in which he had quoted people who "were sharp about Barbara Harris." Hellman writes to inform the readers that Harris refused to gossip about the production after leaving the cast and "such courtesy and unusual restraint have been badly rewarded."

"Miller's Play Closes December 16." *New York Times* 8 December 1972: 37.

News item announcing the close of *The Creation of the World and Other Business* after only twenty performances.

The Archbishop's Ceiling

Critical Essays in Books

Bigsby, Christopher. "Afterword to *The Archbishop's Ceiling*." *The Archbishop's Ceiling*. New York: DPS, 1985. 65–68.

Bigsby examines the political and personal questions posed by "this complex but moving play."

Critical Essays in Journals and Magazines

Schlüeter, June. "Power Play: Arthur Miller's *The Archbishop's Ceiling*." *CEA Critic* 49 (Winter 86–Summer 87): 134–38.

Schlueter offers a close reading of *The Archbishop's Ceiling* as "a sophisticated foray into the epistemological nature of reality and art" that perfectly utilizes the world-stage metaphor "created through the presumed presence of hidden microphones in the Archbishop's ceiling.

Production Reviews

Barber, John. "*The Archbishop's Ceiling*." *Daily Telegraph* (London) 19 April 1985. *London Theatre Record* 5.8 (1985): 375.

Barber faults Miller's script in this negative review of the Bristol Old Vic production, directed by Paul Unwin. "Mr. Miller, though successful a [sic] first in evoking the shuddering apprehensions of the hunted and victimized, seems always about to spring a surprise which never comes. Weak as an action thriller, the play is even weaker in ideas."

Billington, Michael. "*The Archbishop's Ceiling*." *Guardian* (London) 19 April 1985. *London Theatre Record* 5.8 (1985): 375.

While admitting to seeing Miller as a playwright who "has been crucified by American critics for failing to live up to his own genius," Billington praises the European premiere of *The Archbishop's Ceiling* at the Bristol Old Vic as "a complex, gritty, intellectually teasing play."

———. "*The Archbishop's Ceiling*." *Guardian* (London) 31 October 1986. *London Theatre Record* 6.22 (1986): 1198–99.

Positive review of the Royal Shakespeare Company production, directed by Nick Hamm, that Billington says "tends to take you round the track twice over but what it gives you is the sense of a major writer wrestling with the problem of how one preserves personal integrity in a corrupt world."

Coe, Richard. "Arthur Miller's *Ceiling.*" *Washington Post* 2 May 1977: B: 1, 7.

While faulting *The Archbishop's Ceiling* for having too many characters, Coe admits that the play does pick up in the second act.

Edwardes, Jane. "*The Archbishop's Ceiling.*" *Time Out* (London) 5 November 1986. *London Theatre Record* 6.22 (1986): 1194.

Edwardes lauds the Royal Shakespeare Company production, directed by Nick Hamm, as "a powerful exploration of a world in which morality no longer appears to provide easy answers."

Edwards, Christopher. "*The Archbishop's Ceiling.*" *Spectator* (London) 8 November 1986. *London Theatre Record* 6.22 (1986): 1194.

Negative review of Miller's play, produced by the Royal Shakespeare Company and directed by Nick Hamm. Says Edwards, "while there is always a fluent and intelligent piece of writing the vivid balance and engagement so evident in the first half are, unfortunately, not sustained to the end."

Gardner, Lyn. "*The Archbishop's Ceiling.*" *City Limits* (London) 6 November 1986. *London Theatre Record* 6.22 (1986): 1194.

Negative review of the Royal Shakespeare Company production, directed by Nick Hamm. Says Gardner, "while the first half is a brilliant and stimulating cascade of ideas, the debate is over-protracted, and after the interval the play short-circuits into repetitious arguments, leaving the characters to lurch into monstrous self-parody."

Hiley, Jim. "*The Archbishop's Ceiling.*" *Listener* (London) 6 November 1986. *London Theatre Record* 6.22 (1986): 1196.

Says Hiley, in his negative review of the Royal Shakespeare Company production, "Quite simply, *The Archbishop's Ceiling* takes far too long to get off the ground. And Nick Hamm's production doesn't help. Characteristically lucid, it allows everything the same heavily significant pace."

Hirschhorn, Clive. "*The Archbishop's Ceiling.*" *Sunday Express* (London) 2 November 1986. *London Theatre Record* 6.22 (1986): 1196.

Positive review of the Royal Shakespeare Company production, directed by Nick Hamm, that Hirschhorn praises for its "excellent cast" and earnest direction—"You leave the theatre with much food for thought."

Hoyle, Martin. "*The Archbishop's Ceiling.*" *Financial Times* (London) 30 October 1986. *London Theatre Record* 6.22 (1986): 1194, 1196.

Hoyle calls the Royal Shakespeare Company production, directed by Nick Hamm, a "turgidly pretentious piece" with "hoary ideas couched in dully repetitious language."

Hurren, Kenneth. "*The Archbishop's Ceiling.*" *Mail on Sunday* (London) 21 April 1985. *London Theatre Record* 5.8 (1985): 375.

Rave review of the Bristol Old Vic European premiere, directed by Paul Unwin. Says Hurren, Miller's "writing is taut and muscular, Paul Unwin's direction lucid, the performances (Ian Lindsay, Alan Dobie, Ed Bishop, Maureen O'Brien) exemplary."

———. "*The Archbishop's Ceiling.*" *Mail on Sunday* (London) 2 November 1986. *London Theatre Record* 6.22 (1986): 1194.

Hurren likes Miller's play in his review of the Royal Shakespeare Company production, directed by Nick Hamm, but is disturbed by the "shouting"—"If only the company would tone down the decibels, the play might be seen as a near-masterpiece."

Jones, Dan. "*The Archbishop's Ceiling.*" *Sunday Telegraph* (London) 2 November 1986. *London Theatre Record* 6.22 (1986): 1197.

Jones praises the acting in this otherwise "gloomy" production by the Royal Shakespeare Company, directed by Nick Hamm.

Licht, Jonathan. "*The Archbishop's Ceiling.*" *Jewish Chronicle* (London) 7 November 1986. *London Theatre Record* 6.22 (1986): 1196–97.

Mixed review of the Royal Shakespeare Company production, directed by Nick Hamm, that Licht criticizes for its delivery—"Although Miller's dialogue contains many a philosophical depthcharge, I found the impetus of the play theatrically sedentary. . . [but] even an Arthur Miller 'failure' is worth one evening of any questioning human being's time."

Morley, Sheridan. "*The Archbishop's Ceiling*." *Punch* (London) 12 November 1986. *London Theatre Record* 6.22 (1986): 1194.

Without offering either a positive or negative review of the Royal Shakespeare Company production, directed by Nick Hamm, Morley offers a plot synopsis and the opinion that *The Archbishop's Ceiling* presents "real and burning issues of freedom and betrayal."

"New Play by Miller Is Faulted in Washington." *New York Times* 3 May 1977: 50.

News item that summarizes the mostly negative reviews of the Washington, D.C., premiere of *The Archbishop's Ceiling* and reports that there are plans for the play to open in New York in the fall after Miller completes the rewrites.

Peter, John. *Sunday Times* (London) 21 April 1985.

Peter praises the European premiere of *The Archbishop's Ceiling* as "full of a giant and warm humanity, and the uncomfortable honesty of a man who is his own moral inquisitor."

———. *Sunday Times* (London) 2 November 1986.

Peter praises Nick Hamm's production of *The Archbishop's Ceiling* as an experience that "deepens the sense of density, of three-dimensional solidity about both people and arguments."

Ratcliffe, Michael. "*The Archbishop's Ceiling*." *Observer* (London) 28 April 1985. *London Theatre Record* 5.8 (1985): 374–75.

Positive review of the Bristol Old Vic European premiere, directed by Paul Unwin, that Ratcliffe calls an "incisive, well-directed, splendidly acted and designed" production.

———. "*The Archbishop's Ceiling*." *Observer* (London) 2 November 1986. *London Theatre Record* 6.22 (1986): 1197–98.

Ratcliffe blames both the acting and the directing in this negative review of the Royal Shakespeare Company production, directed by Nick Hamm—"it is almost as if [Hamm] has confused the nature of the ideas with the texture of the writing itself."

Rissik, Andrew. "*The Archbishop's Ceiling*." *Independent* (London) 31 October 1986. *London Theatre Record* 6.22 (1986): 1197.

Negative review of the Royal Shakespeare Company production, directed by Nick Hamm, that Rissik says possesses "the illusion of a complex play, where the desire to impress an audience can shape man's beliefs."

Shorter, Eric. "*The Archbishop's Ceiling*." *Daily Telegraph* (London) 21 October 1986. *London Theatre Record* 6.22 (1986): 1198.

In his highly laudatory review of the Royal Shakespeare Company production, directed by Nick Hamm, Shorter recommends that his readers go "and breathe for a couple of engrossing, stifling hours, the air of life for writers behind the Iron Curtain."

Shulman, Milton. "*The Archbishop's Ceiling*." *London Standard* (London) 30 October 1986. *London Theatre Record* 6.22 (1986): 1199.

Positive review of the Royal Shakespeare Company production, directed by Nick Hamm. "Although the plot at times becomes unnecessarily melodramatic, Arthur Miller's sinewy, muscular dialogue, laced with frequent touches of ironic humour, keeps one tingling with intellectual [sic] excitement."

Smith, Joan. "*The Archbishop's Ceiling*." *Sunday Today* (London) 9 November 1986. *London Theatre Record* 6.22 (1986): 1199.

While calling the overall effort by the Royal Shakespeare Company, directed by Nick Hamm, an "interesting play," Smith chides Miller for a weak second act—"the arguments are repeated ad nauseam, and he introduces a superfluous bit of chicanery with a gun to rescue the script."

Tinker, Jack. "*The Archbishop's Ceiling*." *Daily Mail* (London) 5 November 1986. *London Theatre Record* 6.22 (1986): 1194.

Tinker praises the Royal Shakespeare Company production, directed by Nick Hamm, as "an interesting and powerfully performed political curio."

Weales, Gerald. "Come Home to Maya." *Commonweal* 8 July 1977: 431–32.

Negative review of the premiere production of *The Archbishop's Ceiling*. Says Weales, "It is, as usual with Miller, a play heavy with ideas, one that seduces the viewer into the kind of discussion that these paragraphs contain. On the human level, it is less successful. The characters are complex in conception, richly endowed with biography, dangerously articulate, but they are trapped in the play as well as in the imaginary country."

Related Interviews and Profiles (not with Miller)

Lustig, Vera. "Free Space." *Plays and Players* (London) March 1989: 7–10.

Actress Stella Gonet discusses her role in *The Archbishop's Ceiling* at the Royal Shakespeare Company.

———. "The Prague Faust." *Plays and Players* (London) May 1988: 13–15.

Actor John Shrapnel discusses his work in two plays set in Eastern Europe, *The Archbishop's Ceiling* and Havel's *Temptation*, both staged by the Royal Shakespeare Company.

Up from Paradise

Critical Essays in Books

Coen, Edward M. *Working on a New Play*. New York: Prentice, 1988. 187–88.

Brief anecdotal mention of opening night of *Up from Paradise* at the University of Michigan. In their 100-seat theatre, the first two rows, all the way across, were filled with New York theatre critics. Says Coen, "It was like playing to the Berlin Wall."

Production Reviews

Rich, Frank. "Stage: Miller's *Up from Paradise*." *New York Times* 26 October 1983: C22.

Negative review of the fully-staged New York production of *Up from Paradise* at the Jewish Repertory Theatre, directed by Ran Avni. Says Rich, the work is "a casual, warm-spirited and innocuous musical chalk talk whose future is likely to reside with amateur church and synagogue theatre groups."

The American Clock

Critical Essays in Books

Weales, Gerald. "Watching the *Clock*." *The Achievement of Arthur Miller: New Essays*. Ed. Steven Centola. Dallas, Tex.: Contemporary Research, 1995. 125–34.

Culling bits of information from reviews, interviews, and news reports, Weales offers a detailed production history of *The American Clock* and its transformation from an unsuccessful play into a "mural-mosaic-vaudeville."

Production Reviews

Barnes, Clive. "This *Clock* Is a Bit Off." *New York Post* 21 November 1980. *New York Theatre Critics' Reviews* 41 (1980): 81–82.

Mixed review of New York premiere in which Barnes predicts that the play "will probably be a failure" at the box office, but that "it does show the same kind of intimate, inner voice writing that made *The Death of a Salesman* [sic], a masterpiece."

———. "*Clock* Watchers, Rejoice." *New York Post* 20 October 1997.

Barnes praises the Signature Theatre Company revival as a "splendidly spirited and moving production" that "is the memory-play trailer to a time capsule of the decade or so that formulated Arthur Miller and his American generation."

Beaufort, John. "*The American Clock*." *Christian Science Monitor* 24 November 1980. *New York Theatre Critics' Reviews* 41 (1980): 83.

Beaufort praises the New York production, directed by Vivian Matalon, for never failing "to hold the spectator's interest."

Billington, Michael. "*The American Clock*." *Guardian* (London) 8 August 1986. *London Theatre Record* 6.16 (1986): 838.

Overall positive review of the National Theatre Company production, directed by Peter Wood, that Billington calls "a good one even if the balance between the private and public worlds is not always perfectly maintained."

Brantley, Ben. "Tarnished Dreams Hold Painful Lessons." *New York Times* 20 October 1997: E1.

Mixed review of the Signature Theatre Company's production of *The American Clock*, directed by James Houghton—"Seen purely as a piece of theatre, *Clock* is not something to rejoice over. As an event, however, it is."

Canby, Vincent. "*Side Show* Asks, What Is Normal?" *New York Times* 26 October 1997: Sec. 2: 4.

Mostly negative review of the Signature Theatre Company's production of *The American Clock*, directed by James Houghton—"this would-be jubilant reworking of vintage Arthur Miller finally bogs down."

Coveney, Michael. *Financial Times* (London) 7 August 1986. *London Theatre Record* 6.16 (1986): 838.

Coveney praises Peter Wood's production of *The American Clock* at the National Theatre for reaffirming "Miller's reputation at a stroke," which "suggests we may have to look at all his plays of the last decade or so much more carefully."

de Jongh, Nicholas. "*The American Clock.*" *Guardian* (London) 20 December 1986. *London Theatre Record* 6.25–26 (1986): 1399.

Mixed review of the National Theatre Company production, moved to the Olivier from the Cottesloe, and directed by Peter Wood, in which de Jongh says "the production and the cast command admiration for what they make of the play, rather than what the play makes of them."

Edwardes, Jane. "*The American Clock.*" *Time Out* (London) 11 December 1986. *London Theatre Record* 6.25–26 (1986): 1398.

Edwardes praises the National Theatre Company production, moved to the Olivier from the Cottesloe, and directed by Peter Wood, as an "epic production [that] avoids becoming too sentimental."

Edwards, Christopher. "*The American Clock.*" *Spectator* (London) 16 August 1986. *London Theatre Record* 6.16 (1986): 837.

Highly laudatory review of the National Theatre Company production, directed by Peter Wood, that Edwards calls "impressive" and "brilliantly staged. . . . This is a touching, amusing and cleverly wrought piece of theatre."

Feingold, Michael. "Two-Faced Structures." *Village Voice* 28 October 1997: 97.

Mostly negative review of the Signature Theatre's revival of *The American Clock*. Feingold calls it "a not-quite-there play" that is "lively, moving, and flavorsome . . . like a good stein of microbrew."

Freedman, Peter. "*The American Clock*." *Sunday Today* (London) 10 August 1986. *London Theatre Record* 6.16 (1986): 839.

Positive review of the National Theatre Company production at the Cottesloe, directed by Peter Wood, that Freedman calls "an engrossing-enough words-and-music portrait of Depression America."

Henry, William A., III. "Torn Apart and Pulled Together." *Time* 18 August 1986: 70.

Positive review of the London premiere of *The American Clock* that Henry calls "a robust, expressionistic celebration of a time that tore America apart yet paradoxically brought it together."

Hiley, Jim. "*The American Clock*." *Listener* (London) 14 August 1986. *London Theatre Record* 6.16 (1986): 832.

Hiley claims that in the National Theatre Company production, directed by Peter Wood, "we're given too much by way of production values when pace and leanness are required . . . in a show about the Depression, this seems insensitively bountiful, to say the least."

Hirschhorn, Clive. "*The American Clock*." *Sunday Express* (London) 17 August 1986. *London Theatre Record* 6.16 (1986): 832.

Hirschhorn calls the National Theatre Company production, directed by Peter Wood, "lopsided" and a "flawed but fascinating evening" of theatre.

Hoyle, Martin. "*The American Clock*." *Financial Times* (London) 19 December 1986. *London Theatre Record* 6.25–26 (1986): 1399.

In this negative review of the National Theatre Company production, moved to the Olivier from the Cottesloe, directed by Peter Wood, Hoyle attacks the acting choices, accents ("staggering miscalculation"), and the interspersing of popular song throughout the text as serving "to fragment the work's episodic structure even further, to defuse tension and to soften the impact of the harsh social observation."

Hurren, Kenneth. "*The American Clock*." *Mail on Sunday* (London) 10 August 1986. *London Theatre Record* 6.16 (1986): 832.

In this brief review of the National Theatre Company production, directed by Peter Wood, Hurren lauds it as "brilliant."

Kalem, T. E. "Broke and Blue." *Time* 9 June 1980: 65.

Negative review of *The American Clock*. Kalem feels that while the vignettes make for interesting social history, they ultimately diffuse the audience's attention.

Kelly, Kevin. "Miller's *American Clock* Turns Clockwork Pale on Broadway." *Boston Globe* 27 November 1980.

Negative review of the premiere production of *The American Clock*, which details the change in artistic personnel that occurred after the opening at the Spoleto Festival USA. While praising Joan Copeland's performance as "truly extraordinary," Kelly is disappointed by Miller's script, which he says has "all the cheery uplift of *Annie* minus, of course, Sandy, orphans, and Christmas Eve with Daddy Warbucks."

Kerr, Walter. "A History Lesson from Miller, a Social Lesson from Fugard." *New York Times* 30 November 1980: Sec. 2: 5, 14.

Negative review of the New York premiere of *The American Clock*, starring Joan Copeland and directed by Vivian Matalon, in which Kerr praises the work's truths but laments that it ultimately feels "both impersonal and incomplete."

———. "How Playwrights Do—or Don't—Make a Point." *New York Times* 4 December 1980: C17.

While Miller proved with *The Price* that he could write comedy, he failed in *The American Clock* because he was "left suspended between pity and the search for a punch line to make it all better."

King, Francis. "*The American Clock*." *Sunday Telegraph* (London) 10 August 1986. *London Theatre Record* 6.16 (1986): 832.

Positive review of the National Theatre Company production, directed by Peter Wood. Says King, "Since good writing usually brings out good acting, the members of this family are all portrayed with skill."

Kissel, Howard. "*The American Clock*." *Women's Wear Daily* 21 November 1980. *New York Theatre Critics' Reviews* 41 (1980): 82.

Glowing review of New York premiere starring John Randolph and Joan Copeland. Kissel praises *Clock* ("to my mind Miller's best since *A View from the Bridge*") for its "powerful image of the Depression. . . . The sort of evening that revives one's faith in the American theater."

Kroll, Jack. "*After the Fall*." *Newsweek* 1 December 1980: 84. *New York Theatre Critics' Reviews* 41 (1980): 83–84.

Mostly negative review of the New York production of *The American Clock*, which Kroll feels "never finds an effective dramatic shape: it's part play, part chronicle, but mostly it's Miller's last evocation of the images and people that have haunted him more than any other in his life."

Manifold, Gay. "*The American Clock*." *Theatre Journal* 37 (March 1985): 106–107.

Negative review of the Mark Taper Forum's production of *The American Clock*, produced for the Olympic Arts Festival and directed by Gordon Davidson in which Manifold blames Davidson's interpretation that ignored "the darker side of Miller's play, resulting in a production which bears little or no resemblance to Miller's irrational and absurd madhouse."

Morley, Sheridan. "*The American Clock*." *Punch* (London) 20 August 1986. *London Theatre Record* 6.16 (1986): 837.

Lengthy review of the National Theatre Company production, directed by Peter Wood, that Morley praises for its "considerable emotional and documentary power."

Morrison, Blake. "*The American Clock*." *Observer* (London) 10 August 1986. *London Theatre Record* 6.16 (1986): 839.

Morrison calls the National Theatre Company production at the Cottesloe, directed by Peter Wood, "a brisk and entertaining evening with some excellent songs."

Nathan, David. "*The American Clock*." *Jewish Chronicle* (London) 15 August 1986. *London Theatre Record* 6.16 (1986): 838.

While not recognized, says Nathan, "as an important play in America but, having proved to be one over here," *The American Clock* "deserves a transfer to one of the National's larger theatres" from the Cottesloe where it is being performed.

Pascal, Julia. "*The American Clock*." *City Limits* (London) 14 August 1986. *London Theatre Record* 6.16 (1986): 832.

After calling Peter Wood's direction "soft," Pascal berates Miller for his script—"There is something obscene about making glossy entertainment about the suffering of the Depression: it should have an uncomfortable edge."

Pearce, Edward. "*The American Clock*." *Daily Telegraph* (London) 22 December 1986. *London Theatre Record* 6.25–26 (1986): 1398.

Negative review of the National Theatre Company production, moved to the Olivier from the Cottesloe, directed by Peter Wood. Says Pearce, "Supposedly about Jewish life in New York, it had all the Presbyterian qualities—a sermonette three hours long, and Arthur Miller being nostalgic about the bad old days can make three hours seem like six."

Peter, John. "*The American Clock*." *Sunday Times* (London) 10 August 1986.

Lauding the Peter Woods's production of *The American Clock* as "a spellbinding theatrical event," Peter notes that the play "lacks the tight composition and distilled moral indignation of his best-known work," but concludes, "theatrically, it's a treat."

Rich, Frank. "In Political Theater, Soft Campaign Is Best." *New York Times* 26 December 1980: C3.

Rich laments that the "once-promising" *The American Clock* has been ruined in its most recent production by "counter-productive sets."

———. "Play: Miller's *American Clock*." *New York Times* 21 November 1980: Sec. 3: 3. *New York Theatre Critics' Reviews* 41 (1980): 80–81.

Rich bemoans the changes that have been made to Miller's script since its world premiere at the Spoleto Festival in 1979, changes that make the "once beautiful pieces . . . smashed almost beyond recognition . . . he also has injected too much sentimentality, thematic signposting and slapdash comedy." *The American Clock* is a "potentially soaring play that . . . has arrived on Broadway unwound."

———. "Play: Miller's *Clock* at Spoleto U.S.A." *New York Times* 27 May 1980: C7.

Mixed review of the Spoleto premiere of *The American Clock* in which Rich praises the Baum family scenes but expresses his hope that Miller will "cut away the clutter" before the play's New York opening.

Ridley, Clifford A. "An Expansive Tribute to a Nation's Soul." *Philadelphia Inquirer* 20 October 1997: D6.

Favorable review of the Signature Theatre Company's revival of *The American Clock*, directed by James Houghton, that Ridley calls "exhilarating" and "splendid" with "an exemplary cast."

Rissik, Andrew. "*The American Clock*." *Time Out* (London) 13 August 1986. *London Theatre Record* 6.16 (1986): 832.

While there are "some fine and subtle performances from an excellent cast," Rissik dislikes the National Theatre Company production, directed by Peter Wood, as "muddled and tear-stained . . . the characters are vague and generalized, and what they feel comes at us in an absurd wash of pain and disenchantment."

Shorter, Eric. "*The American Clock*." *Daily Telegraph* (London) 9 August 1986. *London Theatre Record* 6.16 (1986): 831.

Shorter laments, in this mixed review of the National Theatre Company production, directed by Peter Wood, that "by showing us so many sides to the thing, Mr. Miller denies himself a chance to rise dramatically above a racy, retrospective run through of the world he knew as a young man."

Shulman, Milton. "*The American Clock*." *London Standard* (London) 7 August 1986. *London Theatre Record* 6.16 (1986): 840.

Mixed review of the National Theatre Company production at the Cottesloe, directed by Peter Wood. Says Shulman, "Miller's saga of people discovering society does not want them has had its didactic painful edges softened by Peter Wood's tactful, fast-moving production."

Siegel, Joel. "*The American Clock*." ABC. WABC, New York. 20 November 1980. *New York Theatre Critics' Reviews* 41 (1980): 84.

Calling the New York production of *The American Clock* "touching, moving, often quite funny," Siegel remarks that it "is not the kind of play you expect from Arthur Miller."

Simon, John. "Agitprop." *New York* 3 November 1997: 54.

Negative review of the Signature Theatre Company's production of *The American Clock*, directed by James Houghton, that Simon feels was "directed with an unstable mixture of artistry and artsiness at a slack pace" with the overall effect 'a blur."

Watt, Douglas. "*American Clock* Ticks Away at Past." *New York Daily News* 21 November 1980. *New York Theatre Critics' Reviews* 41 (1980): 80.

Negative review of premiere production directed by Vivian Matalon and starring Miller's sister Joan Copeland in the role of Rose, a character fashioned on Miller's mother Augusta. While complimenting Copeland for her "warmly engaging performance," Watt decries what he sees as an "oddly unsatisfactory play" that "doesn't work."

Wilson, Edwin. "New Drama by Miller." *Wall Street Journal* 21 November 1980. *New York Theatre Critics' Reviews* 41 (1980): 82.

Wilson explicates the plot of *The American Clock*, praises the acting of Joan Copeland, and muses that the play is "Mr. Miller in a mellow mood. Despite the bleakness, there is a warm glow that suffuses the play."

Winer, Linda. "A Familiar Tick-Tock." *Newsday* 20 October 1997: B2.

Negative review of the Signature Theatre Company revival of *The American Clock*, directed by James Houghton, that Winer says "seems more like good intentions than good theatre."

Wren, Celia. "Miller Time." *Commonweal* 13 February 1998: 21.

The first part of this review is devoted to the Signature Theatre's revival of *The American Clock*, which Wren finds "beautifully directed by the Signature's artistic director, James Houghton," with "writing so concentrated that personalities spring to life in the briefest of spaces." See Wren for review of *A View from the Bridge*.

News Reports, Letters to the Editor, and Related Matter

Calta, Louis. "News of the Stage." *New York Times* 9 September 1973: 58.

News item reporting that Miller will be attending rehearsals of *The American Clock* at the University of Michigan.

“Closing of *The American Clock*.” *New York Times* 2 December 1980: C7.

Brief item announcing that *The American Clock*, directed by Vivian Matalon and playing at the Biltmore Theatre, will be closing after only twelve performances and eleven previews. The play was capitalized with $500,000 and lost the entire investment.

Nathan, David. “*The American Clock*.” *Jewish Chronicle* (London) 26 December 1986. *London Theatre Record* 6.25–26 (1986): 1399.

Brief item announcing that the “superb production” by the National Theatre Company that had been playing at the Cottesloe had moved to the larger Olivier Theatre.

Some Kind of Love Story/Elegy for a Lady

Production Reviews

Billington, Michael. "The Contours of Passion." *Guardian* (London) 25 January 1989: 46. *London Theatre Record* 9.1–2 (1989): 64–65.

Positive review of the London premiere of *Some Kind of Love Story* and *Elegy for a Lady* at the Young Vic, directed by David Thacker and starring Helen Mirren and Bob Peck, that Billington praises for the economy of language—"Miller has lost none of his gift for the resonant phrase"—and elegant design.

Brantley, Ben. "Miller, Mamet and Much in between in Festival of One-Act Plays." *New York Times* 11 May 1996: A11.

Positive review of *Elegy for a Lady*, directed by Curt Dempster and starring Christina Haas and James Murtaugh, produced at the nineteenth annual marathon of one-act plays by the Ensemble Studio Theatre.

Coveney, Michael. "*Two-Way Mirror*." *Financial Times* (London) 14 January 1989: 23. *London Theatre Record* 9.1–2 (1989): 66.

Positive review of *Some Kind of Love Story* and *Elegy for a Lady* at the Young Vic, directed by David Thacker and starring Helen Mirren and Bob Peck. Says Coveney, "At the heart of both plays is the persistent Miller quest for truth in defiance of impertinent interrogation."

Edwardes, Jane. "*Two-Way Mirror*." *Time Out* (London) 1 February 1989. *London Theatre Record* 9.1–2 (1989): 61.

Mixed review of the London premiere of *Some Kind of Love Story* and *Elegy for a Lady* at the Young Vic, directed by David Thacker and starring Helen Mirren and Bob Peck. Says Edwardes, "this is an evening of fragile insights, fleetingly glimpsed, but, like the reflection in the *Two-Way Mirror* of the title, always, in the end, frustratingly just beyond our reach."

Edwards, Christopher. "*Two-Way Mirror*." *Spectator* (London) 28 January 1989. *London Theatre Record* 9.1–2 (1989): 65.

Calling the London premiere of *Some Kind of Love Story* and *Elegy for a Lady* at the Young Vic, directed by David Thacker and starring Helen Mirren and Bob Peck, "a very interesting and dramatically accomplished evening," Edwards praises Miller's plays for their "departure from the kind of plays that made Miller's reputation 40-odd years ago."

Gardner, Lyn. "*Two-Way Mirror*." *City Limits* (London) 2 February 1989. *London Theatre Record* 9.1–2 (1989): 61.
Gardner lambastes the London premiere of *Some Kind of Love Story* and *Elegy for a Lady* at the Young Vic, directed by David Thacker and starring Helen Mirren and Bob Peck, for containing "only high school profundities and a no-man's land of Pinteresque left-overs."

Gener, Randy. "Love Tracks." *Village Voice* 8 May 1996: 71.
Positive review of *Elegy for a Lady*, directed by Curt Dempster and starring Christina Haas and James Murtaugh, produced at the nineteenth annual marathon of one-act plays by the Ensemble Studio Theatre, that Gener calls "exquisite."

Hiley, Jim. "*Two-Way Mirror*." *Listener* (London) 2 February 1989. *London Theatre Record* 9.1–2 (1989): 67.
Negative review of *Some Kind of Love Story* and *Elegy for a Lady* at the Young Vic, directed by David Thacker and starring Helen Mirren and Bob Peck, that Hiley calls "sketchy, introspective material."

Hirschhorn, Clive. "*Two-Way Mirror*." *Sunday Express* (London) 19 January 1989. *London Theatre Record* 9.1–2 (1989): 65–66.
Brief positive review of *Some Kind of Love Story* and *Elegy for a Lady* at the Young Vic, directed by David Thacker and starring Helen Mirren and Bob Peck. Says Hirschhorn, "Minor Miller, to be sure—but that's no cause for complaint."

Hurren, Kenneth. "*Two-Way Mirror*." *Mail on Sunday* (London) 29 January 1989. *London Theatre Record* 9.1–2 (1989): 63.
Hurren praises the plays' fascinating mysteries and brilliant performances in this positive review of the London premiere of *Some Kind of Love Story* and *Elegy for a Lady* at the Young Vic, directed by David Thacker and starring Helen Mirren and Bob Peck.

Jones, Dan. "*Two-Way Mirror*." *Sunday Telegraph* (London) 29 January 1989. *London Theatre Record* 9.1–2 (1989): 66.
Highly laudatory review of *Some Kind of Love Story* and *Elegy for a Lady* at the Young Vic, starring Helen Mirren and Bob Peck.

Says Jones, "These are haunting, poetic plays, and the director, David Thacker, must be congratulated on his handsome, respectful production."

Kelly, Kevin. "Arthur Miller's New Work a Double Disaster." *Boston Globe* 18 November 1982.

Negative review of *2 by A.M.*, directed by Miller at the Long Wharf Theatre. Kelly calls the pair of one-acts and "entirely gratuitous exercise from a dramatist once considered a craftsman," and Miller's directing full of "cheesy grandeur."

Kemp, Peter. "*Two-Way Mirror*." *Independent* (London) 25 January 1989. *London Theatre Record* 9.1–2 (1989): 62.

Negative review of the London premiere of *Some Kind of Love Story* and *Elegy for a Lady* at the Young Vic, directed by David Thacker and starring Helen Mirren and Bob Peck. Says Kemp, the double bill "promises depth, but its lustre—done handsome justice in this highly polished production—is all on the surface."

Morley, Sheridan. "*Two-Way Mirror*." *Herald Tribune* (London) 1 February 1989. *London Theatre Record* 9.1–2 (1989): 64. Rpt. in *Playbill* 31 March 1989: 89.

While conceding that "Miller is the greatest living American dramatist," Morley feels the plays presented at the Young Vic would be better suited as motion pictures.

Nathan, David. "*Two-Way Mirror*." *Jewish Chronicle* (London) 27 January 1989. *London Theatre Record* 9.1–2 (1989): 62.

Positive review of the London premiere of *Some Kind of Love Story* and *Elegy for a Lady* at the Young Vic, directed by David Thacker and starring Helen Mirren and Bob Peck. Likening *Some Kind of Love Story* to a Raymond Chandler mystery and *Elegy for a Lady* to a Pinter conversation piece, Nathan praises Miller for his own "clear, unmistakable" voice—"He uses the influences, they do not use him."

Paton, Maureen. "*Two-Way Mirror*." *Daily Express* (London) 24 January 1989. *London Theatre Record* 9.1–2 (1989): 65.

While Paton laments that the double bill of *Some Kind of Love Story* and *Elegy for a Lady* at the Young Vic, directed by David Thacker and starring Helen Mirren and Bob Peck, is not "exactly vintage Miller," she still recommends the evening as "a marvelous excuse for watching the miraculous Mirren in action."

Piette, Alain. "*Elegy for a Lady* and *Some Kind of Love Story*." *Theatre Journal* 35 (December 1983): 554.

Negative review of both one-acts of the double bill that Piette says "lacks credibility." *Elegy for a Lady* is "poorly developed" and while in *Some Kind of Love Story* "the tempo is quick, the situation original, the language brilliant," Miller has not developed the argument of the play.

Ratcliffe, Michael. "*Two-Way Mirror*." *Observer* (London) 29 January 1989. *London Theatre Record* 9.1–2 (1989): 61.

Positive review of the London premiere of *Some Kind of Love Story* and *Elegy for a Lady* at the Young Vic, directed by David Thacker and starring Helen Mirren and Bob Peck. Says Ratcliffe, the one-act plays "display a masterly craftsmanship and direct human understanding throughout."

Rich, Frank. "2 by Arthur Miller." *New York Times* 10 November 1983: C21.

Rich dislikes Miller's "sledgehammer staging" of his own plays at the Long Wharf Theatre and calls the production, starring Charles Cioffi and Christie Lahti, "a worthy, though unsuccessful experiment in esthetic simplicity by a writer who's prone to big thinking."

Shorter, Eric. "Arthur Miller at New Haven." *Drama* 147 (Spring 1983): 41.

Positive review of the double bill of one-acts, that Shorter says shows at once Miller's "range of talent as a theatrical technician; and the range of his humour as a student of character."

Shulman, Milton. "*Two-Way Mirror*." *Evening Standard* (London) 24 January 1989. *London Theatre Record* 9.1–2 (1989): 67.

In an otherwise positive review of the London premiere of *Some Kind of Love Story* and *Elegy for a Lady* at the Young Vic, directed by David Thacker and starring Helen Mirren and Bob Peck, Shulman laments the order of their presentation.

Spencer, Charles. "*Two-Way Mirror*." *Daily Telegraph* (London) 15 January 1989. *London Theatre Record* 9.1–2 (1989): 63.

Negative review of the London premiere of *Some Kind of Love Story* and *Elegy for a Lady* at the Young Vic, directed by David Thacker and starring Helen Mirren and Bob Peck. Says Spencer, "Throughout the performance one feels there must be more here than meets the eye. It is only later that one suspects that there might actually be a great deal less."

Tinker, Jack. "*Two-Way Mirror*." *Daily Mail* (London) 24 January 1989. *London Theatre Record* 9.1–2 (1989): 62.

Tinker thinks that while the works contained in *Some Kind of Love Story* and *Elegy for a Lady* at the Young Vic, directed by David Thacker and starring Helen Mirren and Bob Peck. are not Miller's greatest achievements, they do, nonetheless, "weave an insistent spell quite beyond their apparent ambition."

Watson, Suzanne. "*Two-Way Mirror*." *What's On* (London) 8 February 1989. *London Theatre Record* 9.1–2 (1989): 63–64.

Negative review of *Some Kind of Love Story* and *Elegy for a Lady* at the Young Vic, directed by David Thacker and starring Helen Mirren and Bob Peck. Their flaw, says Watson, is that "they are undramatic, being dialogues in the mind rather than on the stage. Although gamely performed, they fail to hold the attention and carry the audience on, in the way of his earlier work."

Clara **and** ***I Can't Remember Anything***

Critical Essays in Books

Centola, Steven R. "Temporality, Consciousness, and Transcendence in *Danger: Memory!*" *The Achievement of Arthur Miller: New Essays*. Dallas, Tex.: Contemporary Research, 1995. 135–42.

Offering a Sartrean reading of the double bill of one acts that make up *Danger: Memory!*, Centola concludes that Miller's plays "embody a moral code that celebrates self-determinism and the possibility to live an authentic existence."

Production Reviews

Beaufort, John. "Memories Infuse Two Miller One-Acters." *Christian Science Monitor* 11 February 1987. *New York Theatre Critics' Reviews* 48 (1987): 347.

Even-handed review of premiere production of the double bill of one-acts in which Beaufort remarks, "Whether smooth or rugged, the path down memory lane achieves its destination within the limits the playwright has set himself."

Brustein, Robert. "Danger: Manipulation." *New Republic* 9 March 1987: 26.

While *I Can't Remember Anything* is a "simple and appealing genre piece," *Clara* is a "crude work." Miller, says Brustein, "was so intent on illustrating the frailty of liberalism that he neglected characterization and plot."

Collins, William B. "Arthur Miller's New Plays Explore Memory's Frailties." *Philadelphia Inquirer* 10 February 1987: C5.

Mixed review of the Lincoln Center production of the double bill of one-acts entitled *Danger: Memory!*, directed by Gregory Mosher, starring Geraldine Fitzgerald, Mason Adams, Kenneth McMillan, and James Tolkan. Says Collins, Miller's "voice is muffled, his presence attenuated. And his intentions are not altogether clear."

Curry, Jack. "Miller's *Memory* Isn't Memorable." *USA Today* 9 February 1987. *New York Theatre Critics' Reviews* 48 (1987): 348.

While calling the double bill of one-acts as "disappointing," Curry remarks that *Danger: Memory!* "occasionally recalls the playwright's past brilliance. But in large part these pieces are far from unforgettable."

de Jongh, Nicholas. "*Danger: Memory!*" *Guardian* (London) 8 April 1988. *London Theatre Record* 8.7 (1988): 430.
Negative review in which de Jongh remarks that "no real dramatic flashes, no fresh illuminations, are sparked from this damp-squibbed double bill which reveals Miller playing the amateur psychiatrist."

Edwards, Christopher. "*Danger: Memory!*" *Spectator* (London) 16 April 1988. *London Theatre Record* 8.7 (1988): 429–30.
Edwards feel that the first play in the double bill of one-acts, directed by Jack Gold at the Hampstead Theatre, "fails to find sure rhythm," but that *Clara* "bears the touch of the master in both construction and tone."

Henry, William A., III "Cry from the Heart." *Time* 9 March 1987: 88. *New York Theatre Critics' Reviews* 48 (1987): 347.
Brief essay that favorably reviews the double bill of one-acts, "their contemplative voice is well worth hearing."

Hiley, Jim. "*Danger: Memory!*" *Listener* (London) 21 April 1988. *London Theatre Record* 8.7 (1988): 427.
Hiley finds the double bill of one-acts, directed by Jack Gold at the Hampstead Theatre, to contain "obvious, if inconclusive ideas" with scripts that are not "vintage" Miller.

Hirschhorn, Clive. "*Danger: Memory!*" *Sunday Express* (London) 10 April 1988. *London Theatre Record* 8.7 (1988): 428.
Positive review in which Hirschhorn finds the double bill of one-act plays to be "tightly directed by Jack Gold and well interpreted by its two male leads."

Hurren, Kenneth. "*Danger: Memory!*" *Mail on Sunday* (London) 10 April 1988. *London Theatre Record* 8.7 (1988): 431.
Brief positive review of the British premiere of one-acts that Hurren says, "like everything else Miller writes, it is illuminated by an implacable liberalism underpinned with innate compassion."

Jones, Dan. "*Danger: Memory!*" *Sunday Telegraph* (London) 10 April 1988. *London Theatre Record* 8.7 (1988): 430.
Jones praises the acting of the double bill of one-acts, directed by Jack Gold at the Hampstead Theatre, as "so brilliant as to be educational," but laments that both plays "are hard to put on."

Kissel, Howard. "Good Work in a Lost Cause." *New York Daily News* 9 February 1987. *New York Theatre Critics' Reviews* 48 (1987): 344.

Kissel dislikes both one-act plays but praises the actors and director Gregory Mosher for "surmounting" the challenges presented by Miller's plays.

Lida, David. "*Danger: Memory!* —A Review." *Women's Wear Daily* 9 February 1987. *New York Theatre Critics' Reviews* 48 (1987): 346.

Lida praises the acting and the directing of the double bill of one-acts but criticizes both of Miller's plays for their didactic nature—"Throughout his career, one of the marks of Miller's work has been his compulsion to preach—to tell and not show what his plays are about. It is as if he doesn't trust his audience to get it if they aren't told."

Maxwell, Sharon. "*Danger: Memory!*" *Jewish Chronicle* (London) 22 April 1988. *London Theatre Record* 8.7 (1988): 428.

Maxwell laments that usually "a new play by Arthur Miller is always an event," but "sadly, *Danger: Memory!* at the Hampstead Theatre, which is, in fact, two plays fails to live up to expectations."

Morley, Sheridan. "*Danger: Memory!*" *Punch* (London) 22 April 1988. *London Theatre Record* 8.7 (1988): 427.

Morley labels the two one-acts, enjoying their British premiere at Hampstead, directed by Jack Gold, as having "the fascination of late sketches by a master painter of the human condition."

Morrison, Blake. "*Danger: Memory!*" *Observer* (London) 10 April 1988. *London Theatre Record* 8.7 (1988): 431.

Positive review of the British premiere of the double bill of one-acts, directed by Jack Gold. Says Morrison, "In both pieces characters with a compulsion to forget are brought up against unpleasant truths by a friendly accuser: from this simple Freudian premise Miller constructs two complex realist dramas which show his creative powers, at 73, still in full spate."

Radin, Victoria. "*Danger: Memory!*" *New Statesman* (London) 14 April 1988. *London Theatre Record* 8.7 (1988): 429.

In this mixed review of the double bill of one-acts, Radin says that *I Can't Remember Anything* is "elliptical and strange" and "has a kind of raw, unshaped honesty that nearly always captures the grain of lived experience," while *Clara* is "thicker and more endearing but less frank."

Rich, Frank. "The Stage: Arthur Miller's *Danger Memory!*" *New York Times* 9 February 1987. *New York Theatre Critics' Reviews* 48 (1987): 343–44.

Mostly negative review of the double bill of one-acts (*I Can't Remember Anything* and *Clara*) staged at the Mitzi E. Newhouse Theatre by Gregory Mosher. Rich calls Miller's writing "studied and ponderous" and "an evening in which the pontificator wins out over the playwright."

Richards, David. "Memory & the Message." *Washington Post* 22 February 1987: F1.

Mixed review of Lincoln Center premiere, directed by Gregory Mosher at the Mitzi E. Newhouse Theater, in which Richards concludes that the double bill of one-act plays "may not stand very tall on its own, but it does not violate a career. It belongs."

Robinson, Tim. "*Danger: Memory!*" *City Limits* (London) 14 April 1988. *London Theatre Record* 8.7 (1988): 428.

Robinson feels that Miller's new double bill of one-acts, currently enjoying its British premiere at the Hampstead Theatre, directed by Jack Gold, is not up to the playwright's past level of accomplishment. Says Robinson, "Both deal—entertainingly, it can't be denied—with lives diminished, which in the light of Miller's past achievements, seems uncannily to hold up a mirror to a talent diminished."

Rogoff, Gordon. "Treadmiller." *Village Voice* 17 February 1987: 99.

While finding Gregory Mosher's production at the Newhouse "respectable enough," Rogoff laments that the double bill of one-acts is "neither here nor there." It contains "realism without reality, [and] sincere acting from everyone without explosions into clarity that might conceivably rescue the plays from the prevailing murk."

Romain, Michael. "*Danger: Memory!*" *What's On* (London) 13 April 1988. *London Theatre Record* 8.7 (1988): 428.

Highly positive review of the British premiere, directed by Jack Gold at the Hampstead Theatre, that Romain says shows Miller "to be writing in a new, more austere and abstract style. *Clara* is his most concentrated play since *The Prince* [sic], and is indeed worth the price of admission in itself."

Rose, Helen. "*Danger: Memory!*" *Time Out* (London) 13 April 1988. *London Theatre Record* 8.7 (1988): 427.

Mixed review of the British premiere of Miller's double bill of one-acts, at the Hampstead, which Rose feels owes its success to its director—"Jack Gold's clear, unfussy direction balances the uneven weight of the plays, bringing a combined sense of understanding to both."

Sauvage, Leo. "*Danger: Memory.*" *New Leader* 9–23 February 1987: 17.

Sauvage considers the double bill on one-acts, appearing at Lincoln Center, to be "poorly directed" by Gregory Mosher. *I Can't Remember Anything* has vague symbolism and *Clara* is "spoiled by Miller's irrelevant preoccupation with ethics and ethnicity."

Simon, John. "*Danger: Memory.*" *New York* 23 February 1987: 127–28.

Simon calls Miller's double bill of one-acts "so flaccid and lackluster that one questions whether they are about anything beyond Miller's desire to maintain his undeserved reputation as a dramatist."

Stasio, Marilyn. "Miller at Grips with Memory." *New York Post* 9 February 1987. *New York Theatre Critics' Reviews* 48 (1987): 346.

In a negative review of both one-act plays, Stasio remarks that "neither one has been filled in with characters or ideas of sufficient substance."

Taylor, Paul. "*Danger: Memory!*" *Independent* (London) 8 April 1988. *London Theatre Record* 8.7 (1988): 428–29.

Taylor lauds the double bill of one-acts as "beautifully directed" by Jack Gold, but admits that the structure of *Clara* "feels false," and *I Can't Remember Anything* treads "a wobbly line between the broad comedy of a review sketch and something much darker and more ineffable."

Tinker, Jack. "*Danger: Memory!*" *Daily Mail* (London) 12 April 1988. *London Theatre Record* 8.7 (1988): 427–28.

Tinker admits to a certain amount of confusion over the British premiere of one-acts, directed by Jack Gold, and partly blames the "woefully miscast" actors and particularly Betsy Blair who "consequently can do little for a role for which Nature had intended the likes of Katherine Hepburn."

Wallach, Allan. "Miller's New One-Acts Evoke Memories." *Newsday* 9 February 1987. *New York Theatre Critics' Reviews* 48 (1987): 345.

Negative review of both plays—"Neither play has the texture or specificity that would make its subject fresh and arresting. . . . We're reminded of the days when Miller wrote with an authority that these sketchy and insubstantial plays approach only in sporadic phases."

Watt, Douglas. "Another Round of Miller Light." *New York Daily News* 19 February 1987. *New York Theatre Critics' Reviews* 48 (1987): 344–45.

Mixed review of the "two slight playlets under the blanket title *Danger: Memory!*" in which Watt remarks that while the twin bill "hardly makes for a stimulating evening," "both works are effortful . . . but this is low-key Miller and probably deserving of no more than the four weeks allotted it in the cozy underground Newhouse Theatre."

Related Interviews and Profiles (not with Miller)

Frymer, Murry. "The Delicate Work of Color-Blind Casting Working toward a Universal Theater." *San Jose Mercury News* 7 October 1990: 4.

In an article on Edward Hasting (artistic director of the American Conservatory Theater) and his interest in nontraditional casting, Miller is mentioned as having been approached by Hastings to give permission to cast the part of a New York Jewish policeman in *Clara* with a black man. Miller is reported as being enthusiastic about the idea and even rewrote a few lines to fit the change.

The Ride Down Mount Morgan

Critical Essays in Books

Schlueter, June. "Scripting the Closing Scene: Arthur Miller's *The Ride Down Mount Morgan*." *The Achievement of Arthur Miller: New Essays*. Ed. Steven Centola. Dallas, Tex.: Contemporary Research, 1995. 143–50. Rpt. as "*The Ride Down Mount Morgan*: Scripting the Closing Scene." *Dramatic Closure*. Rutherford, N.J.: Fairleigh Dickinson UP, 1995.

Schlueter offers a close reading of Miller's *The Ride Down Mount Morgan* as a play "preoccupied with (con)testing" its ending, "in which the contours of the real are difficult to define." Further, she states, the main character (Lyman Felt) "stands as a model of a playwright whose artistic options diminish as the play progresses and who finally falls victim to the historical force of the final scene."

Critical Essays in Journals and Magazines

Centola, Steven R. "'How to Contain the Impulse of Betrayal:' A Sartrean Reading of *The Ride Down Mount Morgan*." *American Drama* 6.1 (Fall 1996): 14–28.

In an effort to help clarify "some of the apparent inconsistencies within the play" and to illustrate "how the dialectical tension that underlies and unifies the play's comic and moral elements" to reveal "the depth and magnitude of Miller's artistic vision," Centola offers a Sartrean reading of *The Ride Down Mount Morgan.*

Grecco, Stephen. "Theater." *World Literature Today* 67.2 (Spring 1993): 383.

In this review of the print version of *The Ride Down Mount Morgan*, Grecco praises the work as "Miller's most significant dramatic work in four decades. . . . The play is Arthur Miller at his wittiest and philosophically most profound and adds considerable luster to his reputation as a dramatist of the first rank."

Reitz, Bernhard. "From Loman to Lyman: Arthur Miller's Comedy." *Contemporary Drama in English: New Forms of Comedy*. Trier: WVT Wissenschaftlicher Verlag Trier, 1994. 93–105.

Paper given at the second annual conference of the German Society for Contemporary Theatre and Drama in English. After briefly discussing the similarities in form and content between *The Ride Down Mount Morgan* and *Death of a Salesman*, Reitz explores Miller's use of the tragicomic structure in *Mount. Morgan* to reveal the ethical, societal and psychological dimensions of protagonist Lyman Felt.

Critical Essays in Newspapers

Joffee, Linda. "London Theater Puts New York in the Shadows." *Christian Science Monitor* 13 January 1992: Arts: 10.

Joffee examines the reasons why Miller chose to premiere his new play *The Ride Down Mount Morgan* in London instead of New York.

Production Reviews

Bayley, Clare. "*The Ride Down Mount Morgan*." *What's On* (London) 6 November 1991. *Theatre Record* 11.22 (1991): 1348.

Mixed review of the premiere production, directed by Michael Blakemore. Says Bayley, "A gratuitously complicated set and some peculiar blocking serve as minor irritants in an otherwise pleasurable evening. Despite sticky moments (such as a ridiculous *Iron John*-style moment of masculine initiation with a lion), its smooth-sliding construction, well-oiled with *bon mots*, glides you through this good, but not great play."

Billington, Michael. "*The Ride Down Mount Morgan*." *Guardian* (London) 1 November 1991. *Theatre Record* 11.22 (1991): 1351.

While Billington recognizes that *The Ride Down Mount Morgan* is "a fierce critique" on contemporary values and praises the play for having "plenty of shrewd and pungent things to say about our sanctification of self," he laments that "the narrative is not strong enough to support the ideas."

Brantley, Ben. "Arthur Miller, Still Feeling the Pain After the Fall." *New York Times* 25 July 1996: C13.

A favorable review of the Williamstown Theatre Festival production of the American premiere of *The Ride Down Mount Morgan* directed by Scott Elliott. Brantley finds that the play "offers a fascinating testament to one author's constancy of vision and his abiding willingness to experiment to put it over."

———. "Sure, Devoted to His Wife: Question Is, Which One?" *New York Times* 17 November 1998: E1.

Unfavorable review of the Public Theatre's production starring Patrick Stewart and Frances Conroy. Says Brantley, the play "smells musty, despite the physical elegance of the director David Esbjornson's production and the compelling performances. . . . [it] brings to mind a host of more vivid works about the desperation of male menopause . . . with the attendant sense that Mr. Miller has really brought nothing new to the table."

Brustein, Robert. "The Ride Down Mount Rushmore." *New Republic* 16 September 1996: 30–31. Rpt. as "Aspects of Arthur Miller." *Cultural Calisthenics: Writings on Race, Politics, and Theatre.* Chicago: Ivan R. Dee, 1998. 78–81.

Favorable review of the American premiere production of *The Ride Down Mount Morgan* presented at the Williamstown Theatre Festival. Brustein seems genuinely surprised by the play's loose structure and humor, and calls Miller's work "engaging" and "an exhilarating journey."

Canby, Vincent. "A Modest Star Shines Brightly." *New York Times* 22 November 1998: Sec. 2: 8.

Positive review of the Public Theatre production of *The Ride Down Mount Morgan* that Canby calls "the most thoroughly involving new Miller play that I have seen in years" that "deserves your attention, and soon."

Cassidy, Suzanne. "Miller Play Divides the Critics in London." *New York Times* 5 November 1991: C13.

News item reporting the various mixed reviews that the London premiere of *The Ride Down Mount Morgan* has received thus far. Excerpts of various critical commentary are included.

Christopher, James. "*The Ride Down Mount Morgan*." *Time Out* (London) 6 November 1991. *Theatre Record* 11.22 (1991): 1352.

Negative review of the premiere production, directed by Michael Blakemore. Says Christopher, "It's a fascinating and not unmoving play with many disparate themes and emotions rippling beneath the skin; but as it stands emotional catharsis doesn't come much more confused than this."

Coveney, Michael. "*The Ride Doun Mount Morgan*." *Observer* (London) 3 November 1991. *Theatre Record* 11.22 (1991): 1348-49. Rpt. as "Arthur Miller Disappoints His Faithful British Fans." *San Jose Mercury News* 10 November 1991: 9.

Negative review of the London premiere of *Ride Down Mount Morgan* at the Wyndham Theatre, starring Tom Conti, Gemma Jones, and Clare Higgins, directed by Michael Blakemore. Says Coveney, "the writing is flat, the dilemmas and arguments stupefyingly banal."

Dodd, Ian. "*The Ride Down Mount Morgan*." *Tribune* (London) 15 November 1991. *Theatre Record* 11.22 (1991): 1352.

Highly negative review of the premiere production, directed by Michael Blakemore. Says Dodd, "The play's underlying ambiguity is deliberately destabilizing, so that the hospitalized, semi-conscious Lyman, and by extension the audience, is uncertain whether what he is actually experiencing is real or imagined. Well it's real and it's called boredom."

Eck, Michael. "WTF's *Mount Morgan* Is Pure Arthur Miller." *Times Union* (Albany) 24 July 1996: D6.

Mixed review of the Williamstown Theatre Festival production, directed by Scott Elliott and starring F. Murray Abraham and Michael Learned. Says Eck, "*Mount Morgan* is impressive, but not in the same league as his best plays. It is a good play, not a great play, and perhaps unfairly we have come to expect greatness from our legends."

Edwards, Christopher. "*The Ride Down Mount Morgan*." *Spectator* (London) 9 November 1991. *Theatre Record* 11.22 (1991): 1352.

Mixed review of the premiere production, in which Edwards praises *The Ride Down Mount Morgan* as "a telling, at times very funny examination of spiritual emptiness" but decries that "Miller tries to spin it out beyond its dramatic foundations."

Feingold, Michael. "Felt and Unfelt." *Village Voice* 1 December 1998: 137.

Mostly negative review of the Public Theatre's production starring Patrick Stewart and Frances Conroy. Faulting the script while praising the acting, Feingold remarks, "All it says morally is that a dishonest man can be a charmer. This isn't exactly hot news, and Miller has, disquietingly, structured his play to go no further."

Goldfarb, Michael. "Mixed Reviews in London." *Newsday* 4 November 1991: II: 53.

Synopsis of mixed reviews for the premiere production of *The Ride Down Mount Morgan* at the Wyndham Theatre in London. Of note is Miller's comparison of his collaboration with director Michael Blakemore with the working relationship he had with Elia Kazan several decades earlier.

Goldstein, Herbert. "*The Ride Down Mount Morgan*: Arthur Miller's Transcendent Masterpiece." *The Arthur Miller Society Newsletter* (June 1999): 14–15.

Goldstein praises the American premiere of *The Ride Down Mount Morgan* at the Williamstown Theatre Festival as a "masterpiece" that has "transcended his earlier work." Says Goldstein, "Miller brings us a powerful, resolute, and clear-eyed depiction of not one or two characters, but a group of people who search the destructiveness of their own exploitive living, and suffer the impact of sudden and forceful recognition."

Greer, Herb. "*Mount Morgan* a Bumpy Ride." *Washington Times* 24 November 1991: D8.

Greer dislikes *The Ride Down Mount Morgan*, premiering in London at the Wyndham Theatre, starring Tom Conti, because "it does not have a plot. Rather, it has a situation—a man with tow wives—that Mr. Miller tries to expand with solemn moral commentary while working the material for laughs."

Gross, John. "*The Ride Down Mount Morgan*." *Sunday Telegraph* (London) 3 November 1991. *Theatre Record* 11.22 (1991): 1350.

Gross admits to being pleasantly surprised by the premiere production of *The Ride Down Mount Morgan*, a play with "a good deal of humour, some frisky dialogue, even quite a few respectable wisecracks. Still, Miller is Miller. He cannot help taking his characters seriously, and on the whole—on this occasion, at least —I was rather glad of it. Their moral dilemmas may not be as gripping as he intends, but the details of the story are undeniably interesting. You are never deeply moved but you are almost always absorbed."

Henry, W. A., III. "Arthur Miller, Old Hat at Home, Is a London Hit." *Time* 11 November 1991: 100–101.

Highly laudatory review of the West End premiere of *The Ride Down Mount Morgan* that Henry calls "Robustly funny, full of fantasy and hallucination yet easy to follow, it is free of the world-weary, elegiac tone of the four slight one-acts that had been Miller's sole stage output in the previous decade."

Hirschhorn, Clive. "*The Ride Down Mount Morgan*." *Sunday Express* (London) 3 November 1991. *Theatre Record* 11.22 (1991): 1352.

Mixed review of the premiere production that Hirschhorn says is "non-vintage Miller, but definitely worth seeing."

Hurren, Kenneth. "*The Ride Down Mount Morgan*." *Mail on Sunday* (London) 3 November 1991. *Theatre Record* 11.22 (1991): 1347.

While admitting that the play has "nagging flaws" such as "the situation's dependence on money (it wouldn't work if Lyman were not rich) and its implicit sexism (it wouldn't work, either, with the sexes reversed"), Hurren praises the premiere production, directed by Michael Blakemore and starring Tom Conti, as "consistently entertaining" and "certainly Miller's funniest play."

Kaufman, David. "Peak Performance: What a *Ride*! Arthur Miller's *Mount Morgan* Is Funny & Profound." *Daily News* 17 November 1998.

Positive review of the New York debut at the Public Theatre of *The Ride Down Mount Morgan*, directed by David Esbjornson and starring Patrick Stewart and Frances Conroy. Kaufman lauds all aspects of the production, calling it "some of Miller's best writing in decades."

Koenig, Rhoda. "*The Ride Down Mount Morgan*." *Punch* (London) 13 November 1991. *Theatre Record* 11.22 (1991): 1351.

Negative review of the premiere production, directed by Michael Blakemore, that Koenig calls "a sort of bad-taste rerun of *Whose Life Is This Anyway?* that "settles down to a cosy evening of rambling harangues and flashbacks that tell us what we already know or add nothing of interest."

Kuchwara, Michael. "Less Tragic, Willy Loman-Like *Ride*." *Washington Times* 29 November 1998: D4.

Kuchwara praises the off-Broadway production at the Joseph Papp Public Theatre, starring Patrick Stewart, as a "robust if occasionally overdone play" with a "terrific cast" and a "fluid, carefully crafted production."

Morley, Sheridan. "*The Ride Down Mount Morgan*." *Herald Tribune* (London) 6 November 1991. *Theatre Record* 11.22 (1991): 1347.

Mixed review of the premiere production directed by Michael Blakemore. Says Morley, "In the Miller canon this is the closest we have come back to *After the Fall*," but the play "lacks the range and passion of that earlier semi-memoir. There is elegance and wit and shrewd analysis here, but a feeling also that the action is taking place in another part of that 14-room house."

Nathan, David. "*The Ride Down Mount Morgan*." *Jewish Chronicle*(London) 8 November 1991. *Theatre Record* 11.22 (1991): 1350–51.

Nathan praises the premiere production, directed by Michael Blakemore, for providing "comforting reassurance that it is possible to be 76 years old and not be ossified under a carapace of smug certainties."

Nightingale, Benedict. "*The Ride Down Mount Morgan*." *The Times* (London) 2 November 1991. *Theatre Record* 11.22 (1991): 1348.

Calling Tom Conti's performance as Lyman Felt "far too casual and relaxed," Nightingale criticizes the premiere production, directed by Michael Blakemore as "sadly lacking" and for not taking seriously "the feelings of the female characters." Says Nightingale, "the prime problem is the play. Under the pretension, all Miller is doing is putting the familiar excuses for adultery. Despite the *frisson* given by bigamy, the only real difference is that this man has married his mistress. Peter Nichols wrote much better about essentially the same conflicts in *Passion Play*. Why not revive that?"

Paton, Maureen. "*The Ride Down Mount Morgan*." *Daily Express* (London) 1 November 1991. *Theatre Record* 11.22 (1991): 1347–48.

Calling *The Ride Down Mount Morgan* "the most sexually explicit play of Arthur Miller's distinguished career," Paton praises the work for its depth—"Here he confronts the eternal verities: Love, death, sex and insurance. The drama is painfully funny, suffused with sadness and sometimes scandalously acute."

Peter, John. "A Change of Scene for Mellow Miller." *Sunday Times* (London) 3 November 1991. *Theatre Record* 11.22 (1991): 1350.

Peter praises Tom Conti for his "superb portrait of a man in search of both guilt and salvation," and Miller for writing "with all the vigor and agility of the commercial theatre at its most irresistible."

Shulman, Milton. "*The Ride Down Mount Morgan*." *Evening Standard* (London) 1 November 1991. *Theatre Record* 11.22 (1991): 1348.

Positive review of the premiere production, directed by Michael Blakemore and starring Tom Conti, that Shulman praises for Miller's "skill and wit to make these characters intriguing, in spite of their small-minded possessiveness, and compelling, in spite of their stubborn faith in the omniscience of social standards. He turns an American tragedy into an ironic and amusing paradox."

Shuttleworth, Ian. "*The Ride Down Mount Morgan*." *City Limits* (London) 7 November 1991. *Theatre Record* 11.22 (1991): 1352.

Brief negative review of the premiere production, directed by Michael Blakemore and starring Tom Conti, that Shuttleworth says "feels like standing in a stone circle: impressively majestic, but the runes are indecipherable and probably not that profound anyway."

Siegel, Ed. "Miller Goes on *Ride* of Mirth, Morals." *Boston Globe* 23 July 1996: D1.

Positive review of the Williamstown Theatre Festival's production of *The Ride Down Mount Morgan*, directed by Scott Elliott and starring F. Murray Abraham, Michael Learned, and Patricia Clarkson. Siegel finds the play "an accomplished, forceful piece of playwriting. It feels thoroughly funny and contemporary without giving in to some of the drearier, smirkier conventions of postmodern playwriting."

Simon, John. "Queasy Rider." *New York* 30 November 1998: 124.

Negative review of the American premiere of *The Ride Down Mount Morgan* at the Public Theatre, starring Patrick Stewart and directed by David Esbjornson. Says Simon, "Miller can write effective lines—atrocious grammar aside—but these are balanced by others that are no more than senescent masturbation." A production that is "equally desperate and dull."

Spencer, Charles. "*The Ride Down Mount Morgan*." *Daily Telegraph* (London) 1 November 1991. *Theatre Record* 11.22 (1991): 1350.

Negative review of the premiere production, directed by

Michael Blakemore, in which Spencer admits to having "high hopes" that the play "would display a fine late flowering of Arthur Miller's talent," but acknowledges that, instead, it only "serves as a painful reminder of just how long ago he wrote the plays on which his reputation rests."

Stearns, David P. "Arthur Miller's Wry View from *Mount Morgan*." *USA Today* 25 August 1996: B9.

Favorable review of the Williamstown Theatre Festival production of *The Ride Down Mount Morgan*, directed by Scott Elliott and starring F. Murray Abraham, Michael Learned, and Patricia Clarkson. Says Stearns, Miller's play is "a wise, provocative, salty, above all funny new play."

———. "Missing the Mark on *Mount Morgan*." *USA Today* 16 November 1998: D3.

Stearns praises the Public Theatre's New York debut of Miller's play as "a vigorous, barbed comedy encompassing nearly everything wrong with the male gender," but laments that it "is crippled by an eye-rollingly broad production . . . and yet another badly misjudged stage performance by Patrick Stewart."

StClair, William. "My Book of the Year." *Financial Times* (London) 7 December 1991: 16.

In a list of books nominated as good reads by writers and critics, StClair recommends the published version of *The Ride Down Mount Morgan*. Says StClair, "In the hands of the master dramatist the action shifts effortlessly between words and thoughts, through past and present." Of note is the large black-and-white photograph of Miller from *Passage*, a retrospective of the work of American photographer Irving Penn.

St. George, Andrew. "*The Ride Down Mount Morgan*." *Financial Times* (London) 2 November 1991. *Theatre Record* 11.22 (1991): 1349.

Positive review of the premiere production, directed by Michael Blakemore and starring Tom Conti. Says St. George, "The writing is lighter than vintage Miller, rarely political, less visceral and more attuned to the surfaces of life. The plot never stirs, for the situation is everything: comedy if one thinks, tragedy if one feels. The result is an immensely satisfying evening's theater."

Sutcliffe, Thomas. "*The Ride Down Mount Morgan*." *Independent* (London) 2 November 1991. *Theatre Record* 11.22 (1991): 1349.

Negative review of the premiere production, directed by Michael Blakemore and starring Tom Conti. Says Sutcliffe, "What's missing is the sturdy simplicity of Miller's great plays, their willingness to risk banality. With its brisk one-liners and fretwork of moral conflicts, *The Ride Down Mount Morgan* is studiously self-conscious, busy with its own thoughts as though none of Miller's marginal calculations have been excluded from the final work."

Usher, Shaun. "*The Ride Down Mount Morgan*." *Daily Mail* (London) 1 November 1991. *Theatre Record* 11.22 (1991): 1351.

Usher says that Miller's first new work in a decade, "if not miraculous, is a mildly startling, extremely entertaining, mind-flexing surprise," and urges his readers to "hurry to share a notoriously serious dramatist's fresh incarnation as architect of a laughter-filled maze in which frail humans are laid low by selfishness and paradoxes."

Wardle, Irving. "*The Ride Down Mount Morgan*." *Independent on Sunday* (London) 3 November 1991. *Theatre Record* 11.22 (1991): 1346.

Wardle chides the premiere production, directed by Michael Blakemore as "stupefying" and "but for Miller's artistic rank and personal popularity, *Mount Morgan* would not have found a theatre."

Weber, Bruce. "Arthur Miller Takes a Poke at a Devil with 2 Lives." *New York Times* 10 April 2000: E1.

Calling the Broadway production of *The Ride Down Mount Morgan*, starring Patrick Stewart and directed by David Esbjornson, a "seriously discomforting comedy," Weber paises the work as "a pretty good poke in the side."

Winer, Linda. "A Daring *Ride Down Mt. Morgan*." *Newsday* 17 November 1998: B2.

Highly laudatory review of the American premiere of *The Ride Down Mount Morgan* at the Public Theatre, starring Patrick Stewart and directed by David Esbjornson. Says Winer, "Everyone is vulgar and hilarious, selfish and giving, ridiculous and quite grand in this generous play about the tragic and wondrous unknowability of the human creature."

Wolf, Matt. "Miller and Hare in Less than Top Form." *American Theatre* (January 1992): 52–53.

Critiques of the London productions of *Ride Down Mount Morgan* and David Hare's *Murmuring Judges*.

Related Interviews and Profiles (not with Miller)

Pacheco, Patrick. "Arthur Miller and the Life of a Playwright." *Newsday* 12 November 1998: B9.

Patrick Stewart, opening as Lyman Felt in *The Ride Down Mount Morgan* at the Public Theatre, is asked to comment about Arthur Miller's number one rank in the National Theatre survey of English Language Dramatists.

Rothstein, Mervyn. "Patrick Stewart's Unfinished Business." *New York Times* 2 April 2000: Sec. 2: 7.

Interview conducted on the occasion of the opening of the Broadway premiere of *The Ride Down Mount Morgan*. Stewart responds to questions regarding his approach to the role of Lyman Felt, his accident while playing the role at the Public Theatre in 1998, and his feelings regarding doing the play a second time.

Shewey, Don. "How to Be a Producer, in One Instant Lesson." *New York Times* 14 July 1996: Sec. 2: 5.

This article details the summer theatre festival in Williamstown, focusing on the American premiere of *The Ride Down Mount Morgan*. Shewey quotes director Scott Elliott, star F. Murray Abraham, and Miller who each offer a positive spin on the production.

News Reports, Letters to the Editor, and Related Matter

Barron, James. "Public Lives." *New York Times* 22 October 1998: B2.

Brief news item reporting that Blythe Danner has quit the New York premiere production of *The Ride Down Mount Morgan* (starring Patrick Stewart) due to "a personal family matter."

McKinley, Jesse. "Patrick Stewart in Miller's *Ride*." *New York Times* 19 November 1999: E2.

Item reporting that actor Patrick Stewart has agreed to return as Lyman Felt in Miller's *The Ride Down Mount Morgan* in March of 2000 for a limited run. Inspired by the previous year's sold-out run at the Public Theatre, Miller was inspired to revive the play.

"The enthusiasm was so high," he said, "We're all a little nutty about it."

"New Miller Play on the Way." *Atlanta Constitution* 14 August 1991: B3.

Brief news item announcing that the world premiere of Miller's "latest work" will take place in London at the Wyndham Theatre, starring Tom Conti. Miller's explanation for the non-American first showing is that there is more of a theatre culture in London as well as "actors of a certain caliber."

"Patrick Stewart Takes Curtain Call." *Sunday Mercury* 10 January 1999: 40.

News item reporting that during the final seconds of a performance of *The Ride Down Mount Morgan*, Patrick Stewart was struck on the head by a falling metal bolt that cut his scalp. Stewart, unaware that he was bleeding profusely, had taken his curtain call in order to show his girlfriend in the audience that he was all right. Unfortunately, because of the gruesome bleeding, his curtain call startled and frightened the audience instead.

Pogrebin, Robin. "Shuberts Turn to Union In Dispute with Stewart." *New York Times* 3 May 2000: B1.

News item announcing that the producers of *The Ride Down Mount Morgan* have filed charges against Patrick Stewart and the stage actors union for the curtain speech that Stewart made the prvious Saturday "accusing the producers of failing to promote the play adequately."

The Last Yankee

Critical Essays in Journals and Magazines

Abbotson, Susan C. W. "Reconnecting and Reasserting the Self: The Art of Compromise in Arthur Miller's *The Last Yankee*." *South Atlantic Review* 63.4 (Fall 1998): 58–76.

Abbotson offers a close reading of the two-scene version of *The Last Yankee* to expose its urgent central message that seeks to explode "false myths of American society (materialism, complete happiness, and the easy life) and tries to lead people toward a truer American spirit which [Miller] sees evidenced in the Constitution and the Bill of Rights."

Production Reviews

Corliss, Richard. "Attention Must Be Paid." *Time* 8 February 1993: 72. *New York Theatre Critics' Reviews* 54 (1993): 25–26.

Positive review of the Manhattan Theatre Club's production and Miller's script as "poignant." Corliss concludes that "it is just a sketch, really—some lines that reveal the contours of a soul. In his final days, Matisse did work like this."

Edwardes, Jane. "*The Last Yankee.*" *Time Out* (London) 12 May 1993. *Theatre Record* 13.9 (1993): 489.

Positive review of London production, directed by David Thacker, and starring Peter Davison, Helen Burns, David Healy, and Margot Leicester (playing at the Duke of York's), that Edwardes says "is a frustrating slither of a play barely an hour and a half long with an abrupt ending, but Miller's slither is more potent than many other playwright's weighty chunk."

Feingold, Michael. "Post-Miller Time." *Village Voice* 2 February 1993. *New York Theatre Critics' Reviews* 54 (1993): 27.

Negative review of *The Last Yankee* (Manhattan Theatre Club production) in which Feingold faults Miller's play as "a leftover cry from a world that has long ceased to exist."

Gerard, Jeremy. "*The Last Yankee.*" *Variety* 25 January 1993. *New York Theatre Critics' Reviews* 54 (1993): 26.

Mixed review of the Manhattan Theatre Club's production that Gerard calls "Sketchy, oddly selective about the details of these four characters' lives and somewhat trapped in a '50s social sensibility, *The Last Yankee* nevertheless feels dead right in its depiction of two marriages a generation apart."

Hart, Steven. "*The Last Yankee*." *Theatre Journal* 46 (May 1994): 277–78.

After reviewing the "univocal and negative" critical response to the original production of *The Last Yankee* by the Manhattan Theatre Club, Hart investigates the Spoleto Festival's production, which "offers a different view of the play's central images."

Hasell, Graham. "*The Last Yankee*." *What's On* 1(London) 2 May 1993. *Theatre Record* 13.9 (1993): 489.

In this otherwise positive review of the London production, directed by David Thacker and playing at the Duke of York's, Hasell questions Miller's treatment of women in the script—"what I missed here was any suggestion that patriarchal society may be to blame: asked why the two depressives in the play were both women, Miller has said it's 'because the people I know with depression are women.' He gives no credence to the fact that the women's problem is to do with having to live their lives vicariously through their husbands."

Hemming, Sarah. "Worth Getting Out of Bed for." *Independent* (London) 12 May 1993: 14. *Theatre Record* 13.9 (1993): 488.

Positive review of London production of *The Last Yankee*, directed by David Thacker, that Hemming calls a "fine production" of "a play full of uncomfortable truths and brilliantly observed humour."

Kingston, Jeremy. "*The Last Yankee*." *The Times* (London) 6 May 1993. *Theatre Record* 13.9 (1993): 489.

Kingston praises the London production, directed by David Thacker and playing at the Duke of York's, as "finely paced . . . the effect of watching these troubled lives is far from dispiriting."

Kirkpatrick, Melanie. "Arthur Miller, Alive and Home Again." *Wall Street Journal* 27 January 1993: A14. *New York Theatre Critics' Reviews* 54 (1993): 23.

Highly laudatory review of the Manhattan Theatre production, starring John Heard and Frances Conroy, directed by John Tillinger, that Kirkpatrick calls "simultaneously funny and tragic, sobering and uplifting . . . the work of a master craftsman and is testament to Mr. Miller's genius at elevating ordinary events into poetry."

Kissel, Howard. "*Yankee* Explores Rebirth of Nation." *Daily News* 22 January 1993. *New York Theatre Critics' Reviews* 54 (1993): 29.

Kissel praises Miller's *The Last Yankee* (Manhattan Theatre Club production) as "fitting" and "especially remarkable. . . . For most of his career, Miller has written symphonies. It is nice to see that, rather than abandoning composition, he can fashion a well-wrought piece of chamber music."

McNeil, Helen. "Pictures from an Institution." *Times Literary Supplement* (London) 5 February 1993: 17.

McNeil lauds Miller's play, directed by David Thacker and playing at the Young Vic in London, as "the most moving of all the recent lessons by the master, and one well worth seeing in David Thacker's vivid production."

Morley, Sheridan. "In *Last Yankee* Miller Is Taking American Pulse." *International Herald Tribune* (London) 3 February 1993: n.p.

Positive review of the David Thacker production, starring Peter Davison, Zoe Wanamaker, David Healy, and Helen Burns at the Young Vic, that Morley calls a "thoughtful, resonant production with an immaculate cast."

Nightingale, Benedict. "Dark Side of the American Dream." *Times* (London) 28 January 1993: n.p.

Nightingale has mixed feeling regarding the David Thacker production playing at the Young Vic Theatre. While the work is "not very well constructed," a "bit sketchy," and "somewhat underwritten," Nightingale admits to being left "impressed and moved; and not, I think, just because of the deft, concentrated acting of David Thacker's cast."

Oliver, Edith. "Yankee Doodling." *New Yorker* 1 February 1993: 102. *New York Theatre Critics' Reviews* 54 (1993): 25.

Negative review of the Manhattan Theatre Club's production in which Oliver admits to being confused by the script. "Much of *The Last Yankee* is beyond me; I'm not sure—and not for the first time—that I see Mr. Miller's point."

Peter, John. "America the Grave." *Sunday Times* (London) 31 January 1993: Sec. 8: 21.

Positive review of the London production, directed by David Thacker and presented at the Young Vic Theatre, that Peter calls "masterful" with performances by Zoe Wanamaker, Helen Burns, David Healy, and Peter Davison that are "each exquisitely crafted, luminous and hard, like diamonds."

Richards, David. "Funny or Dour, It's Depression All Right." *New York Times* 31 January 1993. *New York Theatre Critics' Reviews* 54 (1993): 28.

Negative review of the Manhattan Theatre Club production of *The Last Yankee* that Richards calls "discreet and a little dour."

Ridley, Clifford A. "Two Men and Their Depressed Wives in Arthur Miller's *The Last Yankee*." *Philadelphia Inquirer* 23 January 1993: D9.

In this negative review of the Manhattan Theatre Club's production of *The Last Yankee*, directed by John Tillinger and starring John Heard and Frances Conroy, Ridley faults Miller's script for being "less a play than a sketch of a play" that "feels like a first act, an introduction to four characters who might be worth getting to know."

Scheck, Frank. "Thoughtful *Yankee* Could Use a Bit More Miller of Yore." *Christian Science Monitor* 28 January 1993: NOW: 13.

Mixed review of the Manhattan Theatre Club production of *The Last Yankee*, directed by John Tillinger, starring Frances Conroy and John Heard. Scheck praises Miller's dialogue and vivid characterizations but wishes it had more bite.

Simon, John. "Coming Apart Together." *New York* 1 February 1993: 61-62. *New York Theatre Critics' Reviews* 54 (1993): 24.

Simon praises the Manhattan Theatre Club production of *The Last Yankee* as a "pleasant surprise."

Spencer, Charles. "Victims of the Dream." *Daily Telegraph* (London) 28 January 1993: 19.

Mixed review of the London production, directed by David Thacker at the Young Vic Theatre, that Spencer says "at its best it is good-hearted, sympathetic and touching. Nevertheless, at 80 minutes, it is an insubstantial work, and its themes sometimes seem over-familiar and simplistic."

Stearns, David Patrick. "Off-Broadway Show on Love among the Disenchanted." *USA Today* 28 January 1993: D8. *New York Theatre Critics' Reviews* 54 (1993): 29.

Positive review of the Manhattan Theatre Club's production of *The Last Yankee*, starring Frances Conroy, that Stearns calls "a highly promising [play] that showcases Miller's ability to present an everyday scene that effortlessly crystallizes basic human truths."

Stuart, Jan. "At Odds with the American Dream." *Newsday* 22 January 1993: 62.

Positive review of the Manhattan Theatre Club production, directed by John Tillinger and starring John Heard, Frances Conroy, and Tom Aldredge, that Stuart says "sits with you, pleasingly, revealing its nourishments with quiet confidence over the days to come."

Tai, Stefan. "Arthur Miller's *Last Yankee*—A Male Depressive." *Contemporary Review* 264 (March 1994): 147–48.

Review of premiere production at the Duke of York's, before its move to the Young Vic, directed by David Thacker. Tai praises Miller's newest work as a "comic but deeply moving and poignant play."

Taylor, Paul. "Miller's Winter Windfall." *Independent* (London) 28 January 1993: 23.

Taylor rates the production, directed by David Thacker and playing at the Young Vic, as "superbly acted."

Torrens, James S. "*The Last Yankee*." *America* 27 February 1993: 16.

Mixed review of the Manhattan Theatre Club production that Torrens says "seems unfinished,"

Watt, Doug. "Theatre Club's *Last Yankee* Is Not so Doodle Dandy." *Daily News* 29 January 1993. *New York Theatre Critics' Reviews* 54 (1993): 27.

Negative review of Manhattan Theatre Club production of *The Last Yankee* in which Watt faults Miller's dialogue as "easy and natural, but only occasionally interesting and never revealing enough. The acting, under John Tillinger's sharp direction, is better than the play it serves."

News Reports, Letters to the Editor, and Related Matter

Sherrin, Ned. "*The Last Yankee*." *Sunday Express* (London) 9 May 1993. *Theatre Record* 13.9 (1993): 488.

Brief item announcing that the "excellent" production of Miller's *The Last Yankee*, directed by David Thacker, has moved from the Young Vic to the Duke of York's.

Broken Glass

Critical Essays in Journals and Magazines

Abbotson, Susan C.W. "Issues of Identity in *Broken Glass*: A Humanist Response to a Postmodern World." *Journal of American Drama and Theatre* 11 (Winter 1999): 67–80.

While set in 1938 during the period of "Kristallnacht," Abbotson reads *Broken Glass* as "a humanistic response to the contemporary world we inhabit" and "an artist's efforts to redefine the postmodernist trend toward disjunction and otherness into a culture of connection and self."

Antler, Joyce. "The Americanization of the Holocaust." *American Theatre* February 1995: 16–20+.

Discusses Miller's play *Broken Glass* as "one of a number of recent stage works that break new theatrical ground by linking the Holocaust directly and profoundly to the American psyche."

Bigsby, Christopher. "Miller's Journey to *Broken Glass*." Program for premiere of *Broken Glass*. Long Wharf Theatre 1 Mar.–3 Apr. 1994: 21, 23, 25.

Essay in which Bigsby contexualizes Miller's play as history, as social commentary, as psychological study, and as personal statement.

Brustein, Robert. "Separated by a Common Playwright." *New Republic* 30 May 1994: 29–31. Rpt. as "Aspects of Arthur Miller." *Cultural Calisthenics: Writings on Race, Politics, and Theatre*. Chicago: Ivan R. Dee, 1998. 75–78.

Brustein comments on what he sees as Miller's virtual status as England's playwright-laureate and posits that Miller may have wished he had opened *Broken Glass* there instead of New York. "*Broken Glass* may very well dazzle the critics and delight the public when it is eventually produced in London. Here it seems like just another spiral in a stumbling career."

Kanfer, Stefan. "Mysterious Time Machines." *New Leader* 6–20 June 1994: 38–39.

Questioning the reasons behind producing *Broken Glass* on Broadway, Kanfer says, "Granted, Miller remains a marquee name, and at 78 he has turned out a full-length play with bona fide stars.

Yet we are not in the presence of a durable, aging giant on the order of Verdi or Chaplin or Picasso. We are, rather, witnesses to fading powers that, in truth, were never very strong to begin with."

Lyons, Donald. "Angry Women & Furious Machines." *New Criterion* 12.10 (June 1994): 45–51.

Lyons discusses four recent London imports (*Carousel, Medea, The Winter's Tale*, and *An Inspector Calls*) and three recent American plays (*Picnic, Three Tall Women*, and *Broken Glass*). Of *Broken Glass*, Lyons laments that the new work "did not receive an ideal production"—"John Tillinger's direction chose to emphasize a laborious and ungainly set at the expense of any dramatic urgency or build"—and criticizes Miller for his characteristic "multiplicity of focus: is the play about Nazis or about marriage?"

Critical Essays in Newspapers

Armitstead, Claire. "Double Visionaries." *Guardian* (London) 27 July 1994: Sec. 2: 4.

Lengthy essay discussing Miller's close working relationship with David Thacker for the London production of *Broken Glass*.

Production Reviews

Barnes, Clive. "Fear and Self-Loathing Amid *Broken Glass*." *New York Post* 25 April 1994. Rpt. in *New York Theatre Critics' Reviews 1994* 55 (1994): 123.

Positive review of the Broadway production of *Broken Glass*, starring Amy Irving and Ron Rifkin, that Barnes finds a "striking yet ambiguous" drama that " reveals the shrewd theatricality of a master."

Billington, Michael. "Putting the Pieces Together." *Guardian* (London) 6 August 1994: Sec. 2, p. 26. *Independent on Sunday* (London) 7 August 1994. *Theatre Record* 14.16 (1994): 975–76.

Favorable review of the London production (Lyttelton Theatre) starring Margot Leicester and Henry Goodman that Billington calls "a wise, humane and moving play."

Canby, Vincent. "Arthur Miller Still Holds to His Moral Vision." *New York Times* 1 May 1994: Sec. 2: 5.

In this favorable review of *Broken Glass* starring Ron Rifkin and Amy Irving, Canby finds it "intense," "deceptively prosy," and "meticulously constructed," and containing "a poignance so rare these days that it's almost old-fashioned."

Coveney, Michael. "*Broken Glass*." *Observer* (London) 7 August 1994. *Theatre Record* 14.16 (1994): 976–77.

Negative review of *Broken Glass*, directed by David Thacker at the Lyttelton Theatre. Coveney calls the play "the work of a great playwright reduced to prophetic, finger-wagging abstractions. As in his last two plays, *The Ride Down Mount Morgan* and *The Last Yankee*, Miller relates a trite fantasy of national malaise to feebly imagined histories of physical and mental disintegration."

Darvell, Michael. "*Broken Glass*." *What's On* (London) 10 August 1994. *Independent on Sunday* (London) 7 August 1994. *Theatre Record* 14.16 (1994): 975.

Darvell praise David Thacker's direction as "inspired," the performances of Margot Leicester and Henry Goodman as "wringing every ounce of pathos from this most plangent of themes," and Miller's play as having "internal rhythms" that "provide the meanings between the lines, and what is left unspoken is every bit as telling as the words themselves."

de Jongh, Nicholas. "*Broken Glass*." *Evening Standard* (London) 5 August 1994. *Theatre Record* 14.16 (1994): 979–80.

de Jongh laments in this mixed review of the David Thacker production of *Broken Glass* that the play "does not really rise to [Miller's] own theatrical standards."

Doughty, Louise. "Shard Time: Night and Day." *Mail on Sunday* (London) 14 April 1994: 30. *Theatre Record* 14.16 (1994): 979.

While admitting that *Broken Glass* "feels a little underdeveloped and towards the end it lurches into melodrama," Doughty lauds the work for bristling "with ideas and, every now and then, there is an insight which makes you catch your breath."

Edwardes, Jane. "*Broken Glass*." *Time Out* (London) 1 March 1995. *Theatre Record* 15.4 (1995): 225.

Mixed review of the David Thacker production at the Duke of York's, transferred from the National, in which Edwardes praises the production for its "fascinating subject matter and the extraordinary emotional pitch which the actors sustain throughout" the play, but wishes "that the life of the play hadn't so clearly eluded" Miller.

Feingold, Michael. "Schema Things." *Village Voice* 10 May 1994: 101. Rpt. in *New York Theatre Critics' Reviews 1994* 55 (1994): 122.

In a mixed review of the Broadway production of *Broken Glass*, starring Ron Rifkin and Amy Irving, that Feingold calls "interesting at every moment except its turning points, Feingold compares Miller's drama with J.B. Priestley's work *An Inspector Calls* in an effort to expose the "schematic matrix" inherent in both dramas.

Gerard, Jeremy. "*Broken Glass.*" *Variety* 25 April 1994: 38.

With "heartfelt" performances and a "remarkable unity of presentation" thanks to director John Tillinger, the Broadway premiere of *Broken Glass*, starring Amy Irving and Ron Rifkin, is "a serious work" that "takes risks few playwrights muster the nerve to take."

Gore-Langton, Robert. "*Broken Glass.*" *Daily Telegraph* (London) 27 February 1995. *Theatre Record* 15.4 (1995): 227.

Brief mixed review of *Broken Glass*, directed by David Thacker and playing at the Duke of York's, that Gore-Langton calls "a complex, but never boring psychiatric sleuther marred by an implausibly miraculous final scene. It has astonishingly good acting to recommend it."

Grant, Steve. "*Broken Glass.*" *Time Out* 10 August 1994. *Independent on Sunday* (London) 7 August 1994. *Theatre Record* 14.16 (1994): 974.

Grant criticizes *Broken Glass* for David Thacker's "top-heavy production" and Miller's "attempt to revive memories of the prewar Nazi persecution" that "is prescient enough" but "it's just a pity that too much of the rest remains anecdotal, a dramatised true story doomed to be judged by the 'So what?' factor, locked in the mind of the author but not truly made flesh."

Gross, John. "*Broken Glass.*" *Sunday Telegraph* (London) 7 August 1994. *Theatre Record* 14.16 (1994): 976.

Calling the dialogue of *Broken Glass*, directed by David

Thacker at the Lyttelton, "clumsy and off-target," Gross laments that "historical realities are lost sight of in a fog of humanistic rhetoric."

Henry, William A., III. "Sylvia Suffers." *Time* 9 May 1994: 76.

Favorable review of the Broadway opening of *Broken Glass* that Henry admires not only for the longevity of its author but for the work itself with is "complex, a little mysterious, full of arresting incident, grippingly played."

Hirschhorn, Clive. "*Broken Glass*." *Sunday Express* (London) 7 August 1994. *Theatre Record* 14.16 (1994): 978–79.

Calling *Broken Glass* "Miller's best play since *The Price*," Hirschhorn praises Miller for succeeding "triumphantly in creating a truly complex, believable character in Philip."

Hopkinson, Amanda. "A View from the Bridge." *New Statesman and Society* (London) 5 August 1994: 31–32.

Despite its title, the subject of this piece is the London premiere of *Broken Glass*, the genesis of the drama and its themes, and the factual basis of the hysterical paralysis that effects Sylvia Gellburg.

Hulbert, Dan. "*Broken Glass*." *Atlanta Constitution* 26 April 1994: B9.

While admitting that *Broken Glass* is not one of Miller's strongest plays, critic Dan Hulbert praises the work for succeeding "in illuminating how the personal and political landscapes are one. . . . In any case, *Broken Glass*, like most important drama, goes beyond self-therapy to skilled healing of the national body politic."

King, Robert L. "All American." *North American Review* 279.4 (July–August 1994): 45–46.

While admitting in his review of *Broken Glass* that Miller has an "admirable commitment to serious issues," King laments that Miller "seems fearful that an audience might miss his moral point," so the playwright" tends to spell out conclusions, underline significances, and thrust symbols forward."

Kingston, Jeremy. "*Broken Glass*." *The Times* (London) 27 February 1995. *Theatre Record* 15.4 (1995): 226.

Mixed review of the 10-week run of the David Thacker production of *Broken Glass* at the Duke of York's in the West End, transferred there after its sold-out run at the National Theatre. Kingston calls it "a deeply felt work" that "nevertheless stirs thoughts more insistently than it provokes feelings." Despite "acting as powerful as any currently on offer in all London . . . the play is not as good as it thinks it is.

Kissel, Howard. "Miller's *Broken Glass* Doesn't Crystallize." *Daily News* 25 April, 1994. In *New York Theatre Critics' Reviews* 55 (1994): 131.

Concluding that the Broadway production of *Broken Glass*, starring Amy Irving and Ron Rifkin, "seems more like the outline for a play than the finished product," Kissel decries what he sees as Miller cluttering his play "with naturalistic touches that have little vitality of their own and do not amplify his main concerns."

Koenig, Rhoda. "Nothing to Understand." *Independent* (London) 6 August 1994: Weekend Arts: 28. *Theatre Record* 14.16 (1994): 977.

Negative review of the London production, directed by David Thacker at the Lyttelton Theatre, that Koenig calls a "limp and unconvincing narrative. [Miller's] characters are wooden and inarticulate, city yokels afflicted with galloping naivity."

Lahr, John. "Dead Souls." *New Yorker* 9 May 1994: 94–96. In *New York Theatre Critics' Reviews* 55 (1994): 124–25. Rpt. in *Light Fantastic: Adventures in Theatre*. New York: Delta, 1996. 194–98.

Positive review of the Broadway premiere of *Broken Glass*, starring Ron Rifkin and Amy Irving, which includes portions of an interview with Miller concerning the production, that Lahr calls "a brave, big-hearted attempt by one of the pathfinders of postwar drama to look at the tangle of evasions and hostilities by which the soul contrives to hide its emptiness from itself."

Leon, Masha. "Masha Leon." *Forward: Ethnic News Watch* 27 May 1994: 5.

Inventive and negative review of *Broken Glass*, starring Amy Irving, Ron Rifkin, and David Dukes, that questions the logic of the events of the play's ending and bemoans Miller's characterization of Jews in the play—"Sorry to tread on hallowed ground and author, but once again a Jewish male character has been portrayed as a negative, self-hating, impotent, obsequious Jew. kvetch, kvetch, kvetch. Genug! Enough already!"

Macaulay, Alastair. "*Broken Glass*." *Financial Times* (London) 6 August 1994. *Independent on Sunday* (London) 7 August 1994. *Theatre Record* 14.16 (1994): 975.

Macaulay criticizes *Broken Glass*, directed by David Thacker, as possessing messages "that thud around like so many missiles; but they do not constitute serious drama."

———. "*Broken Glass*." *Financial Times* (London) 1 March 1995. *Theatre Record* 15.4 (1995): 225–26.

Macaulay calls *Broken Glass*, directed by David Thacker at the Duke of York's, following its move from the National, as confirmation "that Arthur Miller is the most overrated playwright of our time." Macaulay also asserts that Margot Leicester was "miscast" for having "neither the beauty nor the vigor that are attributed to Sylvia," and that Henry Goodman's performance as Philip is "as unyielding, narrow and ponderous as the play."

Morley, Sheridan. "Miller's Crossing." *Spectator* (London) 13 August 1994: 31. *Theatre Record* 14.16 (1994): 977.

Morley lauds *Broken Glass*, directed by David Thacker at the Lyttelton, as "a breathtakingly brilliant exploration of the paralysis that overtook America in November 1938 as news of the Nazi persecution of the Jews just after Kristallnacht reached their Brooklyn cousins."

Nathan, David. "*Broken Glass*." *Jewish Chronicle* (London) 12 August 1994. *Theatre Record* 14.16 (1994): 977–78.

Positive review of *Broken Glass*, directed by David Thacker. Nathan asserts that he doubts "if Jewish anxieties have ever been so expressed in the theatre" and praises the work as play that "springs from the core of Miller's unequivocal Jewishness."

Nightingale, Benedict. "Smashed Certainties." *The Times* (London) 6 August 1994. *Theatre Record* 14.16 (1994): 978.

Lengthy positive review of *Broken Glass*, directed by David Thacker at the Lyttelton Theatre. Nightingale praises "Miller's passion for his theme" and concludes that "you won't see a more sympathetic yet less sentimental piece of characterization anywhere in London."

Paton, Maureen. "*Broken Glass*." *Daily Express* (London) 5 August 1994. *Theatre Record* 14.16 (1994): 978.

Mixed review of the David Thacker production at the Lyttelton in which Paton criticizes the play as "a sketchy, predictable piece" and asserts that "only Arthur Miller could write—and get away with—the longest doctor's note in the history of the theatre."

Peter, John. "A Raw Slice of Humanity." *Sunday Times* (London) 14 August 1994: Sec. 10: 21. *Theatre Record* 14.16 (1994): 980.

Lengthy positive review of the David Thacker production at the Lyttelton Theatre. Peter praises *Broken Glass* as a "grand, harrowing play, deeply compassionate and darkly humorous," and "one of the great creations of the American theatre."

Richards, David. "A Paralysis Points to Spiritual and Social Ills." *New York Times* 25 April 1994: C11.

Mostly negative review of the opening night performance of Miller's play, *Broken Glass*, at the Booth Theatre. Richards calls the play "a spiritual detective story," and finds the Miller's writing "predictable"—"there's something vaguely mathematical about Mr. Miller's excavation of the past. Each scene dutifully yields up its bit of exposition, reveals the telling personality trait or spills a little more of the dark secret. . . . this is Ibsenism by the book."

Scheck, Frank. "Grains of a Good Play Exist in Arthur Miller's Strained *Broken Glass*." *Christian Science Monitor* 27 April, 1994: 17.

Praising the John Tillinger production of *Broken Glass* as "elegant," "dignified," and "heartfelt," Scheck faults Miller's "melodramatic" ending and "problematical" characters. Says Scheck, "You can feel that there's a great play buried within *Broken Glass*, but like its heroine, it can't seem to rise to its feet."

Simon, John. "Whose Paralysis Is It, Anyway?" *New York* 9 May 1994: 80–81.

Calling Miller "the world's most overrated playwright," Simon offers a scathing review of the Broadway premiere of *Broken Glass*, starring Amy Irving and Ron Rifkin. Says Simon, *Broken Glass* "gives the epithet *shattering* a theatrically new, and wholly undesirable, meaning."

Smith, Neil. "*Broken Glass*." *What's On* (London) 1 March 1995. *Theatre Record* 15.4 (1995): 226.

Smith praises *Broken Glass*, directed by David Thacker, as "an important play" and "a vibrant and compassionate discourse on personal and global morality from a playwright who has made it his business to marry the two."

Spencer, Charles. "*Broken Glass*." *Daily Telegraph* (London) 5 August 1994. *Theatre Record* 14.16 (1994): 974–75.

Spencer lauds *Broken Glass*, directed by David Thacker at the Lyttelton Theatre, as Miller's "strongest play in many years, a gripping and at times powerfully affecting drama."

Stearns, David Patrick. "A Glistening *Broken Glass*." *USA Today* 25 April 1994: D4.

Mixed review of *Broken Glass*, directed by John Tillinger and starring Ron Rifkin, David Dukes, and Amy Irving. Says Stearns, "Stark realism collides with enigmatic, extrasensory matters in ways that even a master like Miller can't quite bring off, though that doesn't stop him from a fascinating attempt."

Taylor, Markland. "*Broken Glass*." *Variety* 14 March 1994: 63.

Negative review of the Long Wharf Theatre production of *Broken Glass*, starring Amy Irving and Ron Silver, that Markland says "has yet to make the crucial leap from page to stage"—"There's a massive task ahead, and it goes without saying that Miller himself must spearhead the major work needed to be done on his play."

Taylor, Paul. "*Broken Glass*." *Independent* (London) 27 February 1995. *Theatre Record* 15.4 (1995): 227.

Taylor lauds the David Thacker production, playing at the Duke of York's after its sold-out run at the National, for "exploring the psychological connections between the marriage and the wife's fears about matters close to home." Says Taylor, "the play is both convincing and produces tremendous moral and emotional impact."

Tinker, Jack. "*Broken Glass*." *Daily Mail* (London) 5 August 1994. *Theatre Record* 14.16 (1994): 976.

While Tinker applauds the "highly accomplished acting" of *Broken Glass*, he criticizes David Thacker's direction as having a "somnolent pace" and Miller's script for being "remorselessly remote."

———. "*Broken Glass*." *Daily Mail* (London) 3 March 1995. *Theatre Record* 15.4 (1995): 227.

While admiring the performances of Margot Leicester and Henry Goodman, Tinker decries that the David Thacker production at the Duke of York's made him feel "cut off constantly from any real involvement with [the characters] by a glass wall of disbelief. Not even a cello's melancholy accompaniment could move me at the Jews' plight. This in itself was something of a first."

Wardle, Irving. "*Broken Glass*." *Independent on Sunday* (London) 7 August 1994. *Theatre Record* 14.16 (1994): 974.

Wardle praises the David Thacker production at the Lyttelton for "its ferocious emotional energy" and "a return to [Miller's] old territory, full of echoes from the past."

Wilson, Edwin. "Miller Resurfaces at Tony Time." *Wall Street Journal* 5 May 1994. In *New York Theatre Critics' Reviews* 55 (1994): 132.

Glowing review of the Broadway production of *Broken Glass*, starring Amy Irving and Ron Rifkin, that Wilson calls "beautifuly acted" and Miller's "best play of recent years"— "a production that brings home the Holocaust not with the direct impact of other recent works, but indirectly, through nuance and reverberation. It is therefore all the more powerful."

Winer, Linda. "Arthur Miller's Morality Soaper." *Newsday* 25 April 1994: B2. In *New York Theatre Critics' Reviews* 55 (1994): 131–32.

While finding the first third of the Broadway production of *Broken Glass* engrossing, Winer laments that "Unfortunately, the situation becomes more and more artificial, the connections between the wife's symptoms and Hitler's rise get increasingly tenuous, the psychological revelations are mostly pedestrian, and despite the playwright's well-publicized revisions of the last scene, he has not found a satisfactory way out."

Winn, Steven. "A Woman's Personal Holocaust." *San Francisco Chronicle* 25 April 1994: E3.

Negative review of *Broken Glass*, directed by John Tillinger, that Winn calls seriously intended but seriously flawed.

Wolf, Matt. "Splintered Factions: *Broken Glass*." *Times Literary Supplement* (London) 19 August 1994: 18.

Wolf praises David Thacker's production of *Broken Glass* as the sole reason for the play's success, noting that Miller's "larger concerns, sadly, cannot compete with the cruder specifics of Miller's sextet . . . the doctor, in particular, is not credible on any level beyond his status as another highly-sexed Miller male."

Related Interviews and Profiles (not with Miller)

"Acting against Type: The Self-Hating Jew." *New York Times* 24 April 1994: Sec. 2: 6.

Lengthy interview with Ron Rifkin in which the actor discusses the various Jewish characters he has played, including his current role of Philip Gellburg in Miller's *Broken Glass*.

Benedict, David. "David Benedict on Theatre." *Independent* (London) 29 July 1994: Entertainment: 10.

Brief interview with David Thacker in which the director discusses the production of *Broken Glass* at the National Theatre. Says Thacker, "It's a masterpiece. It's as good as anything [Miller] has ever written."

Pacheco, Patrick. "The Amy Chronicles." *Los Angeles Times* 17 April 1994: Calendar: 5.

Interview with Amy Irving, star of the Long Wharf Theatre premiere of *Broken Glass*. Irving discusses her approach to the role of Sylvia Gellburg, favorable family influences on her career, her marriage and subsequent divorce from Steven Spielberg, her marriage to Brazilian film director Bruno Barreto, and her film credits.

Rizzo, Frank. "She's Not So Delicate in Miller's *Glass*." *Los Angeles Times* 22 March 1994: F2.

Interview with Ron Rifkin and Amy Irving, stars of the Long Wharf Theatre premiere of Miller's *Broken Glass* that includes their comments regarding their approaches to their roles and the modern relevance of the play, which is set in 1938.

Simonson, Robert. "Backstage with Amy Irving." *Theatre Week* 13 June 1994: 19–21.

Interview with Amy Irving in which she discusses her approach to her role of Sylvia Gellburg in *Broken Glass* and the themes of anti-Semitism in the play.

Smith, Harry. "Amy Irving on Her Current Roles on Broadway and Television." *CBS This Morning* 19 May 1994. Broadcast transcript.

Irving briefly discusses working with Miller on *Broken Glass* in New Haven.

News Reports, Letters to the Editor, and Related Matter

Blowen, Michael. "For Sirkin, It's Miller Time." *Boston Globe* 5 March 1994: Living: 66.

Brief item that reports the enthusiasm of producer Spring Sirkin who is working with Robert Whitehead and Miller at the Long Wharf Theatre's production of *Broken Glass*, starring Amy Irving, Ron Rifkin, and Frances Conroy.

"Letters to the Editor." *Los Angeles Times* 3 July 1994: 79.

Two letters to the editor written in response to Jan Breslauer (June 19) review of *Broken Glass* ("The Arthur Miller Method"). One letter writer asserts that the play was "boring, unfocused and too long," while the other wished Breslauer had mentioned Marilyn Monroe in her essay.

Klein, Alvin. "*Broken Glass*, The New Haven Tryout That Isn't." *New York Times* 3 April 1994: 13CN: 10.

Article examining the Long Wharf Theatre's denial that their production of *Broken Glass* is a "tryout," even though the world premiere is scheduled to begin previews at the Booth Theatre in New York City nine days after the play's closing in New Haven. Of note is the inclusion of details relating to script revisions, including work on several endings, and casting changes that have taken place both pre- and post-production at the Long Wharf.

"Olivier Awards." *USA Today* 4 April 1995: A9.

News item announcing Miller's *Broken Glass* as Best Play at the 1995 Laurence Olivier Awards in London.

"Ron Silver Leaves Cast of New Play by Miller," *New York Times* 30 March 1994: C22.

Short news item announcing the departure of Ron Silver from the cast of *Broken Glass* at the Long Wharf Theatre in New Haven. No reason is given.

Weber, Bruce. "On Finding Just the Right Ending." *New York Times* 22 April 1994: C2.

Reports on the reception celebrating the fiftieth anniversary of Miller's Broadway debut and his recent opening of his thirteenth work *Broken Glass*. Miller remarks on his writing process and the evolution of the play's many endings.

The Ryan Interview

Production Reviews

Brantley, Ben. "Wilder and Miller in One-Act Festival." *New York Times* 6 May 1995: Sec. 1, p. 17.

Brief mixed review of the premiere production of *The Ryan Interview*, starring Mason Adams and Julie Lauren, directed by Curt Dempster for the eighteenth annual festival of new one-acts at the Ensemble Studio Theatre. While Brantley finds the play about an old Connecticut Yankee being interviewed by a young reporter on his 100th birthday "conventional," he praises what he call the work's "engagingly easygoing pace" and dialogue possessing "an effortless ring of accuracy."

I Can't Remember Anything* and *The Last Yankee

Production Reviews

Brantley, Ben. "They Converse but Do Not Speak to Each Other." *New York Times* 12 January 1998: E3.

Negative review of both one-acts (*I Can't Remember Anything* and *The Last Yankee*), directed by Joseph Chaikin at the Signature Theatre Company. Says Brantley, the dialogue "often suggests a protracted series of acting exercises, and the performers only rarely achieve a convincing sense of familiarity with one another. There's an oddly stilted and tentative air throughout that makes the production feel disjointed in ways that go beyond its thematic intentions."

Canby, Vincent. "Big and Beautiful, *Ragtime* Never Quite Sings." *New York Times* 25 January 1998: Sec. 2: 7.

Favorable review of the double bill of Miller one-acts presented by the Signature Theatre Company, directed by Joseph Chaikin, that Canby calls "lively" and "a quiet, moving, informal evening of theater."

Feingold, Michael. "Clarity Cases." *Village Voice* 20 January 1998: 113.

Faulting previous productions of both *I Can't Remember Anything* and *The Last Yankee* as "dull, muddled, vague works trying to say something 'interesting' while evading the obvious," Feingold praises the Signature Theatre's revival, directed by Joseph Chaikin, as a "refreshing" surprise.

LeSourd, Jacques. "Signature Offers Miller in Minor Key." *Gannett News Service* 13 January 1998.

Negative review of the Signature Theatre Company production of the double bill of *I Can't Remember Anything* and *The Last Yankee*, directed by Joseph Chaikin, that LeSourd calls "a wan and dispiriting theatrical experience."

Lyons, Donald. "Theater: Miller Time." *Wall Street Journal* 14 January 1998: A17.

Negative review of the Signature Theatre Company production. Says Lyons, "The problem is that there's no drama here. Much that the two people say is touching and lifelike, but Mr. Miller's refusal of context means that *I Can't Remember Anything* amounts to a frustrating amalgam of the cryptic and the cranky."

Winer, Linda. "Minor Miller Is a Major Moment." *Newsday* 12 January 1998: B2.

Calling the double bill of one-acts "beauties," Winer praises the Signature Theatre Company's production of *I Can't Remember Anything* and *The Last Yankee* as "subtle, engaging, personable and shaded with the sort of moody emotional detail that can elude Miller's more declarative statements."

Mr. Peters' Connections

Critical Essays in Journals and Magazines

Barbour, David. "Dens of Iniquity." *TCI* 32.8 (August/September 1998): 7–9.

Detailed description of English set designer Francis O'Connor's vision for the world premiere production of *Mr. Peters' Connections*, including O'Connor's "interesting decision to give such an abstract play a specific, detailed setting."

Weales, Gerald. "American Theatre Watch, 1997–1998." *Georgia Review* (Fall 1998): 529–41.

Weales makes brief mention of *Mr. Peters' Connections*, offering details regarding the play's plot and themes, concluding that "the strength of the play lies in the journey, not its end."

Critical Essays in Newspapers

Preston, Rohan. "Between a Role and a Hard Place." *Minneapolis Star Tribune* 12 November 1999: 16.

Essay that examines the character of the black bag lady Adele in Miller's *Mr. Peters' Connections*. Preston interviews the actress playing the twenty-one line role (who reveals that Miller told her he wrote the part in order to get to know African Americans better) and explores the stereotyped construction of the character, concluding, "Ultimately, Miller ends up trapping her in a stick-figure malaise, and Adele is less a dreamy exploration of something unknown than a projection of a one-dimensional death."

Production Reviews

Barnes, Clive. "Not Quite Miller Time." *New York Post* 18 May 1998. http://206.15.118.165/051898/1819.htm (4 April 1999).

Negative review of the premiere production of *Mr. Peters' Connections*, staged by the Signature Theatre Company and starring Peter Falk. Says Barnes, "It's a good play. That much I know from reading the script. How good, I'm not sure, for this first production seems to me to be very bad. I suspect something of a travesty."

Buford, Bill. "Miller Export." *Guardian* (London) 26 May 1998: 17.
Buford remarks on the mostly negative criticism that Miller's plays have received in the United States and comments that his newest play, *Mr. Peters' Connections*, has some problems.

Brantley, Ben. "Peter Falk's Search for Meaning." *New York Times* 18 May 1998: E1.
Mostly negative review of the Signature Theatre Company's world premiere production of *Mr. Peters' Connections.* Says Brantley, "The work is an example of the experimental, ruminative style the dramatist has adopted of late, an approach that is by no means his most effective."

Brustein, Robert. "Still Searching for Theatre." *New Republic* 3 August 1998: 29–30.
Mostly negative review. "It is windy, tiresome, self-conscious, and full of moody maundering. Miller is so eager to get things off his chest that he hasn't bothered to provide his new play with a plot, a form, or even much effort at characterization, though there's more than enough in the way of theme. . . .Still, one has to respect the aging author's courage in baring his own lack of inspiration (momentary, let us hope) and his expectation of death."

Canby, Vincent. "This Time, Peter Falk Is Part of the Mystery." *New York Times* 24 May 1998: Sec. 2: 4.
Mixed review of the Signature Theatre Company's world premiere production of *Mr. Peters' Connections*, directed by Garry Hynes and starring Peter Falk. "It is an anti-dramatic reverie written, it would seem, for the playwright's own pleasure and shown to us with that unstated understanding."

Feingold, Michael. "The Old Miller Stream." *Village Voice* 26 May 1998: 147.
Negative review of the Signature Theatre's premiere production, starring Peter Falk and Anne Jackson, that Feingold calls "the least interesting, and the most intriguing, work to come from Arthur Miller in many years. . . . How I wish he'd had a director who could approach his discontinuous universe more daringly."

Kuchwara, Michael. "Classic Comebacks Peter Falk Returns in an Off-Broadway Show." *Buffalo News* 29 May 1998: GUSTO section.
Negative review of the Signature Theatre Company premiere that Kuchwara says is "oddly uninvolving despite some pungent

dialogue. . . . In the end, Peters does discover what the subject is but it is an answer he and the audience knew right from the minute the curtain went up on this lightweight piece of work."

Lyons, Donald. "Theater: Miller's Grumpy Old Man." *Wall Street Journal* 20 May 1998: A12.

Negative review of the premiere production, starring Peter Falk, that Lyons calls a "retrospective meditation by the one-time husband of Marilyn Monroe."

Melton, Robert W. "Book Reviews: Arts & Humanities." *Library Journal* 15 September 1999: 83.

Calling *Mr. Peters' Connections* "Miller's strongest play in 30 years," Melton praises the work for "effectively using absurdist techniques" and giving existential questions "stunning dramatic shape and force."

Preston, Rohan. "*Mr. Peters' Poetically Questions Reality, Illusion*." *Minneapolis Star Tribune* 5 November 1999: B4.

Highly laudatory review of the Guthrie Theater Lab production of *Mr. Peters' Connections*, directed by James Naughton, that Preston calls a "poetic and gutsy new play" that "shimmers as it distills its jazzy poetry."

Ridley, Clifford A. "*Mr. Peters'* Raises Many Questions, Enjoyably." *Philadelphia Inquirer* 18 May 1998: D6.

Positive review of the premiere production of *Mr. Peters' Connections* at the Signature Theatre Company, starring Peter Falk and directed by Garry Hynes. Says Ridley, "It is a play in which you needn't be aware of where you are in order to feel you're definitely going someplace. . . . By play's end, with its sense of cautious optimism, you feel you've been on a journey with an eloquent guide. . . ."

Stearns, David Patrick. "Miller's Play Lacks *Connections*." *USA Today* 18 May 1998: D2.

Negative review of premiere production of *Mr. Peters' Connections* at the Signature Theatre Company, starring Peter Falk and Anne Jackson. "It's so nonlinear, so opaque that you're never sure who's dead or alive—or even why you should wonder about such things."

Winer, Linda. "Old Coat, New Shoes, Bared Souls." *Newsday* 18 May 1998: B2.

Winer calls the Signature Theatre Company production, directed by Garry Hynes and starring Peter Falk, a "strange and beguiling" play, and priases Miller's work as "filled with enough unusually graceful wit and wisdom to make its own collectible volume."

Related Interviews and Profiles (not with Miller)

Hooton, Amanda Jane. "For Peter Falk, Mysteries of a Deeper Sort." *New York Times* 17 May 1998: Sec. 2: 9.

Profile of Falk and his role in Miller's new expressionistic play in which he plays a retired Pan Am pilot who has recently bought a pair of shoes. He appears to be sitting in an abandoned nightclub waiting for his wife. "Before she arrives, he encounters an assortment of mysterious characters who may be real or may be phantoms from his past."

Preston, Rohan. "Arthur Miller's Cathy-May: An Actor Reflects on a Tough Role." *Star Tribune Online* (Minneapolis) 18 November 1999. http://www2.startribune.com/stOnLine/cgi-bin/article?thisSlug=MAYVAR&date=18-Nov-1999&word=miller&word=arthur (18 November 1999).

Interview with Kali Vernoff who plays Cathy-May (a four-line part) in the Guthrie Theater Lab production of *Mr. Peters' Connections*, directed by James Houghton. Vernoff says that, while she loves working with Miller on the play, she had to give her acceptance of this role of a scantily clad woman who is "throttled" by her husband (one hand up her skirt, the other around her neck) a great deal of thought.

News Reports, Letters to the Editor, and Related Matter

Lyman, Rick. "On Stage and Off." *New York Times* 6 February 1998: E2.

Item detailing the new full-length play for the Signature Theatre company, *Mr. Peters' Connections*, and Miller's comments on his leading man Peter Falk and director Garry Hynes.

Smith, Liz. "For Art's Sake, Falk Joins Cast of Arthur Miller Play." *Philadelphia Inquirer* 12 February 1998: E2.

Gossipy news item announcing Miller's completion of *Mr. Peters' Connections*, which will star Peter Falk and be produced by the Signature Theatre Company.

6. Film, Radio, and Television Plays

All My Sons

1948

"*All My Sons*." *Magill's Survey of Cinema* 15 June 1995. *Electric Library* (3 December 1999).

Section on *All My Sons* that includes an abstract, summary, analysis, production credits, and review sources for the film.

Barnes, Howard. *New York Herald Tribune* 29 March 1948.

Barnes praises the acting of *All My Sons* but laments that this does "not off-set [the] fabricated situations and blurred characterizations."

Crowther, Bosley. "Screen in Review." *New York Times* 29 March 1948: 17.

Crowther praises the film for landing "a fairly staggering right-hook on the jaw of the genus profiteer" and Edward G. Robinson for his "superior job of showing the shades of personality in a little tough guy who has a softer side."

"Father and Sons." *Newsweek* 12 April 1948: 89.

Mixed review that praises the film for bringing Miller's "personal narrative into closer focus," but admits that the play is a better telling of the story of the Keller family.

Hatch, Robert. "A Matter of Ethics." *New Republic* 22 March 1948: 33–34.

While Hatch dislikes the contrived nature of the film's ending, he praises the acting of Burt Lancaster and Edward G. Robinson and lauds the story's serious and important themes.

McCarten, John. "The Current Cinema: The Disinherited." *New Yorker* 3 April 1948: 58–59.

Brief mixed review that chides the contrived storyline of the film version of *All My Sons* while praising the movie's "effective melodrama."

"New Pictures." *Time* 12 April 1948: 100, 103.

While the film has a heartfelt theatrical intensity, the film is "tainted with self-righteousness" and its dialogue is better suited to the stage.

Parish, James Robert, and Alvin H. Marill. *The Cinema of Edward G. Robinson*. South Brunswick, N.J.: Barnes, 1972. 169–70.

Brief chapter on *All My Sons* that includes production credits, a synopsis of the film, and excerpts of film reviews. Three black-and-white production stills accompany the text.

Whitebait, William. "The Movies: *All My Sons.*" *New Statesman and Nation* 4 September 1948: 193.

Whitebait finds the story of the Keller family and the themes of greed and guilt quite effective, but overall, the film is not emotionally engaging.

1987

O'Connor, John J. "Arthur Miller's *All My Sons* on 13." *New York Times* 19 January 1987: C16.

O'Connor praises the *American Playhouse* production of *All My Sons* as a "a good solid revival" whose final moments veer off "rather sharply into melodrama. But the passion holds, and the play survives."

Siegel, Ed. "*All My Sons* a Sign of Hope." *Boston Globe* 19 January 1987: 23.

Mixed review of the *American Playhouse* presentation of *All My Sons* starring James Whitmore, Aiden Quinn, and Michael Learned. Says Siegel, it "isn't the best play you'll ever see, but its power and force make it a welcome return . . . and a sign of hope that television and theater may not have irreconcilable differences."

The American Clock

Goodman, Walter. "Brooklyn Then and Now, in Arthur Miller's Eyes." *New York Times* 23 August 1993: C14.

Negative review of the TV production of *American Clock*, adapted by Frank Galati and directed by Bob Clark, starring Eddie Bracken, Darren McGavin and Estelle Parsons (shown on TNT on 23 August 1993 as part of the TNT *Screenworks* series). Says Goodman, "Miller's try at capturing the spirit of the Depression in 90 busy minutes" is "a touch scattered" and "never does make a stimulating connection between America today and in the 1930s or between viewers or anyone on the screen."

King, Susan. "Miller Time on TNT." *Los Angeles Times* 22 August 1993: TV Times: 7.

Feature article that discusses the genesis of the TNT *Screenworks* television production of *The American Clock*, starring Mary McDonnell, John Rubenstein, Estelle Parsons, Darren McGavin, and Rebecca Miller, including comments by McDonnell and screenwriter Frank Galati, who discusses the relevance of the depression-era drama to America's current condition.

Korzen, Annie. "Casting with More Chutzpah Might Help." *Los Angeles Times* 6 September 1993: F3.

Korzen blasts the TNT production of Miller's *American Clock* as "yet another example of 'white-washing' the casting of Jewish characters—a common practice of Jewish writers, directors and producers."

Loynd, Ray. "Miller's *American Clock* Ticks on Screen." *Los Angeles Times* 23 August 1993: F10.

Positive review of the TNT *Screenworks* production of Miller's *American Clock*, "a rare example of a major playwright's work finding its more natural form on the TV screen."

Roush, Matt. "A Slow *Clock*." *USA Today* 23 August 1993: D3.

Mixed review of the TV adaptation of *The American Clock*, that Roush calls "an elliptical epic, meandering on a broad social canvas."

Schaefer, Stephen. "Right Time for Mary McDonnell." *USA Today* 23 August 1993: D3.

Profile of actress Mary McDonnell, star of the television production of *American Clock*. McDonnell discusses the resonance of Miller's play as well as her feelings on good acting roles for women.

Broken Glass

Cohn, Ellen. "Paralyzed by Fear." *Jewish Week* 18 October 1996: PG.
Cohn calls the *Mobil Masterpiece* television production "soapy."

McCabe, Bruce. "Gripping Tale of *Broken Glass*." *Boston Globe* 20 October 1996: 4.
Highly laudatory review of the *Mobil Masterpiece Theatre* production that McCabe calls "one of the most cathartic theatrical experiences you'll ever have in front of the TV."

Miller, Ron. "*Broken Glass* a Fractured Vision for Masterpiece Theatre." *San Jose Mercury News* 18 October 1996: E1.
While finding PBS's *Mobil Masterpiece Theatre* production of *Broken Glass* "well-acted," critic Ron Miller says "It never became real to me, and I found the theatricality of it off-putting."

O'Connor, John J. "A World and a Wife Collapsing." *New York Times* 18 October 1996: D22.
Review of *Masterpiece Theatre*'s production of *Broken Glass*. O'Connor finds it "troubling in way that the playwright undoubtedly didn't intend" with Miller's "exploring of Jewishness" derailed "by too many distractions."

Rose, Lloyd. "*Broken Glass*; Kristallnacht through an American Prism." *Washington Post* 20 October 1996: G8.
Rose calls the television production of *Broken Glass* "an odd work, messier and less didactic than the playwright usually is. He doesn't box up his themes neatly inside this drama—they squirm loose and thrash around, unresolved. It's a play about awful, unanswerable questions."

Roush, Matt. "'Talk' Is Cheap, but *Broken Glass* Shatters." *USA Today* 18 October 1996: D3.
Positive review of the *Masterpiece Theatr*e television production of *Broken Glass*. Says Roush, "Miller's play is elusive, mysterious, and in its final moment, breathtakingly tragic."

Sheckel, Michael. "*Broken Glass* Translates Well to TV." *Jewish Advocate* 24 October 1996: PG.

Mixed review of the *Mobil Masterpiece* production, directed by David Thacker. "While personally dissatisfied and confused by the play's loose ends, I still recommend *Broken Glass*. Not the greatest of Miller's works, it is by far superior to most television productions and worth two hours on a Sunday night."

Shirley, Don. "Grim *Broken Glass* on Stage, Not on Small Screen." *Los Angeles Times* 19 October 1996: F18.

Negative review of the *Mobil Masterpiece Theatre* production, directed and co-written by David Thacker. Says Shirley, "The intense close-ups and lugubrious music emphasize everything that's soap-operatic about this play—and there's a lot of that. Still, it's always important, if not necessarily energizing, to take a look at the latest from America's playwright laureate."

Siegel, Ed. "Miller's *Broken Glass* Splinters into Pieces." *Boston Globe* 18 October 1996: D18.

Mixed review of the *Mobil Masterpiece Theatre* production, directed and co-written by David Thacker. While "a worthy attempt," Siegel faults Miller's script as "spotty throughout" with "an ending so melodramatic that one can only say 'Oy vey.'"

Taitte, Lawson. "Miller Drama Translates Well on Television." *Dallas Morning News* 19 October 1996: C1.

While Taitte finds *Broken Glass* "Miller's most interesting work in decades," he criticizes the television version for its "abrupt, schematic ending."

Clara

Kelly, Kevin. "*Clara*: A Muddled Mess from Miller." *Boston Globe* 5 February 1991: 54.

Negative review of the television version of *Clara*, the first offering on *General Motors Playwrights Theatre*. Kelly calls Miller's one-act "a play so bad every word mocks the blurb behind the sponsorship: the bumper shining GM Mark of Excellence."

Loynd, Ray. "*Clara* a Wrenching Work by Arthur Miller." *Los Angeles Times* 5 February 1991: F9.

Positive review of the A&E *Playwrights Theatre* production, starring Darren McGavin and William Daniels, directed by Burt Brinckerhoff, that Loynd calls "spare and unwavering and, curiously, it even has the tone of 1950s Golden Age television drama in its hermetic focus, which is refreshing on the small screen."

O'Connor, John J. "A Play by Arthur Miller and a Talk with Him." *New York Times* 5 February 1991: C16.

O'Connor reports on the premier of the *General Motors Playwrights Theatre* presentation of *Clara* that evening on the Arts & Entertainment Network, offers details of the film's plot, and comments on the taped interview that will follow the film, recorded in 1980 for the *South Bank Show* on London Weekend Television with Melvyn Bragg as the interviewer. Miller discusses the Great Depression and growing up in Harlem.

Warshawski, Morrie. "TV Review: Arthur Miller Dramatizes Obsessions of N.Y. Jews in '38." *Jewish Bulletin of Northern California* 18 October 1996. http://jewishsf.com/bk961018/ettv.htm (10 March 2000).

Warshawksi praises the acting of Margaret Leicester and Henry Goodman in the David Thacker television production as "superb" and Miller's play "emotionally wrenching."

Winfrey, Lee. "A Murder Case by Arthur Miller." *Philadelphia Inquirer* 5 February 1991: C7.

Entertainment feature detailing the plot, characters, and situations in Miller's play *Clara*, filmed as part of the second season of *Playwrights Theatre* on the Arts & Entertainment cable network, starring Darren McGavin and William Daniels.

The Crucible

1967 Television Production

Gould, Jack. "Arthur Miller's High Pitched *The Crucible*." *New York Times* 5 May 1967: 79.

Gould dislikes the television version of Miller's *The Crucible* because it has become "cold and remote" on the small screen, with camera cuts cutting the necessary tension.

Les Sorcières de Salem 1958 French Film Version

Crowther, Bosley. "Screen: French *Crucible*." *New York Times* 9 December 1958: 54.

Crowther praises this "persistently absorbing film" for its

"outstanding performances" and it ability to slowly unreel "a staggering vista of social disintegration while making its characters as near and sentient as closeups can be."

Hartung, Philip T. "The Screen: Many Things to Many People." *Commonweal* 2 January 1959: 363–64.

While the French film version of Miller's *The Crucible* is overtold, Hartung believes that the script about the dignity of man in opposition to society works better as a movie than a stage play.

Kauffmann, Stanley. "Torture, New and Old." *New Republic* 22 December 1958: 21.

With a Marxist political allegory, Kauffmann denounces the French film version of *The Crucible*, adapted by Jean-Paul Sartre, as a distortion of Miller's drama.

McCarten, John. "The Current Cinema." *New Yorker* 13 December 1958: 209–10.

Mixed review of the French film version of *The Crucible*, adapted by Jean-Paul Sartre, that McCarten feels has some strong moments but is ultimately a film that distorts Miller's story into a revolutionary tract about political agitation.

McDonald, Gerald D. "*Witches of Salem*." *Library Journal* 1 January 1959: 70, 88.

McDonald finds the French film version of *The Crucible* "compelling," although Jean-Paul Sartre gave Miller's story about social injustice and witch-hunting a Marxist/Socialist reading.

Quigly, Isabel. "Sabbath Witches." *Spectator* (London) 6 September 1957: 310.

Quigly finds Sartre's adaptation of Miller's play to an "appalling politically pointed tale" that is both forbidding and insightful.

Sartre, Jean-Paul. "Jean-Paul Sartre nous parle de théâtre." *Théâtre Populaire*. 15 (September–October 1955): 1–9. Excerpt rpt. as "On *Les Sorcières de Salem*." Trans. Nora L. Magid. *"The Crucible": Text and Criticism*. Ed. Gerald Weales. New York: Viking, 1971. Penguin, 1996. 421–22.

Lengthy interview in which Sartre is asked to define the existence and need for a truly popular theatre. Of note are Sartre's comments regarding his adaptation (for the film *Les Sorcières de*

Salem), in which he discusses being troubled by the play's ambiguous ending and his desire to make Proctor's death "like a free act which he commits to unleash the shame, effectively to deny his position, like the only thing which he can still do."

Walsh, Moira. "*He Who Must Die* and *The Witches of Salem*." *America* 17 January 1959: 480–82.

Brief commentary of the Jean-Paul Sartre adaptation of *The Crucible*. Walsh believes Sartre changed the focus of the story by stressing the sacrificial nature of the innocent townspeople and eliminating all contemporary parallels.

Weber, Eugene. "*The Crucible*." *Film Quarterly* 12 (Summer 1959): 44–45.

Negative review of the French film version of *The Crucible*, adapted by Jean-Paul Sartre, that Weber finds "poorly contrived." "Miller's original material has been stretched beyond its endurance"—"the script twisted away from the original point. . . ."

Whitebait, William. "Witch Doctors." *New Statesman* (London) 7 September 1957: 276.

Whitebait feels that Sartre's adaptation of *The Crucible* is a distortion of Miller's distorted understanding of the Salem witch trials of 1692. While "the story—on paper—might seem excellent, but it leaves us cold when it means to be humanly astringent."

"*Witches of Salem*." *Time* 5 January 1959: 84.

Negative review of the French film version of *The Crucible*, adapted by Jean-Paul Sartre. While Miller also misses the point of the Salem witch trials of 1692, Sartre's work confuses the issue entirely by identifying "the witch burners as colonial capitalists and the hero as a son of the suffering masses."

1996 American Film Version

Ackerman, Jerry. "Hollywood-on-Hog." *Boston Globe* 29 August 1995: 39.

Lengthy and detailed article on the financial benefits to the community of filming Miller's *The Crucible* on Hog Island, Massachusetts.

Andrews, Jeanmarie. "Getting It Right." *Early American Homes* 27.6 (December 1996): 80, 74.

Article that details the research that went into creating an authentic look and feel to the American film version of *The Crucible*, including locations, designs, props, furniture, fabrics, and arts and crafts.

Ansen, David. "That Wicked Witchcraft." *Newsweek* 2 December 1996: 80.

Positive review that expresses reservations about Miller's treatment of Puritan Salem. Says Ansen, "The author has little curiosity about what made these settlers the way they were, what role the church played in binding them together. Miller's strength, and his weakness, has always been his tendency to see things in black and white, which is what makes *The Crucible* moving, and also suspect. I recommend Hytner's movie highly, but a part of me resists a work that makes the audience feel as noble in our moral certainty as the characters it invites us to deplore. Some part of its power seems borrowed from the thing it hates."

Beck, Marilyn, and Stacy Jenel Smith. "Cast of *The Crucible* Gets into Character." *San Jose Mercury News* 7 October 1995: E3.

Item reporting the filming of *The Crucible* on Hog Island, Massachusetts, including comments by actor Bruce Davidson (Rev. Parris).

Blake, Richard A. "Convictions." *America* 15 February 1997: 24–26.

Lengthy essay praising Miller's film for its ability to stand on its own "as an incisive examination of the human condition."

Bowman, James. "*The Crucible*." *American Spectator* 17 January 1997.

While criticizing Miller's use of dialect, Bowman praises the film version of *The Crucible* as "quite well done with strong performances."

Butler, Robert W. "Stage Is a Better Setting for Metaphoric *Crucible*." *Kansas City Star* 20 February 1996: P10.

Negative review of the film version of *The Crucible* that movie critic Butler says "that probably never should have been made into a movie." The film's parallel to 1950s politics "is largely lost on contemporary audiences."

Carr, Jay. "*Crucible* Bewitches." *Boston Globe* 20 December 1996: E1.

Positive review of the film that Carr calls a "high-impact" production that is "more electrifying than ever, boldly focusing as much on repressed sexuality as on political paranoia and conflagration."

———. "Witchy Woman." *Boston Globe* 15 December 1996. Rpt. as "That's the Spirit." *San Jose Mercury News* 20 December 1996: 3.

Profile/interview of Winona Ryder in which she discusses her experiences in making *The Crucible*, her approach to the role of Abigail, and incidents from her past that lead her to acting as a career.

Clark, Mike. "Tale of Witch Trials Casts a Powerful Spell." *USA Today* 27 November 1996: D1.

Highly favorable review of the film version of *The Crucible* that Clark calls "screen champagne" and "a bang-up movie."

Coe, Jonathan. "*The Crucible*." *New Statesman* (London) 28 February 1997: 43.

Coe praises the film version of Miller's play for its "impeccable" production design, but laments that "what the film has gained in pseudo-verisimilitude it has lost in universality. . . . what they end up with is a decent, occasionally moving, historically very specific movie about the Salem witch trials."

Coolidge, Shelley Donald. "On-Site Filmmaking: A Boon to States' Coffers." *Christian Science Monitor* 25 September 1995: 9.

Lengthy feature article reporting the financial boost to the local economy that will come from the filming of *The Crucible* in Massachusetts, including the unusual package of incentives offered by the state to lure the filmmakers there.

"*The Crucible*." *Entertainment Weekly* 23 August 1996: 62.

Short feature reporting various "events" during the filming of *The Crucible*: Hytner and cast watching Demi Moore's *The Scarlet Letter*, filming on Hog Island, a chance encounter between Hytner and Ryder, and Miller's frequent appearances on the set.

"*The Crucible*." *People* 2 December 1996: 20.

Brief favorable review of the film, which calls it "passionate, engrossing, and invigoratingly intelligent."

Curtis, Quentin. "Witch Trials and Errors in Salem." *Electronic Telegraph* 1 March 1997. http://www.telegraph.co.uk:80/et?ac=001557312925871&rtmo=Vw3g8qJK&atmo=YYYYYYYp&pg=/et/97/3/1/bfquen01.html (11 April 1999).

Calling the American film version of Miller's play "resolutely unmoving," Curtis surmises that "the problem is that the play is brilliant but hollow, more rhetoric than drama. For a movie that mainly consists of people shouting at each other, there is surprisingly little real conflict."

Decter, Midge. "The Witches of Arthur Miller." *Commentary* March 1997: 54–57.

While questioning the value of Miller's stage play ("it is hard to believe that audiences have ever really been moved by this play"), Decter praises the film version as "good and gripping entertainment." Also discussed are the thematic concerns of McCarthyism and the characters' embodiment of innocence and guilt.

Denby, David. "*The Crucible*." *New York* 2 December 1996: 114–15.

Denby criticizes the American film version of *The Crucible* for being a "distant, rushed, and confused" production of a "frenetic modern play let loose on pristine and obviously constructed sets."

Diaz-Balart, Jose, and Mark McEwen. "Actress Winona Ryder Discusses Her Role in the New Film *The Crucible* and Her Career." *CBS This Morning* 19 December 1996. Broadcast transcript.

Ryder discusses the character of Abigail, her memories of reading *The Crucible* as a youngster, her response to the era of the film, and her early acting interests.

Gates, David, and Yahlin Chang. "One Devil of a Time." *Newsweek* 2 December 1996: 76–79.

Glib essay on the processes that went into the making of the film version of *The Crucible*, subtitled "Here's How a Classic Went Hollywood but Kept Its Virtue." Of note is Miller's producer-son Bob pitching the script to Twentieth Century-Fox as "a story about sex."

Gleiberman, Owen. "Bewitching Hour." *Entertainment Weekly* 29 November 1996: 68.

Positive review of the "joltingly powerful" film version of *The Crucible*, directed by Nicholas Hytner, that Gleiverman praises for the addition of the opening sequence of teenage girls in the woods—"it sets a mood of eroticized fear and delirium that reverberates throughout the movie."

Gordinier, Jeff. "Best Supporting Actress." *Entertainment Weekly* 28 February 1997: 62.

Feature article on Joan Allen's role of Elizabeth Proctor in the film version of *The Crucible* in which she admits that she had never read the play before being cast. According to director Nicholas Hytner, this turned out to be an advantage for she did not play the part "like a stern, judgmental shrew on the stage. This Elizabeth Proctor would have to try a little tenderness."

Gritten, David. "Trials and Tribulations: A Timely Return for *Crucible*." *Los Angeles Times* 30 April 1995, Calendar: 25.

Interview with Nicholas Hytner regarding the soon-to-be filmed version of *The Crucible* and his "excitement" with working with Miller. Says Hytner, "Reading Miller's first draft . . . was like reading English again."

Guthmann, Edward. "A *Crucible* for All Time." *San Francisco Chronicle* 20 December 1996: C1.

Gutherman praises the film version of *The Crucible*, directed by Nicholas Hytner, as "at once stunningly cinematic and perfectly faithful to Miller's text."

Karger, Dave. "Witches Brewing." *Entertainment Weekly* 10 May 1996: 42.

Short item offering quotes by director Nicholas Hytner and Miller's wife Inge Morath on the film production of Miller's *The Crucible*. Of note are Hytner's comments of his first meeting with Miller—"It was like going to Shakespeare and asking for amendments to *King Lear*."

Kauffmann, Stanley. "Latter-Day Look." *New Republic* 16 December 1996: 30–32.

Kauffmann praises the American film adaptation of Miller's work as "the best Miller work that I know." He adds that the film has been helped by the passage of time and "actually helped by the fact that no topical analogy applies. . . . With no need to weather the political-analogy test, freed too of the gratitude of an audience hungry for McCarthyism, the play stands on its own and is better for it."

Kempley, Rita. "The Devil Made Them Do It." *Washington Post* 20 December 1996: N45.

Mixed review of the American film version of Miller's play, directed by Nicholas Hytner, that Kempley calls "handsome and well acted" but too dependent on "the heat between Ryder and Day-Lewis, and it simply isn't there. The attraction is fatal allright, but it certainly doesn't seem mutual."

Luscombe, Belinda. "Why, It Hath Hit Writ All over It." *Time* 29 July 1996: 87.

Short blurb describing Miller's feelings regarding the film version of *The Crucible* and the choice of casting Winona Ryder in the part of Abigail Williams.

Maslin, Janet. "The Bewitching Power of Lies" *New York Times* 27 November 1996: C9.

Maslin offers a positive review of *The Crucible* [film], calling it a "handsome and impassioned" movie that "now speaks to subtler forms of dishonesty and opportunism than it did before."

McCormick, Patrick T. "Don't Make the Devil the Fall Guy." *U.S. Catholic* 62 (April 1997): 37–40.

Essay detailing the historical use of the devil as a literary device. Of Miller's *The Crucible*, McCormick states, it "is not about demons, but some deep and ugly need to find others guilty for the crime of being human, a need to hold somebody else responsible for the messiness and frustration of our lives."

McEwen, Mark. "Actor Daniel Day-Lewis Discusses His New Movie *The Crucible*." *CBS This Morning* 16 December 1996. Broadcast transcript.

Day-Lewis discusses the role of Proctor, working with Winona Ryder, and missing the "way of life" of filming Miller's play.

"Miller's *Crucible* is Clan-Do Effort." *USA Today* 18 November 1996: D2.

Gossipy news item that quotes Miller as being pleased by the outcome of the American film version of his *Crucible*. "This is the only time when what I imagined while writing actually showed up on the screen."

Morgan, Edmund S. "Bewitched." *New York Review of Books* 9 January 1997: 4, 6.

Historian Morgan favorably reviews Miller's film *The Crucible* and discusses the process and advantages of turning the play into a movie. With attention to detail, he examines the historical record of the Salem witch trials and compares it to Miller's interpretation of events.

Morgan, Marie. "*The Crucible*." *New England Quarterly* 70.1 (March 1997): 125–29.

Morgan, an historian of antebellum America, compares the text of Miller's 1953 play with the screenplay of *The Crucible* and finds that while the playwright has opened up his story, the film also "creates its own puzzles, mysteries that are not resolved by resource to the screenplay."

Navasky, Victor. "The Demons of Salem, with Us Still." *New York Times* 8 September 1996: Sec. 2: 37.

Lengthy review of the film version of *The Crucible*. Navasky, publisher and editorial director of *The Nation* and the author of *Naming Names*, a seminal study of Hollywood blacklisting, pronounces the film true to the storyline of the play—"a parable of paranoia." Says Navasky, "And so the final irony may well be that the movie it was thought impossible to make during the McCarthy years because it was about McCarthyism . . . turns out not to have been about that particular social deformation at all. Rather it was about something more universal—fear of forces one can't understand and control."

Novak, Ralph. "*The Crucible*." *People Weekly* 2 December 1996: 20.

Positive review of the film. Says Novak, "Audiences can attend this movie and enjoy the rare sensation of being treated with respect by the people who made it."

Rose, Lloyd. "*The Crucible*: Guilt Tripping." *Washington Post* 20 December 1996: D7.

Rose criticizes director Nicholas Hytner for using his all-star cast "in obvious ways" and treating the script "as if it were Shakespeare. [Hytner] doesn't seem to understand that what he's directed could be subtitled Blood-Crazed Teen Bimbos from Inner Space."

Rothstein, Edward. "On Naming the Names, in Life and Art." *New York Times* 27 January 1997: C13.

Rothstein discusses the links between *The Crucible* and the anti-Communist fervor of Sen. Joseph McCarthy. Also mentioned is the denial by the American Film Institute and the Los Angeles Film Critics Association of honor to Elia Kazan for his naming of names and his relationship to Miller.

Seiler, Andy. "Miller Recharges *Crucible*." *USA Today* 27 November 1996: D1.

Feature article in which Miller discusses the differences between the film and the stage versions of *The Crucible*, his original conception for the play, and its modern relevance. Also quoted are Winona Ryder, Daniel Day-Lewis, and director Nicholas Hytner.

———. "Ryder Possessed by *Crucible* Role." *USA Today* 3 January 1997: D4.

Profile of Winona Ryder, star of the American film version of *The Crucible*, in which the actress discusses her approach to the role of Abigail. Miller is quoted as praising Ryder's ability, insight, and energy.

Shribman, David M. "Salem's Past in Fact, Fiction." *Boston Globe* 13 December 1996: A3.

Shribman criticizes Miller's film for its inaccurate depiction of the Salem witch trials based upon his reading of the records in the Peabody Essex Museum, but predicts that the movie will play to huge audiences and be loved because "we are all the children of Salem"—"wicked, misled, zealots for bad causes. . . . We are all from Salem, and we fly to conclusions with the winds."

Simon, John. "Play Rach 3 for Me." *National Review* 27 January 1997: 56–57.

Mixed review of the film in which Simon praises the fact that Miller "sensibly" dropped "his half-hearted attempts at period diction that hurt the play, but ultimately dismisses the production: "The plot affords the actors ample opportunities to be vertiginously noble or dizzyingly wicked, but, somehow, the bloom is off the venture; perhaps we have seen the stage version too many times."

Sterritt, David. "*The Crucible* Tells Old Story with Modern-Day Relevance." *Christian Science Monitor* 27 November 1996: 15.

Positive review of the film, directed by Nicholas Hytner. Sterritt praises the impressive production and the 1950s play that "relates surprisingly well to today's versions of the bias and scapegoating that Miller rightly deplores."

Travers, Peter. "The Devil Made Them Do It." *Rolling Stone* 12 December 1996: 89–90.

Favorable review of Miller's film version of *The Crucible.* Travers calls it a "seductively exciting film that crackles with visual energy, passionate provocation and incendiary acting."

Turan, Kenneth. "Hysteria Resides at Heart of Frantic *Crucible.*" *Los Angeles Times* 13 December 1996: F12.

Negative review of the American film production of *The Crucible*, directed by Nicholas Hytner. Says Turan, "Rife with screaming fits and wild-eyed rantings, this film is too frantic to be involving, too much an outpost of bedlam to be believable."

Vaillancourt, Meg. "Massachusetts Wins Bid for Movie Site." *Boston Globe* 7 July 1995: 19.

News article announcing that Twentieth Century-Fox has chosen Massachusetts for the location of the American film version of Miller's play. Massachusetts offered the producers free office space and set construction (using prison inmates), transportation provided by the National Guard. In return, the filming will generate millions of dollars for the local economy.

Weales, Gerald. "What Sartre Saw in Salem." *American Theatre* April 1997: 51.

Weales remarks on Sartre's adaptation of Miller's play (*Les Sorcières de Salem*), and includes the argument that Miller's current film version of his play seems "to have been drawn from the French film, the most obvious of which is Abigail's love-happy-ever-after ending."

Weintraub, Bernard. "In New Films, Facts Get Some Assistance." *New York Times* 3 December 1996: C13.

While movie studios are increasingly drawn to fact-based dramas, there is a blurred and often controversial line between fact and fiction. The events that inspired *The Crucible* are "both murky and startling."

Winer, Linda. "*The Crucible* Helps Define 'monicalewinsky.'" *Newsday* 25 September 1998: B2.

Positive review of the American film version of *The Crucible* in which Winer compares the 1953 play about the Salem witch trials to the more current controversy regarding President Clinton's sexual scandal and its implications regarding personal freedom.

"Winona Ryder." *People* 12 May 1997: 133.

Brief profile on the star of *The Crucible* that includes Miller's comments on her as an actress.

Death of a Salesman

1951

Alpert, Hollis. "Mr. Miller's Indignant Theme" *Saturday Review of Literature* 22 December 1951: 34.

Alpert blames Stanley Roberts's screenplay, Laslo Benedek's direction, and Fredric March's miscasting as Willy Loman for the failure of the film version of *Salesman*, but acknowledges the "honesty and the dignity of the attempt."

Crowther, Bosley. "*Death of a Salesman*." *New York Times* 21 December 1951: 21.

Mixed review that praises March's performance but criticizes the story as "dismally depressing."

"Current Feature Films." *Christian Century* 20 February 1952: 231.

Favorable review of the film version of *Death of a Salesman* that faults the mentally unbalanced portrayal of Willy Loman for weakening the film's moral argument.

"*Death of a Salesman*." *Life* 14 January 1952: 63–64, 66.

Brief mixed review that applauds the directorial talents of Stanley Kramer and his "impressive movie adaptation," but faults the film for following the play "almost too literally."

"*Death of a Salesman*." *Magill's Survey of Cinema* 15 June 1995. *Electric Library* (3 December 1999).

Section on *Death of a Salesman* that includes an abstract, summary, analysis, production credits, and review sources for the film.

"*Death of a Salesman*." *Newsweek* 31 December 1951: 56–57.
Brief positive review that calls the adaptation of Miller's play "admirable."

"*Death of a Salesman*." *Variety* 12 December 1951: 6.
Highly laudatory review that praises Fredric March for "perhaps the greatest performance of his career . . . a memorable if exhausting film experience."

Hartung, Philip. "It Comes with the Territory." *Commonweal* 28 December 1951: 300–301.
Hartung suggests that the film adaptation of Miller's play needs some "softening humor to relieve the play's lengthy tension."

Hatch, Robert. "Movies." *New Republic* 31 December 1951: 22.
Hatch focuses on Linda Loman as the true focal character in both the film and the play and praises Fredric March as an actor who "melodramatizes the emptiness of the role and will probably win an Oscar."

Hine, Al. "*Death of a Salesman*" *Holiday* March 1952: 14, 16, 18.
Hine praises the film version of *Salesman*, starring Fredric March and directed by Laslo Benedek, as "one of the greats." Not only does the film hold its own, but "it seems to make a special category for itself."

Kass, Robert. "Film and TV" *Catholic World* February 1952: 386.
Negative review of the film version of *Salesman*, starring Fredric March and Kevin McCarthy, that Kass says "suffers from an overemphasis on Willy's mental deterioration. . . . He is a small man, really, and a faintly unpleasant one so that it is impossible to be very stirred when, at last, he is downed by circumstance."

McCarten, John. "The Current Cinema." *New Yorker* 22 December 1951: 62.
While a significant play, the portrayal of the Loman family on the screen turns them into a ridiculous sight.

"The New Pictures." *Time* 31 December 1951: 60.
Mixed review of the "bravely uncommon" film adaptation of *Death of a Salesman* that, regrettably, clings too closely to the play to be truly successful, and portrays a mentally unbalanced Willy Loman that ruins the reality of the story.

Quirk, Lawrence J. *The Films of Fredric March*. New York: Citadel, 1971. 201–3.

Chapter that includes production credits, plot synopsis, excerpts from reviews, and eight black-and-white photographic stills from the film.

Spoto, Donald. "'There's Something Emotionally Wrong Here. . . .'" *Stanley Kramer: Film Maker*. New York: Putnam, 1978. 73–82.

Brief chapter offering details on the production of the film of *Death of a Salesman*, starring Fredric March and Mildred Dunnock. Spoto lauds director Laslo Benedek's direction, particularly his "brilliant technique" of handling the film's "flashback" transitions, but severely criticizes Miller's story as based on "an improper understanding of what constitutes tragedy" and "emotionally sterile." Three black-and-white photographs, one a production still, the others rehearsal shots, accompany the text.

Warshow, Robert. "The Movie Camera and the American." *Commentary* March 1952: 275–81.

While the film adaptation of *Death of a Salesman* has a certain power and effect, it is, ultimately, inferior to the stage play.

1966

Dallos, Robert E. "*Death of a Salesman* Wins Emmy as Best Drama." *New York Times* 5 June 1967: 87.

News item reporting that *Death of a Salesman* was awarded the Emmy for television's best dramatic program of the 1966–67 season. Other awards went to director Alex Segal as best director and Miller for his adaptation.

Gent, George. "CBS Seeks Out Original Dramas." *New York Times* 22 June 1966: 95.

News item reporting that CBS has announced plans to spend $500,000 to encourage authors to write original and "significant" scripts for television, paying up to $25,000 per script. The president of CBS is quoted as crediting the CBS Playhouse production of *Death of a Salesman* as "creating new enthusiasm" for serious drama on television.

Gould, Jack. "New Life of a Salesman." *New York Times* 15 May 1966: II: 15.

Gould praises the CBS production of *Death of a Salesman*,

starring Lee J. Cobb and Mildred Dunnock, for bringing back the "excitement and dignity" of the early 1950s. Says Gould, "The little box in the parlor suddenly stopped its raucous blabbing and spoke with power and beauty."

———."TV: *Death of a Salesman*." *New York Times* 9 May 1966: 79.

Highly laudatory review of the television version of *Death of a Salesman*, starring Lee J. Cobb and Mildred Dunnock, that Gould calls "a veritable landmark in studio drama, an occasion of power so shattering and poignancy so delicate that there is no earlier parallel to cite."

1985

Canby, Vincent. "*Private Conversations* on Filming of *Salesman*." *New York Times* 7 October 1985: C16.

Review of *Private Conversations*, the documentary on the making of the television production of *Death of a Salesman*, starring Dustin Hoffman, appearing at the New York Film Festival. Canby says that the film "offers some revealing moments, though not enough to keep it from looking like a promotional film of somewhat higher quality than most."

Feingold. Morris. "An American Tragedy, Like It or Not." *Village Voice* 24 September 1985: 41.

Feingold praises the television version of *Death of a Salesman* for having a vitality that "reinforces the sense of the play being irrevocably stuck in our culture, like it or not, its weak points and its strokes of brilliance both precise reflections of our national identity."

O'Connor, John J. "*Death of a Salesman* Doubles 1966 Audience." *New York Times* 17 September 1985: C17.

News item reporting that the CBS-TV broadcast of *Death of a Salesman*, starring Dustin Hoffman and John Malkovich, had a viewership of 20–25 million, just about double what the 1966 production, starring Lee J. Cobb, had earned with its 10–15 million viewers. Also noted is the fact that there were more television sets in 1985 (84 million) than in 1966 (54 million) that might account for the increase.

———. "Hoffman in *Death of a Salesman*." *New York Times* 13 September 1985: C26.

Positive review of the television production, directed by Volker Schlondorff and starring Dustin Hoffman, that O'Connor calls "as powerful and magnificent a performance of the play as is likely to be seen in this generation."

Shewey, Don. "TV's Custom-Tailored *Salesman*." *New York Times* 15 September 1985: Sec. 2: 1, 23.

Article that details the process by which the stage play of *Death of a Salesman* was adapted, redesigned, restaged, and reinterpreted for the small screen.

Siegel, Ed. "*Death of a Salesman* Is Brilliant Television." *Boston Globe* 15 September 1985: Arts and Film: 83.

Lengthy positive review of the television version of *Death of a Salesman*, starring Dustin Hoffman, that Siegel calls, "one of the highlights of the 1985 television season and just one step short of a masterpiece."

Zacks, Richard. "This *Salesman* You'll Welcome to Your Home." *San Jose Mercury News* 13 February 1987: 10.

Positive review of the video release of Miller's *Death of a Salesman* starring Dustin Hoffman and John Malkovich. Zacks says it is "stupendous because the audience is not given a front-row seat. It's given a much better angle instead."

Zorn, Theodore E. "Willy Loman's Lesson: Teaching Identity Management with *Death of a Salesman*." *Communication Education* 40 (April 1991): 219–24.

Zorn details his use of the film version of *Death of a Salesman*, starring Dustin Hoffman, to teach interpersonal communication concepts and "to illustrate the reciprocal relationship between self-concept and communication in the negotiation of identities."

2000

Marks, Peter. "The Mythic Glad-Hander on TV? It's a Deal." *New York Times* 9 January 2000: Sec. 13: 4.

Interview with actor Brian Dennehy on the occasion of the television production of *Death of a Salesman*. Dennehy was heavily involved in the Showtime filming—acting the part of Willy Loman, serving as executive producer, and assisting in the editing of the film. Dennehy says his approach to the role was one "that hasn't really been explored before, which was the idea of his emotional illness. I did a lot of work on bipolar personality and manic-depressives, and it's interesting: I got letters from psychiatrists about the accuracy of the medical aspect of the performance."

Stearns, David Patrick. "*Salesman* Rings Better than Ever." *USA Today* 7 January 2000: E13.

In a television production that "has captured all the right moments" of the acclaimed Broadway revival, Stearns highly praises *Death of a Salesman* as "more than a play, but an inkblot with which we examine ourselves."

An Enemy of the People

"*American Playhouse* Collaboration, Arthur Miller Embraces *Enemy*." *Los Angeles Times* 12 June 1990: II: 9.

In an news article that reports Miller's presence at a read-through at Fox Studios for the PBS *American Playhouse* production of *An Enemy of the People*, starring John Glover and George Grizzard, Miller is quoted as praising director Jack O'Brien and remarking on his dissatisfaction with film versions of his *Death of a Salesman* and *All My Sons*.

Frymer, Murry. "Version of Ibsen Play Is Enemy of Subtlety." *San Jose Mercury News* 13 June 1990: F6.

Negative review of the PBS *American Playhouse* television version of Miller's adaptation of Ibsen's work, starring John Glover and George Grizzard. Says critic Frymer, not only are the actors unbelievable characters, but "the story really lacks credence."

Jaffee, Miriam. "Miller's *Enemy*." *Los Angeles Times* 23 June 1990: F2.

Letter to the editor in which Jaffee protests Miller adapting Ibsen's *An Enemy of the People* "as a format to express his own views." Miller and others, says Jaffee, "should struggle through the creative process and formulate their own ideas instead of attaching themselves like lampreys to suck the guts out of other playwrights' efforts."

Loynd, Ray. "A Viewer-Friendly *Enemy*." *Los Angeles Times* 13 June 1990: F1.

Calling Jack O'Brien's direction dynamic and John Glover's

performance "burnished," Loynd praises the KCET production for *American Playhouse* for its "surging, topical vitality in an Americanized adaptation by Arthur Miller."

Marin, Rick. "Miller Goes for Green with *Enemy*." *Washington Times* 13 June 1990: E3.

Marin praises the *American Playhouse* production of *An Enemy of the People* for its production values but complains that overall the play is dated.

McCabe, Bruce. "A Doctor's Struggle for Truth." *Boston Globe* 10 June 1990: TV Week: 2.

Positive review of the *American Playhouse* television production of Miller's adaptation. McCabe compliments the script, which "is as topical as it was when Miller wrote it in 1950."

O'Connor, John J. "*Enemy of the People* Set in Maine." *New York Times* 13 June 1990: C18.

O'Connor details the plot of Miller's adaptation of *An Enemy of the People* and praises the television production as "a powerful depiction of social corruption and selfishness" and "a fascinating signpost to one major direction that theatre and literature are likely to take in the 1990s: anger is back in fashion."

Roush, Matt. "A Self-Defeating *Enemy of the People*." *USA Today* 13 June 1990: D3.

While finding the play "timely," critic Roush faults the television production of *An Enemy of the People* for its lack of "dramatic coherence" and "self-righteousness. The characters seem to spout lugubrious rhetoric about authority, truth, society and revolution at a haywire, high-speed pace."

Wood, Daniel B. "Ibsen's Still-Valid Views of Pollution and Politics." *Christian Science Monitor* 13 June 1990: Arts: 11.

Positive review of the PBS *American Playhouse* production of *An Enemy of the People*, starring John Glover and George Grizzard, directed by Jack O'Brien, that Wood finds "eminently watchable." Included is a phone interview with the director in which he discusses the play's relevance to modern audiences.

Everybody Wins

Ansen, David. "Doing the Very Wrong Thing." *Newsweek* 5 February 1990: 72.

Calling Miller's film a "joyless fiasco," Ansen blames the screenplay "which, had it borne the name Arnold Miller, would probably never have been produced."

Arnold, Gary. "Ironic Title Can't Aid *Everybody Wins*." *Washington Times* 22 January 1990: E3.

Arnold calls *Everybody Wins* "a losing proposition for an exceptionally reputable collection of people" that "appears to be the victim of a faulty game plan, aggravated by many a busted play."

Barnes, Harper. "Surprisingly, Arthur Miller's Script Is Film's Flaw." *St. Louis Post Dispatch* 22 January 1990: D6.

Negative review of *Everybody Wins* that Barnes calls a "fairly entertaining, strangely uninvolving small-town mystery" that "ought to be better."

Canby, Vincent. "A Heroine Fixated on Everything." *New York Times* 20 January 1990: 13.

Calling *Everybody Wins* a "mess," Canby criticizes the film for having "lapses in continuity" and "introducing singular information, such as Angela's personality changes and Jerry's religious obsession, which is left undeveloped."

Clark, Mike. "The Audience Loses on *Everybody Wins*." *USA Today* 22 January 1990: D4.

Clark finds *Everybody Wins* a "quirky/murky mess that even in-the-trenches moviegoers might well avoid."

"*Everybody Wins*." *Magill's Survey of Cinema* 15 June 1995. *Electric Library* (3 December 1999).

Section on *Everybody Wins* that includes an abstract, summary, analysis, production credits, and review sources for the film.

"*Everybody Wins*." *Time* 5 February 1990: 73.

Brief negative review of *Everybody Wins* that says the film fails "to sustain the viewer's attention."

James, Caryn. "On Film Credits List, That Miller Is Arthur." *New York Times* 22 November 1988: C: 17, 21.

Profile of Miller's first original movie (*Everybody Wins*), a story loosely based and inspired by Miller's real-life involvement in the Peter Reilly murder case.

Kael, Pauline. "*Everybody Wins*." *New Yorker* 17 December 1990: 120–21.

Positive review in which Kael praises Debra Winger as one of the two or three most fearless screen actresses in America and finds Miller's screenplay "surprisingly cool, quirky." Kael urges her readers to see it.

Kauffmann, Stanley. "*Everybody Wins*." *New Republic* 5 March 1990: 26.

Overall, Kauffmann finds *Everybody Wins* "disappointing." While Debra Winger does deliver "a convincing portrayal of Angela" the film "fails to achieve even mediocrity."

Kelleher, Terry. "Arthur Miller Is Whodunit in This Mystery." *Newsday* 20 January 1990: II: 15.

Negative review of *Everybody Wins*. "The whodunit is routine, the character study underdeveloped and the moral treatise sketchy. The ending aims for cynicism and achieves only anticlimax." Adds Kelleher, the film is "as satisfying as a plea bargain."

Lovell, Glenn. "The Audience Loses in *Everybody Wins*." *San Jose Mercury News* 3 February 1990: C1.

Mostly negative review of *Everybody Wins* that Lovell calls "as suspenseful as watching paint peel."

Rainer, Peter. "*Everybody Wins* Falls a Bit Short of Victory." *Los Angeles Times* 22 January 1990: F4.

Rainer dislikes *Everybody Wins* from the first scene—"Literal mindedness in a movie is almost always a tip-off that things aren't going to get any better."

Ringel, Eleanor. "*Everybody Wins* Is Another Loser for Talented Co-Stars Nolte, Winger." *Atlanta Constitution* 7 March 1990: C5.

Negative review in which Ringel states, "Nobody wins in *Everybody Wins* . . . certainly not the audience, which deserves more for its money than this painfully botched curiosity."

Ryan, Desmond. "Stars and an Arthur Miller Script." *Philadelphia Inquirer* 7 February 1990: F5.

Negative review of *Everybody Wins* that blames Miller for his sophomoric script and "stiff and stilted" dialogue. Says Ryan, "Quite frankly, if this script had been submitted by a film-school student, the teacher would have handed it back with a demand for a major overhaul or the suggestion that the kid might want to change majors."

Sterritt, David. "Mega-Talents Veer Off Target in *Everybody Wins*." *Christian Science Monitor* 12 February 1990: Arts: 11.

Negative review of *Everybody Wins*. Sterritt blames the dialogue that sounds "artificial and stagy," and the script that "lurches along, surrounding occasionally good scenes with others that are clumsy and lifeless."

Travers, Peter. "*Everybody Wins*." *Rolling Stone* 22 February 1990: 39.

Travers feels that the fault with *Everybody Wins* lies not with the director or the actors, but with Miller's "overblown dialogue" and massive script problems.

Fame

O'Connor, John J. "TV: *Fame* Comedy by Arthur Miller, on NBC." *New York Times* 30 November 1978: C22.

Review of the *Hallmark Hall of Fame* television production, starring José Ferrer and Richard Benjamin, due to air this evening, which O'Connor states "wastes too much time getting started, making the sixty minutes seem like a three-hour epic. But there are compensations in that second half."

The Golden Years (Radio Broadcast BBC 1987)

Davalle, Peter. "*The Golden Years*." *The Times* 6 November 1987.

Davalle praises the first-ever broadcast of Miller's forty-seven-year-old radio play as possessing "flashes of psychological insight (and certainly of poetry) that are worthy to stand alongside anything in later Miller."

Ryan, Alan. "*The Golden Years*." *Sunday Telegraph* (London) 8 November 1987: 18.

Respectful review of Miller's radio play, written in 1940 for the New Deal Federal Theatre Project. Ryan calls the BBC radio production "interesting on several levels" but "propagandist in his aims."

Young, B. A. "*The Golden Years*." *Financial Times* (London) 7 November 1987.

Young calls *The Golden Years* "a baroque piece, with proper attention given to excitement and tension."

The Misfits

Alpert, Hollis. "Arthur Miller: Screenwriter." *Saturday Review* 4 February 1961: 27, 47.

After having read the book of *The Misfits*, seen the movie, and talked with Miller about both, Alpert studies their differences and similarities in an effort to examine "the writer's problem when he has the desire to say something in terms of film." While the book deserves credit for inspiring Miller to make the film, the movie "captures the attention and holds it unflaggingly, helped by the actors, the direction, and excellent, spirited photography."

Angell, Roger. "The Current Cinema: Misfire." *New Yorker* 4 February 1961: 86, 88.

Angell lambastes *The Misfits* "as a dramatic failure of considerable proportions" due to Miller's screenplay, "which seems to me obtrusively symbolic and so sentimental as to be unintelligent."

Beckley, Paul. "Graphic Reality in Miller's Film." *New York Herald Tribune Lively Arts and Book Review* 5 February 1961: 10.

Praises Monroe's performance as "dramatic, serious, accurate," and Clark Gable's as "little less than great."

"Cinema: New Picture." *Time* 3 February 1961: 68.

While lauding the mustang hunting sequence for its exciting dramatic action, the reviewer finds the film "loaded with logy profundities."

Conway, Michael, and Mark Ricci. *The Films of Marilyn Monroe*. New York: Cadillac Pub., 1964. 153–57.

A chapter on *The Misfits* that includes a listing of cast and production credits, film synopsis, and excerpts of critical reaction to the film. Seven black-and-white production stills accompany the text.

Corrigan, Robert. "The Soulscape of Contemporary American Drama." *World Theatre* 11 (Winter 1962–63): 316–28.

Corrigan argues that *The Misfits* represents a significant change in Miller's dramaturgy in that it is about "each man's sense of his own loneliness and the impossibility of communication even with one's closest fellows."

Crowther, Bosley. "Last of a Legend." *New York Times* 5 February 1961: II: 1.

Crowther discusses the "hypnotic" nature of watching Clark Gable in *The Misfits* with the "foreknowledge that Mr. Gable is dead" and this was his last film, for "this is the old familiar Gable, very much alive."

———. "*The Misfits.*" *New York Times* 2 February 1961: 24.

Negative review of *The Misfits* in which Crowther praises the direction as "dynamic, inventive, and colorful" and Gable as "ironically vital," but ultimately dislikes the film because "characters and theme do not congeal. There is a lot of absorbing detail in it, but it doesn't add up to a point . . . the picture just doesn't come off."

Davidson, Bruce. *Portraits.* New York: Aperture, 1999. 58. 60–61.

Four black-and-white full-page candid photographs taken on the set of *The Misfits* in 1960.

Dent, Alan. "Alien Values." *Illustrated London News* (London) 10 June 1961: 992.

Negative review of *The Misfits* that Dent calls a "messy and disappointing film" that has Marilyn Monroe playing her "usual character—a luscious little half-wit who trades all the time on the fact that all men, everywhere, find her irresistible."

Dudek, Louis. "Arthur Miller and *The Misfits.*" *Delta* 15 (August 1961): 26–27.

Dudek dislikes the film for its incomprehensible theme—that "men are alone, homeless, and miserable because they are incapable of compassion."

Essoe, Gabe. *The Films of Clark Gable.* N.J.: Citadel, 1970. 250–55.

Chapter on *The Misfits* includes production credits, film synopsis, and review excerpts. Eight black-and-white production stills from the film, some full-page, accompany the text.

Fiedler, Leslie A. *Waiting for the End.* New York: Stein and Day, 1964. 87–88.

Brief mention of Miller's film in which Fiedler assesses the playwright's success at adapting "the classical American Western to new times and new uses." As Fiedler notes, "the woman is no longer the pious and pretty but flat-chested schoolmarm that Gentile Americans know their actual grandmothers to have been, but the big-busted, dyed blonde, life-giving and bursting with animal vitality; she is all that the Jew dreams the *shiksa*, whom his grandmothers forbade him to mate."

Goode, James. *The Story of "The Misfits."* Indianapolis: Bobbs-Merrill, 1963. Rpt. as *The Making of "The Misfits."* New York: Limelight, 1986.

Objective, journal format account of the filming of *The Misfits*, inter cut with interviews from principals and production personnel. Note: photographs in second edition are different than those in the first—mostly stills from the film instead of the first's candid Magnum shots. No index in either edition makes use as source a challenge.

Grauman, Lawrence, Jr. "*The Misfits*." *Film Quarterly* 14 (Spring 1961): 51–53.

Negative review of *The Misfits* that Grauman says "is so strainingly serious, in fact, on so many different levels at once, that it ultimately collapses under its own ponderous weight."

Hamilton, William. "Of God and Woman: *The Misfits*." *Christian Century* 5 April 1961: 424–25.

Hamilton praises Miller for daring to use the Western for serious purposes, to express the competing myths of "freedom and conformity."

Hammen, Scott. "*Misfits*." *John Huston*. Boston: Twayne, 1985. 97–99.

Brief overview of the history of the production. Hammen praises Huston's work as a noble effort, "obviously undertaken with sincerely high aspirations and strove toward admirable goals." Ultimately, however, the film fails because it had "been weighted down by its celebrity cast and Miller's compulsion to embalm it in pseudoprofundity."

Hartung, Philip. "The Screen: Woe, Woe, Whoa." *Commonweal* 17 February 1961: 532–33.

With a "corny ending" and "occasional lapses in taste," *The Misfits* gives us a "fascinating study of maladjusted people who deserve understanding."

Hatch, Robert. "Films." *Nation* 18 February 1961: 154–55.

Criticizing the film for its "hollow sound," Hatch blames Miller's screenplay—"there is no truth, or at least no credibility, in the story Mr. Miller has devised. He has put together the ingredients for a total smash-up, and extricated his victims by main force of narrative."

Johnson, William. "Movie Viewer." *Modern Photography* May 1961: 24–25.

With "settings especially well conceived," this positive review of *The Misfits* works, says Johnson, because "the stars melt into their character, so that we forget they are stars."

Kass, Judith. *The Films of Montgomery Clift*. N.J.: Citadel, 1979. 191–96.

Chapter that includes production credits, plot synopsis, behind the scenes anecdotes, and nine black-and-white photographic stills from the film.

Kauffmann, Stanley. "Across the Great Divide." *New Republic* 20 February 1961: 26–27. Rpt. in *A World on Film: Criticism and Comment*. New York: Harper, 1966. 99–102.

While praising the movie for its promising premise and a screenplay that is "several universes above most American films," Kauffmann faults what he sees as essentially a "talked out" film that is "unsuccessful both in its treatment of its subject and as a use of the film form."

Leonard, John. "Who's a Misfit?" *National Review* 20 May 1961: 321–22.

Negative review of *The Misfits* that Leonard calls "a confused attempt to grapple with the Big Questions," that owes its unrealized sense of meandering to the character of Roslyn—"She isn't real, but the movie is all about her: all about Marilyn Monroe. Arthur Miller was thinking out loud about his wife, trying her out locked in the top of all sorts of fairy towers, standing back, taking a look, trying a new castle, always unsuccessful."

McIntyre, Alice T. "Making *The Misfits* or Waiting for Monroe or Notes from Olympus." *Esquire* March 1961: 74–81.

Lengthy first-hand account of the filming of *The Misfits* that quotes Miller, Monroe, Gable, and John Huston on issues relating to the script, the difficulty of the shoot, approaches to character, and Monroe's now-legendary and expensive tardiness and illnesses, which caused many delays in shooting.

McLaughlin, Richard. "*The Misfits* by Arthur Miller." *Springfield Republican* 12 March 1961: 5.

Highly negative review of *The Misfits*, which McLaughlin calls a "rather lugubrious attempt on the part of Miller to psychoanalyze his own misfitted marriage to Marilyn Monroe."

Magnum Cinema. London: Phaidon, 1995. Cover and 158–71.

Photographic essay by members of Magnum on the set of *The Misfits*, including those by Bruce Davidson, Dennis Stock, Eve Arnold, Ernst Haas, Elliott Erwin, Erich Hartman, and Henri Cartier-Breson.

Mayne, Richard. "Shoot the Moralist." *New Statesman* (London) 28 April 1961: 678.

Brief negative review of *The Misfits*, which Mayne says is lacking the "knotted quality of truth that would make it more than a good film."

Meyer, William R. "The Making of *The Misfits*." *The Making of Great Westerns*. New Rochelle, New York: Arlington House, 1979. 298–313.

Chapter on the film that includes production credits, film synopsis, and essay on the making of the film. The essay, based mostly on gossip and innuendo and has factual errors, covers the genesis of the script, production woes, salaries of stars, and Monroe's personal problems. Five black-and-white photos, mixed shots of individuals and production stills, accompany the text.

The Misftis: The Story of a Shoot. London: Phaidon, 2000.

Dozens of black-and-white photographs, some never seen before now, by Magnum photogrpahers Eve Arnold, Henri Cartier-Bresson, Inge Morath, Bruce Davidson, and Cornell Capa, among others, dominates this book on the making of *The Misfits*. Included is a lengthy interview with Miller and Inge Morath on their memories regarding the film and an essay by Serge Toubiana on the production details, controversies, relationships, and problems of one of Miller's most unpleasant personal and professional experiences.

"*The Misfits*." *Magill's Survey of Cinema* 15 June 1995. *Electric Library* (3 December 1999).
Section on *The Misfits* that includes an abstract, summary, analysis, production credits, and review sources for the film.

"*The Misfits*." *Newsweek* 6 February 1961: 84.
Mixed review that blames director Huston for failing "to instill an even tempo" producing "some unaccountably awkward passages."

"*The Misfits*." *Variety* 18 October 1961: 6.
Positive review that especially praises the mustang sequence as "a gem of filmmaking."

"Mosaic of Marilyn." *Coronet* February 1961: 58–69.
Brief interviews with John Huston, Eli Wallach, Montgomery Clift, Clark Gable, and Arthur Miller on the occasion of the release of *The Misfits*. Each man describes her differently as "each comments on the Monroe character riddle as he alone views it." Six Magnum photographs from the filming, as well as thumbnail shots of each man interviewed, accompany the text.

"Movies." *McCalls* April 1961: 6, 21.
Brief positive review of the film version of *The Misfits* that lauds the acting of Clark Gable and Marilyn Monroe, the direction of John Huston, and the writing of Arthur Miller.

Popkin, Henry. "Arthur Miller Out West." *Commentary* 31 (May 1961): 433–36.
Lengthy and valuable essay that examines the theme of communication in *The Misfits*, "a theme that Miller has hitherto expressed only in passing and almost inadvertently."

Pratley, Gerald. *The Cinema of John Huston*. New York: A. S. Barnes, 1977. 126–30.
In a book compiled from interviews with John Huston, the director of *The Misfits* offers his brief first-hand account of the production of the film, dwelling on the now-infamous experience of working with Marilyn Monroe.

Press, David. "Arthur Miller's *The Misfits*: The Western Gunned Down." *Studies in the Humanities* 8.1 (1980): 41–44.

Press offers a close reading of *The Misfits* as an affirmation of "the Western as debilitated, exhausted myth which misshapes experience, cripples consciousness, and masks meaning in layer upon layer of self deception."

Quigly, Isabel. "The Light That Never Was." *Spectator* (London) 9 June 1961: 840–41.

Highly negative review of *The Misfits* that Quigly calls "morbid" and "pretentious triviality" that sounds "in spite of a sentimental story and much weird, battered symbolism about masculinity and mustangs, only too true to life."

Signer, Stefan. "Pyramid Lake, Nevada, 1956: Poem for 6 Percussionists, 1988." Stuttgart: Musikkontor, 1989.

Musical score (51 pages), inspired by a text by Arthur Miller printed on page 3. First performance on 27 April 1989. Score located in the Performing Arts-Music Department of the New York Public Library. Also in the Library of Congress Performing Arts Reading Room.

Walker, Alexander. "Body and Soul: Harlow and Monroe." *The Celluloid Sacrifice: Aspects of Sex in the Movies*. New York: Hawthorn, 1966. 129–30.

Brief mention of Miller's screenplay of *The Misfits* in the context of an essay on Marilyn Monroe. Says Walker, "in the hindsight of their separation and divorce, it is *The Misfits* rather than the play he subsequently wrote, *After the Fall*, which seems like his attempt to exorcise her spirit."

Walsh, Moira. "*The Misfits*." *America* 18 February 1961: 676, 678.

Negative review of the film that faults the "accidental overtones of tragedy" that surrounding its release, including the death of Clark Gable and breakup of the marriage of Miller to its star.

Weales, Gerald. "Tame and Woolly West." *Reporter* 2 May 1961: 46–47.

Weales feels the film fails due to the poor acting, directing, and Miller's "abandonment of tragedy."

Weatherby, W. J. "*The Misfits*: Epic or Requiem?" *Saturday Review* 4 February 1961: 26–27.

After Weatherby traces the genesis of Miller's screenplay, *The*

Misfits, and details the plot of the film, he examines what he sees as the reasons for "the film's promise," including the accurate casting of the stars into roles they naturally understand and the fact that this production "is not a Hollywood product in the usual sense."

Whitcomb, Jon. "Marilyn Monroe—the Sex Symbol Versus the Good Wife." *Cosmopolitan* December 1960: 53–57.

In this interview given on the set of *The Misfits*, Marilyn Monroe discusses her career, her marriage to Miller, working with Clark Gable, her shyness, and her interest in gardening and cooking. Miller is quoted as commenting on his considerable involvement with the picture, from casting to daily rewrites to ensuring that "all the story values are kept in."

Playing for Time

Ferretti, Fred. "Critics of Redgrave Casting as Jew Ask Equal Time." *New York Times* 7 November 1979: C30.

News item reporting the efforts of the Committee for Equal Time, whose members include Martin Balsom, Mel Brooks, Tony Lo Bianco, and Larry Gelbart, to force CBS to grant an equal amount of broadcast time "for the presentation of a dramatic program of the same length in an equal time slot, by a top dramatic writer, emphasizing the other side of the question." CBS is reported to stand by their casting decision and had denied the group their request. Miller is quoted as defending the casting of Redgrave ("She is not an anti-Semite, I'm certain of that.") and his adaptation of Fénelon's book ("I'm going to rely on what I wrote.").

Lewis, Anthony. "After Auschwitz." *New York Times* 2 October 1980: A23.

Opinion piece praising Miller's television movie of *Playing for Time* for passing "the essential test of dignified faithfulness to the meaning of the Holocaust."

Mann, Judy. "Art Is Long, But Life, Politics Are Short." *Washington Post* 26 September 1980: B1, 6.

Feature article on author and Auschwitz survivor Fania Fénelon's efforts to have Vanessa Redgrave replaced in the television production of Fénelon's book *Playing for Time*. The film's producer, Linda Yellen, is quoted at length defending the decision and speaking out against what she perceives as yet another form of blacklisting in Fénelon's attempts to fire the actress for her political beliefs.

McLean, Robert A. "Amid the Horror Emerges a Heroine." *Boston Globe* 30 September 1980.

Highly laudatory review of the CBS teleplay of *Playing for Time* starring Vanessa Redgrave. McLean praises Redgrave's portrayal of Fania Fénelon, "an individual tour de force which vindicates the controversial Redgrave casting." and Miller's script as "a triumphant hymn to the human spirit."

———. "Redgrave Drama Has No Sponsors." *Boston Globe* 11 September 1980.

News item detailing the controversy surrounding the casting of Vanessa Redgrave in the role of Fania Fénelon in the CBS teleplay of *Playing for Time*, including the network's difficulty in obtaining commercial sponsorship and Fénelon's own personal protest against the Redgrave casting decision.

"News." *Boston Globe* 13 December 1979.

News item reporting that the film's director Joseph Sargent has "quit in a huff over what the network calls 'creative differences'" during the production of Miller's adaptation of Fania Fénelon's memoir *Playing for Time.* He had previously replaced the former director Tony Richardson (Redgrave's husband) who had quit the project before shooting began "because he said his personal standards on the production weren't being met." The new director is Daniel Mann and is being shot in Fort Indiantown Gap in central Pennsylvania.

O'Connor, John J. "TV: Vanessa Redgrave, Inmate." *New York Times* 30 September 1980: C9.

After recounting the controversy surrounding the making of *Playing for Time*, O'Connor praises the film for being "totally uncompromising in its depictions of hope and despair, of generosity and viciousness, of death and survival in the bizarre, nightmare world of a concentration camp."

"*Playing for Time*." *Boston Globe* 30 September 1980.

After reviewing the controversy surrounding the decision to cast Vanessa Redgrave, supporter of the PLO, as Fania Fénelon in Miller's *Playing for Time*, the critic praises Redgrave's performance as "nearly flawless."

Shales, Tom. "The Scar That Binds." *Washington Post* 30 September 1980: B1, 7.

Highly lauditory review of the televison film of *Playing for Time*. After relating the controversies surrounding this producion, Shales remarks, "This is one of those rare seious works of television tha deserve special treatment."

The Price and *A Memory of Two Mondays*

Gould, Jack. "Miller's *The Price*." *New York Times* 4 February 1971: 71.

Gould praises the television version of *The Price* as perfect for the small screen with an excellent cast headed by George C. Scott and Colleen Dewhurst.

Novick, Julius. "Arthur Miller: Does He Speak to the Present?" *New York Times* 7 February 1971: II: 17.

Novick enjoyed the television production of *A Memory of Two Mondays*, calling it "a gentle, lyrical, Chekhovian evocation of the past with a special unpretentious charm," but disliked *The Price*, a play that "seems to be written out of an impulse long since exhausted. . . . If only Solomon had more to do than hold up the action with his monologues, if only Miller would invest more of himself in the unpretentious, idiomatic, comic side of his play, it would be possible to look forward to Miller's future work with more enthusiasm."

Williams, Raymond. "Remembering the Thirties." *The Listener* (London) 8 April 1971: 460–61.

Mistakenly thinking the play was written around 1950, Williams praises the NBC-ITV production of *The Price* as "memorable" and "very powerful"—"a precise experience in a precise rhythm."

A View from the Bridge

Crowther, Bosley. "Questions of Choice" *New York Times* 28 January 1962: II: 1.

While the film version of *A View from the Bridge* is sincere, Crowther laments that the main character is not the tragic figure that Miller intends, but instead, a boorish stubborn brute.

———. "*A View from the Bridge*" *New York Times* 23 January 1962: 36.

Crowther praises the excellent acting of the film version of *A View from the Bridge* but finds Eddie Carbone an unsympathetic character who deserves his fate.

Gill, Brendan. "The Current Cinema" *New Yorker* 27 January 1962: 82.

Gill lauds the film version of *A View from the Bridge* as brilliant and a highly effective piece of cinema.

Hartung, Philip. "The Screen: Mother Wins, Uncle Loses" *Commonweal* 9 February 1962: 518.

While Hartung praises the film version of *A View from the Bridge* for its acting, direction, and writing, he laments that it "strains too hard to be great tragedy."

Hatch, Robert. "Films" *Nation* 10 February 1962: 125.

Blaming Miller for the morbid, not tragic, quality of *A View from the Bridge*, Hatch asserts that the playwright can't seem to "locate his drama in individuals of sufficient complexity or stature to make the narrative absorbing."

Kael, Pauline. "*The Innocents* and What Passes for Experience." *Film Quarterly* 15 (Summer 1962): 27–29. Rpt. as "*A View from the Bridge*, and a Note on *The Children's Hour*" in Kael's *I Lost It at the Movies*. Boston: Little, Brown, 1965. 172–76.

Kael lambastes the film version of *View*, directed by Sidney Lumet, as a portrait of "a man behaving so insanely and stupidly that we keep wondering why he isn't put away or treated. . . . It's not so much a drama unfolding as a sentence that's been passed on the audience. What looks like and, for some people, passes for tragic inevitability is just poor playwriting."

Kauffmann, Stanley. "The Unadaptable Adapted" *New Republic* 12 February 1962: 26–27.

Negative review of the film version of *A View from the Bridge* that Kauffmann finds uninteresting, unoriginal, and unnecessarily longer than the stage play.

———. "Movies: Miller Agonists." *Show* January 1962: 5. Rpt. as "*A View from the Bridge*." in *A World on Film: Criticism and Comment*. New York: Harper, 1966. 102–106.

Citing Miller's consistent "bad luck with the films made from his plays," Kauffmann laments that *A View from the Bridge* "could have been a tense shocker," but "has been puffed and bloated until, in the second half, even its good cast cannot interest us any longer in its battered, repetitive story."

Knight, Arthur. "Runaway!" *Saturday Review* 27 January 1962: 28.

Negative review of the film version of *A View from the Bridge*, directed by Sidney Lumet, that Knight finds "an odd, uncomfortable mixture of styles" that "fails to jell."

McDonald, Dwight. "Films" *Esquire* February 1962: 22, 24.

Brief positive review of the film version of *A View from the Bridge* that McDonald finds "modest" but possessing "real virtues."

"Oedipus in Flatbush" *Time* 19 January 1962: 55.

Praising the screenplay, direction, and acting, this review faults Miller's misuse of Greek tragedy in the creation of a character in Eddie Carbone, who is a pathetic "Oedipus in a gorilla suit."

Rosten, Norman. "Scenarist Eyes His *View from the Bridge*" *New York Times* 21 January 1962: II: 9.

Rosten details his adaptation of Miller's play *A View from the Bridge*, including his dropping of the narrator character and cutting and/or rearranging sequences—all with an eye to keep the characters intact and consistent with the play.

Somers, Florence. "New Movies" *Redbook* February 1962: 29.

Brief positive review of *A View from the Bridge* that compares the film to *Marty* and *On the Waterfront* in its "honesty and authenticity."

"*A View from the Bridge*." *Magill's Survey of Cinema* 15 June 1995. *Electric Library* (3 December 1999).

Section on *A View from the Bridge* that includes an abstract, summary, analysis, production credits, and review sources for the film.

"What's Eating Eddie?" *Newsweek* 22 January 1962: 80–81.

Negative review of the film version of *A View from the Bridge* that suffers from an implausible story that confuses both the main character and the audience.

7. Fiction and Nonfiction

Focus

Barry, Iris. "Look through This Glass." *New York Herald Tribune Weekly Book Review* 18 November 1945: 4.

Barry calls Miller's novel "a first-rate horror story, cleverly as well as passionately devised from the first premonitory nightmare touch, apt by it mere story-telling proficiency to enlist one's interest and thereby to plunge one inextricably in its sinister sequence of events, right through to the unexpected emergence of its hero from his intolerable dilemma."

Bellow, Saul. "Brothers' Keepers." *New Republic* 7 January 1946: 29.

Bellow finds Miller's first novel "implausible" and a failed attempt to express the transformation of the main character from Jew-hater to Jew.

Butterfield, Alfred. "*Focus*." *New York Times Book Review* 18 November 1945: Sec. 7: 15.

Mixed review of Miller's novel that Butterfield calls a "strong, sincere book bursting with indignation and holding the reader's attention dispite its many faults." Later, he comments, "As the case history of a very strange human experience this novel has high merit. As a book of substantial meaning, it does not succeed."

"*Focus*." *Booklist* 1 December 1945: 111.

Brief positive review of *Focus* that is described as "an artistic, dramatic, and uncompromising portrayal of the social and personal irony of racial intolerance. . . . The author bars no holds and calls the Christian front by name."

"*Focus*." *Kirkus* 15 September 1944: 345–46.

Mixed review of Miller's first novel that the critic finds "interesting" and "telling" but faults for using mechanical plot devices to help tell its story.

"*Focus*." *New Yorker* 3 November 1945: 102.

Negative review of *Focus*, a novel with a predictable ending that the critic figures out "long before Mr. Miller has finished belaboring it."

Keefe, Edward. "*Focus*." *Commonweal* 7 December 1945: 219–20.

Brief unfavorable review that criticizes Miller's first novel as colorless and contrived.

Kennedy, Leo. "*Focus*." *Chicago Sun Book Week* 11 November 1945: 28.

Highly lauditory review of *Focus* that Kennedy calls an "indictment of bigotry and social irresponsibility" using a "consumately skillful literary form." Kennedy likens Miller's first novel to *Uncle Tom's Cabin* in its indictment of anti-Semitism.

Liptzin, Sol. *The Jew in American Literture*. New York: Bloch, 1966. 228–30.

Very brief analysis of *Focus* as a counterattack to anti-Semitism in its exposure of bigotry.

Lob, Ladislaus. "'Insanity in the Darkness': Anti-Semitic Stereotypes and Jewish Identity in Max Frisch's *Andorra* and Arthur Miller's *Focus*." *Modern Language Review* 92.3 (July 1997): 545–58.

Lob analyzes the similarities and differrences between the two works, finding that both are based on mistaken identity and work as investigations of issues of personal identity and social responsibility. The two works depart from one another in their endings, reflecting, perhaps, their authors' differening temperaments and personalities.

Mesher, David R. "Arthur Miller's *Focus*: The First American Novel of the Holocaust?" *Judaism* 29.4 (1980): 469–78.

In this unique comprehensive essay, Mesher offers a close reading of Miller's neglected, only novel, *Focus* (1945), as an important and "accurate contemporary expression of the American Jew's reaction to the destruction of European Jewry, and as one of the few attempts, in the entire generation of Jewish-American writers, to bear witness to the fate of their people."

Ross, Jean. "*Focus*." *Kirkus* 15 August 1945: 345–46.

Negative review in which Ross calls Miller's book "not wholly successful, but interesting and with a certain challenge" and a "telling" first novel.

———. "*Focus*." *Library Journal* 15 October 1945: 979.
Brief mention of Miller's novel, notable for its advice to libraries to use caution before ordering as the book contains attacks on the "Christian Front."

Smith, G. Harrison. "The Shape of a Human Face." *Saturday Review of Literature* 17 November 1945: 11.
Positive review of *Focus* that Smith finds an eloquent and significant work that deals with fears rather than action.

Situation Normal

Basseches, Maurice. "'Tenshun!" *Saturday Review of Literature* 2 December 1944: 64, 66.
Positive review of *Situation Normal* that Corporal Basseches calls "one of the most important books about America and the war" published.

Duffield, Marcus. "Whys and Wherefores." *Nation* 13 January 1945: 50.
Brief positive review of *Situation Normal* that Duffield calls a "provocative piece" of journalism.

Kupferberg, Herbert. "Touring Training Camps." *New York Herald Tribune Weekly Book Review* 17 December 1944: 3.
Highly laudatory review of Miller's fist book of reportage. Says Kupferberg, "Mr. Miller is an excellent reporter: he has an eye for the little things that give meaning to the big ones."

Maloney, Russell. "Jottings for a Movie." *New York Times Book Review* 24 December 1944: 3.
Fairly positive review of *Situation Normal* that applauds Miller's ability to "describe actual happenings rather than stalking ideas or impressions."

"*Situation Normal*." *Booklist* 1 January 1945: 133–34.
Positive descriptive review of *Situation Normal* that the critic calls an "authentic G.I. reaction to the war" by [erroneously] one of Hollywood's "ablest reporters."

Tobin, James. *Ernie Pyle's War: America's Eyewitness to World War II*. Kans.: UP of Kansas, 1997.
Tobin uses anecdotal information, mostly culled from Miller's

autobiography and *Situation Normal*, to relate Miller's work on the screenplay for *The Story of G.I. Joe* and his association with Ernie Pyle. "Miller yearned to say what the war ought to be; Ernie aimed to say what it was."

Arthur Miller's Collected Plays

Atkinson, Brooks. "Five by Miller." *New York Times* 9 June 1957: Sec. II: 1.

Atkinson critcizes Miller's preface as "forbidding," "humorless and a little pretentious," but lauds the playwright's refusal to "turn his private conscious over to administration by the State. . . . That is the measure of the man who has written these "high-minded plays."

Brien, Alan. "There Was a Jolly Miller." *Spectator* (London) 8 August 1958: 191–92.

Brien recounts both critical response to Miller and Miller's response to his critics in this favorable review of his *Collected Plays*. While criticizing Miller's "Introduction to the *Collected Plays*" as "painfully and often clumsily written" and "full of polysyllabic words, untidy sentences, snippets of sociological jargon," Brien admits that the essay is also "one of the most important texts in the modern theatre."

"*Collected Plays*." *Booklist* 15 June 1957: 523.

Brief positive review that recommends Miller's *Collected Plays* to "readers who can accept a realistic, tough-minded approach to play writing."

Mortimer, John. "Beyond Politics." *Encounter* October 1958: 87.

Positive review of Miller's *Collected Plays* that Mortimer calls "a book which contains some of the best writing to have been done in any medium and surely one of the great plays of this century [*Death of a Salesman*]."

Newman, William J. "The Plays of Arthur Miller." *Twentieth Century* 164 (November 1958): 491–96. Rpt. as "Arthur Miller's *Collected Plays*" *Two Modern American Tragedies: Reviews and Criticism of "Death of a Salesman" and "A Streetcar Named Desire."* Ed. John D. Hurrell. New York: Scribner's, 1961. 68–71. Excerpt rpt. as "The Role of Family in Miller's Plays" in *Readings on Arthur Miller*. Ed. Thomas Siebold. San Diego, Calif.: Greenhaven,

1997. 90–94.

It is Newman's thesis that the characters in Miller's plays are ultimately left without a sense of self because they mistakenly look toward the family and family relationships to provide that meaning.

"Our Colossal Dad." *Times Literary Supplement* (London) 29 August 1958: 482. Rpt. in *Two Modern American Tragedies: Reviews and Criticism of "Death of a Salesman" and "A Streetcar Named Desire."* Ed. John D. Hurrell. New York: Scribner's, 1961. 72–75.

Lengthy essay that essentially recounts the subjects discussed in Miller's "Introduction to the *Collected Plays*," compares Miller to O'Neill and Ibsen, and traces the father-son theme in the works presented in the volume.

Worsley, T. C. "American Tragedy." *New Statesman* (London) 23 August 1958: 220.

Worsley praises Miller's "undoubted and remarkable talent" for "simple strong emotional scenes brilliantly expressed in the highly vivid realistic dialogue of his country and his time," but criticizes the playwright for his "somewhat tortuous prose style" of his prefaces, which "tell us that we have got Mr. Miller all wrong. As he explains [it] . . . he is after things he considers altogether more important."

The Misfits

Freedley, George. "*The Misfits*." *Library Journal* 15 March 1961: 1155.

Brief positive review of the "cinema-novel" version of *The Misfits*, that Freedley praises for its inner meaning.

Hutchens, John K. "*The Misfits*." *New York Herald Tribune Lively Arts and Book Review* 5 February 1961: 27.

Negative comments regarding the printed version of the film. While Hutchens concedes that that idea is spirited, the story remains dormant on the printed page.

"*The Misfits*." *Booklist* 15 April 1961: 519.

Brief negative review of the "cinema-novel" version of *The Misfits* that concedes that "the book will be needed, not so much for the story as for the author's name and interest in the motion picture which was the end result."

Mitgang, Herbert. "Books of the Times." *New York Times* 8 February 1961: 29.

Mixed review of the "cinema-novel" version of *The Misfits,* that Mitgang lauds for the quality of its intentions and themes but criticizes for the lack of description of incident and character that is necessary in fictional works. Concludes Mitgang, "Regardless of whether the film is liked, or well liked, it can be said that Arthur Miller's artistry is present everywhere in the book."

O'Grady, Gerald. "The Dance of *The Misfits*: A Movie Mobile." *Journal of Aesthetic Education* 5.2 (1971): 75–89.

O'Grady closely compares the short story to the cinema-novel version of *The Misfits* in an effort to demonstrate Miller's ability [to quote Miller] to "create a fiction which might have the peculiar immediacy of image and the reflective possibilities of the written word."

Rolo, Charles. "Reader's Choice." *Atlantic Monthly* March 1961: 115–16.

Rolo dislikes the new "cinema-novel" form of *The Misfits,* which he finds less effective than the novel.

"The Written Film." *Times Literary Supplement* (London) 12 May 1961: 296.

Praising the written work over the film version, this mixed review disdains the manner in which Miller has depicted Roslyn and finds her contempuously created.

I Don't Need You Any More

"At Another Distance." *Times Literary Supplement* (London) 30 November 1967: 1125.

Mixed review of the collection of short stories that praises "A Search for a Future" as the best of the bunch, claiming that some stories seem "plotty" while others are "pure anecdote."

Atkinson, Brooks. "A Theatre of Life." *Saturday Review* 25 February 1971: 53.

Atkinson compares the short stories of Tennessee Williams and Arthur Miller, finding that while some of Miller's stories do nothing to enhance his reputation as a writer, "The Misfits" proves to be a "masterpiece of impromptu life."

Bone, Larry Earl. "*I Don't Need You Any More*." *Library Journal* 1 February 1967: 596.

Bone finds "Please Don't Kill Anything" an example of "a memorable selection that shines a beautiful light on a brief but happy moment in the lives of two people."

Charyn, Jerome. "Arthur Miller Off Stage." *Book World* 12 February 1967: 4, 17.

Charyn praises the title story "I Don't Need You Any More" as a "masterpiece," and concludes that "in spite of minor defects, Mr. Miller has shown a formidable talent, and whatever the vagaries of the theatre, whether his plays are *in* this year or not, I don't think his best stories will easily go out of style."

Cook, Roderick. "Books in Brief." *Harper's* March 1967: 136.

Mostly negative review of *I Don't Need You Any More*, that will not enhance Miller's reputation as a great writer. Of note is that Cook feels that the "cinema-novel" version of "The Misfits" reads better than it plays on the screen, mainly because the character of Roslyn is not present in the written work.

Goldman, Arnold. "*I Don't Need You Any More*." *Listener* (London) 2 November 1967: 580.

Goldman likes this collection of short stories better than Miller's first novel *Focus*, which he calls "awkward." While some of the stories are excellent, Miller focuses too much on the "doggedly irrepressible" characters who retain "a characteristic sense of wonder."

Handlin, Oscar. "Old Pros." *Atlantic* March 1967: 143.

Brief negative review that faults the collection of short stories for its lack of "dramatic elements or conversational passages."

"*I Don't Need You Any More*." *Choice* 4 (July–August 1967): 532.

Positive review of the collection of short stories that shows us a Miller who can express his vision "favorably in another medium and dimension."

Jacobson, Irving. "The Vestal Jews on 'Mont Sant' Angelo.'" *Studies in Short Fiction* 13 (1976): 507–12. Rpt. in *Critical Essays on Arthur Miller*. Ed. James J. Martine. Boston: G. K. Hall, 1979. 206–11.

Jacobson offers a close reading of "Mont Sant' Angelo" as a

unique story in the Miller canon in which "an adult comes to feel himself at home in the larger world outside the family structure."

Koven, Stanley. "*I Don't Need You Any More*, Arthur Miller." *Commonweal* 17 March 1967: 686–87.

Negative review that finds Miller's shift in distance "ineffective." Says Koven, what we have is a "bunch of flurry dilemmas."

Lask, Thomas. "Mr. Miller Offstage." *New York Times* 18 March 1967: 27.

Mixed review of the collection of nine short stories published as *I Don't Need You Any More*. Says Lask, Miller "is not an easy or graceful writer, although it is not easy to say why. The writing is clear, precise and unambiguous, yet we are conscious of it. I think it is because Mr. Miller sqeezes so much 'meaning' into his prose. It never relaxes."

"Playwrights in Print." *Time* 10 March 1967: 102.

Negative review of *I Don't Need You Any More*, that faults the works for not being as good as Miller's plays, and containing an "incessant search for identity so common to American writers."

Sheffer, Isaih. "Storytelling Dramatists." *New Leader* 5 June 1967: 24.

Sheffer praises "Fitter's Night" as the best in this collection of short stories that possess "variety, skill, and feeling."

Vince, Thomas L. "*I Don't Need You Any More*." *Best Sellers* 1 March 1967: 436.

Negative review in which Vince finds Miller's collection of short stories "dull" that would have been better served by being authored by a lesser-known writer.

Wakeman, John. "Story Time." *New York Times Book Review* 2 April 1967: 4.

Wakeman praises Miller's collection of short stories as "exact, humane, knowlegeable writing, free of affectation and self-congratulation."

Zimmerman, Paul. "Offstage Voices." *Newsweek* 27 February 1967: 92.

Zimmerman praises what he sees as a Miller who can "relax" in this collection of short fiction that effectively blends "insight and outlook."

In Russia

Burg, Victor. "Arthur Miller *In Russia*." *Christian Science Monitor* 8 January 1970: 17.

Positive review of Miller and wife Morath's book of reportage that Burg calls "strictly personal and concernedly honest."

"The Chemistry of Travel." *Times Literary Supplement* (London) 22 January 1970: 76.

While applauding Miller's probing questions of Russian life and cultural politics, the reviewer admits that "no visitor to the Soviet Union can expect a better time than an acceptable playwright."

Gentleman, David. "In Russia with Inge Morath." *New Statesman* (London) 5 December 1969: 826.

Gentleman praises Miller and Morath's book as the "most penetrating and convincing picture of both the good and bad aspects of an artist's life in such a society."

Reeve, F. D. "*In Russia*." *Book World* 4 January 1970: 11.

Highly negative review that attacks Miller and Morath's book of reportage as pretentious and drab, devoid of the character and humor of the Russian people.

Robotham, J. "*In Russia*." *Library Journal* 1 February 1970: 496.

Robotham praises Miller and Morath's book as "one of the most interesting of Russian travel books."

Salisbury, Harrison E. "*In Russia*." *New York Times Book Review* 14 December 1969: 1, 57.

Positive review of *In Russia* that Salisbury finds especially "accurate" because of Miller's own experiences with "persecution and harrassment" in the United States.

In the Country

Broyard, Anatole. "A Calder on Every Lawn." *New York Times* 10 February 1977: 37.

Positive review of Miller and Morath's photographic journal in which Broyard expresses his agreement with Miller's views that the current nostalgia for the rural life is based on a mistaken understanding of the country as "the last stronghold of a vanished individualism" when in actuality rural life depends on communal needs. Says Broyard, nostalgia, however, is a "yearning for the vanished communal feeling."

"*In The Country*." *Booklist* 1 April 1977: 1138.

Brief positive review that make note of the sense that the country has both mellowed and softened the playwright.

"*In The Country*." *Kirkus* 15 March 1977: 344.

Brief positive review of *In the Country* that the reviewer finds a "rambling and free-associating . . . gentle history" of the Connecticut community in which he has lived for many years.

Johnston, Albert. "*In The Country*." *Publisher's Weekly* 24 January 1977: 321.

Positive review of *In The Country*, that Johnston finds a "muted, thoughtful, and sometimes witty" collection of stories of rural life in New England.

Massie, Allan. "Land of Lost Content." *Times Literary Supplement* (London) 17 June 1977: 722.

Massie finds *In The Country* a sad work that shows a dispairing Eden and a decaying view of a rural community, a once "innocent world where the American Dream, the Protestant ethic, were unchallenged."

Otness, Harold. "*In The Country*." *Library Journal* 15 March 1977: 722.

Otness praises Inge Morath's photographs as provocative and Miller's text as nostalgic, with a sense of deep sadness and quiet desperation at the changes that have taken place in this rural community of New Englanders.

The Theater Essays of Arthur Miller

Brater, Enoch. "*Theater Essays of Arthur Miller*." *New Republic* 6 May 1978: 32.

Brater lauds Miller's essays on the theatre for being not "isolated pieces of experience," but works that succeed "in theatricalizing experience itself."

Havener, W. Michael. "*Theater Essays of Arthur Miller*." *Library Journal* 1 March 1978: 582.

Mixed review of Miller's theatre essays that Havener praises for their "valuable insights" but chides for the collection's "regrettable omissions."

Johnston, Albert. "*Theater Essays of Arthur Miller*." *Publisher's Weekly* 2 January 1978: 60.

Positive review of this collection of cogent and eloquent essays that speak "to the problems of the contemporary theatre and to the ills of our society."

Schlueter, June. "*Theater Essays of Arthur Miller*." *Bestsellers* 37 (February 1978): 345.

Negative review that faults the *Theater Essays* editors for not framing the collection with a thesis or providing evidence of Miller's "maturing playwright's vision." Says Schlueter, "With a few exceptions, the essays and interviews which constitute this book are singularly unnoteworthy. Miller's views on the state of the theatre reflect a professional's, not a literary critics', awareness; his ideas concerning form are anachronism offered as innovation; and his prefaces, while helpful as such, are incomplete in isolation."

Styan, J. L. "A View from the Crucible; or, the Compleat Playwright." *Michigan Quarterly Review* 18 (1979): 509–15.

Praising Robert A. Martin's introduction and editing, Styan offers a positive review of *Theater Essays* that he finds "argumentative, stimulating, challenging," and includes an essay ["Introduction to the Collected Plays"] that "is doubtless among the important pieces of critical writing about drama in our time."

Sullivan, Jack. "*Theater Essays of Arthur Miller*." *Saturday Review* 1 April 1978: 36.

Sullivan lauds the latter essays over the earlier ones and praises Miller's foreword to the *Collected Essays* for its attack on what he calls the "stylized reduction of human suffering to a groan and a cough."

"*Theater Essays of Arthur Miller*." *Booklist* 15 February 1978: 971.

Brief review that praises Miller's "serious and consistent assessment of the theatre's nature and aims."

"*Theater Essays of Arthur Miller.*" *Kirkus* 1 December 1977: 1308.

Highly lauditory review that finds Miller's opinion that the "drama rises in intensity and stature in proportion to the weight of its application to all manner of men" a pertinent and valuable message.

Salesman in Beijing

Adams, Phoebe-Lou. "*Salesman in Beijing.*" *Atlantic* June 1984: 124.

Adams finds Miller's journal of his travels to China to direct *Death of a Salesman* "highly interesting" and filled with "affection, humor, and admiration."

Collins, William B. "For the Chinese, *Salesman* Was a Cross-Cultural Journey." *Philadelphia Inquirer* 7 May 1984: E4.

Collins reccomends Miller's book "to everybody who has more than a superficial interest in the theater."

Hayford, Charles. "*Salesman in Beijing.*" *Library Journal* 1 April 1984: 730.

Positive review of Miller's book of reportage, *Salesman in Beijing*, that Hayford calls a "tough, sensitive exploration" and "a rewarding book."

Houghton, Norris. "Understanding Willy." *New York Times Book Review* 24 June 1984: 37.

Houghton calls Miller's book about his journey to China to direct *Death of a Salesman* with an all-Chinese cast a "remarkable document," not only as a study of the "reactions of a superior stage craftsman," but also as a "highly sensitive and thoughtful" record of Miller's experiences abroad.

Spender, Stephen. "Willy Loman Takes on New Territory." *Washington Post* 13 May 1984: X4.

Positive review of *Salesman in Beijing* in which Spender recounts the high points of Miller's journey (creatively and personally) to China to direct his *Death of a Salesman* with an all-Chinese cast.

Timebends: A Life

Anderson, David E. "A Writer's Reflections on His Life." *Philadelphia Inquirer* 19 November 1987: C5.

Highly lauditory review of *Timebends: A Life* that Anderson finds a "fascinating" "touching and straighforward" story that Miller tells "with a modesty that belies his importance in American cultural life."

"Arthur Miller: Life of a Salesman." *Economist* (London) 14 November 1987: 104.

Complimentary review of *Timebends: A Life* that calls Miller's work "engrossing" and "as an autobiogrpahy, it is complex and testing."

Bawer, Bruce. "A Salesman's Old Line." *American Scholar* (Winter 1989): 140–46.

Bawer finds Miller's autobiography a "remarkable document in self-celebration and political self-justification, as discursive, repetitious, and intellectually simplistic as many of his plays."

Caldwell, Gail. "Arthur Miller at Center Stage." *Boston Globe* 8 November 1987: Books: 103.

Mixed review of *Timebends: A Life* that Caldwell calls "uneven" with a selective chronology that "seems capricious. Like an eloquent, avunculur dinner guest, he can go on far too long about some events and entirely omit others, leaving his host to wonder about all those elliptical pauses."

Collins, William B. "Playing Up the Life of Arthur Miller." *Philadelphia Inquirer* 15 November 1987: S1.

Lengthy review of *Timebends: A Life* by the *Inquirer*'s theatre critic. Collins calls Miller's work "long, engrossing, and occasionally gassy."

Cryer, Dan. "Arthur Miller, Undisturbed by Regret." *Newsday* 1 November 1987: Ideas: 20.

Cryer finds Miller's autobiography "intriguing" and, "despite the jumble of chronology, the book possesses a shapeliness that only a writer of Miller's gifts could give it."

Denby, David. "Arthur Miller, America's Connoisseur of Guilt: All My Sins." *New Republic* 8 February 1988: 30–34.

Mostly negative review in which Denby criticizes Miller's choice to dispense with a chronological sequence and cut "back and forth in time," as well as his "long and rambling sentences," which makes the work "unwieldy." While Miller deserves credit for his stand against HUAC, Denby argues that this work suffers "from overweening moralism" and Miller's "failure to transcend the bleak aesthetics that animated the Left in the 1930s."

Frymer, Murry. "A Playwright of Dilemmas, Arthur Miller's Dramas of Choices Are Unequaled." *San Jose Mercury News* 13 December 1987: 5.

Lengthy mixed review of *Timebends: A Life* that Frymer finds "fascinating" but full of pontification—Miller "seems always bent on making a telling observation, on anything and everything, as if this book was to be the final repository of all his ideas."

Gilman, Richard. "Honest Art." *American Theatre* (February 1988): 29–31.

Gilman discusses *Timebends: A Life*, its anecdotes and gossip.

Grecco, Stephen. "Autobiography." *World Literature Today* (Autumn 1988): 664.

Positive review of Miller's autobiography that Grecco calls "searingly honest (and surprisingly witty) . . . [Miller] does his best to illustrate the universal nature of his drama."

Henry, William A., III. "Books: A Life of Fade-Outs and Fade-Ins." *Time* 23 November 1987: 88.

Mixed review of Miller's autobiography that Henry says is "often muddled, even mawkish."

Hirson, David. "*Timebends: A Life*." *Times Literary Supplement* (London) 25–31 December 1987: 1425.

Negative review of *Timebends: A Life* in which Hirson believes that "Miller is unable or unwilling to recognize that it is . . . this solemn grandiloquence which began long ago to diminish his plays."

Prescott, Peter S. "Arthur Miller Tells His Life." *Newsweek* 16 November 1987: 110.

Prescott finds Miller's autobiography "digressive and overlong, occasionally stumbling . . . into awkwardly constructed sentences."

"*Timebends: A Life*." *Magill Book Reviews*. New York: Grove Press, 1987.

Mixed review of Miller's autobiography. "Omissions and evasions prevent *Timebends: A Life* from being a definitive account of Miller's life. This self-portrait of the playwright in a world where theaters are going dark, however, is the testimony of a decent, thoughtful, occasionally sanctimonious man."

Yardley, Jonathan. "Arthur Miller's Tale." *Washington Post* 8 November 1987: Book World: 3.

Mixed review of *Timebends: A Life* that Yardley calls "earnest and passionate, but also ponderous and artless. . . . In describing his life's work he gets no closer than has anyone else in explaining the inner sources of his art."

Homely Girl, A Life, and Other Stories

Fame (1966), ***Fitter's Night*** (1966), and ***Homely Girl, A Life*** (1992).

Harris, Michael. "3 by Miller Underscore His Certain Talent." *Los Angeles Times* 26 November 1995: Book Review: 14.

Favorable review of the collection of Miller's stories that Harris says reminds "us that the distinguished playwright is a good writer, period."

Henderson, David W. "*Homely Girl, A Life, and Other Stories*" *Library Journal* 1 October 1995: 122–23.

A favorable review of the collection of three short stories, published to commemorate Miller's 80th birthday. "While prose is not what Miller will be remembered for, he exhibits in this collection an adroitness with the medium."

Nathan, Jean. "How a Painting Inspired a Novella & Other Stories." *ArtNews* 92.7 (September 1993): 160–63.

Details the collaboration between artist and writers in the production of fine-press editions of literary works. Mentioned is how Miller's *Homely Girl, A Life* inspired sculptor Louise Bourgeois to create ten drawings and eight collages.

"Notes on Current Books: *Homely Girl, A Life, and Other Stories*." *Virginia Quarterly Review* 72.2 (Spring 1996): 63–64.

Brief notes detailing the individual stories that make up the collection by Miller.

Shapiro, Nancy. "Many Happy Returns to You, Arthur Miller." *St. Louis Post-Dispatch* 15 October 1995: C5.

Shapiro remarks that she had trouble taking "Homely Girl" seriously because it reminded her of the old joke about the unattractive girl and the nearly blind man with the punch line "with my face and your eyes, we make a perfect pair," but enjoyed the other two "strong" stories in the collection.

Steinberg, Sybil S. "*Homely Girl, A Life, and Other Stories*" *Publisher's Weekly* 28 August 1995: 101–2.

Favorable review that "demonstrates [Miller's] mastery of literary realism."

Walton, David. "Miller's Tales." *New York Times Book Review* 24 December 1995: Sec. 7: 10.

Brief positive review of *Homely Girl, A Life, and Other Stories*, which Walton calls "gracefully written" and "makes the reader wish these stories were longer and that there were more of them."

8. Conference Papers (unpublished)

First International Arthur Miller Conference
"The Many Faces of Arthur Miller"
Millersville University, Millersville, Pa. 10–11 April 1992

Braun, Andrea England. "Eddie Wrecks: Probing the Author's Unconscious in *A View from the Bridge*."

Chetta, Peter. "Arthur Miller: Theory and Practice."

Davis, Rocio. "'Make Your Peace with It': The Conscience on Trial in *The Crucible*."

Feldman, Robert Lee. "The Horror of the Holocaust: Miller's *Playing for Time*."

Jacob, George. "The Nature of Enlightenment in Miller's Tragedies."

Lawson, Don. "Brecht and Miller."

Oikawa, Mashiro. "A Transformed Hero: Dr. Stockmann in Arthur Miller's Adaptation of *An Enemy of the People*."

Thomas, Gregory. "The Dynamics of Escalating Crisis: *The Crucible* and Victor Turner's Social Drama."

Tuttle, Jon. "The Families as Corporate Entity in Arthur Miller."

Willis, Robert J. "Arthur Miller's *The Crucible*: Relevant for All Time."

Second International Arthur Miller Conference
Millersville University, Millersville, Pa. 7–8 April 1995

Bigsby, Christopher. "Keynote Address: Arthur Miller and His Contemporaries."

Dominik, Jane. "Arthur Miller and Neil Simon: Tragic and Comic Viewpoints of the American Family."

Jenckes, Norma. "Making Connections between Arthur Miller and Edward Albee."

Johnsey, Jeanne. "General Subversion and the Magistrate of the Heart: De-Politicizing Evil and the Witch Hunt in Arthur Miller, Caryl Churchill, and Robert Coover."

Kozikowski, Stan. "The Death and Life of Willy Loman: A Re-examination of Miller's Theory of Tragedy, the Play, and Their Significance."

Pettigrew, Todd. "*Timebend*ing Elia Kazan: Arthur Miller's Tragic Autobiography."

Sterling, Eric. "Broken Glass, Shattered Ideals: Sylvia's Unconscious Fear of Helping in Miller's *Broken Glass*."

Wang, Qun. "The Dialogic Richness of the Timeless World of Tennessee Williams' and Arthur Miller's Drama."

Third International Arthur Miller Conference
"Arthur Miller: Celebrating a Lifetime of Achievement"
Utica College of Syracuse University, N.Y.
18–19 September 1996

Barber, Jeffrey A. "'Nobody Dast Blame This Man': Willy Loman's Struggle for Male Identity."

Carpenter, Charles A. "Carping about *Death of a Salesman*: Willy's Incongruous Suicide and Some Lesser Disparities."

Centola, Steven. "*All My Sons* and the Paradox of Denial."

Dominik, Jane. "A Specific 'Common' Man: Arthur Miller's Tragedy of the American Working Class."

Feldman, Robert. "The Problem of Evil in *After the Fall*."

Goldstein, Herb. "The Proctors' Drive to Heal Themselves: Counterpoint and a Major Strength against Destructiveness in *The Crucible*."

Johnsey, Jeanne. “Marilyn through *Broken Glass*: Sylvia Gellburg as a Vindication of Miller’s Chaotic Female Protagonists.”

Kavadlo, Jesse. “Marriage and Montage: A Defense of *After the Fall*.”

Kozikowski, Stan. “Miller Deconstructing Aristotle.”

Langsteau, Paula. “Deadly Self-Deception: The Bigotry of Albert Kroll in *Clara*.”

Marino, Stephen. “Poetry and Politics in *The Crucible*.”

Murphy, Brenda. “*You’re Next*: Miller’s Anti-HUAC Poster Play.”

Wang, Qun. “Arthur Miller and the Poetics of Tragedy.”

Fourth International Arthur Miller Conference “Arthur Miller’s Dramatic Theory and Strategy” Millersville University, Millersville, Pa. 13–14 March 1998

Abbotson, Susan. “A Whimsical Dramatic Exercise or Serious Social Drama: Responsibility and Connection in *Elegy for a Lady*.”

Balakian, Janet. “‘Are You Now, Or Have You Ever Been Guilty?’: Dramatic Form and the Problem of Power, Guilt, and Vengeance in *The Crucible*.”

Castellitto, George. “Demirep or Pre-modern Woman: Abigail Williams in 1953 and 1996.”

Centola, Steven. “Reflections of the Mind: Arthur Miller’s Dramatic Strategy in *Two-Way Mirror*.”

Cherciu, Lucia. “The Failure of Simulation and the Economics of Gender in *Death of a Salesman*.”

Cook, Kim. “‘Raising Up a Whore’: The Dramatic Construction of Abigail Williams.”

Dominik, Jane. “Dramatic and Symbolic Uses of Settings and Properties in Arthur Miller’s Drama.”

Egerton, Katherine. "The Lunatic's Ball: Redemption and the Aesthetics of Mental Illness in *The Last Yankee*."

Marino, Stephen. "The Destruction of Myth in *A View from the Bridge*."

Otten, Terry. "Coming to Roost Again: Tragic Rhythm in Arthur Miller's *Broken Glass*."

Porter, Thomas. "The Outside in *The Archbishop's Ceiling*."

Ratliff, Gerald Lee. "The 'Tragic Fallacy' of Arthur Miller's *Death of a Salesman*."

Ribkoff, Fred. "Shame, Guilt, Empathy, and the Search for Identity in Arthur Miller's *Death of a Salesman*."

Sampson, Michelle. "Ethics, Anti-Semitism, and Tragedy in Arthur Miller's *Broken Glass*."

Shulman, Robert. "Left Politics in *Death of a Salesman*: From *Waiting for Lefty* to *Death of a Salesman*."

Fifth International Arthur Miller Conference
"The *Salesman* Has a Birthday"
St. Francis College, Brooklyn, N.Y. 16–17 April 1999

Abbotson, Susan. "From Loman to Lyman: The *Salesman* Forty Years On."

Bigsby, Christopher. "Keynote Address: Arthur Miller: Time Traveler."

Callow, Heather. "Masculine and Feminine in *Death of a Salesman*."

Castellitto, George P. "Willy Loman: The Tension between Marxism and Capitalism."

Centola, Steven. "'The Condition of Tension': Unity of Opposites as Dramatic Form and Vision in Arthur Miller's *Death of a Salesman*."

Dominik, Jane. "Absent Characters in Miller's Drama."

Egerton, Kate. "'Getting Sorry': Truth and Alcohol in *The Archbishop's Ceiling*."

Goldstein, Herb. "Hap Loman's Evolution into Lyman Felt."

Levine, Peter. "'Attention Must Be Paid': Arthur Miller's *Death of a Salesman* and the American Century."

Lindsay, Lewis. "Willy's Mystified Failure to Attain Identity in *Death of a Salesman*."

Marino, Stephen. "'It's Brooklyn, I Know, but We Hunt, Too': The Image of the Borough in *Death of a Salesman*."

Murphy, Brenda. "*Salesman* at 50: The 1999 Broadway Production."

Roudané, Matthew. "Celebrating *Salesman*."

International Symposium on Arthur Miller
Evansville, Ind., April 1998

Murphy, Brenda. "*Death of a Salesman's* Cultural Legacy."

American Library Association Conference
Baltimore, Md. 23–25 May 1997

Centola, Steven. "Miller's Women and the Roles They Play."

Dominik, Jane K. "*The Price*: The Continuing Fraternal Tragedy."

Murphy, Brenda. "'The Hook, the Bridge, and the Waterfront': Miller, Kazan, and Informers."

American Literature Association Conference
San Diego, Calif. May 1998

Balakian, Jan. "The Holocaust, the Depression, and McCarthyism Haunt Miller in the Sixties."

Cook, Kim. "'Raising Up a Whore': The Dramatic Construction of Abigail Williams."

Egerton, Katherine. "'Of Course It Isn't, but That's Where It Comes From': Creation of Hysteria and Other Business in Arthur Miller's *Broken Glass*."

American Literature Association Conference
San Diego, Calif. May 1999.

Marino, Stephen. "*Death of a Salesman*: The Poetic of the Colloquial."

Shulman, Robert. "The Cold War on the Waterfront: Miller's *A View from the Bridge* and Elia Kazan's *On the Waterfront*."

Tuttle, John. "Living the Wrong Life: Arthur Miller's *Danger: Memory!*"

American Literature Association Conference
San Diego, Calif. 30 May 1996

Balakian, Jan. "The Holocaust, the Depression, and McCarthyism Haunt Miller in the Sixties."

Dominik, Jane K. "Who's the Enemy Now?: The Relevance of *An Enemy of the People* a Century, and a Half, Later."

Roudané, Matthew. "*Death of a Salesman* and the Poetics of Arthur Miller."

"Miller and the Holocaust"
Kean University, Union, N.J. February 1999

Abbotson, Sue. "The Contemporary Relevance of Arthur Miller's *Playing for Time*."

Bigsby, Christopher. "Keynote Address: The Shearing Point: Arthur Miller and the Holocaust."

Centola, Steven. "Arthur Miller's *Playing for Time*: The Soul's Self-Portrait."

Marino, Stephen. "Metaphors of Survival in *Incident at Vichy*."

Murphy, Brenda. "Possession, Responsibility, and the Holocaust in Arthur Miller's Plays."

PART III
MEDIA RESOURCES

1. Film and Television Productions of Miller plays

After the Fall. Perf. Faye Dunaway and Christopher Plummer. NBC. 10 December 1974.

All My Sons. Dir. Irving Reis. Perf. Edward G. Robinson, Burt Lancaster. Universal. 1948.

All My Sons. Prod. Iris Merlis. Dir. Jack O'Brien. Perf. James Whitmore, Aidan Quinn, Joan Allen, Michael Learned. PBS. *American Playhouse*. 19 January 1987. MCA Home Video, 1987.

The American Clock. Prod. Michael Brandman. Dir. Bob Clark. Perf. Mary McDonnell, Darren McGavin, David Strathairn, John Randolph, and Rebecca Miller. TNT Cable Network. 23 August 1993.

Broken Glass. Prod. Fiona Finlay. Dir. David Thacker. Screenplay by David Holman and David Thacker. Perf. Mandy Patinkin, Henry Goodman, Margot Leicester, and Elizabeth McGovern. Narr. Russell Baker. BBC and WGBH/Boston. *Mobil Masterpiece Theatre*. 1997.

Clara. Dir. Burt Brinckerhoff. Perf. William Daniels, Darren McGavin, and Jennifer Parsons. A&E Cable Network. *General Motors Playwrights Theatre*. 5 February 1991.

The Crucible. Prod. and dir. Raymond Borderie. Screenplay by Jean-Paul Sartre. Perf. Simone Signoret, Yves Montand, Mylene Demongeot. Kingsley International. Films Borderie, Pathe Cinema. 1957. Hen's Tooth Video. 1995.

The Crucible. Prod. and dir. Harvey Hart. Adapt. Mavor Moore. Perf. Leslie Nielsen and Diana Maddox. Canadian Broadcasting Corporation. 27 October 1959.

The Crucible. Dir. Henry Kaplan. Adapt. Stanley Mann. Perf. Sean Connery, Susannah York, Hugh Latimer, and Barbara Chilcott. Granada TV, Manchester, England. Independent Television. 10 November 1959.

The Crucible. Prod. David Susskind. Dir. Alex Segal. Adapt. Arthur Miller. Perf. George C. Scott, Colleen Dewhurst, Tuesday Weld, Will Geer, Fritz Weaver, Cathleen Nesbit, Henry Jones, and Melvyn Douglas. CBS. 4 May 1967.

The Crucible. Prod. Robert Miller and David V. Picker. Dir. Nicholas Hytner. Perf. Daniel Day-Lewis, Winona Ryder, Joan Allen, Bruce Davidson, Frances Conroy, Paul Scofield. Twentieth Century-Fox, 1996.

Death of a Salesman. Prod. Stanley Kramer. Dir. Laslo Benedek. Screenplay by Stanley Roberts. Perf. Fredric March, Mildred Dunnock, Cameron Mitchell, and Kevin McCarthy. Columbia Pictures, 1951.

Death of a Salesman. Prod. David Susskind. Dir. Alex Segal. Perf. Lee J. Cobb, Mildred Dunnock, James Farentino, and George Segal. CBS. 8 May 1966.

Death of a Salesman. Dir. Volker Schlondorff. Perf. Dustin Hoffman, Kate Reid, John Malkovich, Charles Durning, and Stephen Lang. CBS, 15 September 1985. Anchor Bay Entertainment, 1998.

Am Enemy of the People. Prod. David Griffiths. Dir. Jack O'Brien. Screenplay by Arthur Miller. Perf. John Glover, William Anton, George Grizzard. PBS. *American Playhouse*. 13 June 1990.

Everybody Wins. Prod. Jeremy Thomas. Dir. Karel Reisz. Screenplay by Arthur Miller. Perf. Nick Nolte and Debra Winger. Orion Pictures, 1990.

Fame. Dir. Marc Daniels. Perf. Richard Benjamin, José Ferrer, and Linda Hunt. Television production of short story "The Recognitions," revised into one-act play entitled "Fame." NBC. *Hallmark Hall of Fame*. 30 November 1978.

Incident at Vichy. Prod. Norman Lloyd. Dir. Stacey Keach. Perf. Richard Jordan. PBS. 1973.

A Memory of Two Mondays. Prod. Jaqueline Babbin. Dir. Paul Bogart. Perf. Kristoffer Tabori, Dick Van Patten, Estelle Parsons, and Jack Warden. PBS. *NET Playhouse*. 1971.

The Misfits. Dir. John Huston. Perf. Marilyn Monroe, Clark Gable, Montgomery Clift, Thelma Ritter, Eli Wallach. Seven Arts/United Artists, 1961.

Playing for Time. Prod. Linda Yellen. Dir. Daniel Mann. Perf. Vanessa Redgrave, Jane Alexander, Shirley Knight. CBS. 30 September 1980. Telecast in the United Kingdom on 11 January 1981 on the Independent Television Network by London Weekend Television. Media Home Entertainment, 1984.

The Price. Prod. David Susskind. Dir. Fiedler Cook. Perf. George C. Scott, Barry Sullivan, David Burns, and Colleen Dewhurst. NBC. *Hallmark Hall of Fame*. 3 February 1971.

The Reason Why. Dir. Paul Leaf. Screenplay by Arthur Miller. Perf. Eli Wallach, Robert Ryan. Phoenix/BFA Films and Video, 1962.

An allegory which examines whether or not man is a violent animal and wants to kill.

Les Sorcières de Salem. (*The Witches of Salem*). Prod. Raymond Borderie. Dir. Raymond Rouleau. Screenplay by Jean-Paul Sartre (based on Miller's play). Perf. Yves Montand and Simone Signoret. Films Borderie-Pathe Consortium-DECA, Films de France, 1958.

A View from the Bridge. French title: *Vu du Pont*. Dir. Sidney Lumet. Screenplay by Norman Rosten Perf. Raf Vallone, Carol Lawrence, Maureen Stapleton, Jean Sorel, Morris Carnovsky, Ray Pellegrin. 1962.

2. Documentaries, Tributes, and Biographical Films

American Theatre. Producer/director, Richard Breitman. 5 video cassettes, 300 min. Minneapolis: University Media Resources, University of Minnesota, 1976.

"A general overview of how the theatre developed its peculiar American flavor and why; what economic, cultural, religious, and artistic factors materially affected it; and how and why it ultimately became a theatre of international importance."

Arthur Miller Reads from a New Play. 1 videocassette, 90 min. Authors in Residence Program [series 2, no. 6], NY: Yeshiva University, 1998.

Taped on 26 April 1998 at the Stern College for Women, Louis Koch Auditorium, Midtown Center, Yeshiva University, New York. Miller reads from a new play, a work in progress.

Death of a Salesman by Arthur Miller. 1 videocassette, 45 min. Richmond, Va.: Video Classroom.

Alan Dilnot and Jennifer Strauss of Monash University discuss the play set in the 1950s. Topics include major themes, characters, stage craft, and social commentary of the play.

Intimate Portrait: Marilyn Monroe. Lifetime Original. Narr. Lauren Hutton. Writ. Thomas Yaroschuk. Dir. Elizabeth Jane Browde. Lifetime Channel. 16 April 1997.

The Kennedy Center Honors. Prod. George Stevens Jr. and Nick Vanoff. Dir. Don Mischer. Kennedy Center Television Productions, 2 December 1984.

Marilyn Monroe. Prod. Clak Studio 88. Dir. Donatella Baglivo. Ex. Prod. Adriano Zonin. Host Jack Perkins. A&E Television. 1995.

Spotlight: Focus on Contemporary American Theatre. 7 video cassettes. A production of City University Television (CUNY-TV) and the Center for Advanced Study in Theatre Arts (CASTA) and the CUNY Graduate School. PBS. 1990.

Video recordings of programs broadcast through the PBS Adult Learning Service beginning 5 February 1990.

The Statue of Liberty: A Film by Ken Burns. Prod. Buddy Squires and Ken Burns. Florentine Films. Direct Cinema, 1985.

Archival photographs, paintings, and drawings tell the story of the Statue of Liberty's construction and installation. Miller provides his voice in readings from diaries, letters, and newspaper accounts.

A Tribute to Arthur Miller. Exec. Prod. Bob Banner. Dir. Lynn Gartley. Perf. Charles Durning, John Dillinger, Jack O'Brien. SMU, Dallas, Tex. 9 March 1991.

Friends from the theatre world appreciate Arthur Miller on the occasion of his receiving the Algur H. Meadows award for excellence in the arts. Program includes excerpts from performances of *The Crucible*, *All My Sons*, and *Death of a Salesman*. Held at Rice University, Fondren Library.

Witch City. Video. Prod. Picture Business and Ferrini. Picture Business, 1996.

Fifty-minute documentary about Salem, Massachusetts, including a focus on Miller for his writing of *The Crucible*. For grades 7 and up.

3. Sound Recordings

After the Fall. Perf. Jason Robards, Barbara Loden, Faye Dunaway, directed by Elia Kazan. Caedmon TRS 326, CDL 5326, 1968.
Contains four long playing albums. Text of play included.

After the Fall. Dir. Elia Kazan. Perf. Jason Robards, Barbara Loden. Mercury Records OCS 4–6207, OCM 4–2207 (MG 21000–21003), 1968.
Contains four long-playing albums. Harold Clurman's "Arthur Miller: Theme and Variations" and notes on the play by Robert Pasolli (19 p. illus.) reproduced in album holder. "Original cast recording" by the Repertory Theater of Lincoln Center.

All My Sons. Perf. James Farentino, Arye Gross, Julie Harris. LA Theatre Works #WTA7, 1999.

"The American Challenge." Walter Cronkite. CBS. 22–23 June 1974.
Recording held by Michigan State University.

"Arthur Miller Delivering the Theodore D. Spencer Lecture at Harvard University, February 18, 1953." Introduced by Professor Morrison. WGBH, Boston (radio).
Miller discusses contemporary drama and the techniques of the dramatic form. Located at the Archive of Recorded Poetry and Literature, Library of Congress.

"Arthur Miller Explains His Life and Work in a Segment of a Canadian Broadcasting System Production of *On Home Ground*." Canadian television. 24 October 1979. PBS 8 October 1980.
With the voices of George C. Scott, Clark Gable, and Marilyn Monroe in Miller plays. Held by Michigan State University Library.

"Arthur Miller Speaking on and Reading from *The Crucible* [and] *Death of a Salesman*." Distinguished Playwright Series. Spoken

Arts 704, 1956.

Contains one long-playing album and autobiographical statement on slip case.

Arthur Miller's Adaptation of Henrik Ibsen's "An Enemy of the People." Dir. Jules Irving. The Repertory Theater at Lincoln Center. Caedmon TRS 349, 1971.

Contains three long-playing albums. Notes by Paul Kresh on album, historical and biographical notes (15 p. illus.) laid in album.

Bailie, Gil. "Sacramental Sensibilities in Literature and Life: Reflections on the Poetry of W. H. Auden and *Death of a Salesman*." Florilegia Institute, 1993.

Bailie reads Auden poetry and discusses Christian themes found in them. Also discusses Willy Loman as a type of modern American, a person who has a crisis of the will, and who lacks a center.

Broken Glass. Prod. LA Theatre Works. Dir. Steve Albrezzi. Perf. David Dukes, Linda Purl, JoBeth Williams, Lawrence Pressman. 1996.

Recorded live at the Guest Quarters Suite Hotel, Santa Monica, California, as part of LA Theatre Works' performance series, "The Play's the Thing." Located at the Library of Congress.

The Crucible. Dir. John Berry. Perf. Jerome Dempsey, Alexandria Stoddard. Caedmon TRS 356, CDL 5356, 1972.

Contains four long-playing albums. Repertory Theater of Lincoln Center. Program notes on container.

The Crucible. Prod. LA Theatre Works/BBC/KCRW. Perf. Michael York. 1994.

Recorded at Culver Studios, 2 sound cassettes. Located in the Library of Congress Recorded Sound Reference Center.

The Crucible: An Opera in Four Acts. By Robert Ward, libretto by Bernard Stambler. Perf. Patricia Brooks, Frances Bible, and Chester Ludgin. Chorus and orchestra of the New York City Opera; Emerson Buckley, conductor. Composers Recordings, Inc., CRI 168–SD, 1962.

Opera in four acts, based on play by Miller. Biographical notes, synopsis, and libretto (12 p.) laid in container.

The Crucible. Recording excerpt. Read by Arthur Miller. Spoken Arts 704 (long playing album), and SPOA 8045 (audio cassette).

Death of a Salesman. Perf. Thomas Mitchell, Arthur Kennedy, Mildred Dunnock, Cameron Mitchell. Narr. Arthur Miller. Decca, DL 9006/7, DNA/DXA 102, 1950.

With notes [2 p, inserted] "About the Play," by Louis Untermeyer, and "On the Nature of Tragedy," by Arthur Miller. Two long-playing records.

Death of a Salesman. Dir. Ulu Grosbard. Perf. Lee J. Cobb and Mildred Dunnock. Music by Alex North. Caedmon TRS 310, 1966. Also CDL 5310 (3 audio cassettes).

Three long-playing albums. Text of drama and portion of Miller's "Introduction to the *Collected Plays*" reprinted in accompanying booklet. Spoken introduction by Miller. Author's introduction, biographical sketches, review of the original production, 1949, by John Mason Brown, and text of the play (34 p.) laid in container.

Death of a Salesman. Recording excerpt. Educational Audio Visual, A5F 0906 (audio cassette).

Death of a Salesman. Recording excerpt. Read by Miller. In anthology Spoken Arts 704, also in 8045.

Death of a Salesman. Lecturer: Lois G. Gordon. Deland, Fla.: Everett/Edwards, 1971.

One cassette, modern drama series, cassette curriculum. Gordon lectures on Miller's play. Available at the Library of Congress.

Gross, Barry. "A Survey of American Jewish Literature." Perf. Budd Shulberg, Abraham Kahn, Herbert Gold, Saul Bellow, Philip Roth, Bernard Malmud, and Arthur Miller. WKAR. 16 November 1975.

Horosko, Marian. *Interview with Gerald Arpino*. WBAI, New York City, as part of its series Dance, New York. 1970.

Arpino discusses his latest work for the City Center Joffrey Ballet, entitled "The Poppet." Based on Miller's *The Crucible*, the ballet utilizes film clips, narrative, and theatre elements. Located in the Performing Arts-Dance collection at the New York Public Library.

Incident at Vichy. Dir. Harold Clurman. Perf. Jack Waltzer, Michael Strong, Hal Holbrook, David Wayne. Caedmon, TRS 318, 1967. Also CDL 5318 (2 audio cassettes).

Director's notes and text of play printed in booklet that accompanies two long-playing records.

Incident at Vichy. Dir. Harold Clurman. Perf. Hal Holbrook, David Wayne, Joseph Wiseman. Cast of Lincoln Center Repertory Theater production. Mercury Records, OCM2–2211, 1967.

With illustrated folder and program notes. Contains two long-playing records.

"John Ferres Talks about the New Arthur Miller Comedy *Fame*, and Miller's Career and Appeal." NPR, December 1978.

Recording held at Michigan State University Library.

A Memory of Two Mondays, II. Perf. Estelle Parsons and Jack Warden. Center for Cassette Studies, 1979.

Performance of the play reflecting the mood and depression of the 30s. Recording held at North Dakota State Library.

"Susan Charlotte Seminars for the Playwright, Screenwriter, and Fiction Writer." Prism Playhouse, 1992.

Charlotte presents four creative writing lectures that analyze the texts of four dramas, including *Death of a Salesman* (seminar 2). Lectures are designed to be used in a manual: "Tension: You Can't Live with It and You Can't Write without It." Located in the Library of Congress Recorded Sound Reference Center.

A View from the Bridge. Dir. Ulu Grosbard. Perf. Richard Castellano, Robert Duvall, Linda Eskenas, Jeanne Kaplan. Caedmon, TRS 317. Also CDL 5317 (2 audio cassettes).

Contains two long-playing albums. Text of drama, "Introduction to *A View from the Bridge*," and "About Drama's Relevance" are reprinted in booklet (54 p.) that accompanies records. Located in the Library of Congress Recorded Sound Reference Center.

A View from the Bridge. Dir. Ulu Grosbard. Perf. Robert Duvall. Mercury OCM 2 2212 (MG 21055–21056), 1966.

Original cast recording. Contains two long-playing albums. Miller's "About Drama's Relevance" and biographical sketches (12 p.) laid in container.

4. Internet Sources and CD-ROM Products

Arthur Miller. http://www.gonzaga.edu/faculty/campbell/enl102/miller.htm (10 March 2000).

Site that is made up of a list of Internet links to other Miller sites, including audio clips and essays.

Arthur Miller. http://www.geocities.com/~curtainup/miller.html (10 March 2000).

Site that not only offers some basic information about Miller, but also presents personal statistics, play chronology, trademarks of Miller's plays, links to plays reviewed, and a list of quotes from Miller's plays.

Arthur Miller Author Sheet. http://www.clpgh.org/clp/Humanities/millera.html (10 March 2000).

Site that is made to look like a page out of a notebook containing twenty-seven Miller sources with links to card catalog entries for each item.

Arthur Miller Centre for American Studies. http://www.uea.ac.uk/eas/american/miller.htm (28 November 1999).

Established in 1989 to "encourage the study of all aspects of the United States in Britain." Current Director: Chris Bigsby.

Arthur Miller Society. http://metalab.unc.edu/miller/index.htm (10 March 2000).

Official site of the Arthur Miller Society. Includes infomation on the Society plus an extensive Miller chronology, current Miller events worldwide, a listing of Miller's major works, the Society's newsletter, and Miller links on the Internet.

Arthur Miller's *The Crucible*. http://www.orgam.org/17thc/miller.shtml (10 March 2000).

Huge collection of *Crucible* links, including teacher resources and activities, biographical information, articles, and reviews.

Celebrity Lounge Archive. http://showbiz.starwave.com/showbiz/mouthoff/celeblounge (28 May 1999).

Archive of the Celebrity Lounge that includes an interview with Miller and information on his life and career.

Concordance to Arthur Miller's *Death of a Salesman*. http://www.konbib.nl/dutchess.net/18/06/info-0289.html (10 March 2000).

Complete text of *Death of a Salesman* that includes complete alphabetical word list, alpahbetical word list by frequency, and search capabilities by word, phrase, or character name.

The Crucible Project. http://204.165.132.2:90/crucible/main3.htm (28 May 1999).

Presents an outline student project on *The Crucible*. Contains the text of the play, information on Puritan society, witch hunts, and historial information about Salem, Massachusetts, in 1692.

Death of a Salesman. http://www.deathofasalesman.com (10 March 2000).

Offical site of the 1999 fiftieth anniversary revival of *Death of a Salesman* at the Eugene O'Neill Theatre in New York. Includes a wealth of information regarding this production, including biographies of cast and creative team and production stills. In addition, this site offers production reviews from all major revivals, including the 1949 original, a study guide for students and teachers, transcripts of on-line chats with Miller and Brian Dennehy, and Miller information such as a chronology, biographical sketch, and bibliography.

Death of a Salesman. http://www.performanceworkshop.com.tw/html/drama-eng-13.html (10 March 2000).

Site dedicated to the 17 April 1992 production of *Death of a Salesman* at the National Theatre in Taipei, including reviews, comments, production information, and photographs.

Time/Life Gallery. "Elia Kazan and Arthur Miller." http://www.pathfinder.com/photo/gallery/people/cap20.htm (10 March 2000).

Photograph of Miller and Kazan in 1949, taken on the set of *Death of a Salesman*.

The Kennedy Center. "The Kennedy Center Honors: Arthur Miller." http://kennedy-center.org/honors/years/miller.html (28 November 1999).

Overview of Miller's literary career for a web page devoted to one of the 1984 winners of the Kennedy Center Honors.

The Kennedy Center. "Honorary Committee—The Kennedy Center Fund for New American Plays." http//kennedy-center.org/fnap/committee.html (3 April 1999).

Biographical information on Miller, one of eight prominent theatre artists on a committee supporting new American plays.

Miller, Arthur. *The Crucible.* CD-ROM. N.Y.: Penguin, 1995.

Outline of American Literature: Arthur Miller. http://odur.let.rug.nl/~usa/LIT/miller.htm (28 May 1999).

Features information on Miller and a discussion of his works, provided by the Department of Humanities Computing at the University of Groningen in the Netherlands.

Reuben, Paul P. "Chapter 8: American Drama—Arthur Miller." *PAL: Perspectives in American Literature—A Research and Reference Guide.* http://www.csustan.edu/english/reuben/pal/chap8/miller.html (28 November 1999).

Site that includes Miller Internet links, a bibliography, study questions, chronology, and information on Kazan and Miller's professional and personal relationship.

William Inge Theatre Festival. "Arthur Miller." http://www.ingefestival.org/miller.htm (5 July 2000).

Site that features Miller as the 1995 winner of the William Inge Playwriting award. Includes lengthy Miller biography, festival details, schedule of Miller's involvement in the festival (interview and panel discussion), award ceremony, and scholarly attendees and the papers they presented.

PART IV
APPENDIXES

1. Premiere Stage Productions and Cast Lists

They Too Arise

Lydia Mendelssohn Theatre, The University of Michigan, Ann Arbor, 12 March 1937. Directed by Frederic O. Crandall

The Great Disobedience

The University of Michigan, laboratory production, 1938

The Man Who Had All the Luck

Forrest Theatre, N.Y.; 23 November 1944, 4 performances. Previewed in Wilmington, Delaware. Staged by Joseph Fields; Settings by Frederick Fox

SHORTY	Grover Burgess
J.B. FELLER	Forrest Orr
HESTER FALK	Eugenia Rawls
DAVID BEEVES	Karl Swenson
AUNT BELLE	Agnes Scott Yost
PATTERSON BEEVES	Jack Sheehan
AMOS BEEVES	Dudley Sadler
DAN DIBBLE	Sydney Grant
GUSTAV EBERSON	Herbert Berghof
HARRY BUCKS	James MacDonald
AUGIE BELFAST	Lawrence Fletcher

All My Sons

Coronet Theatre, N.Y.; 29 January 1947, 328 performances. Previewed at the Colonial Theatre in Boston. Produced by Harold Clurman, Elia Kazan, and Walter Fried; Directed by Elia Kazan; Set and Lighting by Mordecai Gorelik; Costumes by Paul Morrison

JOE KELLER	Ed Begley
KATE KELLER	Beth Merrill
CHRIS KELLER	Arthur Kennedy

ANN DEEVER	Lois Wheeler
GEORGE DEEVER	Karl Malden
DR. JIM BAYLISS	John McGovern
SUE BAYLISS	Peggy Meredith
FRANK LUBEY	Dudley Sadler
LYDIA LUBEY	Hope Cameron
BERT	Eugene Steiner

Death of a Salesman

Morosco Theatre, N.Y.; 10 February 1949, 742 performances. Previewed at Locust Theatre in Philadelphia. Produced by Kermit Bloomgarden and Walter Fried; Staged by Elia Kazan; Set and Lighting by Jo Mielziner; Costumes by Julia Sze; Incidental Music by Alex North

WILLY LOMAN	Lee J. Cobb
LINDA	Mildred Dunnock
BIFF	Arthur Kennedy
HAPPY	Cameron Mitchell
BERNARD	Don Keefer
THE WOMAN	Winnifred Cushing
CHARLEY	Howard Smith
UNCLE BEN	Thomas Chalmers
HOWARD WAGNER	Alan Hewitt
JENNY	Ann Driscoll
STANLEY	Tom Pedi
MISS FORSYTHE	Constance Ford
LETTA	Hope Cameron

An Enemy of the People

Broadhurst Theatre, N.Y.; 28 December 1950, 36 performances. Produced by Lars Nordenson; Directed by Robert Lewis; Settings and Costumes by Aline Bernstein; Lighting by Charles Elson

MORTEN KIIL	Art Smith
BILLING	Michael Strong
MRS. STOCKMANN	Florence Eldridge
PETER STOCKMANN	Morris Carnovsky
HOVSTAD	Martin Brooks
DR. STOCKMANN	Fredric March
MORTEN	Ralph Robertson
EJLIF	Richard Trask
CAPTATN HORSTER	Ralph Dunn

PETRA	Anna Minot
ASLAKSEN	Fred Stewart
THE DRUNK	Lou Gilbert
TOWNSPEOPLE	Lulla Adler, Barbara Ames, Paul Fitzpatrick, James Karen, Michael Lewin, Salem Ludwig, Gene Lyons, John Marley, Arnold Schulman, Robert Simon, Rod Steiger

The Crucible

Martin Beck Theatre, N.Y.; 22 January 1953, 197 performances. Previewed in Wilmington, Delaware. Produced by Kermit Bloomgarden; Directed by Jed Harris; Setting by Boris Aronson; Costumes by Edith Lutyens

REVEREND PARRIS	Fred Stewart
BETTY PARRIS	Janet Alexander
TITUBA	Jacqueline Andre
ABIGAIL WILLIAMS	Madeleine Sherwood
SUSANNA WALCOTT	Barbara Stanton
MRS. ANN PUTNAM	Jane Hoffman
THOMAS PUTNAM	Raymond Bramley
MERCY LEWIS	Dorothy Joliffe
MARY WARREN	Jennie Egan
JOHN PROCTOR	Arthur Kennedy
REBECCA NURSE	Jean Adair
GILES COREY	Joseph Sweeney
REVEREND JOHN HALE	E. G. Marshall
ELIZABETH PROCTOR	Beatrice Straight
FRANCIS NURSE	Graham Velsey
EZEKIEL CHEEVER	Don McHenry
MARSHAL HERRICK	George Mitchell
JUDGE HATHORNE	Philip Coolidge
DANFORTH	Walter Hampden
SARAH GOOD	Adele Fortin
HOPKINS	Donald Marye

A Memory of Two Mondays and *A View from the Bridge* (one-acts)

Coronet Theatre, N.Y.; 29 September 1955, 149 performances. Produced by Kermit Bloomgarden and Whitehead-Stevens; Directed by Martin Ritt; Designed by Boris Aronson; Costumes by Helene Pons; Lighting by Leland Watson

A View from the Bridge

LOUIS	David Clarke
MIKE	Tom Pedi
ALFIERI	J. Carrol Naish
EDDIE	Van Heflin
CATHERINE	Gloria Marlowe
BEATRICE	Eileen Heckart
MARCO	Jack Warden
TONY	Antony Vorno
RODOLPHO	Richard Davalos
1st IMMIGRATION OFFICER	Curt Conway
2nd IMMIGRATION OFFICER	Ralph Bell
MR. LIPARI	Russell Collins
MRS. LIPARI	Anne Driscoll
TWO "SUBMARINES"	Leo Penn, Milton Carney

A Memory of Two Mondays

BERT	Leo Penn
RAYMOND	David Clarke
AGNES	Eileen Heckart
PATRICIA	Gloria Marlowe
GUS	J. Carrol Naish
JIM	Russell Collins
KENNETH	Biff McGuire
LARRY	Van Heflin
FRANK	Jack Warden
JERRY	Richard Davalos
WILLIAM	Antony Vorno
TOM	Curt Conway
MECHANIC	Tom Pedi
MISTER EAGLE	Ralph Bell

A View from the Bridge (two-act version)

Comedy Theatre, London; 11 October 1956. Directed by Peter Brook.

LOUIS	Richard Harris
MIKE	Norman Mitchell
ALFIERI	Michael Gwynn
EDDIE	Anthony Quayle
CATHERINE	Mary Ure
BEATRICE	Megs Jenkins
MARCO	lan Bannen

TONY	Ralph Nossek
RODOLPHO	Brian Bedford
1st IMMIGRATION OFFICER	John Stone
2nd IMMIGRATION OFFICER	Colin Rix
MR. LIPARI	Mervyn Blake
MRS. LIPARI	Catherine Willmer
A SUBMARINE	Peter James

After the Fall

ANTA-Washington Square Theatre, N.Y.; 23 January 1964. Produced by Robert Whitehead; Directed by Elia Kazan; Set and Lighting by Jo Meilziner; Music by David Amram; Costumes by Anna Hill Johnstone

QUENTIN	Jason Robards, Jr.
FELICE	Zohra Lampert
HOLGA	Salome Jens
DAN	Michael Strong
FATHER	Paul Mann
MOTHER	Virginia Kaye
NURSES	Faye Dunaway, Diane Shalet
MAGGIE	Barbara Loden
ELSIE	Patrica Roe
LOU	David J. Stewart
LOUISE	Mariclare Costello
MICKEY	Ralph Meeker
MAN IN PARK	Stanley Beck
CARRIE	Ruth Attaway
LUCAS	Harold Scott
CHAIRMAN	David Wayne
HARLEY BARNES	Hal Holbrook
PORTER	Jack Waltzer
MACGIE'S SECRETARY	Crystal Field
PIANIST	Scott Cunningham
OTHERS	Clint Kimbrough, John Phillip Law, Barry Primus, James Greene

Incident at Vichy

ANTA-Washington Square Theatre, N.Y.; 3 December 1964, 99 performances. Directed by Harold Clurman; Set by Boris Aronson.

LEBEAU	Michael Strong
BAYARD	Stanley Beck
MARCHAND	Paul Mann
POLICE GUARD	C. Thomas Blackwell
MONCEAU	David J. Stewart
GYPSY	Harold Scott
WAITER	Jack Waltzer
BOY	Ira Lewis
MAJOR	Hal Holbrook
FIRST DETECTIVE	Alek Primose
OLD JEW	Will Lee
SECOND DETECTIVE	James Dukas
LEDUC	Joseph Wiseman
POLICE CAPTAIN	James Greene
VON BERG	David Wayne
PROFESSOR HOFFMAN	Clinton Kimbrough
FERRAND	Graham Jarvis
PRTSONERS	Pierre Epstein, Stephen Peters, Tony Lo Bianco, John Vari

The Price

Morosco Theatre, N.Y.; 7 February 1968, 425 performances. Preview in Philadelphia. Produced by Robert Whitehead; Directed by Ulu Grosbard; Set and Costumes by Boris Aronson; Lighting by Paul Morrison

VICTOR FRANZ	Pat Hingle
ESTHER FRANZ	Kate Reid
GREGORY SOLOMON	Harold Gary
WALTER FRANZ	Arthur Kennedy

Fame and *The Reason Why*

New Theater Workshop, N.Y.; 1970

Eli Wallach and Anne Jackson

The Creation of the World and Other Business

Shubert Theatre, N.Y.; 30 November 1972, 20 performances. Previewed at Eisenhower Theatre, Kennedy Center, Washington, D.C. Produced by Robert Whitehead; Directed by Gerald Freedman; Settings by Boris Aronson; Lighting by Tharon Musser; Costumes by Hal George; Music by Stanley Silverman

ADAM	Bob Dishy
GOD	Stephen Elliott
EVE	Zoe Caldwell
CHEMUEL, THE ANGEL OF MERCY	Lou Gilbert
RAPHAEL, AN ANGEL	Dennis Cooley
AZRAEL, THE ANGEL OF DEATH	Lou Polan
LUCIFER	George Grizzard
CAIN	Barry Primus
ABEL	Mark Lamos

Up From Paradise (A Theater Piece Spoken and Sung)

Powell Center for the Performing Arts, University of Michigan, Ann Arbor, 23 April 1974. Directed by Arthur Miller; Music by Stanley Silverman; Settings by Alan Billings; Costumes by Zelma Weisfeld; Lighting by R. Craig Wolf

NARRATOR	Arthur Miller
GOD	Bob Bingham
ADAM	Allan Nicholls
EVE	Kimberly Farr
LUCIFER	Larry Marshall
CAIN	Seth Allen
ABEL	Dennis Cooley

The Archbishop's Ceiling

Eisenhower Theatre, Kennedy Center, Washington, D.C.; 30 April 1977, 30 performances. Produced by Robert Whitehead, Roger L. Stevens, and Konrad Matthaei; Directed by Arvin Brown; Scenery by David Jenkins; Costumes by Bill Walker; Lighting by Ron Wallace

ADRIAN	Tony Musante
SIGMUND	John Cullum
MAYA	Bibi Andersson
MARTIN	Josef Sommer

MARCUS	Douglas Watson
IRENA	Bara-Cristen Hansen

The American Clock

Spoleto Festival's Dockside Theater, Charleston, S.C.; 24 May 1980. Previewed at Harold Clurman Theatre in New York. Directed by Dan Sullivan

Biltmore Theatre, N.Y.; 20 November 1980, 12 performances. Directed by Vivian Matalon; Scenery by Karl Eigsti; Lighting by Neil Peter Jampolis; Costumes by Robert Wojewodski; Incidental Music by Robert Dennis

LEE BAUM	William Atherton
MOE BAUM	John Randolph
CLARENCE, WAITER, ISAAC, JEROME, PIANO MOVER	Donny Burks
ROSE BAUM	Joan Copeland
FRANK, LIVERMORE, MAN IN WELFARE OFFICE, STANISLAUS	Ralph Drischell
GRANDPA, KAPUSH	Salem Ludwig
FANNY MARGOLIES, MYRNA	Francince Beers
CLAYTON, SIDNEY MARGOLIES, RALPH	Robert Harper
DURANT, SHERIFF, PIANO MOVER, TOLAND	Alan North
TONY TAYLOR, DUGAN	Edward Seamon
WAITER, BICYCLE THIEF, RUDY, PIANO MOVER, RYAN	Bill Smitrovich
JOE, BUSH	David Chandler
DORIS, ISABEL, GRACE	Marilyn Caskey
IRENE	Rosanna Carter
JEANETTE RAMSEY, EDIE, LUCILLE, ATTENDANT	Susan Sharkey

Elegy for a Lady and *Some Kind of Love Story* (*2 by A.M.*)

Long Wharf Theatre, Conn.; 26 October 1982. Directed by Arthur Miller; Music by Stanley Silverman; Set by Hugh Landwehr; Costumes by Bill Walker; Lighting by Ronald Wallace

Elegy for a Lady

MAN	Charles Cioffi
PROPRIETRESS	Christine Lahti

Some Kind of Love Story

ANGELA	Christine Lahti
TOM	Charles Cioffi

Playing for Time

Studio Theatre, Washington D.C; 22 September 1985

Clara and *I Can't Remember Anything* (one-act plays presented under title *Danger: Memory!*)

Mitzi E. Newhouse Theater, Lincoln Center, N.Y.; 8 February 1987 . Produced by Bernard Gersten; Directed by Gregory Mosher; Sets by Michael Merritt; Costumes by Nan Cibula; Lighting by Kevin Rigdon

Clara

ALBERT KROLL	Kenneth McMillan
DETECTIVE FINE	James Tolkan
TIERNEY	Victor Argo
CLARA	Karron Graves

Some Kind of Love Story

LEO	Mason Adams
LEONORA	Geraldine Fitzgerald

The Golden Years

BBC Radio, *6* November 1987

MONTEZUMA	Ronald Pickup
GUATEMOTZIN (his nephew)	Kim Wall
CUTTLAHUA (his brother)	John Samson
CAGAMA (Lord in Council)	Brian Hewlett
TECUICHPO (the King's daughter)	Victoria Carling
PARACH (thc High Priest)	Hugh Dickson
TALUA (the history boy)	Stephen Rashbrook
TAPAIA	Tim Reynolds
QUAUHOPOCA, JUDGE	Norman Jones
ASTROLOGER	David Timson
SACRIFICIAL BOY	Stephen Tompkinson
COURIER	Paul Sirr
HERNANDO CORTES	John Shrapnel

DONNA MARINA	Hannah Gordon
PEDRO DE ALVARADO	John Hollis
VELASQUEZ DE LEON	Paul Sirr
FRANCISCO DE MONTEJO	Paul Gregory
CRISTOBAL DE OLID	Michael Deacon
DIEGO DE ORDAZ (older)	John Bott
KING XICOTENGA	David Timson
ARBENGA	Steven Harrold
R. OLMEDO	Norman Bird
MESA	Steven Thompkina
PANFILO NARVAEZ	John Samson

The Last Yankee (one-scene play)

Emsemble Studio Theater, N.Y.; June, 1991. Directed by Gordon Edelstien

LEROY HAMILTON	John Heard
JOHN FRICK	Biff McGuire

The Ride Down Mount Morgan

Wyndham's Theatre, London; 11 October 1991. Produced by Robert Fox; Directed by Michael Blakemore; Set by Tanya McCallin; Lighting by Stephen Watson; Sound designed by Paul Arditti; Music by Barrington Pheloung

LYMAN FELT	Tom Conti
NURSE HOGAN	Marsha Hunt
THE FATHER	Harry Landis
THEO FELT	Gemma Jones
BESSIE	Deirdre Strath
LEAH FELT	Clare Higgins
TOM WILSON	Manning Redwood
HOSPITAL PORTER	Colin Stepney

The Last Yankee (two-scene play)

Manhattan Theater Club, N.Y.; 21 January 1993. Directed by John Tillinger; Set by John Lee Beatty; Costumes by Jane Greenwood; Lighting by Dennis Parichy

LEROY HAMILTON	John Heard
JOHN FRICK	Tom Aldredge
UNNAMED PATIENT	Charlotte Maier
PATRICIA HAMILTON	Frances Conroy
KAREN FRICK	Rose Gregorio

Broken Glass

Long Wharf Theater, Conn.; March 1994

Booth Theater, N.Y.; 24 April 1994. Produced by Robert Whitehead, Roger L. Stevens, Lars Schmidt, Spring Sirkin, Terri Childs, Timothy Childs, and Herb Albert; Directed by John Tillinger; Set and Costumes by Santo Loquasto; Lighting by Brian Nason; Sound by T. Richard Fitzgerald; Music by William Bolcom

PHILLIP GELLBURG	Ron Rifkin
MARGRET HYMAN	Frances Conroy
DR. HARRY HYMAN	David Dukes
SYLVIA GELLBURG	Amy Irving
HARRIET	Lauren Klein
STANTON CASE	Geroge N. Martin

The Ryan Interview or How It Was Around Here

Ensemble Studio Theatre One-Act Play Marathon 1995. Directed by Curt Dempster

RYAN	Mason Adams
INTERVIEWER	Julie Lauren

Mr. Peters' Connections

Signature Theatre, N.Y.; 28 April 1998 to 21 June 1998, limited run of 40 performances. Produced by the Signature Theatre Company; Directed by Garry Hynes; Set by Francis O'Connor; Costumes by Teresa Snider-Stein; Lighting by Beverly Emmons; Sound Design by Red Ramona

CALVIN	Jeff Weiss
HARRY PETERS	Peter Falk
ADELE	Erica Bradshaw
CATHY-MAE	Kris Carr
LARRY	Daniel Oreskes
LEONARD	Alan Mozes
ROSE	Tari Signor
CHARLOTTE	Anne Jackson

2. Standard Reference Guides Consulted

Print Sources

Aelman, Irving, and Rita Dworkin. *Modern Drama: A Checklist of Critical Literature on Twentieth Century Plays*. Metuchen, N.J.: Scarecrow, 1967.

Bailey, Claudia. *A Guide to Reference and Bibliography for Theatre Research*. 2nd ed. Ohio: Ohio State University Libraries, 1983.

Beacham, Walton, ed. *Research Guide to Bibliography and Criticism: World Drama*. Washington, D.C.: Research Pub., 1986.

Belknap, S. Yancy, ed. *A Guide to the Performing Arts, 1958–1968*. Metuchen, N.J.: Scarecrow, 1959–1969.

Biography Index: A Cumulative Index to Biographical Material in Books and Magazines. Vols. 1, 2, 4, 5, 7–22. New York: Wilson, 1949 –.

Breed, Paul, and Florence Sniderman, eds. *Drama Criticism Index: A Bibliography of Commentaries on Playwrights from Ibsen to the Avant Garde*. Detroit: Gale, 1972.

Carpenter, Charles A. *Modern Drama Scholarship and Criticism, 1966–1980: An International Bibliography*. Toronto: Toronto UP, 1986.

Carpenter, Charles A. *Modern Drama Scholarship and Criticism, 1981–1990: An International Bibliography*. Toronto: Toronto UP, 1997.

Coleman, Arthur, and Gary R. Tyler. *Drama Criticism: A Checklist of Interpretations since 1940: English and American Plays, 1966–1997*. Vol. 1. Denver, Colo.: A. Swallow, 1998.

Connor, John M., and Billie M., eds. *Ottemillers Index to Plays in Collections Published Between 1990 and 1985*. 7th ed. Metuchen, N.J.: Scarecrow Press, 1988.

Current Biography. New York: Wilson, 1947, 1973.

Dramatic Index, 1909–1949. Boston: W.W. Faxon, 1910–1952.

Eddleman, Floyd E., ed. *American Drama Criticism: Interpretations, 1890–1977*. 2nd ed. Hamden, Conn.: Shoe String, 1979.

Edwards, Christopher, ed. *World Guide to Performing Arts Periodicals*. London: British Centre of International Theatre Institute, 1982.

Encyclopedia of World Drama: An International Reference Work. 2nd ed. New York: McGraw, 1984.

Fidell, Estelle, ed. *Play Index, 1961–1977*. New York: Wilson, 1968–1978.

Hurley, Paul, ed. *American Drama, 1900–1970: A Guide to Information Sources*. Detroit: Gale, 1971.

Index to Personal Names in the National Union Catalog of Manuscript Collections, 1959–1984.

Keller, Dean H., ed. *Index to Plays in Periodicals, 1977–1987*. Revised ed. Metuchen, N.J.: Scarecrow, 1990.

Litto, Frederic, ed. *Theatre Dissertations*. Kent, Ohio: Kent State UP, 1969.

London Theatre Record. 1981–1991. *Theatre Record*. 1991–1999.

MacNicholas, John, ed. *Dictionary of Literary Biography: Twentieth Century Dramatists. Part 1 and Part 2*. Vol. 7. Detroit: Gale, 1981.

McGraw-Hill Encyclopedia of World Drama. 2nd ed. 5 vols. New York: McGraw Hill, 1984.

National Union Catalog of Manuscript Collections. Washington, D.C.: Library of Congress, 1959–1993.

New York Theatre Critics' Reviews. 1947+.

New York Times Index.

The New York Times Theatre Reviews. 1947+.

Poteet, G. Howard, ed. *Published Radio, Television, and Film Scripts: A Bibliography*. Troy, New York: Whitston, 1975.

Pownall, David E., ed. *Pownall's Articles on Twentieth Century Literature.* New York: Kraus-Thomson, 1973–.

Rachow, Louis A., ed. *Theatre and Performing Arts Collections.* New York: Haworth, 1981.

Readers' Guide to Periodical Literature, 1900–. New York: Wilson.

Salem, James M., ed. *A Guide to Critical Reviews: American Drama, 1909–1982.* 3rd ed. Metuchen, N.J.: Scarecrow, 1984.

Samples, Gordon, ed. *The Drama Scholars' Index to Plays and Filmscripts, Vols. 1 and 2.* Metuchen, N.J.: Scarecrow Press, 1974 and 1980.

———. *How to Locate Reviews of Plays and Films: A Bibliography of Criticism from the Beginnings to the Present*. Metuchen, N.J.: Scarecrow, 1976.

Shaland, Irene. *American Theatre and Drama Resources: An Annotated Guide to Information Sources, 1945–1990*. Jefferson, N.C.: McFarland, 1991.

Silvester, Christopher, ed. *The Norton Book of Interviews: An Anthology from 1859 to the Present Day*. New York: Norton, 1996.

Social Sciences and Humanities Index, 1970 – . New York Theatre Research Data Center, 1998.

Subject Index to Periodicals, 1915–1961. London: The Library Association. Continued as *British Humanities Index, 1962 –*.

The Times (London) Index.

Vinson, James, ed. *Contemporary Writers of the English Language: Contemporary Dramatists*. New York: St. Martin's, 1973.

Vrana, Stan A., ed. *Interviews and Conversations with 20th-Century Authors Writing in English: An Index*. N.J.: Scarecrow Press, 1982.

———. *Interviews and Conversations with 20th-Century Authors Writing in English: An Index, Series II*. Metuchen, N.J.: Scarecrow, 1986.

———. *Interviews and Conversations with 20th-Century Authors Writing in English: An Index, Series III*. Metuchen, N.J.: Scarecrow, 1990.

Whalon, Marion. *Performing Arts Resources: A Guide to Information Resources*. Detroit: Gale, 1976.

Woodress, James, and J. Albert Robins, eds. *American Literary Scholarship*. Durham, N.C.: Duke University Press, 1962–.

World Authors, 1900–1950. New York: Wilson Co., 1996.

Databases

Arts and Humanities Citation Index

Biography and Genealogy Master Index.

Dialog@CARL

Dissertation Abstracts Online

EBSCOhost

ERIC

FirstSearch
- WORLDCAT
- Article1st
- NetFirst

Humanities Index

Lexis-Nexis Universe

MLA International Bibliography

Online Sources

Archives and Manuscript Repositories in the United States. http://lcweb.loc.gov/nucmc/other.html (10 March 2000).

Library of Congress Online Catalog. http://catalog.loc.gov/ (10 March 2000).

National Union Catalog of Manuscript Collections. 1986 to Present. http://lcweb.loc.gov/coll/nucmc/nucmc.html (10 March 2000).

3. Newspapers and Periodicals Indexed

Advocate
America
American Drama
American-German Review
American Journal of Psychoanalysis
American Literature
American Mercury
American Quarterly
American Record Guide
American Scholar
American Theatre
Anchorage Daily News
Annali Instituto Universitario Orientale (Naples)
ANQ
Antioch Review
Anvil and Student Partisan
Arizona Quarterly
Arthur Miller Society Newsletter
Atlanta Journal Constitution
Atlantic
Audience
Avant Garde

Ball State University Forum
Baltimore Sun
Berkshire Eagle
Best Sellers
Blair and Ketchum's Country Journal
Book World
Booklist
Books in Canada
Boston Globe
Boston Herald
Brigham Young University Studies
British Journal of Psychotherapy
Buffalo News

Canadian Forum
Cardozo Studies in Law and Literature
Catholic World
Central States Speech Journal
Chicago
Chicago Sun Book Week
Chicago Tribune
Chinese Literature
Choice
Christian Century
Christian Scholar's Review
Christian Science Monitor
Christopher Street
Cimaise
City Limits (London)
Coastlines
College English
Colliers
Colorado Quarterly
Comment
Commentary
Commonweal
Communication Education
Comparative Drama

Comparative Literature Studies
Connecticut Review
Conradinia
Continental Review
Contrast (South Africa)
Coronet
Cosmopolitan
Cresset
Critical Quarterly
Criticism

Daily Compass
Daily Express (England)
Daily Mail (England)
Daily Telegraph (England)
Daily Worker
Dalhousie Review
Dallas Morning News
Delta
Denver Post
Detroit News
Drama (England)
Drama Criticism
Drama Critique
Drama Survey
Drama and Theatre
Dramatics
Dramatists Guild Quarterly

Economist
Educational Theatre Journal
Emory University Quarterly
Encore (London)
Encounter
English Journal
English Record
English Studies
Entertainment Weekly
Esquire
Essays in Literature
Essays in Theatre
Eugene O'Neill Review
Evening Standard (London)

Film Quarterly
Financial Times
Fortune
Forum (Houston)
Forward: Ethnic News Watch
Furioso

Georgia Review
Guardian (London)

Harper's
Harper's Bazaar
Hibbert Journal
History Today
Holiday
Horizon
House and Garden
Houston Chronicle
Hudson Review
Humanist
Hungarian Quarterly

Illinois Quarterly
Illustrated London News
Independent (London)
Index on Censorship
Indian Review of Literary Studies
International Herald Tribune
International Theatre Journal
Interview

Jewish Chronicle
Jewish Currents
Jewish Quarterly
Jewish Survey
Journal of Aesthetics and Art Criticism
Journal of American Culture

Journal of American Studies
Journal of American Drama and Theatre
Journal of Counseling Psychology
Journal of Dramatic Theory and Criticism
Journal of Evolutionary Psychology
Journal of Imagism
Journal of Popular Culture
Judaism

Kansas City Star
Kenyon Review
Kirkus

Language and Literature
Les Lettres Nouvelles
Library Journal
Life
Listener
Literary Cavalcade
Literary Criterion
Literary Half-Yearly
Literary Review
Literature and Theology
Lock Haven Review
Look
Los Angeles Times
Lugano Review

Maclean's
McCalls
McNeese Review
Mail on Sunday (London)
Miami Herald
Michigan Daily
Michigan Quarterly Review
Michigan Today
Midwest Quarterly
Minneapolis Star Tribune
Modern Drama
Modern Language Review
Modern Photography
Modern Review
Modern Sprak
Mother Jones

Nation
National Review
New Criterion
New England Quarterly
New Leader
New Masses
New Republic
New Statesman
New Theatre Review
New West
New York Daily Mirror
New York Daily News
New York Herald Tribune
New York Herald Tribune Lively Arts and Book Review
New York Herald Tribune Weekly Book Review
New York Journal American
New York PM
New York Post
New York Review of Books
New York Sun
New York Theatre Critics' Reviews
New York Times
New York World-Telegram
New Yorker
Newsday
Newsweek
North Dakota Quarterly
Notes & Queries
Notes on Contemporary Literature

Observer (London)
Omni

Panjab University Research Bulletin: Arts
Paris Review
Partisan Review
People Weekly
Personalist
Philadelphia Inquirer
Playbill
Playboy
Players Magazine
PM
Postscript
Prairie Schooner
Prooftexts
Psychoanalytic Review
Publishers Weekly
Punch

Quarterly Journal of Speech
Queen's Quarterly
Quest

Ramparts
Reader's Digest
Record (Bergen, N.J.)
Redbook
Renascence
Reporter
Resources for American Literary Theory
Rolling Stone

San Francisco Chronicle
San Jose Mercury News
Saturday Evening Post
Saturday Review of Literature
Scandinavian Studies
Scholastic
School and Society
Serif
Sewannee Review
Shenandoah
Show
South Atlantic Quarterly
South Atlantic Review
South Central Bulletin
Southern Humanities Review
Southern Review
Spectator
Sphere
St. Louis Post Dispatch
St. Louis University Research Journal
Studies in American Drama: 1945-Present
Studies in American-Jewish Literature
Studies in the Humanities
Sunday Times (London)

Tamarack Review
Texas Studies in Literature and Language
Theater (Lincoln Center)
Theatre Annual
Theatre Arts
TCI (Theater Crafts International)
Theatre Journal
Théâtre Populaire
Theatre Record
Theatre Time
Theater Week
Theatre World
Time
Time and Tide
Time Out
Times (London)
Times (London) *Literary Supplement*

Times Union (Albany)
Tomorrow
Transactions of the Wisconsin Academy of Sciences, Arts and Letters
Transatlantic Review
Transition
Translation
Tri-Quarterly
Triveni: Journal of Indian Renaissance
Tulane Drama Review
TV Guide
Twentieth Century
Twentieth Century Literature

University College Quarterly
University of Denver Quarterly
University of Toronto Quarterly
USA Today
U.S. News and World Report

Vanity Fair
Variety
Village Voice
Virginia Quarterly Review
Vogue

Wall Street Journal
Washington Post
Washington Post and Herald
Washington Times
Western Humanities Review
Western Ohio Journal
Western Review
Western Speech
What's On (London)
Wisconsin Library Bulletin
Wisconsin Studies in Contemporary Literature
Women's Wear Daily
World Literature Today
World Theatre

Xavier University Studies (Louisiana)

Yale Literary Magazine
Yale Review
Yale/Theatre

INDEXES

Name Index

Title and Subject Index

Except when indicated, all title entries in quotation marks are nonfiction essays by Miller and all entries in italics are full-length play titles.

About the Author

Stefani Koorey holds a Ph.D. in theatre history and dramatic criticism, an M.F.A. in theatre management, and an M.A. in theatre arts—all from Penn State University. She has enjoyed a varied professional life as a dramaturg, storyteller, writer, editor, professor, box office manager, and librarian. She recently revised and edited a new edition of *Story Programs: A Source Book of Materials* (Scarecrow Press, 2000) and is a regularly contributing reviewer of young adult literature for *VOYA* (*Voice of Youth Advocates*). Currently, she is a professor of humanities at Valencia Community College, teaching theatre, screenwriting, film, acting for the camera, and humanities.